SUBMERGED

SUBMERGED

HOW A COLD CASE CONDEMNED AN INNOCENT MAN TO HIDE A FAMILY'S DARKEST SECRET

HILLEL LEVIN

CRIME INK • NEW YORK

Dedicated to Mary Jo, Adam, Aaron, Jill, and Gabe
for their love, support, and the occasional sanity check

Submerged
How a Cold Case Condemned an Innocent Man
to Hide a Family's Darkest Secret

Crime Ink
An Imprint of Penzler Publishers
58 Warren Street
New York, N.Y. 10007

First Crime Ink edition

Interior design by Jeff Wong

Library of Congress Control Number: 2024941963

ISBN: 978-1-61316-574-4
eBook ISBN: 978-1-61316-575-1

10 9 8 7 6 5 4 3 2 1

Printed in the United States of America
Distributed by W. W. Norton & Company

CONTENTS

PROLOGUE: THE WRONG PERSON

That Friday in August 2013 looked like another nice day for Jason Tibbs. It was bright and sunny in northwest Indiana and not expected to be too hot or humid. His partner, Leslie, had left the house early for her job, so Jason woke their two young daughters up and prepared them for school. This responsibility was never a chore for Jason, and the girls rarely gave him any trouble. According to their teachers, his "Irish twins"—seven-year-old Kindal and eight-year-old Tatum—enjoyed being back in class and were doing well. One usually sat up front with Jason in his Ford F-150 truck while the other was in the back. He loved listening to their happy chatter during the ten-minute drive down the hilly, tree-lined state highway.

Life could not have been going better for Jason. After some fits and starts, his rocky relationship with Leslie finally settled down. Already married and divorced, they were back on good terms and planned to remarry—a decision partly prompted by their newfound financial prosperity. Both had landed good jobs at Bruno Enterprises, a thriving family-owned chain of fast-food restaurants. Leslie had gone from managing one outlet to supervising other managers. Jason oversaw the mechanical maintenance of all their restaurants across several states. As the Brunos' businesses expanded, the couple's income grew, with each eventually earning an annual salary of $75,000.

Meanwhile, on the side, Jason was making another forty to fifty thousand a year repairing cars in his garage—doing everything from replacing brake pads to rebuilding engines. He had just added a swimming pool and a deck to their backyard and was ready to purchase more land behind them. With that property, he could build a shop for his auto work and a stable for his daughters to start riding horses. There would even be space left over for a pasture. A few years before, after losing what he thought was lifetime employment at a foundry, Jason had been scrambling to find a job—any job. Now, at thirty-eight, he looked at prosperity he had never even dreamed about.

Usually, if Jason had an early start with the girls, he would stop to pick up fresh donuts at a gas station down the street from the school, but there was no time for that on this day. Still, even as he rushed, Jason noticed something different about the usual scenery—a burgundy Crown Victoria parked in front of the fire department with two black SUVs behind it. After his years as an auto mechanic and someone who watched a lot of cop shows, he could easily spot a law enforcement vehicle. These had tinted windows and idled at an angle that appeared poised for pursuit. Jason remembers thinking, "It looks like someone was about to have a bad morning."

The elementary school's long driveway was only a few hundred yards up the road. The principal, a cheery woman, waited outside the building to greet each arriving student. Jason parked the truck and opened the door for his daughters to get out, giving each one a hug and a kiss before letting them go. More than a decade later, he has yet to touch them again.

Jason took the driveway back to the main road and turned toward downtown La Porte. Typically, his first stop would be the Bruno offices to hand in receipts for supplies he had purchased the previous day and get marching orders for his day ahead. Jason didn't travel far from the school before seeing that Crown Victoria in his rearview mirror. When lights started flashing on its dashboard, the car proved to be the police vehicle he suspected. At first, he figured they were after him for doing a few miles above the speed limit, but he knew something else was up when he pulled the truck over, and the unmarked squad car stopped alongside. Next, an armada of SUVs closed in from the front and back. When Jason was ordered from the truck with his hands up, officers surrounded him with their pistols drawn. One of the first to approach was the boyish-looking La Porte police detective Brett Airy. Five years before, Jason had tangled with him over a charge of stealing metal from the foundry. Prosecutors would ultimately drop the case; undoubtedly, an embarrassment Airy had not forgotten. It would be another officer who shouted out, "We have a warrant for your arrest."

"For what?" Jason asked.

"For murder," he answered.

"Then you have the wrong person," Jason replied.

"Are you Jason Tibbs?" he asked. When Jason nodded, he said, "Then you're the one we want. For the murder of Rayna Rison."

Jason Tibbs was not the first or the last man accused of homicide to claim the police had arrested the wrong person. But his response had particular resonance for the murder of Rayna Rison. Jason was the wrong person as far as several prosecuting attorneys and police detectives were concerned. In 1998, five years after Rayna Rison's death, the La Porte County prosecuting attorney, Cynthia Hedge, indicted Rayna's brother-in-law, Ray McCarty, for her murder.[i] That charge was no rush to judgment. Rather than take the indictment directly to the judge, as La Porte County prosecutors did with most cases, Hedge empaneled a six-member grand jury, interviewing more than seventy witnesses over a month—prime among them Rayna's friend, Jason Tibbs. But Hedge was defeated for reelection soon after the indictment. Her successor, Robert Beckman, dropped all charges against McCarty eight months into his term.[ii]

Among those outraged by Beckman's decision was Hedge's chief deputy prosecutor, Scott Duerring. "I have handled a lot of murder cases, death penalty cases, double, triple, and even a quadruple homicide," he told reporters at the time. "No case I have ever worked on was as extensively investigated as Rayna's case was. I worked on that case for over three years before presenting it to a grand jury that lasted four weeks. . . . We employed some of the top forensic experts from the FBI Laboratory in our investigation. The physical evidence we had linking Ray McCarty to the murder was substantial. And then the case was dropped by a prosecutor who never took the time to contact the investigators and experts who knew the case firsthand to get their side."[iii]

Given the extensive nature of the McCarty investigation, it is remarkable that the La Porte County prosecuting attorney's office took thirteen more years to charge another man who happened to be one of the key witnesses before the grand jury. Even more remarkable is the comparatively flimsy evidence the prosecutor used for his indictment.

• • •

On its business development web page, the City of La Porte touts itself as Indiana's "best-kept secret."[iv] Indeed, with a population of twenty thousand, it boasts attributes most larger municipalities would envy. A substantial industrial base bolsters a picturesque historic downtown. Factories and warehouses are arrayed along the state highways that radiate out of the city center. Chicago is only two hours away, and half that distance are the steel mills of Gary.

Still, the city and the surrounding La Porte County are a study in contrasts. Their names translate to "the door" in French because early eighteenth-century settlers saw the area as the gateway to an untamed wilderness of rolling hills, forests, and lakes.[v] A good part of that pastoral countryside remains, with plenty of places for fishing, hunting, and boating. But it is crisscrossed by freight train tracks and lies only a few miles from gritty factories or expansive farmed fields. In some rural outskirts, a sprinkling of mansions and tony horse ranches are interspersed with homes that are double-wide trailers or dilapidated shacks.

Two La Porte County residents were hardly a secret in the state or beyond. Charles O. Finley parlayed his success as an insurance broker into owning professional sports franchises, most prominently the Oakland Athletics. Although he had luxurious apartments in Chicago and San Francisco, he proudly proclaimed La Porte his hometown. Finley built a mansion alongside an eleven-room Colonial manor house and several barns, some of which the flamboyant executive converted to giant party rooms. When his teams played in Chicago, he proudly trooped the athletes to his ranch, showing them off to the locals like thoroughbred racehorses.[vi]

But in the late eighties, the Finley spread would be dwarfed by the La Porte holdings of a new age magnate, Oprah Winfrey. With 160 acres in the county's northeast corner, she had a 9,700-square-foot mansion, an eight-bedroom guest house, caretaker homes, a ten-stall horse barn, indoor and outdoor riding rings, a swimming pool, tennis courts, and an orchard. Although the property was more discreetly tucked away from public view than the Finley Ranch, it was prominently featured in Winfrey's *O* magazine. [vii] Nothing would illustrate La Porte County's contrasts more than her public complaints about the poorly maintained county roads. At times, the ruts and potholes prevented Oprah and her guests from visiting the majestic estate and often required wheel realignment when they did. (Winfrey sold the property in 2003 when she moved her operations to Los Angeles.)

But for many Hoosiers, especially those living in northwest Indiana, La Porte's notoriety is not due to the celebrities or anything the city would tout in promotional materials. Instead, in recent decades, the city is most known for the long-running drama surrounding the 1993 death of Rayna Rison. The sixteen-year-old first went missing when she was supposed to return home from work. Her car was found along a country road the next day. A frantic search ended a month later when police were directed to a body submerged under dead tree trunks along the marshy banks of a pond—only a few miles from where Rayna's car was abandoned.[viii]

With her cherubic face and mop of unruly curly hair, Rayna's yearbook photo went from "missing" posters on telephone poles and bulletin boards to "unsolved case" articles in newspapers and an often-repeated segment on the syndicated television show *America's Most Wanted*.[ix] The national press barely noticed her brother-in-law's indictment. Even though McCarty stayed in jail sixteen months before charges were dropped, Rayna's case was not pulled from the rotation of unsolved murder mysteries until the arrest of Jason Tibbs.

Today, with any Internet lookup, Rayna's angelic photo is paired with the mug shot of burly Jason in his orange jailhouse scrub. His big round head is shaved, and the reddish-brown hair on his Vandyke beard and mustache is neatly trimmed. There is no expression on his face, and his heavy-lidded eyes are half-open—a look that can be read as cold, callous indifference. But according to Jason, it was instead a look of total mental and physical exhaustion.

From the moment he was arrested, his day became a blur. "Everything moved superfast," he remembers. "I was in front of the school at eight with my kids, and I was in court by eight thirty." As he went through booking at the county jail across from the courthouse, his mind was racing. He needed to talk to Leslie to make sure someone would be there to pick up the girls after school, and she had to tell the Brunos why he didn't show up at work. Then they had to decide on a lawyer to hire. "There was just so much to do," he says. Meanwhile, the guards had shuffled him into a special holding cell for the weekend where someone could watch him twenty-four seven. "Because I was charged with murder, they had to keep me there for my personal safety to make sure I wouldn't harm myself."

He couldn't get to sleep until early morning, but they woke him up at 3:00 A.M. to retake his mug shot. He figured that if half asleep he looked weird or menacing, that was fine with the police. "It was clear from the start that they wanted to sensationalize everything about my arrest."

Whether intended by the La Porte authorities or not, Jason's arrest received far more attention than McCarty's in the local media and nationwide. Much of the added attention came from the police cracking such an old and infamous cold case. But for the 2013 arrest—as opposed to the one in 1998—the Rison clan was readily available for interviews. Rayna's father, Bennie, told reporters he was happy to see "the perpetrator being served the justice." He added, "It's good we can clear Ray McCarty's name."[x]

By the end of the day, TV station satellite trucks and vans from across the region besieged the streets of La Porte. Some camped out in front of the courthouse for the weekend. Others trolled the nearby streets to give their reporters stand-up shots in front of landmarks related to the crime: the animal hospital where Rayna worked and was last seen before the abduction, her family home where a boyfriend was kept waiting, and the pond where she was finally found.

Overnight, Jason had been transformed from a hardworking family man to a monster—all the more hideous when his burly mug shot was juxtaposed next to a photo of the sweet young girl he allegedly killed. Worse yet, his supposed victim had been one of his best friends, even a girlfriend for a few months in middle school. He would soon learn that their feelings for each other would be twisted into his motive for killing her—if he couldn't have her, no one else would.

As he sat in the holding cell while everything in his life was falling to pieces, the one thing Jason did not worry about was his ultimate exoneration. "I had that first investigation," he explains, pointing to the multiple law enforcement agencies that swarmed around Rayna's case within days of her disappearance. They did not just incriminate McCarty. They also cleared Jason. "It wasn't only the La Porte city police that looked into my alibi. The State Police verified it, and so did the FBI. Each of them went out and talked to the people I was with the night Rayna disappeared. When they all got the same story, they backed off me." Afterward, Jason remembers, his lawyer at the time told him, "'It's over. You're good. Don't worry about this anymore.' And I never looked back after that."

Over the next few days, his confidence grew as Jason learned about the State's evidence against him. A considerable part of the case rested on testimony from two questionable characters. One, Eric Freeman, barely knew Jason. After years of prodding by police detectives, he confessed to being Jason's accomplice in the disposal of Rayna's body. The other, Rickey Hammons, was serving a forty-five-year sentence for shooting his roommate in the face seven times. One could only assume he was a classic jailhouse snitch, looking to say anything to reduce his sentence. Jason barely knew him either. Hammons claimed to have seen Rayna's dead body in the trunk of a car that Freeman and Jason backed into a barn where he was smoking dope. His story was outlandish on several levels, and like the sworn testimony from Freeman, there was no forensic evidence to back it up. If anything, the forensic evidence disputed it.

But unlike the case with McCarty, the charges against Jason Tibbs were not dropped. His jury trial was held in 2014, a little more than a year after his arrest. Despite his confidence that he would prove his innocence in court, today Jason sits in an Indiana prison serving a forty-year sentence for the murder of Rayna Rison.[xi] His family, flourishing on the day of his arrest, has fallen apart. His mother, who had been so proud of his accomplishments and steadfast in his defense, lived long enough to see his conviction but died before she could see his vindication.

For now, Jason has exhausted his appeals in the Indiana courts. As he pores through his voluminous case files, he admits, "I've just lost faith in the entire legal system. When I go through the paperwork I have and look at what's been argued in my appeals, I ask myself, 'How can a judge look at this and not do something about it?'"

His only hope for a retrial now is pinned to an appeal in the federal judicial system—what he sees, at best, as a very long shot. "At the federal level, you have to come up with new evidence that wasn't considered in your trial," he says. "The old evidence was strongly in my favor, but the jury couldn't hear it all. That's what's so hard for me to understand."

When all the evidence surrounding the Rayna Rison homicide is considered, it does make a compelling case for Jason's innocence. It also raises serious questions about the criminal justice system that convicted him. These questions start with misconduct in the police investigation and the detective's testimony at Jason's trial. They extend to the courtroom and the judge's questionable decisions to block evidence from the first police investigation that incriminated Ray McCarty and cleared Jason. Appeals courts would later question some of the judge's calls but still found the witness testimony against Jason "overwhelming." Undoubtedly, the evidence the judge kept from the jury would have impacted their deliberations.

The judicial errors were further exacerbated by what legal authorities call an "ineffective defense." Jason's lawyers, who started the case supremely confident about his prospects, were unprepared for the prosecutors' tactics and the judge's rulings. In the process, they missed opportunities for additional evidence that could have swayed jurors in Jason's favor or would have thoroughly discredited the prosecution's central witnesses.

With the Rayna Rison homicide, as is often the case with other notorious crimes in America, there were factors involved that went beyond the legal issues. To start, there is considerable debate in the La Porte legal community as to why the murder charges were brought against Jason in the first place—and why they were dropped against McCarty. Those decisions appear to pivot around the election and defeat of the La Porte County prosecuting attorneys. Some local attorneys believe that both the McCarty and Tibbs prosecutions were affected by grudges between former colleagues and political opponents—one of whom ended up as the judge in Jason's case.

The Risons' impact on the prosecution is an even more sensitive issue, especially since a family member had previously been a prime suspect. Highly publicized cold cases put immense pressure on law enforcement to find a resolution. A community's sympathy for the victim's family gives them undue influence—even when they attempt to shield a prime suspect. Finally, La Porte's complicated socioeconomic tensions also played a role. As a high school dropout with a defiant attitude and multiple—if mostly minor—run-ins with the law, Jason Tibbs made a convenient and expendable target for police detectives looking to close a case.

Since Jason's conviction, developments involving key players in the Rison case should lead to a new trial and further support his defense. There is also significant new evidence uncovered in this book that further incriminates Ray McCarty—most of it from police records that detectives and prosecutors overlooked during their lengthy investigation.

After more than ten years of incarceration, Jason Tibbs does not expect to gain his freedom soon. He fights constantly to prove his innocence to anyone who listens. "The system works so slowly and seems so slanted against giving you a new trial that I can't get my hopes up about that," he says. "But I want to get the truth out—to clear my name if nothing else. To clear my name for my kids and the rest of my family."

RAY AND RAYNA

RAYNA RISON

FAMILY
- Bennie (father)
- Karen (mother)
- Lori (sister)
- Wendy (sister)

FRIENDS
- Matt Elser (boyfriend)
- Lisa Dyer
- Jenni McCleland (cousin)

JASON TIBBS

FAMILY
- Rachel (mother)
- Ray Allen (father)

LORI AND RAY McCARTY

FAMILY
- Adrienne (daughter)
- Hunter (son)
- Carolyn (Ray's mother)
- Gerald (Ray's father)

FRIENDS
- Gayla (Holt) Moreau
- Charlie Allen, Cindy Brewer
- Martin Holt (Gayla's ex-husband)
- Gary Marshall (Gayla's son)
- Garry Bucher
- Lois Bucher (Garry's wife)
- Brenda Pegg

RAY AND RAYNA

INTRODUCING RAYNA

For Jason Tibbs, the most fateful meeting of his life occurred in 1988, during the first days of sixth grade. It would happen just outside the Paul F. Boston Middle School cafeteria when one of Jason's new friends, a big beefy guy named Mike Bishop, introduced him to a former girlfriend. She had brown hair in a mullet style, oversized tinted glasses, and a big smile. As Jason remembers, "Mike said, 'This is Rayna Rison. She's a great person, and you guys should get along fine.' Then he kind of giggled and took off."

Jason says he and Rayna just stood in the brightly lit corridor, staring at each other for a few minutes. "It was one of the most awkward moments ever. Here I am, trying to figure out what to say to some girl that a buddy of mine dumped on me." Rayna—still with baby fat in her cheeks—was no raving beauty, but Jason wasn't looking for that. "The drop-dead gorgeous girls were in a different world from mine." Rayna was attractive in another way, he says. "She was just so easy to talk to."

Jason definitely needed someone to talk to. While all the sixth graders were new to Boston Middle School, he was also new to La Porte, having arrived a few weeks before—the third time his family had moved in the last four years. Jason loved the last place they lived in, a little resort community with a big lake outside his back door. He could ride his bike anywhere without his parents worrying about his safety. But then, after only a year, he was yanked

3

out of his kid paradise when his grandmother grew ill, and they relocated to her home in the rural outskirts of La Porte County. He had gone from a close-knit community with endless recreational opportunities to an isolated cluster of houses on a state highway. At first, Jason wasn't even allowed to cross the street alone, let alone ride his bike on it. His middle school, in the City of La Porte, was a twenty-minute car ride away. From the perspective of a sixth grader, it was hard enough to make friends. It would be harder still when he needed an adult to drive to kids' homes or hangouts.

Although Jason didn't know what to say, Rayna was ready with a few questions to open him up. When they talked about where he was from, Jason explained how much he liked his old home and how the new one made him feel like he was in the middle of nowhere. Rayna lived only a few blocks away from school and had already signed up for a lot of activities. She said she knew other students who lived near him. If he got involved in clubs, she could help him get rides home from their parents.

After that first meeting, Jason and Rayna did not become an item as Mike had hoped. But gradually they did grow closer, initially saying hi as they passed each other between classes. Then, after a while, they would stop for a brief chat. Before long, they spent more time with each other when a group of mutual friends hung out. One of Jason's best buddies also lived in the city, and Rayna joined them for a few blocks while they walked to his house after school. Eventually, she or Jason—he doesn't remember who—asked if just the two of them could go out the following weekend.

After that first date, Jason and Rayna became a couple, spending most Friday nights, weekends, and even some school nights together. If Jason had any competition for Rayna's company, it was her myriad extracurricular activities. She played flute and piccolo in the band, managed the girls' basketball team, was on the volleyball squad, and even found time to write for the school newspaper. Rayna encouraged Jason to join the band as a way to make more friends and share some of her passion for music.[1] The school had an ambitious program for newbies like Jason where they would first learn how to read sheet music and then graduate to the instrument of their choice. "I didn't get past the sheet music," he says. "Then she convinced me to try choir, but I couldn't carry a tune in a bucket."

4

Although she didn't get Jason to share any of her extracurricular activities, Rayna introduced him to a circle of friends that mirrored the La Porte schools' demographically diverse population. Future factory workers rubbed shoulders with future executives, and future career criminals shared classrooms with their future lawyers and prosecutors. Some students lived in rural areas like Jason, while others grew up in city neighborhoods like Rayna or newer upper-middle-class subdivisions. It was natural for cliques to form as they do at any public school—like the jocks, the brainy nerds, and the social butterflies. But no class or geographic distinction mattered to Rayna, Jason says. "She got along with everybody."

While Jason and Rayna referred to their six-month relationship as boyfriend and girlfriend, Jason remembers, "There wasn't a lot of romance involved at that age." Holding hands and an occasional kiss good night was as physical as it got. "We were together more as a status thing. All our friends were paired off, and if you went out with them and didn't have a date, it was like you were the third wheel."

La Porte's biggest attraction for young teens was Fun Night, hosted on alternate Fridays by the city's two middle schools.[2] There was dancing in the cafeteria, open basketball in the gym, Ping-Pong tables in the hall, and plenty of snack concession stands. Once they were dating, Jason and Rayna would go to the movies at the Cineplex close to the Risons' house. Another option, if they could get a ride, was the La Porte Casino Roller Rink. It had a funky red brick exterior with glass brick windows that could have housed a factory. Inside, they skated around a perpetually darkened floor under a lattice of wooden rafters or sat on the bleachers in one corner.[3] "It was a place to go where you really didn't have to worry about anything," Jason remembers. "When you weren't skating, you could drink pop, sit around, joke and bullshit, and have a good time. It was something you did as a couple. You never went to the skating rink by yourself."

But with the warm spring weather, their divergent interests would soon pull Jason and Rayna apart. Jason's idea of an after-school activity was roving with newfound friends who lived close to his home. His parents had loosened their reins about crossing the street. They even bought him a dirt bike, which he raced so recklessly with the neighbors' kids that sometimes they were pulled over by the county cops. With the new freedom that his wheels brought him, he did not want to program every bit of his weekend time, which Rayna felt she had to do to accommodate her busy schedule. "More and more, we were blowing each other off," Jason says. "It wasn't like we had some big argument or discussion. We just drifted apart."

Meanwhile, another boy had caught Rayna's eye, with pursuits more aligned with hers. Matt Elser had a high forehead, glasses, and an ever-present toothy smile. They met on the first day of middle school when they shared the same homeroom and sat near each other in social studies. "I thought she was pretty," Matt remembers, "and fun loving." Both liked coming up with witty cracks or puns that made other kids and teachers laugh.[4]

While she mainly got As and some Bs, he got all As and was pretty much considered "a brain," especially when it came to math. In one area, Rayna was superior. She won her elementary school spelling bee, and Rayna came out ahead of him in the Boston competition. Matt still qualified for the county bee, and while they were technically competitors, they studied together for the contest. "Ironically, we were the first two out in the county bee," Matt says. "Our parents joked they wouldn't allow us to study together anymore."

Unlike Jason, Rayna did not have to convince Matt to join the band. He played the trumpet and was not as proficient as she was with the flute, but as time went on, the activities surrounding the music groups would pull them closer together. At first, one girl stood in the way of their relationship. She was someone Matt had known since kindergarten, who played the trumpet too. When Rayna had her sixth-grade birthday party at the roller rink, she invited Matt and his girlfriend. "I think Rayna invited her to the party because she wanted to make sure I would be there."

Still, Matt got the message, and after Rayna broke up with Jason, he asked her to go out to Fun Night. In a pattern that would repeat over the next few years of middle school, they would see each other for a few months and then part ways. "She was very jealous of my time," Matt says. As the years went by, no rival aggravated her more than the basketball teams he helped manage. "You had a few months in the fall and winter where every Friday or Saturday was a game, and she really didn't like that."

No matter where she stood with Matt, Rayna never stopped seeing Jason. "Our relationship evolved from romance to friendship," Jason says. "If we didn't have dates for Fun Night, we would go together, but there were no holding hands or kissing. That stuff was over."

But there were still things they would tell each other about friends and family that they wouldn't tell anyone else. It was a bond that few of Rayna's friends understood. Matt, an admitted "Goody Two-shoes," felt that Tibbs was a "troublemaker." Over the next few years, Jason's behavior would justify that tag. But Rayna only saw Jason's strong points. She argued that he was more intelligent than people thought, and through middle school and his first year at LPHS, he had the grades to justify her assessment. He could also fix mechanical things that dumbfounded most boys his age. There was something else about him that was even more important, as she told a coworker years later. When she was with Jason, "she felt he would protect her, and nobody would ever hurt her."[5]

In sixth grade, even her best friends would be surprised that anyone would want to hurt sweet, gentle Rayna. Jason—her confidant and so-called protector—would have also been mystified. But in the summer of 1988, a few months before they started seventh grade, Jason was introduced to darkness in her life that Rayna had never told him about. It started when she began to babysit her niece for her sister Lori.

One weekday, Rayna called Jason to see if he could keep her company. She had agreed to watch her niece for the afternoon while her sister worked a shift at a video store. Lori drove to Jason's house to pick him up—the first time he met her. Although the two sisters were separated by nine years, they still had a striking resemblance, especially with their high cheekbones and prominent chins. "Lori wasn't happy and chatty like Rayna," Jason recalls, "but she wasn't annoyed about picking me up. She knew Rayna liked and trusted me and had no problems with me being in their house."

Lori and her husband Ray lived on the first floor of a two-flat house across the street from the sprawling sandstone-colored foundry where he worked.[6] The entrance to their unit was from the kitchen at the rear of the house. Inside, Jason could hear Rayna watching the TV in the front room, and he walked down a dark, narrow hall to join her. It wasn't long before they heard someone else come in. It was Ray.

"He must not have been aware that I was gonna be there," Jason remembers, "because at first, he was kind of startled to see me. Then he got irate and kept asking what I was doing there." He was not tall but had broad, muscular shoulders. With his helmet of thick, dark hair, black mustache, and blazing eyes, Jason says, "There was a menace about him. I knew he wouldn't hit me or anything, but he was acting close to that." When Jason turned toward Rayna, expecting one of her spiky comebacks, she was silent.

Ray stomped into the kitchen, where he called Lori at work. "We could hear him yelling and screaming about what I was doing there." The baby was napping, as Rayna said she usually did at that time, and Jason expected that the shouts would soon wake her. But Ray didn't make another appearance. He rattled around in the refrigerator and left, slamming the door behind him. Shortly after that, Lori returned to take Jason home.

"He never gave a reason why he was so mad," Jason says. "Now I realize he had other plans for Rayna after work. But back then, I figured he was just one of those overbearing asshole husbands who had to rule over everything that happened in his house."

THREE SISTERS AND A SON-IN-LAW

For any friend of Rayna Rison, it wouldn't take too long before they heard about her sisters. When it came to Wendy Sue, who was two years younger, they mostly heard her complaints. "It was like she was always underfoot, always nosing around," Jason remembers. "Rayna would be yelling at her, 'Stay out of my makeup, stay out of my stuff, quit following me around.'" Matt witnessed similar arguments. "I think Wendy's relationship with her was just that annoying little sister type of thing. There was nothing extraordinary about it. But it was there."[7] Rayna especially resented how her sister got preferential treatment from their parents. As one close confidant put it, Rayna "didn't know whether it was because [Wendy] was the youngest of the family, but Rayna seemed to think that Wendy got everything she wanted."[8] From Wendy's perspective, Rayna was always getting up on the wrong side of the bed.[9]

The relationship could not have been more different with her sister Lori Ann, who was nine years older. "They talked a lot," Jason says. "When she was young, if she needed someone to talk to, it would be Lori and not her mother." At the time, several of Rayna's girlfriends described Lori as "the cool big sister."[10] For her part, this older sibling did not complain about the younger one getting in her way. Instead, Lori would tell friends how Rayna was "worldly" and mature beyond her years.[11] There could have been no greater compliment for a little sister, although the remark would later have a more sinister meaning.

Comparing their respective yearbook photos, it's striking how much Rayna resembled Lori at the same age. The mini-me later followed in many of her elder's footsteps by joining the school band (both played the flute) and the German Club.[12] But the cool older sister provided some negative influence as well. "Lori got her smoking in the fourth grade," Matt says. "Growing up and seeing how hard it was for my father to quit, I was always trying to get [Rayna] to stop. That was the one thing we would argue about."[13] According to Jason, Lori also introduced her sister to drinking alcohol by serving her wine coolers.

"You have to understand one thing about Lori," says Gayla Moreau, once one of Lori's close friends. "She's always been bossy, and she got that way because her parents let her boss around those little sisters."[14]

The Rison parents' role in their daughters' lives remains the most mysterious part of the family's story for Rayna's confidants. The boyfriends saw Bennie and Karen as yin and yang. Of Bennie, Matt says, "He was an awkward dude. Kind of goofy and trying to be funny all the time."[15] He wore a thin dark toupee that barely covered the top of his head and contrasted with his natural gray hair. When he spoke, his eyes closed. After each crack, he'd tilt his head, pursing his thin lips, and look over the top of his narrow-framed glasses. Jason remembers, "His dad jokes could get pretty crude and would embarrass Rayna. One time, he asked Rayna and me to walk down to the gas station to get 'skid paper.' As we were going out the door, I asked her, 'What does he want us to get?' She just shook her head and answered, 'Toilet paper.' It made me chuckle, but she didn't think it was funny. I'm sure she heard it a hundred times."

Prim and proper, Karen probably did not appreciate those jokes either but would not have spoken up to say so, according to Rayna's boyfriends. "Bennie ran the household," Matt says. "She was just always at home. She was there at any time of day or whenever you dropped by." In fact, unbeknownst to Matt, she worked part-time as a teacher's assistant at an elementary school around the corner but would be done with work before her daughters returned home from their classes. When they did talk, Matt found Karen to be bright and well educated.

Jason didn't remember Karen talking to him at all other than the occasional hello and goodbye. "It impressed me as one of those fifties-era households," he says, "with the wife always in the kitchen. We could all be watching TV in the living room, and she'd still stay in the kitchen. I don't even remember her answering the phone. It was always Ben or one of the girls." But behind the scenes, Karen could show she had the ultimate veto power with matters she deemed important. No one knew that better than Lori, and at critical moments during family crises, she turned to her mother when she wanted to overrule her father.[16]

Both Bennie and Karen came from families that migrated from out-of-state farming communities, no doubt attracted by La Porte's plentiful blue-collar jobs. Karen McCleland grew up with four younger brothers in Rolling Prairie township, the rural northeastern corner of La Porte County. Her father, who described his job to census takers as a tool cutter,[17] spent most of his career making auto and aircraft parts at the Bendix Corporation factory in South Bend, a few miles from their home.[18] Karen attended the tiny Rolling Prairie High School with only fifty-seven students in her graduating class. The nickname "Red" appears next to her senior yearbook photo and may refer to her hair color, which she wore in the same sensible bouffant style she kept through adulthood. Like her daughters, she was involved in the school's extracurricular activities, including the Latin Club, where she was an officer for one year.[19] Bennie's yearbook entry does not show him to be so ambitious either academically or socially. He went to the much larger La Porte High School as a "general course" student with no activities listed. He later described his high school degree as "industrial arts."[20]

Born in Kentucky,[21] Bennie moved with his family to La Porte as a child. His father became a millwright, maintaining heavy equipment at construction sites. Despite his performance in high school, Bennie did not want to see himself stuck in the same gritty occupation as his father.[22] For his older brother, the military offered a path to upward mobility, where he became a "nuclear weapons specialist" and paved the way for side gigs as a Realtor and gift shop owner.[23] Bennie would bank his future on the burgeoning world of information technology. He took night school courses at the South Bend branch of Indiana University, ultimately focusing on computer-aided design.[24]

Bennie was only twenty when he married Karen in 1964—she was twenty-one.[25] Lori was born three years later, and the family eventually settled into an apartment over a storefront on the industrial corridor of La Porte. By 1975, they had moved to a solidly middle-class neighborhood on A Street, near the town center, where Bennie and Karen have remained.[26] As the bulk of computer work moved from mainframes to PCs, Bennie acquired the skills necessary to become a graphic artist.[27]

Like her parents, Lori sought a professional path in her work life, judging from the clubs she joined in high school—for teaching[28] and health[29] careers. Then, before graduation, she met Raymond Clayton McCarty.

Although his family had deep roots in the northern part of La Porte County, Ray grew up ten miles southwest of the city in the unincorporated township of Union Mills, a tiny hamlet of homes surrounded by massive farm fields and crisscrossed by rail lines. His father, Gerald, moved there in 1957 when he was hired as the town's postmaster. A veteran of World War II and the Korean War, McCarty became a big fish in a little pond of two thousand inhabitants. He led several local civic groups and held prominent positions in two postmaster associations.[30] His wife Carolyn was equally active, often with the ladies' auxiliary groups where her husband was a member. She was also a dedicated teacher at La Porte and Michigan City elementary schools. Her devotion to the outdoors made her an active conservation club member, and she fought to preserve a Union Mills pond from nearby construction. During summer nights, she built a campfire in her backyard and served soft drinks to anyone who stopped by.[31] Gayla Moreau, a neighbor for several years, says, "Carolyn was the nicest, sweetest lady. Nobody had a bad word to say about her ever."[32]

The McCartys had one daughter shortly before they moved to Union Mills, but Carolyn could not give birth to another child. Six years later, the couple decided to adopt, first a daughter, and three years later, in 1965, Ray.

Carolyn, the assiduous teacher, soon found that her son had trouble reading. Although his parents held him back a year, he remained a poor student despite his mother's unending efforts to help with his homework, and in sixth grade, he was diagnosed as dyslexic. In addition to his learning issues, he also had trouble fitting in with other students.[33] A teacher in South Central elementary school remembers that Ray had problems being a bully or being bullied by someone else. "Once the parents found out," he says, "they dealt with it quickly."[34] Ray later described himself as a "loner" in school, explaining he didn't trust other people, even friends. He told a therapist, "You have to watch them closely."

Ray did not find much sympathy for his social and academic struggles from his father, whom he described as "stern."[35] But one night in 1978, when Ray was twelve, Gerald had a heart attack at home and died before the ambulance reached La Porte Hospital, twenty minutes away. He was forty-nine.[36] However strained their relationship, Ray believed he suffered greatly from Gerald's absence. He explained to the therapist that he missed "fatherly guidance on subjects such as cars, mechanics, and working on projects."[37]

By the time McCarty reached high school, it was clear that college prep courses would not do him much good. Instead, he participated in a vocational program where he could spend half the day getting work experience.[38] Garry Bucher served on the school board with Carolyn and provided the job at his hog farm.[39] Although McCarty would call him a father figure, the experience did not necessarily endear McCarty to his boss. While Bucher considered Ray a hard worker, he complained about his tardiness and never trusted him to feed his hogs.[40]

As a senior, Ray made an impressive appearance in South Central high school's 1984 *Orbit 22* yearbook (the athletic teams are known as "The Satellites"). Like the sixty-six others in his class, he had a professionally shot color photo that showed him smiling in front of a cloudy backdrop. His brown hair was carefully combed over his forehead, and a slight adolescent mustache was visible above his lip. He wore a perfectly pressed three-piece white suit, white shirt, and a flower-print tie framed by the era's long pointed collars.[41] Unlike most students, his mother, Carolyn, also appeared in the *Orbit*—sitting in a group shot with other school board members.[42]

But as Ray would tell a therapist years later, behind those yearbook images of propriety was a single-parent household in turmoil. McCarty "reported a deterioration in [the] relationship [with his mother] when he turned 18," the therapist wrote in her assessment, "because he 'didn't like her ways, time limits, and having to pay rent.'"[43] He said he soon left home and moved to La Porte, where his uncle and two aunts lived.[44]

But there may have been another reason for his departure—an incident that mixed sexual obsession with physical violence, revealing a disturbing side of Ray's personality. According to a police report, he had one date with Audrey (not her real name), an eighteen-year-old who had graduated from La Porte High School the year before. She did not want to see McCarty again, but she told the police that he continued to call and stalk her. In April 1984, he followed Audrey from her job at McDonald's to her boyfriend's house. When the boyfriend went to Ray's car to ask him why he was bothering Audrey, the boyfriend told police, Ray "proceeded to get out of the car and struck me in the jaw with his fist six times, which resulted in my going to the emergency room [in] considerable pain." McCarty warned him that he'd break his jaw "the next time." Two weeks later, the police tracked down Ray at his new place of employment, a plant that processed gardening materials in La Porte. McCarty agreed to surrender at the county courthouse with his mother, who posted his bond.[45] He later pled guilty to a battery misdemeanor, and Carolyn paid his victim's hospital bill.[46]

During the summer or fall, Ray met Lori Rison, one of Audrey's younger high school classmates at La Porte High School. Their relationship got serious enough for her to use a Union Mills post office box as an address, but she continued her classes in La Porte and graduated in 1985.[47] A few months later, in August, she wed Ray in the same Rolling Prairie Methodist Church where Karen and Bennie had been married. The groom now lived in an apartment around the corner from the Rison home on A Street. The marriage certificate listed his occupation as "tree trimmer–forester." Lori put down hers as "waitress."[48]

Ray's employer, Davey Tree Expert, typically sent crews to remove dead trees or trim branches above utility lines. Although the job could be dangerous, Ray enjoyed working outdoors. As he later told his therapist, his workplace became the primary source of friends,[49] but for the most part, McCarty's social life—away from his young wife—revolved around hunting. As a child, his mother often took him camping, and he shared her love of nature, but no more so than slaying its winged and cleft hoof denizens. Friends remember him always wearing some camo clothing, usually a jacket in the striped tree bark pattern. Although he had little interest in fishing, he hung out at a bait shop that also carried hunting equipment.[50] During the weekends and after work, he scouted fields where he could use a 20-gauge shotgun to bag pigeons, getting permission first from the landowners. His favorite spots included an area behind South Central and around the Bucher hog farm feed silos.[51]

Ray's greatest joy was hunting deer, using either rifles or bows and arrows to kill them. He often stalked his prey in the forested hills of northern La Porte County. As ubiquitous as his camo wear was the bloody green blanket he used to hold the deer he bagged and kept in the trunk of his cars.[52] Among McCarty's few childhood friends was Martin Holt. He married Gayla Moreau after she divorced her husband in La Porte, and she moved with her children to Union Mills. Once, when Holt went hunting with Ray, he took along Gary Marshall, Gayla's son from her first marriage. Today, Gary vividly remembers the experience, especially the behavior of Ray, who was nine years older. "He terrified me," Marshall says. "Everything he did was aggressive. The way he spoke and acted." After the trio bagged a doe, they hung it from a tree. "Ray pushed me in front of the carcass, handed me a knife, and told me to skin it. I hadn't done that before, and I didn't want to do it anyway, but then he stood behind me, grabbed my hand with the knife, and plunged it into the deer. That was the last time I went hunting with him, and it's probably why I never enjoyed hunting all that much since."[53]

THE "AFFAIR"

In the eyes of her closest friends, Rayna Rison's life took a sudden turn in December 1989, shortly before the Christmas holidays. "It's hard to describe," Jason says, "but from then on, it was like some of the sunny parts in her got dim. She wasn't as bubbly. Wasn't as quick to crack a joke."

Her school counselor also noticed her "abnormal behavior." In particular, she appeared "more depressed and down." He grew so concerned that he called the Risons and learned that Rayna had also been fighting with Karen.[54]

The counselor had no clue about the real cause of her trouble, which started a few weeks before when she felt sick at night and didn't know the cause. Finally, Bennie sent Rayna to the family doctor and, later that day, learned why she was nauseated. His thirteen-year-old daughter was nine weeks pregnant.[55] A fraught family conference followed, with Karen pressing Rayna to identify the perpetrator. While his wife suspected one of the boyfriends—Jason or Matt—Bennie would later tell police he feared it was Ray from the start, given how much time Rayna spent babysitting at the McCartys' home. When Rison confronted his son-in-law, Ray admitted he could have been responsible but claimed that Rayna had been the one to initiate the sexual contact, and it happened only once.[56]

Three days after the disturbing discovery, Bennie scheduled an abortion at a South Bend clinic recommended by the family doctor.[57] The experience would haunt Rayna for the rest of her life. Years later, she would describe it in a letter to Matt:

> I was lying on a table in a bright room. . . . [The doctors and nurses] didn't even wait for the drugs to take effect, and when they finally did start to take effect, they laughed at me. . . . I was so scared, and they were laughing at me.

But for Rayna, her family's behavior was even more traumatic than the medical procedure. Bennie was the only one who accompanied her, and "he was more interested in going to lunch [afterward] than he was helping me." The one she expected to help her was Lori.[58]

Although the true nature of Rayna's relationship with the newlyweds would become a topic of fierce debate among the Rison family and friends, there's no doubt that the little sister enjoyed their company initially. When older siblings marry, it can be disruptive for younger brothers and sisters, especially when it takes a "best friend" out of the household. But as Rayna confided to some of her girlfriends, she thought Ray was cute and even had a crush on him,[59] and Lori did not exclude her from the relationship. She was invited to share wine coolers and cigarettes at the young couple's apartments.[60]

But after the McCartys' daughter Adrienne was born in 1986,[61] Rayna became even more of a presence in their lives to help babysit. In 1988, Ray found a better job than tree trimming at the Teledyne Casting Service. While it was grimy and sometimes backbreaking, the foundry job was also convenient.[62] The couple rented an apartment in a two-flat house across the street[63] so Ray could walk to and from Teledyne while Lori used the car for shopping or driving to her afternoon job at a downtown video store.[64] She could also use it to pick up Rayna at middle school to babysit while she worked or stay the weekend so the married couple could go out at night.

Once she learned her little sister was pregnant, Lori, like Bennie, knew who was responsible. She walked out on her husband, taking the baby with her.[65] Lori was sleeping at her parents' house on A Street when Rayna got up for her appointment at the abortion clinic. As Rayna later wrote to Matt,

> The one time I needed [Lori], she turned her back on me, too. She promised me that she'd go, and then when the day came, she decided that going to talk to [Ray] was more important. She just left me. She didn't even get up in the morning to see me before I left. On top of that, she didn't ever come over or call when I got home to see if I was okay.[66]

But the abortion would not quietly put an end to the crisis. Instead, it touched off a cascade of other consequences that threatened to tear the family apart, further traumatizing Rayna and putting Ray in extreme legal jeopardy. State law required that the clinic learn the identity of the aborted fetus's father. Because the mother was underage, Bennie had to notify the La Porte police department about Ray's involvement in the pregnancy. Three days after the abortion, he went to the station at 6:55 A.M. before he left for work and made his report to the dispatch officer. Lori went with him instead of the victim, who Bennie said was home "recuperating" from the procedure. According to the detective, the big sister was "still upset." Lori explained she had moved out of their house because Rayna told her that Ray had threatened to beat his wife and harm their baby if she told anyone he was molesting her.[67] Still, no matter now upset she was with her husband, Lori's presence at the station and the victim's absence also indicated the big sister's desire to control the situation as best she could.

But the police insisted that they had to hear from the victim. A few hours later, Rayna's "recuperation" was over, and she appeared at the police department to make a detailed statement. As recorded by a female detective, she claimed the sexual encounters with her brother-in-law started a few weeks after she turned twelve and spent most weekends sleeping in the McCartys' apartment.

> In June of '87, during the course of the night, Ray would come into the living room area where l was sleeping. He would get on top of me . . . and rubbed my private areas. Ray said that if I didn't do as he asked of me, he would hurt me, and he said that if I ever told, he would KILL me. As time went on, Ray began putting his fingers up . . . my vagina. By August of 1987, we were having sexual intercourse.

As Lori indicated, Rayna was not just concerned about herself but also about Ray's behavior with her sister. "Lori would be beaten by Ray," she told the detective. Although the sisters were "close," Lori became angry when Rayna tried to talk about the abuse. "She wouldn't talk to me for a while. After that, I kept quiet. I didn't want Lori mad at me." However, her big sister did divulge that "Ray's had affairs with other women. [Lori] can't understand what she has done to cause this."

When asked if someone else could have made her pregnant, Rayna was adamant. "Ray is it. He's the only one I've had intercourse with." But until recently, she explained, he had been careful to "always pull his penis out before he ejaculated." Then, in September, he had a vasectomy. The following weekend, he was in too much pain to assault Rayna. Two weeks later, he had sex with her, ejaculating before he pulled out, assuring her that after the surgery, he was no longer "potent."[68] He probably provided Lori with the same assurance, too, because she was impregnated at the same time and would go on to give birth to their second child, a boy they named Hunter.[69]

As Rayna provided her statement with all its graphic details, her parents sat beside her, no doubt mortified. All three signed the detective's transcript. As it turned out, the abortion clinic did not properly store the fluids from the abortion that could have identified the fetus's father with the technology of the time. But then again, Ray admitted his guilt when confronted by Bennie.[70]

At 9:13 P.M. on the same day the Risons provided their reports, Ray submitted to interrogation by another La Porte city detective at the police station. When asked about Rayna's age, he replied, "I think fourteen years old." He also waffled on the number of times they had sexual intercourse, saying, "A few times, but I don't know how many exactly." However, he did admit one instance of oral sex, which he described as "kissing on her vagina." While he admitted knowing that the sexual relations with a minor "was against the law," he denied that he threatened Rayna or anyone else if she told. But before the session finished, he asked to add: "I told her that it wouldn't be a good idea for her to come over so much because she turned me on. She used to be bold in front of me and my wife." As an example, he said there was one time she exposed her naked breasts to the couple while saying, "My tits are bigger than yours, Lori."

When the detective asked if he knew his confession could be used in court, Ray replied, "Yes."[71] At the time, Indiana's laws were relatively mild regarding sexual intercourse with a child under sixteen. The offense was typically considered a Class D (now known as Level 4) felony with a maximum of eighteen months in prison unless there was an "aggravating circumstance." By reporting how McCarty threatened to kill her, Rayna had accused him of the most aggravating circumstance. According to Indiana's criminal code, if a rape victim "is compelled by force or imminent threat of force," the offense can be escalated to a Class A felony. The La Porte County prosecuting attorney did not choose to go that far, but when he did charge Ray, it was with a Class C felony, which called for a minimum sentence of four years.[72]

With the potential of losing her husband for years, Lori now dropped all pretense of supporting her sister. Soon, Lori moved back in with Ray. According to Bennie, Lori "hated Rayna's guts [and] blam[ed] Rayna for what happened."[73] As Lori now explained to anyone who asked, Rayna was at fault, enticing Ray at a time when the young couple had "marital difficulties."[74] She implied this led Ray to seek a sexual outlet elsewhere. Although she claimed the difficulties were partly due to her own pregnancy, Ray's admitted assaults on Rayna long predated that period.[75]

Once the sisters' solidarity about the pregnancy dissolved, any bond they previously had was irreparably broken. As Rayna wrote to Matt, the two couldn't discuss the abortion and its manifold ramifications.

Every time I tried to talk to her about that, she'd be too busy talking to Ray. I wanted to yell and scream and kick her and tell her how much she'd hurt me, but I couldn't. I couldn't hurt her like that because she was my sister, and I loved her. Instead, I blame myself for getting raped and having to go through all of that, and I forgive her so that she can go back to her husband and be happy. My sister loves the man who betrayed her and raped me repeatedly. He took away my ability to trust other people and my self-pride. But I forgave her because she was happy. She told me that she'd always be there for me. I guess that was another one of her lies. Maybe I deserved all that I got. Maybe I did.[76]

It wasn't long before the rest of the family fell in line behind the big sister's spin. What Rayna called rape, they called "an affair."[77] Ray was a hapless victim of a "worldly" twelve-year-old's wiles, and Lori was a wife scorned by her sister. Even Karen would come to disbelieve Rayna's side of the story—or so she said. For Rayna, her family's failure to back her would be the worst part of the experience.[78]

But the Risons could not make her a total outcast. Rayna's cooperation would be essential in reducing Ray's sentence. Bennie hired an attorney with extensive experience defending sexual offenders, and for nearly a year, the case wound through the system as the lawyers haggled over a plea deal. With Rayna's consent, in December 1990, McCarty was allowed to plead guilty to child molesting, a Class D felony. Instead of incarceration, he was given a suspended sentence of three years of probation.[79] However, in return for this lenient treatment, the court required him to satisfy two requirements. First, he had to attend sex offender treatment sessions. "More than three unexcused absences from any counseling will result in automatic suspension from [the counseling] program and possible action to revoke probation." Second, he was to have "no contact or restricted contact with minor children" unless monitored by adults whom the probation officer had approved. To hammer home the significance of these requirements, the court included the following above McCarty's signature:

I understand the court may revoke the suspended sentence and impose an executed sentence [i.e., prison] if:

1. I fail to complete any counseling activities required.

2. I violate, in any way, the "no contact" or "restricted contact" terms of this probation.[80]

19

Once Ray's order of probation for child molesting was filed in January 1991, the family feared the repercussions of the conviction hitting the press. No one worried more than Rayna. After years of fits and starts, her relationship with Matt Elser had finally landed on solid ground. They talked about seriously going steady without any more disruptions. But unlike the Risons, the Elser family was active in their church. With this news, would Matt consider Rayna fatally tainted?

Matt remembers when she called to break the news before he saw it in the paper. "She was very upset and crying," he says. "When I asked what was wrong, she couldn't talk. Her best friend got on the phone, and that's when I learned about everything that happened with Ray. Until then, I didn't know about any of that stuff. She was trying to keep it away from me, but now she wanted me to know before we started dating again, basically giving me a chance to back out."

Despite his naivete and how scary the situation sounded, Matt didn't back out. "In hindsight," he says, "I don't know why I didn't back out. But I'm proud that I didn't."[81]

Meanwhile, Ray reached out to friends and coworkers with his side of the molestation story, even if they didn't ask first. Among those he approached was Lois Bucher, the wife of the hog farmer who gave him the vocational job in high school and was a good friend of his mother. McCarty found her in the post office where she had worked for his father. As Lois remembered, he was very apologetic and promised, "This will never happen to me again. You will never see my name in the paper again." But he then went on to explain "that Rayna came on to him, and she was twelve going on eighteen."[82]

He told another friend, "Rayna got into bed with him and began to mess around with Ray while he was asleep . . . and Lori was asleep on the couch, and that one thing just led to another. [Ray] said that after it was over, he told her to get out of bed and leave him alone, and she became pregnant from the ordeal." For others, he embellished the story by saying that Rayna enticed him first by "parad[ing] around in front of him in only her bra and panties," but when this individual reminded him that "he was thirty at this time and she was only twelve. He should have known better. Then he said Ray looked him straight in the eye and told him that this only happened two times."[83]

Ray would finally admit to the full scope of his sexual relations with Rayna when he had to undergo court-ordered treatment. As a first step, he spent three sessions in early 1991 with Melissa McDermott, a clinical social worker, who prepared an assessment for his probation officer. He had told his friends of a one-time encounter and modified that to a "few times" when he confessed to the police. But with McDermott, McCarty admitted to having intercourse with Rayna *twenty-five to thirty times* over the previous six months. However, he objected to Rayna's account that it was forced, saying, "She didn't tell the truth because she wanted her parents' backing."

Instead, he claimed the sexual activity progressed after "we fooled around a little bit." It went from "mutual scratching of backs, kissing, rubbing stomachs and [his penis], fondling of Rayna's vaginal area, oral sex performed on Rayna (one time), and [then to] intercourse."

While Rayna reported that Lori was sleeping when the rapes and molestation occurred, Ray implied that Lori may have been partly complicit by permitting her little sister to join them while they watched pornographic films. He insisted that Rayna "kept coming on to [him] . . . and [would] do things like grab [his] ass. . . . She was coming on to [him], so [he] came on to her." McCarty "elaborately described" how Rayna would undress for him and minimized their nine-year age difference [actually closer to eleven years], saying she was "not too little. She's not childish, as you can see by her build and the way she acts. Her breasts are larger than Lori's. She was a girl with an itchy pussy, so I itched it."

Unlike Lori, Ray did not speak of marital problems pushing him into bed with Rayna, but he did admit to two extramarital affairs that he saw as an "eye for an eye" response to one premarital liaison his wife had. During his assessment, Ray denied ever having beaten Lori, and when McDermott spoke to Lori, "she seem[ed] supportive and allied with Ray."

Despite all he confessed, McDermott was most alarmed by how McCarty "rationalized his abuse of Rayna" and wanted to see her "damaged by the abuse." He claimed that "guys" told him abuse was common and "if they were in the same situation, they'd go for it." Ray also minimized his crime because it apparently did not make the victim suffer. "She doesn't show any hurt. She's not tore up," he told her. "They say she's emotionally scarred and depressed, and she isn't."

As far as Ray was concerned, he was the only victim in the case. While he repeatedly took credit for confessing his crime to the police, he did not know why a judge had to get involved. "I should have been slapped on the hand by my father-in-law, not by the court," he said. "Having it in the paper was enough punishment." He felt further victimized by therapists like his assessor. "I feel like I'm getting stereotyped. You all think I'll do it again, and it won't happen again. What happened, happened."

This attitude did not put McDermott at ease. On the contrary, she wrote, "Ray's continued distorted thinking about his ability to control himself from re-abusing places him at higher risk to abuse."

Consequently, her recommendations for McCarty's treatment were harsh. In line with his order of probation, she wanted him to have individual and group therapy with sexual abuse specialists. However, she wanted to ensure they addressed his "thinking errors" and defensiveness. They could then formulate his "relapse prevention plan," which she felt should include marital counseling. McDermott echoed the court order regarding his future interactions with the victim: "Ray should not have contact with Rayna, even in a supervised setting, until approved by his probation officer, her therapist, and his therapist." But she did not want this edict to penalize Rayna, so she added, "If a family gathering should occur, it should be Ray's responsibility to excuse himself, not Rayna's." McDermott was so alarmed by McCarty's behavior during the assessment she specified two others in his no-contact condition: "Ray should not have contact with minor children, *including his own*, unless supervised by an approved adult" (italics added).[84]

As it turned out, virtually all McDermott's recommendations and the special probation conditions would be flouted, ignored, or frittered away. While Ray was not supposed to be alone with either of his wife's sisters during the sentence (Bennie claimed these were "mutual promises" *he* cut with Ray), these restrictions ended up hurting the victim more than the victimizer. As Rayna told her friends, when the McCartys visited with their two infants, she and Wendy were asked to leave the house[85]—precisely what McDermott wanted Ray to do. After a year, the Rison family let this requirement slip. Meanwhile, there is no evidence that McCarty's contact with his children was ever restricted or even monitored. While McDermott assumed Rayna was provided counseling, she had only two sessions and, with her parents' consent, refused to attend anymore.[86]

Even more startling, Ray was ultimately allowed to reject therapy as well. His probation officer had referred him to a clinic in Michigan City, where he began sessions in May 1991. But in September, the officer received a letter from the program's director informing him that McCarty was "discharged" for "non-compliance with treatment." Ray had attended eight individual sessions but missed three others—violating his probation terms on attendance. When he did appear for therapy, he refused to discuss his sexual behavior. McCarty "continues to minimize the importance of the molestation and to emphasize the victim's responsibility for his sexual acting out," the psychologist wrote. "If he continues not to be cooperative with therapy, weekend or nightly incarceration may motivate him to confront his behavior."[87]

The probation officer next placed Ray in a South Bend program that required him to attend a weekly group therapy meeting and two to four individual sessions a month. If he were to skip sessions again, he would be required to spend his weekends in jail. While this warning improved his attendance, it did little to change Ray's attitude, as the program's director informed his probation officer in December 1991.

> Although Mr. McCarty is keeping his appointments, it would be a mistake to construe that this means he is compliant with the process. He continues to maintain his belief that the only problem he has in life is having to go to counseling. He has been extremely argumentative with this therapist and with the other members of the therapy group. His idiosyncratic thinking process fosters his beliefs that the sexual abuse was only legally wrong, his victim was an equal partner, and that he is the true victim of the process.

He was now instructed to "keep his mouth closed" during group therapy, and despite his "oppositional behavior," the therapist was not ready to terminate him. "If we maintain a united front," he wrote, "we can make some progress with him."[88]

But in July 1992, the therapist wrote McCarty's probation office again to notify him that Ray "was being discontinued from the program for failure to participate in a meaningful manner." Although he kept his appointments, he continued to insist he "did not need therapy." For the therapist, his failure to "participate in treatment for sexual offenders" was "in violation of his sentencing order" that he received as part of his plea bargain.

McCarty amplified his resistance by making "indirect threats" to his therapist with comments like "your day will come." He had a similar threatening manner during group sessions and refused to participate in any way. Besides throwing Ray out of the program, the therapist provided his probation officer with a foreboding analysis:

> His failure to meaningfully participate in this program and his dismissal from the [previous] program . . . have only reinforced Mr. McCarty's belief that he is "a law unto himself." This is the same type of thinking which led him into the molestation of his 13-year-old sister-in-law. In his refusal to meaningfully participate in treatment [and] to meet the most basic requirement of his sentence order . . . Mr. McCarty has thumbed his nose at the court. . . . Sadly, Mr. McCarty's belief that he is above the law appears to be confirmed.[89]

There is no evidence that Ray's probation officer committed him to another sexual offender program. Eight months later, on January 5, 1993, he petitioned to terminate Ray's probation, falsely asserting he "complied with all the rules and regulations" and should be "discharged from probation satisfactorily."[90]

RESTARTING

Forged by the personal tragedy of her abuse, along with the ambition that set her apart from the rest of her family, Rayna launched herself into high school with an adultlike drive that both students and teachers couldn't help but notice. "She was extremely focused on her goal," Jason remembers, "and that was to go to college. She used to say that extracurricular activities were important for her resumé when the time came for her to apply, and it's why she got so involved with so many things."

From the start, Rayna let friends know she wanted to pursue something in medicine or scientific research. The school required all freshmen to take biology, which became an early indicator of what Rayna could achieve. "She

24

was really good at science and loved biology," Matt says. "That put her on track for the anatomy and physiology class in our junior year. I was really good at math, so they steered me to chemistry and physics."[91]

Although the academic paths for Rayna and Matt diverged, music sealed their relationship. It also became a hub of their social life and a source for most friends. As a freshman, Rayna took up the oboe for the first time and was promptly picked to play the challenging instrument in the school's highest-level band. But she continued with the flute in the marching band along with Matt, who stuck with the trumpet.[92] The group's one hundred fifty members were as close-knit as any club or sports team, and their outfits were as distinctive as the school's mascot name—the Slicers for the Berkel deli meat–slicing machines that were then manufactured in La Porte.[93] The musicians wore black slouch hats with the brim folded on one side. Their uniform tops were red with a black cursive *LP* over the heart and a black diagonal slash offsetting white right shoulders and sleeves.[94]

Although Rayna loved the camaraderie, she did not love the marching, which aggravated an ankle condition that made the joint swell. She stuck it out to keep her friends and stay close to Matt. Their band director could be a demanding taskmaster but delivered enticing rewards in return for the hard work. Besides winning various regional competitions, the band marched in Orlando's Citrus Bowl Parade, the high school highlight for all who attended. However exciting the event, the sixteen-hour bus trip—each way—was a bonding experience that made the Slicer Corps even closer.[95]

At fifteen and with their parents' permission, Indiana students could get a permit to work after-school and summer jobs. Rayna eagerly took advantage to start saving money for her college tuition. She worked one or two days on weekends at the Hot 'n Now fast-food hamburger stand a mile from her home.[96]

During the week, Rayna was a "kennel girl" at a veterinary clinic—what she saw as another step in her career path. After doing so well in biology, she set her sights on becoming a veterinarian. Bennie suggested she first work for one to see what the job was like, and she got hired at the nearby Pine Lake Animal Hospital. The kennel girl was to arrive each afternoon at four with the principal responsibility of cleaning the kennels and waiting room. She could also assist with the pets' examinations and surgical procedures, which proved more an exception than the rule. She typically left when the clinic closed at six.[97]

But two jobs were not enough for Rayna. Soon after she turned sixteen in her senior year, she started tutoring a family's elementary-age children. They lived in rural La Porte, near Jason, so she needed a car to drive there right after she finished work at the animal hospital on Wednesdays.[98] Once she got her driver's license, Bennie let her have his 1984 Ford LTD Crown Victoria. It was a cream-colored boat of a car[99] with one set of doors that didn't lock. It also had custom horn sounds that the previous owner installed. If she touched the steering wheel in a certain way, they would embarrass Rayna at inopportune times, suddenly blaring out "Dixie" or "La Cucaracha" while she tried to park at the high school.[100] Still, Bennie felt the car was big enough to protect his skittish daughter should she blunder into any fender benders or other minor mishaps. True to form, Rayna backed off the driveway and into a ditch after one of her first tutoring sessions and needed to be towed out.[101] Still, despite her anxiety behind the wheel, Rayna loved the independence the LTD brought her.

Besides using the car for her various jobs, she could also drive to the oboe teacher she saw one night a week—another sign of how serious she was about her music.[102] While her involvement with the bands may have helped her college resumé, as she explained to Jason, it may have also been one of the few bonds she shared with Bennie. Jason points to how much Bennie spent on the oboe and the private lessons before Rayna could pay for them. That expense, he says, was no small matter for the Risons. "Obviously, Bennie took it seriously if he spent so much. He wanted her to play well, and she did."

Still, Bennie's support for his middle daughter's extracurricular activities was controversial among her friends. One later commented that he was a "shadow" because she seldom saw him attending any of Rayna's myriad performances.[103] Matt disagrees. "His job was an hour away," he argues. "He couldn't get home in time for most things that happened after school." Bennie claimed he never missed home games on Saturday when the marching band played—even if that interfered with work assignments.[104]

Rayna used her wheels for another purpose that surprised many friends. She would visit Jason after her Tuesday tutoring sessions. It wasn't something Rayna tried to hide. As usual, she called her parents to tell them where she was and when she would return home.[105]

In the previous two years, Jason's life had veered off in the opposite direction from hers, giving him the sort of bad reputation with county police that would linger long after. The trouble started in June 1991, after he finished his freshman year in high school. He had been doing chores for the seventy-two-year-old next-door neighbor, whose husband had died the year before. The couple was known to be eccentric,[106] and although the husband had earned a good living at US Steel before retirement,[107] his wife would later describe him as "a miser and a saver [who] would save a piece of string four inches long and scraps of paper."[108] The property looked run-down from the outside, and inside, it was crammed with the hoarder's piles of newspapers. The widow was not as stingy as her husband and paid Jason well for his work. When her requests for help grew, he decided to share the wealth with Blake (not his real name), a friend who lived a few houses away and rode dirt bikes with him.

One day, after he had finished raking, Blake went inside the widow's house to get paid. He saw her reach into a lockbox and pull out an eye-popping wad of cash. According to Jason, his friend rushed back to Jason's house with a plan to steal some of that money. Blake said they could leave half of it behind, and the old lady wouldn't even notice it was missing. Jason went along with the plan, and the two waited until they knew the widow, who lived alone, would be away from home for an extended time. They entered the house by removing the hinges from a door in the breezeway to the garage. Jason followed Blake inside and watched him locate a key hanging under the phone, open the lockbox, and extract all the cash. He put a portion back, locked it up, and returned the key.

They ran back to Jason's room and peeled off bill after bill from their haul, counting up nearly $30,000. They stashed half the cash inside one of Jason's stereo speakers and took the rest to fuel a gluttonous shopping spree of recreational gear that most teenage males could only dream about. It included Jet Skis, a Kawasaki motorcycle, CB radios, and top-of-the-line mountain bikes. Along the way, Blake enlisted some adults as their straw purchasers for expensive items that would have made cashiers suspicious.

At the bike store, Jason was the one who pulled the cash from his jeans at the register. When a friend stopped by to make a layaway payment, Jason gave him a hundred dollars to pay the balance. This all seemed strange to the store's owner. When he asked where Jason got all that cash, he replied it was from a trust fund bequeathed to him by his grandfather. As soon as the boys left, the merchant reported them to the police.[109]

According to Jason, Blake was not done with the heist. He returned to the widow's house with some adults to steal antique guns and coins, smashing through a window to enter. Although alerted to this break-in, it took their victim weeks to figure out how much she had lost, given how her husband squirreled away his possessions. With a tip from the bike store owner, the police tracked down Jason and found the cash in his room. Besides confessing his part in the crime, Jason told the police who else had broken into his neighbor's home. Although most of the cash was returned and the sheriff auctioned off their purchases, a balance of $10,000 remained. The emotional impact of the theft on the boys' elderly victim was far worse than the financial one. She told the court, "I am scared to leave my home. When I hear a strange noise, I start to shake and feel like I want to throw up. I am on Xanax and Tagament [*sic*]." Although Blake may have been the mastermind, she felt most betrayed by her next-door neighbor and angry at Jason's parents for not doing more to supervise him.[110]

As his case wound through the juvenile court process that fall, Jason made matters worse when he drove his father's pickup to meet some friends at a downtown parking lot. They had broken out the windows of several nearby cars to steal electronic accessories and were loading them into the truck's cargo bed when a squad car headed their way, sirens screaming. Jason started to run off with his friends but decided he couldn't leave his father's truck behind. He returned to face the music. Looking back, he says, "There are no excuses for my behavior. I knew what was going on. I was trying to fit in with the wrong guys at school. It was stupid and immature."

It also convinced the juvenile authorities that he had not shown sufficient "remorse" for the next-door burglary. Now, besides paying restitution to the widow, Jason was made a ward of the Department of Corrections and ordered to serve some time at the Indiana Boys School in Plainfield, Indiana.[111] According to state records, Blake was spared that consequence and has yet to commit another crime.

In their preliminary investigation, the juvenile probation officers reported a stable environment in the Tibbs home with attentive, hardworking parents. They described their son as "caring, helpful, outgoing, quick-tempered, and sometimes impatient with his family." To start paying his restitution, his mother got him a job as a dishwasher at the restaurant she managed.

However, the investigation revealed other surface cracks that indicated deeper troubles for Jason. The C average in the first semester of his sophomore year was the most apparent. As the probation officers noted, his grades had previously been much higher. But shortly after returning to school in September, his plans to join the US Air Force were dashed when Jason learned that his eyesight was too poor to fly a jet plane. He had dreamed of one day becoming a pilot after visiting an Air Force base where his uncle's dad worked. When that was no longer possible, poor grades and reckless behavior followed.[112]

Rayna remained one of his last links to positive peers. Perhaps sensing that his life could go awry, he attempted to start dating her before his downward spiral. Jason wrote her letters that years later would take on significance vastly out of proportion with the impulsive adolescent feelings that motivated them. As Jason remembers, he and Rayna were "hanging out" during basketball season when her relationship with Matt tended to hit the skids. Rayna was annoyed with Matt, and he was irritated by her "hanging out" with Jason—perhaps as his wily girlfriend intended. Rayna told Jason, in an offhanded way, that Matt often wondered if Jason was still serious about her. Although Jason did not respond when they were together, in his letter, he wrote, "To answer Matt's question, tell him, 'Yes. I do love you. I always have and will forever.' I will love you forever because you were my first true love. I owe all the good things I am to you because you showed me that you don't always get what you want in life." At another point, he added, "I would go to almost any extreme to get back out with you. . . . Being with you Monday made me realize that I FUCKED UP when I broke up with you."

But Jason tempered his ardor with the realization that her love for Matt was stronger. In a letter he penned the next night, he wrote, "I know my chances of going back out with you are one in a million, and my luck sucks big dicks, so the only time I feel real hope is when things are not real steady between you and Matt."

As it turned out, Rayna returned to a steady state with Matt soon after she read Jason's missives. Although she gently rebuffed his advance, she still found a reason to keep the letters that proposed it. Beyond the romance, Jason may have also pursued another benefit from their companionship—that it kept him out of trouble. He wrote, "As far as me spending time with my friends, I'd rather spend time with you!"[113] Without Rayna, those friends led him in the opposite direction.

In December 1991, after Jason received his disposition (the juvenile equivalent of a sentence), he invited Rayna to his house and lifted his pants leg to show her an ankle monitor. He was on "house arrest" for a few weeks before his transport to Boys School. To that point, Jason had not shared the trouble he was in. This news, he says, made her sad. As always, Rayna did not judge him. Instead, she tried to find a bright side. She said he would be away for only a few months and was sure the time would fly by. She also promised to write.

Although Jason worried about how he'd be treated at Boys School, he says, "It was like a camp more than anything else." There were classes like the ones he took at high school, but also an elective course in auto repair, which convinced him he could pursue that trade as a career. In addition to the schoolwork, there were dances with the female delinquents at Girls School and outings like seeing the Harlem Globetrotters. "They even let us smoke," he remembers, "which was kind of weird, but they treated us like adults as long as we didn't step out of line."

He returned home by May. "My mom and dad weren't happy at all," Jason remembers. "They were disappointed in me but tried to take everything in stride. Once the punishment was doled out, they wanted me to focus on my future, which included getting a job to pay them back for the restitution."

Although Jason returned to LPHS, things there had irreparably changed. Without the goal of being a pilot, he lost the motivation to grind away at his studies. Besides, he says, the stint at Boys School, "gave me a reputation. The guys I hung out with didn't help my reputation either. I wasn't in that crowd of achievers."

Rayna was one old friend who kept in touch. True to her word, she had written him a few letters while he was away. They steered away from his predicament and focused instead on updates in her life, especially all the fun she had in Orlando at the Citrus Parade. When he was back in school, if they passed each other in the hall, they would stop to chat for a few minutes. That's when Jason dropped the next big bombshell. "I told her, 'I'm over all of this,'" he remembers. After school was over that summer, he wasn't coming back in the fall.

"That's a big decision," Rayna replied. "Make sure you think about it some more, so if you do quit, it's something you really want to do."

Back home, Jason's decision did not meet many objections from his parents. His father admitted to the probation officer that he hated school when he was a teen and had dropped out.[114] Ray Allen Tibbs felt it was more important to develop a trade, much like he did at the aerospace plant. Good jobs were always available in La Porte if you knew how to do something. Jason's mother was more disappointed. Although Rachel's post–high school education never rose above an associate's degree, her intelligence helped her climb the ladder at every job. She often worked her way up to managerial positions. She was also an avid reader, a habit she passed on to her son, and she expected him to do well in college. But Rachel wouldn't fight Jason about staying in school if his heart wasn't in it. Instead, she hoped he would find work that paved the way to a career.

For Jason, that meant bouncing around various restaurant jobs until he was eighteen and old enough to enter auto repair courses in technical school. In the meantime, he had already started to work on friends' vehicles. Some people paid him what they could afford. Others let him borrow the cars he fixed. He gave Rayna a freebie when she brought him her LTD after tutoring in the early spring of 1993. She pulled up next to his driveway, and he got under the hood to disconnect the custom sounds for her car's alarm and horn. Bennie couldn't figure out how, but Jason needed only a few minutes to switch wires back to the OEM horn. As he leaned against the LTD, an object inside his pocket dug into his hip. He pulled out a gaudy ring that a friend had given him as payment for working on his car. It caught Rayna's eye. Jason let her keep it, and she eventually hung it from her rearview mirror.

Usually, when Rayna stopped by, they would go to the enclosed back porch of the Tibbses' house. For Jason, it had become his own living room. During Rayna's visits, which usually lasted under an hour, they would idly chat while watching TV or as Jason clacked through the screen of a video game.

Among their topics of conversation was Jason's new passion, a game called Fox Hunt. Players paired up in vehicles with CB radios and gathered at the Pineapple, a bank's downtown parking lot beneath a large sign with the tropical fruit. The Fox team would be given twenty minutes to park in a place visible from a public street. Hunters then searched for them while using their CBs to ask the Fox team questions about the hiding spot. The quarry's signal on the CB grew stronger as they got closer. The first team to find them would get to hide for the next game. On some evenings, the game could extend into the early morning hours. Players would then decamp to a truck stop and spend another hour or two dissecting that night's hunts while drinking coffee and eating pie. It all sounded like fun to Rayna, and at one point, after leaving Jason, she asked Bennie if she could borrow his car one night to play since he had a CB.

Rayna never tried to hide the visits with Jason from Matt, although she knew they annoyed him. One time, when she wasn't tutoring, she had Matt drive to Jason's house. Jason remembers they all had a playful snowball fight. A coworker later said that Rayna saw Jason as a way "to keep Matt honest,"[115] but by then, Jason says, any romantic interest between the two "was well and over with." He had moved on to dating other girls, with the fringe benefit of sex, which he was uncomfortable having with Rayna.

As far as Jason was concerned, Rayna was happy with Matt. But the turbulence returned to their relationship at the start of spring in 1993. Basketball season was over, but Rayna felt her boyfriend was still not showing her enough attention. In a letter he wrote to win back her affection, Matt promised Rayna he would do "anything, ANYTHING," to "keep" her. This included cutting his part-time job to two days a week. It was a gesture that must have made a difference for Rayna.[116] Friends who had heard she was about to split with Matt would soon learn they were closer than ever.[117] This time around, the boyfriend would take the initiative in planning the dates. He talked of them having dinner at Dairy Queen and then seeing a movie with him footing the bill for both. He says, "It was supposed to be kind of a restart."[118]

But there was one disturbing quirk to their romance that had suddenly returned. It had been a problem when they first dated seriously in high school. Although there were times when Rayna wanted to be sexually intimate, Matt, like Jason, was not ready for intercourse with her. Knowing the distress she experienced during the abortion, he didn't want to be responsible for putting her through that again. While they still did plenty of petting and kissing, that intimacy could lead to a response in Rayna that terrified both of them. "We would park somewhere dark to make out as teenagers do," Matt remembers, "when suddenly it was like a switch would flip in her brain, and she would push me away and start bawling for me to leave her alone. I realized, 'She's thinking I'm Ray trying to get at her again.' Sometimes, she would try to get out of the car, even if we were parked in the middle of nowhere. Eventually, I figured out a way to calm her down. It was never easy, but if I held her as tight as I could and kept talking in her ear, she would come out of it. It might have only been five minutes, but it felt like an hour, and it happened multiple times."

Although the term post-traumatic stress disorder (PTSD) had yet to come into vogue, looking back, Matt now sees her behavior at the time as a symptom of the syndrome. One incident occurred in the hallway before the first-period band class. Matt pulled Rayna into a stairwell, hoping she'd get through the episode before class started, but an assistant principal found them first. After Rayna regained her senses, they followed him into his office, and Matt explained what had happened. "They called her parents, and she was supposed to get counseling," Matt says, "but I don't know if that ever happened."[119]

By March 1993, Rayna had not had a panic attack for several months, but then, Matt says, they were making out while sitting together on a swing when it started again, and she shoved him away from her. After she calmed down, Matt asked if Ray was doing something to her, but she didn't want to talk about it. The next time they were together, Rayna was more open. The week before, she had been babysitting for her niece Adrienne, she said, when

Ray put his hands under her blouse and groped her breasts. "He attempted to do more with her," Matt says, "but she told him to stop, and he did."

While hearing about the incident with Ray was deeply disturbing for Matt—especially since it had prompted a return of her PTSD symptoms—Rayna was still shielding her boyfriend, perhaps fearful that the whole truth would chase him away. She had a more traumatic story to tell her best friend, Lisa Dyer,[120] and then Jason the next time she visited after tutoring. He was playing a video game while she sat on his couch. "She seemed down," Jason remembers. "Withdrawn and different. I asked her, 'What's wrong?' and she said, 'It's happening again. Ray has been raping me again.'"

Jason was shocked and outraged that McCarty thought he could get away with assaulting Rayna so soon after his suspended sentence. But this time, Tibbs had a direct line to law enforcement—his mother. Rachel worked at the county's juvenile justice center and interacted daily with the sheriff's deputies. "Let me go tell my mom," Jason said, but Rayna stopped him. She didn't want to get her involved.

"You have to do something," he told her, and she replied, "I'm working on it."

This time, Rayna did have an eyewitness to Ray's abuse—his six-year-old daughter, Adrienne. She reported the incident to Brenda Pegg, a neighbor who occasionally looked after the little girl. According to Pegg, Adrienne told her, "One time she saw Aunt Rayna had come out of the bathroom with a sheet wrapped around her. . . . Her daddy was there and said to [Adrienne], get [your] f'n ass back to bed."[121]

Meanwhile, a new family crisis would erupt for Rayna, touching off a catastrophic confrontation with her big sister. A few days after she told Jason about Ray's assault, she learned of another unwanted pregnancy. Jennifer McCleland was not just Rayna's first cousin but also one of her best friends. On Saturday, March 13, the two sixteen-year-olds met privately to discuss the steps involved in getting an abortion. Jenni did not want her father and stepmother to know she was pregnant because they disliked her boyfriend. While Jenni's birth mother had offered to pay for the procedure, they needed to have it done in Michigan, where parental consent was not required. As Rayna would later confide to a teacher, talk of abortion brought back all the bitter memories of what she went through at thirteen and the lack of support she received from her family. Rayna would not abandon her cousin as her parents and sister had done to her, and she promised to accompany Jenni to the clinic. While she felt uneasy about making the hour-long trip in the LTD without telling her parents, she was sure that Jason would drive them in his car.[122]

But Rayna never did approach Jason for his help. Instead, she took Lori into her confidence the next day and asked her to help. Rayna then got shoved aside when her big sister insisted on making all the arrangements. But nothing bothered her more about the big sister's intervention than Lori's decision to tell Ray what they were doing. He, in turn, called Bennie. McCarty claimed that his molestation sentence required him to share that information with his father-in-law so no one would suspect him of impregnating another teen. However, Ray had once told a therapist about his visceral aversion to abortions, and he may have been trying to stop Jenni from having one. Bennie did not intervene by calling her parents, but when Rayna told him she might miss school the following Monday, he told her he knew why. In a rage, Rayna dashed off a letter to Matt.

> Remind me never to trust anyone. I'll remind you. If you can't trust the people close to you, who can you trust? My older sister, who I used to look up to and trusted with all my heart and soul, the sister to who I found it in my heart to forgive, is a two-faced bitch. She promised me so many things, but she's never been there when I needed her the most. I would have died for my older sister, I loved her that much. She was my best friend. So much for all of that shit. Jenni and I both trusted her. I guess I should have believed my instincts. She's been telling my dad everything when she knew that Jenni didn't want anyone in the family to know. She was specifically asked not to say anything to Ray, but she told him, too. . . . I guess Lori is gonna drive up there, so I don't know if I want to go or not. I can't believe her. . . . I just don't understand why she has to backstab everybody all the time. Well, I'd better go finish crying now. I'm sure that my eyes will be nice and puffy tomorrow.[123]

But Rayna did not just write a letter to Matt. She also sent one off to Lori, igniting what would become known as "the fight." After reading the letter, Lori called her sister and started yelling at her about what she had written. According to Lori, Rayna charged she had "ratted [her] out" when she told

Ray and Bennie about the plans for Jenni's abortion.[124] But the letter contained another charge, according to one friend—that Ray was "molesting" her again.[125]

Further enflamed by something Rayna said over the phone, Lori hung up and drove to the Risons' house to confront Rayna face-to-face. The dispute spilled onto the front lawn, and their screaming prompted one neighbor to call the police. Beyond the raised voices, there was physical contact, too, as Lori confessed to a good friend, Pat Walters. "Lori said that she was yelling at Rayna, and all Rayna said was, 'You're right. You're right. You're right.' Lori said that this made her even more mad, and [she] slapped Rayna."[126]

The next day, Rayna walked into her second-period class "visibly upset and crying," according to another student. When asked what was wrong, she replied, "Things better get better at home."[127]

In a call to Jason—who already knew that Ray was raping her—Rayna had more to say. She had a plan and wanted him to meet her after school one day with Matt and her best friend, Lisa. Jason was racing out the door and expected her to call back, but she never did, so he didn't learn what she intended to do.

Meanwhile, due to something Rayna said during the fight, Lori made her own plans. "Rayna was starting her shit again," she told her friend, Gayla Moreau. "After what she put us through the past three years, we're not going to let her do it again.'"[128]

DARKNESS BEHIND THE BRIGHT AMBITION

La Porte—a city and county of contrasts: from gritty urban industrial to bucolic lakes and forest preserves, from celebrity ranches to double-wide trailers and dilapidated shacks. Photo: LAPORTECOUNTY.LIFE

Jason Tibbs and Rayna Rison in middle school (1988). A friend tried to set them up. Jason remembers, "She was just so easy to talk to." Photo: Paul F. Boston Middle School, 1987–1988 *Bostonian*

Matt Elser, another sixth grader, would become Rayna's steady boyfriend. Their mutual interest in music became their strongest bond. Photo: Boston Middle School, 1987–1988 *Bostonian*

Nine years older, with a striking resemblance to Rayna, Lori was her "cool" but "bossy" big sister, who introduced her to cigarettes and wine coolers. Photo: La Porte High School, *El Pe*, 1985

Ray McCarty met Lori soon after he graduated from high school, when she was in her senior year. Rayna thought he was cute, but Jason sensed "a menace about him" when they met. Photo: South Central high school, *Orbit 22*, 1984

The molestation began at this two-flat house across the street from Ray's foundry job. Rayna spent afternoons and weekend nights babysitting the McCartys' first child. Photo: La Porte County Assessor Property Report

LOST AND FOUND

RAYNA RISON

FAMILY
- Bennie, Karen (parents)
- Lori, Wendy (sisters)

FRIENDS
- Matt Elser (boyfriend)
- Lisa Dyer
- Jenni McCleland (cousin)

EMPLOYER, COWORKER*
- Dr. Gerald Wagner
- Cheryl VanSchoyck

FBI
- Elvin "Bill" Keith*

CITY OF LA PORTE POLICE DEPARTMENT*
- Chief Gene Samuelson
- Corporal Larry Mitchell
- Detectives John Miller (Chief), Bob Schoff, Harold Hahn

JASON TIBBS

FAMILY
- Rachel (mother)

FRIENDS*
- Vic Montorsi
- James Amor
- Angie Vogel
- Misty Smith, Jamie Swisher (sisters); Peggy Johnson (their mother)
- Chad Green
- Josh Jordan
- Scott Combs

LA PORTE COUNTY SHERIFF'S DEPARTMENT*
- Sergeant Joe Pavolka
- Patrolman Jim Jackson

LORI AND RAY McCARTY

FAMILY
- Adrienne (daughter)
- Hunter (son)
- Carolyn, Gerald (Ray's parents)

FRIENDS, ACQUAINTANCES
- Charlie Allen, Cindy Brewer
- Leah Pepple*
- Gayla (Holt) Moreau
- Martin Holt (Gayla's ex-husband)
- Gary Marshall (Gayla's son)
- Garry, Lois Bucher
- Brenda Pegg
- Denise Stout*

WITNESSES*
- James McWhirter*
- Lorn "Brent" Glassman
- Beth York; sons Kyle, Austin
- Jane Lindborg
- Richard Lancaster

*INTRODUCED IN THIS CHAPTER

LOST AND FOUND

FOG

From some angles, Dr. Gerald Wagner's animal hospital, with its sloping brown roof and tan brick facade, appeared to be a quaint, lonely outpost on Pine Lake Avenue. A relatively wide semicircular driveway set it back from the road, and on one side of the lot, there was nearly an acre of grass and trees. Usually, during the week, receptionist Cheryl VanSchoyck was the last to leave after she wrapped up the accounting books for the day. But on March 26, she told the veterinarian she wasn't feeling well. Instead of waiting for Rayna to finish sweeping the lobby, she was outside a few minutes before or after the hospital's 6:00 P.M. closing time. It would then be up to the kennel girl to turn out the lights, which Cheryl knew Rayna didn't like to do. Even on the busy street, she hated being alone in the hospital, especially after dark.[1]

Affectionately known as "Weenie,"[2] magpie Rayna made herself an open book to her coworkers at the animal hospital. They were all aware of each up and down in the relationship with her boyfriend, Matt. They knew she was still close to a boy named Jason, a middle-school heartthrob, who hovered in the distance. They also became acquainted with her niece and nephew. She'd bring them in to play with the puppies and kittens in the kennel while she cleaned up and then take them home to babysit. Sometimes, she stayed late to play with the animals on her own but was careful to sign out first so she wouldn't be paid for that time.

The staff knew intimate things about Rayna other than her love life. As she revealed more than once, she had been raped a few years back by a "friend of the family." Even worse, her parents and sisters blamed her for the incident.[3] This disclosure made most of the adults at Pine Lake even more protective of their Weenie. It also explained why she feared the Mexican immigrants in rental houses down the street who made passes at her or the drunks who stumbled outside from the strip club next door.[4]

Dr. Wagner may have been the one person at the hospital who was not a Weenie fan. With a shock of dark hair flopping over his forehead and a rubbery ear-to-ear smile, he bore a passing resemblance to Will Rogers. Like the vaudeville comedian, he also had his own brand of dry humor, which he dispensed over the backs of the pets he examined. Still, the veterinarian did not find Rayna amusing, and the feeling was mutual. He complained that she never seemed to finish her chores. Also, he did not like seeing her boyfriend—Matt—doing his homework on the desk in the kennel. The one time he got a look at Jason, he scolded Rayna for hanging around such "trash." To Wagner's surprise, the usually timid teen told him she was offended by the comment and did not speak to him the rest of the day.[5] According to her mother, Rayna said they shouted at each other first.[6] While Weenie's rebuke to the big boss may have surprised some of her coworkers, the receptionist would have expected it. The teenager often told Cheryl that Jason made her feel safe.[7]

As one of the last people to see Rayna alive, Cheryl would later become an essential witness for the investigators. The precise time she left the Pine Lake Animal Hospital on March 26 planted the first stake in the timeline that led to the teenager's death. She figured Rayna had only five more minutes of sweeping before she followed her out the door and would have been scrupulous about leaving no sooner than six.

Weenie was also anxious to go. She knew Matt was waiting back home to take her on their "restart" date—Dairy Queen Grill for dinner and then the Disney movie *Homeward Bound, the Incredible Journey*, a live action film featuring two dogs and a cat on a cross-country trek to be reunited with their owners. It was ideal fare for the pet-loving Rayna.[8]

Even after Cheryl got in her car, there was no quick escape from the animal hospital parking lot. Thick fog was rolling off the lake, and the traffic backed up on Pine Lake Avenue's poorly lit two lanes. As she waited for someone to let her in, Cheryl saw a client's car near the other entrance to the parking lot. If it turned in and they were there to pick up a pet, she'd have to go back to process their check—something Rayna couldn't do. But the car did not turn. Cheryl could hurry home, and Rayna was left on her own.[9]

Matt patiently waited for Rayna back at the Risons' house, all dressed and ready to go. He had been there earlier when he drove Rayna home after school. He then left for track practice. After it was over, he changed his clothes in the gym rather than return to his house, twenty minutes away. By 5:15, he was in the Risons' living room with an unexpected companion. Usually by that time, Karen would have been secluded in the kitchen, but she had been sick all day and stretched out on the living room couch. As they watched TV, she kept half an eye on her two-year-old grandson, Hunter, while he played with his toys.[10]

The fog did not dampen the rest of the Rison family's activities. Earlier in the evening, Lori had taken little sister Wendy and her boyfriend to a mall in Michigan City thirty minutes away. Her six-year-old daughter, Adrienne, went along for the ride. When they returned to the Rison house shortly after Matt arrived, Lori grabbed some slices of reheated pizza out of the microwave, scooped up Hunter, and then rushed home, she said, because Ray was waiting with a full meal he had cooked for the family. Bennie showed up shortly after Lori left. Wendy soon enlisted him to take her and her boyfriend to the movie theater a few miles away, assuring him that his parents would do the pickup.[11]

Matt became increasingly concerned about Rayna as he watched the Risons bustle in, out, and around the house. It was not unusual for her to work late, but when it got to 6:30, he decided to call the hospital's private line. There was no answer. At first, he figured she didn't answer the phone because she was on the way home. She had still not arrived when Bennie and the kids left for the movie theater.

After a few minutes passed, Matt decided to check for himself. The parking lot was empty when he arrived at the animal hospital. He got out of his car to check the clinic's side door. It was locked. From the corner of his eye, he could see traffic snaking along Pine Lake Avenue and glimpsed red brake lights, like the ones on Rayna's LTD, headed up the viaduct bridge toward the Risons' house. Matt got into his car, figuring she would be home soon.

Matt returned to the Risons', but Rayna had yet to arrive. Now, her parents started to show more concern. This wasn't like her at all. Whenever her plans changed, she would call to let them know, even if she made a brief stop to see a friend, like she did when she saw Jason after tutoring. Matt next called him, but Jason wasn't home. Matt got in his car and headed downtown to start a more frantic search. He went first to the DQ, where they were going to eat. He saw Vic Montorsi working behind the counter, a friend he had in common with Jason. Vic had not seen Rayna or Jason that night but told Matt he'd get into his pickup during his break and try to track down Jason with the CB. Matt next drove down Pine Lake to Hot 'n Now, the hamburger stand where Rayna worked on the weekends. Again, no one had spotted either Rayna or Jason that night.

He completed his search on the other side of town, closer to the Rison home, where the cinema, Quick's bowling alley, and the Maple Lane Mall shared adjoining parking lots. Matt's circuit of teen hangouts encompassed only a few square miles, but on a typical Friday night in La Porte, traffic slowed to a crawl, adding to his frustration. Although Rayna bowled in a league at Quick's, there was little chance she'd be there, but Matt took a stab, to no avail.

He called on pay phones between his various stops to check back with the Risons. There was still no news when he returned to their home after eight o'clock. Her parents believed there must have been a miscommunication about the time or day of the date.[12] In her more understated way, Karen got on the phone to call around, dialing Lori first. She was surprised when Ray answered the phone, a little out of breath. He told her he had not seen Rayna and that Lori was out shopping at the grocery store.[13] The Risons and Matt next called Rayna's friends—all were stunned to learn she was missing.[14] Around nine o'clock, Bennie reached Dr. Wagner at his home. As far as he knew, Rayna left work shortly after closing time. He had just returned from the hospital, where he had put his son's dog in the kennel and had seen nothing amiss.[15]

When all the calls proved fruitless, Bennie grew more anxious. Finally, he drove to the La Porte City Police Department a few blocks away. At

10:30 P.M., the dispatch officer took his missing person report. "She always let the family know where she was going or where she was at if she wasn't coming home," he told the officer. "Today, she didn't." When asked if there had been any "family problems," Bennie replied that there were none. If she had run away for some reason, he was "uncertain" why she hadn't contacted them by now. On the Missing Person form, it asked for him to describe her car, which he knew intimately from the front to rear bumpers. He wrote: "Tan 1984 LTD, four doors," and added, "cracked windshield."[16]

CROC

For Jason, March 26 drifted along like most unmoored days in his dropout year. A time would come when seemingly inconsequential events that evening would take on the utmost importance, but Jason's activities on that Friday night were nothing out of the ordinary. They started with a plot to introduce his good friend James Amor to a cute sixteen-year-old named Misty Smith, who lived in a trailer park on the other side of La Porte. Another one of Jason's friends, Angie Vogel, was Misty's neighbor. Over the phone, she and Jason hatched a scheme where he would pretend to help Misty's younger sister, Jamie Swisher, with her homework while James got to know Misty better. Jason had tutored Angie in the past, and her mother would attest to his proficiency at math if the neighbor girls' mother had misgivings about the arrangement.

There was only one hitch in Jason's plans. He had not filled up his father's pickup the last time he drove it, and now his parents wouldn't allow him to take it out again. Stranded at his house without a vehicle, he phoned Angie, who had become a regular in the Fox Hunt games. She used her CB to find Jason's erstwhile friend, Chad Green, who was a cousin by marriage. Unlike Jason, Green had his own car and did not have to borrow one from his parents. Chad was already riding around with James in his gray Ford Tempo. They drove to Jason's house, where they all hung out for an hour or so and then headed to the trailer park. Along the way, they passed the Pine Lake Animal Hospital. Jason figured it was around 5:40 P.M. He could see the lights on in the lobby and Rayna's LTD in the parking lot next to another car. "I thought it was odd that she was working so late," he remembers, but nothing else seemed unusual.

When the boys arrived at the Swisher trailer around six, the girls' mother was not yet home from work, but Angie was there, ready for a sleepover. Meanwhile, Chad took off. Not much homework was getting done when Peggy Johnson pulled in shortly after six o'clock. Instead, her daughters were doing flips and cartwheels in the front yard while a boy she didn't know stood watching. Peggy quickly sent James packing but let Jason stay when Jamie insisted he was really there to help her and Angie with their math. James used Angie's CB to call Chad, who was riding around with Jason's best friend, Josh Jordan. They soon arrived at the trailer park to pick up Amor.

Jason remembers that over the next few hours, there was probably more goofing off than tutoring, but by nine o'clock, he was ready to leave and join the nightly game of Fox Hunt. He caught a ride downtown with Angie's older brother, Jeff, and their cousin.

As they drove, Jason could see the fog had started to lift, but enough remained to make that night's game more of a challenge—especially in less populated areas. For Jason, Fox Hunt had introduced him to a new set of older friends—most in their twenties and thirties—and could provide a harmless, inexpensive diversion. He was likelier to know players by their CB handles than by their given names. His handle was Crocodile, but he was also known as Croc.

When Jason arrived at the Pineapple, he hopped into an older four-wheel-drive truck owned by Scott Combs, one of his new Fox Hunt friends. Combs told him that he heard over the CB that Kid Wicked—Vic Montorsi—was trying to reach him, but he didn't know why. Jason tried to get Kid Wicked on the CB, but Vic was already back at work behind the counter at Dairy Queen. Thinking it was nothing serious, Jason immersed himself in that night's Fox Hunt, which went on for several games. Friday nights tended to be the most popular, and couples could come from South Bend or southwest Michigan to play. Jason figures there must have been at least ten teams because the game lasted more than three hours.

After it was over, he met back up with James Amor. Because it was so late, no group headed out for a truck stop. Instead, they all just broke up and went their separate ways. Jason and James still needed a ride. A CB friend suggested they first go to his place to hang out. Once there, they threw darts and watched TV for another two hours. The friend's roommate drove them home between three and four in the morning.

Back in his room, Jason fell into a deep sleep on his expansive waterbed, curled up in one corner while James slept on the other. Only a few hours later—what seemed like moments after he shut his eyes—Jason's mother knocked on his door. She said a few kids from the high school band were there looking for Rayna because she hadn't come home on Friday night. His mind still bleary, Jason dismissed the urgency of their visit. "I figured maybe she was trying to ditch Matt," he remembers. "I just rolled over and went back to sleep."

But after another few hours, his mother knocked again, this time much louder. "I could hear that there was some urgency in her voice," Jason says. "I popped out of bed and asked, 'What is going on?' And she said, 'Rayna is missing, and they can't find her. You need to get up.'"

Jason woke James, and they stepped outside onto the porch, where they saw a group of high schoolers milling around the front lawn. He recognized several from the marching band. Some carried stacks of *Missing* posters with Rayna's yearbook portrait on them. As Jason learned later, Bennie printed them at the packaging company where he worked and passed them out earlier that morning to band members and their families at LPHS.

Matt arrived with Wendy Rison in his car. After leaving the high school parking lot, the two had conducted another fruitless search around one side of Pine Lake. Matt hardly slept the night before and spent the day in a haze, at one point rear-ending a car on Pine Lake Avenue. When he heard about Rayna, the other driver, who happened to be a classmate, let him go, and they settled up for the minor damage later.

After Jason emerged from his house, Matt joined him and Rayna's best friend, Lisa Dyer, on the porch. Lisa immediately gave Jason the third degree. "She can be very headstrong," Jason says, "and she got right into it with me about where I was on Friday night. I just told her I was out with my friends last night and that James was with me for most of it. Then James said, 'Yeah. He was with us.'"

But Jason didn't feel much need to defend himself. His primary concern was finding Rayna. He told Matt and Lisa he would get his Fox Hunt crew to help. With their CB radios, they could organize and monitor their search more efficiently with their vehicles. But even as he stood on the porch, Jason had little hope they would find Rayna alive. From the grim looks on their faces, he could see that Matt and Lisa had the same fear. For most of Rayna's friends, the thought that any danger could come to the sunny young woman was as unexpected as a lightning strike. But for her closest friends, Rayna's peril was not so random, nor was the person who probably perpetrated it.

THE MISSING PERSON

From the start, the City of La Porte's police commanders saw that a sixteen-year-old's sudden disappearance from their streets would bring unprecedented attention to their force. Early on Saturday, they marshaled all possible internal and external resources to assist in the search and bring it to a quick conclusion—whether joyous or tragic. They summoned patrolmen and even undercover cops to help detectives and expand their canvass of Rayna's friends, family, and potential witnesses. Because Rayna was missing and could be the victim of a kidnapping—a federal crime—La Porte also called in the local office of the FBI to further supplement their interviewers with highly trained and experienced special agents. Meanwhile, state police helicopters buzzed the sky, and county sheriff's officers cruised rural roads. All looked for a five-foot, five-inch teenager with a full head of frizzy light brown hair, wearing blue jeans and an oversized high school letterman jacket with the name Matt Elser on the back. They also had the description and license plate of her tan 1984 LTD.[17]

For many of the first interviews, the city police commanders dispatched Corporal Larry Mitchell, a big, imposing officer with a barrel chest and full black mustache. He had been on the force for ten years and would soon be made a captain. Mitchell was on the scene at 10:00 A.M. when Bennie Rison and the marching band's music director assembled nearly one-hundred people in the school's parking lot. Most of the students who turned out had played with Rayna in the marching band or concert band, and many of their parents showed up too. Bennie passed out the *Missing* posters hot off the press. He spread a county map over the hood of a car and used it to organize search parties. Still, as the police reported, he periodically became emotionally overwhelmed—tearfully grateful about the turnout and visibly worried about his daughter. Officers had to assist "in calming down Mr. Rison when required."[18]

The gathering also allowed Corporal Mitchell to ask for the names of friends the police should contact. But in following up on some of those leads, officers soon learned that there was an unexpected dynamic in the victim's relationship with her family. The most explosive revelations would come from Matt—before Rayna had been missing twenty-four hours. Early Saturday morning, he happened to be in the animal hospital when an LPPD officer dropped by to ask Rayna's coworkers some quick questions. Even then, the teen felt the need to disclose information about Rayna's cousin, Jenni, and her upcoming abortion. (He thought he was Rayna's only friend who knew but wasn't aware it had already happened.) The officer asked him to go to the police station later to sit with him and Corporal Mitchell for a more extensive interview.[19]

Matt brought along his mother, but the fireworks began after the officers asked her to leave the room so they could discuss sexual matters with her son in more graphic detail. While Matt said he was "intimate" with Rayna, he had not "had sex" with her. Mitchell wrote in his report that when asked if Rayna had any problems the police should know about, Matt "brought up the 1988 incident in which Rayna was a victim of child molestation." But then Matt went on with more disturbing information: "He added that since [an] incident approximately one month ago, Rayna was bothered by Ray McCarty (her brother-in-law and the man who molested her in 1988). McCarty reportedly put his hand up her shirt during this incident. This upset Rayna for several days after the incident."[20]

While the police tried to reach out to more of Rayna's family and friends, volunteer search parties—including Jason's Fox Hunt friends—fanned out across the city and its rural outskirts. Jason figured the most logical place to look was the vast wilderness area known to locals as the Kingsbury Ordinance Plant, or KOP (kay-oh-pee). During World War II, the federal government set aside some 13,000 acres of plains and forested hills in the southeast corner of La Porte County to manufacture missiles and other explosive devices. Most of the area was abandoned after the Korean War, and later, small portions were carved out for industrial development. The rest of the preserve was deemed the Kingsbury Fish & Wildlife Area, but much of it looked like a strange postapocalyptic park. While there were streams and woods for hunting and fishing, there were also grassy expanses with abandoned huts of corrugated metal, cement bunkers overgrown with grass, and piles of rubble.[21] During more carefree times, Jason and his buddies would use their four-wheel drives to tear across the KOP fields or summit the bunker mounds.

They were not looking for thrills that Saturday afternoon, but it didn't take long for them to see the futility of their mission. The hiding places for a body among the abandoned structures appeared endless. As they pulled over to search an empty bunker, a KOP security officer drove up to ask what they were doing. Even after they told him why they were there, he would later report to the police that he found their "activity" to be "very suspicious." He asked for their names but came away with a bunch of CB handles instead, which he also provided in his report.[22]

If KOP looked like a haystack in the proverbial search for the needle, finding Rayna somewhere in the county with all its forests, lakes, and untilled fields seemed exponentially more difficult. But before Saturday was over, that task was significantly cut down in size. La Porte County patrolmen had identified the missing teen's car in a rural area nine miles northeast of the animal hospital.

The police were brought to the scene by twenty-year-old Lorn "Brent" Glassman. Although his father was the one who reported the vehicle to the police on Saturday, his son spotted the car first the night before. He nearly plowed into it, driving home in the Friday fog from dinner downtown— sometime between seven and seven thirty. His passenger remembered that the big tan LTD practically sat in the center of County Road North 200 East—a narrow strip of pothole-ridden asphalt, barely wide enough for two cars, that ran north and south. The Glassman family lived in a trailer one hundred yards from the abandoned vehicle, just below East 600 North, an equally narrow dirt road that ran east and west.

The LTD had the hood up, seemingly on the verge of getting fixed or towed, so Brent was surprised to see it still there on Saturday afternoon. When he walked down the road to get the license plate so his father could report the car to the police, he noticed the driver's window was halfway open. Inside, he saw a vinyl purse with its contents—lipstick, chewing gum, hairpins—spilling across the front passenger seat.[23]

It was not until ten thirty on Saturday night that a La Porte County patrolman arrived to secure the car and the scene for further investigation. On his way, after checking the license plate number with La Porte City police, the dispatcher informed him that the vehicle belonged to the missing girl. As the patrolman drove up North 200 East he saw a large sedan with the hood up and the tiny bulb behind the engine still illuminated. Across the road from the car was a dark sea of farmers' fields, broken only by the lights from the Glassman's trailer. Dense woods loomed over the LTD from the other side of the road. He parked his squad car several yards away and approached on foot. Shining his flashlight through the half-open driver's window, he could see the keys in the ignition, the purse's contents scattered on the passenger seat, and in the back, a black sweatshirt with an orange thunderbolt and red letters spelling "Hot 'n Now." Another county officer soon joined him. The two opened the trunk and found nothing inside. The first patrolman on the scene returned to his cruiser to let the dispatcher know he found Rayna's car but saw no sign of her. He requested a call to the City of La Porte police so their detectives could join him.

A third county patrolman arrived, and they all started taking pictures. On the road nearby, they saw the remains of a gold hair barrette that had been shattered by a passing vehicle. Closer to the car, they spotted two footprints in the muddy shoulder of the road, one larger than the other, and stuck two little evidence flags in the soil to mark them.[24]

A City of La Porte police car soon joined them with the portly chief of detectives, John Miller, and Bob Schoff, one of his crew and a twenty-year veteran on the city's force. In previous years, Miller ran training seminars for all regional law enforcement officers about "crime scene protocol" and evidence collection.[25] The county patrolmen displayed the fruits of Miller's instruction, carefully roping off the area and not touching or otherwise tampering with the car, its contents, or the surroundings. The photos they took of the LTD before it was towed to the city police department would ultimately reveal insights into the crime that were not immediately apparent. Meanwhile, Schoff and another LPPD detective followed up on the flags stuck in the mud by making plaster casts of the footprints—evidence the detectives believed would lead them to their culprits.[26]

But finding the car was just the start of the weekend's revelations. Brent Glassman and his friend were not the only ones to see the LTD on Friday night. Elizabeth "Beth" York and her two sons lived around the corner from the Glassmans' trailer and also had a near-collision with Rayna's car on North 200 East Still, her tip had additional details that were even more compelling for the detectives.

The Yorks were returning from a wrestling meet in South Bend. Beth forgot that the venue was not on central time like La Porte, but eastern time like most of Indiana. As a result, the Yorks missed the event. The low visibility on the way home only added to her aggravation. Driving north on North 200 East, Beth saw the LTD's headlights through the swirling fog and pulled more to the right of the narrow road. But behind the car was a pickup, and she had to swerve at the last second to avoid hitting the truck's open driver-side door. As she passed, she also glimpsed two men—one near the front of the LTD and one between the vehicles. The near swipe with the truck door was the sort of close call that drivers quickly file away since no damage was done.

The following morning, the fog lifted. Beth could have looked across the field through the back windows of her house and still seen the LTD, but she didn't notice it again until she went on some errands in the afternoon. Then, later that night, squad cars descended on the intersection with lights flashing and sirens wailing. Beth and her husband walked a few yards around the corner to see what the commotion was about. Now, the car with the hood up was surrounded by yellow crime scene tape and had become the focus of multiple police cameras. She saw another civilian huddling with officers—a distraught balding man in his fifties, who she later learned was the missing girl's father. But the officers' attention soon turned to Beth when she casually mentioned her encounter with the car and the pickup on Friday night. The detectives did an initial interview and then implored her to file a statement at the City of La Porte police station the next day.

Over several interviews and much reflection on what they saw in the blinks of their eyes, Beth and her sons would add three vital elements to the investigation. The first one was another stake in the timeline. Beth could establish—within a quarter-hour span—when they passed the two vehicles. She was confident about the time because her boys snapped on the TV when they got home. One of their favorite programs, *Married ... with Children*, still had several minutes to go before it finished at seven o'clock. Now, the police did not just have Rayna's car. They could determine that her separation from it came less than an hour after she reportedly left work.

The second element the family contributed was the second vehicle—but all three Yorks differed in their description. Beth thought she saw a smaller-sized pickup like her husband's Ford Ranger. At first, she was unsure of the color but later said it was "blue or black with a wide silver stripe down the side."[27] Fourteen-year-old Kyle, who was in the back seat, could only describe the truck's color as "dark." However, unlike his mother, he believed it had a camper-type cap behind the cab. In the passenger seat next to his mom, twelve-year-old Austin thought he saw a "black or dark green" van—although he later admitted a cap could have made him mistake the pickup for a van.[28]

The Yorks' third and most striking contribution involved the people they saw around the vehicles. Eventually, Beth was confident that she saw a man of medium build with thick black hair standing in front of the LTD as though he was looking under the hood. While she could not describe his clothes in detail, she got a general impression that he was a "hunter" and, as she told one officer, "a real outdoorsman." She had no impression of the other man, whom she remembered standing on the side of the road between the vehicles. Austin thought he was wearing a "hat," but none of the Yorks felt confident they could pick out either individual in a lineup.[29]

It was entirely possible that the truck had stopped to help a driver—with her car's hood up—in apparent distress. But if the two men were Good Samaritans, they would have followed up by taking Rayna home and calling for a tow or the police. Instead, everything about the Yorks' encounter sounded suspicious to the detectives. Only a day later, they went public with what they thought they had learned from the family. The headline in *The South Bend Tribune* read: "2 men reportedly seen near teenager's car." Detective Captain Miller told reporters about a "dark pickup" and "two white men" who were seen near Rayna's car but did not divulge the names of his witnesses. He also added, "There were no signs of a struggle."[30]

In fact, Miller had another report about a pickup possibly associated with Rayna's abduction, which he did not publicize, even though the witness could not have been considered more reliable. But the report was so much at odds with everything else the detectives learned it was not made public and would continue to confound them for the rest of their investigation.

The witness was Sergeant Joseph Pavolka, a patrolman in the La Porte County Sheriff's Department for sixteen years. On Friday at 9:50 P.M., he was headed to work at the foot of the gravel drive on County Road North 150 East that led to his house a few hundred yards away. Before he could turn onto the cross street, East 600 North, two vehicles approached from his right at 25 to 30 miles per hour. He described the first as a "full-size car, tan in color, good condition." Close behind, he saw a "full-size pickup, approximately 1969 Chevy, dark green, with camping type cap on back. The height of the cap was approximately the height of the pickup truck cab."

Although Pavolka admitted that "heavy, thick fog" could have obscured what he saw, he believed he was close enough to the vehicles to describe the occupants. The dark-complected driver of the pickup truck had a "muscular build, [and] dark hair, cropped short at ear line." He believed there to be a passenger in both vehicles but did not get a look at the one in the pickup. In the car, he saw a dark-complected man with a "slender build, and dark hair cropped short at ear line. … Subject was in a slouched sitting position, wearing a bill cap (baseball type)." As for the driver of the car, he saw a "white female driver, blond shoulder length hair (full style, not straight), wearing black jacket with orange-colored patches on sleeve. This jacket, in my opinion, being a school's athletic awards jacket."[31]

The description of the pickup driver could easily fit with Ray. But the detectives were shocked to hear that Pavolka had Rayna driving the car—a possibility that became less likely as more witness testimony poured in.

The city's police couldn't help but think that some inadvertent, wishful thinking drove Pavolka's self-report. The part they most doubted involved his description of the car, which was very much like the LTD. When Pavolka says he saw Rayna's vehicle, other witnesses claimed it was already abandoned on North 200 East, just around the corner. But as time passed, the idea that Rayna was the driver seemed even more outlandish.

Despite the skepticism, Pavolka clung to his initial report and conducted something of his own investigation to corroborate it, first pursuing a truck he later saw in traffic that he thought was the pickup that passed him by and then visiting the Yorks to see if photos of that truck could correspond to the one they saw.[32] Although there was one explanation for the Pavolka sighting that made sense, it was too horrific at this early stage of the investigation for any of the detectives to consider.

LORI'S LIGHT BULBS

Late Wednesday afternoon, five days after Rayna's abduction, Jason met Lori McCarty in her tiny Haviland Street house for the first and last time. The visit had been suggested by Gary Marshall, who, in those days, Jason only knew by his first name or CB handle, Werewolf. While Jason had seen Lori several times with Rayna, Gary knew her better because his mother and stepfather—Gayla and Martin Holt—were such good friends of the McCartys. Gary told Jason he would stop by Lori's house for the latest news on Rayna, and Jason asked if he could go along.[33]

The McCartys' white wood frame home was just 660 square feet[34]—as big as a beach cottage—and sat below street level on the bottom of a little embankment. Jason remembers the sun starting to set as they entered the house and the gloomy darkness inside, barely offset by lamplight. The front door opened directly into a living room with chairs, a couch, and a TV. There were piles of laundry by the chairs, which he thought was understandable. "It looked like taking care of the house wasn't the main priority with everything else they had going on."

Lori brought them coffee but had little time to sit and talk. "She was constantly moving," Jason says, answering a ringing phone or pacing back and forth. Just three days before, she mentioned Jason as "the only person she could think of as being a suspect" in her sister's abduction because he wanted them to "get back together."[35] The next day, when the police interviewed Jason, he was just as explicit that Lori's husband should be the prime suspect. He cited conversations "on several occasions" with Rayna when she told him, "Ray [had] continued to make sexual advances toward her."[36]

But when Lori and Jason spoke at the Haviland house that day, neither knew the other's charges. Consequently, he remembers their chat as "cordial and friendly." All agreed that Rayna was not the type to run away—a prospect that some detectives continued to suggest. Lori shared a call from a psychic who said that Rayna was in Rolling Prairie, an unincorporated community in the northeast section of the county with only a few hundred inhabitants. "It kind of made sense," Jason says, "because there are a lot of wooded areas out there."

At some point, Lori took a few calls and returned looking upset. Jason recalls, "Someone said something about the [molestation conviction] that had happened before. She knew it would be brought up again because [Ray] just got off probation in January."

Lori told Jason and Gary that Rayna's disappearance "was tearing her family apart." It was especially difficult for her young children. "The kids don't really understand what's going on."

Lori could not help but bring up "the fight" with Rayna a few days before her sister disappeared. Although Lori did not explain why they were fighting, she admitted that she should have apologized to Rayna but didn't want her sister to get "all big-headed about it and then [have her] say [back], 'You were wrong, and you know it.'"

When Jason asked where Ray was on Friday night, Lori replied that he was "checking out the pigs at this guy's farm" but called her from a phone in the barn and arrived home soon after. She told her guests that this was the same alibi for Ray she provided to a city detective and FBI agent. Still, Lori was upset about how they questioned her—even though she spent about two hours talking to them. They repeatedly asked her about seemingly harmless details that Lori never managed to keep straight, like when Ray returned to their house on Friday night. While Lori had Ray arriving home at seven o'clock, she later said she herself didn't return until eight. As Lori sat thinking about it, a "little light bulb" came on when she realized she wouldn't have known if he had been there at seven because she hadn't seen him for another hour. Then she got worried about telling the police the "wrong things," which would make her or Ray look like they were lying. The more the police asked these questions, the more light bulbs they created for Lori to worry about.

Lori's first interview was with the veteran City of La Porte detective Bob Schoff.[37] Although very tall, with a prominent lantern jaw, Schoff had a soft-spoken, laid-back manner that Lori and her family never found threatening. He was active in their church, and his children went to the same public schools. As far as the Risons were concerned, he was a good neighbor who wouldn't cause them or the McCartys any problems.[38] While the police had trouble reaching Ray, Lori volunteered to talk to Schoff at the city police station on Sunday without a lawyer.

As expected, the interview was an easygoing affair. Lori got to say how close she was to her sister, who "confided in her a lot." She told the detective she doubted her sister would run away, especially in bad weather. Besides, the sisters had previously planned a shopping trip to a mall on Saturday, and Rayna would not have wanted to miss that. When she described Rayna's clothes, she mentioned Matt's letterman jacket and the green sweatshirt she wore underneath with big, embossed letters spelling "E.U.R.O." across the chest. As for her shoes, she suggested either Nike sneakers or the fashionable ankle boots Rayna continued to favor even though the soles had split across the middle—a TMI detail that would have probably embarrassed her sister.

While feeling at ease with Schoff, Lori gabbed about a few things she would later regret. First, she tried to account for how the McCartys spent their Friday night, providing times that did not sync with other witness reports at this early stage in the investigation. While Lori told Schoff she didn't leave her parents' house until seven o'clock, her sister Wendy and her boyfriend put that time more than an hour earlier. She had Ray working overtime, arriving home at five thirty, and staying home the rest of the night. After returning to 517 Haviland, Lori claimed not to leave again until nine o'clock to help search for her sister. Over the next few days, she and Ray would alter those times considerably.

Lori made one more mistake by introducing Schoff to two of her friends, Pat and Richard Walters, who would ultimately provide some of the most incriminating evidence about the young couple. The Walters did not live far from where Rayna's car was found, and Lori suggested the "highly unlikely" possibility that Rayna had visited them before she was abducted.[39]

Two days after Jason and Gary saw Lori, she went to the La Porte police station to speak to an FBI agent. Again, she did not have a lawyer with her, but this interview did not go as smoothly as it did with Schoff. Ex-Marine Elvin "Bill" Keith III was fifty with a close-shaved head and a dour, pursed-lip expression. He wore steel-rimmed glasses that framed a steely gaze. Like other special agents, Keith first captured all the interviewee's vital stats, including birth date, Social Security number, phone number, and address. He then asked far more probing questions than the police detectives Lori complained about to Jason and Gary. In response, she made significant adjustments to the McCartys' timelines on Friday night. Ray did not just go home after work. He cleaned up and then went to take care of the animals at Garry Bucher's hog farm in Union Mills, where Ray grew up. Describing Bucher as a friend Ray frequently visited, Lori indicated he called from the barn to tell her he would soon be home. When Keith asked if Bucher was there when Ray called, Lori replied that she didn't know. As for her own itinerary, she added a trip to Kroger at 9:30 P.M. for groceries.

Without prompting, Lori then said Ray was worried that the evidence technicians might lift his fingerprints from Rayna's car. A week or so before, "Rayna came to visit him," and it had suddenly occurred to him that he touched her car during that visit. Lori knew this was no big deal but explained that he was "nervous" about the missing person investigation "because of her husband's previous relationship with her sister."

As Lori went on to share her sentiments about Ray's "relationship" with Rayna—a subject she had never broached with Schoff—Keith took them down in detail, no doubt surprised at what he heard. Lori "became more agitated and indicated that, at the very least, her sister Rayna was a willing participant in the sexual activity, and although her husband Ray was charged with a crime and blamed totally, she obviously believes her sister to be partially at fault."

Lori justified Ray's indiscretion by explaining that the McCartys were having "extreme marital difficulties" and charged that her sister "acted in a provocative way towards her husband." Keith notes that the provocateur was thirteen years old (and had actually just turned twelve when it started). Lori continued by telling him Rayna was "much more worldly than people normally believe." She further complained that the molestation charges made Lori a victim too, and "everyone showed sympathy and concern for her sister Rayna, but no one ever asked her how she felt or gave her any sympathy."

Still, Lori's characterization of Rayna's relationship with Ray was not her only knock on the missing person. She also described her as "vindictive and angry." Her example of this behavior was how Rayna blamed Lori for telling Ray about their cousin Jenni's abortion plans, which Ray then disclosed to Bennie. As a result, she said, Rayna was "extremely angry" with her for betraying her confidence.

Lori closed the interview by expressing her belief in Ray's innocence and offering to make him available for an interview whenever the FBI requested. To vouch for his honesty, she explained, "If he ever did anything wrong, such as when he had the sexual relationship with her sister, and his 'back was up against a wall,' he would always tell the truth." Although Lori had named Jason a possible suspect during her Schoff interview, when she was with Keith, she dismissed the idea that Jason or Matt "would have [had] anything to do with Rayna's disappearance."

Hardly anything Lori told Keith was typical for the close relative of a missing person. If anything, it betrayed emotions and rationalizations that could lead Lori to harm her sister or defend her husband for doing so. Although there's no record that Keith directly challenged her comments, he would later indicate how much they appalled him.[40]

However, Rayna's little sister, Wendy, provided the police with a profile of the missing person that was almost as disparaging. Perhaps this would not have surprised Rayna's friends, who reported that the two sisters bickered constantly. Wendy described Rayna's mood as "exceptionally good" the week before she disappeared, adding, "She rolled out on the right side of the bed for a change." When it came to the molestation charge against Ray, she said, "Rayna did not tell the whole truth. She wanted to try sex, and Ray fell for it." The detective writing the report continued, "Wendy thought the affair went on for about six months to a year with [Rayna] over at Ray and Lori's every weekend. She also said, 'Ray hasn't ever been the same since he was charged.'"

Wendy was not so kind to Jason. Much like Lori when she spoke to Schoff, Wendy quickly raised suspicions about the former boyfriend and his desire to get back with Rayna. Wendy then brought up an incident she said occurred when she was in the back seat of her sister's LTD. She said Rayna was driving, and Jason was in the passenger seat. "Jason acted like I wasn't even there and told Rayna that he loved her, that he wanted Matt out of the picture, that he and Rayna belonged together," the detective reported her saying. He added, "Wendy said Rayna did not get upset over this but did not encourage it either."[41]

For those who knew the victim, this tale had a big problem. Rayna, a reluctant driver, would have never been behind the wheel if she had a boyfriend in the car, and Tibbs denies he had ever been a passenger in the LTD. As far as the detective was concerned, Wendy's accusations against Jason were undermined by what she had to say about her brother-in-law. He wrote in his report, "When asked about Ray McCarty, Wendy was very defensive of him and denied that he had ever attempted anything of a sexual nature with her. She felt that in regards to the molesting, Rayna didn't tell the whole truth. That she wanted to try sex, and Ray fell for it."

THE BOYFRIEND GRILL

In the days after Rayna went missing, Jason was among those most actively searching for her, often going out with his Fox Hunt friends. When news broke Sunday that police found her car on North 200 East, Jason and his crew followed up, searching in the surrounding woods and fields. Near the corner with East 600 North, Jason noticed a suspicious tire tread in the mud that looked like it came from a truck that had backed haphazardly off the narrow road. Seeing a trailer home nearby, he knocked on the door to ask if the homeowner could tell him more about it. Lawrence Glassman, whose son Brent first spotted the LTD on their street, did not take kindly to anyone snooping around his property. Jason later went to the LPPD station to report that Glassman's behavior was "suspicious" and "defensive." Lawrence was not too happy with the encounter either, and soon after Jason's visit, he called the LPPD dispatcher to say he had been "bothered" by the nosy teens.[42]

Focusing on a few miles around North 200 East, Jason and two friends began to investigate the nearby abandoned barns and farmhouses. With his suspicions about Ray, the search was deadly serious for Jason. As far as his buddies were concerned, he says, "It was just a thing to do." They treated it like a real-life version of Scooby Doo, the silly/scary cartoon they watched as children and got a few thrills in return. The three stopped at an empty, dilapidated farmstead when they thought they heard a scream. They parked their trucks and followed a long dirt driveway that led to a nearly collapsed barn. As Jason waited outside, a friend ventured through the half-open threshold. He saw holes in the wall and roof that looked like someone had kicked their way in or out. He bent over to swipe at a liquid on the ground and pulled his hand away, convinced he had dipped it in blood. Then they heard two more screams. All scrambled back to their trucks and raced downtown to report the incident to the police.

On Monday afternoon, Corporal Mitchell made the rounds of teen hangouts in downtown La Porte. After talking to Rayna's friends and coworkers, he realized he needed to ask Jason for a more extensive interview. When Mitchell called him, Jason voluntarily appeared at the LPPD station with his mother. After only a few minutes, he echoed Matt's concerns about Ray. Mitchell wrote in his report, when "asked about any problems Rayna has been having, [Jason] stated that she had told him on several occasions that her brother-in-law 'Ray' has continued to make sexual advances towards her. She has said he (Ray) was 'all over her' and that he (Ray) was doing 'the normal.'" Unlike Matt, Jason then added what must have been surprising details about the Risons' response. "Tibbs stated that Rayna has told her family but that they do not believe her. Tibbs also stated that Rayna is 'afraid of Ray' and submits to his (Ray's) advances out of fear." Jason then told Mitchell he was willing to "submit to a polygraph regarding this matter if needed."[43] Jason did not know that Matt had also agreed to undergo the procedure. Evidently, neither understood what they were in for.

Although Jason had pledged to cooperate with further questioning, he was unprepared for the police to pick him up two days later while hanging out with his friends downtown. The first detective to meet him at the station was Harold Hahn. With his curly black hair and mustache, Hahn looked like a compact version of Gabe Kaplan, who played the teacher in the old TV show *Welcome Back, Kotter*. Despite questions other officers had raised about Hahn's investigative skills and his relative lack of experience, Miller made the forty-two-year-old detective his chief investigator on the Rison case. In the eyes of two observers familiar with the department, Miller valued his eagerness to take on the high-profile case more than his proficiency.

When they started speaking, Jason had the same friendly exchange with Hahn that he had with the other police officers. He repeated what he told Mitchell about his whereabouts on March 26 and why he felt the purse in Rayna's LTD suggested that she had been abducted. She was "a smart girl" who would not have abandoned a broken-down car with her purse inside and would have left a note about where she was going. After answering a few more cursory questions, Jason thought he could go, but Hahn reminded him that he had offered to take the polygraph and couldn't leave until he did.[44]

An examiner from the state's department of corrections set up a polygraph on one of the empty desks in the detectives' bullpen and had Jason sit on a chair next to it. He nervously watched as sensors were wrapped around his biceps, chest, and fingertips. For the test, the examiner used a method known as Zone of Comparison, which compared the respondent's physiological results from questions relevant to the investigation with control questions that have known answers (e.g., *What's your name?*). Irrelevant questions are asked as well. For Jason, there were only two relevant questions:

1. Do you know where Rayna Rison is at?
2. Did you have anything to do with Rayna's disappearance?

Unknown to Jason, at some point that evening, Matt Elser underwent his own confrontation with the truth machine, only he was asked two additional relevant questions:

1. Did Rayna tell you where she was going?
2. Have you talked with Rayna since she left?

After his test, Jason sat in front of Hahn's desk and waited for him to return with the results. When the detective got back, his voice took on a new, hectoring tone. The polygraph examiner reported that the responses to Jason's relevant questions "indicated deception." Matt got the same supposedly deceptive results on all four of his questions.[45]

The detectives now believed their investigation had made a hopeful turn thanks to the polygraph. Maybe Deputy Sheriff Pavolka *had* spotted Rayna driving the car at the foot of his driveway. Maybe the abduction was, in fact, a charade stage-managed by Rayna and her friends to bring attention to Ray's assaults.

From across his desk, for more than an hour, Hahn kept hammering away at Jason with the two relevant questions in his polygraph examination: *Do you know where Rayna is at? Did you have anything to do with Rayna's disappearance?* In his report, Hahn noted that Jason looked "nervous" but continued sticking to his supposedly deceptive answers. Hahn concluded that "it was evident that Jason was not being totally honest with answers to these two pertinent questions."[46]

For his part, Jason remembers, "I may have been nervous in the beginning, but the longer the whole thing went, the angrier I got. I had gone there to help them, and the way Hahn approached it, I was being accused of knowing something I wouldn't tell them. I was being accused of *not* wanting to help them, and that got me a little upset."

Next, Hahn insisted Jason sit for yet another interview with his supervisor. What Jason thought would be a quick Q&A at the station had turned into an unending hours-long ordeal. Meanwhile, his mother, Rachel, had become concerned too. Earlier in the evening, one of Jason's friends had told her that the police had picked him up for questioning. When he didn't return home, she went to the station, afraid that he may have inadvertently said something that implicated him in Rayna's abduction. When Rachel asked the dispatcher about her son, she was met by shrugs, even though she could see Jason down a hall behind him, sitting at a desk in the detectives' bullpen.

Rachel returned home and started calling the lawyers she knew from her job at the juvenile justice center. One referred her to Michael Drayton, a shrewd and well-respected defense attorney, whose office was only a few blocks from the police station.[47]

Jason's final interview would be with the chief of detectives, Captain John Miller. Although he could be gruff, Miller was more straightforward than Hahn and prepared with a list of pointed questions and a tape recorder. Hahn hovered in the background as they spoke, occasionally leaving the bullpen to take a phone call.

Although Miller would eventually focus on Jason's activities the night of March 26, he was surprised to hear that the teenager had met with Lori earlier that day at her home on Haviland Street and asked in detail about their conversation. Jason related her concerns about the police questions, her "light bulbs," and what she said about Ray's alibi. Before he spoke with Jason, Miller didn't even know Lori's first name. Still, her version of her husband's alibi would take on increasing importance—especially the bit about Ray's call from the hog farmer's barn, which Miller had Jason repeat.

When Miller asked what Jason thought happened with Rayna, he answered, "Me and a few of my other friends think she was taken. She was abducted." Miller next asked, "By whom?" Jason replied, "Well, we don't know by whom, but some of us tend to think that Ray had something to do with it."

Jason then went on to describe Rayna's calls over the previous month— right up to the last time they talked—when she accused her brother-in-law of raping her again and that he threatened to kill her if she told anyone. He provided the names of other friends, like Lisa Dyer, who had heard the same.

Miller wondered if Rayna might have responded to the attacks by planning her disappearance, and Jason shot back, "No. She's not the type of girl to plan this. No matter what happened."

Jason also gave his best guess as to where Rayna would be found. Like the psychics, he suggested Rolling Prairie, an unincorporated area in the northeastern part of the county where, he said, "there's a lot of woods, and there's a lot of abandoned houses." He further explained that the McCartys had once lived there. Ray knew the terrain well because "he's a real ... avid hunter and knows just about everything there is to know about the woods."

When the interview ended, the chief of detectives let Jason know how impressed he was with the teen's insights. "You probably know Rayna as well as anyone, he said. "You're not only a personal friend or more. ... She confided in you, and she told you many things." But Miller still suspected he might have helped her run away and told him he needed to "research your inner self and find out who you are ... because you are the key to this."[48]

Soon after, Rachel arrived with Drayton, and upon seeing the lawyer, the detectives released Jason. Miller would later report to the state police that by the end of the evening, Jason had become "belligerent" and "would not be interviewed without counsel."[49]

But Jason was not Rayna's only boyfriend to become belligerent. Hahn even managed to push mild-mannered Matt to the breaking point. "I attempted to speak with Matt after the test was concluded," Hahn wrote in his report. "I did most of the talking, and Matt would not respond to any of my questioning. He also would not make any eye contact with me." Finally, when asked again if Rayna had run away, Hahn wrote, Elser "shouted out at me that we did not do anything for Rayna the last time she was in trouble."

Unlike Jason, Matt was not alone with the officers, and at this juncture, Hahn noted, "Matt's father stopped the interrogation-type interview and stated that Matt has been in Chicago all day and is tired and has had enough. Both were allowed to leave. ..." Hahn concludes his report with the observation, "This officer feels that there is more to Matt's knowledge of Rayna than he is responding to now."[50]

AMERICA'S MOST WANTED JACKET

From the start, the detectives never quite knew what to make of Bennie Rison. At times, like most parents of missing children, he could be overcome by waves of emotion and seemed exceedingly vulnerable. Then, at other times, he almost reveled in the power that radiated from the community's sympathy for his misfortune. Interacting with the police, he was sly, even conniving, when trying to bend the investigation to his will.

But when it came to the agents of the FBI, Bennie did not attempt to sway them one way or the other. Instead, like a Catholic penitent to a priest, he endeavored to tell them the whole truth no matter how badly it reflected on him or his family. No investigator impressed him more than flinty Bill Keith—a hard-bitten FBI man out of central casting in a three-piece suit.

Until Keith arrived on his doorstep Monday morning, Bennie's interactions with the police had been fairly limited. Besides the missing person report and the brief encounter with Mitchell in the high school parking lot, he made one quick call to the dispatch desk, suggesting that an individual could have abducted Rayna in revenge for a small claims lawsuit Bennie had filed against him.[51] However, Bennie forgot this charge during his introductory interview with Keith. Instead, he and Karen provided their timeline of the comings and goings in the Rison household on March 26. "Rayna," Karen told the FBI agent, "always called when she was not going to make it home right away."

Her parents had heard that when the LTD was found, the driver's seat was pulled as close as possible to the steering wheel, as Rayna preferred. They suggested this meant that she must have driven the car to the spot where it was abandoned. It did not occur to them that the vehicle could have been operated by someone intimately familiar with Rayna's quirks who adjusted the seat to throw off detectives—much as that person could have raised the hood of the car.

When asked about potential suspects, the parents both professed Matt's innocence. He was with them most of the evening on March 26, but they added he was "sincere and not the type of person who would commit a crime." They were not so sure about the former boyfriend, Jason. Rayna would have let him in her car. They could not "think of anyone else who might be a suspect," but they did say that Rayna "confided" in Jason "a number of years ago when she had some trouble." They did not spell out that "trouble" during the interview and never mentioned Ray's name.[52]

But two days later, Bennie pulled Keith aside while he was in the City of La Porte police station. He asked if they could talk privately, and Keith told the detectives to give him an interview room. Once inside, the agent wrote in his report, "Mr. Rison told SA Keith he wanted to talk about the situation that occurred between his son-in-law Raymond McCarty and his daughter Rayna Rison approximately four years ago."

Bennie described the molestation as a "sexual relationship which occurred over a long period of time when Rayna was 13 years old." He did not mention that it started when she was twelve or that her subsequent pregnancy led to Ray's conviction in state court. Instead, he told Keith, "At the point the sexual situation was made known, [Bennie] spoke to Raymond McCarty and made an agreement. ... [Ray] would admit he made a stupid mistake, take care of his wife and his family, never touch Rayna again, and submit to psychiatric treatment."

Bennie claimed Ray stuck to the agreement but divulged Ray's "strange" behavior since Rayna's disappearance. While everyone else was worried about the situation, Ray had only visited the Rison house once or twice since Rayna went missing and had yet to talk to Bennie about the investigation. Also, when Bennie's mother got on the phone with Ray to ask what he thought about her granddaughter's disappearance, he replied, "Well, you can't tell about Rayna. She's a little weird." Bennie then told Keith, "He has not totally discounted McCarty as a suspect in his daughter's disappearance, but he has a hard time believing it could be possible."[53]

Nothing clouded Bennie's exalted view of the FBI during his interviews with Keith, and he persuaded Ray to go through his own voluntary session with the agents. In preparation for the feds, Ray went to his supervisor at Teledyne to amend the alibi he had previously provided him. As the supervisor later reported to the La Porte police, "Ray stated that he had to get his stories straight before he talked to the FBI. He had to figure exactly where he was that Friday night."[54]

On Thursday morning, April 1, six days after Rayna's disappearance, Bill Keith and another agent appeared at the foundry to pick Ray up and take him to the LPPD station. As Lori and Ray told the police multiple times, Ray was willing to "cooperate one hundred percent." Harold Hahn, the LPPD detective, joined the session and wrote his report with the introduction: "Reason for interview was to establish what Raymond might know about Rayna's disappearance and his whereabouts Friday evening 3-26-93."

Once they sat him down at Hahn's desk in the bullpen, Keith walked Ray through his schedule on March 26, from when he woke up at 4:00 A.M., started work at 4:57 A.M., and then clocked out at "approximately" 4:40 P.M. In his notes, Keith had McCarty employed as a "core assembler" at the Teledyne Casting Service.[55]

Technically, inside the plant, Ray's supervisors referred to him as a "hauler and dipper."[56] None of the investigators ever learned what that job entailed. Instead, they focused on the exact hours he worked and the inconsistencies that arose when they tried to confirm them. He told them his day at Teledyne typically ended at three thirty in the afternoon, but he found out earlier that he had to work overtime and called Lori to let her know. The plant's time card system had him punching out at 4:40 P.M. Ray said he stayed an hour later to clean out his "muller," a machine that mixes the sand compound he used. He named a coworker who would confirm that.[57] Although the man saw Ray return to the plant after he punched out, he did not know if Ray spent as much as an hour cleaning the machine—a task that should take far less time.[58] Even more suspicious, Ray never followed up with the Teledyne personnel department to get paid for that supposed extra hour of overtime.[59]

After work, Ray said he went home to clean up but then went to look at a house for sale on a street that ran perpendicular to the Pine Lake Animal Hospital. From that house, he would have had a full view of the lobby where Rayna was sweeping up. This was yet a new detail that Lori had not included in her version of Ray's alibi and a particularly damning one. Ray now admitted he was near the animal hospital shortly before Rayna left for the day. He also put himself in a location to spy on her when she did.

After checking out the house for sale, Ray remembered getting a soda at McDonald's and returning home. Around 8:30 P.M., he said, he got a call from his mother-in-law, Karen, who was looking for Lori. Ray said his wife did not return home until ten thirty—ninety minutes later than Lori told Keith. By then, concern about Rayna had reached a fever pitch, but Ray said he went to bed at eleven because he had to wake up early Saturday morning.

Most surprisingly, once City of La Porte detectives looked at the McCartys' interviews, they realized Ray did not mention a trip to the hog farm. Instead, he brought up the big fight over Cousin Jenni's abortion. When asked what happened to Rayna, Ray speculated that "someone abducted her" because she left her purse behind in the car, but McCarty denied having anything to do with it. He also denied recently "touching her in a sexual manner," as her friends had charged. He then made the most startling confession of the interview. Keith reported, "McCarty admits that he is a child molester and stated his counselor told him he should always admit to his problem and that he must always watch himself to avoid becoming sexually involved with any other young people." It was an admission that would have stunned virtually all his counselors.

While McCarty claimed he had "become very friendly with Rayna," he said the relationship was not sexual. He may have hugged her on occasion, but Rayna did not object to that. In any case, Ray said he was "rarely" alone with her, but only a few moments earlier, he said that his fingerprints might be found inside the LTD because he had gone with Rayna to the store and no one else accompanied them.

Both investigators made note of Ray's demeanor during the interview. Keith described him as "extremely nervous and shaking and was concerned about being cold."[60] In Hahn's words, "Raymond became very emotional to the point of tears."[61] Still, McCarty offered to undergo a polygraph examination the next day, although Keith wrote he "was concerned that he would tell the truth and the machine would make him out to be a liar."[62]

Hahn arranged for his boss, Captain Miller, to drive McCarty on Friday to the FBI's regional headquarters in Merrillville, Indiana, an hour away. But that was not the last the detective heard from Ray on Thursday. After he returned home, Hahn got a call from the LPPD dispatch desk. Ray was in the station demanding to speak to either Keith or Hahn. Hahn told the dispatcher that whatever he had to say, it could wait until the following day in Merrillville, but Ray insisted that they speak. Lori, he told Hahn, had reminded him that he had gone to the hog farm on the Friday night when Rayna disappeared, a detail he forgot to mention during his interview. "Ray stated that he did not want us to think he was lying." Hahn then told him, "All he had to do is talk to the investigators in the morning and set them straight as to what he did."[63]

Early Friday, after Miller dropped him off at the FBI offices in Merrillville, Keith introduced Ray to the FBI agent who would administer the polygraph examination and then left the room. First, Ray told the examiner he needed to "clarify statements" he had previously given Keith because "he wished to now tell the truth" about his March 26 activities.

This time, Ray was definitive about leaving work at 5:40. He again mentioned looking at the house for sale near the animal hospital but said he talked to *two* men, not just one. The examiner wrote, "McCarty could only provide general descriptions of these individuals and was not sure they lived in the area."

He did not stop at McDonald's for a soda, as he told Keith, but he went to his friend's hog farm in Union Mills. While this story matched Lori's, Ray changed one significant detail. He did not call her from the barn as she thought but from a nearby truck stop, and he arrived home later than he had previously indicated.

Tellingly, one detail did not change. He returned to Haviland Street in time to pick up Karen's phone call at 8:30 P.M. He probably assumed that Karen had already told detectives when she called him, and the McCartys would not ask that she alter her statements.[64]

As for Ray's other changes to his statement, LPPD detectives suspected they resulted from leaks in their department.[65] Somehow, the McCartys were getting updates that forced the couple to align their stories with the detectives' latest witness reports. For example, someone must have told them that Ray's blue Datsun station wagon with its distinctive rust spots was seen on the street perpendicular to the animal hospital. Then, after Ray's interview with Keith and Hahn, the McCartys learned that it hadn't been one person who spotted the car, as Ray said, but two.[66] He must have also found out that the police had interviewed Garry Bucher and his wife earlier in the week. The hog farmer told the detectives that the phone in the barn "had been disconnected for some time."[67]

The polygraph examiner had already studied Keith's report from the previous day and would later write that Ray "changed several significant details." Although he confessed to previously not telling investigators the truth, he still signed two consent forms for the polygraph. One had a waiver of rights, including "I do not want a lawyer at this time."

The first part of Ray's test was like the one administered to Matt and Jason, with the examiner asking several irrelevant questions along with two that were relevant: *Did you cause the disappearance of Rayna Rison? Do you know where Rayna Rison is now?* Like the boyfriends, Ray answered "no" to both, and like the boyfriends, the examiner determined his responses "deceptive."

However, there was another part of the examination that was different for Ray. The agent showed him a map of La Porte County that he had broken into five sections. As controls, he also included Kansas City, St. Louis, and "an area not on this map." The examiner determined Ray had "significant reactions" to one area in the county's northeast corner. It encompassed Rolling Prairie, where Rayna's car was found and where some psychics and Jason were pointing. As the consent forms assured, his response could not be used against him in a court of law, but if it proved correct once Rayna was found, it would have consequences—making investigators much more suspicious about their prime suspect.[68]

Ray left Merrillville without knowing his polygraph results, but the day's stressful events were not yet over. That night at eight o'clock, the Fox network would air an episode of *America's Most Wanted*, which would devote the closing segment to Rayna's disappearance and a request for information leading to her discovery. Making their investigation a part of the show was a Hail Mary pass for the City of La Porte police department, but Chief Gene Samuelson felt he had to exhaust all options to find the missing girl.

The spot featured Rayna's high school portrait with her full head of curly hair. It also focused on her clothes—especially Matt's distinctive letterman jacket, which was displayed along with her photo.[69] The body of the garment was black cloth, and the sleeves were black leather with orange piping around the crew knit cuffs. On the left arm, orange fabric chevrons in a V shape represented his years on the track team, and a musical clef with two chevrons on the right breast showed the years he played in the band. Stitched on the back of the jacket was a cursive *Elser* with *MATT* inside a curlicue.[70]

Jason remembered watching the program with his family. He was surprised that Rayna's segment wasn't longer. In those moments, he says, "They sure made a big deal about the letterman jacket and that she was last seen wearing it." He figured the Risons emphasized that detail when talking to the show's producers.

For most families of missing or murdered persons, such shows as *America's Most Wanted* are a necessary evil that, at best, can help them find closure to their tragedy but also dredge up wells of sadness. Oddly, Ray and Lori made the event a social occasion, inviting several friends to their house to watch the program. Among them was Gayla Moreau. She was then married to Martin Holt, one of Ray's high school buddies from Union Mills. She remembers that the tiny home was packed and had an almost party atmosphere. Once the Rayna segment aired, she was surprised to see no emotion registered on her hosts' faces. "It was like they were watching a show about someone they didn't know."[71]

The mood changed dramatically when a downcast Bennie suddenly appeared. After the program ended, he followed his son-in-law into the children's bedroom and watched while Ray pulled together Adrienne's clothes for a sleepover. According to Keith's report, Bennie first told Ray, "I'm here to help, and we can talk about anything." He then suggested they go for a ride to discuss what he had just heard from the FBI—that Ray had failed the polygraph.

In response to this news, Bennie said, Ray began to "cry and sob bitterly." Keith writes, "Mr. Rison suggested that McCarty go into the [adults'] bedroom to pull himself together, so he did not make a scene in front of the children."

Ray followed that advice but soon returned to the children's bedroom with "a loaded and cocked revolver." Keith writes, "He told Mr. Rison, 'If you don't believe me, shoot me now. [The FBI agents] don't believe me!'"

Bennie pulled the gun away and took it into the kitchen, where he removed the bullets, which he later gave to Keith, and then hid the revolver in the refrigerator. Lori heard her husband carrying on and joined the fray "to scream at Ray." Now, Bennie had to calm them both down.

He then ushered Ray and his granddaughter out of the house and into his car. After they dropped off Adrienne, Bennie finally convinced Ray "to get himself under control."

Bennie told him, "I know the two questions you failed on the polygraph, and there must be some explanation." But Ray denied that there was an explanation and lamented again, "No one believes me."

As they continued to drive, they speculated on what could have happened to Rayna and how she could have been abducted. When Ray asked if he knew where her car was found, Bennie drove to North 200 East He parked where he remembered seeing the LTD in the glare of the police lights, but Ray sat silent.

Bennie took Ray back home and urged him to "talk the whole situation over with his wife," Keith wrote. He suggested they go for another drive the next day along with the family dog, who might pick up Rayna's scent.

"You're a good hunter and a good woodsman," Bennie told him. "The police and the FBI have not been able to find her, so you and I are going to go tomorrow and find her."[72]

Little did Bennie know that even more drama was in store that night when Jim Jackson, a county patrolman, made another critical discovery in their investigation. He had watched *America's Most Wanted* at the LPPD station. Like the McCartys, the city police had a full house. Patrolmen from all departments helped detectives man the phones for tips. Others were ready to hop into their squad cars and follow up on anything that sounded the least bit credible.

Even though Jim Jackson worked on narcotics cases for the county, he still showed up at the station to see if he could help. At thirty-one, Jackson was tall and thin with a beard, shoulder-length hair, and clothes that intentionally looked "scraggly" so he could convincingly pose as a drug dealer or buyer in undercover busts. His car was typically an unmarked Chevy.

The tips had not poured in like Chief Samuelson hoped, and Jackson could see that most of the officers at the station were sitting around talking. He remembers, "I decided it would be more useful for me to go out and check some dump sites again."

During his twelve years as a patrolman, he learned that vital evidence in a crime often ended up in a handful of dumps spread around the county—anything from stolen cars, safes, and vending machines to guns and knives. These were places away from residential areas where cars and trucks could drop unwanted or illicit items and make a quick getaway. During the Rison investigation, he kept his eye on three of them.

After leaving the police station, he stopped for take-out coffee and drove south to one of the more popular disposal spots. It was a clump of woods surrounded by farm fields but not far from the intersection of two main roads. He parked his car and took out his Maglite. Dumpers usually followed the ruts from tire treads into open spaces among the trees, but that night, even from the road, Jackson spied something hanging in branches just five feet off the ground. As he got closer and trained his flashlight on the object, he saw black leather sleeves and orange patches frosted with bits of snow. Jackson says, "I thought, 'Oh my gosh. That's the letterman jacket.'"

Jackson ran back to his car and called the La Porte station. Soon, a convoy of city squad cars was speeding to the scene, sirens screaming.[73] By coincidence, Jason and a few other Fox Hunters were visiting the friend who thought he dipped his hand in blood. He lived in a farmhouse around the corner from the dump site. By the time the boys got there, the cops had roped off the street and illuminated the trees in bright white light as they took pictures of Jim Jackson's find before they moved it.

"You could tell it had been thrown up there hastily," Jackson remembers, "but it was a cold, damp night, and the moisture on the jacket must have frozen it stiff because it just clung to the branches."[74]

In any case, the jacket hadn't been up there for long. Another sheriff's deputy had checked the dump earlier in the day and didn't see it. Later, when police checked the pockets, they found a folded school paper Rayna had written, a paper towel, a single cloth glove, a partial stick of chewing gum, and the inhaler she used for her asthma.[75]

The discovery, so soon after *America's Most Wanted*, made some city detectives suspicious. They suggested Jackson found it elsewhere earlier and then planted it to attract publicity. "Yeah, I was questioned about it," Jackson says, "and I was offended. But eventually, it all came out that I was telling the truth. It was a fluke that I found it when I did."[76]

But another question remained. Why did the person who had the jacket fling it into the trees? Did *America's Most Wanted* suddenly make it too hot to handle? There was no chance that Ray did the flinging on Friday. By then, he knew the La Porte police had him under surveillance, tracking him from home to work and back again. A trip he made the previous day may have told the real story about the jacket—only the police never figured out whom he went to see. That person may have been the one who made the hasty toss.

THE SWAMP

At ninety-one, Jane Lindborg is still spry with a sharp and lively mind. Although she describes the books she writes as "works of fiction," they contain vivid memories of her childhood in La Porte County's rustic Rolling

Prairie community. Among the earliest and most frightening incidents she recalls was when a neighbor's barn caught fire. From the rise where her family's house stood, her father could see smoke billowing upward in the early evening. The only farm in that area belonged to Lewis Wagner. He was an old man who went to bed early and kept all his shades drawn—a family habit dating back to the previous century when they thought local Native Americans would peek through their windows.

Jane's father decided to warn Wagner before the fire consumed the barn and spread to other structures. He told her mother he had to take the quickest route, cutting through the untended fields, woods, marshes, and bogs between their home and the Wagner farm. "My mother and I just sobbed when we heard that," Jane remembers. "In the dark, there was no telling what could happen to him. We just held each other tight until he got home." No part of the terrain worried them more than the marshy bowl at the bottom of a hill that they called "the swamp." It ran along one side of Range Road, the unpaved boundary line between the county's townships. Depending on the time of the year, the swamp could be shallow or deceptively deep, with mud that sucked you down like quicksand. Brambles, bushes, and branches fallen from surrounding trees posed other hazards that could scratch or spear through the thickest dungarees.

Jane's father didn't get to Wagner in time to save the barn, but at least he made it back to his family in one piece. Jane stayed in that house on County Road East 700 North and later bought a house on the same road as a married adult where she remained through the end of the century. Over the decades, she watched Range Road widen and sluice more and more water into the swamp until newcomers started referring to it as a pond. That designation has never appeared on the county's official plat maps— perhaps because the body of water had limited appeal for recreation. It was too shallow for boating, and the deep muck and ice-clearing chemicals running off Range Road created inhospitable conditions for most fish or swimmers.

In later years, Jane made the place a destination for a pleasant stroll from her home on East 700 North—about a mile in each direction. Most of the narrow road was hemmed in by a dense tangle of bushes and foliage that remained unchanged from her childhood. In some places, the high branches of trees on each side leaned together and wove a canopy that could blot out the sun.

Jane remembers leading guests on one walk to the "swamp" during the middle weeks of April 1993. That month, they had enjoyed a particularly pleasant early spring with no rain and warmer than usual temperatures. She told her companions to keep their eyes open. "That young girl was still missing," she says, "and I thought maybe we could spot something useful to the police."[77]

In the weeks after her disappearance, Rayna Rison remained very much on the minds of people in her community and beyond. Besides the daily reminders in local newspapers and national wire services that she was still missing, more publicity came with rewards for her safe return. An anonymous donor put up $5,000 a few days after police found her car. A week later, the ante went even higher after the jacket discovery when La Porte's most famous patron, Charlie O. Finley, offered $25,000.[78]

The search would end on Tuesday afternoon, April 27, in that place where Jane unwittingly led her guests. Like so many other aspects of the Rison case, the discovery would come with initial confusion and lingering questions about how it was made. The first news about the incident appeared in a local paper with the headline, "Anglers Find Body Near Stream." The article did not identify either of the "two fishermen."[79] One day later, another newspaper added further clarification, reporting, "The body was discovered by a family of four fishing in the pond." Again no one in this group was named, but police did identify Richard Lancaster, a dairy farmer whom the family "flagged down." He followed a man into the woods alongside the pond, a few dozen yards from Range Road. The man then pointed out a shape under some tree limbs and asked if that was a body. Lancaster says he replied, "Yeah, it's a body. We better call the sheriff." Although Lancaster described the body as "fully clothed" and "all swollen,"[80] he would later tell the police that it was not immediately visible. His guide had to throw out some stones to show him where to look in the water.[81] More details about the encounter continued to bubble up from the pond, much like the victim's remains. The family comprised a man, his wife, and two children: a ten-year-old son and a fourteen-year-old daughter. Eventually, the reasons for their presence at the pond would evolve from fishing to hunting for turtles.[82]

As it turned out, the man who led Lancaster to the body was known to the police—if anything was too well known—which may be why they kept his name from the press. By 1993, at age thirty-nine, James Flett McWhirter had an extensive rap sheet dating back to 1979, with twelve arrests and ten convictions for offenses including burglary, theft, and possession of stolen merchandise. In those days, the balding McWhirter affected a wispy goatee and mustache that barely covered his cleft lip, making him even more recognizable.[83] Given his checkered past, investigators may have felt it best to leave him out of the story. A surprising party would try to drag him back into it later. But regardless of the rap sheet, McWhirter's behavior that day and in the following weeks should have raised suspicions—namely, that he had "inside" knowledge about where Rayna's killer disposed of her body. His efforts to get Lancaster and someone else he flagged down to witness his sighting was a lame attempt to verify his role in the discovery or, worse yet, cover up his link to the murderer. For whatever reason, detectives chose not to pursue that line of inquiry.

After Lancaster drove to a nearby farm to call the police, three high-ranking members of the La Porte County sheriff's office soon arrived on the scene. Although the body remained under the branches in the water, the officers strongly suspected its identity and notified the City of La Porte police department.[84]

Before long, news leaked out to the local media. One of Lori's old friends, Leah Pepple, who worked at a La Porte radio station, called to tell her that a body had been found but not yet identified. Leah had known Ray when they grew up together in Union Mills. She later became friendly with Lori and spent more time with the McCartys after breaking up with her husband. She watched the upheaval that followed Rayna's disappearance and sympathized as Ray and Lori complained about being harassed by the police. When the two women first met, shortly after Ray's molestation conviction, Lori told Leah that Rayna "was as much to blame" for the crime as her husband. After she went missing, Lori bitterly speculated that Rayna was hiding somewhere. "I'll kill her," she told Leah. "She only did this to get Ray in trouble."

Leah expected her friend's attitude to change once she got the news.[85] But Lori did not rush off to huddle with her parents and sister. Instead, she kept her tanning appointment at the Time and a Half video and tanning store where she worked until the day Rayna disappeared. Before Lori got into the booth, she shared the update matter-of-factly with Denise Stout, who had taken her shift after she quit. Lori asked Denise not to be disturbed. If Ray called, she should ask what he wanted. McCarty called but did not leave a message or have Denise get his wife. Once Lori emerged from the booth, Denise told her about the call, and she left the store. Twenty minutes later, La Porte police detectives arrived looking for Lori.[86]

Just weeks after finding the famous letterman jacket, La Porte County patrolman Jim Jackson again took center stage in the Rayna Rison investigation when he was assigned to pull the body from the pond. A certified scuba instructor, Jackson was on the county's dive team responsible for water rescue and recovery. His diving supervisor was Joe Pavolka, who thought he saw Rayna driving a car at the foot of his driveway on March 26. Pavolka asked Jim to drive the dive truck to the site.[87] By the time Jackson arrived, the area was already teeming with twenty officers from the city and county police departments, including the La Porte County sheriff and LPPD Chief Gene Samuelson. Also in attendance were the county coroner, her assistant, and two EMS workers.[88]

A county detective provided Jackson with instructions for the recovery but needed to point out the body to him before he started. "You couldn't stand fifteen feet away and definitively tell that it was a body," Jim remembers. She was face down in the water under a cross of two tree limbs more than five feet long. Her backside and one leg were exposed, but the blue jeans had blanched into the same beige color as the wood. Jackson says that the submerged part of her body "was covered by leaves and silt. When you put your face underwater, you really couldn't see. The water was that murky."

Pavolka soon joined Jackson, and they both put on their scuba gear, including oxygen tanks. Since the tree limbs and a tangled pile of branches obstructed access to the body from the muddy shore, the officers had to approach from the opposite side of the pond. The water was shallow enough for them to wade without fins but no less dangerous. "It was kind of rough going in there," Jackson recalls. "Very treacherous with all the stumps and branches. I got poked and prodded. At one point, my legs sunk all the way down in the muck to just below my knees. I had to crawl in it to move forward."

Once they got closer, they could see a body inflated like a balloon, with the clothes practically bursting at the seams. "When digestive bacteria build inside the stomach," Jackson explains, "the body becomes extremely bloated and buoyant. Even though they piled all this stuff on top of her, she still forced it all upwards."

From their view in the water, Pavolka and Jackson determined that the two long tree limbs provided most of the weight holding her down. As they worked to remove them, detectives used video cameras to record the activity from two vantage points: the shore and an inflatable boat in the water. Once the divers could move her away from the woodpile, they carefully slid her into a water recovery body bag. While the muddy water and bloating had distorted and blackened the front of Rayna's clothes, Jackson could still tell how her abductors had handled her before they submerged her. Someone grabbed the front of her bra as she was dragged into the water, pulling the straps and the sweatshirt nearly up to her neck. Likewise, he says, one sleeve was yanked halfway off an arm—probably due to a hasty removal of the letterman jacket.

Once onshore, Jackson and Pavolka transferred the body to another recovery bag that would allow some water to drain out.[89] Although her face was bloated beyond recognition, the E.U.R.O. letters stood out against the darkened green sweatshirt for all to see. Later that day, Miller would write his case report on the body recovery and conclude as follows: "From the clothing description given at the time of disappearance, along with jewelry and black ankle top shoes with cracked soles, indications are [that] the body located in the above-mentioned pond is La Porte Case Report 93033517—the missing juvenile, Rayna Rison."[90]

MINORS' EVENTS OF UTMOST IMPORTANCE

Rayna and Matt (in 1993 and 1994 photos) were ready to "restart" their rocky relationship with a Dairy Queen dinner date and *Incredible Voyage* movie on Friday, March 26, 1993. Photos: *La Porte County Herald-Dispatch*; LPHS, *El Pe*, 1994

"Kennel girl" Rayna was the last to leave the Pine Lake Animal Hospital, no doubt anxious to get home for her date, but it was the last place she was seen alive. Photo: Google Street View

That night, Jason asked Chad Green (*right*), an erstwhile friend, for a ride to the Deluxe Trailer Park. The teen antics that ensued would be of ultimate importance twenty-one years later.

Jason's friend James Amor wanted to meet the older sister of Jamie Swisher, a cute girl he had seen at high school. Jason would tutor Jamie in math while James would talk to Jamie. Photos: LPHS, *El Pe*, 1994; New Prairie High School, *Prairie Life* '95

When the girls' mother arrived home from work, she kicked James out but let Jason stay, knowing he had previously helped a neighbor with her math homework. Photo: Google Street View

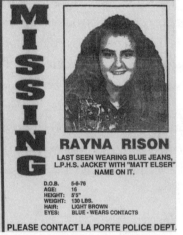

MISSING

RAYNA RISON

LAST SEEN WEARING BLUE JEANS, L.P.H.S. JACKET WITH "MATT ELSER" NAME ON IT.

D.O.B. 5-6-76
AGE: 16
HEIGHT: 5'5"
WEIGHT: 130 LBS.
HAIR: LIGHT BROWN
EYES: BLUE - WEARS CONTACTS

PLEASE CONTACT LA PORTE POLICE DEPT.

On Saturday morning, Rayna's distraught father, Bennie, met her fellow band members in the high school parking lot and asked them to distribute *Missing* posters he printed at work. Photo: Exhibits, State of Indiana

Saturday night, county police learned Rayna's car was left, hood up, on a country road nine miles north of the animal hospital. Photo: Exhibits, State of Indiana

Her purse and its contents were strewn across the front seat, the glove compartment was open, and newspapers were spread under the passenger seat. Photo: Exhibits, State of Indiana

Police Chief Gene Samuelson (*right*) displays Matt Elser's letterman jacket, which Rayna was wearing when she was abducted. It was found in a dump on April 1. Photo: *La Porte County Herald-Argus*

At a church service with his wife, Karen, and Rayna's two sisters, Bennie goes on TV and pledges to keep the name of anyone who can help find his daughter confidential. Photo: *La Porte County Herald-Dispatch*

On April 27, newspapers reported that Rayna may have been found a few miles from where her car was abandoned. Details about who discovered her continued to change. Photo: *South Bend Tribune*

Rayna's body was pulled from a pond that was also known as a swamp by locals, with shallow depths and poor conditions for either fishing or boating. Photo: Exhibits, State of Indiana

Rayna's corpse was submerged under tree limbs and foliage and not discernible from fifteen feet away, according to the county policeman assigned to pull her from the water. Photo: Exhibits, State of Indiana

James McWhirter claimed to find the body—first while fishing, then searching for turtles with his daughter. Ray told a neighbor the career criminal was a friend of his best friend. Photo: La Porte County Jail

THE CASE AGAINST RAY

RAYNA RISON
FAMILY
- Bennie, Karen (parents)
- Lori, Wendy (sisters)

FRIENDS
- Matt Elser (boyfriend)
- Jenni McCleland (cousin)

RISON PRIVATE INVESTIGATORS
- Barry Nothstine*
- Tina Church*

RISON PSYCHICS
- Sue Burzynski*
- Noreen Molnar*

CITY OF LA PORTE POLICE DEPARTMENT
- Stephen Ames, Evidence Technician*
- Chief Gene Samuelson
- Detectives John Miller (Chief), Bob Schoff, Harold Hahn

*INTRODUCED IN THIS CHAPTER

JASON TIBBS
FAMILY
- Rachel (mother)
- Leslie (wife)

LAWYER
- Mike Drayton

LA PORTE COUNTY
- Circuit Court Judge Robert Gettinger*
  Prosecuting Attorney
  - Cynthia Hedge*, 1995–1998
  - Chief Deputy Scott Duerring*
  - Deputy Kathleen Lang*
  - Bill Herrbach, 1991–1994
- Dr. Rick Hoover*, Forensic Pathologist
- Barbara Huston*, Coroner
  Sheriff's Department
  - Sergeant Joe Pavolka
  - Patrolman Jim Jackson

FBI
- Douglas Deedrick*, Trace Evidence Analyst
- Elvin "Bill" Keith

INDIANA STATE POLICE
- Sergeant Arland Boyd

OTHER SUSPECTS
- Larry Hall* (serial killer)
- Ed Logan*

LORI AND RAY McCARTY
FAMILY
- Adrienne (daughter)
- Hunter (son)
- Carolyn (Ray's mother)

FRIENDS, COWORKERS
- Charlie Allen, Cindy Brewer
- Darold, Connie Willis*
- Mark Emerick*
- Mike Kepplin*
- Brian, Tina Townsend*
- Robin Dingman*
- Jeanette Zellers*
- Garry, Lois Bucher
- Brenda Pegg
- Pat, Richard Walters*
- Gayla (Holt) Moreau

WITNESSES
- James McWhirter
- Pam Rosebaum*
- Bryan Durham*
- Rene Gazarkiewicz*
- Kim Hackney*
- Val Eilers*
- Andre Bridges*
- Lorn "Brent" Glassman
- Beth York; sons Kyle, Austin
- Roy West, John Proud

THE SINGING DETECTIVE

Even before the EMS ambulance with Rayna's remains arrived at South Bend's Memorial Hospital for an autopsy and official identification, a La Porte County detective was on the phone with Arland "Arlie" Boyd, a sergeant for the Indiana State Police. Case 93033517 no longer involved a missing person. It was now a murder, a state crime, which meant that the FBI agents Bennie Rison found so formidable would bow out and make way for Boyd, Northwest Indiana's most experienced homicide investigator.[1]

Unlike Special Agent Keith, Boyd did not affect an officious or intimidating outward appearance. Although a trooper for twenty-five years, he had ditched the Stetson, tie, and uniform long ago. Instead, he tended toward modish jackets and turtlenecks to go with his long sideburns and a stringy mustache. But the deep voice and pointed questions that came out of Boyd's mouth were every bit those of a Sergeant Friday. Combined with his piercing stare, it made an unnerving experience for anyone submitting to his interrogations. Boyd admits, "I do tend to make people very uncomfortable."

As Boyd tells it, he initially had other intentions for his baritone. With significant experience singing in his church, he entered Indiana State University as a vocal major, joining a school group that toured extensively. After graduating, he pursued singing as a career, but when he got married and had a few kids, he says, "That got in the way. My family was really

religious and thought my place was at home and not off singing all the time."
His father-in-law was the first to see a TV commercial advertising for state
police candidates and said, "Hey, you'd make a good trooper."

From the start, Boyd's superiors at the ISP could see his predilection for
detective work and sent him to various seminars to improve his investigative
skills, including a program at the University of Baltimore that the police call
Harvard Homicide. Among his teachers was famed forensic pathologist Dr.
Rudiger L. Breitenecker, who led the government's investigation of the Jonestown
massacre and created the first criminal database for DNA analysis.[2] Despite his
advancement in the world of homicide, Boyd never stopped singing. A search
for his clips in newspaper databases finds a jarring juxtaposition between his
roles as the featured soloist in a wedding ceremony and the chief detective in
gruesome courtroom testimony.[3]

By 1993, with hundreds of death investigations under his belt, local
authorities often turned to Boyd to oversee complicated or highly publicized
cases. Although La Porte's county and city police had their share of
interagency rivalries, they did cooperate as part of what they called the
Homicide Team, which the prosecuting attorney could activate when deemed
necessary. The first team meeting on the Rison case occurred Wednesday
morning, just hours after the victim was pulled from the water.[4]

In their pronouncements to the press about the body they found, officials
were careful to remain vague. They did not confirm the victim's identity until
a forensic pathologist matched the teeth with Rayna's dental records. Then,
even more strangely, they were not conclusive about the cause of death. One
paper reported, "La Porte Police Chief Gene Samuelson said it was impossible
to determine if Rison was strangled or drowned because her body was too
badly decomposed." In fact, her remains were intact enough for the autopsy
to determine that "there were no signs of trauma," or as La Porte County
Coroner Barbara Huston put it, "no marks on the body."[5] Huston and her
forensic pathologist never provided a satisfactory answer on the cause of death
and ultimately chose asphyxiation by process of elimination. Yet another
mystery would hover over the Rison case and hamper a potential prosecution.

Samuelson was most circumspect about the state of his detectives'
investigation into Rayna's murder, telling reporters, "There are no strong

suspects."[6] But when the chief briefed Boyd and the rest of the Homicide Team on Wednesday morning, Raymond McCarty was identified as "the prime suspect."[7] Moreover, Detective Hahn had already appeared before the circuit court judge to get a search warrant for the McCarty household later that day.[8]

The Homicide Team decided to hammer their prime suspect with a one-two punch that would commence with a Boyd jab at an interview and then follow with a search team uppercut on the McCarty premises and vehicles. Accompanied by a county detective, Boyd drove to 517 Haviland, where Ray and Lori greeted him. But now, Ray was no longer willing to "cooperate one hundred percent." He had retained the services of Larry Rogers, one of the area's most active and irascible defense lawyers. Boyd reported that the attorney told his client "not to make any statements until he had discussed the situation further with Rogers."[9]

Lori, who had yet to get her own lawyer, proved more cooperative and offered to return to the LPPD station with the officers for an interview. However, Boyd could not stay to talk to her then, and there is no record of any statements she made after he left.

Ray was alone with his kids at 517 Haviland when four city and county officers descended on his home. One more time, county patrolman Jim Jackson was on the case, assigned by the team to read the warrant, which permitted police to search for "all boots or shoes over size 7." They seized eight pairs matching the description, including hip waders and work boots. During the search, in a bedroom cabinet, they found two boxes of ammunition and the Smith & Wesson revolver that Ray threatened to use on himself after hearing he failed the polygraph.[10]

The interest in the boots and shoes was directly related to the plaster cast of footprints in the mud near Rayna's abandoned car. It indicated that one of the individuals that the Yorks saw standing by the LTD had a size ten foot, like Ray. However, evidence technicians also thought that the impression in the plaster cast was consistent with the soles of Eastland work boots. One of the detectives had spotted the brand on Ray's feet before Rayna's body was found. But there was no trace of Eastland boots in either 517 Haviland or Ray's locker at Teledyne, where the police also got a warrant to search.[11] Some detectives believed that word about the warrant had leaked once again to the McCartys, giving them time to dispose of the boots and other clothing before the search.

Hahn did learn something five years later that may have validated those suspicions. The owner of 517 Haviland told him that the people who rented the house after Ray and Lori experienced heating problems in one of the bedrooms. When repairmen arrived to check on the issue, they found "clothing stuffed into the ductwork." The renters threw out what was clogging up the ducts. Evidence technicians did find fibers in the ducts that they sent to the FBI for testing, but they could not be tied to either Ray or Rayna.[12] There's no indication if boots were among the items thrown away, but Lori later told a friend how Ray disposed of the "wanted" footwear by throwing them down a blast furnace at Teledyne.[13]

During the 517 Haviland search, police also seized the family cars, yielding more than a hundred items for further testing, primarily bags of particles vacuumed off the vehicles' carpeted floors and seats. Ray's rusty blue 1980 Datsun B210 was filled with the disordered debris of his habits and passions: various articles of camo clothing, long johns, hunting gloves with the fingertips cut off, bloodstained rags and towels, empty cans and bottles of pop, candy wrappers, and dozens of Skoal chewing tobacco tins. Police found some cigarette butts crushed inside the car's ashtray. Since Ray did not smoke his nicotine, and his wife did not travel in the station wagon, the butts may have provided potential clues about accomplices with the advent of DNA analysis, but that was still years away for most investigations.[14]

One significant item was missing—the green blanket in the station wagon's hatchback where Ray kept the deer carcasses.[15] Evidence technicians commented in their reports that the hatchback area was suspiciously clean. Lori would later admit to a county patrolman that she was the one who hastily vacuumed out the back of the car after Ray called to warn her the police would soon seize it.[16] Among the items removed from the McCarty garage for FBI analysis were "vacuum cleaner attachments."[17]

Lori's 1988 Pontiac Sunbird was pristine by comparison. In addition to the carpet and seat samples, the evidence technicians only found a traffic warning ticket and a local mental health center receipt.[18]

After being rebuffed for an interview by his prime suspect, Trooper Boyd spent the rest of the day on a high-level orientation trip conducted by La Porte County Prosecuting Attorney William Herrbach. With a barrel chest that burst through his ill-fitting suits and a straightforward way of speaking, Herrbach had a common touch that appealed to juries when he was a deputy prosecutor. He often tried cases where Boyd was a key witness, and their respect was mutual. As leader of the Homicide Team, the prosecuting attorney would rely on Boyd to direct the investigation. Herrbach first drove the state trooper to North 200 East, where Rayna's LTD was abandoned, and from there, they walked the short distance to the Glassman trailer, where they met Brent and heard how he nearly collided with the car in the fog. They next saw county patrolman Pavolka, who lived a few hundred yards around the corner on North 150 East.

For Boyd, Pavolka repeated the details of his perplexing late-night sighting. He was more convinced than ever that Rayna was the female in a Slicer letterman jacket who drove the sedan closely followed by the pickup. Boyd remembers that other investigators found Pavolka's story "less likely," but he adds, "I never discounted Pavolka. It all seemed very real to him, and a policeman is the kind of witness that you want in court."

Herrbach closed his orientation with a five-minute drive from Pavolka's home to Range Road and the pond where Rayna's body was found. Although local police had conducted nearly one hundred interviews during the missing person investigation, the prosecuting attorney had concerns that important witness details had eluded them—especially in the reports written by city detectives. Although it might seem redundant, he wanted Boyd to reinterview the key witnesses again to catch any details the local cops may have missed.[19]

Boyd did not take long to prove the wisdom of Herrbach's request. The trooper characterizes his reinterviews as attempts to "reaffirm" essential information. Still, often he brought out nuance that previous interviewers didn't see that added new evidence to the investigation. A good example was his interview with Garry Bucher, the hog farmer who was a father figure to Ray when he was growing up in Union Mills. LPPD Chief of Detectives John Miller had previously talked to him about McCarty's alibi for the evening of March 26 and learned that Ray could not have called Lori from the barn since the phone there wasn't working.

Boyd brought out something else that negated the alibi—Bucher would have *never* asked McCarty to look after his hogs because "he was not skilled in all the working and feeding of the hogs" and was, on occasion, unreliable. The farmer usually asked a neighbor to help while he was out of town and let the man borrow his pickup in return.

Boyd also got Bucher to talk about Ray's suspicious behavior on April 1, after his interview with Hahn and Keith, and a day before his polygraph in Merrillville. He arrived at Bucher's farm between 7:00 and 8:00 P.M., looking "extremely upset," explaining that he and Lori had given the police two different stories about his activities on March 26. He was even more concerned about how he would do with the lie detector "test." Bucher then offered the fatherly counsel that he should "just tell the truth" and "it would be no problem." That advice made Ray feel no better. He left the farm but returned an hour later in better spirits because he claimed to have found people at the local truck stop who would say he called Lori from there. As police later learned, Ray tried to talk the waitstaff into saying they remembered him when they didn't—even more suspicious behavior.

Jason Tibbs was among Boyd's other reinterviews. Besides Ray, he was the only person cited as a potential suspect. On Friday, April 30, Boyd brought Jason, his mother, and their lawyer, Mike Drayton, to a conference room used by the prosecuting attorney's office. Despite Miller's warning about Jason's "belligerent" attitude, Jason sat through his most extended interview yet with the meticulous state trooper. He revisited the six months he dated Rayna in the seventh grade and their continuing relationship as "best of friends." In dismissing the notion that Rayna drove herself to Rolling Prairie on March 26, Jason told Boyd, "She was a very nervous 'skittish' type person. He described her as a very poor driver and one who could not see well. . . . He said that she did not like to drive at night, and [he] could find no reason she would ever leave town to drive to North La Porte County on a foggy night. . . ."

From his notes, Boyd was particularly interested in Jason's views on the prime suspect.

> [Tibbs] described Ray as being a person to himself [who] seemed to be occupied in his own world. He said that McCarty definitely had an attitude problem and knew that, on occasion, he would meet and try to talk with Rayna. Tibbs

told me that when Rayna was in the eighth grade, Ray had raped her and that her parents had never believed that Ray was responsible for the rape and considered her to be the cause of his actions. Rayna said that she was afraid of Ray, and she was terrified at his being so strong and powerful. She said Lori had recently been taking out her frustrations of what Ray had done [to] her, and she too blamed Rayna for Ray's sexual encounters with her. Rayna had told Tibbs that she hated McCarty because of what he had been doing to her and how he had affected her life. He said she would become upset, and every once in a while, she would begin crying, telling him that it was hard for her to just completely forget about what had happened and how Ray had used her.

Jason next told Boyd about his last call with Rayna a few nights before "her disappearance," when she told him, "Ray's doing it again."

In talking to Jason, Boyd did not just focus on Ray. He also took the teenager through his alibi in more detail than the previous interviews—from his faux tutoring escapade to his Fox Hunt, the late-night hangout with CB friends, and his mother's efforts to rouse him the following day. Boyd also revisited what some officers and family members found most suspicious about his behavior. This included his desire for Rayna to get back together with him, which Jason expressed in an old "love letter" that Rayna's family found in her room. Jason told Boyd that Rayna was "very happy" with Matt, "even though they had their problems," and he did not interfere. Although some police, including Jim Jackson, were surprised that Jason appeared near the dump so soon after the letterman jacket was found, Jason explained that his friend lived around the corner. Finally, Boyd asked about Jason's ring that evidence technicians found in Rayna's car. He told Boyd he had worked on her LTD a few weeks before and pulled the ring out of his pocket when he had to lean against the car. Rayna admired it, and "he had allowed her to use it." He added that "no symbolism" went along with the gift.

Looking back on the interview, Boyd remembers that the only thing that bothered him was how Jason went back to sleep after his mother tried to wake him on Saturday morning. If he was supposedly such good friends with the missing girl, why didn't he get right up? However, that sentiment aside, Boyd concluded in his report that he and the county detective "saw no reason to believe that Tibbs was directly involved in the disappearance and/or death of Rayna Rison."[20]

The next day, May 1, Jason planned to attend Rayna's funeral and bought a jacket for the occasion. But a few hours after the interview with Boyd, he received a call from the individual who reportedly got Rayna's cousin Jenni pregnant. While he talked, Jason says, he had two "buddies" nearby. "He told me the family didn't want me at the funeral. They didn't appreciate what I did and told me I should keep my mouth shut. They said it would cause a scene if I showed up, and I'd have to fight all three of them." Their threat proved too much for Rachel. She had her son move out of La Porte and stay an hour away with his aunt until the hard feelings blew over.

Jason assumed that what he "did" was tell police how Ray had started assaulting Rayna again. One more time, a police report leaked to the Rison family, but Jason was not the only one to make the charge about Ray. Matt and Rayna's girlfriends said much the same. But increasingly, the Rison family had singled Jason out as *their* prime suspect: from Lori mentioning Jason as the only possible suspect she could think of to Wendy with her story about Jason professing his mad love for Rayna as she sat in the back seat of the LTD. Then Bennie joined in too. Just hours after Rayna's body was found, he brought a high school boy named Wayne Zeman to the LPPD station. Zeman had a litany of complaints about Jason, from the way he treated a former girlfriend (by not following through on a promise to take her to the prom) to the rough nature of his friends (Zeman said one of them was "involved with the cults and devil worship"). He also claimed that Jason had threatened him, and he filed a police report in response. Taking their report, the officer concludes: "Wayne and Bennie thought the above information could be useful in the apprehension of the person(s) involved with Rayna's death."[21]

Still, the family had to do more than jettison Jason from the funeral to dispel the suspicions that hung over the victim's brother-in-law. The AP wire service recounted that "family members and friends turned out by the hundreds" at Rayna's funeral service to view "her pink and white casket." The reporter added, "A tattered baby doll from her childhood, a teddy bear, and her clarinet were placed nearby." The article then provided a few less sentimental details: "The automobiles of Lori and Raymond McCarty have been impounded by the La Porte County Homicide Investigation Team, but police refuse to say how that is connected to [Rayna's] death. . . . Raymond

McCarty pleaded guilty in January 1991 [actually 1990[22]] to molesting Rison and served a suspended sentence." The story reports, "The Rison family sat in the front rows of the church, including her parents, grandparents, two sisters, and brother-in-law."[23]

Lori would later complain to friends that because of the search warrant, Ray didn't have his own good shoes for the funeral. But Ray's footwear could not have been more head-scratching than the very ambivalent poem that Lori wrote for the occasion to address her dearly departed sister:

> The good times we had,
> I hold in my heart so dear.
> All of the bad times don't seem so bad.
> I don't know where you are.
> You and I may be siblings driving our folks to their wits' ends.
> We can be each other's worst enemies,
> But we're always best of friends.[24]

THE SPOTTED CAR

During the '70s and '80s, Datsun's B210 cars were not necessarily known for their sleek or classic design. When the company added a station wagon to the line, it unartfully elongated the hatchback version and wedged in another row of seats. Owners most appreciated the B210's ability to get forty miles a gallon at a time when gas prices started to spike. However, the thin metal shell that enabled the model's fuel efficiency made it especially susceptible to rust, which would do more to limit the car's longevity than its engine.[25]

Ray got his 1980 B210 station wagon as a hand-me-down from Bennie,[26] and by 1993, it had dozens of weeping rust spots on both sides of the car, all in varying shades of orange against a baby blue body. The distinctive look, combined with a rusted-out muffler's rattle and roar,[27] made a memorable impression on witnesses and provided police with their most incriminating eyewitness evidence about Ray's location on the night of the abduction.

The Datsun's first and most crucial March 26 sighting was on Warren Street, which ran perpendicular to the Pine Lake Animal Hospital. Around 5:30 P.M., Roy West and John Proud, both twenty-nine, were loading their band equipment into a van for a gig that night. They saw, in West's words, "an old beat-up station wagon with a loud muffler" idling across the narrow street in front of a house with a *For Sale* sign. As West told the police, the bandmates became suspicious that someone was either getting ready to steal their instruments or casing the neighborhood for a future robbery. With Proud looking on, West approached the station wagon, but the driver got out first and met him in the street. He asked West if he knew the price of the house for sale. West says he curtly told him to call the agent and then returned to his van. The driver got back in his car, waited a few minutes, and drove off, but fifteen minutes later, West saw the station wagon idling again, farther down the street and closer to the animal hospital. It was still there when he left for his gig shortly before six.

Although West had called in his tip to the sheriff after Rayna went missing, the county detectives followed up with alacrity once her body was found. They talked to both bandmates[28] and taped an interview with West. Although both men positively identified Ray's Datsun B210, they were not as sure he was the one who got out of the car when they saw a recent picture. West remembered someone "thinner . . . kind of tall and thin," wearing sunglasses, even though it was already dark.[29] Ray was not tall and not thin by any standards. Police chalked up West's description as possibly distorted by the foggy night and their brief meeting.

In the first two weeks of May, two other critical witnesses came forward to describe events they saw in the animal hospital parking lot a few minutes after six o'clock. As they slowly drove by in heavy traffic, Pam Rosebaum[30] and Bryan Durham[31] caught what looked like an argument between a young woman in a letterman jacket and a young man. Two cars in the driveway, parked side by side, partly obscured their view. Both would later identify Rayna's tan LTD as one of the cars. The other, they said, was smaller, and Rosebaum thought its color was silver. According to Durham, the girl was backing up toward the hospital, "waving her arms as if to say, 'go get out of here,' or 'I don't want to talk.'" He said he would have jumped out of his car to help if the man—who had his back to him—had swung at her, but he appeared to keep his distance. Also, Durham saw a light on in the hospital and felt others were there to help her.

The memories of Rosebaum and Durham diverged when describing the man. Rosebaum saw someone young and no more than five feet eight or nine inches tall. Durham believed him to be "lanky and tall," with hair that was "light brown or blonde" like the individual West saw earlier. But Durham remembered an additional odd detail about his appearance—that he was wearing "football pants: tight jersey-type pants cut off below the knees" and a "sweatshirt with the sleeves cut off."

Unlike Rosebaum, Durham saw the driver of the smaller parked car, whom he described as "a white male" with "dark-colored hair." He also remembered that this man was wearing sunglasses.

With the testimony of these three witnesses, a timeline was coming into view consistent with the first stake planted by the animal hospital's receptionist. She believed that Rayna left work a few minutes after six. The altercation that Durham and Rosebaum witnessed took place a few minutes later—between 6:05 and 6:10. The light that Durham saw could have been the vet's security light, which was calibrated to turn on and stay lit for a while after employees went through the exit door that led to the parking area.

As to what happened after Durham and Rosebaum drove by Pine Lake Animal Hospital, the detectives turned to Rene Gazarkiewicz. She first contacted them four days after Rayna's abduction. The thirty-six-year-old was a feisty fireplug who would not hold back her opinions about others involved in the case—especially James McWhirter, who found Rayna's body—and retained abundant details about the crime scene. On the night of March 26, she passed by the animal hospital not once but twice—the first time around 6:10 on her way to get cigarettes for a friend.

Gazarkiewicz approached by driving down Warren Street past where West and Proud had seen the station wagon earlier. By this time, the Datsun was parked in the animal hospital lot as though ready to exit. Before she turned left on Pine Lake, Rene looked back to check for oncoming traffic, and the car's brights turned on, nearly blinding her. She "flipped the individual off," but the headlights forced her to look harder at the offending vehicle. She saw two men inside the car—the one in the passenger seat smoking. A female was leaning through the driver's window. Over time, Gazarkiewicz would further claim that the female was leaning so far into the vehicle that "her feet were in the air." Rene's first impression was that the female had leaned in for a kiss, and nothing was amiss. But of greater importance, she believed the female could have been Rayna Rison, who had been her son's classmate and in the same bowling league.

Gazarkiewicz drove less than half a mile up Pine Lake Avenue to purchase the cigarettes. When she returned to the animal hospital a few minutes later, no other person was in sight. The offending car had still not exited, but the headlights were off, and she got a better look at it. Having once worked for her family's auto body repair shop, she knew her cars and remarked that this was an old one—she estimated an early eighties model—with an unusual "medium blue" color. When Rene had looked into the brights, she saw the headlights were square. Now, with a second look, she saw two other characteristics consistent with Ray's Datsun—no hubcaps and damage to a lower body panel where he had extreme, darkened rust. At this point, Gazarkiewicz also noticed Rayna's car, which had the parking lights on and now sat in front of the hospital lobby, parallel to the street.[32]

Another witness added further credibility to her details and her timeline. Kim Hackney was approaching the animal hospital while driving down Pine Lake. Like Gazarkiewicz, she was blinded by a car in the parking lot with its bright lights on. She saw it leaving between 6:10 and 6:15.[33]

But the animal hospital parking lot was not the last Datsun sighting of the night. Some twenty minutes later, nine miles north, Val Eilers and her nine-year-old daughter had left their home on East 600 North, headed to a school play. As Eilers turned right on the corner of North 150 East, she was shocked to see two cars on the side of the road at the base of a little hill. One car had pulled mostly off the road, but a larger car in front had parked at an angle with its rear end jutting into the middle of North 150 East On seeing that, Val later told the police, she uttered a "no-no word," which would be the evening's most memorable moment for her daughter. She remembered thinking, "I wonder what they're doing there on a night like this?"

While Eilers had room to pull around the car, she feared that in the fog, a car coming down the hill from the other direction wouldn't see her in time. She made it by safely, and in the process, she did get a close look at the intrusive vehicle, which she called "a small station wagon" with four doors and a color that was "faded light blue" or "grayish blue." She described the car's condition as "dusty" and "grungy." She could see two heads inside but couldn't say anything more about them.

A county detective was assigned to interview Eilers at the utility company where she worked. Val, forty-one, was a blonde with a big smile who was proud of her organizational skills and eye for detail. To verify that she got the date right, Eilers took out her "Daily Do" appointment book to show the detective that she had written "play at New Prairie" in the calendar square for Friday, March 26. She repeated the description of the cars she had given over the phone but forgot about one thing in the back of the station wagon that caught her attention. Eilers met with the detective at her home later that evening to retrace the few hundred yards from her driveway to the encounter with the cars. When Eilers took him around the corner to North 150 East, he could see tire treads in the grass shoulder where she said the cars were parked, but after a brief search, he couldn't find any other physical evidence.

In the Eilerses' home, the detective took out color photos of Rayna's LTD, Lori's Sunbird, and Ray's B210 Datsun. Val was sure she didn't see the LTD and was less confident about Lori's car, but when Eilers saw the Datsun, the detective wrote, "She began to shiver and was visibly shaken." Noticing "sudden redness in her face" and "watery eyes," the detective feared Val was about to faint and had her sit on the couch. Once she could compose herself, Eilers pointed out the same area of rust on the bottom of the driver-side panels that had caught Rene Gazarkiewicz's eye and explained it was why she called the car "grungy." As for the back of the station wagon, the feature she couldn't remember was the windshield wiper—still a novelty for smaller cars.[34]

The police received another curious report of a Datsun sighting in the vicinity four days *after* Rayna's abduction. This tip came from a woman who lived up a hill on Range Road, one half-mile north of the pond. Sometime around midnight, she could not sleep and went to her living room to turn on the TV. As she started to sit down, she saw the headlights of a car that had pulled into her driveway. Like other homes in the sparsely populated area, she had no neighbors nearby and became concerned about who it was. She tried to get a better view of the vehicle from other windows in her house, but then it pulled far enough forward to trip the motion detector for the light above her garage, which gave her a clear view of the small station wagon, rust spots and all. Moments later, the car backed out of her driveway and slowly headed down the hill toward the pond. If Ray were behind the wheel, why would he have risked appearing so close to where he hid his victim? Perhaps to see if she was still submerged, checking the view from both sides of Range Road.[35]

In any case, revelations from the Datsun spotters would put a severe crimp in Ray's alibi, which had him headed south to Bucher's hog farm instead of north and a half mile—as the crow flies—from Rayna's abandoned car. They would also fly in the face of McCarty's denials that he had ever been close to the pond or where the LTD was found. These discrepancies were not anything State Trooper Arlie Boyd would keep from prime suspects. He preferred to confront them in person to see how they reacted. But Ray, as Boyd recalls, "avoided me at all costs." Lori was different. "If anything," he says, "at the early stage of the investigation, she was anxious to hear what I had to say."[36]

ALIBI FOR AN ALIBI

As Arlie Boyd looks back on his early interviews in the days after Rayna's body was found, none seemed more important than the ones he had with Lori McCarty and Ray's self-described best friend, Charlie Allen.

With Lori, Boyd says, their interactions were more like fencing than a one-sided interrogation. "At the time, I didn't think she had anything really to do with the homicide, so I decided to stay close to Lori to find out—as much as I possibly could—what was going on behind the scenes. But now I can see she was doing the same thing with me, trying to find out what we knew or didn't know."

For their first meeting on May 11, Boyd showed up at 517 Haviland by himself. He usually found a one-on-one interview in the subject's home could make that person feel more at ease and more likely to tell the truth or at least blurt out something that wouldn't be said in a group setting. He started by asking Lori the questions that had become standard in all her previous police interviews. When did she last see Rayna, and what was she wearing? How did Lori spend the rest of her day? When did she first learn that Rayna was missing? When did Ray first call, and when did he say he was coming home? When *did* he come home? Where was Ray later?

If Boyd had looked closely at Lori's previous interviews, he would have seen her answers to the same questions change in subtle ways—especially regarding her activities during the evening hours of March 26. Some of her answers would change again for Boyd. But police were more drawn to any information she could provide about Ray, which they assumed she had gotten from him. As Lori recited the current version of her husband's alibi, the times and places where he claimed to be on March 26 had shifted significantly or had already been contradicted by other witness interviews. Boyd would not let this go unmentioned, as he detailed in his report about their exchange.

"Ray's story was not believable," he bluntly replied after Lori's latest recounting of his alibi. Boyd wrote that he next explained, "We knew that [Ray] had not been to Bucher's that evening and that we knew for sure that he had been at a location very near the animal hospital where he could readily observe the activities across the street. I also told her that we could show that he was in north La Porte County that evening." Boyd then warned her that the investigators "had great concern as to why he was not telling us the truth."

Lori's response was what Boyd would have expected from a wife who had been kept in the dark about her husband's nefarious activities. He wrote, "Lori became very upset with those facts and asked me if [Ray] had a girlfriend."

Boyd said he knew nothing about a girlfriend but "appreciated her being candid with us . . . that Ray was hiding the truth for whatever reason." Boyd reported that he concluded the interview with the following advice: "Her problem was with Ray and not with me."[37]

For Boyd, this encounter with Lori had moved the investigation forward and left him thinking he had gained a valuable ally. "I was hoping that somewhere, I hit the right nerve. As far as I was concerned, she was sincerely taken aback by what I told her, and she had an attitude that appeared helpful."[38]

But Lori's next steps in supposedly assisting the investigation were not directed at Boyd. Instead, much as what happened after Ray's first interview with Hahn and Keith, the McCartys made an after-hours call to the City of La Porte police station. This time, Lori was first to speak to the dispatcher with an "urgent" request that the Risons' old friend, Detective Bob Schoff, return her call that night. By this time, the family's desire to make Schoff their preferred conduit had come under suspicion from other detectives. Hahn, in particular, expressed concern to his superiors that Schoff had "loose lips." The veteran detective's conversation with the McCartys was among his last contributions to the investigation.

Lori would be the first to talk to Schoff when he called the McCartys back. According to the detective's report, she explained "that she had some new information, and that Ray did not tell the correct story because he had lied to me."

Her wayward husband next got on the line. As Schoff wrote, "Ray started out by saying, 'Can we keep this private and off the record,' because he had not spoken to his attorney yet but was going to him tomorrow and talk him into letting him come in and give his statement."

Ray next asked if his phone was tapped, and Schoff replied that, to his knowledge, it was not. McCarty then made even more significant changes to his alibi. Ray not only admitted he was on Warren Street before 6:00 P.M., but he also said he was in the animal hospital's parking lot, where Rayna saw him from the lobby and came out to talk to him. According to the new alibi, he asked Rayna where Lori was. She told him that she went shopping with Wendy, to which Ray said he replied, "Oh, shit. That's right."

Ray next admitted to Schoff that he did not go south to the hog farm in Union Mills but north, on Highway 39 toward South Bend, to see his therapist. Along the way, he spotted "a girl hitchhiking." He could only describe her as having "brown hair." She asked for a ride to a truck stop further up the road. He first stopped to call his wife from a nearby motel. He said he made up the story about the Bucher hog farm because "I didn't want her to know I picked up a girl."

Lori then took the phone back to say that Ray's new account had been prompted by Boyd's visit with her earlier in the day. When her husband returned home later, "Ray could see she was very upset over something. She then told him that he had not told her the truth." Lori assured Schoff she was confident Ray "was telling the truth this time" and that the police "should look [in] another direction."

But the phone call was not yet over. Ray got back on the line to say that the revolver confiscated during the search was not his and should be returned to the rightful owner, a Teledyne supervisor. Hahn would follow up with the supervisor, who told the detective he had sold the gun to McCarty and not loaned it. After the police seized it, Ray asked him to pretend the Smith & Wesson was still his. Once the police returned it to the supervisor, Ray said he would then get it back from him. If the McCartys' call was an attempt to prove that Ray was ready to turn over a new leaf when it came to telling the truth, the gun story was not the way to end his conversation with Schoff.[39]

As Boyd and Hahn soon discovered, the McCartys were not averse to updating their friends about all the changes Ray kept making to his alibi. At Teledyne, he told his coworkers and supervisor that he had really picked up a hitchhiker and gone north instead of looking at the hogs down south. He added a further embellishment for his buddies about pulling off the road to have sex with the hitchhiker before he dropped her at the truck stop.[40]

But Ray's changes to his alibi did not stop detectives from following up, where possible, to verify if they were true. Of course, they could not track down every potential female hitchhiker with brown hair, but they could go to the little roadside Cassidy Motel, where Ray said he called Lori. The owner, Tom Cassidy, did not remember seeing McCarty on March 26 but said a call could have been made from a pay phone outside his motel.[41] A later search warrant for calls from that number did not find any to the Rison or McCarty households.[42]

Once State Trooper Boyd learned about Ray's new alibi, he appeared on Lori's doorstep at 517 Haviland to ask when they could talk so he could hear the details from her instead of having them filtered through Schoff. But Lori had no interest in any more trooper tête-à-tête. She was now taking the advice of her husband's attorney and getting her own lawyer to join all future meetings with the cops. Boyd said he had no problem with that and suggested she get back in touch once she secured counsel.[43]

After Lori, the detectives would focus their inquiries on forty-three-year-old Charles Edward Allen, who they figured to be Ray's most likely accomplice. In the days following Rayna's disappearance, it did not take long for the police to figure out that Charlie was among McCarty's closest friends. The officers surveilling 517 Haviland saw him arrive as many as eight times in a "small blue car" from which he extracted his "heavyset" body.[44] He was tall—six-foot, three inches—but with his corpulent frame and "reddish" hair and beard,[45] he was nothing like the slim blonde accomplice some witnesses placed at potential Rison crime scenes.

When Hahn first interviewed Allen two days after Rayna's funeral, he disclosed little that could have been related to the abduction or murder. He said he met Ray eight years before when they worked for the Davey Tree Expert Company. They continued to be friends even after Ray left Davey for a job at Teledyne, closer to his home. The two would go hunting in places around Union Mills. Among their favorite haunts was the Bucher hog farm, where they would shoot pigeons. Although they had been fishing a few times, he said, "Ray does not really care for fishing."

When Hahn asked Allen about Ray's molestation charge, he wrote, "Charles stated that Ray told him that the reason for him getting arrested was due to the fact that he was sleeping, and Rayna came and got into bed with him one night. Things happened, and Rayna got pregnant."

Allen did not think that incident would have led Ray to kill her. He was confident of that because he was "close to Ray [and] he did not feel that Ray would do anything to harm Rayna."[46]

Two days later, Boyd took a crack at Allen and brought Charlie to the prosecutor's conference room for the first of several interviews. A county detective joined them. Allen recited much the same information he gave Hahn, including the story about how Ray got Rayna pregnant.

When Boyd asked about Ray's movements on the night of March 26, Allen said Lori had told him that after work, her husband had had something to eat at Taco Bell, down the street from the animal hospital, and then went to Bucher's farm to check on his hogs.

But when Boyd persisted in asking about Allen's activities that Friday evening, the friend suddenly had more information to divulge about Ray. He had visited Charlie at 7:00 or 8:00 P.M. "wearing a camouflaged jacket, cap; and driving the blue Datsun station wagon." McCarty asked to use the phone so that he could call Lori. As far as Allen knew, his phone wasn't working. His live-in girlfriend, Cynthia "Cindy" Brewer, directed Ray to a nearby bar to make the call. At 10:00 P.M., Allen took Brewer to her job at a nursing home. When Charlie returned home, about ten minutes later, he got ready for bed but was awakened by his barking dog and found Ray standing in his doorway. By this time, McCarty had changed out of his camo clothes and was wearing blue jeans. Explaining that he had loaned his car to someone else, Ray asked Allen for a ride home, and Charlie obliged, driving him the three miles to 517 Haviland.

Allen's sudden spate of revelations about Ray took Boyd and the county detective by surprise. They later agreed, as Boyd wrote, "that Charles Allen is very impressionable and might be considered 'dull' in intelligence."[47]

Still, they felt he had not told them the whole truth and probably needed to be interviewed again. Boyd explains, "You have to be careful with people [who are impressionable] because sometimes they help you, but they are just as likely to hurt you."[48]

Another county detective interviewed Cindy Brewer, Allen's girlfriend, for a sanity check before Charlie returned home from the prosecuting attorney's office. She was also one of the McCartys' friends and appeared much more careful about saying anything that could incriminate Ray. She claimed to have been sick for most of the day on March 26 and that their only visitor had been Allen's mother, who was looking for money he borrowed. But when asked about their phone, Brewer admitted that Charlie did not think it was working. She told him it was disconnected but hid it because he racked up too many charges with his long-distance calls. She also agreed it was possible that "someone" had come over to their house after she left for work and that "Charles might have given them a ride somewhere but that she doubted it very much." She then told the detective, "She had no reason to lie [about] the situation and just wanted the police to find out what had happened to the little Rison girl."[49]

SPLITTING HAIRS

For the Rison case detectives, as with most modern homicide investigators, analysis of forensic evidence offered their best hope to seal the case against Ray. By June, an increasing number of witness interviews suggested a motive but no smoking gun for why Ray killed

Rayna when he did. While witnesses unknown to Ray put him or his car in incriminating places, police could not assemble a plausible timeline to account for his movements throughout the evening of March 26. Although they knew McCarty had an accomplice, and Charlie Allen emerged as the most likely candidate, he looked nothing like the witness accounts of a slim—even skinny—blonde associate.

On the other hand, with his constantly changing alibi, nobody did more to raise suspicions about Ray than McCarty himself. His attempts to get others to lie about it further betrayed a consciousness of guilt. Still, ironically, his previous bad behavior could explain the shifting stories. Multiple women told police about his philandering ways, how Lori had repeatedly caught him in the act, and his attempts to hit on them. If he had really picked up a female hitchhiker and then drove out of his way to accommodate her, he had every reason to hide that from an already suspicious wife.

Detectives expected more witness interviews would eventually fill in the gaps for circumstantial evidence, but they were also looking for incontrovertible physical evidence linking Ray to the crime. Yet, over and over, analysis from forensic specialists proved paltry or even more confusing.

The fog that engulfed Rayna's cause of death started with the string of confusing statements that La Porte County Coroner Barbara Huston made to the press shortly before the funeral. "Rayna was abducted and fought off her assailants," she said. "It may be that in the process . . . she was knocked unconscious. She may have been dead before she was tossed into the water or was unconscious when she was put in the water, or someone may have held her head under water." To make matters even hazier, she added that Rayna "definitely died as the result of asphyxiation and while it could have been from drowning, we found no water in her lungs."

But moments later, she undercut her previous suppositions by saying, "It couldn't be determined if she had been beaten or how she may have been knocked unconscious." Like the chief of detectives, the coroner blamed the corpse's month of decomposition for their failure to be conclusive. "The body was too badly deteriorated [so that] bruises couldn't be determined."[50]

By the time Huston's comments hit the public, however, Rayna's autopsy was complete, and the findings contradicted most of what the coroner said.

Dr. Rick Hoover, the forensic pathologist who performed the procedure, concluded that there was no "definitive evidence of injury." In other words, Rayna could not have "been beaten," as the coroner told the press. Furthermore, it was unlikely she "fought off her assailants" or that someone had "held her head under water." After close examination, Hoover could see that "the cutaneous [skin] surface demonstrates no evidence of lacerations, hemorrhage, contusion or ecchymoses [large bruises]."[51] In other words, the body was *not* "too badly deteriorated that bruises couldn't be determined," as the coroner and chief of detectives claimed.

Then what exactly killed Rayna? Again, contrary to Huston's statements, Hoover believed drowning was unlikely. Instead, he listed the cause of death as "Asphyxia due to cervical compression"—namely strangling—and the manner of death was "Homicide."

As Hoover later explained, his conclusion was not based on physiologic evidence. There were no signs of bruising around the victim's neck and, internally, there were no fractures in the neck bones—although that's not uncommon for young women who have been strangled. Much more telltale signs of strangulation are little pinpoint spots from broken blood vessels known as petechiae. These appear in the face, eyelids, and the skin around the eye. Hoover could not find the petechiae or perhaps did not look for them. In the autopsy report, he uses decomposition as a partial excuse, explaining that it would "mask any minor hemorrhages" resulting from strangulation.[52]

For Hoover, the only remaining explanation for Rayna's death would be "homicidal poisoning which, upon completion of postmortem toxicological studies, should be ruled out."[53] But later, when those results came in, they were not what the pathologist expected. The volatile drug screen of Rayna's blood revealed an unusually high concentration of isopropanol—commonly known as isopropyl alcohol. The initial test showed 43.8 milligrams per deciliter (mg/dL) or 438 parts per million. The lab wrote that if ingested at that level, the subject "may exhibit slight alcoholic influence," while a 100 mg/dL concentration would be "lethal."[54]

The appearance of isopropyl alcohol in Rayna's system would be another of the mysteries about the homicide that confounded investigators. The first toxicology test also indicated a trace amount of cocaine, which the detectives disbelieved given what they knew about the victim. This one finding made them doubt the isopropanol results as well. Hoover then sent the blood and gastric samples to another lab. While this facility found no cocaine, it returned results showing a similarly high concentration of isopropanol.[55]

The question then emerged: How did it get into Rayna's system? The most common form of isopropyl alcohol is rubbing alcohol. At one point, a clearly mystified detective Hahn asked Matt Elser if his girlfriend was "experimenting with drinking rubbing alcohol"—a question that stunned the boyfriend. He replied that she wasn't drinking anything more potent than wine coolers.[56] Given the pain and damage rubbing alcohol would cause to the sinuses and digestive system, only the most desperate alcoholics swill the substance. It is then metabolized into another chemical, acetone. But then again, no acetone was detected in Rayna's blood screen, something the lab characterized as "ABNORMAL," using all caps to call out the unexpected result and a clear indication that she didn't drink it.[57]

At first, for Hoover, the test results had only one explanation: isopropanol was a byproduct of decomposing organs. He then researched that possibility but concluded in a letter to Hahn, "Standard postmortem decomposition does not include the creation of the volatile Isopropyl Alcohol (Isopropanol)."[58]

Although they continued discussions with Hoover, detectives did not believe his autopsy or subsequent toxicology tests provided them with evidence that could tie Ray to the homicide or even definitively explain how he killed Rayna. Instead, when it came to forensic analysis, they would pin their hopes on much smaller things: hairs and fibers—known as trace evidence. The FBI had an entire lab devoted to analyzing this material in Washington, DC.

At the end of May, the LPPD evidence technician, Stephen Ames, sent the FBI's Trace Evidence Unit items taken from the McCarty home and cars, along with what was found in Rayna's LTD. He included victim hair "standards"—taken from brushes and the corpse—that could be compared with hairs found in the other material. The letterman jacket was already sent and underwent extensive "scraping" to remove all surface debris.

In his introductory letter, Ames revealed preliminary conclusions that homicide detectives had already made in concert with Hoover's autopsy. "Victim was carried into the water, not dumped!" Ames wrote. "No signs of defensive wounds or trauma usually associated with physical force beatings or strangulation."[59]

Douglas Deedrick, the special agent who ran the FBI's trace evidence lab, was considered law enforcement's leading expert in the field. A few years later, for a brief time, he'd become a household name as a central witness for the prosecution in O. J. Simpson's murder trial. In photos and videos from that period, his full head of prematurely gray hair is carefully combed in a preppy style that contrasts with a thin boyish face and gold-rim glasses. Standing before large charts with a pointer like Poindexter, he gave the jury a wonkish introduction to trace analysis and the fiber evidence that incriminated Simpson.[60] Later, during cross-examination, he calmly fended off dayslong grilling from defense counsel.[61] He was precisely the sort of expert witness to impress judges and instill prosecutors with confidence in those minuscule bits of evidence.

Only a couple of weeks after receiving the shipment from La Porte, Deedrick called Hahn with exciting news—two fibers found on Rayna's clothes matched fibers found in the McCartys' cars. One was a light blue color like Ray's B210 carpet materials. As luck would have it, Deedrick used to drive a 1980 Datsun, so the color immediately caught his attention as he examined the debris scraped from the Matt Elser letterman jacket. A black fiber found on Rayna's blue jeans appeared to come from the carpet in Lori's Sunbird. Deedrick wanted to clip relevant standards from each vehicle to confirm the match.

Green acrylic strands found in Rayna's hair, clothes, and both McCarty cars most attracted the FBI analyst's attention. They accounted for the bulk of fibers collected and could have been transferred from one vehicle to the next by a driver or passenger. Since this trace material was so prevalent, it must have come from an item with a relatively large surface area, like a blanket. Several witnesses had commented about a blanket Ray kept in the Datsun's hatch that he used to wrap deer carcasses. He may have done the same with Rayna's body.

The police needed a second search of the McCartys' residence and vehicles to get their carpet standards, find the blanket, and pick up potential additional evidence that had been missed when officers focused on finding Ray's footwear during the first search. Deedrick also wanted samples of the couple's hair to see if it matched unidentified strands they found on the letterman jacket and a clump taken from under the steering wheel of Rayna's LTD.[62]

The potential for the second search was so great that Deedrick went to La Porte himself. His first order of business was to help Hahn and the prosecutor get the warrant by testifying in the probable cause hearing for the search before Judge Robert Gettinger. As it turned out, they did not need to flex their persuasive powers. The judge was as well briefed on the investigation as anyone in the courtroom and inclined to help the investigators.

However, at one point during the hearing, Deedrick did need to address a question about fiber analysis most often asked by skeptics: How can guilt or even a search warrant be predicated on a few nearly microscopic fibers when the victim was exposed to so many other fibers during the course of her day? Deedrick explained, "Because fibers are transitory in nature, they can be lost very quickly." He argued that the ones that remained on Rayna's hair and clothing were among the last she encountered.[63]

One part of the probable cause hearing may have surprised Deedrick as much as it did the judge. The prosecutor asked that the search warrant be kept confidential until after an arrest. While the judge ultimately granted the request, he had to research first to see if that was possible.[64] The only reason to keep the search secret was to protect Ray McCarty from bad publicity. It was strange deference for such a prime suspect. Still, Bennie had vociferously complained that the investigation had focused too much on Ray, and Prosecuting Attorney Herrbach did not want news about the search to increase friction with the victim's family.

Hahn was most concerned that there would be no leak *before* the search at 517 Haviland, as happened the last time. He didn't have to worry. Lori was so unprepared for the warrant she was smoking a joint with a female friend when the police arrived, or so she later scoffed to someone else. She claimed there was still a "roach clip and marijuana in the ashtray," but the cops never noticed.[65]

Deedrick was also part of the team that searched the residence and the vehicles. He was the one who took the standards from the cars' carpets and seat covers. This time, the detectives didn't want anything else to slip through the cracks. Car seats were removed to provide better access to debris underneath. Among the items seized: a red Santa Claus suit to see if its fabric matched with red fibers found in Rayna's clothes (it didn't); the contents and cleaning tools of a Shop-Vac vacuum, which they believed Lori used to vacuum out the trunk of Ray's Datsun; various green-colored clothing including a child's sweatshirt; snowbrushes (they tend to attract loose fibers); and a blue electric blanket found in the backyard.

Deedrick did not find the blanket that he thought was the source of the green acrylic fibers, but he made an unexpected discovery on Lori's dresser—a plastic wand twenty inches long with two metal prongs at one end. The label read: O-Mega Super Baton Stun Gun. Upon activation, the prongs could deliver a jolt of 120,000 volts.[66]

Detectives already knew that Ray had purchased a 46,000-volt stun gun on March 19, a week before Rayna's abduction, and then exchanged it the next day for the much more powerful model.[67] Like other potentially incriminating behavior, neither Lori nor Ray hid the purchase from friends and coworkers. At Teledyne, a few people in the break room noticed a mark on McCarty's biceps that looked like a snakebite. He explained that he had bought a stun gun and asked the cashier to try it on him first. One witness reported him saying, "It knocked the shit out of [my] arm. Imagine what it would do to a smaller person in the right place."[68] When the police tracked down the store where Ray bought the stun gun, the cashier confirmed McCarty's odd request. However, he said he refused to demonstrate it on Ray.[69] Most suspiciously, the McCartys had varying explanations for why Ray got the stun gun. Ray told some people they had trouble with vicious dogs in their neighborhood.[70] He and Lori told others it was for her protection when she left her job at the video store late at night.[71]

Although Ames had asked Deedrick if he could analyze the device, Hahn had forgotten to put it on the search warrant. When the agent showed the stun gun to Lori, she dismissed it as no longer working but said her lawyer hadn't decided whether she should give it to the police. Deedrick could do no more than hand it back to her. Otherwise, Deedrick was not disappointed by his haul and seemed confident it would confirm more connections between Rayna and the prime suspect.

Unbeknownst to Deedrick, Lori had discussed the stun gun only hours before with Arlie Boyd. They had rescheduled their interview once she secured counsel. Again, it fell on the same day as a later search. The trooper and Hahn met with Lori and her lawyer at the City of La Porte police station.

There would be no back-and-forth fencing session like their previous meetings. Boyd expected that the lawyer would rein in her more intemperate remarks. This time, the trooper zeroed in on *her* timeline and focused on areas where she kept changing details or conflicted with the memories of other witnesses.

Once again, Lori had a new piece of information to impart—probably because she knew the police had already found out. At some point during the day on March 26, Lori told Boyd she called the video store where she was supposed to work that night to quit the job—supposedly because she had found a better one. Boyd later learned that with such short notice, the employer begged her to work one more shift or find a replacement. Lori promised she would but did neither.

Lori said she spent the afternoon with her sick mother and never went home to 517 Haviland. But Wendy Rison had told Boyd that her sister wasn't at the family's house when she returned home after school with her boyfriend. She had to call Lori at 517 Haviland to remind her they needed a ride to the mall as promised. When Boyd challenged her on this, he wrote, "Lori could not remember whether she may have gone home during the day or not but did state to us that it was very possible that she drove home for some purpose."

Lori had another memory lapse about when she left the Rison house after they returned from the mall. She said she went home at 7:00 P.M., as in her previous interviews. But in separate interviews with the police, Wendy and her boyfriend had Lori leaving with the kids around six. Both remember her saying Ray was waiting with dinner for them. When Boyd challenged her on the time she left, "Lori said that she could not remember and that she may have gone home earlier."

She did recall Ray was not at 517 Haviland when she got there but that he called to say he was at the hog farm and would be coming home soon. Lori was unaware that Bob Schoff had shared the new hitchhiker alibi with the other detectives. Now, pulling no punches, Boyd stopped the interview.

He went looking for Schoff and brought him back into the room. The city detective then repeated what he heard from Ray while Lori was on the line. At this point, her lawyer interjected that she should not answer any questions about the new alibi, but with Schoff in the room, Lori did not deny what he heard from Ray.

Boyd's following questions were more rapid-fire and reflected the insights that Deedrick's fiber findings had brought to the investigation:

> In the week prior to her disappearance, [had] Ray ever ridden with Rayna in her car?
> She did not think so.
> [Did] Ray ever [drive] her gray Sunbird?
> He probably drove it on Saturday and Sunday after Rayna's disappearance.
> [Did] Rayna ever [drive] her car?
> It was a stick, and she could not drive a stick.
> [Had] Rayna ever ridden in [Lori's] car?
> On occasion.
> [Had Lori] ever driven Ray's car?
> She had not.
> [Had Rayna] ever driven it?
> Not to her knowledge, but [Rayna] had ridden in the car with Ray.
> [Did she have] a fight with Rayna in the last week prior to her disappearance?
> She did have a disagreement with her, but it was all [about] the abortion to be performed upon Jennifer McCleland.
> Was Ray having sex again with Rayna?
> She emphatically said she did not know of any such event taking place.
> [Did] she [have] possession of a stun gun?
> Ray purchased a small stun gun for her approximately one week before Rayna's disappearance.

Lori elaborated more about the stun gun, explaining that Ray bought it for "protection in her work." She mentioned that he originally purchased one he tested on himself and deemed insufficient. He then exchanged it for a more powerful one and asked her to try it on him. "After much coaxing," Boyd wrote, "she put the stun [gun] against him and triggered the mechanism. [It] knocked him completely from the bed and stunned him for some period of time." Despite these revelations, after talking with her counsel, Lori was not ready to turn the stun gun over to Boyd for further examination. The session would end with Lori asking if Boyd was done with her. The trooper said it was likely unless more information was developed.[72]

Ultimately, Lori did turn over the stun gun to City of La Porte police, but only after Hahn fulfilled one of her more macabre requests. According to the detective, she called at the end of July to see if she could "view photos of Rayna the way police found her." Hahn replied, "It is not custom[ary] for police to allow photos such as these to be viewed by family members." But Lori insisted, claiming that it would allay her "nightmares and she can't get it out of her mind that Rayna might still be alive. . . . She understood that the photo we have will not be of a pleasant nature."

While Hahn admitted that he "saw no immediate reason to deny her the opportunity," he still had to run it by other investigators. When he called Boyd, the trooper agreed there was "no harm" in letting her look.

Hahn called Lori back the next day to let her know she could see some selected shots. Lori appeared at the police station thirty minutes later. The detective first showed her a close-up of the rings on Rayna's puffy left hand after she was pulled from the water. Next came a photo of her sister's leg inside the blanched jeans and under the cross of the two long tree limbs. The final, gruesome view was of Rayna's unrecognizable face—bloated and pink like some Cabbage Patch doll—above the E.U.R.O. sweatshirt as she was pulled from the water.

While Hahn noted Lori's "nervousness" as she started looking at the photos, he added, "Other than that, not much emotion was displayed."

Before she left the station, Hahn asked again for the stun gun, and she let him take possession a few weeks later. Hahn packed up the stun gun and shipped it to the FBI for further analysis.[73]

Meanwhile, Deedrick had already compared the standards he took during the second McCarty search warrant. He was now confident that fiber scraped from the letterman jacket could be traced to Ray's Datsun. Likewise, he could connect the black fabric on Rayna's jeans with Lori's Sunbird. The ubiquitous green acrylic from the assumed missing blanket had also cropped up in debris swept from the two vehicles during the second, more thorough search that Deedrick personally supervised.

The agent let the Indiana investigators know that more examinations were in progress, especially those that involved the McCarty hair standards and other strands found in the second search.[74] With that news, Boyd met with Herrbach in early August. They agreed to take a break while waiting for more FBI lab analysis. But as Boyd concluded his forty-eight-page report on findings to date, he didn't want to give the impression that the Rison case detectives were stymied. "The matter is still under investigation," he wrote, "and Raymond McCarty is the prime suspect in this case."[75]

WITH A LITTLE HELP FROM THEIR FRIENDS

As detectives reached out to dozens of the McCartys' friends through the first months of 1994, a few common themes emerged in their interviews. One was the nearly compulsive nature of the couple's gregariousness. They did not just meet people and let the relationship slowly build to something more intimate. Instead, there was an immediate embrace and a deluge of convivial gestures. These gestures applied to distant relatives and childhood classmates who had wandered back into their orbit, neighbors, coworkers, or even clerks at frequented stores. Soon after meeting, there would be more visits at the new pal's home, followed by a stream of phone calls. One recipient of this affection was Gayla Moreau, whose ex-husband, Martin Holt, had been Ray's childhood friend. After they married, the two couples would double date, and Lori would be in constant contact with Gayla. "She would call me almost every day and could talk for hours," Moreau remembers.[76]

Another refrain from the interviews with wives and girlfriends was Ray's inappropriate and highly sexualized behavior. "He would do weird things," Gayla told the police. "Like once we were all eating at a German-style restaurant, and he ordered frog legs. When the waitress came to the table, he started looking between the legs and even asked her, 'Are these all girl's frog legs?' There was another time we were walking into a department store, and they had an underwear display, and he'd pick up the panties and smell them to see if anybody tried them on. You'd think, 'Ewww! Do I really know this guy?'"[77]

Eventually, Ray's loose talk would turn into unwanted advances. Several women who police interviewed reported Ray's attempts to hit on them. "He had a habit of showing up when he knew I was alone with the kids," Gayla says. "It gave me the chills, and the more I rebuffed him, the angrier he got with my kids."

McCarty's lascivious ways even extended to family relations. One in-law told a detective he "would start talking about his sex life" when he was alone with her, including "intimate details" about what he did with Lori in bed. She added, "He has a problem with touching people and especially females. . . . [Our] family is a close and hugging family, but Ray seems to take this a step further." She said other females in the family had also expressed this concern.[78]

With almost all acquaintances—even the ones she didn't know well—Lori brought up Ray's molestation charge, characterizing it as an "affair" and assigning as much or more blame to Rayna.[79] For some, Lori also talked about "the fight" with her sister shortly before her disappearance.[80]

What most interested the detectives was what Lori said "in real time" on March 26 and the following weeks as their investigation intensified. Without prompting, she would bring up Ray's missing boots and the stun gun—sometimes showing great concern that the police were closing in on her husband or laughing off their attempts.

When Arlie Boyd returned to the case in January 1994, these friends and coworkers would be his focus in nearly two dozen interviews over the next ten months. He conducted many with Hahn and others alone after the city detective opened seams for the trooper to probe further. As filtered through their contacts, the couple's comments gave detectives a view inside the McCartys' psyches that could have accompanied every stage of the crime. In some cases, this amounted to critical circumstantial evidence.

Among the friend interviews that may have shown Ray's preparation for the disposal of his victim's body were those conducted with Darold Willis and his wife, Connie. The men used to hang out at the Rod-N-Reel Bait shop, where they bought their hunting equipment. Together, they would shoot pigeons with shotguns and deer with bows and arrows. As he did with so many other friends, Ray told Willis about the molestation charge, blaming Rayna for "parad[ing] around in front of him in only her bra and panties [to] tease him [and] things got the best of him." Willis told police he reprimanded Ray about the [eleven-year] gap in their ages. "[Ray] should have known better." Ray then "looked him straight in the eye and told him that this only happened two times."

Willis says he initially believed McCarty, but their relationship would ultimately fray in the days before Rayna went missing. Darold's wife, Connie, told police that Ray called one night, sounding "very nervous." As he spoke, she recalled, "it seemed like he was out of breath." McCarty wanted to borrow Darold's pickup truck. Connie explained that her husband had it with him for a job he was doing out of state. Ray called the next night, asking if her husband was back yet. Darold knew enough about Ray's womanizing ways to resent the calls to his wife while he was out of town, which ended his friendship with McCarty.[81]

Ray's desperate requests to borrow a pickup the week before March 26 became another theme in interviews with his friends.[82] However, the detectives never determined how he got a truck or from whom.

Twenty-two-year-old Mark Emerick had surprisingly intimate knowledge of the McCarty family and their reaction to the police investigation. Yet, his principal connection to Lori was checking out the videos she rented at a store where the McCartys were frequent shoppers. Video Express, his grandmother's business, was just two hundred feet from the couple's home when they lived across the street from Teledyne. Lori or Ray would appear almost daily to rent a video or buy a snack. Often, Lori stayed to chat with the affable young man behind the counter, and after they moved, she invited him at least once to each of their next two residences. Both husband and wife told Emerick about Ray's "affair" with Rayna at some point in the friendship.

On Saturday morning, March 27, Lori was waiting at Video Express when Mark arrived to open. Appearing distraught, she gave him one of Rayna's *Missing* posters to hang in the store and left soon after. Over the next few weeks, she dropped by with updates on the police investigation but made light of their efforts because "Rayna had just run away." Still, Lori also felt the need to brief Emerick on her March 26 activities in minute detail, along with each change in Ray's hog farm alibi.

Emerick did not consider himself one of Lori's close friends, but after Rayna's body was found, she quickly called to give him the news—the first time she ever phoned him at home. Later, he would get updates on the hitchhiker alibi and the stun gun that knocked Ray off the bed. She confided in Mark about "how angry she had become over Ray and Rayna's relationship" and that "Rayna wasn't innocent like it had seemed." Finally, in full confession mode, she spoke about her fight with Rayna a few weeks before her disappearance, although she added that the two sisters "made up" soon after.

Lori's anger for her sister stood out for the detectives when they interviewed Emerick. They were also struck by her oversharing with such a casual acquaintance.[83] They found that Ray could be just as indiscreet with individuals he had just met. Mike Kepplin was introduced to Ray when he briefly dated Wendy shortly after Rayna's disappearance. The two enjoyed bowhunting deer and, according to Kepplin, "hit it off real good from the start." Soon, the eighteen-year-old would go to the McCartys' house without Wendy, and he remained friends with Ray after breaking up with her. During his visits, Ray would take him into the bedroom or in the backyard to shoot arrows and discuss what he did on the evening of March 26. Each time, McCarty added new details. One was something the police had never heard before. Ray admitted to seeing Rayna in the animal hospital parking lot but told Mike that Rayna got in his car and there was "horseplay."

Lori was with them when Ray offered the alibi about the hitchhiker. The young friend thought this was the first time she heard the story. She seemed very upset. When they were alone later, Ray confided he had sex with the hitchhiker. For Kepplin, the changing alibis only made him more suspicious. At one point, he says, he asked Ray if he killed Rayna. As Hahn reported, "Ray would only say [to Kepplin] that the police are trying to get a coon up a tree, and [Ray] was not going to be that coon. Ray never told [Kepplin] that he didn't kill Rayna."[84]

Brian Townsend was another of Ray's hunting buddies, and Lori latched onto his wife Tina as a confidant. Unlike most of her friends, Tina knew Rayna well. Before the Townsends moved from downtown to the country, they lived only a block from the Risons' home and frequently used their middle daughter as a babysitter. Coincidentally, Lori had gone to the Townsend house on the day Rayna's body was found. The two women chatted while their children were playing. They had not yet heard the news, but according to a Hahn report, Lori shocked Tina by "saying that someone probably threw [Rayna] in the water." She then asked her host, "How long does it take a body to float up out of the water?"

Lori would soon find out. Tina received a call from her grandmother, who had heard that Rayna's body had been found in a pond off Range Road. When Tina relayed the dreadful news, Lori calmly collected her children and said she would head to Range Road.[85] But instead, she returned home, where her friend Leah called to say she also heard that a body had been found at the pond.[86] Even after the second tip, Lori did not go to Range Road to check for herself. Instead, she left the children home with Ray and went for a tan at Time and a Half video.[87]

Two women closer to Lori than Tina gave police conflicting views on her state of mind during the investigation and the state of her marriage. Robin Dingman had been one of Lori's best friends in high school but moved away for nine years after graduating. When she returned to La Porte, now divorced, the friendship was rekindled, followed by Lori's daily calls. Ray's molestation charge had happened while Robin was away, but Lori minimized the impact it had on her sister by saying, "Rayna wanted it and was more than willing to do it with Ray."

One of Lori's calls to Robin came at 6:00 A.M. on Saturday, March 27. Lori cried as she told Dingman that Rayna was missing and explained why something must have happened to her. Robin helped by babysitting Hunter on Sunday while Lori and Ray put up *Missing* posters. Once Rayna's body was found, Ray and Lori expected help of a different kind. McCarty first broached the request at his sister-in-law's wake. He asked Robin, "Let's go for a walk," and then sat down with her to talk in the funeral home lobby. Mostly, he wanted to know what "the police are doing" with their investigation of Rayna's homicide. Lori knew Dingman was good friends with a dispatcher for the LPPD's 911 system. But that person would not have shared sensitive information. Robin repeatedly told Ray she had no idea what the police were doing. Then, as if to earn her confidence, Ray told Robin he had a new alibi. Instead of going south to the hog farm, as McCarty told his wife, he had gone north to repay a friend in South Bend for a loan. He picked up a female hitchhiker along the way and dropped her off at a truck stop. He lied about the hog farm because he didn't want his wife to get angry "that he was with another woman" that night.

Dingman wanted no part of his confession or the conversation—especially at that time or in that place. If nothing else, his hitchhiker story

117

put him near Range Road and contradicted his claim a few minutes earlier that he had "never been in the area where Rayna was found." Robin excused herself to return to the mourners. But Dingman's suspicions about Ray were never echoed by Lori. Instead, she called Robin daily, pressing her to get information from her dispatcher friend. Lori complained "she was being harassed by the police," who were "trying to talk to her all the time." She had gotten a lawyer to stop that, but Lori said she was also getting counseling at a local mental health center to deal with the stress.[88]

Compared to Robin, Jeanette Zellers was one of Lori's more recent and casual friends, which did not prevent McCarty from divulging "intimate details of information related to Rayna's death," according to Hahn's report. The two met while cleaning out factory offices for Service Master—the supposedly better job that Lori took after she quit the video store. Unlike Dingman, Jeanette often heard Lori doubt her husband's innocence. As Zellers put it to Hahn, "Lori is on a roller coaster. . . . One time [she] is convinced that her husband Ray is involved in Rayna's death and the next moment says, 'No way.'" As the first anniversary of Rayna's abduction approached, Lori leaned more fully into *No Way*, telling Zellers that she had sent her kids to a friend in Wisconsin. "If Ray was arrested," she said, "she would not let Ray go without a fight. Even if it meant her going to jail with Ray."

According to Jeanette, as the women worked, Lori talked incessantly about the case, perhaps testing new alibi stories on her or grooming the confidant for an inevitable police interview. But Zellers was listening carefully, noticing the changes in Ray's alibis and how Lori shifted the account of her activities on March 26. Lori first told Jeanette that she left her parents' home at 6:00 P.M. but later said it was at seven. Similarly, the time she quit the video store went from the morning to the afternoon; in fact, the employer's records showed 11:00 A.M.[89] Lori told Zellers this was why Ray didn't know where to reach her later in the day. For reasons Zellers did not understand, Lori talked about Rayna babysitting two days before her disappearance and how the big sister sent her to the store in her Sunbird. As police knew, the story was patently untrue because Rayna couldn't drive a stick, but it may have been concocted to counter forthcoming fiber evidence.

None of the new twists were fooling Jeanette. She figured that Lori fed her all the updates for some ulterior motive. If Zellers needed one more reminder of the couple's moral depravity, it came when Lori showed up at her house after the second police search. She had a box she asked Jeanette to store for them because it contained "adult toys and movies, the X-rated kind" that she didn't want the cops to find. Zellers replied, "Nothing of the such was ever coming into her home."[90]

Like Zellers, Brenda Pegg was another of Lori's acquaintances who watched the McCartys' antics with an increasingly jaundiced eye, usually keeping her opinions about them to herself. The detectives found her a particularly astute source of information as a neighbor, babysitter, and cashier at another place the couple frequently patronized, the Little Saver convenience store and gas station on Pine Lake Avenue. Although she knew Lori and Ray "for some time," the relationship had started to sour shortly before Rayna was abducted. While she was alone with him in the store, Ray had made an awkward pass by grabbing her around the shoulder and asking her out to a nearby bar. He had touched her before in ways that made her uncomfortable, but this time, Brenda pushed him away and told him to stay where he was. She then picked up the phone, and when Ray asked what she would do, she told him she was calling her husband. He ran out of the store, and they never had much to say after that.

As a babysitter and neighbor, Pegg already knew of incidents that made her question the McCartys' parenting skills. Her roommate saw Ray roughly grab his daughter in Pegg's home, and as a result, they no longer let him enter the house. Brenda had concerns, too, about how Lori treated her daughter Adrienne. She told Hahn about meeting the school bus during a recent snowstorm. After collecting her child and starting to walk home, she heard Adrienne call and run after her. Lori had not been there waiting for her, and Adrienne could not get into their house. Pegg took the wet and crying child home with her and called the girl's mother. She had to let the phone ring thirty times before Lori finally answered. She did not walk the few hundred yards to pick up Adrienne for another thirty minutes.

More disturbing were things the six-year-old said while Pegg was babysitting. "Why did Daddy make my Rayna go away?" she asked once.

Also: "Why did Mommy not let my Rayna come back?" Adrienne would also tell her that she saw Rayna emerge from the bathroom with a sheet wrapped around her and was scolded by Ray "to get [her] fucking ass back to bed."

With this knowledge and her contempt for the McCartys, Pegg paid close attention to Ray and Lori whenever they entered the Little Saver to purchase their daily sundries. On March 26, nothing seemed out of the ordinary for Ray. He stopped in after work for the usual can of Skoal chewing tobacco and candy bars. But she remembered Lori acting differently, "very jittery and talking a mile a minute and pacing." During Brenda's shift that night, Lori made three visits, each time buying a pack of cigarettes, candy bars, and a bottle of pop. She asked Brenda a favor during her first stop in the early evening. If she saw Ray later, she should tell him she was going to work. It was a strange message since Lori had quit that job earlier in the day, but she acted like she still had the job, even complaining about the drive across the town to the video store "in this crappy weather." Brenda saw her again around 10:30, this time asking if she had seen Rayna. Then, she returned in the Rison family car instead of the Sunbird at closing time. Pegg had already locked the door, but when Lori waved through the window, she let her in. Lori's pack of cigarettes was the last sale Brenda rang up on the register. Lori asked again if she had seen Rayna and told Pegg her sister was missing.[91]

There was yet another McCarty associate with even more to tell. Ironically, Lori had first mentioned her friend Pat Walters and her husband Richard during an easygoing interview with LPPD detective Bob Schoff. They were the only ones Rayna knew who lived close to where the LTD was found. Lori took for granted that Schoff would let the information pass and never follow up.

But Arlie Boyd was no Bob Schoff. When the investigation resumed in early 1994, Lori was among the first reinterviews the trooper scheduled. This time, probably after consulting with her lawyer, who was in attendance, Lori did not ramble but provided a straightforward recitation of her activities on March 26. She reverted to saying that she left her parents' house at 7:00 P.M., even if that conflicted with what Wendy and her boyfriend remembered. Lori was now vague about Ray's schedule, putting his return home between 4:00

and 8:00 P.M., but she was sure he stayed home for the rest of the evening. She did not comment on her husband's alibis. Instead, her timeline had her leaving the children with him around 9:30 so she could buy groceries at Kroger. Not until she returned home at 10:30 did she get a call from her mother and learn that Rayna was missing. When asked about the stun gun, Lori replied that Ray had bought it for her protection at night. She explained that it might have been broken when she dipped it in a goldfish bowl and killed a sick fish that would have been "flushed" otherwise.

Boyd asked about Pat Walters as they were wrapping up the interview. "Did she know her?" he asked. Boyd wrote that Lori replied, "Pat once worked with [Lori]. They had become very good friends and [talked] almost daily." When she asked why Boyd wanted to know, he reminded her that she had mentioned Walters when Schoff first interviewed her.[92]

The likelihood that Boyd would soon be talking to Pat Walters probably did not sit well with Lori and may have sparked a confrontation with Ray later that day. According to a neighbor across the street from 517 Haviland, "there was a big fight between Lori and Ray. . . . You could hear the screaming from Lori behind [their] closed doors. . . . She was mad about having to be interviewed by the police, and she was blaming Ray for this." Lori then followed up her shouting by "throwing things believed to be Ray's out of the front door." The neighbor said she had witnessed other loud arguments between the McCartys in the past, but "usually it is Ray doing the yelling."[93]

As it turned out, Lori's concerns about Pat Walters were well placed. Her interviews would be among the most significant in the Homicide Team's investigation. Nearly two decades older, Pat and Richard were parent figures for the young couple, who they found more entertaining and simpatico than their birth parents. The McCartys were frequent guests at the Walterses' comfortable brick ranch, with its big picture window overlooking the woods and an enclosed back porch.

Hahn and Boyd arrived at the Walterses' home two days after they talked to Lori. Thinking back to March 26, Walters remembered that she and her husband had ventured through the fog in the early evening for take-out food from Arby's. They returned home between 6:30 and 7:00 when Pat received a call from Lori. As she recalled, McCarty "seemed somewhat concerned" because

Rayna had not come home. As Boyd wrote in his report, "Pat told her not to worry, that it was still very early and she shouldn't be too concerned yet."

This information was stunning for the detectives. Only two days before, Lori told them she didn't learn that Rayna was missing until ten thirty. As Pat said, there should have been no need for concern that early in the evening. Later, Lori would tell Walters she only went to the Little Saver for milk and cigarettes. Lori never talked to Pat about going to the Kroger grocery store, as she had just told the detectives.

Since the investigation started, Pat had gone on the same roller coaster with Lori that McCarty rode with Jeanette Zellers. At first, she learned of Ray's ever-changing alibis and heard Lori's unwavering support. But then, after the first Boyd interview in May, Lori "called crying and telling her how . . . after talking with the police [she] believed that Ray had killed Rayna." Looking back, Pat wondered why she was crying. Was it because her husband killed her sister? Or because she might be implicated in the murder plot? For the detectives, the 6:30 P.M. call to Walters on March 26 indicated complicity or, at the very least, foreknowledge of the crime.

Some detectives questioned why Lori would have confided in Walters that Ray may have committed the crime. However, the McCartys did have enormous trust in the older couple and probably felt the Walterses would never betray them. A demonstration of that trust came when Ray "took all of his weapons" to Richard on April 28 so the police wouldn't find them during their first search at 517 Haviland.[94]

After the Homicide Team reviewed Pat Walters's alarming disclosures, they decided another meeting was necessary to confirm them. To their surprise, more explosive information was to come when Detectives Hahn and Boyd showed up on the Walterses' doorstep three weeks later. They asked again about the first time Lori called Pat on March 26. According to Hahn's notes, "Pat stated that she was sure it was sometime between 6:30 and 7:00 P.M." Since she had older children, she could not understand why Lori would be "very shaken" because "Rayna was only an hour late." It was not unusual for her children to be that late.

When the detectives pressed Pat about Lori's relationship with Rayna, like everyone else, she brought up "the fight." Walters remembers Lori saying it happened only a few days before March 26 and how she slapped Rayna.

According to Pat, Lori "felt really bad [about] the fight," especially after Rayna went missing. But then the older friend dropped her biggest bombshell: "Lori talked about Rayna taking this pregnancy test at Jennifer's house."

When Pat asked if Rayna was worried whether her boyfriend Matt had gotten her pregnant, "Lori said that Rayna said that this was not Matt's baby, and Rayna said that she cannot talk about it now." Lori said she heard this revelation "about a week or two before Rayna came up missing."[95]

What could be more threatening to the McCartys than the chance Ray had gotten Rayna pregnant again? If true, this time, a judge would not go so easy on Ray—no matter what the Rison family said in his defense. It would mean years—even decades—behind bars for him. Did the detectives think Rayna's pregnancy was a motive for Ray to kill her? "Oh yeah," Boyd answers. "Absolutely."[96]

If Rayna had disclosed her pregnancy tests during "the fight," which occurred a week to ten days before her disappearance on March 26, that could have tied into Ray's purchase of the first stun gun on Friday, March 19. The detectives now felt they were closing in. Although they had not heard back from the FBI on the potency of the O-Mega Super Baton, they assumed it could have been the murder weapon.

An open question remained about Ray's accomplice, but Pat even had a tip about that. During one of Lori's confessional phone calls, when she admitted that Ray may have murdered Rayna, Pat told the detectives, "Lori said that this Charlie Allen is involved along with Ray." Lori talked of one particularly suspicious meeting a few days after Rayna disappeared when Allen and Ray went into [the McCartys'] bedroom and were there for more than an hour behind closed doors."[97]

To the chagrin of the Homicide Team, their investigation of the Rison homicide kept circling back to "dull" Charlie Allen. Boyd and Hahn had already interviewed him three times since the beginning of the year. Prosecuting attorney Herrbach thought he was so vital to their case that he asked Boyd to make Allen his first interview after the hiatus.

Two months before the Walters interviews, Hahn and Boyd had cornered Charlie at a work site three hours from La Porte. Whether it was the element of surprise or a neutral location, the interview was the most productive session with Ray's best friend. When asked about the first time he saw Ray on March 26,

Charlie now remembered it was soon after he returned home from work at four thirty. As in previous interviews, he said Ray was in his camouflage hunting outfit and wanted Charlie to go out with him, which he refused. McCarty then asked to use the phone to call Lori, and Charlie's girlfriend, Cindy, directed him to a pay phone outside the tavern a few blocks away.

With this timeline, Ray could have easily called Lori and gone to Warren Street by 5:30 when the two bandmates spotted his car. Again, most suspiciously, Allen said he did not know why Ray wanted him to go out when he appeared for the first time that night.

As before, Allen said Ray returned later that night dressed in different clothes. A barking dog woke Allen, and he found Ray at his door. But in this telling, McCarty was with another man. Ray said they needed a ride to 517 Haviland because he had loaned his car to someone else. Allen claimed he did not ask how or why they got to his door without a car. Allen also told police he could not describe Ray's companion and would not recognize him if he saw him again.

Allen then drove the men to Ray's home in the "blue Chevrolet Chevette" he had borrowed from his girlfriend's brother-in-law. This information, tied to something Allen said in a previous interview, should have helped identify the other man. It was another vital clue that flew beneath the detectives' radar. Despite Ray's comment about loaning out his car, Allen said he saw the Datsun in the street when he dropped off his passengers. As the men left the Chevette, Allen remembered Ray turned and told him that he "should not tell anyone that he had been with [Ray] that night."[98]

With this new information, the detectives felt they had Allen on the brink of becoming a crucial cooperating witness in the case against Ray. They asked him to appear at the La Porte police station for a "detailed interview" and "possibly a polygraph examination." Allen seemed willing to oblige both requests.

But when arrangements were made for the next week, Allen did not show up at the appointed hour. Thinking he had forgotten the time, Hahn went to his house and learned that Charlie had gotten his own lawyer, who wanted to be present before his client made any more statements. Despite the new hurdle, the Homicide Team decided to do what they could to accommodate Allen and the attorney because, Boyd reported, "We all agree that Allen has information that is vital to the case and its overall outcome."

As expected, Charlie's lawyer negotiated an agreement with Herrbach that he would not be prosecuted for anything he told the police.[99] But when he finally appeared at the police station for another interview, Allen did not use his newfound immunity to offer more revelations about Ray McCarty. Instead, Allen backtracked and said that what he previously told Hahn and Boyd was "not accurate." The events with Ray appearing at his house two times in one evening may have happened, but not on March 26. He then proceeded to provide a bizarre mash-up of Ray alibis. These included new details that even Lori had not disclosed but were undoubtedly influenced by the latest breakthroughs in the police investigation. According to Charlie, Ray's latest alibi had him talking to Rayna at the animal hospital to see if she wanted him to pick up something from Taco Bell, where he was getting supper for his family. Then, Allen said, Ray did go to the hog farm but couldn't make a call from the barn. On his way back home, he picked up the hitchhiker. In this telling, Ray pulled to the side of a country road to have sex with her when a truck came up behind them. Ray knew the driver and got out to talk to him.

Throughout this interview, Allen made a point to change specific details he provided previously—especially about the individual who showed up with Ray on some night that wasn't March 26. Suddenly, he could describe him as having "Ray's height and build [with] brown medium-length hair." Also, "the guy was in his late teens or early twenties." Just as telling was his identification of the truck that pulled up behind Ray after he supposedly stopped to have sex with the hitchhiker. At first, he said it was a Chevy S-10 but then took that back. As Hahn notes: "Charlie later changes this to just a small truck."

Like other friends, Allen remembered Ray was looking to borrow a pickup the week before Rayna's abduction. Ray only said he needed it to "move something heavy," but Allen never asked what that was or if he got a truck from anyone else. Although Charlie knew about the stun gun, he believed the McCartys got it because Lori had been "approached" by someone in their neighborhood.

But in this latest interview, Allen did provide one revelation that showed he couldn't be dismissed despite the constant prevarications. When asked about the pond where Rayna was found, Allen replied that he was familiar with it since his son was friendly with the family that owned the property. When asked if he knew where Rayna's body was found in the pond, Allen provided a surprisingly accurate answer: the north side of the lake thirty-five feet from Range Road. This location had not been shared with the public or the Rison family. Boyd did not want to let this go. He drew a map of the pond on a piece of paper and asked Charlie to mark the spot with an *X* and then sign it.[100]

A few days later, Hahn had Allen back again for yet another attempt to pin him down with a straightforward Q&A. Charlie did not back off his previous comments and offered no new details this time. Still, his answers to two questions only added to the intrigue.

"Is there anything Ray can use against you if this goes to trial?" Hahn asked.

Allen replied, "I am not sure."

"Are you afraid of anyone at this point?"

"Yes," Charlie answered. "Ray." He then added, "I am not sure why."[101]

RAY GOES OFF THE RAILS

Although Allen remained a constant source of frustration for the detectives, in the first months of 1994, they were still confident that they were closing in on Ray, and they hoped the next big breaks would come from someone in the Rison family. Like Lori, Bennie seemed to be riding a roller coaster on Ray's culpability in Rayna's murder.

As far as the public was concerned, Papa Rison was unhappy with the pace of the Homicide Team's investigation. In early January, Bennie sent a letter to La Porte school parents and friends asking them to participate in a grassroots postcard campaign that would pressure the authorities to complete their investigations. The letter read as follows:

> I desperately need your help to close the most tragic chapter of my life. Look around at the members of your community. Picture a pretty 16-year-old girl who is actively involved in Marching Band at school. She's smart, popular, and just a wonderful person to be around. She's hardworking (has two part-time jobs) and tutors younger children. She's looking forward to college, and the whole world is at her feet. Do you know this person? Maybe it's your best friend. Maybe it's your neighbor. Maybe it's your sister or daughter.

I knew this person also. She was my daughter, Rayna Rison. Unfortunately, I will never hear her play oboe again, hear her infectious giggle, or see her graduate from High School. She was abducted and murdered on her way home from a part-time job at a veterinary clinic on March 26, 1993. Her body was found on April 27, 1993, in a pond only a few miles from home. I am sure you are saying to yourself that something like that will never happen to me or to my friend or to my daughter, but the number of these incidents are increasing at an alarming rate. I am pleading for your help. Help me let our Political and Community leaders know we are outraged that our young people are dying and their murderers are not being brought to justice. Here's what you can do. Write a short note on a postcard to Governor Evan Bayh, Indiana State Attorney General Pamela Carter, U.S. Attorney General Janet Reno, and First Lady Hillary Clinton. Make sure you ask them to reply to your postcard. Please ask your friends and neighbors to write postcards to the above people and mail them on January 17, 1994, to these Political leaders.

Your help is greatly needed to grab the attention of these Public officials. It will be a great opportunity for us to let them know our concerns and fears. Let's get the message out!

Thank you,

Bennie Rison and Family

To make his recipients' follow-up as easy as possible, Bennie suggested "messages" for the "political leaders." These included:

Rayna Rison was murdered in La Porte, Indiana. I would like to know who murdered her and why.

Rayna Rison's murder investigation is a prime example of our justice system in action. How can we let this continue?

Why was Rayna Rison murdered? When will her killer(s) be brought to justice?

We can not [sic] let Rayna Rison's murder case go unresolved. Why hasn't the case been solved?

Is Rayna Rison's murder investigation the rule rather than the exception in Indiana's justice system?

I would like to know why Rayna Rison's murder has not been solved. Does Indiana want to be known as a State where children can be murdered, and the perpetrators go unpunished?

How is the hard-earned tax money we pay for protection being spent? Are murders like Rayna Rison's an example of what we can expect?

I am a ____-year-old student, and I am extremely concerned about my safety after what happened to Rayna Rison. Why hasn't this case been solved?

To rachet up his pressure one notch higher, Bennie asked his campaigners to send him back the replies they got from the political leaders. He could then present the numbers at a rally on January 22.

Probably in response to Bennie's campaign, on January 23, the LPPD issued a press release with an update on the investigation and a bold prediction. In previous briefings, the police had blamed the slow progress in the case on delays in receiving results from the FBI labs. However, now they announced, "All evidence has been received from the FBI, and their lab investigations have been concluded." Although they would not yet share test results, they could say, "Investigators feel confident that an arrest will be made in the near future."

Before the police issued the press release, Hahn asked Bennie to come into the station to hear it from him first. The detective promised it was only the first of many that would "keep the public interest in this case [and put more] stress on the person or persons responsible for Rayna's death."[102]

But to Hahn's surprise, Bennie also had news for him—something that would have stunned those who wrote postcards to help him find Rayna's killer. As Hahn wrote in his report:

> Bennie wished to relate an incident that [happened] this past week. . . .
> Ray had been to [Bennie's] home to pick up an extension cord in the evening hours. When Ray went to leave, he stopped in the doorway for a moment and turned around and said that he had something to tell him. Bennie stated that a few moments went by with Ray just standing there. Ray then said . . . that he had been to the animal hospital to talk to Rayna that Friday night. Ray stated that he went there to ask Rayna if she knew where Lori was at. . . . [Rayna] said that Lori was with Wendy shopping, and Rayna then said that she had more work to do in the back and went back into the animal hospital. Bennie stated that he offered no reply to what Ray had just said, and Ray stated that he needed to tell this to him. Ray then left.
> Bennie stated that this was a shock to him but knew [that with] this information, police could put Ray at the animal hospital that Friday night. Ray seems to be trying to cover his tracks. . . .
> Bennie stated that he is concerned with Lori and the kids when Ray is arrested. He wanted to be advised before the arrest to prepare his family. . . . I advised that [he could not know before], but he will be advised as soon as it happens.[103]

By relating the "incident" and talking about his son-in-law's imminent arrest, Bennie finally revealed how obvious Ray's guilt now appeared to him. But in truth, the detectives had nothing new to incriminate McCarty. The FBI had not given them any forensic silver bullets to help solve the case. The cause of death mystery continued to linger—so much so that Herrbach and the chief investigators went to South Bend to personally grill Dr. Rick Hoover, the forensic pathologist who conducted Rayna's autopsy.

In his report about the meeting, Boyd wrote that "numerous factors were discussed." Among them was "the possibility of a 'stun gun' causing death to an individual." Hoover agreed it could, but he had no research to support his opinion.[104] Special agent Deedrick had already told Hahn that the FBI analysts considered the stun gun a "non-lethal weapon."[105]

Another topic of discussion with Hoover was isopropyl alcohol. Hoover was still mystified about how the chemical got into her body. All he knew for sure, he told the detectives and prosecutor, was that it happened "prior to death."[106] In sum, the forensic pathologist could not deliver the rock-solid evidence they needed to tie Ray to the crime.

For Boyd, their best hope for a quick resolution lay with Lori McCarty. When Bennie came forward with Ray's admission about seeing Rayna on March 26, he appeared primed to help. In early March, the detectives approached Papa Rison for a meeting. Boyd was his usual blunt self. As he wrote in his report, "Bennie was asked to talk with his daughter, Lori, and to have her contact us with the truth in the matter. We told him we knew Lori had not been truthful with us but did not believe Lori was involved in Rayna's death. We told him that we believed Ray was definitely involved and that Lori was concealing information about her activities that night to aid Ray in his stories."

But a few days later, when the detectives heard back from Bennie, he told them he "was not in a position to talk candidly with" Lori and would call them once he did. In addition, he asked Hahn to arrange a meeting with the prosecuting attorney. Later in the week, Bennie and Karen appeared in Herrbach's office and were joined by Boyd and Hahn. The Risons had nothing new to say about Ray or Lori. Instead, Bennie tried to pump the prosecutor about the investigation. But Herrbach was not about to take the bait. He now had both feet in the detectives' camp. As Boyd wrote in his report, "Mr. Herrbach told [Bennie] that he should try to convince Lori to talk with us and tell the truth."[107]

Despite the prosecutor's advice, Bennie did not push Lori to cooperate. As more than one friend told the detectives, the Risons' oldest daughter tended to be "bossy," which extended as much to her parents as anyone else.[108] While Bennie sincerely wanted to find Rayna's murderer, he also told friends that he feared losing his oldest daughter and her children.[109] Lori continued to threaten her parents with various types of Rison family ruptures should Ray get arrested.[110]

With the first anniversary of Rayna's disappearance approaching, Bennie decided to strike out in another direction. He hired a South Bend firm to help him conduct his own investigation. They subcontracted with two moonlighting licensed private detectives who worked during the day at the Indiana State Prison in Michigan City. One had been with the South Bend police department for more than twenty years; the other, Barry Nothstine, had a similar tenure at the Michigan City police department and served twice as chief of the force. In addition to his pedigree as a police officer, the fifty-three-year-old Nothstine was well known in Northwestern Indiana as a spokesman for the prison system—especially during such highly publicized events as executions and riots.[111] For Bennie, Nothstine had more than enough stature in the community to compete with La Porte's mild-mannered police chief, Gene Samuelson, should his investigation point in an opposite direction from Ray.

But from the start, Nothstine made it clear to Bennie that he would not clash with local law enforcement. Should he find any new evidence during his investigation, he would take it directly to the cops. The prospective client claimed he had no trouble with that. However, Bennie would not have been happy with one of the first calls that Nothstine made—to Arlie Boyd. Rison had made it clear that he hated and distrusted the trooper, but Nothstine had worked with Boyd on multiple homicide cases and had ultimate respect for his investigative skills. He was not about to get involved with an active investigation without his old friend's permission. Boyd remembers having no problem with Nothstine taking the job. The respect was mutual, and he didn't mind having another experienced hand on the case.

As Nothstine told Boyd, Bennie most wanted him to focus on leads that the police had been quick to dismiss.[112] One was Jason Tibbs, and the other was an ex-convict named Eddy Logan. A former live-in girlfriend called Rison to say Logan had bragged about killing Rayna. She also claimed he had the same type of truck police were looking for and a bracelet he took off Rison's body. Like the LPPD detectives before him, Nothstine could not verify her charges or tie Logan's truck or the bracelet to the crime. Instead, he and his partner determined that the relationship was marked by heavy drinking and a breakup that the informant didn't see coming. Also, unlike Ray, Logan had alibi witnesses and documentation for his whereabouts that checked out.[113]

Meanwhile, at even the earliest stages of their investigation, the private eyes couldn't help but trip over Ray. As Boyd hoped, Nothstine even contributed to the evidence against him, finding additional witnesses near North 150 East and North 200 East who heard the Datsun's loud muffler. As he promised, Nothstine was on the phone with Boyd after each discovery. Besides the muffler noise, most of what the private detectives found had already been logged by the police. Finally, after only a few weeks on the case, Nothstine told Bennie he could no longer take his money. His private investigation only confirmed the same prime suspect identified by Hahn and Boyd—something he knew the client didn't want to hear.[114]

Contrary to the pronouncements made earlier in the year, the prosecuting attorney, Bill Herrbach, appeared no closer to an arrest in Rayna's case by the fall of 1994. An upcoming reelection campaign may have influenced his reluctance to make a move. As a Democratic incumbent in a heavily Democratic county, Herrbach should have been a heavy favorite against Cynthia Hedge, the candidate who emerged from the Republican primary. Although a deputy prosecutor, she mainly worked with juveniles and had no experience with adult criminal trials. An attractive, understated brunette, mostly known for her involvement in civic groups, Hedge offered a soft-spoken counterpoint to the garrulous, backslapping incumbent. But Herrbach barely scraped by his Democratic opponent for the nomination. He probably did not want to risk his reelection on a controversial indictment, and Bennie Rison gave him every indication that he would make his son-in-law's arrest controversial.[115]

However, Ray's behavior was not making it easy to ignore him. As Boyd and Hahn continued to reach out to the McCartys' friends for interviews, their prime suspect decided he had had enough. One Friday evening in late September 1994, he drove over to the home of Harold Hahn. The detective had left earlier in the day for a vacation in Florida, and his wife, Trudy, was alone. At first, she didn't recognize McCarty, confusing him with a neighbor who lived down the street. He asked if Harold was home, and when Trudy said he wasn't, Ray asked if he'd be home later. When she told him her husband was on vacation, he smiled, and she realized he was not her neighbor. She asked his name. He answered, "Ray." She replied, "You're Ray McCarty, aren't you?" He started smiling again.

But the encounter would get stranger when McCarty said, "The real reason I came was to ask if you would babysit my kids tomorrow." Trudy told him she would not because she would be with her own family. Ray then got into his rusted Datsun and left. When Trudy drove to the La Porte police station to report the incident, she noted that his car had a "loud muffler."

The officer on the dispatch desk saw nothing funny about Ray's visit, and because Trudy was home alone, he strongly recommended that she stay elsewhere. The officer then called prosecuting attorney Herrbach, who called Arlie Boyd to inform him about the incident.

A policeman accompanied Trudy Hahn back home so she could pack for a few days' stay and arrange for someone to feed her cats. While the Hahns were gone, the LPPD's night shift patrol would check on their house. They would also keep an eye on the home that Ray and Lori had just purchased three blocks away from the Hahns.[116]

Arlie Boyd was not about to let Ray's stunt go unanswered. A few days later, he showed up at Teledyne and met with McCarty's supervisor, who knew Ray had gone to Hahn's house because he was "upset at Harold about something." Boyd asked him to call McCarty into his office. It was the first time the trooper and the prime suspect met face-to-face. After introducing himself, Boyd let Ray know he was not there for an interview, but McCarty still said he had nothing to say and that the detective should talk to his attorney instead. "I told him we were not going to go away because he had an attorney," Boyd wrote in his report about the meeting. "[I] then told him that if he needed a babysitter, I would be happy to sit for him. McCarty angrily left the room."[117]

Lori informed her older friend Pat Walters about Ray's visit to the Hahns, adding that her husband thought it was "cute." However, the McCartys found nothing cute in Boyd's visit to Teledyne, as Walters reported to the trooper. More defiant than ever, Lori told Pat that her lawyer would soon hold a press conference proclaiming the couple's "complete innocence."[118]

But in the next few weeks, Ray's behavior appeared anything but innocent to the detectives. Indeed, they believed they had caught him, practically red-handed, grooming another teenager for sexual activity. They first heard about Nancy (not her real name) as their interviews radiated out to more marginal acquaintances of the McCartys. One, an occasional babysitter, told them that Lori was very angry when she arrived home after work to find Ray alone with the sixteen-year-old Nancy. McCarty had met the girl when he was helping out on a friend's dairy farm. She worked there after school milking cows.[119]

Hahn and Boyd had Nancy come into the La Porte police station soon after they got the tip. Since she was not with her parents, the city detective secretly recorded the session in case anyone would later question how the policemen dealt with a minor. To their surprise, Nancy did admit to her friendship with Ray and the incident when Lori discovered them in the McCarty home. Although she said Lori threatened her, "she did not take [her threats] seriously." The teen was defiant about her relationship with Ray, denying any sex was involved. She, too, was aware of his hitchhiker alibi and could not believe he was involved with Rayna's death.

Disturbed by Nancy's attitude, the detectives decided to talk to her parents as soon as possible. Hahn started with her mother. Although Nancy told her parents about going to the police station, they did not believe she had been candid about what she discussed with the detectives. Early the following day, Nancy's parents appeared at the La Porte police station, at first angry that their daughter had been dragged into the investigation and questioned without them present. But then Hahn played his recording of the interview, and their attitude changed. Nancy had told them that she met with Ray after she left the police station, something that did not disturb them before but now looked like an active attempt to manipulate their daughter.

Coincidentally, Nancy's father had worked with Rayna at Hot 'n Now. He often commented on the similarities between the two teens—even in their appearance—and thought they would become good friends if he could introduce them. After knowing why Ray had become the detectives' prime suspect, Hahn wrote that her father was "greatly afraid for his daughter's welfare." The parents discussed sending Nancy to stay with a relative who lived out of state "until this matter gets straightened out."

With her parents' permission, the detectives arranged for Nancy to join them later that day. When asked about the meeting with Ray the last time she left the station, Nancy again became defensive and insisted that it was "by accident" when she walked past the city park and saw McCarty with his children. He then took the kids home to stay with Lori so he could talk to Nancy alone at the mall. They saw each other two more times, she admitted, at the farm. Again, Nancy insisted they were only friends and nothing more. But the detectives then conducted what Hahn called "a counseling session on [Nancy's] behalf," presumably filling her in on Ray's previous conviction and witness reports about his behavior with women. Nancy and her parents finally left the station at 3:00 P.M.

But Hahn's day about Ray had not finished and was about to make a bizarre turn. After 4:00 P.M., when the detective left work and returned home, he spotted McCarty in his new vehicle, a blue Dodge pickup with the temporary paper license taped in the rear window. Based on a "strong professional guess," Hahn believed Ray was headed for Nancy's home. At first, he started to follow him, but when McCarty spotted him and veered into a more circuitous route, the detective stopped the pursuit. Instead, Hahn went directly to the anticipated destination, driving at the speed limit without using flashing lights. When he arrived, he found Nancy's little brothers playing in the front yard. They told Hahn he had just missed a man in a blue truck who asked if their father was home. They told him he wasn't, but the man didn't leave his name and said he'd return later. Hahn gave the boys his card and told them to dial 911 if they saw the truck again.

As the detective started backing out of their driveway, Nancy and her parents arrived. Hearing that Ray had dropped by only moments ago, the parents needed no more convincing about the danger he posed to their daughter. Meanwhile, the boys spotted Ray's truck in the distance, parked on the other side of an empty field. Hahn wrote in his case report, "I advised [Nancy's father] I will make every attempt to locate and stop Ray to tell him to stay away from his property, family, and [Nancy]."

The detective then took off in the direction of Ray's truck. Seeing him approach, McCarty started up his vehicle and drove away at high speed. But after going a distance, he stopped, did a U-turn, and headed back toward Hahn, who was waiting with his car in the center of the narrow road. Ray had to slow down to pass, and Hahn yelled at him to stop. With their driver's-side windows down, the detective told McCarty "not to have any further contact" with Nancy or her family. Ray claimed that he just wanted to tell her father he was friends with Nancy and would now stay away from her so as not to "jeopardize her job at the farm." Hahn replied he would be better off writing a letter or making a phone call. If he showed up on their property now, "the possibility of someone getting hurt is very good."

The middle-of-the-road talk then took another turn as Ray lamented how "unfair" the police had been with him. Hahn replied that they had not said anything about him that could not be proved, but McCarty still had an opportunity to "challenge its validity" if he allowed the detectives to question him. "I advised Ray that I know that he has a story to tell," Hahn wrote in his report, "and I wish we could sit down and talk [with or without] his attorney." Unless he talked, the detective told him, they would have to rely on what his friends had said, and "we do have enough information and evidence now to effect an arrest."

With that, Hahn expected Ray to drive away, but instead, he parked on the side of the road and pulled down the tailgate of his new truck. Ray invited him to hop up for a seat because he had a long story to tell "if [Hahn] could keep it a secret." But first, he asked if the detective had a recorder. The detective replied that he did not. Ray then lifted his jacket to show he didn't have a weapon. The detective opened his coat to show he *did* have a gun. "Ray said he [was] not going to cause any type of problem," Hahn wrote. "I advised it would not resolve anything if he did."

As the two sat on the pickup's tailgate, Ray told the latest version of his hitchhiker alibi with, as usual, some new details. This version had him going to Warren Street to look at the house for sale and then talking to Rayna in the parking lot to find out where Lori was. His added detail was that a pickup pulled in after he left and had the brights on.

Another new detail would be why he traveled to South Bend: to see a Black security guard at the hospital where he was getting therapy. He only knew that the guard's first name was Andre, but he had borrowed money from him and wanted to pay it back. The detective asked if he had called first since the round trip would take three hours. Hahn wrote that Ray replied, "He is a spontaneous person. He makes no plans and does everything on the spur of the moment."

Ray also had more details about the hitchhiker, saying she told him she had to get out of La Porte "because there was nothing but trouble for her here." His description now went beyond her long brown hair. She was "slim in build" and "wore a black leather biker's jacket with chains on the shoulders. [He] did not get a good look at her face and did not think he would be able to recognize her if he saw her again." He could not tell Hahn if she was "attractive" or where he dropped her off at the truck stop. But Hahn told him, "If we know [the] exact place where you dropped off this woman, I guarantee someone will have noticed because people notice such things. I advised Ray that if this is the truth, then there is no way we are going to shake him from it."

But after Ray provided his revelations, Hahn offered a few regarding Charlie Allen. McCarty had not heard that his best friend had told the police about the early evening visit where Ray was looking to make a phone call and the late-night visit when McCarty came looking for a ride with an unknown companion. Hahn wrote, "Ray stated after thinking [for a while] that this never happened. . . . He had no idea what Charlie was talking about."

Hahn asked Ray if he had ever been near the pond where Rayna was found. He answered that Bennie or Lori had taken him there later, but it was the first time he had seen it. The detective next asked if he let anyone borrow his Datsun in the few days after Rayna went missing, and Ray replied, "No." Hahn told him the Range Road homeowner spotted his car in her driveway between 12:30 and 1:00 A.M. on the Sunday after the abduction.[120]

When the two men separated, neither one could have been satisfied with what they heard from the other. But the Homicide Team was ready to give Ray every benefit of the doubt and act as though he was telling the truth about his hitchhiker and Andre. Two weeks later, *The South Bend Tribune* reported, "Investigators are attempting to locate a female hitchhiker who reportedly was given a ride on March 26, 1993, by a suspect in the slaying of 15-year-old [actually sixteen-year-old] Rayna Rison." Herrbach described her precisely as Ray did in his impromptu interview with Hahn, right down to the chains on her black leather jacket. Herrbach told reporters, "We are looking for this person who may be able to corroborate certain evidence."

The reporter concluded the article with a line that reflected the skepticism of the investigators. He reported that the person they sought was wanted only as a witness and not a suspect "if the woman exists."[121]

Meanwhile, Boyd and Hahn drove to South Bend's Memorial Hospital in search of Andre. They found that he did exist. But Andre Bridges did not know Ray McCarty or even recognize his photo. Since he was at the security desk where patients signed in, and his name was sewn on his uniform, he expected Ray would have been familiar with it. However, he emphatically denied loaning him money, which would have been against hospital policy.[122]

Like a fish thrashing on the line, Ray's efforts to wriggle away from the investigation only drove the detectives' hooks deeper. But the decision to indict him was no longer a headache for Herrbach. Against the prognosticators' predictions, he lost the general election to Cynthia Hedge. Republicans swept all the countywide offices in the anti-Democratic fervor that overtook Indiana midway through President Bill Clinton's first term.[123]

GOING COLD

If Bennie thought Ray would get a pass from the new prosecuting attorney, he was in for a surprise. Her campaign manager, Scott Duerring, was an experienced trial attorney who had been a prosecutor for two of her predecessors and tried dozens of homicide cases. Upon Hedge's election, he returned to the office as her chief deputy prosecuting attorney and relied on his previous experience to drive several initiatives in the new administration. "Rison was one of the open cases I wanted to see fully investigated and brought to a conclusion. Frankly, I became very committed to that. [Hedge] pretty much let me do what I felt was necessary as long as I kept her in the loop."[124]

Duerring's pursuit of Rayna's killer could also pave the way for his own political ambitions. No doubt prosecuting Ray McCarty would bring massive publicity, and most of Duerring's colleagues figured it was only a matter of time before he ran for office. With his carefully coiffed ringlets of silver hair, cleft chin, and fitted suits, he cut a crisp figure in court distinctly at odds with the rumpled Democratic prosecutors before him.

But the Rison investigation barely crawled forward under the Hedge administration. The two years before her November 1994 election, police conducted nearly two hundred fifty interviews. There were just another six interviews in the next three years.[125] Soon after Hedge was elected, Boyd met with Duerring. "The case was going cold," Boyd remembers. "I told Scott we have to make a decision and move forward on it, or we should close it. My feeling was that we had enough evidence to make it winnable. Of course, he did, too. Other people didn't feel the same way, though."[126]

Those opposed to proceeding without more evidence were undoubtedly affected by how Ray's family closed ranks around him. For Boyd, the Rison family's defensiveness about Ray was not unusual. "It's only natural for them to believe their relative didn't do it. Then you have to prove [the case] to them within reason. If they're still against you, you're gonna have a problem.[127]

Duerring also remembers the difficulty of proceeding against a prime suspect whom the victim's family so intensely defended. He says, "It was a very unusual, strange dynamic."

With the case nearly two years old, Duerring could no longer convene a Homicide Team, which was supposed to focus on more recent crimes. Instead, he set up an ad hoc group that met monthly to review the case, including detectives, prosecutors, and his office's investigators. Duerring, for one, had not been in office or otherwise involved in the investigation. He and the other new prosecutors first needed to get up to speed. "We literally pulled out all of the evidence that had been obtained. Hundreds of pages of reports and even the logs they put on top of her."

Because the trace evidence had become so important, Duerring organized a trip to Washington, DC, where his group could meet with the FBI analysts to understand their findings better and see what more new technology might yield.[128] The prosecutors needed something concrete to counter the ambiguity of the autopsy and the conflicting testimony they got from Charlie Allen. More than ever, the detectives believed he was Ray's accomplice in the murder.[129]

Among those most hesitant to proceed against Ray was the genial City of La Porte Police Chief Gene "Sam" Samuelson. Sam worked his way up the ranks from patrolman, but with his constant smile, thinning gray hair, and oversized glasses, he looked more like a minister than a law enforcement officer. Samuelson was the rare chief who talked about the social conditions that fostered crime and not just the equipment or laws needed to break it.[130] He also expressed genuine sympathy for the families of the victims, which he extended to the Risons. Given their attitude toward the prime suspect, Samuelson felt they needed unassailable evidence before indicting him. When asked about his failure to close the case, he blamed the inconclusive autopsy and how long Rayna's body was submerged in water. "A lot of evidence was lost during those thirty days we couldn't find her," he told one reporter.[131]

As the investigation wore on, Bennie, at the invitation of Samuelson, became a constant presence in the LPPD station, often plopping himself down on an empty chair in the detectives' bullpen and putting his feet on the desk—much to the annoyance of the officers around him.[132] At some stage, Bennie lost the toupee and modish, tinted glasses. He kept the fringe of gray hair around his bald head cut short and wore wire frames instead. Those involved in the case had gotten sick of how he blew hot and cold on Ray's guilt. They also believed that he looked at Samuelson's kindness with contempt. Behind the chief's back, Bennie lamented that the county sheriff should have been the one to run the investigation.[133]

Hahn heard about Bennie's attitude toward Samuelson in July 1995 when he received a complaint about Lori at yet another job—this time as an aide at the Fountainvew Terrace nursing home where Allen's girlfriend Cindy worked. The previous month, a nurse had complained to the police about Ray. He had barged into the nursing home to confront the charging nurse when she asked Lori to pull an extra shift. She said Ray "began shouting and pointing his finger and making threats." He did not leave until she picked up the phone to call 911. The following month, a licensed practical nurse at the facility told the police that Lori harassed her after she learned the LPN's husband was a Chicago cop. Lori wanted him to "get information as to what the police are doing and what knowledge they [have regarding] the death of her sister Rayna." What struck the nurse was that "Lori seemed more interested in what the police have on her and her husband, Ray," than the killer.

She explained to Lori that her husband "has no jurisdiction in La Porte" to find out about an LPPD investigation. But after Lori went home, she called the nurse again, saying she'd "pay for any information" and then put her father on the line. Bennie reiterated the offer to pay and "offered to make her husband the chief of police of La Porte if he wanted it."

Nothing the nurse said stopped Lori and Bennie from demanding her help. Lori gave her a deadline to reply, which she wouldn't do. Lori even appeared at the nursing home during her vacation to follow the nurse for an hour. The LPN then called Hahn, "concerned as to what might happen" should Lori return. The detective told her to alert other coworkers to Lori's behavior and for them to call the police "if anything remotely begins to get out of hand."[134]

In desperation to learn more about what the police knew, Bennie tried interviewing some of the detectives' most vital witnesses. Prime among them was Rene Gazarkiewicz, who passed by the animal hospital twice on March 26. The second time, she saw Rayna with her head inside the Datsun and her feet off the ground. There is no way that Duerring would have consented to that meeting with its potential to taint Rene's future testimony in court. But to his credit, Bennie recorded every minute. He did not try to alter what she saw that night, which she recounted almost precisely as she did for the police. The two went on to swap political gossip and their complaints about local law enforcement. To Bennie's surprise, Gazarkiewicz provided unsavory details about James McWhirter, who found Rayna's body. It was information, she claimed, that the police did not want to hear.[135]

As 1994 drew to a close, Bennie finally decided to reach out to another private investigator, Tina Church. She had previously worked with other families who sought counseling from Parents of Murdered Children. At forty-one, with long, flowing blonde hair and blue eyes, Tina worked as an investigator for defense counsel in some of the area's most notorious crimes. An empathetic listener, she could elicit information from rebuttal witnesses that enraged prosecutors, who often questioned her tactics.[136] But Church also had a feisty side that dated back to when she filed suit against an employer for sex discrimination.[137] Church had no trouble directly challenging anyone she thought was lying or taking advantage of her.

To start the Rison investigation, Church spent considerable time with Bennie and Karen, listening to their complaints about the police detectives and offering to plunge into the rabbit holes of other suspects who were not their son-in-law. But like Nothstine, the other private investigator, it did not take her long to see Ray's culpability. And like Nothstine, she kept in touch with the police every step of the way, at points calling State Trooper Arlie Boyd for his feedback and even Chief Deputy Prosecuting Attorney Duerring. But most of all, she frequently talked with Harold Hahn, permitting him to record their conversations.[138]

Unlike Nothstine, Church had an unwanted partner in her inquiry named Sue Burzynski. Calling herself a "Tele-psychic," Burzynski actively peddled her services at sixty dollars an hour to the police in South Bend and surrounding communities. A matronly young woman with swept-back blonde hair, she claimed "special powers" that enabled her to find missing persons, especially deceased ones. "I can feel the person when they are dead," she told *The South Bend Tribune*. "I just know."[139]

When Rayna disappeared, Burzynski went to the La Porte County sheriff's office asking if she could touch a photo of the missing girl. She later met with county and city detectives and told them the vibrations she felt could help locate Rayna. They agreed to have officers drive her around the county to see if any location would reverberate for her. Undercover narc Jim Jackson from the county sheriff's office and a detective from the City of La Porte police department pulled the assignment in their unmarked car.

Jackson remembers that they wanted to give Burzynski the benefit of the doubt. "You can't help but hope and dream that she's legit, but obviously, that was never the case." In short order, the chauffeurs' nickname for their passenger went from Psychic Sue to Psycho Sue. "She drove us crazy," Jackson says, "making us run like chickens with our heads cut off all over the county. Like up to East 800 North, where she had a vision that Rayna was rolled up inside a carpet. Then, down south, where she had a vision, she was dumped by the side of Fail Road. Finally, we figured we got the assignment because no one else wanted to be around her."[140]

Once Rayna's body was found, Burzynski told Bennie he could still use her psychic powers and interviewing skills to help find the *real* killer. She became even more involved after Nothstine quit the case. It didn't take long for Tina Church to call Burzynski Psycho Sue too. But Church did not summarily dismiss her like the county patrolmen. Instead, she tried to keep her close, paying her to help with another investigation, which took Sue out of state and out of Tina's hair.

Burzynski got close enough to Church to reveal the Risons' mole inside the City of La Porte police station—namely, the good old boy detective Bob Schoff. When Tina told Hahn, the detective couldn't hide his anger. Having already suspected Schoff as a leaker, Hahn assured Church he'd crack down harder on his colleague. "We'll make the corrections there [with Schoff]. I have the authority to do that." As for Burzynski, Hahn told Tina, "We've had a lot of weird people come in here . . . trying to help us, and it really set us off on some wild goose chases."

In time, Church realized that the most valuable role she could play was to help the police build a case against Ray with the cooperation of Bennie and maybe even Karen. Her first goal was to sit down with McCarty. She asked Bennie to arrange a meeting with her in South Bend, but as she told Hahn, that made Lori very upset. One Friday in January 1996, they tried another ploy. Bennie stopped off at the McCartys' home and asked that Ray come by his house on Saturday to help with a project. Although he did not tell his son-in-law, Church would be waiting there for an interview.

But the next morning, Lori, not Ray, appeared at the Rison house, asking what her dad wanted her husband to do. As Church related to Hahn, Bennie decided to drop the ruse. "He then says, 'The person working with me would like to talk to Ray. . . . There's a possibility that maybe he could be exonerated.' And Lori says, 'He's not talking to anybody.'"

As Tina told Hahn, she had to scramble for a plan B. First, she had to calm down Bennie and Karen. She told them, "Obviously, [the McCartys'] feathers are ruffled a little bit." But then she reminded Bennie how Ray had said, "He would talk to you and not anyone else. I said, 'Go over and talk to him.'"

Church did not just buck up Bennie's courage. Before he left, she outfitted him with the concealed tape recorder she would wear if Ray had shown up at the Risons' house. "So Bennie went over there," she told Hahn. "And right away, Ray is, 'I'm not supposed to be talking to anybody.' And this is his father-in-law."

But to her surprise, Bennie persisted with his questions. "And Bennie is saying, 'Well, what time were you at the clinic?' [Ray replies,] 'Well, between five of six [o'clock] and five after, but I'm not supposed to talk to anybody.' Now, Bennie says, 'Right, but you and I need to talk.' Then Ray raced across the room, saying, 'Get out of my house. I'm gonna have to throw you out.'"

At this point in her account, spunky Tina marveled at Ray's cowardice. "I don't know about you, Harold," she told Hahn, "but if I was to throw somebody out of the house, I'd get up in their face. Anyway, he's pacing back and forth like a caged animal. . . . [Bennie] couldn't determine for himself where that fear was coming from, other than he was just flat-out scared to death of Bennie."

But at that point in Bennie's interrogation, Lori appeared on the scene to intervene again. This time, she threatened to call the police on her father if he didn't leave. After Bennie returned home, Church encouraged him to return to the McCarty household and try again. This time, Lori threw him out and made good on her threat. As Bennie drove home, a police officer responding to her call stopped Rison's car and warned him to stay away from his daughter's house.

After hearing about Bennie's police stop, Church recalled, "I simply said to Bennie, 'What do you think? Are those the actions of innocent people?' And he said, 'No, no, no.' And Bennie broke down, and he cried."[141]

Still, for a while, Bennie was determined not to give up. That Saturday night, at 9:15, he called Hahn's home, as the detective wrote in a report. Rison said he could see "no reason [for Ray] not to at least talk to this private investigator to get suspicion off him." But then he asked Hahn what penalty he'd suffer if he returned to the McCarty house and got arrested. The detective told him the cost of a cash bond to get out of jail but recommended that he not go, and Bennie hung up the phone. Alarmed by the call, Hahn left a message for the LPPD's Sunday street patrols, warning that there would be "a potential of violence" if officers were dispatched to either the

McCarty or Rison homes. In his opinion, he wrote, "Bennie Rison will go to [the McCarty home] to confront Ray McCarty."[142]

A few days later, when discussing his report with Tina Church, Hahn speculated whether Bennie "wanted to get himself arrested just to bring the attention back onto the case again because it's been quiet for quite some time."

Church agreed that might have been a smart tactic, saying, "The one thing that Lori can't stand is the press. Let the press get wind that she has a restraining order [against her dad]. Let her explain why."

But Church doubted Bennie would follow through, given the opposition from the rest of his family. "Karen has already told him [if] you get arrested, I'm not bailing you out." Lori also prevailed on her little sister Wendy to back her up. Like Bennie, Wendy had shown Church, in flashes, that she thought Ray was responsible for Rayna's death. But she had also been combative with police and defensive about her brother-in-law, pointing at Jason Tibbs as the more likely suspect. Now, according to Church, Wendy "got right in both Bennie's and Karen's faces" to tell her parents to stop bothering Ray.

But what most worried Bennie was Lori's response as he continued to push for the truth. According to Church, "Lori ends up going ballistic. She goes over [to the Risons' house], throws the key [to the Risons' house] at Mom, and says, 'I'm done. You're not seeing my kids anymore.'" Tina believed this threat kept Karen on Ray's bandwagon, making her increasingly angry when Bennie questioned his innocence.

"I think Bennie is very concerned about Lori because Lori is on the verge of flipping out," Church told Hahn. "And he kept saying, 'She's gonna snap. She's gonna snap.' I said, 'Bennie, Lori's not a rubber band. People don't snap. She may sit down, start crying, and may have to get on some medication or go somewhere to rest for a few days. But she's carrying a lot of shit that needs to come out. And she's never going to be well until that stuff is out of her.'"

Bennie later explained that the worries about Lori extended to her children, the ultimate leverage Lori had on their grandparents. At one point, he told Church that Lori threatened to kill her children and herself if she were arrested.

Despite the flak from his family, Bennie tried to keep Church working on the investigation. He had an hour-long commute home from his job at the packaging plant in Elkhart, and Church's home office in Mishawaka was on the way. Church complained to Hahn that there were times when Rison stopped by her office almost every day.[143] Back in 1993, he did much the same with Noreen Molnar, a young woman who also lived near his workplace. She originally called him about premonitions she was having while Rayna was missing. But Bennie kept dropping by even after his daughter was found. He shared his fears that Ray was the culprit and he'd "lose another daughter" and, at other times, defended him. But then she said Bennie would share information that seemed too intimate about Rayna and "weird." He also confided in her that he didn't have any friends. His visits to Molnar were before work and came earlier and earlier while she was still in her pajamas. Finally, Noreen asked him to stop coming over and threatened to call the police if he did. Even after Bennie stopped the visits, she did get in touch with the La Porte police and talked to Bob Schoff.[144]

Tina Church did not need the police to intervene for her. She saw no good end to her involvement in Rayna's case or Bennie's constant visits and wanted nothing more to do with Psycho Sue. By the end of March 1996, she let Rison and Hahn know she was off the case.

Finally, Sue Burzynski was left alone to run Bennie's investigation. She followed up on all the leads Nothstine and Church had quickly discounted. Prime among them was Jason Tibbs. He remembers getting her call in February 1997. "She started by being nice," he says. "But then she kept asking questions in a very aggressive way, like she was the police. I told her I had better contact my lawyer before I answered. Then she stopped being nice and said, 'I think you have something to hide, and you should know you're a suspect in this murder.'"

Little did Jason know that Burzynski had taped their conversation and shared it with Bennie. Evidently, he didn't like what he heard. "A few days after that lady called," Jason says, "Bennie came to our house and apologized for how she acted." But in the meantime, Jason got back in touch with Mike Drayton, who talked to his contacts at the police department and learned that Tibbs was not a target.

Burzynski pursued Rison's other leads just as aggressively, but before long, she decided who was really at the center of Rayna's murder plot—the two long-haired undercover cops, Jim Jackson and his partner from the LPPD, who had politely chased after each and every one of her premonitions when Rayna was still missing. Their coconspirators, she claimed, included other officers, Rayna's cousin Jenni, and her girlfriends. All were part of a giant sex and drugs ring. She even found a way to wrap Ed Logan into the scheme. No matter how wide she spun her outlandish web, it did not snare Ray McCarty. As a result, Bennie continued to pay for her services.[145] Coincidentally, a few months later, in 1997, in an article titled, "Detectives try psychics when all else fails," *The South Bend Tribune* sent a reporter to follow up on notorious cases where detectives sought help from people who claimed paranormal powers. "La Porte city police used several psychics in the case of Rayna Rison, who was killed in 1993," the paper reported. "Police there said they were of little help." Detective Hahn was even more emphatic in an earlier article on the subject, declaring, "They haven't helped us one bit."[146] Among the psychics cited was Burzynski, referred to as "Sue B" by the reporter, who added that the Rison case "remains unsolved."[147]

Other than the psychics article, a brief piece with the headline, "La Porte Police Seek Leads in Rison Slaying," was the only 1997 *Tribune* story devoted to Rayna's case.[148] For the first time, nothing appeared on the anniversary of her disappearance or when her body was found. As her murder investigation faded from view, the clock was running out on Cynthia Hedge's efforts to try Rayna's killer before she was up for reelection. The police and Scott Duerring believed they had enough to prosecute Ray McCarty, but the politics in the face of the Rison family opposition demanded just a little more. By the end of the year, the detectives decided to take two cracks at a breakthrough.

For the first crack, they returned to Charlie Allen. He no longer had a lawyer and was willing to talk again. Hahn videotaped a lengthy session this time, retreading all the ground traveled in previous interviews. Still, Allen stuck to his story about Ray and the stranger appearing on his doorstep at some time other than March 26. Hahn also brought up the letterman jacket, clearly suspecting that Allen had something to do with its appearance in the dump when Rayna's *America's Most Wanted* segment aired. But this line of inquiry seems odd since Allen and his girlfriend, Cindy Brewer, were at 517 Haviland watching the show with the McCartys—as Hahn knew since the

LPPD patrolmen were surveilling the house. The only news from this interview was that girlfriend Cindy would soon be Charlie's wife. Another new wrinkle was Hahn's passive-aggressive approach. He warned if Allen had anything to do with the letterman jacket, "You possibly will see charges at that point. . . . I have no intentions of wanting to ever arrest you, okay? And especially related to this. And it would break my heart to have to do that."[149]

The second crack at resuscitating the case proved more productive. The evidence technicians reviewed all the material sent to the FBI labs to see what could be resubmitted for analysis with new technology. Duerring remembers this process turned up even more of the green fibers that detectives connected to Ray's carcass blanket. "Excuse my terminology," he says, "but there were just a shit ton of those fibers in her hair. That, to me, was the actual physical evidence we were looking for. It made me feel very confident about our case."[150]

But the evidence audit turned up something else as well. The detectives realized that debris from Rayna's car had never been submitted in the first place. It was an embarrassing oversight that the prosecuting attorney's office would not freely admit. Once Douglas Deedrick got this material, it didn't take long before he struck gold. As he reported to La Porte detectives, "A brown Caucasian head hair that exhibits the same microscopic characteristics as the known head hairs of Raymond McCarty was found in . . . debris from driver's floor of victim's car." Deedrick referred to the head hair he removed from Ray during the second search as his standard for comparison. However, his report added a cautionary note: "It is pointed out that hair comparisons do not constitute a basis for absolute personal identification."[151]

But that caveat did not prevent Duerring and Hedge from talking about a significant "new" development without mentioning what it was. With the green fibers and the head hair, the police felt they finally had enough physical evidence to tie Ray to the crime.[152]

Deedrick made other discoveries in February and March, but not as conclusive as Ray's head hair in Rayna's car. Looking through the rest of the LTD debris, he discovered pubic and nose hair. He also reexamined the letterman jacket and found "light-colored blonde hair."[153] None of these samples matched Rayna's standards, but they did provide an excuse for a new search warrant directed at the body of Charlie Allen. Once again, a probable cause hearing was held before the amenable and well-informed Judge Gettinger, who asked Hahn at one point, "Could Charlie Allen, in fact, be one of those people that would have been able to assist Mr. McCarty in potentially disposing of the body?"

The detective answered in the affirmative. Although Hahn admitted that Allen's hair was more "reddish-colored" than blonde, he was granted the search warrant.[154] A few hours later, he tracked Charlie down near his home and drove him to the hospital to draw blood and then to the LPPD station, where evidence technicians could pluck hairs, do a cheek swab for DNA, and take fingerprints. In reporting on the body search, Hahn wrote, "Mr. Allen did not have the appearance of being traumatized or upset over what had just been done to him."[155]

WHEN JURIES ARE GRAND

As the Rison investigation dragged on, nearly consuming Cynthia Hedge's entire first term, her chief deputy Scott Duerring had one last trick up his sleeve to bring matters to a head—convening a grand jury. This would mean presenting evidence to six community members who could decide to indict a suspect. In January 1996, he had batted away a report—probably floated by Bennie—that their office was about to convene a panel. The account, he said, "shocked" him.[156] But by January 1998, preparations for the procedure had already begun in earnest.

The use of grand juries varied widely among the region's prosecuting attorneys. There were no grand juries in Porter County, just east of La Porte. In Lake County, east of Porter, they met weekly for all sorts of crimes. La Porte leaned far closer to Porter than Lake. Before Hedge, Duerring had served as a prosecutor for fourteen years and remembered only four grand juries.[157]

But unlike her Democratic predecessors, Hedge was willing to shake things up in her office. The most dramatic change had been making Duerring and two other prosecutors full-time staff members instead of part-time hires from local firms. She imported one of those attorneys, Kathleen Lang, from Cook County, Illinois, a vast jurisdiction encompassing

Chicago. As an assistant state's attorney, Lang prosecuted the serious street crime and gang activity that had become more of a problem in La Porte during the nineties.[158]

To prepare for a Rison grand jury, Duerring sent Lang and another prosecutor to Lake County to see the panels in action and to learn how best to organize one for La Porte. In a later article in *The Muncie Times*, Duerring explained that laying the groundwork for grand juries required extra hours that weren't possible under the previous part-time regimes in the La Porte prosecuting attorney's office. Ironically, in the same article, a Porter County prosecutor argued that a grand jury "offers [victims'] families some solace. When people are killed, relatives are entitled to some kind of impartial hearing."[159]

As Duerring knew well, a grand jury investigation of Rayna's murder would offer her family anything but solace. On the contrary, he saw it as a tool for prosecuting Ray against their objections. Still, he did try to make his grand jury something of an "impartial hearing" by presenting evidence related to other suspects. "My approach was to throw everything we had at this grand jury," Duerring remembers, "and let them sort through it to determine what was legitimate."[160]

Early in 1998, La Porte evidence technicians sent the FBI fingerprints for Ed Logan, whose ex-girlfriend had claimed he bragged about killing Rayna. They also submitted the finger- and palm prints for Larry Dewayne Hall.[161]

Four years before, when Hall was arrested as the suspected killer of a teen in an Illinois town that bordered Indiana, media reports flared with the possibility that he had murdered dozens of other young victims. Alleged Hall homicides were scattered across the country, but most were clustered in the Midwest, a few hours from his home in Wabash, Indiana. Bringing added notoriety to the case was his strange appearance. In some cases, his suspected victims lived near parks that had recently hosted Civil War reenactments. Hall would attend those events dressed as a Union soldier from Indiana. To appear more authentic, he had grown bushy "burnsides," sideburns that extended to his chin, reminiscent of the famed Union General Ambrose Burnside. Local police at first dismissed him as a "wannabe"— someone with the perverted desire to kill pretty young girls but otherwise harmless. However, an investigation spearheaded by an Illinois deputy sheriff found sufficient evidence to convict him for murdering the young woman in the border town and to implicate him in many more killings.

Rayna's death would have occurred at the height of Hall's suspected homicide spree, and he lived only ninety miles away from La Porte.[162] The physical evidence tying him to her murder were two items seized from his van. One was a handwritten list of names, places, and dates, including: "Rayna Rison 1993 La Porte Gas Station." The other was a bottle of birth control pills with "Rayna Rison" written on the label.[163] When first informed about Hall and sent his mug shots, Hahn wrote in a report, "I was amazed [at] the likeness between Larry Hall and Ray McCarty." Indeed, absent the burnsides, with his mustache and thick black hair, he was a pudgier version of Hahn's prime suspect.[164]

The supposed Rayna-related material in Hall's possession was among an array of objects that could be considered mementos from his crimes. These included articles of women's clothing, newspaper clips reporting on a missing or murdered young woman, things taken from the crime scene, or just notes scrawled on scraps of paper. Like other serial killers, Hall could have used these souvenirs to remind himself of the sexual assault that usually accompanied his suspected homicides.[165]

Eventually, the Hall evidence relating to Rayna did not hold up to closer scrutiny. Of the names that could be made out on his list,[166] most were associated with women he may have killed,[167] but not all. One was murdered by a man who confessed to the crime. The victim was pregnant with his child when she died.[168] As for the birth control pills, the label was handwritten in Hall's scrawl, and the bottle could not be found at local pharmacies.[169]

Although Hall would have seemed like a miraculous fall guy for Ray, the Rison family quickly dismissed the evidence that most incriminated him. Karen and Lori told the press that Rayna was not "sexually active" in the months before her death and did not need birth control pills. However, her friends told police that Rayna was so paranoid about getting pregnant after Ray's assaults that she was taking contraception. Indeed, among the items in her purse strewn across the seat of the abandoned LTD was a "gray vinyl pouch" containing a "birth control pill dispenser" with Rayna's fingerprints. The package in Hall's possession with Rayna's name on it did have Triphasil contraceptive tablets inside, but only his prints were on the sheet with the pills, not hers.[170]

During the spring of 1998, as Duerring and Lang sent out scores of subpoenas to witnesses and organized their presentation to the grand jury, no news about their efforts leaked to the press. The secrecy was undoubtedly due to the harsh warnings about disclosure accompanying the judge's order to testify. Sharing any information about the proceeding would violate the law and be subject to a severe penalty.

In early April 1998, clueless that a resolution might soon be at hand, *The South Bend Tribune* penned a five-year-anniversary story on Rayna's unsolved murder with the headline, "1993 slaying investigation continues." Duerring kept a straight face when the reporter asked him if the case was at a dead end. "We don't feel we're at a dead end at all," he replied, adding that the investigation was "very active" and pointing to "new scientific procedures designed to uncover previously undetected evidence."

Of course, those words had been used before by multiple prosecutors and detectives. When asked to weigh in, Bennie told the reporter that he was "not convinced authorities are doing all they can," which was why he continued to "spend a bundle" on private investigators. He was frustrated that detectives had not used the "information" he gave them to make an arrest and continued to deny that Ray or Lori could have been involved. "I would think if there was any evidence that went in that direction, the case would be resolved."

In a rare interview, when asked how she handled the grief, Karen Rison answered, "I handle it most of the time. You have to go on, but it's not easy." As she spoke, the reporter wrote, "her voice [was] quivering with emotion."

Although Duerring refused to predict when an arrest would be made, he said he was "hopeful" about solving the case. "If I weren't, we would not be spending this amount of time and resources."[171]

Four weeks later, on Wednesday, May 6, 1998, La Porte Prosecuting Attorney Cynthia Hedge announced a grand jury had been convened earlier that day in the Rayna Rison homicide investigation. For most of her constituency, it was a welcome milestone. But it put Hedge on the defensive over two issues. First, why did it take so long to bring the case to court? Hedge replied, one reporter wrote, that "it was 'additional information' that pushed prosecutors to make the grand jury decision." But when asked later whether it was new or old "additional information," the prosecuting attorney said that grand jury secrecy forced her to "draw the line" on providing more details.

Hedge was also asked about the upcoming election, which was only six months away. Did that prompt her to call the grand jury? She answered, "When I was elected to be prosecuting attorney, I was elected to a four-year term, not a three-year term and not an election-year term. Whether it's an election year or not, we need to do what we need to do. The bottom line is in any of our decisions, we have to do what is right, and this was the right thing to do."[172]

Jason Tibbs would hear about the grand jury from his lawyer, Mike Drayton. Hahn approached the attorney first, afraid there were still some hard feelings about how the police kept Jason in the station without telling his mother. Rachel Tibbs had contemplated a lawsuit later, but Drayton talked her out of it, given the community's interest in solving the case, and she settled for an apology instead. In the interim, much had changed for Jason. He had met Leslie Ann Dean, the daughter of a good friend, and found someone he thought could be a life partner. They had their first child, Duston, in October 1996 and married two months later.

By 1998, Jason had given up hope that anything would come of Rayna's murder investigation. "I thought they found some reason to sweep everything under the rug," he says. But once he heard about the grand jury, Jason wondered whether they might pull him back into the case as a suspect. Drayton was quick to dismiss that idea. "He told me, 'The only reason they're calling you as a witness is that they think you're telling the truth.'"

Although Jason cannot divulge anything he said before the grand jury, he doesn't remember in any case. "It was a blur," he says. "At first, they had me out in the hall with my mother and Drayton," he says, "but only Mike was allowed to go into the room with me. It was like a huge conference room, and there were big windows. I was told Hedge was in there, but I had no idea who was who. A man asked me most of the questions [probably Duerring], but a thin woman with glasses [probably Kathleen Lang] asked some, too. Mike said if any question made me uncomfortable, I could motion to him, and we could walk out of the room to talk it over. That never happened, but I couldn't tell you a thing they asked me, even if I was allowed to do it."

Despite the secrecy, the Risons were no doubt intimately aware of the grand jury's process. Rayna's parents and sisters must have been called to testify. Only Ray, as a potential target for indictment, would have been exempt.

The McCartys awaited the panel's determination from yet another address—nine miles out of town near the Fish Lake recreational area. It had been among the couple's favorite places for summertime recreation, and for a few years, they owned a cottage near the water. Their new abode was a little thousand-square-foot ranch on the corner of a tilled farm field. They had moved in a month before, knowing that the grand jury would soon be upon them, with the potential to disrupt their lives as never before.[173] The little house near the lake may have seemed like a vacation-style refuge where they could weather any bad publicity.

As the grand jury continued in session throughout the month, more information did slip out in the press. The panel met three times a week and had been scheduled to hear seventy witnesses. Finally, on Wednesday, May 27, they began deliberating at 4:00 P.M. and agreed on a unanimous decision six hours later.[174]

Early the next day, as Ray left through the front door of his new home for work, he was greeted by a SWAT team comprised of La Porte city and county police who had surrounded the house and roped off the road from both directions. An LPPD captain had him lie down on the driveway and put his arms behind his back so he could be handcuffed. As he lay there, the captain showed him the arrest warrant for the murder of Rayna Rison.

The police took Lori into custody too, but as the captain explained to *The South Bend Tribune*, she was not under arrest. "We just didn't want her in harm's way." Then, indicating that he also had a search warrant, he added, "We didn't want her returning to the house right away. We asked her if she would accompany us to the police station, and she said, 'Yes.'"[175]

By this time, Jason Tibbs also had a job at Teledyne. When he arrived for his afternoon shift, he was informed that the police had arrested Ray and then came to the factory to search his locker. His coworkers had heard that Jason testified to the grand jury a week before and thought he would be happy to get the news.

Over the next few days before Ray's arraignment, more information about grand jury evidence leaked to the press. Reporters learned about Rayna's abortion and Ray's three-year suspended sentence for molesting her in 1990. As one paper put it, "Lori reportedly was outraged when she learned of her husband's affair with her younger sister."[176] A reader would later complain that the reporter referred to statutory rape as "an affair."[177] Other leaks included testimony that Ray assaulted Rayna again before she disappeared and threatened to kill her if she told anyone else.[178]

Now, with the grand jury indictment in hand, Hedge was more outspoken about her pursuit of Rayna's killer from the start of her administration. "When I was elected, I had resigned myself to this case," she told the *News-Dispatch* of Michigan City. "We felt very strongly this was a case we wanted to see come to a resolution for everyone: the victim, the family, and the community."[179] As to why it took so long, she explained to the *Post-Tribune* of Merrillville that they had to review all the evidence "slowly but methodically. [After going] through that long process," she said, "we reached a point where we had enough evidence to proceed."[180]

Hedge and LPPD's detective captain singled out one person for particular praise, thanking Detective Sergeant Harold Hahn for his "extraordinary efforts" in leading the investigation. Hahn "just didn't let go," Hedge said.[181]

But was Ray's indictment the "resolution" that Rayna's family wanted? When McCarty was arraigned a few days after his arrest, the *News-Dispatch* reported, "Lori McCarty wept and was comforted by her mother and sister before entering the courtroom." Once inside, she composed herself but clutched Wendy's hand.[182] Meanwhile, TV cameras recorded her husband taking a security-conscious circuitous route through the courthouse basement, wearing a gray jail jumpsuit over his squat wrestler's physique. His thick black hair with brown highlights was combed with an off-center part, and his mustache drooped into a Fu Manchu.[183] He sat in the courtroom in front of his wife and mother-in-law, and the bailiff permitted them to exchange a few words. Bennie was nowhere in sight and unavailable for comment, a most unexpected absence for a man who had continually thrust himself into the center of his daughter's homicide investigation.

Once the court was in session, the judge scheduled a trial for eight months from that date. As was typical for Indiana homicide cases, Ray would not be released before trial. Also not out of the ordinary, the *News-Dispatch* reported that Larry Rogers, Ray's pugnacious defense counsel, asked "for a gag order to prevent authorities now active in the investigation from disclosing specifics about the case to reporters before the trial."[184] However, more unusually, he asked for it to cover "past investigators"[185] involved in the investigation. To everyone's surprise, Hedge's chief deputy, Scott Duerring, agreed.

The "past investigator" who concerned both the prosecution and the defense was Cynthia Hedge's predecessor, folksy Bill Herrbach. He would be quoted in virtually every article about the case, defending his administration for not bringing charges because he did not have sufficient evidence.[186]

For all their pronouncements about new evidence or new technology to analyze old evidence, Hedge and Duerring never specified what that new evidence was—and nothing they said was enough to muzzle Herrbach. As a result, uncertainty hung over their indictment of Ray McCarty like a cloud. It considerably darkened after Hedge lost her reelection bid.[187] Eighteen months later, in what the *News-Dispatch* called "a shocking move," La Porte County's new prosecuting attorney dropped the charges.[188]

THE CASE THAT SHOULD HAVE BEEN MADE AGAINST RAY

RAYNA RISON

FAMILY
- Bennie, Karen (parents)
- Lori, Wendy (sisters)

FRIENDS
- Matt Elser (boyfriend)

COWORKERS
- Cheryl VanSchoyck

RISON PRIVATE INVESTIGATORS
- Tina Church

CITY OF LA PORTE POLICE DEPARTMENT
- Patrolman Barry Aftowski*
- Chief Gene Samuelson
- Detectives John Miller, Bob Schoff, Harold Hahn

LA PORTE COUNTY

Prosecuting Attorney
- Bill Herrbach, 1991–1994
- Cynthia Hedge, 1995–1998
- Chief Deputy Scott Duerring (for Hedge)
- Dr. Rick Hoover, Forensic Pathologist

Sheriff's Department
- Sergeant Joe Pavolka
- Patrolman Jim Jackson

FBI
- Douglas Deedrick, Trace Evidence Analyst

INDIANA STATE POLICE
- Sergeant Arland Boyd

WITNESSES
- Mike Keeling*
- Douglas McGarvey*
- John Mitchell*
- Lorn "Brent" Glassman
- Beth York; sons Kyle, Austin
- Jane Lindborg
- Roy West, John Proud
- Bryan Durham
- Rene Gazarkiewicz
- Kim Hackney
- Val Eilers

LORI AND RAY McCARTY

FAMILY
- Adrienne (daughter)
- Hunter (son)
- Carolyn (Ray's mother)

RAY'S FRIENDS, COWORKERS
- Scott Scarborough*
- Sandra Salat*
- Chris Wallen*
- James McWhirter, Gayla (Holt) Moreau
- Gary Marshall (Gayla's son)
- Charlie Allen, Cindy Brewer
- Garry, Lois Bucher
- Brenda Pegg
- Darold, Connie Willis
- Mike Kepplin
- Pat, Richard Walters

*INTRODUCED IN THIS CHAPTER

157

THE CASE THAT SHOULD HAVE BEEN MADE AGAINST RAY

In his statements to the press after the grand jury indictment, Bill Herrbach did not attempt to dispute the panel's decision. Looking back on the two years he presided over the Rison investigation as La Porte County prosecuting attorney, he said, "Everyone who was on our Homicide Team at the time believed it was Ray McCarty [who killed Rayna]."

But in multiple interviews, Herrbach claimed that he never had "sufficient" evidence to convict Ray in a jury trial. He implied that his successor faced the same dilemma—no matter what the grand jury decided. When pressed about holes in the investigation, Herrbach focused on three areas.

First was the cause of death, an endless source of frustration for his Homicide Team. Duerring admitted it remained unresolved under Hedge and blamed an inconclusive autopsy on the body's decomposition underwater. As a result, the prosecution did not know how the victim died, let alone have a murder weapon connected to Ray. At best, they had a receipt for the stun gun purchased just after Rayna's big argument with Lori and just before her abduction, and Ray's changing reasons for why he got it. But there was no physical proof that Ray ever used the O-Mega Super Baton on Rayna or that it would have killed her if he had.

The second problem for Herrbach was a gap in the witness testimony on March 26. While Ray's constant changes to his alibi raised suspicions, he said, the detectives could find no one "to put him with Rayna that night." Beth York was the closest the police came when she described someone who looked like Ray peering under the LTD's hood on North 200 East. But when it came to the eyewitnesses near the Pine Lake Animal Hospital, they described someone who did not have Ray's stature or hair color. Instead, he was tall and thin with blonde hair. In other words, they saw McCarty's accomplice, who was certainly not big and fat like Charlie Allen. The detectives' failure to identify one or more accomplices in line with witness testimony left another gaping hole in the investigation.

Finally, because of these gaps, Herrbach argued, and the uncertainty about the Allen testimony, the prosecution could never establish a plausible timeline for Ray's activities on Friday night. "McCarty was in the vicinity of the animal hospital at the time of her disappearance," he told reporters, "but we couldn't account for his whereabouts for a period of time after that."

With comments like that, it's understandable why Duerring wanted to gag his former boss. Herrbach wished to defend his failure to act in such a notorious case with such an obvious culprit.

Still, despite the skepticism Herrbach expressed about an indictment, he did have sufficient evidence for a jury trial—even before he left office. His staff and the detectives just overlooked it. The murder weapon was always front and center in the forensic toxicology and would have been connected with Ray if the police had asked what he did at Teledyne. Ray's male accomplice was inadvertently identified by Charlie Allen, who tellingly tried to edit his previous mention of the man's name, which went unnoticed by the detectives. Ray himself revealed his connection to James Flett McWhirter, the man who found the body, and another tip connected McWhirter to the pickup truck used during Rayna's submersion. Most importantly, a close reading of the McCartys' interviews and critical witness testimony reveals the centrality of Lori in the plot, its execution, and attempted cover-up.

In retrospect, an outsider could wonder how La Porte city and county detectives missed so many crucial clues in assembling their case against Ray. But in fairness, this was not just any crime. When a teen is abducted and murdered like Rayna Rison, the public puts tremendous pressure on police. The all-hands-on-deck approach to capturing initial interviews and tips means officers must get involved who are not fully versed in the case and may miss the significance of a reported incident or individual. As the central figures in the murder plot were interviewed and reinterviewed, answers changed in subtle ways that should have been revealing but seemed to have slipped by the detectives. What is most remarkable about the Rison case is all the evidence the prosecutors had at hand to prosecute Ray McCarty that, for various reasons, they couldn't see.

THE DIPPER

The sand-colored complex of Teledyne Casting Service played two roles in Rayna Rison's tragic life and death. Soon after Ray started work there in 1987, Rayna would go to the house and babysit for their infant, Adrienne, so Lori could leave for her job. Ray only had to walk home a few hundred yards to find Rayna alone with his daughter. Often, she would spend the night. As he would later admit, this is when the molestation of his sister-in-law began and did not end until she became pregnant at the age of thirteen in 1989.

The role of Teledyne in Rayna's 1993 murder came with a chemical integral to Ray's job. When asked what McCarty did at the plant, one supervisor told detectives it was "hauling and dipping" in the core room.[1] From the police records, it does not appear that detectives fully understood what that meant, perhaps because it would have required some knowledge about foundries.

Once one of La Porte's largest employers, with as many as four hundred workers, Teledyne manufactured a wide range of cast iron parts, including locomotive engine blocks, automotive stamping dies, and printing presses.[2] An essential element of the plant's metal casting process was sand. It could be molded into different shapes when mixed with binders like clay. Properly treated, the mixture could not be penetrated by molten iron. Sand packed on top of patterns inside wood frames formed the outer shells of parts. Sand cores shaped the internal holes and passages.[3] Creating and treating the sand—"core assembly"—was Teledyne's most labor-intensive job, and the "core rooms" employed the most workers.[4]

McCarty handled smaller cores in an area known as the green sand room, which referred to the type of sand that was used for this purpose. As a *hauler*, Ray would move dollies with wooden boxes that had core patterns inside. He would open the boxes, pack them with the sticky sand compound, and then remove the resulting cores for treatment. As a *dipper*, McCarty submerged the core into a resin paint solution that would give it a hard shell and keep out any moisture that molten metal could penetrate. He used a basket to lower several small cores into a tub with the solution or put on gloves to dip a piece by hand.

The dipping solution needed a precise thickness or viscosity to make the proper shell. Ray would check the viscosity several times daily with a glass instrument resembling a fat thermometer. Should the reading show the solution was too thick, he would pour in a chemical to make it thinner. That chemical was isopropyl alcohol—the substance found in Rayna Rison's system that the forensic pathologist, Dr. Rick Hoover, could not explain. Although Hoover said it was most commonly used in rubbing alcohol, that application only requires a 70 percent solution.[5] The industrial isopropyl alcohol—also known as IPA—that Ray used was far more concentrated and toxic, with a 99.9 percent solution.[6]

Today, the US Government's Occupational Safety and Health Administration requires all IPA containers to display brightly colored labels declaring, "Health Hazard." A typical IPA warning reads: "May be poisonous if inhaled or absorbed through the skin. Vapors may cause dizziness or suffocation."[7] The 1993 core room workers remember dispensing the IPA from a tabletop tank. It had no warning label since those were not mandated back then, but Chris Wallen, a "Lead Man" who trained new core room staff, said that practical experience alone would acquaint a dipper with the dangers of IPA. Workers in those days did not wear respiratory equipment and poured the substance from the tank into an open five-gallon bucket. "You put your head too close to that bucket," Wallen says, "and you got lightheaded real quick."[8]

In the *Clinical Toxicology* textbook chapter on isopropyl alcohol, medical toxicologist Dr. Marsha Ford describes how the substance can lead to severe illness or death. "The predominant toxic effect," she writes, is "depression of the CNS [central nervous system]." Slight exposure to IPA can lead to dizziness. Prolonged or concentrated exposure can result in unconsciousness or coma.[9] In the early days of surgery, physicians saw the initial blackout from IPA as a good thing and used it as an anesthetic. Until recently, veterinarians did the same with their operations on cats.[10] But besides the impact on the brain stem, Ford writes, "severe [IPA] toxicity" can lead to "respiratory depression and hypotension [excessively low blood pressure]." Ford cites research showing that suffocation is "usually the cause of death" in IPA-related fatalities.

According to Ford, it is not clear how much IPA is fatal. Her view is at odds with the toxicology lab that Hoover used, which indicated a more than 100 mg/dL concentration was "lethal." Rayna's system showed 48.3 mg/dL, which could have been reduced while her body was submerged in water. But for Ford, these amounts are immaterial. She writes, "In 31 fatalities, Isopropanol levels ranged from 10 to 250 mg/dL, and two patients with coma had levels of 20 and 30 mg/dL."[11]

If Ray had soaked a rag in IPA and held it over Rayna's nose and mouth, it would have quickly incapacitated her. As he held it against her face, the substance would have been absorbed through her skin and inhaled. Ford points to studies that show this dual absorption "can produce significant toxicity."[12]

Wallen, who instructed Ray at Teledyne, says manufacturers now have more sensitivity to the dangers caused by occupational chemicals. IPA is no longer a component of dipping paint. But back in 1993, he says, isopropyl alcohol would have been readily available to Ray. "You definitely had that big tank [of IPA] in the Core Room. Everybody there could have access to it every day."[13]

Ray inadvertently revealed when he last got access to IPA on March 26. In all his alibis, he made a point of saying that he walked back inside the plant after he punched out. He claimed he did so to clean out the machine where he mixed his sand. While he had a coworker confirm he returned to the plant, the man did not see what he did inside the core room.[14] Rather than clean the machine, McCarty could have soaked several rags with IPA or simply filled a bottle with IPA and walked out of Teledyne with the murder weapon inside his duffel bag.

When an eyewitness, Rene Gazarkiewicz, saw Rayna leaning into Ray's Datsun with her feet off the ground, Ray could have been holding a rag soaked in IPA over her face. As Jason Tibbs told the police, Rayna was always "terrified" by McCarty's strength,[15] and that night, he could have been using it to hold her suspended half-inside his car while the IPA suffocated her. Perhaps afraid that someone saw Rayna in his clutches, Ray told Mike Kepplin, his young hunting friend, that she got in his Datsun that night for "horseplay."[16]

But if McCarty stayed in the driver's seat, he needed someone else to entice or drag Rayna to the car's window. This was the accomplice so essential to the State's case against Ray, but someone the detectives never managed to identify.

THE TREE TRIMMER

Anyone who helped Ray abduct Rayna and then hide her body would have had some identifying characteristics in his background. First, he had to have been a very close or longtime friend of McCarty to put his future in such jeopardy should he be caught. Second, he would need to be unusually cruel and morally depraved to assist in killing a defenseless young woman.

It was not hard for the police to identify all Ray's closest friends. Despite the McCartys' efforts at conviviality, the truth was that Ray had very few intimates. Most were males he grew up with in Union Mills. An exception was Charlie Allen, who described himself as Ray's best friend. They met while working at Davey Tree Expert Company. In one of his first interviews, Charlie mentioned another coworker from that firm who was with him on the morning of March 26. His name was Scott Scarborough.[17] Besides being Allen's coworker, Gayla Holt told the detectives he was also one of Ray McCarty's closest friends. He was not home when Boyd went to interview him in Union Mills. Hahn was supposed to follow up but never did.[18]

In 1993, at thirty, Scarborough was a masterful and fearless tree cutter. He had no problem climbing a towering tree; whatever the surrounding hazards, he could find a way to take it down. At six feet, one inch tall and around 150 pounds, he was skinny but also wiry and exceptionally strong for his weight, able to wrangle tree limbs his coworkers would have preferred he cut into pieces.[19]

Scarborough had a narrow face, oversized glasses, and an impish smile in yearbook pictures from his tiny Union Mills grade school.[20] A teacher remembers "Scottie" as hyperactive and challenged by most of his classes, much like McCarty, who was two years behind him.[21] To get to Scarborough's house, Ray had to walk a few hundred yards around the corner, down a hill, and under a rail viaduct. Scott's family lived in a large, rambling home across the street from a block of bars. According to Gary Marshall, who also grew up in Union Mills, the Scarboroughs had a reputation for generosity and hard drinking. "If your car broke down, they were the first ones to help you fix it," he says, "but you didn't want to go to the bar with them later."[22]

As a young man, Scarborough had his share of scrapes with the cops. At eighteen, he was arrested for stealing a license plate and then for theft a few months later. Most of the charges that followed were traffic related: reckless driving, operating while intoxicated, and speeding with trucks and motorcycles, which he came to love.[23] But he got into the most trouble with his love life. He was married in 1984, but his twenty-two-year-old wife was killed two months later when a hit-and-run driver struck her.[24] Over the next fourteen years, he had at least four children by women he did not marry[25]—two from one-night stands.[26] Court records show he paid child support, but they also indicate several charges related to domestic battery.

One longtime lover describes the two sides of Scarborough's Jekyll and Hyde personality. "Scottie could be extremely charming, helpful, and very resourceful," she remembers. By his midtwenties, he had moved into his grandmother's nineteenth-century home across the street from the house where he grew up. Bit by bit, he expanded and modernized it without help, and the girlfriend moved in with her two children. "He was a very talented carpenter and could fix anything," she says, "and had so much energy, he could stay up a couple of days without sleeping if he decided he wanted to finish a project.

"But behind closed doors, he was different. He would get quite violent, especially after he was drinking. Although I wasn't hospitalized from his beatings, I had black eyes and broken ribs. Sometimes, he would grab me by the throat and choke me out. I wouldn't say anything [to the authorities] because I was terrified of what he could do to me. I left several times, but he always begged me to come back and promised to change. At one point,

I got him to stop drinking. I also got him to see a psychiatrist who diagnosed him as bipolar. He took medication for a while but eventually refused because of the side effects. Then, the beatings started again. The last straw came when he took sewing scissors and stabbed me in the leg. My children saw it, and I left that night."

Rayna's abduction and murder occurred while this woman was living with Scarborough. "I knew they grew up together," she says of Scarborough and Ray McCarty, "but Scottie thought he was odd. When he came over to the house, they usually talked outside. I don't ever remember Scottie asking him in. I do recall Scottie talking about the Rison girl's murder and Scottie basically saying that he thought Ray did it."[27]

Scarborough's son Lucas was born a year before Rayna's death. He lived briefly with his mother until her husband threw him out, and then he stayed off and on with Scott. Now an adult, he is not as tall as his father, but he says, "I'm just as skinny." Lucas followed Scott Scarborough into tree-trimming, runs a crew, and has plans to start his own business someday.

Growing up, he witnessed his father's violent episodes and, at times, was on the receiving end. But he also saw another side—someone who tried to wrestle with his demons and continually improve. After several years of applying, Scarborough got into the Laborers' Union in the early 2000s and worked for a company that built scaffolding at construction sites. With the union, Lucas says, "He told me he went from a paycheck to a career."

Lucas never heard Scarborough mention anything about Rayna Rison or Ray McCarty, but he adds, "I know there was something real dark in his past that he didn't want to talk about. It turned him into a loner. He knew everybody in town, but he'd say, 'I don't have friends. I have acquaintances.' It's possible he did something bad with one of those guys he felt guilty about."

By the time Lucas was sixteen, in 2008, he was living with his father. The house, he says, was always "a work in progress," but it had plenty of room for him and the occasional girlfriend. There were still times when Lucas had to weather Scott's rages, which were always worse when his father drank. "He had an anger switch, and if it was clicked, he was just pissed off at the world." One morning, Lucas woke up to find Scott face-planted in their front yard after a bender from the night before. "He could have frozen to death if it was any colder. When he got sober, we had one of our biggest arguments. I begged and cried for him to stop drinking, and when I told him I'd leave, he promised he wouldn't drink anymore. He said if he ever wanted to drink, he'd ask my permission first."

For a while, it looked like father and son Scarborough could settle into a normal domestic life. They went fishing together, puttered around with engines, and planned cross-country car trips. Scott reconciled with an old flame who needed a place to live. Robin (not her real name) had become a surrogate mother to Lucas as he bounced from his birth mother to various Scarborough relatives. "I call her Mama R," he says. She had a baby the year before her reconciliation with Scott, but had broken up with the child's father.[28]

The household was briefly peaceful, but Scarborough became physically abusive again and Robin moved out. As usual, charming Scottie begged her to come back. Finally, one night, hoping they could patch things up, she brought her baby over for Lucas to watch. She then hopped on the back of Scarborough's beloved Harley-Davidson, and they roared off to some nearby bars. When they returned, Robin remembers, "We were in the bedroom with the baby, and it was like he snapped. When he got that way, he wasn't just mean. He was crazy."[29] What followed would later be detailed in a police report by a La Porte County deputy sheriff. He wrote, Scarborough "became very angry towards victim and started punching the victim about the face while [she] was holding her year-and-a-half daughter."[30]

Lucas recalls, "I could hear Mama R screaming, and I knew they had the baby with them. When I got up there, he kept yelling, 'She stole my money,' but it had just fallen out of his pocket."

Lucas could not stop his father from beating Robin, so he took the baby from her arms and went downstairs.[31] According to the police report, "The accused continued punching, smacking, biting and choking the victim for some time before falling asleep. The victim was able to sneak out of the accused's residence with her daughter and then sought medical treatment at the La Porte Hospital for severe bruises to both of her eyes, face, neck, chest, and arms."

The hospital notified the police, and two sheriff's deputies responded. In addition to taking photos of Robin's injuries, they retrieved a handful of hair Scarborough had torn out of her head. She had put it into a baggie to preserve as evidence. Robin's mother and aunt were also there, and when she had second thoughts about reporting him, they convinced her to cooperate with the police so they could get a warrant for Scott's arrest.[32] The charges included strangulation, battery, and domestic battery in the presence of a child.[33] A conviction on all three could bring him years in prison. Robin was advised to get an order of protection as well.

It took another ten days to issue the arrest warrant,[34] and Robin went into hiding. Two weeks later, the police had yet to arrest Scarborough. As far as Lucas knew, hard feelings from the fight had blown over, and his father was working out-of-town jobs. One day, Scott called to say some "work buddies" had asked him to go to a bar, and he wanted to know if it was okay with his son. Lucas gave his approval.[35]

Soon after, Scarborough started calling Robin. "He was blowing up my phone," she says. "Finally, I picked it up, and he said he knew where I was hiding and was going to come over and kill me."

Robin frantically called the police.[36] One sheriff's deputy would later say he caught sight of Scott on his Harley and started a pursuit.[37] Scarborough sped away, but as he rounded a notorious bend in a road known as Pinhook Curve, he collided with a deer and lost control of his bike. He flew off, headfirst, into the curb.[38] An autopsy would later find his blood alcohol content exceeded the level for legally drunk.[39]

Robin never discussed Rayna Rison with Scarborough, but when asked if he could have assisted Ray in Rayna's murder, she replies, "He definitely had it in him to do it. Several times when he was beating the shit out of me, he said, 'I'm going to kill you. I'm going to kill you, and no one will ever find your body.' I used to wonder where that came from."[40]

Several compelling clues tie Scarborough to the crime, starting with Charlie Allen. Although Boyd and Hahn characterized him as "dull" and "impressionable," in retrospect, Allen's replies to their questions look wilier and more deceptive if, at times, bumbling. The deception may have been coached by his future fiancée, Cindy Brewer, who was also friendly with the McCartys. While she appeared to stick to her story consistently,[41] Charlie stumbled in some ways that frustrated the police, but in others they never noticed. Nothing would have done more to encourage Charlie's evasiveness than his complicity in Rayna's murder. If he had prior knowledge or offered any assistance to Ray, he could go to prison too—a risk that Cindy and a lawyer may have drummed into his head after his first interviews.

While the detectives always saw Allen as part of the murder conspiracy, they also came to believe he participated in the abduction and disposal of Rayna's body. But another scenario is more plausible: he got cold feet. During his out-of-town interview with Boyd and Hahn—probably the most truthful of the lot—Allen said that when Ray first came to his door on Friday night, "McCarty asked him to go with him, but Charles told him it was 'too foggy' to go out." Boyd's report continues, "Allen told us McCarty never stated where he was going or what he was going to do, nor did Allen ask."

How could Ray ask him to go out on such a foggy night and not tell him where he was going? Given McCarty's tendency to blab, it would be hard to believe he wouldn't say where. It would be even harder to believe he wouldn't tell his best friend.

But Allen's account took an even more suspicious turn with his failure to identify Ray's companion when he returned later that night.[42] Again, it was not like McCarty *not* to have introduced this man or given him a name. More likely, it was someone that Charlie knew—someone he knew so well he wanted to protect him from the police investigation. In fact, Allen divulged this person's name during his first interview with Boyd. When the trooper asked Charlie how he started the day, "Allen stated that he believed he would have been in the Monterey area working with a subject he knew from Union Mills known as Scott Scarborough."

Allen then made it clear that Scarborough was not just another coworker. When Boyd asked what kind of vehicle he drove, Allen "said that Scarborough drove a blue Chevrolet Chevette that belonged to an Elmer Schreve, [Allen's girlfriend] Cindy Brewer's brother." (Actually, he was her brother-in-law.) Allen would later reveal that he, too, borrowed this car when his own broke down.

During that first interview, Allen further connected himself to Scarborough by telling Boyd how "his normal practice" would have been to drive to "Scott's house in Union Mills" after he got off work— perhaps to drop him off if they were sharing the same car.[43]

But nothing Allen said did more to incriminate Scarborough than what he *didn't* say in later interviews. He participated in some of these with a lawyer by his side and, sneakily, tried to take back some of the information he first gave the detectives. This is especially noteworthy in his third interview when he identified the people on his March 26 Davey Tree crew and substituted "Jim Harness" for Scarborough.[44]

The most compelling accounts tying Scarborough to the crime come from the eyewitnesses, particularly Bryan Durham and Roy West. Durham drove by the animal hospital when Rayna was backing away from a man he described as "lanky and tall" with hair that was "light brown to blonde in color." He also remembered this individual was wearing unusual clothing: "football pants, tight jersey-type pants cut off below the knee."[45] What he might have seen instead were arborist pants. These have black leather chaps below the knees to protect a tree trimmer's calves while climbing trunks or cutting limbs. The brightly colored material from the waist to the thigh is tight-fitting. The chaps may have made the pants legs look cut off below the knees in the darkness from a distance.[46]

As for the encounter on Warren Street, the eyewitness testimony had always baffled the detectives. While Roy West and John Proud, the two bandmates loading their equipment in a van, spotted the spotted Datsun across the street from Roy's house, the individual who got out of the car was definitely not Ray. When word leaked out that two men had seen his car on Warren Street, Ray came up with the story about looking at a house for sale. But then he further embellished the tale by saying he talked to both observers. John Proud says he watched from across the street as Roy West approached the Datsun and never exchanged words with the suspicious stranger.[47] This confirms that McCarty did not get out of the car and didn't know who Scarborough talked to. He must have remained inside.

For his part, Roy West has always been adamant about describing the man he saw from a few feet away. "He was kinda tall," he told a La Porte County sergeant. "Tall and thin." When shown a photo of Ray McCarty, he replied that the man he talked to was "thinner."[48] At six feet, one inch, and 150 pounds, Scarborough was that much taller and thinner.[49] And also Scarborough wore tinted aviator glasses, as West observed on the individual on Warren Street. Today, when shown a color mug shot of Scarborough from 1989,[50] West admits that many years have intervened but says, "It's hauntingly familiar."[51]

While Rene Gazarkiewicz did not see Scarborough standing outside the Datsun, she saw someone smoking in the passenger seat when the brights turned on, which almost blinded her. While Ray got his nicotine fix from chewing tobacco, Scarborough was a chain smoker.[52]

Scarborough could have also filled in one more missing piece of the puzzle that involved the letterman jacket. On April 1, 1993, a day before Rayna's segment on *America's Most Wanted*, the LPPD had a surveillance team of patrolmen monitoring everyone who went in and out of 517 Haviland. Shortly after he returned home after work, McCarty "ran out" of 517 Haviland and jumped inside Lori's Sunbird. He then drove to a county road and, "at speeds between 65–75 MPH," headed south toward Union Mills. He was being tailed by City of La Porte patrolman Barry Aftowski, who would rise to chief in years to come. In his report, Aftowski wrote that on the deserted road, "I had to stay back a little ways, but I feel he knew that I was following him." Aftowski lagged behind but then lost sight of the Sunbird. Aftowski checked at Bucher's hog farm, but Ray did not appear there for another few hours.[53] What McCarty did during the interim remained a mystery for the police, but he could have used that time to meet up with Scarborough. By then, the Risons knew that the letterman jacket was a focus of the *America's Most Wanted* segment featuring Rayna. Ray could have given the hot commodity to Scarborough, and together, they may have decided to dump it far from the pond. Although the police were watching Ray on April 2, Scott had no one observing him during the few hours before the broadcast when police believed the jacket had been tossed.

All these decades later, much of Scarborough's participation in Rayna's homicide requires speculation. But some evidence can tie him more definitively to the crime. After Bennie reviewed the items recovered from Rayna's LTD, he belatedly mentioned that his daughter typically carried a few hundred dollars in her purse in case of emergency. It appeared to be missing. FBI analysis found two unidentified smears of male DNA on that purse. One could have come from Scarborough if he had snagged her cash.

Although the DNA was a mixture of two unknown males, advances in probabilistic genotyping can separate the profiles. A match would be more likely with male DNA taken from the jacket collar, which was not a mixture.

Similarly, Deedrick removed strands of blonde hair from the letterman jacket that he could not connect to anyone through visual analysis. Today, DNA analysis can tie hair to individuals if the roots are intact. Although Scott Scarborough is dead, he has at least four heirs with DNA that could identify him as the source for those specimens.

When asked if he would contribute a swab from his cheek, Lucas replies, "Sure. I want to know if he did it."[54]

THE FINDER

A mong the sideshows in the Rison investigation, none was more suspicious than the discovery of her body by James Flett McWhirter on April 27, 1993. His behavior suggested prior knowledge of where Rayna was submerged in the pond. His actions in the following weeks revealed his efforts to collect reward money in return. But there is no sign that detectives looked closely at his background and connections to McCarty or his associates.

Among the tantalizing tips that slipped through the investigation's cracks was one from Ray's neighbor on 517 Haviland. According to the police report, she saw him the day after Rayna's body was found and, without showing much emotion, Ray told her, "Somebody had slung her body into a pond." But then, she said, McCarty added, "as if he were bragging, it was a friend of one of Ray's best friends that had found the body."[55]

If the police had paid attention to this information, they would have had an obvious candidate for the "best friend"—Charlie Allen. But the most surprising source of information about McWhirter came from star eyewitness Rene Gazarkiewicz, who had seen Rayna suspended half-inside Ray's Datsun. In her interview with Bennie, she said she attempted to warn the police and prosecutors about McWhirter to no avail. Her bad experiences with him dated back to 1989 in Michigan City when McWhirter became her "neighbor from hell."[56]

At that point in his life, McWhirter had already been arrested more than ten times for charges that included theft, burglary, and criminal mischief.[57] The son of immigrants from Scotland,[58] he never seemed to fit in. One La

Porte High School classmate remembers how McWhirter was bullied over his cleft lip and nasal-sounding speech.[59] By the time he was nineteen, police had arrested him for possessing a dangerous weapon and burglary.[60]

McWhirter moved to Michigan City after meeting Sandra Salat, who grew up there.[61] He worked making furniture at InterRoyal Corporation,[62] where his future father-in-law was a longtime employee.[63] The couple married in 1976[64] and lived together next door to Gazarkiewicz.[65] From 1979 through the eighties, police records show that McWhirter bounced back and forth to his hometown, continuing a sideline as a petty thief. Once, when arrested in La Porte, he used 1408 D Street as his address.[66] The four-bedroom house, owned by his sister, was also where his widowed mother lived, and McWhirter stayed there on occasion when he wasn't bouncing around homeless shelters.[67]

In Michigan City, during the early eighties, Rene Gazarkiewicz was friendly with McWhirter's wife, Sandy, and would help babysit their four children. It didn't take long for her to encounter their father's illicit lifestyle. "I found out real quick what cocaine looks like," she told Bennie. "I walked into the kitchen one day, and the [two-year-old] twins were playing with white powder . . . in these little lines. Sandy came in and had a fit." Rene also saw signs that McWhirter was booking illegal bets and trading in amphetamine pills.

Gazarkiewicz says she kept the McWhirter household's secrets to herself. Still, when her brother-in-law, a Michigan City police officer, arrested McWhirter, the perp may have believed Rene had provided the tip. McWhirter then determined to wreak revenge on his next-door neighbor. As Gazarkiewicz told Bennie, "He just shot bullets in [our] car, he ripped the [aluminum] siding off my house, broke into our house a couple of times . . ., threw rocks at my children if they were in the backyard." He even cut her dog's chain with wire cutters and chased it into traffic.[68] Ultimately, the police did arrest McWhirter for absconding with Rene's siding and attempting to sell it for scrap. He had to spend sixty days in jail as a result.[69]

That hardly ended his criminal career or harassment of Gazarkiewicz, who eventually moved to La Porte partly to escape him.[70] To date, McWhirter has been arrested more than fifty times and served nearly five years in prison. His longest sentences have been for dealing heroin and cocaine, but most charges against him have been for public intoxication and resisting arrest during those incidents.[71] Many of his arrests appeared in the press, but he was also a victim. One article had him getting stabbed in the neck with a pen.[72] While delivering pizzas and driving under the influence—of too much caffeine, his sister told reporters—his car swerved across traffic on Pine Lake Avenue and plowed into a concrete porch. Had firefighters not given him CPR after pulling him out of the wreck, he might have died on the spot.[73] McWhirter suffered an even more severe injury when Sandy blasted him with a shotgun in 1981. She is named only as his "estranged wife" in *The South Bend Tribune*, which reported that the shooting "resulted from a domestic quarrel."[74] There is no record that charges were filed against her, so she may have fired in self-defense, but a scar on his abdomen remained one of the identifying marks on his arrest reports.[75]

By April 1993, Sandy had divorced McWhirter and remarried.[76] But she was with him when he found Rayna's body. Why would she have pulled her two children out of school in Michigan City and gone fishing with her ex-husband in an isolated pond on an unpaved country road twelve miles away? McWhirter, who had his driver's license revoked, needed a ride.[77] Still, Sandy must have had some other motivation to disrupt her kids' schedule and take them to this unlikely destination for a family outing.

McWhirter may have thought his children would have provided cover for why he was at the pond. But his behavior after the discovery was hardly slick. If he had truly stumbled on Rayna's body, why would he have felt the need to flag down strangers to confirm what he saw instead of going directly to the county sheriff or the city police? He knew both well.

McWhirter left no doubt about his motive for staging the discovery when he approached Charlie Finley later and asked for the $25,000 in reward money. After being rebuffed, he even sought out Bennie at his job. The Elkhart packaging company had been using hourly workers from homeless shelters, and McWhirter had joined one of the contingents. Once he arrived at the firm, he asked the foreman to take him to Rison's office, where he complained about not getting his reward. As Bennie told Gazarkiewicz, McWhirter "was really upset with Charlie Finley because he put a stipulation in there for her safe return, and I explained to him that . . . was my wife's idea."[78]

If the police discovered how McWhirter learned where Rayna was submerged, they could have opened another door to the conspiracy behind her murder. McCarty did most of the spade work when he identified McWhirter as a friend of Allen's. Charlie had previously shown police that he knew where Rayna was submerged by putting an X on Boyd's hand-drawn pond map.[79]

However, it's unclear how Allen came to know McWhirter, although the homes where they stayed in La Porte were very close. In 1993, the backyard of Charlie's residence on Circle Drive was a few hundred feet behind the D Street house where McWhirter's mother lived. While the tidy tree-lined D Street could have been in a middle-class suburb, the neighborhood around Allen was a jumble of mostly trailer-park homes with gravel pads and driveways. The only drinking establishment within walking distance was the I Street Family Tavern, where Ray was directed to call Lori.[80] It was a longtime area hangout with an inexpensive restaurant and a smoke-filled bar—the sort of place that McWhirter liked to patronize and where he might have introduced himself if Allen was drinking there too.

Another connection may have been made through Allen's then-live-in girlfriend (and future wife), Cindy Brewer. Her brother-in-law, who loaned his blue Chevette to Allen and Scarborough, had a home one block from McWhirter at another La Porte address listed in his arrest records.[81]

While Ray did not disparage McWhirter to his neighbor, it's hard to believe that he and the others in the murder plot were too thrilled with his "discovery" or when he made a play for Finley's reward money. But then again, McWhirter may have served a role in the conspiracy that made his coconspirators reluctant to crack down on him.

In July of 1994, La Porte County patrolman Joe Pavolka received a call from a woman whose ex-husband had sold a pickup truck to McWhirter "shortly before the [Rison] homicide." According to Pavolka's notes, as recorded by an LPPD patrolman, "Just after the homicide, McWhirter junked the truck even though the *only* thing wrong with it was a dent in one of the fenders. [Her] ex-husband was supposedly upset over the fact that she was thinking of passing this information on [to the police] and told her to mind her own business."[82]

Police were well aware of McCarty's frantic efforts to find a pickup truck in the days before Rayna's abduction. Multiple friends and acquaintances reported his desire to borrow their trucks.[83] His repeated calls to Darold Willis's wife about his pickup—while he was out of town—fractured their relationship.[84] Meanwhile, given his sketchy background, McWhirter was probably a last resort for Ray and Charlie to obtain a truck. He would have needed money from them to make the purchase—perhaps why he was so quick to junk the pickup once the police announced they were looking for it.

However, while there's a good chance McWhirter supplied the truck, there is no possibility that he participated in any nefarious activity on March 26. According to records from the La Porte Police Department, he was still serving a thirty-one-day sentence for theft.[85] But Ray and Scarborough could have parked the truck in a prearranged spot near the home of McWhirter's mother and sister on D Street. They then walked the few hundred yards to Allen's home on Circle Drive when his barking dog announced their presence on Charlie's doorstep.

THE MASTERMIND

The actual role that Lori McCarty played in her sister's death remains one of the touchiest subjects in the Rayna Rison investigation and appears to have divided the La Porte County Homicide Team. In the eyes of State Trooper Arlie Boyd at the time, any lies she told the police were to protect her husband and not to hide her participation in the plot.[86] Hahn did not seem so sure and, during multiple interviews, probed whether anyone was taking care of the McCartys' children that Friday night.[87] The former prosecuting attorney, Bill Herrbach, was indirectly direct. He repeatedly told reporters that "every potential suspect . . . was eventually eliminated except for McCarty *and* his wife, Lori."[88] (Italics added.)

We can understand why the authorities, for the most part, were skittish about implicating Lori, let alone indicting her. They had trouble enough going after her husband in the face of the Rison family's opposition. The blowback against arresting Lori would have been exponentially worse. There was something distinctly monstrous about a sister plotting her younger sibling's death that the public would have had trouble contemplating. Besides, a capital sentence against both parents would have left their children de facto orphans.

But there is significant material in the police records to implicate Lori in the crime—not the actual murder, but the conspiracy with Ray and his friends to commit it, hide the evidence, and then cover up their involvement. Even more disturbing are the indications that Lori was far more than a helpmate. Instead, she appears as the instigator after what she heard during "the fight" with Rayna about her taking pregnancy tests.[89] At crucial points leading up to the killing and the aftermath, Ray looked for her input, if not her direction. Her decision to quit her video store job that day strongly indicates her willingness to be available for help during the evening when she typically worked.[90] The shifting accounts she gave police of her activities—that counter other witnesses—point like laser beams to the moments she was most concerned about them investigating. Moreover, the shifts in Ray's alibis reveal her role in orchestrating what her husband told the police after the murder.

For Gayla Moreau, whose husband Martin was among Ray's closest friends, it was inconceivable that Ray would have killed Rayna without Lori leading the way. Her certainty is partly due to the power dynamic in their marriage that flipped after the molestation charge. Previously, Gayla told Boyd that Ray would hit his wife and "push her around."[91] Pat Walters made a similar comment to Boyd, saying that *before* the "rape charge . . . Ray had been mentally and physically abusive to Lori," and she had seen bruises from where he hit her.[92] After his conviction for the molestation, Lori told Gayla her husband was no longer so rough with her. She credited the counseling sessions that were part of his sentence—the sessions he was ejected from for lack of compliance.[93] More likely, the relationship changed when Lori wielded power inside her family that helped keep him out of prison.

In the days before and after the abduction, two incidents solidified Gayla's views on Lori's involvement. The first was the call Gayla got after "the fight" with Rayna. This is when police believe Rayna told Lori she was taking pregnancy tests. According to Moreau, Lori "said, 'Rayna was starting her shit again. After what she put us through the past three years, we're not going to let her do it again.'"

At the time, Gayla says, she didn't fully understand what Lori intended as the consequences for Rayna's "shit." Even after Rayna disappeared, Gayla did not want to think the McCartys had anything to do with it. She bought the first alibi about Lori and the kids eating at her parents' house while Ray went to the hog farm because he had nothing better to do. In her eyes, this was typical behavior for Lori's vapid husband. "Then we went out [with Lori and Ray] to eat one night," Gayla recalls, "and they say, 'Guys, we've got to tell you. This is really what Ray did.'"

It was not just Ray who told the Holts about the new alibi. Lori chimed in as well. Gayla says, "I remember thinking, 'And now they're changing his alibi. That's not good.'" She was especially skeptical when Ray claimed to have seen the motel pay phone from the road and decided to call Lori from there. "I know the Cassidy Motel, and you can't see the pay phone from [the road], especially in the fog. 'And then I went to myself, 'Oh my God, they killed her. They really killed her.'"

From what she saw at the dinner table, Gayla believed the murder was a team effort, and given Lori's vitriol about Rayna, she wondered if she hadn't tortured and killed her sister somewhere inside the motel. "That thought freaked me out," she says.[94]

Lori's involvement in the planning, if not the actual murder, was substantiated by another unexpected informant—Ray's cellmate in the La Porte County Jail, where he waited for his trial before charges were dropped. Mike Keeling was a career criminal with multiple charges against him, including theft, armed robbery, resisting arrest, and carjacking. But like Gayla, he was also freaked out by Ray. In a letter he wrote to a deputy prosecuting attorney, he called McCarty "very sick . . . with a split personality or something."

During their incarceration, the jail had several lockdowns, keeping the men cooped up in their cells for days. As was his wont, Ray blabbed in self-destructive ways, perhaps to impress his tough-looking cellmate. At the top of his letter, Keeling wrote, Ray "talks to me as [if] I'm his best friend. . . . He talks to me about his case all the time in which he admitted to me that he did murder that girl."

Like other jailhouse snitches, Keeling did not just provide this information out of the kindness of his heart. He expected an early release in return, which may have undermined what he had to say about Ray in the eyes of the prosecutor. But for detectives, his comments would have echoed themes from their interviews with the McCartys' friends, as Keeling recounted in one conversation: "I specifically asked him if he killed her, and he was like, 'Yeah, Mike. But she deserved it.' He said that Rana [*sic*] tried messing up him and his wife's life together. I'm pretty sure that his wife had something to do with it as well as him, but he's protecting her name."

Keeling continued, "When I asked him if his wife helped him, he said that they had it planned good and even had the spot picked out where to put her [where] he said he was going to bury her."[95]

With this context from Keeling, another police tip takes on even greater significance. Like some others, it slipped through the cracks of the investigation but put a chilling perspective on Lori. The day it was phoned in to the police—March 30—further adds to its credibility. Rayna's body had yet to be found in the pond on Range Road, and police had no idea where she was. The tipster reported an incident two days before her Friday, March 26 abduction. The officer took down the call as follows:

[The caller] stated that last Wed., 3/24/93, at 1755 hours [5:55 P.M.], she was driving on Range Rd. near US 20 and observed a smaller-sized P-U [pickup] truck stopped in the roadway with (2) large subjects in the vehicle, both believed to be males. [She] stated that she then observed a W/F [white female] subject standing behind the rear of the P-U, looking out over a field. [She] stated that the truck was by a large tree on the NE corner, and the W/F was looking to the East. [She] stated that the P-U then started moving ahead at a slow pace, and the W/F was walking behind same.

[She] stated that she pulled ahead and off the side of the roadway to observe further what they were doing. [She] stated that the driver of the P-U was a Mexican male with broad shoulders. [She] stated that he had black hair, and the hair was very full but not longer than shoulder length. [She] stated that she did not get a good look at the passenger but thought that he was a large-built male, unk [unknown] race. [She] stated that the girl kept looking over the field as she was walking as if she was looking for something. . . .

The girl walking behind the P-U was described as a W/F large build, light-colored hair, straight, and appeared to be tied back. . . . [She] stated that she appeared to be rather tall.[96]

Apparently, the woman who called in this tip had witnessed the planning for the burial spot that Ray talked about with Mike Keeling. Her description of the pickup driver is very much in keeping with the way other witnesses described Ray—Mexican-looking with black hair, swarthy skin, and broad shoulders. Her description of his passenger makes him look more like Charlie Allen than Scott Scarborough. If so, Ray's best friend was much more involved with the plot than he ever let on, which may be why he belatedly decided to lie about Ray's March 26 visit to his home. The description of the woman as "rather tall" does not fit with Lori, but the "large build" with "light-colored hair" would have matched her at that time.

If this scenario is true, Lori's role in the plot appears more critical than the detectives ever imagined. It also explains her activities on Friday night and why she tried relentlessly to hide them. But if she was involved, one unanswered question complicated her potential complicity—what did she do with her children?

Lori's usual go-to for childcare was Karen Rison, but as all could attest, her mother was ill and in no condition to care for her kids that night. Furthermore, Bennie, Wendy, and her boyfriend consistently told police they saw Lori leave the Rison house with the two children. Police considered another possibility—that she locked Adrienne and Hunter inside 517 Haviland, as Brenda Pegg and Gayla Moreau accused her of doing in the past. But Karen—of all people—inadvertently debunked that theory during a conversation with Bennie's private investigator, Tina Church, who then repeated it to Hahn. When she first became concerned about Rayna on Friday night, Karen told Church she called Lori. Karen "says it was around 8:30. And Ray answered the phone, out of breath. And [Karen] says, 'It was so odd because I didn't hear any background noise. . . . I can remember thinking to myself . . . Where are the kids? Why is it so quiet?' She said there was no TV noise. There was nothing. And I said, 'Why would that bother you?' [Karen answered,] 'Well, I've never heard that.'"[97]

If the children weren't with Karen and not at 517 Haviland, where were they? At one point, one of the detectives asked Adrienne, who was just six years old. She replied that she spent the evening at her grandmother's house—an answer the police did not find credible because all the other witnesses had her leaving the Rison house with her mother and brother.

But Adrienne had another grandmother, Ray's mother, Carolyn McCarty, in Union Mills. According to Arlie Boyd, the detectives never considered the possibility that Lori went directly from her parents' home to her mother-in-law's house, ten miles south. If she had left the Risons around 5:50, there would have been plenty of time to drop off her children with Carolyn and then meet Ray at North 150 East where Val Eilers almost smashed into them.[98]

However, if the police had called Carolyn to confirm this possibility, they would have been unlikely to get any satisfaction. Although Gayla calls her "the sweetest, kindest lady,"[99] the retired schoolteacher was intensely and combatively protective of her son. According to private eye Church, when her associate tried to talk to Carolyn about why the police suspected Ray, "She was real nasty and [replied], 'This is bullshit. Rayna asked for it.'"[100]

Ironically, the police did not need Carolyn's help to confirm that her grandchildren were in Union Mills on Friday night. Lori's movements the next day revealed everything they needed to know. While she spent Saturday morning distributing the *Missing* posters to a few friends and local businesses like the video stores, she then picked up Ray at Teledyne shortly after 1:00 P.M. and drove to Union Mills. She told Boyd her purpose was to "post posters." But the real reason could have been to collect the children. During that interview, the state trooper focused on the holes in her husband's alibis and did not find anything suspicious about the Union Mills trip.[101] But he did wonder why Ray and Lori went out of their way to put up posters in the tiny agricultural town instead of concentrating their efforts on the much more populated area in downtown La Porte where Rayna went missing. Boyd says, "I thought that just made no sense at all."

Chances are Lori's decision to leave her kids with Carolyn and race out to North 150 East was prompted by the call Ray made from the tavern near Allen's house. For some reason, McCarty wanted his wife to be physically present. Perhaps to weigh in—either on a change of plans or to provide the help he was expecting from Charlie before he got cold feet. More likely to deliver his hip waders.

The weather conditions forced Ray and Scarborough to reconsider their burial spot. County patrolman Jim Jackson remembers that March 26 was not just foggy. He says, "That fog was some of the worst I've seen in my career. It was heavy, soupy fog. You could hardly see across the hood of your car. I remember because I was driving that night. When I heard [Rayna] was missing the next day, I thought she had driven over an embankment into the water somewhere because of that fog."[102]

One of Scarborough's girlfriends suggests the possibility of how the fog could have interfered. "If they were doing it with Scottie, they had to have a plan," she says. "He wouldn't go out that night and dig a hole. He would have already dug the hole."[103] Just as likely, the pre-dug grave chosen by Lori—according to the tip—was significantly off-road, which could be why Ray needed a truck.

By the time Lori met with Ray on North 150 East, the men may have realized it was too treacherous to reach the grave site in the fog and muddy ground conditions. They needed a plan B. The pond was just up the road from where the tipster saw the white female walking behind the pickup. If Ray and Scarborough harbored second thoughts about venturing into a field or woods, they may have seen the pond as a much more accessible option. A dirt trail ran alongside the water where the pickup wouldn't get stuck, and there was a pile of branches and brambles they could use to cover her body. Wearing his hip waders, Ray could have dragged Rayna by the bra into the few feet of silty water. Scarborough, the tree trimmer, may have also had the hand tools to chop off the cross of long, heavy limbs that they thought would keep her body submerged.

We cannot know what was discussed during the meetup on North 150 East, only that Ray felt Lori's presence was essential—if only to bring the waders—before he and Scarborough could proceed. Parking his spotted Datsun and Lori's Sunbird so close to Rayna's abandoned LTD on North 200 East was a considerable risk. It did have consequences because Val Eilers ultimately identified both the McCartys' cars at a critical time.

After a brief interlude, Lori left North 150 East and returned to downtown La Porte, where she had to start helping in the search for her sister. A little later, around 7:30 P.M., Brenda Pegg, the cashier at the Little Saver, sold Lori a pack of cigarettes, noticing that she was "very jittery and talking a mile a minute and pacing."[104]

But Lori's contribution to the plot was not yet complete. She did something in the evening hours that she tried to conceal with differing accounts of her movements to friends and detectives. At first, Lori told Pat Walters that she couldn't remember what she did—only that she came home after leaving her parents' house and did not go out again until she picked up Wendy at 10:30 P.M. to go searching for Rayna.[105] But then, when pressed by the police, her memory became less hazy, and she talked about picking up groceries at the Little Saver convenience store where Pegg worked. When Boyd interviewed her, the shopping destination had changed to the much larger Kroger supermarket. Lori now remembered leaving her home at 9:30 and spending exactly forty-five dollars at the store. Since she paid in cash, she didn't have a credit card receipt and could not verify what she said.[106]

If the Kroger shopping was a ruse, what other trip was she trying to hide? One answer solved two mysteries hovering over the Rison investigation: what happened to Matt Elser's infamous letterman jacket after Rayna's death, and who patrolman Joe Pavolka saw driving the car at the foot of his driveway.

Some clues were found in the disarray of Rayna's clothing, which was visible even after she was submerged for a month. Besides her bra being yanked, her sweater was pulled halfway up one arm in a hasty effort to remove the letterman jacket, which would have impeded her submersion.[107] In their haste, Ray and Scarborough could have thrown the jacket inside the pickup. Scarborough perhaps only realized he still had it after Ray returned in his Datsun to 517 Haviland where he breathlessly answered the eight-thirty call from his mother-in-law and changed out of his camo clothes.

If this is true, Lori next made her most brazen decision that night—to don the letterman jacket herself and put it back in Rayna's abandoned LTD on North 200 East. Although a few inches taller than Rayna, Lori had her sister's flowing curly hair and high cheekbones—the perfect replica to fool anyone into thinking she was the missing person. In the process, she might even propagate the mirage that Rayna was a runaway. Friday night, at 9:50 P.M., when Officer Pavolka looked to his right and saw two vehicles coming his way, Lori could have been at the wheel of her Sunbird with Scarborough in the passenger seat and Ray riding close behind in the pickup.

But if the patrolman was surprised to see that convoy cruising through the foggy night, the drivers had to be even more shocked to see the La Porte County squad car. They were not about to pass by Pavolka and turn the corner at North 200 East, a few hundred yards away. If they had made the policeman suspicious, he was likely to follow, and if he saw them stopped by the LTD, the jig would be up. As a result, Lori and Ray most likely continued east on East 600 North, past North 200 East, where they almost collided with another resident who lived nearby and was on his way to a night-shift job.[108]

After the close call with Pavolka, Ray and Lori had no choice but to return home with the letterman jacket. Thanks to *America's Most Wanted*, they would be forced to dispose of it a few days later. But by wearing her sister's cherished token of Matt's affection, Lori showed she was not a dupe or a hands-off cheerleader in her sister's demise. She was literally up to her neck in a scheme to hide vital evidence.

In the following months, Lori continued to demonstrate her leadership of the conspiracy by orchestrating Ray's alibis. Twice, when it looked like he flubbed his part by forgetting significant storylines or had to amend previous statements that were upended by new witness testimony, it was Lori who intervened with city detectives so Ray could renege or revise.

For the police, one faulty detail most undercut Ray's first alibi about going to Bucher's hog farm. They never realized that this supposed flub revealed who was weaving his fabrications. It involved how he first called Lori to say where he was and when he would return home. Supposedly, he contacted her from a phone in the hog barn. When LPPD chief of detectives John Miller visited the farm to interview Garry Bucher on March 31, he learned the phone had not been working when Ray claimed to have used it. Miller went to the barn himself to confirm it was still not working. The detectives thought they had caught McCarty in a lie that intensified their suspicions about his guilt.[109]

But a close reading of the police reports shows that Ray never said he called from the barn. At this stage of the investigation, he had not even sat for an interview. Lori was the one who first mentioned the call from the barn when she spoke to FBI Agent Bill Keith on March 30.[110] She said the same to Jason Tibbs and Gary Marshall when they dropped by 517 Haviland to visit the next day, which Jason reported to Miller.[111]

THE TIMELINE

Looking back on the revelation about the barn phone, State Trooper Arlie Boyd says, "That was a huge thing for me at the time," but he admits the source could have been Lori and not Ray. He explains it would have been difficult to parse because so many different detectives and agencies were collecting information at that point. Besides, Boyd recalls, "It was hard to determine where her heart was in this whole thing." Whenever he thought he had her cornered, he says, "She was smart enough to be pliable and not put herself in a hole."[112]

But Boyd points out another problem with fixing Lori's culpability. When told about Ray's access to isopropyl alcohol, Scarborough, and the Range Road witness supporting the letter from Ray's cellmate, Boyd responds, "Much of this information you're giving me never got to me. Literally. I'm sitting here thinking, 'Wow, I'd like to have known that. I'd like to have been told that.' For some reason, many of these facets were kept from me. Now remember, there's a number of people or policemen working in unison . . . . Once in a while, you don't get all the information because someone else was on that particular lead and it didn't funnel back to you. If I had known some of this stuff, it would have really concerned me."

THE TIMELINE

Ultimately, for the naysayer prosecuting attorney Bill Herrbach, the case against Ray could not be made unless the State "account[ed] for his whereabouts" throughout Friday night, March 26. He felt this was a significant gap the detectives never managed to fill. It would have shown how Ray could have abducted and killed Rayna, disposed of her body, and then returned to 517 Haviland by eight thirty when his mother-in-law called. The police had other stakes in the timeline with the first sightings of Rayna's car on North 200 East and then the Sunbird and Datsun on North 150 East. But a substantial piece was still missing from the puzzle. Ideally, it would account for how all the steps in the crime were accomplished in some two hours, in such foggy conditions, and with two men moving around three vehicles.

As with so much else in the Rison case, the solution lay with a tip that investigators ignored. The caller was Douglas McGarvey, then thirty-eight years old. Because of what he saw in such exacting detail, it helps to know more about his background. A native of La Porte, McGarvey graduated from Purdue University with majors in math and physics. By 1993, he had started an engineering career that took him to the upper ranks of Raytheon, Indianapolis, the defense contractor's Internet Information Services division. McGarvey died in 2017,[113] but when asked about his powers of observation, his daughter, Amy Bishop, replied, "My dad was extremely smart and had talent/knowledge in math, physics, engineering, and management. So, it's safe to say he had good powers of observation." She adds that he was not an auto mechanic but was interested in cars, able to do minor repairs, and enjoyed scouting out parts at the local junkyard. He also always drove a truck.[114]

An LPPD patrolman took down McGarvey's call at 10:05 P.M. on March 29. His report reads as follows:

> [McGarvey] said that Friday night (3-26) at approximately 1845 hrs. [6:45 P.M.], he was southbound on US 35, north of the [Charlie] Finlay [sic] residence, and in that area, on the east side of 35, he saw a car matching the description of Rison's car, sitting on the side of the roadway with the hood [up]. Approximately twenty yards south, on the west side of 35, was a bright blue 70s model Nova or Duster sitting with its rear end partially jacked up with nobody around it. The car matching Rison's had two males working under the hood. One was approximately 6-02, slim build and light brown hair. The other was about 5-10, 180 lbs, very dark complected [with] dark hair.
>
> [McGarvey] said that there was also an unoccupied tan Chevy S-10 sitting near the curve (by the Mobil station) just off the roadway that he thought to be strange.[115]

In essence, McGarvey witnessed the staging area Ray and Scarborough used before submerging Rayna in the pond. Her body was probably in the Datsun or truck. This location is vital in establishing a plausible timeline for the two men. Forced to juggle three vehicles without Charlie Allen, they needed a spot with easy access to the state highways.

Bolstering McGarvey's observations were coincidental factors from his personal life. His daughter explains that he had family on Highway 35, so he was intimately familiar with landmarks along that stretch.[116] None were better known in the La Porte community than Charlie Finley's expansive white party barn, which was distinctively topped by a press box and gold-roofed belfry. It stood out from a hill overlooking the two-lane highway and, for decades, was host to a live animal manger scene during the weeks leading up to Christmas.[117] Because cars turning left into the property could create a jam for southbound traffic, La Porte eventually added an asphalt apron to that shoulder in the road so other drivers could get around the turners. This is where McGarvey saw the blue vehicle, mostly likely Ray's blue Datsun which resembled the Nova hatchback. It was probably jacked up to make it look like the owner was in the process of changing a tire.

McGarvey's identification of Rayna's LTD across the road from the Datsun helped solve another mystery that nagged at the detectives—whether her car had been moved from North 200 East at some point and later returned to almost the same spot. McGarvey's tip confirms the memories of witnesses who said it was practically in the middle of the road when they first saw it early in the evening. By the time it was towed, the county detectives' photos show it was parked off to the side.[118]

Nothing about the McGarvey tip is more striking than his description of the two men looking under the hood. He has Scarborough's height within an inch, along with his slim build and blonde hair. McGarvey was uncannily accurate about Ray's height, weight, dark complexion, and hair. Much as he had on North 200 East, McCarty pretended to look under the hood, and Scarborough joined this time.

As for McGarvey's identification of the pickup down the road, his daughter says he should have known this because "he definitely had a Chevy S-10 at some point." The stripe along the side that Beth York remembered was consistent with the model's color configuration from that era. It was the smaller pickup that she said was comparable in size to a Ford Ranger. The S-10 was also the model pickup that Charlie Allen first said had stopped behind Ray while he was supposedly having sex with his supposed hitchhiker. Allen then tried to take that back to say it was just a "small truck."

How McGarvey has the S-10 positioned at the gas station, three-quarters of a mile south of the other two vehicles, reveals the plan Ray and Scarborough devised for coping with the fog. Their various destinations were north, but the pickup was pointed south toward an intersection that led to Highway 39. Rather than take the most direct route, they went a little out of their way to stick with the better-lit and paved thoroughfares. They could more than make up for the added distance by traveling faster.

Using McGarvey's report along with other police tips that were discounted or ignored, it's possible to construct a plausible timeline for Ray, Lori, and Scarborough that evening of March. Travel times are determined by faster speeds on the highways and much slower ones on the county roads. A few issues do arise that need special consideration. These include:

Witness times. Unless pinned to events like TV shows or punch clocks, these must be given five or ten minutes' leeway. For example, at first, Cheryl VanSchoyck was sure she left the animal hospital at 6:02 P.M.[119] but later said it may have been as early as 5:45.[120] Meanwhile, it's assumed that Rayna would not have left sooner than six because she was careful not to cheat on her time card. In the case of Val Eilers, her encounter with Ray's Datsun and Lori's Sunbird took place only a few hundred yards from her home, so the time she provided needs little leeway. With Beth York, her near-collision with the pickup and the LTD happened soon enough for her sons to see *Married . . . with Children* before it ended at 7:00 P.M. central time.

Why did they retrieve the LTD? The most confounding aspect of the conspirators' night was the decision for the three to meet on North 150 East and then retrieve Rayna's car. This erratic move could not have been part of the master plan but a response to the unexpected weather conditions. If the pickup got stuck on the way to the off-road, pre-dug gravesite, the LTD could be parked on firm ground nearby for them to escape with the body. Their only option was to retrieve the LTD they had previously abandoned. But later, the pond emerged as a safer plan B. First, Ray had to use the waders Lori brought to see if he could get deep enough to submerge Rayna. Once that checked out, he put the waders in front of the passenger seat of the LTD, where police later found wet newspapers. He drove it to North 200 East with Scarborough in the S-10 following close behind. Meanwhile, we can assume that Lori was not about to further incriminate herself and her Sunbird by letting them use her car. Besides, she needed to return to town to establish her alibi.

Their route in returning the LTD. Given the tight window between the McGarvey Highway 39 sighting of the pickup and LTD and the York family's report about seeing the vehicles on North 200 East, twelve miles away, it's apparent that Ray and Scarborough made a quick stop to check out the pond. They then proceeded up Range Road and took the first right a few yards away. As they were speeding east on East 700 North, they passed Jane Lindborg's home, making enough noise for her to call the police the next day. LPPD chief Samuelson picked up the phone. When Jane complained that the speeders were an accident waiting to happen on such a foggy night, good old Sam replied, "It's just some guys dicking around."[121] After Ray and Scarborough turned the corner at North 200 East, they sped past the home of John Mitchell, who later reported, "they were traveling too fast for the foggy conditions." (Three hours later, while driving to work, Mitchell almost crashed into Ray and Lori on East 600 North after their close call with Pavolka.)[122]

The submersion. In this timeline, Ray and Scarborough would have had more than an hour to return to the pond and submerge Rayna under the branches and tree limbs. They still had enough travel time before and after to appear in all the credible witness sightings and for Ray to get back home to answer the call from his mother-in-law and change his clothes.

The jacket fiasco begins. When Scarborough and Ray split up sometime after 8:00 P.M., they probably did not expect to see each other for the rest of the evening. Ray rushed back to 517 Haviland to fulfill his alibi role as a stay-at-homebody, and Lori was waiting for him. But soon, the couple would learn that their work was not yet done. Scarborough told them in person or by phone that Matt Elser's letterman jacket had been left in the S-10. At that point, they could have let Scarborough dispose of it—much as he ultimately did—but Lori did not see that as an acceptable solution. Instead, she took the tremendous risk of putting on the jacket to impersonate her sister while leading the late-night caravan of S-10 and Sunbird back to North 200 East. Why did she take that risk? The deed was done, and they had all seemingly gotten away with murder. Maybe Lori thought that if she were seen and mistaken for Rayna, it would only confuse the police that much more. In any case, it was an act of supreme self-destructive overconfidence, but it did confuse the cops more than she ever hoped.

Circling back to 540 Circle Drive. Among the missing puzzle pieces in Ray's "whereabouts" on March 26 was how and why he appeared on Charlie Allen's doorstep asking for a ride around 10:30 P.M. What makes the most sense is that Scarborough got in the pickup with Ray after the abortive effort to deposit the letterman jacket in the LTD. They drove back to the house on D Street where James McWhirter—the pickup procurer— occasionally stayed with his mother and sister. They could have left the S-10 at a prearranged parking spot nearby. Then, they only had to walk a few hundred feet to Allen's house on Circle Drive.

Nothing about Charlie Allen's account of that night was more suspicious than his willingness to drive Ray back home the second time he came to his door. If the evening started with Charlie backing out because of foggy driving conditions, it made no sense why, so late at night, he was now willing to go out with Ray and the so-called stranger.

Ray McCarty timeline, Friday evening, March 26, 1993

Time (P.M.)	Address	Location Name	Distance (miles)	Activity
5:15	540 Circle Dr.	Charlie Allen		Ray McCarty (RM) leaves after Allen refuses to join him.
5:20	1508 I St.	Tavern	0.5	RM calls Lori from the pay phone to meet him at N. 150 E.
5:30	117 Warren St.	Surveil Spot	2.4	RM starts surveillance of Pine Lake Animal Hospital (PLAH). Scott Scarborough (SS) encounters Roy West.
5:55	330 Pine Lake	PLAH	0.1	Cheryl VanSchoyck leaves PLAH. Rayna is alone.
6:00		PLAH		As Rayna leaves, Bryan Durham sees her confronted by SS. She gestures to tell him to get away, but he somehow brings her to the Datsun driver's side window, where RM pulls her inside.
6:07		PLAH		Rene Gazarkiewicz sees Rayna halfway inside the car as she passes by. After RM suffocates Rayna with an IPA-soaked rag, he wraps her in the green blanket he uses for his hunting quarry.

THE TIMELINE

Time (P.M.)	Address	Location Name	Distance (miles)	Activity
6:10		PLAH		The Datsun's brights blind Kim Hackney as the car exits the PLAH parking lot.
6:20	5754 N. 200 E.	Glassman	9.8	RM and SS hastily abandon Rayna's LTD outside the Glassmans' trailer, where Brent almost collides with it.
6:25	5856 N. 150 E.	Eilers	0.9	RM and SS in Datsun meet with Lori in her Sunbird to get RM's waders. Val Eilers almost collides with them.
6:30	5754 N. 200 E.	Glassman	0.9	RM and SS retrieve the LTD as a backup for the offroad site if the pond does not check out.
6:38	2707 US-35	Staging	9.0	RM and SS drive Datsun, LTD to the staging area, where the two cars are seen by Douglas McGarvey on Highway 35, along with the S-10 pickup farther down the road. RM and SS jack up the Datsun and transfer Rayna to the pickup.
6:50–6:55	5754 N. 200 E.	Glassman	12.0	RM and SS return north via Range Rd., check out the pond, and decide no need for the LTD. Take E. 700 N. to go east past Jane Lindborg's. Arrive moments before Elizabeth York passes with her sons.
7:00	6855 N. Range Rd.	Pond	3.2	RM and SS return to the pond with pickup and submerge Rayna.
7:50		Pond		RM and SS leave the pond and return to the staging area.
8:10–8:25		Staging	8.1	RM takes the Datsun off the jack and goes home; SS realizes the letterman jacket is still in the pickup.
8:15–8:30	517 Haviland	RM Home	2.1	RM arrives home in time to receive a phone call from Karen Rison. She later says he sounds out of breath.

Time (P.M.)	Address	Location Name	Distance (miles)	Activity
9:30				After hearing from SS, Lori decides to put the jacket in the LTD. Takes RM in her Sunbird to reconnoiter with SS at staging area.
9:35		Staging	2.1	Lori puts on the letterman jacket and drives her Sunbird with SS as a passenger. RM drives the S-10 pickup.
9:50	6301 N. 150 E.	Pavolka	9.0	Lori and RM see Pavolka's squad car at corner of N. 150 E. and E. 600 N. Drive past N. 200 E. Decide to go home with jacket. At some point, SS gets out of the Sunbird and into the pickup with RM.

Ray McCarty and Scott Scarborough, from 9:50 to end of the evening

Time (P.M.)	Address	Location Name	Distance (miles)	Activity
10:15	1408 D St.	McWhirter's Sister's Home	14.8	They return the pickup to a parking spot near the home of McWhirter's mother and sister.
10:20–10:30	540 Circle Dr.	Charlie Allen	0.09	After parking pickup, SS and RM walk 500 feet through backyards to Allen's home.
10:30–10:40	517 Haviland	RM Home	2.9	Charlie drives RM home in Blue Chevette and then takes SS home to Union Mills.

Lori McCarty, from 9:50 to end of the evening

Time	Address	Location Name	Distance (miles)	Activity
10:15 P.M.	517 Haviland	LM Home	14.8	After a brush with Pavolka, Lori continues on E. 600 N. past N. 200 E. Later, SS gets in the S-10 with RM, and she drives home alone. Lori hides the letterman jacket and calls the Risons' house.

THE TIMELINE

Time	Address	Location Name	Distance (miles)	Activity
10:25 P.M.	613 Pine Lake Ave.	Little Saver	2.9	Buys cigarettes from Brenda Pegg and, for the first time, asks if she's seen Rayna.
10:30 P.M.	202 A St.	Rison	1.8	Switches to Risons' car, and Wendy joins her.
10:30 P.M.–1:00 A.M.	Areas around Pine Lake		?	She searches areas where Rayna could have supposedly turned and driven off the road into Pine Lake.
1:00 A.M.	613 Pine Lake Ave.	Little Saver		Lori buys cigarettes again from Pegg at the Little Saver for the day's last sale. She tells Pegg that Rayna is missing.
1:05 A.M.	202 A St.	Rison	1.8	Lori and Wendy return to the Risons' in their parents' car.
1:10 A.M.	517 Haviland	LM Home	1.8	Lori goes home in her Sunbird for the night.

AN INCOMPLETE INVESTIGATION

The Datsun's hatchback looked "suspiciously clean" to evidence technicians. Lori admitted Ray asked her to vacuum it before police seized the car after Rayna's body was found. Photo: Exhibits, State of Indiana

Multiple witnesses identified Ray's "spotted" 1980 B210 Datsun on the night of the abduction. Pictured here parked in front of the McCartys' house at 517 Haviland Street. Photo: Exhibits, State of Indiana

Soon after Rayna's abduction, Lori's 1988 Sunbird with the black "bra" was seen parked by Ray's car a mile from the pond—perhaps when Lori brought him his waders. Photo: Exhibits, State of Indiana

This 1988 Chevrolet S-10 with a silver stripe was likely the pickup seen with Ray's Datsun. A police tip claimed McWhirter purchased it, then junked it after Rayna was found. Photo: Reddit.com/RegularCarReviews

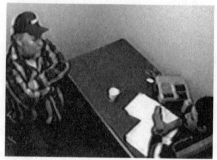

Detective Harold Hahn once again interrogated Ray's best friend Charlie Allen (left). Police believed Allen assisted McCarty in some way with Rayna's murder and submersion. Photo: City of La Porte Police Department

Left: More likely, the tall, skinny accomplice spotted with Ray was Scott Scarborough, McCarty's childhood friend, and Allen's coworker. He beat and threatened to kill multiple girlfriends. Photo: La Porte County Jail

Right: One witness saw someone wearing "tight jersey-type [football] pants cut off below the knee." But it could have been Scarborough, wearing arborist pants for trimming trees. Photo: Solidur Felin Chainsaw Pants, Bartlett Arborist Supply

ISOPROPYL ALCOHOL

POTENTIAL HAZARDS

FIRE OR EXPLOSION
Flammable/combustible material; may be ignited by heat, sparks or flames.
Vapors may travel to a source of ignition and flash back.
Container may explode in heat of fire.
Vapor explosion hazard indoors, outdoors or in sewers.
Runoff to sewer may create fire or explosion hazard.

HEALTH HAZARDS
May be poisonous if inhaled or absorbed through skin.
Vapors may cause dizziness or suffocation.

Fire may produce irritating or poisonous gases.
Runoff from fire control or dilution water may cause pollution.

EMERGENCY ACTION
Keep unnecessary people away; isolate hazard area and deny entry.

Withdraw immediately in case of rising sound from venting safety device or any discoloration of tank due to fire.

The forensic pathologist who conducted Rayna's autopsy could never account for the isopropyl alcohol found in her system—overlooking a critical clue in identifying her killer. Photo: Brady Hazardous Material Label

Left: Rob Beckman, whom Hedge fired as a deputy prosecuting attorney, beat her in the general election. Nine months later, he dropped the murder charges against Ray McCarty. Photo: Ott/Haverstock Funeral Chapel and Cremation Services

Ray was filmed walking through the jail basement on the way to his arraignment for Rayna's murder. Photo: WSBT-TV, Channel 22

Right: Ray was in tears after Beckman dropped his charges and released him from jail. The decision took him by surprise, but the stigma of his alleged involvement with the murder remained. Photo: WSBT-TV, Channel 22

LIFTING THE STIGMA

RAYNA RISON
FAMILY
- Bennie, Karen (parents)
- Lori, Wendy (sisters)

FRIENDS
- Matt Elser (boyfriend)

CITY OF LA PORTE
POLICE DEPARTMENT
- Detective Brett Airy*

MICHIGAN CITY
POLICE DEPARTMENT
- Detective Mark Lachmund*

LA PORTE COUNTY
- Dr. Rick Hoover, Forensic Pathologist
  Prosecuting Attorney
    - Bob Szilagyi*, 2011–2014
    - Rob Beckman*, 1999–2010
    - Cynthia Hedge, 1995–1998
    - Bill Herrbach, 1991–1994
    - Chief Deputies Christopher Fronk*, 2006–2014
    Scott Duerring, until 1998

JASON TIBBS
FAMILY
- Rachel (mother)
- Leslie (wife, ex-wife)
- Duston, Tatum, Kindal (children)
- Peggy, Billy Ray Hurt (in-laws)*

LAWYERS
- Scott Pejic*
- Mike Drayton
- Craig Braje

FRIENDS AND COWORKERS
- Jim, Nancy Bruno; daughter Jennifer, son-in-law Paul Delrio (employers)
- James Milich*
- Josh Jordan
- Chad Green

INDIANA STATE POLICE
- Sergeant Al Williamson*

*INTRODUCED IN THIS CHAPTER

LORI AND RAY McCARTY
FAMILY
- Adrienne (daughter)
- Hunter (son)

1ST INVESTIGATION WITNESSES
- Beth York; sons Kyle, Austin
- Rene Gazarkiewicz

2ND INVESTIGATION WITNESSES
- Rickey J. Hammons Jr.*
- Eric Freeman*
- Rickey Hammons Sr., Judith (parents)
- Jennifer Hammons (sister)
- Tom Wiman (Hammonses' tenant)

HAMMONS INVESTIGATION*
- Daniel Jemiolo Cassidy (DJC): Victim
- Joseph, Janet Jemiolo (DJC parents)
- John, Janice Cassidy (DJC grandparents)
- Julie Cassidy (DJC sister)
- Robert Sheridan (DJC coworker)

LIFTING THE STIGMA

OFFICE POLITICS

When the La Porte prosecuting attorney Robert Beckman dropped the murder charges against Ray McCarty in August 1993, no one was more surprised than the beneficiary. The decision had been a secret until it was announced on a Friday, a few hours before the court closed. Upon hearing the news, McCarty asked his lawyer, "Does this mean I get to go home?" When the attorney answered, "Yes," he told the *News-Dispatch*, his client cried. The lawyer added, "I think he's still in shock."[1]

Two weeks later, after having some time to collect himself, Ray was interviewed for a Merrillville *Post-Tribune* article titled "Stigma of Murder Still Sticks." As he shared with the reporter, getting out of jail was not quite vindication. He could see "in some people's eyes [that] they think he's guilty of murdering his 16-year-old sister-in-law." Lori, the reporter wrote, was "very bitter" at this state of affairs and blamed "the authorities for single-mindedly focusing on her husband." Ray felt police should have been looking at "other suspects" when the evidence against him was lacking. "I'm just glad we have a new prosecutor that can look a little closer and see through what was being done."[2]

But Beckman's decision was not so welcomed by the public at large. *The South Bend Tribune* had heralded McCarty's indictment with an editorial titled, "Murder charge restores community confidence."[3] Now that confidence was ripped away. "It was a shock to the community," one prominent attorney remembers. "People felt that if the grand jury indicted him, he should go to trial, and the State should let the chips fall where they may."[4]

Inside the courthouse, feelings about McCarty's release were more complicated. Defense lawyers and some prosecutors saw it as a gutsy, principled move by that rare prosecutor who would let the evidence and not public pressure affect his determination. As Beckman told the press, "It's the obligation of the prosecutor-elect to do what is right and not what is popular."[5] But for other attorneys familiar with county politics, something else was at play in Beckman's move on the Rison case: a deep-seated grudge against two people he blamed for depleting his livelihood two years before.

Rob Beckman never fit into neat categories throughout his legal career. Rail-thin with large wire-frame glasses, a trimmed mustache, and a crescent moon of hair combed over one side of his bald pate, he was usually photographed with a wry smile, but as one opponent remembers, he was "tightly wound," and prone to sudden outbursts of anger.[6] Beckman could also be extremely generous, advising young attorneys even if they were on opposing sides in a trial.[7] While a proponent of the death penalty[8] who could slap a child molester with a hundred-year sentence,[9] Beckman was also among the first prosecutors in the state to propose the legalization of marijuana[10] and supported youth activities to reduce delinquency.[11] A civic pillar in his hometown of Michigan City, he was a prolific fundraiser for the zoo and fairgrounds. Although he was strictly suit and tie during the day, at night he probably earned some double takes from convicted drunk drivers when he popped up in his jeans and a work shirt playing electric guitar for rock 'n' roll bar bands.[12]

Beckman served ten years as a public defender for the county before he became a prosecutor in 1990 and then worked primarily on traffic offenses and misdemeanors.[13] Despite his affiliation with the Democratic Party, four years later his new Republican bosses, Cynthia Hedge and her chief deputy, Scott Duerring, promoted him to the major felony team at Michigan City's Superior Court. There, he could cut his teeth on high-profile prosecutions for murder, child abuse, and drug dealing. They also chose to keep his wife, Priscilla Jo Beckman, as a juvenile court deputy prosecutor.[14]

Despite their confidence in him and his wife, Beckman could not keep quiet about how Hedge and Duerring ran the prosecuting attorney's office. Of most concern was their initiative to hire more full-time staff.[15] Until then, the county's prosecutors were part-time, which benefited the multitasking Beckmans. Rob also served as the corporate attorney for Michigan City, a part-time position. Meanwhile, he and Jo shared a private practice built around cases that wouldn't conflict with their prosecutorial roles.[16]

For Duerring, the part-time prosecutor was a quaint holdover from when the county caseload was much smaller. He says, "We weren't a little office any longer, and there were problems with people paying attention to their part-time job as a prosecutor versus their private practice and things like that. I felt we needed to go with more full-time prosecutors, and [Hedge] listened to my input."[17]

However, it was hard to find experienced trial attorneys who wanted to work full-time for the county, which meant hiring candidates out of law school. As far as Beckman was concerned, these rookies "botched" criminal cases. He also continued to harp on Hedge's lack of trial experience influencing what he saw as her poor decisions.[18] For Duerring, that lack of experience brought a fresh perspective. When it came to familiarity with trying criminal cases, he argues, "She surrounded herself with people who knew what they were doing. And she listened to their advice rather than thinking that suddenly, because she was elected, she knew everything."

Beckman was never one of those people in the prosecuting attorney's circle, and he let other lawyers in the office know his concerns.[19] Duerring remembers, "Rob was undermining [Hedge's] authority very vocally, which I thought was affecting the morale of other deput[y prosecutors]." The chief deputy says he was the one who recommended Beckman's termination, and Hedge followed through. In August 1997—without warning—Beckman was fired. News of his termination came through the mail and fax. "I had just opened the letter and read it when a fax came across that [said the same thing]," Beckman told a reporter for the Michigan City *News-Dispatch*. "I was never contacted in person about this. I haven't had any verbal communication with [Hedge] in the last nine months."

He said the reasons for his dismissal cited in the letter were "nebulous." When reporters asked for more detail, Hedge called the firing a "tough decision" but declined to give the reasons for it, explaining, "I think the most responsible thing to do on personnel issues is to not make a comment."

Beckman was not so reticent, professing shock and admitting to the delicate nature of his family's financial condition with one child entering college and another wearing orthodontic braces. He explained that he could not just fall back on his private practice to pay the bills because his work as a prosecutor had limited the clients he was allowed to represent. "If [Hedge] had intended to hurt me, my wife, my children, she has done it," he told the reporter. "She has thrown my life into turmoil."

At another point in the interview, when lamenting how difficult it would be to build back his private practice, Beckman said, "They knew that when they did this."[20] By putting the onus on "they," he meant not just Hedge but her chief deputy, Duerring, who he suspected was behind the firing. "Scott and Rob used to be good friends," another prosecutor remembers. "After Rob was fired, I don't think they spoke to each other again."[21]

A surprising contingent derided Hedge's decision once news of the firing got out. Calling the move a "travesty," a prominent defense attorney proclaimed how Beckman was respected by his side of the bar even though he was "a very tough, hard-nosed prosecutor." He added, "There were no sneaky things with him as there are with others on the prosecutor's staff now." Another called him "beyond reproach." Even the Michigan City police chief chimed in to say, "From our perspective, Rob did an excellent job. . . . It's going to be a huge loss for us."[22]

Despite the tributes from courthouse allies and foes, Beckman reflected on his career with remorse. Pointing to the financial hardship ahead, he ruefully concluded, "It really makes me wonder why I have spent seventeen years in public service."[23]

But then, true to his contradictory and unpredictable nature, Beckman threw himself into public service as never before, announcing his candidacy in the following year's race for La Porte County prosecuting attorney. From the start, courthouse insiders and reporters saw his campaign as more an act of revenge than ambition.[24] But his firing left enough blood in the water for Hedge to appear vulnerable and make for a crowded Democratic primary.[25] If nothing else, Beckman's years of public service gave him ample chits he could cash in for endorsements. But his zeal to oppose Hedge in the general election left nothing to chance, and he raised an unprecedented amount of campaign funds by La Porte County standards.[26]

Although Beckman assured the press that his candidacy was not a "vendetta" against Hedge,[27] she became the focus of the Democratic primary debates rather than the records of the three opponents.[28] Beckman emerged victorious with 42 percent of the vote, 10 percent higher than his closest rival, while Hedge ran unopposed in the GOP primary. It set the stage for a general election contest that one of Beckman's Democratic opponents predicted would be a "nasty, vindictive campaign."[29]

But Hedge would prove no pushover, raising $37,000 for the race against the Democrat's $31,000. Beckman had already spent $25,000 in the primary. While the year before, after he was fired, he pled poverty, more than 40 percent of his campaign funds came from a personal loan. For her part, Hedge kicked in 52 percent of her total.[30]

The two candidates could not have presented a more striking contrast in their handful of debates. As he did from the start, Beckman attacked Hedge for not appearing enough in the courtroom, and he charged that the transition to fourteen full-time lawyers was a waste of taxpayer funds. He even promised to forgo his private practice and city attorney job in Michigan City to try the most challenging cases on his own. As he did in the primary, Beckman touted himself as the most experienced trial attorney in the race. Hedge countered that her staff included prosecutors like Duerring, who had more major felony cases under his belt than her opponent. She could also argue that in moving to full-time staff, she was emulating a national trend to modernize the office with prosecutorial specialists who would not be distracted by private affairs. Portraying her position as more of an administrator than a litigator, she pointed to programs dealing with drugs and domestic violence that she couldn't have initiated if she had been bogged down in a trial.[31]

Turnout for La Porte County "off-year" elections typically hovered around 30 percent. Still, thanks to the fireworks and campaign cash generated by the prosecuting attorney race, a shocking 45 percent of the electorate showed up at the polls in November 1998.[32] Throughout the evening of election day, the lead seesawed back and forth between the incumbent and the challenger. Finally, when the last votes were counted, Beckman emerged as the winner, eking out a victory by 280 votes, fewer than 1 percent of the total cast.

In his victory speech, the winner declared, "Obviously, every decision, every action that happens to you happens for a reason." It didn't take inside knowledge to know what "decision" he referred to, but the woman who made that decision accepted her loss graciously and did not file for a recount. Even before the final results were known, she hoped the election would bring back "cohesiveness" to La Porte County's legal community. The victor was not ready for kumbaya. True to his campaign promise, he announced that at least eleven of the fourteen full-time prosecutors would be let go. Beckman said it was too soon to say whom he would choose to remain, but he would only pick "the best of the best," irrespective of their political affiliation.[33]

Hedge's chief deputy, Scott Duerring, did not wait for the new boss's determination, knowing he'd never make the cut. He resigned. After letting nearby counties know he was available, he was quickly scooped up for the superior court in South Bend.

There is no newspaper report that the Rayna Rison case was a prime topic during the feverish debates surrounding Beckman's campaign. The judge had scheduled the trial for February 1999, which would have given the new prosecuting attorney only a month to review the voluminous files. It was precisely the high-profile case that Beckman promised to try as the lead prosecutor. He requested a continuance, and the judge complied, posting a new date for the fall, giving Beckman enough time to get up to speed.

Everyone involved expected the case to proceed in October[34] before the prosecuting attorney's bombshell August announcement that he was dropping the charges against McCarty. Beckman's curt explanation of why echoed his predecessor Bill Herrbach's assessment without any details. "The case is not right," he told reporters. "The case is not ready to be given to a jury." He also claimed the reasoning was not his alone and shared by his "senior staff."[35]

But for veterans of the previous administration, the decision was one more act in Beckman's vendetta against his former bosses. The grand jury indictment of Ray McCarty was *the* hallmark achievement of Hedge's term and monopolized Duerring's time like no other case. Beckman would later drop charges in another highly publicized indictment associated with the former chief deputy, further supporting the theory that vengeance trumped jurisprudence in those decisions.[36]

Hedge, who had remained out of the spotlight since her defeat, would not let Beckman's McCarty call go unchallenged. "When I was elected in 1994, I made a commitment to do what I could do to get [the Rison] case processed, and I felt very strongly about it," she told reporters. "I cannot begin to tell you how distressful this is, not only for the community but the Rison family and for Rayna. The system let Rayna down today."

Of course, investigators would have questioned whether the Rison family was so distressed by Ray's release, but all those who worked on the case were disgusted to see him let off the hook—no one more so than Scott Duerring. When asked for his response, he defended the grand jury process against charges that it was slanted against McCarty. "We presented every piece of evidence we had both pro and con to let jurors have a fair and objective outlook of what we had as prosecutors."

Duerring also charged, "Mr. Beckman never reviewed this case with an open mind, with justice in mind. He had other motives for dismissing this case." He implied that politics were behind those motives, based on "his comments during the campaign."[37]

Today, Duerring is more pointed about the flaws in Beckman's decision-making process. "I reached out to a number of people who were intimately involved in that case as investigators," he says, "and I asked them, 'Did Rob ever talk to you about this case? Did he ever get your input?' And they all said, 'No. Rob never called us.' In my opinion, if you're considering an extreme measure of dismissing a very touchy case with high-profile, sensitive matters where the State has poured a lot of resources, you don't sit in a vacuum and make that decision. You do your homework and sit down with the chief investigators and people involved in the case to get information before you make that drastic move."[38]

But in August 1999, when asked about Beckman's decision to dismiss, Duerring didn't just criticize the move. He also laid down a gauntlet that Rob could not ignore. "At least nine people worked on this case every day of every week for three years to get it to the grand jury," he told reporters. "I would like to know how [Beckman] plans on investigating it further. I would give a month's pay [if] Rob Beckman, in six months, [could tell me] what's new in this case. . . . He is the third prosecutor who has touched this thing [and] I would like to know how he plans on investigating it further."[39]

The six months would come and go without an answer about "anything new in the case," and then for the rest of Beckman's debut term. However, the mystery surrounding Rayna Rison's death did not threaten his tenure. Beckman ran unopposed for the next election and a second one[40] before finally seeing a slim chance to meet Duerring's challenge. There was just one problem with the new investigation. It originated with one of the most despicable perpetrators his office ever convicted.

IN THE CARDS

To fully understand the tragedy of Daniel Cassidy's life, do not stop at the day in October 1999 when Rickey Hammons ended it by shooting him ten times. Instead, go back twenty-one years before, when the victim was four years old and known as Danny Jemiolo and he watched as his father shot his mother multiple times with a pistol as he sat in the back seat of the family car. His parents had recently separated, and Janet Cassidy Jemiolo had come to pick up Danny and his infant sister from Joseph Jemiolo after they had spent a night with him. Upon shooting his wife, Jemiolo pulled his terrified son out of the car, brought him back to the house, and sat him on his knee. He explained that he killed Janet so she wouldn't keep him apart from his children.[41]

According to a relative, Janet Cassidy had dropped out of La Porte High School to pursue a "hippie lifestyle." She met Jemiolo during her backpacking travels,[42] and they stopped in Denver to get married when she was seventeen.[43] Danny was born a year later, and they returned to her hometown to settle down. At twenty-three,[44] Janet was a beautiful young woman with long brown hair, and her relative says Joseph was intensely jealous when she decided to leave him.[45] But Jemiolo had been drinking heavily before he killed her and pled guilty to manslaughter. He served only nine years and was released from prison. Twenty-five years later, he killed his second wife, this time with a baseball bat.[46]

Janet's parents, Janice and John Cassidy, adopted Danny and his little sister, Julie, and raised them like their own children. Eventually, they explained what happened to their mother, and although her killer tried to contact them while he was in prison and out, they refused to have anything more to do with him.[47] Danny grew to six feet tall, with thinning sandy brown hair and a peach fuzz complexion.[48] He wore glasses in his junior yearbook picture and looked studious and more mature than his peers,[49] but he was also a year older, having been held back by his October birthday. He left La Porte High School as a senior to join the Marines when he turned eighteen. (Rayna would die later in that school year.)

Danny's tour peacekeeping in the Balkans[50] lasted four years, which he told friends he did not enjoy. After an honorable discharge,[51] he took his grandfather's advice to sell cars. It was a career that had been good to John Cassidy and nurtured a nest egg that hatched into his purchase of a La Porte motel.[52] He introduced Danny to Robert Sheridan, the sales manager at Harbor Chevrolet, one of the area's fastest-growing dealerships. Sheridan not only hired him but, as a favor to John, took Danny under his wing to show him the ropes, and it wasn't long before he proved himself worthy of the attention. Sheridan liked to call him a "hustler." The sales manager watched with pride as Danny ran in and out of the dealership to get keys for a test drive rather than keep a prospective customer waiting. In return, his protégé would jokingly call Sheridan "Dad."[53] Over one year, Danny sold 110 vehicles, an impressive number for newcomers.[54] Sheridan would say if he had a drawback, it was keeping up with his paperwork.[55] Still, Harbor's owners saw Danny as management material and started teaching him the back-office skills he'd need to help run an auto superstore on land they purchased near the highway.[56]

In 1998, while looking ahead to a prosperous future, Danny decided the time had come to address the grimmest incident of his past. He officially changed his last name from Jemiolo to Cassidy, the moniker of his mother's family and the grandfather who had done so much to secure his prospects.[57]

But suddenly, his career in cars came to a crashing halt. While running across the road to help a customer, he was hit by a driver who fled the scene.[58]

The accident caused significant leg damage, requiring major reconstructive surgery on both his knees and an ankle.[59] Sheridan and the Harbor owners often visited during his long weeks in the hospital. They had no hard feelings about his lawsuit against the dealership and offered a reward to find the driver who hit him.[60] But as Danny soldiered through a lengthy and painful rehabilitation, he began to get second thoughts about his career choice. His cousin, one of his best friends, was studying on the main campus of Purdue University in West Lafayette, Indiana. He often visited to party, and college looked like a lot of fun. It could also give him a more stable career than selling cars. The newly minted Cassidy decided to give it a shot by applying for admission. To his surprise, he was accepted. Rather than live in a dorm, he talked to his cousin and another friend about putting a down payment on a more luxurious off-campus apartment, and the three of them signed a lease for a year.

Danny then broke the news to "Dad," but Sheridan and Harbor's owners were not about to let him go so easily. They gave him a $300 monthly raise and a check for $5,000 to stay.[61] Just as important, they promised to groom him to become the general manager of the new superstore. No longer would he need to hustle on his mangled legs. Still, Danny felt he had to decline the offer, no matter how enticing their retention package. If he backed out of the lease in West Lafayette, his roommates couldn't swing the rent on their own, and it was too late for them to find an acceptable alternative. In response, the bosses took the ante up another notch. A partly furnished three-bedroom house was on the property they purchased to build the superstore. They planned to knock it down once they completed construction and paved the parking lot. Danny could stay there rent-free for the next year as long as he kept it neat and clean for the occasional out-of-town vendor. In the biggest mistake of an already traumatic life, Danny accepted the generous offer and decided to stay.[62]

A young woman he met at a Purdue party probably played a big part in his decision. Soon after, she accepted a job in Texas, but stayed in touch on the phone and made occasional visits. She later described Cassidy as "intelligent, spontaneous, passionate, cocky, and liked to joke." She appreciated his long-distance pursuit of her but admitted she wouldn't be surprised if he went out with another woman because he "liked to flirt and liked the chase." Danny turned out to be more serious about their relationship than she thought. By the summer of 1999, he kept broaching the idea of marriage, and she kept rebuffing him by saying they both weren't ready for that commitment. With a much better salary and a clear career path to even greater affluence, Danny felt he was ready and started proposing again.[63]

Trouble for Cassidy arrived in the pint-sized, seemingly harmless guise of Rickey Joseph Hammons. As a teen, he was known by the Fox Hunt crowd as the annoying little brother who tagged after his more popular sister during games. In return, he took the apt CB handle of Mouth.[64] As he approached his twenty-first birthday, he grew even more mouthy, especially after too many bottles of Heineken, a couple of joints, or a losing hand at cards. While his friends considered him good for a laugh, his parents no longer got the joke. Rickey never found steady work after he dropped out of high school, and they now demanded that he get a job and move out of their house with Patton, his oversized, unruly Bernese mountain dog mix.[65] Danny's cousin, who would have been his roommate at Purdue, swooped in for the rescue. With Cassidy's support, Hammons replaced him as a car washer and porter when he left for Purdue. As for a place to stay, Danny let him take one of the empty, unfurnished rooms in his house.[66] No doubt anxious to get her son to move out, Hammons's mother contributed a bedroom set.[67] For rent, Cassidy only asked that Rickey help keep the place clean.[68] When his tenant proved too lazy and sloppy to hold up his end of that bargain, the landlord let him stay for just fifty dollars a month.[69] Danny's generosity did not stop with the job and the housing. Using his connections to a local bank, he got Hammons a loan to purchase a red Chevy Lumina from Harbor's used car lot.[70]

In the beginning, Danny seemed fine with the housemate. As he did with his sister during Fox Hunt games, Hammons tagged after Cassidy when he made his nightlife rounds. These usually started at the Blue Chip Casino, then a Michigan City riverboat, followed by local bars and the occasional strip club. Comparatively flush with his car-selling bucks, Danny always played the part of the generous older brother with his younger friends, picking up the tab for their drinks or food. When their benefactor had a little too much to drink, they could sit back and laugh as he tried unsuccessfully to pick up attractive women.[71] Cassidy's biggest splurge was a speedboat moored at a nearby marina. He first met Hammons when he came along with his cousin for a ride.[72] Generous to a fault, Danny had no problem with the younger friends taking out the boat on their own.[73]

But as the summer wore on, Cassidy's relationship with Hammons began to fray. While Danny was visiting his girlfriend in Texas, Hammons hosted a wild party in the house that put a gaping hole in one of the walls. The Harbor bosses expected Cassidy to make it presentable until the demolition, and Sheridan sometimes dropped in to ensure his protégé was complying. When Danny returned, he had to dip into his wallet to pay for a quick repair.[74] While Cassidy was away, Hammons also drove around in Danny's new model Oldsmobile Intrigue, at one point leaving Patton locked inside. Before he got back to the car, the monstrous mutt had torn up the leather interior.[75] The total for the damage in the house and the Oldsmobile amounted to $1,500, and Danny expected to be paid back.[76] When no money was forthcoming, he kicked Rickey out of the house and held his mother's bedroom set hostage until Hammons reimbursed him for the repairs.[77]

Perhaps expecting Danny to garnish the funds from his Harbor check, in mid-September 1999, Hammons abruptly quit his job at the dealership after only four weeks of pay.[78] He arrived at the Army Recruiting Office in Michigan City a few days later. Hammons had always proclaimed his interest in following his father's footsteps into the service. He enjoyed shooting pistols and rifles, wearing close-cropped hair, and sporting green Battle Dress Uniform (BDU) clothing. One close friend described him as a "military type."[79] Another thought the BDU wear was no more than cosplay.[80] But Hammons's intentions to enlist turned out to be authentic. He expected to report to training camp by the end of the month, which could stymie Cassidy and his other collectors for years to come. That dream would be shattered soon after he enlisted, when he was informed his "entry was denied." The urine from his physical had shown traces of illegal drugs—cocaine and marijuana.[81]

In the next few weeks, Hammons would exhibit more frenetic behavior than usual. One Saturday evening, he showed up briefly at a friend's home and could not keep still. Another guest thought he was high on something and remembered, "He was jumping all around like he was all paranoid." At one point, he pulled a handgun from his waistband. The observer described it as the same size as a Glock and "old and beat up." Before he left, Hammons told the others, "I just gotta keep moving. I'm worried something will happen to me."[82]

On Tuesday night, October 5, he showed up at three different friends' homes, kitted out in his BDU shirt, pants, and combat boots, pounding his Heinekens.[83] One of those friends had recently bumped into Danny, who had said, "Tell Rickey the next time you see him that if he doesn't pay me my money, I'm going to kick his ass." When told what Cassidy said, Hammons replied, "Fuck him. I ain't paying him."[84]

That evening, while Rickey paid his social calls, Danny was at the dealership, helping complete all the paperwork for a busy day of sales. He didn't leave until eleven thirty.[85] At home, he kept wearing his Harbor polo shirt but got out of his dress slacks and pulled on sweats to relax. No longer able to run to stay fit after the accident,[86] he still ate like he did and had gained almost fifty pounds since the accident.[87] He mixed macaroni and cheese in a pot and dropped a half-chicken in a frying pan before he abruptly stopped cooking.[88]

At one o'clock the next morning, a woman living in a sparsely populated area eight miles away from the future dealership reported hearing what she thought were several rapid-fire gunshots. Seven hours later, a driver on his way to work spotted a man's body on a nearby country road that bounded a little lake. He lay face up in the tall grass. Michigan City police and La Porte County evidence technicians soon arrived.[89] In the crime scene report, the sheriff's deputy noted "blood droplets" on the top of the victim's shoes—dressy wingtips that seemed at odds with his sweatpants. The drops indicated that he was first shot in the chest. The officer then reported, "High-velocity blood splatter was documented near and around the victim's head, indicating that the victim was repeatedly shot in the face while on his back, on the ground." Eventually, the evidence technician counted ten bullet wounds in the victim's body: three in the chest and seven in the face. Powder burns suggested the facial shots were made at close range. The .380 caliber bullet casings were from ammunition used for a semiautomatic handgun.[90]

Although the victim carried no wallet, his polo shirt prompted the police to call Harbor Chevrolet, where a general description of the corpse was enough for the manager to identify him as Danny Cassidy. The manager and "Dad" Sheridan went to the hospital to confirm the identification by looking at a photo of Danny's bullet-riddled face. Calls then went out to his grandparents and the Texas woman he recently called his fiancée.[91]

Word about Cassidy's murder spread quickly through La Porte County. Shortly after it was reported on the radio, an eavesdropping valet at the Blue Chip Casino heard a coworker say over the phone in their booth, "Oh my God. I gave him the bullets." The coworker was Jennifer Hammons, Rickey's older sister. The informant also heard her say words to the effect that her brother owed the victim money.[92]

Two days earlier, La Porte County police had picked up Rickey for a preliminary taped interview. He professed shock at hearing the news about Cassidy's death but otherwise appeared calm and convivial during the half-hour session. Given their questions, the officers did not know enough to suspect his involvement.[93] But on October 8, when two detectives picked up Rickey Hammons at his parents' La Porte home and took him downtown for questioning, they were armed with information about his dispute with Cassidy and his sister's exclamation about giving him the bullets. Although chatty about his personal history and not hiding his youthful indiscretions, Hammons clammed up when asked about his activities in the hours leading to Danny's death. The detective wrote in his report, "Hammons seemed agitated and claimed he couldn't remember."

At the same time, two other detectives were interviewing Rickey's big sister, Jennifer, who said she had handed her brother ten rounds of .380 caliber bullets a few days before Cassidy's shooting. Hammons had told the police he did not have a gun, but the police learned his father, Rickey Hammons Sr., had bought four semiautomatic pistols for his family and turned two of them over to the officers. He said two others had been stolen.[94] They were Russian-made Makarov handguns known as the "AK of the pistol world." The magazine[95] could hold nine bullets with one more loaded in the chamber—ten shots were emptied into Danny. Hammons confidently told his inquisitors that if a ballistic examination were done on the Makarovs they got from his parents, they "would find neither of the guns was used to kill Dan Cassidy." Before the police let him go three hours later, the detectives told him "that they suspected he was involved in the murder."[96]

A week later, the Michigan City *News-Dispatch* reported, "Rickey Hammons, 21, La Porte, was formally charged with murder, battery by bodily waste, and public intoxication during his initial appearance in La Porte Circuit Court. He allegedly shot Daniel Cassidy, a 25-year-old car salesman at Harbor Chevrolet in Michigan City, nine times." Besides the number of shots, there were several other errors in the reporting that grated on the victim's family. Instead of Hammons's landlord, Danny was identified as his "ex-roommate," and they were characterized "as friends, who at one time lived together." Perhaps more eye-catching and indicative of Rickey's bizarre behavior were the other charges of "battery by bodily waste and public intoxication." As the article explained, these counts were unrelated to the murder but the suspect's interaction with detectives the day before his arrest.[97] As future articles would report, he was intoxicated when he entered the La Porte County sheriff's office in the early morning hours of October 12 to confess his role in the murder. He later fought with a detective by punching him in the chest and spitting at him.

However strange that seemed, none of the reporting would even hint at the wild, convoluted goose chases where Hammons sent investigators before he finally confessed to the crime. He also pointed them to where he threw the Makarov pistol used as the murder weapon.

Like other Indiana homicide suspects, Hammons languished in the county jail until his trial, his conviction a foregone conclusion. But within weeks after his arrest, his court-appointed defense attorney filed a motion to suppress his confession, arguing it was extracted under duress while he was still intoxicated. Claiming he was "physically assaulted" by sheriff's deputies and "sleep deprived," the motion charged he then "suffer[ed] a psychological breakdown" that rendered anything he said as "inadmissible."[98] The motion was denied, and on June 9, 2000, Hammons signed an agreement to plead guilty to murder in return for forty-five years in prison.[99]

The sentencing two months later was a formality but would allow Danny's survivors to confront his murderer in court and let him know what his crime had done to impact their lives. Even after his guilty plea, Rickey was not done with his misdirection, using the hearing to publicize a new twist to Danny's murder and heap yet more misery on his grieving relatives. After telling the judge that a homosexual rape had provoked the murder, Hammons turned to the family and said, "I just want you to understand what happened. Danny was a good person, but he had another side to him you all didn't know."[100]

Danny's younger sister, Julie, was outraged. She had sat in the car with her brother when their father shot their mother. In her victim impact statement, she wrote, "I do not know how to explain the impact Danny's death has had on me. My life has been forever changed. I have now lost my entire immediate family to gun violence. . . . My life without Danny will never be the same. My brother, my childhood companion, my hero. Gone forever."[101]

Now, she had to suffer the indignity of hearing that her brother was responsible for his own murder. Outside of court, she told reporters, "What would you say if you murdered somebody and then realized you were going to jail or prison for a good portion of the rest of your life? I think you would make up whatever you could make up to make people think you were the victim, not the criminal."

A reporter wrote that she believed Hammons had killed Danny "because [Cassidy] wanted to inform the police about crimes Hammons allegedly committed." Still, she had nothing specific to say about the nature of those crimes.

La Porte County Prosecuting Attorney Rob Beckman could have set reporters straight, but his response to Hammons's charge of rape was tepid and legalistic. Despite the evidence detectives had uncovered about the $1,500 debt, he told reporters that a motive for the murder "could not be proven." However, he added, "There simply was no physical evidence to support what Hammons had said [about the rape]."[102] As Beckman also knew but did not say, no witness testimony supported what Hammons said. Detectives had interviewed their mutual friends within hours after Rickey made his rape charge.

But from behind bars, Hammons insisted on this version of his story. At one point, he wrote to the judge, requesting "a full mental and medical evaluation done by a fully trained medical doctor in the field of rectum analysis, sexual related diseases, and sexual transmitted diseases. This has a lot to do with the motive in my case! I also need the mental psychologist that is trained paceficically [sic] in the field of rape and molestation (also has something to do with the motive in my case). I am also asking that these doctors be out of the county of La Porte if any way possible."[103]

Over the next seven years, Rickey would continue to litigate his case, producing prodigious amounts of legal paperwork.[104] Most of his early efforts involved requesting new court-appointed counsel, even though Craig Braje, the attorney who wrote his motion to suppress, was considered among the best defense lawyers in the county (and most expensive when paid by private parties). Eventually, Hammons represented himself, churning out demands pro se to review proceeding transcripts and police reports. He sought post-conviction relief for Braje's "ineffective counsel" because "counsel did not investigate, interview or properly prepare himself to defend petitioner."[105] After attempts to modify his sentence were denied, he moved to "change venue from judge," charging he had "a personal bias and prejudice against [Hammons]."[106]

Meanwhile, Hammons did not prove to be a model prisoner, losing good conduct credit for "refusing a drug or alcohol test" and "possession, introduction, use of unauthorized substance." He was also written up for "insolence, vulgarity, or profanity" and "disruptive, unruly, rowdy conduct."[107] This included pranks directed against inmates who crossed him—such as signing them up for gay porn magazine subscriptions or using their ID numbers for excessive commissary purchases.[108]

But in late February 2008, Hammons's behavior and legal strategy took a sharp turn after an article appeared in *The South Bend Tribune* titled, "Will inmates put cards on the table?" It reported on a deck of playing cards that would be sold to Indiana state prisoners. Each card had a victim's photo from an unsolved homicide. A contact number for the state's TIPS Hotline was below. The *Tribune* reported that Rayna Rison was one of the deck's four La Porte cold cases. A blurry rendition of Rayna Rison's high school yearbook photo graced the Six of Clubs with the description: "Age 16, was last seen alive March 26, 1993, wearing blue jeans, a La Porte High School Letter Jacket with 'Matt Elser' on the back. Her body was located in a pond off of Range Road in rural La Porte County, Indiana." A spokesman for Indiana's Department of Corrections told the paper that inmates responding to the hotline "might seek to cooperate in the hopes of receiving a sentence modification or other reward."[109]

In the days after the article was published, Rickey made multiple attempts to contact Michigan City detective Mark Lachmund, a principal investigator in the Cassidy case and the one who arrested him for Danny's murder. In a letter, Lachmund reported, Hammons "was requesting to speak with me about a 'cold case' from 1993."

Hours after opening the envelope, Lachmund arranged for a phone call with the authorities of Hammons's prison. He later wrote, "In speaking with Rickey on the telephone, Rickey advised that he had observed the deceased body of Rayna Rison in the trunk of a vehicle what he thought to be several days after she was reported missing. Rickey was willing to advise several names of subjects that he thought were involved and was willing to give me the information but not over the telephone."

Few other Michigan City detectives had been as privy to Rickey's behavior during the Cassidy investigation as Lachmund, which may be why he added in his report, "Rickey gave me his word that the information he was going to reveal was honest and truthful."[110]

BEATING A DEAD HORSE

After Rayna Rison's death, Jason Tibbs was tossed into a churning sea of personal turmoil. For the next fifteen years, like a man swimming against a riptide, he would thrash toward calm waters, only to be sucked back into turbulence by an undertow of poor judgment and bad luck.

The choppy nature of this life would commence on May 1, 1993, the day of Rayna's funeral, when threats from Rison family friends convinced Jason's mother to get him out of town for a few weeks. When he returned, they worked on a plan to have him leave for a more extended time and start a new career. Thanks to his class at Boys School, Jason realized he had an aptitude for auto repair. Once he turned eighteen in June, he could move to Indianapolis and enroll in the Lincoln Tech trade school there. He had no trouble passing the GED exam as a first step.[111]

After Jason received his Automotive Standard of Excellence diploma from Lincoln Tech, he returned to La Porte in 1994 and went through a series of odd jobs and girlfriends. He would get more serious about his work and love life in the summer of 1995 when he met Leslie Ann Dean. Jason had first become friendly with her stepfather, Billy Ray Hurt, who had moved to Indiana from Kentucky a few years before. Leslie decided to join them after he and his wife Peggy had settled in La Porte. Jason first saw her on the back of Billy Ray's motorcycle and was immediately smitten. She was, he says, "curvy in the right places," with a heart-shaped face, hazel eyes, and long blonde hair she kept in a ponytail. Although he was with another woman at the time, he was able to pull Billy Ray aside to ask about his passenger. The friend replied, "Never mind because she's absolutely off limits." His wife, Peggy, wanted her daughter to have nothing to do with Jason.

At seventeen,[112] Leslie was only three years younger than Jason, but Peggy was more concerned about the suspicion that still hung over Tibbs from his association with Rayna Rison. Although Billy Ray had enough contact with Jason by that point to vouch for him, his wife did not want to tempt fate.

Despite Peggy's best efforts, the two did come into close contact at a particularly painful moment for Jason after he fell off his friend's motorcycle. Skidding across the asphalt road left him with severe road rash on his back. A few days later, it was aggravated when a friend inadvertently slapped him there while he hung out at Billy Ray's house. Peggy brought him inside to pull off his old bandages that were bleeding through and replace them with new ones. As the others watched, Jason bent over an ironing board, bracing for the adhesive to be torn from his ravaged skin. He didn't notice that Leslie had snuck below to tie his shoelaces together. With a yank, Peggy pulled off the bandages, and when Jason bolted up to shriek, his feet locked together, and he fell backward on his butt. Everyone laughed, including Jason. It was the kind of prank he might have pulled on someone else, making Leslie even more desirable. They would soon sneak around her mother's back to see each other. Beyond the physical attraction for Jason, Leslie was also bright and liked to read. He could have the kind of conversations with her that he hadn't had with other women since he talked with Rayna. "When Peggy found out we were seeing each other," Jason says, "she had a big argument with Leslie and, for a while, kicked her out, but eventually, she let it go."

Tibbs may have helped matters by showing how serious he was about this relationship. He buckled down by getting a job with a company that serviced heavy-duty trucks, bringing home a decent paycheck, and learning about diesel engines and hydraulics. A few months later, Leslie was pregnant.

Now, the future step-grandfather wanted to see Jason in a job with benefits, better pay, and upward mobility. While at Teledyne, Billy Ray had built a reputation as a valuable jack-of-all-trades. He had the clout to get Tibbs a foundry job a month before their baby Duston was born. Ray McCarty was still working at Teledyne but during a different shift. If they saw each other, it was in passing and at a distance. In December 1996, two months after he started the job, Jason and Leslie were married.

But the next few years would not be all domestic bliss for the young couple. Although Teledyne did offer advantages over the vehicle repair jobs, it also had periodic layoffs—two in the next two years. Infidelity compounded the financial insecurity. Jason says she started it, and he only had his affairs in retaliation. Leslie took matters to a new level in 2000. She was managing a toll road gas station when Jason says, "She fell for a guy flashing big wads of money." She followed the paramour to Massachusetts and a supposed life of luxury. Jason filed for divorce, but then, a few months later, Leslie started calling Rachel Tibbs. She wanted Jason to bring her back to La Porte.

By then, Tibbs wanted nothing more to do with her. Instead, he offered to pay a friend to make the trip, but his ex held out until he agreed to come along. "I knew why," he says. "She wanted to spend all that time in the car convincing me to get back together."

Jason says he initially resisted, but ultimately, the couple did reconcile. Nine months later, in February 2004, their second child, Tatum, was born. Before the year was out, Leslie gave birth to her younger sister, Kindal.

During all the upheaval in his family life, Jason continued to be shadowed by legal difficulties, most of his own making. The ridiculous ones spiraled up from traffic violations. He felt an officer unfairly ticketed him for driving 35 mph in a 25-mph zone on an overpass when he was going no faster than the other vehicles around him. He refused to pay the fine and then lost his license. He was pulled over five times for driving while suspended[113] until he agreed to serve forty-five days in jail to have all his charges dismissed. The county let him go after one week, but bit by bit, Jason was adding to his reputation as a troublemaker with the court and the police.

He had two more serious charges after he split from Leslie and during one of his periodic layoffs from Teledyne. He was working at an auto parts store where, he says, the manager suggested he help her inflate sales numbers so they could qualify for a bonus. Some of that phony bookkeeping included the bogus payment for an engine that was never recovered. Jason believed it went to her boyfriend, but he took a guilty plea to felony theft, and court records show he paid $4,800 in restitution.[114] His sentence was supposed to be suspended, but a little more than a year later, he was caught up in another crime. As he had as a juvenile delinquent, he got in trouble by hanging around with the wrong people. This time, he answered a call from two friends who needed a ride during a snowstorm. When he picked them up, they were covered with snow and lugging a stuffed hockey bag. A few blocks later, a squad car pulled Jason over. When the officer asked about the bag, no one spoke up, and he opened it to find merchandise stolen from a nearby body shop. "I didn't know what was in it, and he could see I wasn't covered with snow like those other guys and their bag, but it was my car, so I took the rap." With a second felony theft in two years under his belt, the judge ratcheted up the punishment.[115] His sentence of one year was suspended, but he had to wear an electronic monitor around his ankle for 180 days. He still had it on when he reunited with Leslie.

Despite his brushes with the law, Jason's truck and auto repair skills were in demand, and he had no trouble finding work at local service shops. Still, after the girls were born, he wanted the benefits he got at Teledyne, and Jason jumped at an opening in the foundry's maintenance shop where he would service and rebuild production equipment. He had to take a test first but had no trouble passing it. After two years, he was promoted to management and assured he had a bright future with the company.

But then, out of the blue in July 2007, Jason faced the most life-altering charge yet—that he stole from the employer where he had staked his future and expected to spend the rest of his working life. He had no warning that anything was amiss when, early one afternoon, the woman in charge of Teledyne's human resources came to his office with a young man in tow. "Someone would like to talk to you," she said.

With his short, military-style haircut and boyish face, Brett Airy looked like he was barely out of high school, so Jason was surprised to see a business card identifying him as a City of La Porte police detective. "He was very easy-going," Jason remembers. "He said he had a few questions for me if I could come down to the station to talk to him. I had some things to finish up, and he said, 'No rush. Come down when you're done.'"

But once Tibbs and Airy were face-to-face downtown, the tone changed. The detective told Jason that someone married to a coworker said she saw him and his best friend, Josh Jordan, outside the maintenance shop stealing barrels of nickel balls while she was waiting to pick up her husband. She claimed that Jason was driving a forklift and loading the barrels on the back of Josh's Chevy Suburban. Jason laughed. He would have had to break down walls to get the barrels from the storage area through the maintenance shop. Besides, the time she saw the theft would have been during a shift change for most workers and lunch for his crew. "You would have had all kinds of people moving around," he said. "That charge is just as false as false can be."

But Airy did not appreciate Jason's answers to his questions. "He started to get snide with me," Tibbs says, "and I responded by getting smartass with him. Finally, he says, 'If you're innocent, why don't you take this voice stress analysis on my computer?' I asked, 'Why are you wasting my time on this stupid story?' And he's like, 'Just humor me.'"

According to the US Department of Justice, voice stress analysis (VSA) tests are accurate only 50 percent of the time, but Jason felt he had nothing to fear. He took the test and failed. "I didn't think anything of it," Tibbs remembers. "The whole thing seemed like a big joke." As for the detective, once he challenged him, Jason says, "He acted like a whiny kid." It was hard to take Airy seriously, let alone see him as a nemesis who could ruin his life.

But before Jason returned to Teledyne, Airy was back on the phone with the HR director, telling her the employee had failed the VSA test. When she pulled Tibbs into her office, the company president was waiting. Their reason for firing him left an indelible mark. "They told me they were letting me go," he says, "because 'my integrity had become suspect.'"

Jason and Josh soon learned the identity of their accuser. She was the ex-wife of a good friend of theirs who once worked at Teledyne. When she started an affair with one of her coworkers, they informed their friend, which probably led to their divorce. Her retaliation had a devastating impact on Jason but cost Josh in legal fees as well. But neither man contemplated copping a plea. Other than her accusation, the police had no evidence.

For help, Jason turned again to Mike Drayton, the attorney who pulled him out of the police station after Rayna disappeared. He, too, was incredulous at the charges. "I just did the math on the weight of those barrels," he remembers. "There's no way you could have moved them around like that woman said."[116] Jason put him on retainer, but ultimately, Drayton gave it back. Jason says, "He told me he checked his sources inside the police department and learned they had nothing."

A week after getting fired from Teledyne, Jason had another job with a mobile truck repair service. It did not have anywhere near the promise of his work at the casting plant and would barely pay their bills. Leslie got work managing an Arby's restaurant to keep them afloat. Little did they know that this would be the luckiest break of their tumultuous relationship.

Meanwhile, counter to Drayton's sources, Jason heard that Airy continued to contact his former coworkers about the nickel theft. A few months later, in April 2008, he was not surprised when Leslie called him at work to say that Airy and another detective were on her doorstep with a "warrant" for her husband. In his report, Airy wrote that Jason's black Camaro was in the driveway, implying Tibbs was hiding somewhere on the property.[117] Actually, Jason's employer had him commute with his service truck in case he had to leave directly from home for an emergency repair.

When Leslie called, Jason believed Airy had a warrant for his arrest in the supposed nickel theft. He called Drayton, who told his client to go directly to his office while he called around to see what the warrant was about. Jason arranged to meet Leslie when she dropped off their toddlers at her mother's. They then took the Camaro downtown to find that Drayton had been stymied in his inquiries. "No arrest warrant has been filed in any court in the county," he told them. The lawyer had no idea why Airy had shown up at Tibbs's door, and Jason figured the young detective was overreaching again. But as they left Drayton's office building and started to get in their Camaro parked outside, Jason heard someone call out his name. He turned to see Airy standing by an unmarked car with another officer. Jason grabbed Leslie. They ran back inside and up the flight of stairs to Drayton's law firm. His secretary directed them to his private office while the attorney confronted the detectives in the hall. Jason could hear Drayton demanding to know why they were arresting his client. The officers replied that they had a search warrant, not an arrest warrant. Now, Drayton was confused. They could have searched Tibbs's home without Jason being present, but then they explained that the search was for his person and not his premises. Jason and Leslie could hear Drayton laugh. "You think he has nickel in his pockets?"

"No," Airy replied. "This is for the Rison investigation." He then handed the warrant to the attorney, who couldn't hide his disbelief. "Are you still beating that dead horse?"[118]

Drayton brought the papers back to Leslie and Jason in his office. He explained that they now wanted a DNA swab and what are known as major case prints, which involve getting impressions from every part of the palm and hand beyond the tips of the fingers. Typically, these are only taken from the prime suspects in a crime. To comply with the warrant, Jason had to walk a few blocks to the city's police station, where a state trooper evidence technician would take the necessary specimen. As Jason left Drayton's office, he saw Airy waiting outside with another officer—not to accompany him to the jail, but to taunt him. "What would you say if we had someone who saw you with the body?" he asked.

Jason replied, "I'd say he was probably as high as you are now."

THE POLE BARN

On Monday, March 10, 2008, eleven days after receiving Rickey Hammons's letter, Detective Mark Lachmund drove four hours from his Michigan City office to the Wabash Valley Correctional Facility,[119] a compound of low-rise buildings housing prisoners from minimum to maximum security levels. It is in Carlisle, at the southern tip of Indiana, only a few miles from Kentucky.[120] Given the distance for La Porte's inmate families to visit, it might as well be in Siberia.

Accompanying Lachmund for the ride was State Trooper Al Williamson. Rob Beckman had hoped the detective would give him a breakthrough in the Rison investigation that would absolve the prosecuting attorney for dropping the charges against Ray McCarty.[121] Around lunchtime, the two met with Hammons in one of the little rooms where prisoners can confer with their attorneys.

As the detectives fumbled with the tape recorder, Hammons must have sized up his visitors. Forty-five-year-old Williamson had a poker face and the honed stare of an experienced interrogator. With a mass of gray brushed-back hair and glasses that slipped to the end of his nose, fifty-three-year-old Lachmund was more the genial good cop. Considering his previous experience with Hammons, which he was unlikely to forget, Lachmund was, if anything, surprisingly genial upon confronting the felon again. As the transcript shows, neither man could conceal their desperation for a new development in the cold case, and Hammons realized he was in control. The chumminess and cockiness that Cassidy detectives found so off-putting now returned to this new interrogation. Rickey insisted on calling the detectives by their first names and made light of his disorderly conduct back in the La Porte County sheriff's office.

As he set up an audio recorder, Lachmund said they wanted the interview to be "a real laid-back conversation" and hoped Rickey would not be "intimidated by the taping." Hammons assured him he was not. Almost apologetically, the detective explained that they needed to read him his Miranda rights so Hammons could acknowledge with his signature that he was willing to talk to them without having a lawyer present, which he did.

Hammons cut to the chase after providing background information on himself and admitting that he did not know Rayna personally. "The one guy's name that you are looking for is Jason Tibbs," he told the detectives.

Lachmund was not familiar with him. "White guy, Black guy?" Lachmund asked. "How old would he be right now?"

"Oh, Mark," Hammons replied, "I couldn't give you an exact date. I'd say he's about, had to be, midthirties."

Lachmund's ignorance about Tibbs must have surprised his informant. Even a quick perusal of police files would have shown him to be a prominent suspect—perhaps the most prominent after McCarty. Williamson remained silent.

But Hammons then provided another name to the detectives that had never come up in the previous investigation—not in all the witness interviews or hundreds of tips from outsiders. His sister, Jen, he said, "dated this Eric Freeman guy. He lived in our house." Hammons described Freeman as Jason's "running partner," adding, "I guess they'd been friends for some time. They seemed to be pretty tight, you know, run around together, whatever."

In clearing Tibbs as a suspect, previous investigators had made an extensive canvass of Jason's friends, especially the close ones who were with him the night of Rayna's abduction and the days after. Freeman was never swept up in their net or even mentioned by third parties.

Perhaps stunned by Lachmund's cluelessness and Williamson's silence, Hammons asked, "Either of those two names ring a bell to you guys?"

Lachmund answered, "Nuh-uh," but Williamson said, "Yeah, sure do."

Hammons replied, "Well, I'm gonna give you a whole lot more, and it might set off some more alarm bells."

What he had to give centered around a pole barn[122]—a low-cost shed popular in the Midwest that uses poles sunk into the ground for structural support instead of a traditional cement foundation.[123] In 1993, the Hammons family had such a structure in their backyard. It was approximately fifty by thirty feet with blue corrugated metal siding.[124] Lachmund said he remembered the barn when he searched the Hammonses' backyard for remnants of Rickey's murder weapon but never went inside. "Bringing back memories?" Hammons asked.

"Yes," Lachmund replied. "Thank you."[125]

At one end of the longer side were sliding doors that could open for a vehicle.[126] Hammons explained that the space was primarily used for his parents' dog breeding business but held some barnyard animals as well. Kitty-corner from the sliding doors was a wood structure that housed the dog kennels. Rickey called the top of the kennels a "loft," where he could climb up to "hide" among bales of hay, look at "girlie books," and smoke dope.

On the evening of March 26, 1993, Hammons told the detectives he was on top of the kennels. "I was smoking some weed, you know, got high, Mom and Dad catch me, and you know my ass is hit, right. Well, in pulls Eric and Jason in that car."

"That car" was Hammons's sister's 1986 Buick Century. Although Freeman was not supposed to drive his girlfriend's car without her parents' permission, he often did. Anticipating that Freeman would deny getting behind the Buick's wheel, Hammons cited a downtown accident where the boyfriend was listed as the driver in the police report.

According to Hammons, Freeman backed the car through the sliding doors. "Anyway, so they get out of the car, they start arguing, 'What the fuck, da, da, da, da.' I'm like, what the hell's going on, so I cast [throw away] the joint. I'm like, man, what the hell? I'm freaking out, right? I don't want them to catch me 'cause I know [Freeman will] go tell, right?"

Then, Hammons told the detectives, Freeman went behind the car. He opened the trunk to reveal Rayna's body.

"And you could see her in the trunk from where you're at?" Lachmund asked.

"I can see her from up here," Hammons replies, later estimating he was thirty to thirty-five feet away. Although her face was up, he said he did not realize it was Rayna Rison until a few days later. But Hammons went on to provide more details about the corpse than its identification, revealing intimate knowledge of the autopsy, probably learned from archive newspaper reports. "Now I didn't see no blood on her face or nothing like that. Her face, it wasn't, it wasn't blue, but it wasn't white neither. It had a, like a, I don't know how to describe it. I mean, we've seen dead bodies before, me and you. I mean, she didn't look nothing like Danny. . . . I mean, she didn't have no massive trauma or nothing. I'm not trying to be cold when I say that or nothing."

"No," Lachmund interjected. "I understand."

Williamson concurred that he was not put off by the description either. "I do homicides, so . . ."

But there was other intimate information he divulged that should have raised suspicions. Showing his hand, Hammons prefaced his comment by saying, "I know that you can't tell me no details." Then he asked, "Did you guys find a blanket?"

"A what?" Lachmund asked.

Hammons clarified, "Maybe you found some fibers like this or something on her body."

Later, Williamson confirmed, "To answer your questions, yeah, we found fibers."

The fiber evidence uncovered in the first investigation was never publicized. Other than the police, the prosecutors, and the grand jury, the only ones who would have known about it were the McCarty and Rison families. But the prepping was incomplete, or Hammons forgot what he was told. However, when Williamson asked him about the color, he answered, "I believe it was red, black, and white, but I can't be one hundred percent sure on that." In fact, the telltale fibers were green.

Hammons also claimed to remember what the two culprits said to each other. "Jason said back to [Freeman], he was like, 'Well, what are we gonna do? What are we gonna do?' And Eric says, 'I don't know, but she can't stay here.' Like that, he said, 'She can't stay here,' and I'm thinking to myself, what the fuck?"

But Rickey realized his view of the dead body was not enough to satisfy the detectives. He also needed to deliver a motive. "Eric said something to Jason about some pussy. He said, 'Over some pussy,' like . . . , 'You did this over some pussy.' Over some jealousy, or over some uh, maybe she wouldn't give him some pussy or, I don't know."

He later elaborated, referring to Jason's CB handle of Croc. "I believe that Jason, Crock of Shit, killed her. Intentionally, nonintentionally, I don't know. And that's because Eric was making comments like, 'What the fuck were you thinking, over some pussy?'"

"That's how you took it?" Lachmund asked.

Williamson interjected, "Your perception?"

"That's my perception of how the conversation was," Rickey replied. "Whether or not that's true or not, I can only speculate, right? And I don't want to give anything other than facts, so I'm just telling you those are the parts of the conversation that I recall hearing."

Then, Hammons added another critical element to his story, saying, "They stayed there for like twenty minutes, twenty maybe thirty minutes, right? And the whole time I'm up there like this, like, 'Please leave.' Right? 'Please leave.'" He said he could hear scraping noises as though they were gathering shovels to help in the burial. Then they left, and he could watch them drive away through a bullet hole in the wall.

In context with all the known evidence in the case, Rickey's claim about the time Jason and Eric spent in the pole barn shattered everything else he had to say. However, the detectives did not know enough about that evidence to challenge him. Instead, they raised a few other issues that would have made his story suspect, starting with why Hammons was supposedly hiding.

"Mark and I can attest," Trooper Williamson said, "when somebody walks in a room, you can tell if somebody's been smoking weed or not. We stop a car, and we can tell if somebody is smoking weed." The detective wondered why Freeman and Jason wouldn't have smelled it.

In response, Hammons tried to back up and modify what he had told them moments before when he said he "got high" before the Buick arrived. Now, he replied, "I had just fired it up." Then, he pointed out the little vents on either side of the barn and that his mother would "have fans running in there, like during the summer—fans, you know, for ventilation, for the dogs or whatnot."

Hammons also stretched credulity by describing Rayna's face inside the trunk down to the blue tinge of her skin color.[127] Although the detectives were unfamiliar with the barn's interior, the headspace in the loft would have made their informant's sightline highly suspect. There was barely three feet beneath the rafters[128]—not enough room to stand or even sit up in most places; hardly a location to relax or get an angle to look into a trunk thirty feet away.

Still, even if that were possible, what light could have been available to see the skin on her face was blue? Hammons claimed the car backed into the pole barn around 5:00 P.M., but all the other witness testimony would have pointed to a time no earlier than 7:00 P.M.—an hour after sunset.[129] Here, the detectives were clueless about the timeline but still wondered about the lighting, even if Rickey's story were true. "While you're up on the loft and this car pulls in," Lachmund asked, "are you able to see and see clearly over the natural light?"

Hammons replied by pointing to the strip of translucent fiberglass siding that topped the wall behind the loft. "There's plenty of light in there. . . . At the top—it's not sheet metal. . . . It lets all this natural light in. So there's plenty of light in there to see. . . . I mean, unless it's midnight out, you know, dark in there, that's the only time you can't see. . . . If the sun is up, you can see in that pole barn."

"Without the lights on?" Williamson asked.

Hammons replied, "Without the lights on. Yeah."

With this answer, implying that the sun was still up when he saw the body in the trunk, Hammons definitely doubled down on an early bird timeline. Multiple witnesses had testified that Rayna was abducted in the Pine Lake Animal Hospital parking lot when it was already dark enough for cars to have their headlights on. Furthermore, the dense fog and cloud cover made things darker than usual for that time of day.

But the detectives did not quibble further about the lighting. They were most concerned by why he didn't report his sighting sooner. In response to that question, Hammons explained, "I've never been a big fan of authority, so for me to go run and tell on him. . . ."

"That wouldn't be like you to do that," Lachmund concurred sympathetically.

Hammons continued, "Uh, I don't want to say my dad's a criminal, but he always told me, you know, if you see something, keep your mouth shut. . . . It ain't your business."

But once again, with this comment, Hammons contradicted another theme of his statement—how much he hated Eric Freeman and wanted him gone. During the interview, he called him a "rat" and a "shady person" and described a fight where he pulled a gun on Freeman. "I don't trust Eric," he explained. "'Cause me and Eric done had words a few times. You know, arguments, this, that, and the other. He'd tell on me for everything, every little thing I did, you know, 'Rickey skipped school,' or 'Rickey did this.' Trying to score points with Mom and Dad, you know."

If Hammons had seen Freeman with a dead body in the trunk of his sister's car, why would he hide such a monumental offense from his parents? Whatever he thought about the authorities, it would have guaranteed the rat's immediate ejection from his household.

But as Hammons could see, the detectives were not there to find holes in his story. They desperately wanted to believe it. They overlooked other aspects of his recital that should have made them suspicious. Although he was asked to remember a night fifteen years ago, Rickey did not lack for minute details like the color of Freeman's shirt or the cap that Jason was wearing.

For Lachmund, this should have been reminiscent of the stories that Hammons spun around Cassidy's death. The Michigan City detective brought up his multiple confessions on the day he was arrested. In response, like the two were veterans sharing war stories, Hammons asked, "Remember I got in a fight with the jailers? First, I got in a fight with Kintzele?"

"In the bathroom?" Lachmund replied. "Kintzele still talks about that to this day."[130] Hammons had initiated the fight by punching the police sergeant in the chest.[131] But now, in the topsy-turvy world of a needy detective, Lachmund asked Hammons to forgive the man he hit. "You shouldn't hold it against him," he said.

"No," the felon generously replied. "I don't hold no grudges."

In time, there would be much speculation about why Rickey Hammons came forward. Detectives and prosecutors would adamantly insist that he asked for nothing in return. But during this first interview, as they were about to start the session, Hammons asked, "Before we start recording, can I speak to you off the record, or is that possible?"

Williamson replied, "I don't have a problem with that."

"You don't have a problem with that?" Lachmund asked his partner, seemingly incredulous. But the tape recorder was then turned off.[132] Later, when asked, under oath, what Rickey said off the record, Williamson replied: "He didn't want anything for the information he was about to give. He said he wanted nothing. He just gave me a reason why he wanted nothing. He was doing the right thing for the right reasons. . . . He did not want to memorialize that on the recording."[133]

Given everything else Hammons went on to share with the detectives—including intimate information about himself and his family—it strains credulity that he would have wanted to keep his righteous selflessness off the record. Unsurprisingly, after Jason's conviction, Hammons did admit that he had been promised a reduced sentence in return, although he didn't specify when this offer occurred.

However, it did not take long before he asked for a special favor. Three days after the interview, he wrote Lachmund, claiming another prisoner had spotted him with the officers and was now charging that Hammons was "telling on something to the police. . . . Mark, I'm not playing you at all, but I need your help. I'm asking that you either call or have one of your boys to make a call to Central office and have me moved." He added, "Please help me." And again, under his signature, "Please help ME!!"[134]

Beyond the help he supposedly didn't want, the letter reveals something else prosecutors may have found inconvenient. Hammons thanked Lachmund for "how you people have treated my family." In time, this statement, which indicated back-channel conversations with the Hammons family, could emerge as critical evidence for Jason's defense.

THE RAT

While Rickey Hammons and Mark Lachmund had become fast friends during their ninety-minute confab at Wabash Valley Correctional Facility, the Michigan City detective was not allowed to stay on the case. State Trooper Williamson had to find a partner from the City of La Porte police department, which had jurisdiction. Detective Brett Airy gladly leaped at the assignment. He had already been entangled with Jason on the Teledyne nickel theft, which was not gaining much traction. Now, he could nail Jason with a capital crime in the region's most notorious cold case. Given the taunt Airy sent Jason's way at his lawyer's office, it was a challenge he tackled with relish.

A day after he met with Hammons, Williamson called the young detective to debrief him. They were both on the phone when they reached the Hammons family. Airy reported, "Neither Rickey's parents or sister found any discrepancies with Rickey's story."[135]

Actually, there were plenty of discrepancies between what the family remembered and what Rickey told the detectives in his rambling interview. When they found out, the family had to paper over some of those inconsistencies quickly. Others emerged over time as they learned the extraneous details of his stories, which created awkward situations for Airy and Williamson. But the parents and big sister Jen were "all in" on convicting Jason Tibbs. Whether it was wishful thinking or under-the-table assurances by the police, they believed a successful prosecution could win an early release for "Little Rickey." (Big Rickey was his father, Rickey Hammons Sr.)

Oddly enough, the Hammons and Tibbs families had previous connections, which is how Rickey might have learned that Jason had once been a Rison murder suspect. Like Judith Hammons, Rachel Tibbs was a dog breeder, and according to Jason, "They interacted quite a bit about raising dogs and selling them—especially around the time when Rayna first disappeared. I'm sure my mother commiserated with Mrs. Hammons when they held me that time at the police station." Also, Judith and Big Rickey both worked with Jason's sister at the Indiana Department of Transportation.

While Jason Tibbs may have been familiar to detectives from the first investigation, Eric Freeman was another story. He was not among the web of Rison and Tibbs friends that the police questioned, perhaps because he was two to three years older and had grown up—like Ray McCarty—in Union Mills. His name did not appear once among all the interviews conducted by investigators. While Rickey characterized Eric as Jason's "running buddy," Jason remembers him as a marginal figure in the group that played Fox Hunt and never saw him outside the presence of Jen Hammons, Eric's girlfriend.

A child of divorce, Freeman had bounced back and forth between his father's home in Union Mills, his mother's house in La Porte, and sometimes her father's farm outside of town. A fight with his stepmother sent him to La Porte High School in his senior year.[136] After he graduated in 1992, he lived at the Hammons house, sleeping on a couch in their living room.[137] Freeman asserted on multiple occasions with the police that his relationship with Jen—three years his junior—was chaste. When Judith Hammons did Eric's wash and found a condom in his pocket, she assumed he was having sex with another girl, not her daughter. Judith and Freeman told police it was why he was kicked out of the family's house and had to live with his grandfather.[138]

With a high forehead, deep-set, raccoon-like eyes, and a toothy smile, Freeman had a demeanor that one friend took as "goofy"—not unlike the SNL comedian Pete Davidson.[139] But Jason remembers him as mostly "pissed off" and in a sour mood. He could also be jealous and possessive when it came to Jen. Jason and another friend remember an incident at the Hammons house when he waved a .22 rifle at someone he thought was making a pass at her.

Jason says he was never alone in the Buick with Freeman. If they were together in the car, it was with Jen. One such excursion was documented. In November 1992, Jason was also accompanied by a girlfriend when they passed a house that James Milich was visiting. He was one of Jason's erstwhile friends and Freeman's rival for Jen's affections. "James had a two-door Cadillac," Jason remembers. "I sold him the tires for that car and never got paid for them and got tired of asking him for it, so I told Eric to stop, got out, and slashed the tires. Little did I know that just up the block was a big old crusty cop named Kabacinski. When we started to leave, he turned on his lights and siren and pulled us over. He had me get out and said, 'Kid, you're making me do my job. If you're going to do something like that, you should learn to look over your shoulder or get a new career path.'"

The officer arrested the still-juvenile Tibbs for criminal mischief. He went to jail briefly until he was released to his father, and the charge was dropped.[140] It was a minor incident, but prosecutors later used it to confirm that Jason did, in fact, ride with Freeman in the Buick, who was identified as the driver by the arresting officer. However, other details in Kabacinski's report proved inconvenient for the State's case since Jen did not remember that Jason was arrested. Although the prosecutors tried to enter into evidence every other Tibbs offense—juvenile and adult—this was not one of them.

After his breakup with Jen and ejection from her family's house, Freeman soon had another girlfriend he would eventually marry. They lived a peripatetic life together, working on horse farms in Indiana, and then moved, in 1994, to Gastonia, a city in south-central North Carolina, to be closer to her family.[141]

A cycle of breakups began that mirrored the one with Jen Hammons. Freeman started his Carolina sojourn living in his first wife's family home.[142] While there, he commenced a relationship with a married woman. They had a son in July 1995.[143] As their marriages broke up,[144] he joined his paramour in a home owned by her parents.[145] They married after their divorces were finalized in 1999.[146] For Freeman, another split and marriage would follow.[147]

Eric's employment proved as rocky as his love life. He had flings as a salesman with several small firms on either side of the border with South Carolina.[148] His big break came in 2000 when Freeman met an elderly local home builder with a soft spot for young couples who were first-time buyers. Freeman began working for the builder, which he described as "doing odd jobs on houses."[149] In return, for just $18,000, he purchased a new two-bedroom ranch in Clover, South Carolina, surrounded by an acre of land on a road named for his employer.[150] In 2008, he took out a mortgage for $160,000 on the same property.[151]

Nine months before that transaction, City of La Porte Detective Brett Airy contacted Freeman through the York County police in South Carolina. A few days later, on March 18, 2008, a little more than a week after State Trooper Al Williamson met with Rickey Hammons, he and Airy sat down with Eric in the York sheriff's interview room. Freeman agreed to be tape-recorded, assured by Williamson that he wasn't "under arrest" and was "free to leave at any time."[152]

In setting up his sister's former boyfriend, Hammons told the detectives that Freeman would pretend to know nothing about Rayna's murder but would flip if they "apply enough pressure." He advised, "Just go out and say, 'Look, we know that you know about this. We have such and such evidence.' [You] ain't even got to show [it to] him. He will buckle and give you Jason."[153]

As Hammons predicted, Freeman appeared clueless about Hammons's alleged events that incriminated him and Jason. However, he confirmed his relationship with Jen Hammons and that he stayed with her family during the summer of 1992 after graduating from La Porte High School.[154] He talked about Fox Hunt, and "Croc" was among the first CB handles he remembered.[155] But Eric cited Chad Green as his best friend from the Fox Hunt crowd and did not mention Jason.[156] In line with what Rickey said, Eric admitted to driving the Buick Century and getting into an accident downtown.[157] When asked if Jason was ever with him in the car, he answered, "less than a half a dozen [times] that I recall," and indicated Jen was with him all those times.[158]

As for the pole barn, Freeman had no idea anything significant happened there on the night of March 26 and did not remember ever backing into the structure with the Buick.[159] He did talk about cleaning up the "dog poop" from the kennels under the loft, which was part of his price in living with the Hammons, and sometimes he would do so with Little Rickey.[160]

When the detectives probed into his relationship with Jason, Eric could recall giving him a ride only once—when Tibbs slashed the tires on James Milich's Cadillac.[161]

All told, Freeman made no effort to portray Tibbs in a positive light. He reported that despite her dog-breeding alliance with Rachel Tibbs, Judith Hammons "wasn't a big fan of Jason's [and] Jennifer wasn't a big fan either."[162] However, the detectives did not get any satisfaction regarding the most pertinent question. Williamson asked, "At any point in time, did you or were you in that vehicle along with Jason Tibbs and Rayna Rison . . . ?"

"Not that I recall," Freeman replied. "No."[163] When the detectives asked whether he ever rode in Rayna's car, Eric answered, "I didn't know she had a car."[164]

Later, Airy pressed further. "Is it possible, though, that you saw her in the trunk [of the Buick], and you don't remember?" he asked.[165]

"I really don't remember anything in the trunk. I don't," Eric answered, perhaps not understanding what was at stake with the question, because he added, with a stab at humor, "[The trunk is] not one of my hang-out places."[166] Not only did Freeman not see anything in the trunk, but he also said, "I don't recall opening the trunk for any reason."[167]

If Williamson felt any frustration with the session when it concluded forty-five minutes later, he didn't show it. "I appreciate your cooperation with us," he told Freeman. "It means a lot to us that you have taken the time away from your family. That's very important to us. . . . As I know your quality of time to family is important to you also, I'll conclude this interview."[168]

But the detectives were not quite done with Freeman. Upon returning to La Porte, Airy went through police reports from the first investigation to identify mutual friends in the social circles of Eric and Jason. While they found one individual who repeated that Tibbs and Freeman were best friends,[169] most who knew Jason did not know Eric or had vague memories about him.

Another Freeman development involved Craig Braje, the lawyer who represented Rickey Hammons in his motion for post-conviction relief. Although the lawyer's submission to the court for Hammons was well researched and thorough, Rickey later accused him of offering "ineffective counsel."[170] According to Airy's reports, after the interview with the detectives in Clover, Freeman had hired Braje as his attorney. Given his past relationship with Rickey, who was now Eric's accuser, his representation could be seen as a conflict. Even more curious, the La Porte court could not appoint Braje as a public defender for a South Carolina resident. Freeman or a benefactor would have to be paying his reputed high fees.

Nevertheless, Braje became the conduit for Williamson's communications with Freeman. By June 2008, the state trooper had asked the lawyer for Eric to take a polygraph in the York County sheriff's office and provide cheek swabs to see if he was linked to the unidentified male DNA on Rayna's purse. Surprisingly, Braje agreed for Freeman to take the polygraph as long as the examiner didn't ask follow-up questions, and he gave his okay for the sheriff to collect the swabs at that time. Like Matt Elser and Jason before him, Freeman took a Zone of Comparison polygraph with the relevant questions: "Did you see Rayna's dead body?" and "Did you see Rayna's dead body in the trunk of the car?" Like Matt and Jason, Eric failed.[171]

LULL

In the weeks following Rickey Hammons's pole barn epiphany, Airy and Williamson pursued their investigation at a torrid pace. Once they served the warrant on Jason for his major case prints and a DNA swab, they conducted fourteen interviews in the next six weeks. They zeroed in on Jason's mutual friends with Rayna, finding most had hazy memories of events that transpired fifteen years ago. Some completely forgot what they told the police in the days after Rayna disappeared. Airy also tracked down the tips in 1993 and 1994 that pointed toward Jason—even talking to Leslie's sister after hearing an erroneous rumor from Bennie Rison that Leslie said something to her about the murder that incriminated her husband. The sister scolded Airy for calling her, and Leslie followed up with a voicemail asking him to talk directly to her if he had any questions about what she said to her family.[172]

In November, Williamson and Airy traveled to Indianapolis to interview Matt Elser at his workplace. As Airy reported, Matt's comments mostly incriminated Ray. He repeated his accounts about Rayna's PTSD "fits" that he thought were related to McCarty's abuse and her complaints that Ray was assaulting her again, which she made a few days before her disappearance. Although Elser said he didn't trust Jason then, Matt confirmed to the detectives that Rayna wanted to visit Tibbs and considered him a friend.[173]

In the first two months of 2009, Airy delved into other testimony against Ray to see if there was a way to turn it against Jason or make it conform to the pole barn story. He started with the eyewitnesses who saw Rayna's abduction from the Pine Lake Animal Hospital. The detective also spoke to those who later spotted her LTD and Ray's Datsun in the northern part of the county. He showed them the Hammonses' Buick Century and asked if the big gray sedan could have been the car they saw in the parking lot—not the midsized, rust-spotted blue Datsun.

No doubt, Rene Gazarkiewicz was most frustrating for him. When she first passed the parking lot shortly after 6:00 P.M. on March 26, she saw Rayna leaning halfway inside Ray's car. After Rene picked up a pack of cigarettes, she got a second look at the Datsun as she drove home. When Airy interviewed her fifteen years later, Rene still had unshakable memories about the station wagon's color, the rust at the bottom of the passenger side door, and the wheels without hubcaps. In other words, a car that looked nothing like the gray Buick Century sedan.

But Airy soon discovered a way to blot out her inconvenient testimony. After Rayna's abduction, in their desperation to learn her whereabouts or find her abductor, La Porte police sent eyewitnesses like Rene to a retired Michigan City cop who practiced hypnosis. The hypnotist did not glean much more information from Gazarkiewicz during his session, but anything she did say while under the trance could be blocked from evidence by a judge since the technique has been known to induce false memories.[174]

Airy could not use hypnosis sessions to edit the memories of the York family. Beth and her two sons lived around the corner from where Rayna's car was abandoned on North 200 East. They provided two pieces of evidence that popped the plausibility of Rickey's story like a soap bubble. Most devastating was the time when they would have first seen Rayna's abandoned LTD. They knew it was at some point before 7:00 P.M. because the kids could still watch a few minutes of *Married . . . with Children*. If Jason and Eric had stopped at the Hammonses' pole barn and then returned to the animal hospital to pick up Rayna's car, they would have never made it to North 200 East by then. The Yorks also reported seeing a pickup parked behind the LTD—something Airy did not want to hear. During his interview with Beth, he mentioned that one of her sons thought the vehicle was a van. Referring to himself in the third person, he wrote in his report, "This detective then stated to Beth that it was possible then that it was a sedan and not a truck, and Beth advised that it was possible that it was a sedan, but she thought it was a truck." She added that her other son thought it was a truck too.

Although Beth and that son had been hypnotized, Airy could not use hypnosis to hide their testimony about the pickup.[175] The police had immediately released the news about the truck when the Yorks came forward, and it was many weeks before the two had their session with the hypnotist.

After meeting with the Yorks and probably realizing that he had to work with their truck sighting, Airy followed up with the Hammons family and learned they had a pickup on their property. It belonged to Tom Wiman, an old friend of Big Rickey who was staying in their basement bedroom while Freeman was sleeping in their living room. But there were problems with melding his vehicle into Little Rickey's story and the York family's sighting. First, the truck was a full-size, dark blue Ford F-150. It looked nothing like the smaller pickup that Beth remembered. Second, as even Little Rickey later told the detectives, Wiman hated Freeman—the two nearly got into a fistfight—and he would have never let Eric borrow his truck. But in response to that, Airy fixated on the idea that Freeman could have copied Wiman's key to drive the pickup without his permission.

The detective then embarked on a three-month phone odyssey to find Wiman and his truck, using insurance companies and police departments to track the two through Missouri and Arkansas. A convicted drug dealer, Wiman was not anxious to talk to a cop, but Airy convinced his brother that he only wanted information about the truck. Wiman then called back to confirm his contempt for Freeman and that "he would never let him borrow his truck." In any case, the pickup was later wrecked in an accident and junked by the insurance company. Airy still tried to find the truck by calling all the junkyards where the F-150 could have met its demise. He was finally told it had been crushed for recycling.[176]

A few months after Airy came up short on Wiman's truck, he and Williamson visited forensic pathologist Dr. Rick Hoover. As other detectives did before them, they tried to find answers to the autopsy's perplexing anomalies. Once again, Hoover asserted that Rayna was asphyxiated "due to cervical compression," even though her hyoid neck bone was not broken and there were no other signs of physical trauma. As for the isopropyl alcohol, his theories had now evolved in two questionable ways. First, "Isopropanol levels were low for ingestion, so . . . it would have not been enough to kill Rayna or for her to appear to be intoxicated." Hoover compounded this misinformation by adding he now believed isopropanol "levels were present only through decomposition." In 1993, he told detectives that he could find no research supporting this theory, and it was unlikely that he found any since.

But the detectives persisted with their questions, looking for more clarity than Hoover was willing to give. Airy asked if Rayna could have died of a heart attack, and Hoover answered that there was no "circumstantial evidence" to support that conclusion. Williamson wondered if she had been "accidentally smothered," but Hoover explained it would have taken three to five minutes of "cervical compression" to lose consciousness. Airy finally suggested drowning, and Hoover shot that down too.[177]

The detectives met with the forensic pathologist on September 2, 2009, which Airy summed up with three paragraphs in his supplement report. But then, in the next paragraph, he wrote, "After this detective and Detective Williamson met with Deputy Prosecutor Christopher Fronk in regard to presenting an immunity agreement to Craig Braje for Eric Freeman, this detective contacted Eric at [telephone number] on **3/19/13** to verify his address before the immunity agreement was presented to Mr. Braje."[178] (Italics and bold added.)

In one sentence, the detective's report leaped from 2009 to 2013, but Airy did not explain the yawning gap of four years in his investigation. He also did not report why the detectives felt the need for an immunity agreement, although he did confirm that Braje was still on the job for Freeman. As happened the first time around, the investigative case went cold for an extended period, and just like before, politics probably played a role in both the delay and the decision to proceed.

While Rickey Hammons emerged in 2008 with a story that could have vindicated Rob Beckman's decision to drop the charges against Ray McCarty, the sensational new witness presented the prosecutor with a Hobson's choice. No matter how tempting it was to put the Rison case behind him, Beckman was intimately familiar with the details of Hammons's crime and his behavior during the weeks that followed Cassidy's death. Beckman—often tagged as self-righteous by opponents—was not the kind to clear his name with the likes of Rickey Hammons or a shady immunity deal.

But in May 2010, in his bid for a fourth term, La Porte County's prosecuting-attorney-for-life was ousted in a stunning Democratic primary upset. The giant killer was Robert "Bob" Szilagyi, then sixty-one.[179] With a fringe of gray hair around his bald head, steel-rim glasses, and a gray mustache, Szilagyi could have been mistaken for a kindly neighborhood grocer. However, his bitter rivalry with Beckman dated back to the days when both were junior La Porte County prosecutors. From the start of his campaign, Bob went after Rob with both barrels blazing. His first line of attack was Beckman's support for the legalization of marijuana. After plucking a statement out of context ten years before, he charged that the incumbent wanted to make cocaine legal too.[180] When Beckman touted his successful drug prosecutions and referred to himself as the toughest "gunslinger" in the courtroom, Szilagyi shot back at him from the left, saying, "Beckman seems to want a reputation as a Western bully with a badge and a gun."[181] In a blow considered "below the belt" by other lawyers in the tight La Porte legal community, the challenger also focused on Beckman hiring his daughter as his deputy prosecutor after his son had served in that position.[182] Before the primary was over, Szilagyi went to an even more incendiary level, calling his opponent a racist because he once referred to a defendant as "a big black buck" during a murder trial and rehashing the incumbent's record of "threats and intimidation" that did not make him "fit to serve."[183]

Indeed, in the extrajudicial area of temperament, the longtime prosecutor was most vulnerable, and his behavior outside the courtroom probably proved his undoing. As he had been when Hedge fired him, Beckman was brutally honest about his personal travails, admitting he was moodier and less patient after his wife Jo's agonizing terminal illness in 2008. He told the press, "I was angry at the world for putting my wife through such misery." Beckman was most furious at a noisy construction project down the road from his family home where Jo spent her last days. He had fought bitterly to stop it and was caught on tape upbraiding a Michigan City officer attempting to police traffic in the area.[184] Worse yet, after a plan committee meeting on the project, he confronted a highway engineer and warned him that he had "an arsenal of weapons at his residence." The engineer claimed the prosecutor referred to a recent mass shooting and "vowed to make 'Virginia Tech look like nothing' at the next plan committee meeting."[185]

Despite Beckman's bad temper and all the resentments that had piled up against him in the three terms he served, the challenger could only squeak out a 400-vote victory in the primary.[186] Szilagyi had a much more solid win in the general election, beating an opponent Republicans scrambled to find when Beckman lost.

After the county clerk announced his election, the winner admitted to reporters, "I feel kind of numb at hearing this."[187] But with his hard-won office came the troublesome Rison cold case—the cat in the basement of his newly acquired house. Given the hard feelings with his predecessor, Bob was probably in no hurry to bail Rob out of the most dubious decision of his long tenure. Szilagyi would first need to appoint his own chief deputy prosecuting attorney, assign him to the case, and get him to review the voluminous documents and the associated convoluted evidence.

But early in his reign, Szilagyi, who ran as a paragon of virtue, had to confront a personal peccadillo that complicated any decision. During a contentious divorce before his election, he had forged his ex-wife's signature on a document to refinance what had been their family home. Szilagyi claimed to have done so with her permission. However, once she discovered what he did, his ex brought the forgery to the Indiana Supreme Court Disciplinary Commission (ISCDC) for a "disciplinary review."

The case only went downhill from there after the commission learned that Szilagyi used his secretary's stamp to notarize the application and did not receive her permission either. After a brief investigation, La Porte County's prosecuting attorney was suspended from practicing law for sixty days in an extraordinary reprimand. The humiliation was compounded by his ex-wife's civil suit and a criminal investigation requiring a special prosecutor that dragged on throughout his term of office.

As a result, by March 2013, when asked to consider an immunity agreement for Eric Freeman, Szilagyi was in a vulnerable position. The Democratic primary was just a year away. A formidable opponent was already on the horizon who Szilagyi believed was funding his ex-wife's lawsuit.[188] He needed a massive distraction and a Hail Mary touchdown pass like a break in a notorious cold case if he had a prayer of winning the primary. Although the McCarty indictment had not saved Cynthia Hedge, this time around, the State would have Rayna's family on its side. From a political perspective, it was a no-brainer for Szilagyi to dominate the headlines by arresting a new prime suspect. (He still ended up losing the primary in a landslide.[189])

For Jason Tibbs, there was a deceptive five-year lull after the State took his major case prints and DNA swab. It seemed like the Rison investigation had finally left him behind. Meanwhile, his family and work lives had come together in ways he could have never imagined.

When Leslie found work managing a local Arby's, she and Jason hoped at best that the job would make up the difference from his reduced salary after Teledyne fired him. Instead, it was an introduction to a thriving family business that would pull the couple on board as it rapidly expanded. In managing a tiny Arby's outlet, Leslie had to focus on expenses as much as sales. When minor electrical and plumbing repairs were needed, she'd ask Jason to stop in to make them after he finished his shift repairing trucks. It could mean rewiring a heat lamp or toaster, maybe welding broken parts back together. With management permission, his pay was a milkshake and roast beef sandwich.

Word of Jason's acumen spread through the company, and when a cooler went down at the family's liquor store, which also housed the firm's administrative office, Jason went in to try his hand. He had not been trained to fix the broken part but had no fear about looking through manuals or calling the manufacturer for help. Standing in the aisle as he thumbed through diagrams, he felt a punch in the shoulder and heard, 'Get out of the way.' He turned to see a short, older man with a deep tan, a full head of brushed-back silver hair, and a neatly trimmed mustache. "He wore something like a floral silk shirt and khaki pants," Jason remembers. "He was very well put together, but nothing too flashy. At first, I was a little cross, thinking, 'Why is this guy hitting me?' But he had a twinkle in his eye with a little smile, and you could tell he was joking. Then he asked, 'What are you doing?' I told him, 'I'm trying to fix this damn thing,' and he said, 'Let me know if you need any pointers.'"

Before long, sixty-three-year-old Jim Bruno, founder and CEO of Bruno Enterprises, was on the floor with Jason, poring through the diagrams. A high school graduate who started employment as a steelworker, Bruno saved money to have a few small shops on the side. Eventually, he and his wife, Nancy, realized they were best suited to the restaurant business, first with a supper club and then a rapidly expanding portfolio of fast-food outlets that included Arby's, Pizza Hut, Dunkin' Donuts, Baskin-Robbins, and Brown's Chicken. His investment in several Buffalo Wild Wings restaurants across the country played a role when Arby's merged with the chain in a multibillion-dollar deal.[190]

In January 2009, Jim's son-in-law, Paul Delrio, who served as Bruno's vice president for operations, called Jason to see if he'd work for them full-time. They had added thirteen more units to their restaurant portfolio and would have more than enough repairs to keep Jason busy. In time, Jason would become the company's director of maintenance.

Although they seemed at opposite ends of the org chart, Jason still had plenty of face time with Jim, who was happy to share the keys to his success in the franchise business. "He told me he was always looking at the percentages," Jason says. "When he considered buying a property, he had goals for each cost area against the revenues." In the beginning, Bruno did many repairs himself to lower his expenses, and he remained in touch with the nuts and bolts even as he expanded his empire.

Jim found a can-do kindred spirit in Jason as his chief DIY officer. At times, Jason had to call in an outside expert—but he knew he had the boss's approval if he met certain conditions. "Pay attention when they show up," Bruno instructed Jason. "If you learn how they did it, I don't have to pay them again." The CEO would add, "Then tell me, and we'll both know."

After a while, Jason's mandate expanded beyond the stores. "Jason could fix anything," Jim's daughter, Jennifer Delrio, says. "If an employee told us they had a problem with a washing machine or hot water heater, we'd send Jason to fix it."[191]

Like other Bruno staff, Jason and Leslie soon discovered they had also joined the family. This meant barbecues and birthday parties at Jim's house. The young couple became close friends with Jennifer and Paul, who were about the same age and had a young child. They would all drive to Chicago for kid shows or the zoo and dinner afterward at the Rainforest Café.

While Paul was officially his superior, Jason took him under his wing to introduce the "city boy" to rural recreation. "He was the kind of guy who always looked like he came off the cover of *GQ* magazine," Jason remembers. "I got him to put on some jeans and boots and his work shirt to go four-wheeling through the mud. In the winter, we did snowmobiles."

Still, for Jason, nothing about his job or social life was more cherished than his relationship with Jim. "I had the utmost respect for him," he says, "and he made a big impact on my life."

Bruno died in 2022, but Jennifer attests that the feeling between her father and Tibbs was mutual. "Dad treated Jason like a son," she says.[192]

Yet, early in their relationship, Jim's trust in Jason was tested by a phone call from a former employee. Afterward, Bruno asked Jason into his office, saying, "I just heard something important, and I want you to answer honestly." The day before, Jason had spent thirteen dollars on the company credit card to replace a toolbox he had broken. He hadn't written it up yet in his expenses. Sometimes, details like that didn't escape Bruno's notice, and Jason thought the boss wanted to discuss it. Instead, Jim told him that an individual who had worked for him in school had become a La Porte detective. He called to say Bruno should fire Jason because "he was bad" and had two warrants out for his arrest—one for theft and the other for murder. "It caught me completely off guard," Jason remembers. "I said, 'Jim, that's some old bullshit. I can't believe they keep bringing it up.'"

Bruno replied, "Just find out what he's talking about. If you need anything, call me, and I'll help you take care of it."

Over the next three days, Jason made multiple trips to the clerk's office at the county courthouse to see if there were any outstanding warrants for his arrest. Nothing could be found. Finally, a secretary took pity on him and said she'd give him a printout as long as he wouldn't tell where he got it. The warrant was for the nickel case. From what he could see, the detectives had held off on the arrests until they could locate all three individuals indicted. Jason called Leslie to join him and bring his wallet back home. He then walked down to the bailiff stationed by the courthouse entrance. "I handed him the printout and asked him to get Airy," Jason says. "He laughed and said, 'This is a new one on me. Nobody turns themselves in.'"

When Airy arrived, Jason was outside the courthouse door smoking a cigarette with the bailiff and Leslie. The detective's partner had been with him outside Drayton's office and was the former employee who called Jim. "I could see Airy was all pissed off," Jason says. "He probably wanted to make a big spectacle about arresting me at the Bruno offices."

Although they were only a few yards from the county jail, Airy insisted on handcuffing Tibbs. "I had hurt my shoulder a few days before and told him I couldn't put that arm behind my back, but Airy started clipping on the cuffs. Then, according to Jason, the bailiff said, "'What are you doing that for? He's not going to run. He's been waiting for you.' Airy told him to mind his own business, and he'd conduct the arrest the way he wanted."

But as the detectives marched Jason to the jail, the bailiff followed behind. Once Jason entered the county facility and was no longer in the custody of the police, the bailiff had Airy's partner take the handcuffs off immediately. After the detectives left, he turned toward Jason and said, "I don't know what you did to those guys, but they sure have an attitude about you."

Airy's nickel investigation would soon be doomed by the discombobulated answers the accuser gave during a deposition conducted by Josh Jordan's lawyer. Still, the indictment continued to drag through the court. Jason could no longer turn to attorney Mike Drayton for help. He had his hands full representing Prosecuting Attorney Szilagyi in the various cases brought by the ex-wife and had stopped working on criminal defense cases.[193] Tibbs tried a Michigan City lawyer who, it seemed, could never make any progress. At last, he turned the case over to Scott Pejic, an ambitious young attorney specializing in drunk driving defense who wanted more experience in other criminal cases. Jason met him through a friend and did a few repairs at his house. Tall, with chipmunk cheeks and a clean part through his preppy haircut, Pejic was perpetually polite and pleasant in a way that appealed to Jason and Leslie. He did not brush off the nickel theft like the other lawyer and quickly returned their calls. Although Pejic actively pursued a resolution, Jason had no interest in taking a plea, and Airy and the prosecutor did not want to let go. Finally, in June of 2012, the judge dismissed the case without prejudice—meaning he could open it again if new evidence were uncovered.[194] While a *"with* prejudice" would have been a far more satisfying outcome, the Tibbses had no complaints about Pejic or his diligence.

As far as Jason was concerned after the nickel case was dismissed, he had escaped Airy's clutches and left his legal travails behind. He had no idea he was still a target in the Rison investigation. That is, until his arrest on a balmy Friday morning in August 2013.

As Jason rode back to the county courthouse complex in a squad car, he ticked off who he had to call with the few minutes left on his cell phone battery. First would be Leslie, but he wanted someone to represent him at the arraignment, which an officer told him would happen as soon as he was processed.

Once he arrived and the cuffs were off, he saw Scott Pejic in his recent call list. When he reached out, the affable attorney promised to race to the courthouse to help him get through the arraignment and see what the State had against him in the probable cause affidavit for his arrest. Although Jason liked Scott, he had asked Leslie to follow up with Mike Drayton to serve as his trial lawyer. He had extensive experience defending clients in notorious murder cases and was wired with the county's legal establishment to get fair treatment from the prosecution and the judge. However, when Leslie called, Drayton said a homicide defense required a $50,000 retainer. "That may seem like a lot of money," Drayton explains, "but I never made money on homicide cases. If done right, they're incredibly time-consuming."

Meanwhile, after Pejic left the jail, he called Leslie to say he could represent Jason. The young lawyer was so anxious to cut his teeth on a big homicide case that he did not require a retainer. He also promised to bring in an experienced, well-regarded attorney from Indianapolis as the lead attorney.

"I think Scott's offer had a big impact on Leslie," Jason says. "She wasn't thinking about his experience. She was thinking about the money side because she had the kids and no help paying the bills with me in jail. Besides, as far as we were concerned, Scott did a good job on the nickel case. From what she heard, he was the only lawyer willing to work with me without an upfront payment."

But the couple never had a chance to discuss the momentous decision before Leslie hired Pejic. Over the weekend, the county kept Jason in a holding cell under the courthouse with no access to a phone. By the time they talked on Monday, Pejic had been hired.

However, there was something Leslie did not tell Jason. She met with Jim Bruno and Jennifer Delrio the day after Jason was arrested. "Leslie was in a panic and wanted to hire a lawyer in the worst way," Jennifer remembers. "We said we'd give her a loan for all the legal fees, but when he saw how much that would be, my dad took it over. I told her, 'It is really important for you to interview several attorneys. You can't just hire anybody for a murder case.' We had a list of lawyers from Illinois and Indiana to call. But she did not do what I asked and hired this guy who represented Jason in some comparatively minor stuff. Maybe later, Jason said that was fine because he didn't know we were involved. We would have hired a much better attorney for him, but there was nothing we could do. It was Leslie's decision."

In time, Leslie's choice of a lawyer was not the only thing she did that disturbed Delrio and her parents. Jennifer says, "I don't think Jason was in jail two months before she started dating another man."[195] She quit from Bruno Enterprises soon after.

THE CASE AGAINST JASON TIBBS

RAYNA RISON

FAMILY
- Bennie, Karen (parents)
- Lori, Wendy (sisters)

FRIENDS AND COWORKERS
- Matt Elser
- Lisa Dyer
- Cheryl VanSchoyck

CITY OF LA PORTE POLICE DEPARTMENT
- Detective Brett Airy
- Detectives John Miller, Bob Schoff, Harold Hahn (retired)

MICHIGAN CITY POLICE DEPARTMENT
- Detective Mark Lachmund

LA PORTE COUNTY
- Circuit Court Judge Thomas Alevizos*
- Prosecuting Attorneys Cynthia Hedge; Rob Beckman
- Chief Deputies Scott Duerring; Christopher Fronk
- Sheriff's Deputies Mark Ludlow* (retired); Jim Jackson (retired)
- Dr. Rick Hoover, Forensic Pathologist

JASON TIBBS

FAMILY
- Rachel (mother)
- Leslie (wife, ex-wife)

LAWYERS
- John Tompkins*
- Scott Pejic

FRIENDS AND COWORKERS
- Josh Jordan
- Jim, Nancy Bruno; daughter Jennifer Delrio (employers)

FBI
- Douglas Deedrick, Trace Evidence Analyst
- Elvin "Bill" Keith

INDIANA STATE POLICE
- Sergeant Al Williamson
- Sergeant Arland Boyd (retired)

*INTRODUCED IN THIS CHAPTER

LORI AND RAY McCARTY

FAMILY
- Adrienne (daughter)
- Hunter (son)

CIVILIAN WITNESSES FROM 1ST INVESTIGATION
- Beth York; sons Kyle, Austin
- Rene Gazarkiewicz
- Lorn "Brent" Glassman
- Val Eilers
- Roy West
- Bryan Durham
- Vic Montorsi
- Angie Vogel
- Misty Smith, Jamie Swisher (sisters); Peggy Johnson (mother)
- Chad Green
- James Amor

CIVILIAN WITNESSES FROM 2ND INVESTIGATION
- Patricia Umphrey*; Lonnie Garner (son)*
- Tracy Manns* (McWhirter's daughter)
- Rickey J. Hammons Jr.
- Jen Hammons
- Eric Freeman
- Mike Keeling

THE CASE AGAINST JASON TIBBS

THE SLAM DUNK DEFENSE

In American jurisprudence, there is no charge as binary as homicide. While thin lines separate the type of murder—say, manslaughter versus first-degree or second-degree—the verdict still boils down to whether the defendant took another person's life. With Rayna Rison, the evidence that her brother-in-law killed her is incontrovertible. Jason Tibbs has the misfortune of showing how the flaws in his county's justice system could permit an innocent person to be convicted of that crime. A combination of factors had to converge. They started with a judge, perhaps biased, who blocked critical evidence from the jury. Compounding his decisions were questionable tactics by the prosecutor and his investigators. Some bordered on the edges of professional propriety and even legality—especially regarding the treatment of key witnesses and exculpatory evidence hidden from the defense. Despite all those obstacles, an acquittal should have been possible, if not for Jason's team of bungling, overconfident attorneys.

The first time Jason heard about John L. Tompkins was from his mother, Rachel. He was the experienced trial lawyer from Indianapolis that Scott Pejic promised to bring on the team. Rachel was very impressed when she saw on the web that he was designated as a Super Lawyer [a certification bestowed by peers and licensed by the designees], and then even more impressed by his record and competence when she spoke to him and Scott on the phone. "I have a really good feeling about John," she told her son.

Jason met Tompkins in the conference room the jail provided for attorney conferences. It had one door for inmates and another for lawyers to enter from the public area. Jason remembers Tompkins, then fifty, bounding into the room with Pejic following behind. "He was a bundle of energy and positivity." Just five feet tall, Tompkins had the sculpted broad shoulders of a weight lifter. He wore a suit and a porkpie hat, a personal trademark, with a shaved, bald head underneath and gold steel-rimmed glasses. An infantry captain in the army, he maintained the bulldog demeanor that would have helped him prosper in the military. Although much taller than Tompkins, Pejic slunk into the background. "Tompkins took command of the room," Jason says. "He told me, 'This is what we're going to do and what we have to do.'"

With the arrest papers in his hand, he proceeded to pick apart the probable cause, sneering at the amateurs they were up against. "You're not even being charged properly," he explained. "You should be charged with manslaughter and not murder. The case is just a witch hunt, and we can show these charges are demonstrably false.'"

Jason had questions about whether he could get out on bond, but Tompkins quickly shut them down. "He told me, 'We won't approach bond now.' It was the end of the discussion, but I took that in stride. He seemed to know what he was doing."

At some point during the meeting, Jason remembers Tompkins saying, "This is a slam dunk case. If I were you, I wouldn't worry about this."

As the months passed, Pejic was the one who usually showed up to talk, get paperwork, and ask questions as many as three times a week. Often, they spoke through the thick glass teller-like windows in the visitors' room. When Tompkins came, the lawyers booked the conference room. "John would sit there and go through the evidence," Jason remembers. "He couldn't believe all the stuff we had, and he'd say, 'It's just a matter of time before you're home.'"

Although everything about Tompkins's manner instilled confidence, Jason had concerns about the defense strategy they described. "Their focus was on Ray: show that he was arrested, show he had the motive to kill Rayna, show how he kept lying about where he was at on March 26. I tried to tell them we needed to focus on my alibi—where I was at and what time I was there. But they were so convinced McCarty did it. They weren't worried about showing I *didn't* do it."

In January 2014, nearly five months after Jason's arrest, the circuit court judge, Thomas Alevizos, held his bond hearing—which became a little preview of the upcoming trial. In Indiana, homicide defendants are seldom released, no matter how high the bond. Tompkins and Pejic did not let Jason get his hopes up, but it was an effort Jim Bruno wanted them to make, and since he was paying their bills, they complied. Tibbs explains, "Jim was going to do whatever it took to get me home and care for my family."

As expected, Alevizos did not set a bond, but Jason's lawyers did not see the hearing as a total loss. "They told me it allowed us to see their hand," he says, "and they were not impressed." Detective Airy had to take the stand and appeared shaky when asked whether it was "impossible" for Jason to do the things charged by Freeman and Hammons in a "time frame" set by other witnesses. It also got headlines in the press like, "Former suspect's alibis were faulty." Airy admitted he had not followed up on all the evidence incriminating Ray McCarty.[1]

However, red flags did appear in the hearing that should have been of more concern to the defense counsel. Deputy Prosecuting Attorney Fronk featured testimony from a woman Jason barely knew who came forward after his arrest, claiming he had confessed to her that he strangled Rayna. The prosecutor also mentioned some of Jason's alibi witnesses who, understandably, could no longer remember what happened on that Friday night twenty years ago. But all of them had been clear about Jason's whereabouts when interviewed by the police in 1993.[2]

According to Jason, the one witness during the hearing who made the biggest impression was Jim Bruno. According to an account from one local paper, "Bruno said Tibbs was his maintenance supervisor and a trusted employee who even had keys and the code for an alarm to Bruno's home in La Porte. He said customers and employees have never complained about Tibbs."

On the stand, Bruno recounted the call from Airy's partner, who had once worked at one of his franchise restaurants, and told him to fire Jason because he murdered Rayna "and the police were going to get him." Jim said Jason denied it when he talked to him, and that was all he had to hear.

According to the article, Bruno said, "Tibbs is not a threat and, if released, he would allow Tibbs to continue working for him. Bruno said he would call the court if Tibbs was released and violated any conditions. 'I'm not going to let him break the law,' said Bruno."[3]

Perhaps smarting because Jim pushed them into the hearing, the lawyers let Jason know they were not happy with his testimony. "He told the judge that he would pay the bond whatever the amount," Jason recalls. "The lawyers didn't like that. It looked like I had access to too much money, which wouldn't look good to a future juror."

Besides financial support, Jim and his wife Nancy were also there for moral support. They visited Jason twice in jail. He mostly stayed connected over the phone weekly with the couple, their daughter Jennifer, and office staff. "Sometimes I called Jim's cell phone just to check in and see what's going on," Jason says.

"We definitely got some customer backlash for supporting Jason," Jennifer remembers. "Even from some of the people who work in our stores. But that wasn't going to stop my dad from helping him."[4]

RULING OUT THE EVIDENCE

B uilt in the 1890s with eye-catching red sandstone, the Romanesque county courthouse is still the most prominent edifice on the City of La Porte skyline. The third-floor courtroom that became a chamber of horrors for Jason is an object of local civic pride and is considered among Indiana's most architecturally distinguished halls of justice. With its high arching, stained glass windows, cathedral ceilings, and scrolled, dark wood moldings, the La Porte Circuit Courtroom appeared as much a church as a legal venue. The light shines through Roman-style goddesses in flowing robes or geometric patterns painted on crystalline facets. Dominating the back of the room, an almost life-size Goddess Justitia—the personification of divine law—emerges from a rosy penumbra, with eyes pointing to the heavens and a voluminous open tome in her arms.[5]

Presiding from on high in this jewel-box court, more potentate than priest, was Judge Thomas Alevizos. At fifty-three, with glasses and a Humpty-Dumpty bald head, he could look down on the lawyers and their clients as either a benign, smiling presence or a snarling Louie De Palma in his *Taxi* dispatch cage. He spoke openly about his struggles with diabetes and kept courtroom staff on edge with updates about his medical condition and diet. One attorney who frequently appears before Alevizos says, "I always try to find the bailiff first to see if the judge has had breakfast. If not, I try to schedule for another day."[6]

Before his election to the bench in 2006, Alevizos had been a fixture in the Michigan City Democratic party and county legal circles. He served on the city council and then the Indiana House of Representatives for three terms until he announced he was running for La Porte county prosecutor to unseat Cynthia Hedge.[7] A few weeks later, Rob Beckman joined the race, and Alevizos eventually backed out, telling a reporter "he had a good relationship" with Beckman.[8] They were both on the same page regarding the issues and personalities involved with the office. Like Beckman, Alevizos criticized Hedge for putting too many full-time prosecutors on the payroll. He also criticized her for hiring deputies who lived outside the county—a shot at chief deputy Scott Duerring, a longtime resident of Porter.[9]

Once Beckman won the election, the "good relationship" paid dividends for Alevizos. The former state rep was among the first deputies Beckman hired. On paper, Alevizos was well qualified for the job. He had served three years as a deputy prosecutor before running for the state legislature. During his tenure in Indianapolis, he focused on committees related to law enforcement.[10]

Then, seven years later, one good turn deserved another when Alevizos was elected to preside over the court where the county waged its most high-profile battles.[11] Unlike his predecessor, the new judge did not lock horns with Beckman. Despite the prickly sides they could show others, the judge and the prosecutor appeared to work well together until Beckman's shocking defeat.[12]

Even though Beckman was no longer in office, the judge did not forget his old friend's griefs and grudges when the Tibbs trial fell into his lap. Alevizos could not hide his contempt for Hedge's case against Ray McCarty. "There is nothing to that indictment," he said at one point, dismissing the grand jury's verdict. Citing an old adage about how easy it is for prosecutors to manipulate those panels, he said, "You can indict a ham sandwich [with a grand jury]."[13] He also suggested the previous prosecutors' "motive" for indicting Ray was winning the upcoming election.[14]

But the judge did more than express his opinions in sidebars. Five days before the trial started, he held the motions in limine hearing, which determined the evidence to be presented to jurors. After hearing arguments from each side, he later ruled that the defense counsel could not reference Ray's arrest or indictment or even mention the words "grand jury" during the trial.[15] It was a shocking development for Tompkins and Pejic, who argued they had a compelling case for "third-party guilt"—that McCarty and not Jason was the real killer. But in response, Alevizos disparaged the grand jury indictment as no more than the "opinion" of "six people."[16] He referred to the upcoming election in 1998 as more of an incentive for Cynthia Hedge than McCarty's guilt.[17] While Ray's conviction for child molestation could not be disputed, Alevizos believed his indictment for murder should not be used against him. As he later instructed the lawyers during the trial, "If you have specific evidence within the rules of evidence that you can link up to this case that points towards Mr. McCarty's guilt, you can bring that in."[18] But if the State's two key witnesses—Hammons and Freeman—concocted their testimony to convict Jason, how could any of that be tied to McCarty?

The only option that Jason's lawyers had for fighting against the judge's rulings on evidence was to conduct an offer of proof hearing outside the jurors' presence. These procedures were unlikely to change Alevizos's mind, but they preserved the record for appellate courts that could use the judge's decisions as the basis for overturning a conviction.

STAR WITNESSES

On October 29, 2014, Judge Thomas Alevizos opened Jason's trial with standard instructions for the jury about maintaining confidentiality, refraining from conversations with outsiders, or conducting independent research. He then solemnly intoned the reason they were all gathered in La Porte's ornate courtroom:

> This is a criminal case brought by the State of Indiana against the defendant, Jason Tibbs. The case was commenced when an information was filed charging the defendant with murder, a felony. That information, omitting the formal parts, reads as follows:

STAR WITNESSES

> Detective Brett Airy, being duly sworn upon his oath, says that on or about the 26th day of March 1993, in the County of La Porte, State of Indiana, one, Jason Tibbs, did unlawfully, knowingly, or intentionally kill another human being, to wit, Rayna Rison, by choking or strangling her causing her to die.

A few minutes later, he added the obligatory admonition that Tibbs was still innocent until proven guilty. "The fact that a charge has been filed and that the defendant was arrested and brought to trial is not to be considered by you as any evidence of guilt. . . . The burden is upon the State to prove beyond a reasonable doubt that the defendant is guilty of the crime. It is a strict and heavy burden."

But to a great extent, Jason's guilt had already been decided in the press. The trial became an object of regional fascination. Chicago TV stations, which usually ignored events south of the state's border, turned out in force, as did those from South Bend, Northwestern Indiana's biggest market.

On that first day, the media attention did not seem to faze Jason's lawyers, who brimmed with confidence. Scott Pejic's family included a few attorneys, and they attended to watch their young scion perform in a high-profile proceeding. They sat near Jason's mother, Rachel. Wearing a dark suit, Jason was ushered in by court officers before the jury or the judge appeared. He was impressed by the preparations made around the defense table. "They had stacks of color-coded files," he remembers, "and paralegals to run back and forth to the parking lot where they had a van full of them. They had two legal pads for me and all these instructions about how I should act, like leaving the top page clear and taking notes so it looked like I had questions and concerns about the testimony."

With a melodramatic opening line, Christopher Fronk, La Porte County's chief deputy prosecuting attorney, assumed his unaccustomed role in the media spotlight. He proclaimed to the jury, "If I can't have her, nobody can." He then explained, "That's the reason this defendant gave to Eric Freeman when Freeman asked why he was looking at the body of a sixteen-year [-old] girl in the trunk of his car. If I can't have [her], nobody can. That's the reason this defendant gave for strangling Rayna Lynn Rison to death, physically choking the life out of her, and then dumping her body into a rural pond in La Porte County."[19]

255

As Fronk expected, "If I can't have her, nobody can" became the headline or first line for much of that day's press coverage.[20] But the actual origin of the quote is in question for anyone familiar with the second investigation of Rayna Rison's homicide. As with most of his case, the prosecutor exercised considerable artistic license to tell the State's version of Rayna's murder.

One part of the emotional appeal to the jury in his opening remarks was real—Jason's love letter that the Rison family turned over to the police after Rayna's abduction. (Fronk did not mention Matt Elser's equally overwrought letter, which the detectives had to discover on their own after they asked to search the victim's room. [21])According to Fronk, using more artistic license, "The defendant professed his love for Rayna and asked Rayna to be done with Matt."[22] Of course, the letter repeatedly states that Jason wants her to get back with him only if she is no longer happy with Matt.

His other opening remarks offered a preview of the State's case that would have surprised detectives from the first investigation. While it featured some witnesses they had interviewed, Fronk made it sound like their testimony would diverge radically from things they said twenty-one years before, especially those who had provided Jason with an alibi. Supposed new testimony incriminating Jason related to Matt Elser's letterman jacket and the gaudy ring Jason gave to Rayna. As far as old evidence was concerned, Dr. Rick Hoover, the forensic pathologist who frustrated detectives and prosecutors in 1993, had become more definitive after two decades, ready to testify that "Rayna had been strangled."[23]

Most surprising for anyone previously involved with the investigation was the new hero in the cold case—Rickey Hammons. As Fronk admitted, he was "a convicted murderer but someone who has never asked for anything in return for his testimony nor has he been promised anything" (a claim that would later be disputed, but long after the verdict). Moreover, Fronk declared Hammons was risking life and limb to testify. "Point in fact," he told the jurors. "In prison, if you cooperate with law enforcement, you're labeled a snitch, and that could [have] serious consequences. . . . Snitches get stitches."[24]

Although nowhere as noble as Hammons in Fronk's pantheon, Eric Freeman was another exemplar of the truth the jury needed to heed. While he supposedly did lie when police first interviewed him in 2008 and needed a 2013 immunity agreement before he fully disclosed his participation in Rayna's homicide, he was now being "honest" to hold up his end of the bargain. "You know," Fronk conceded, Freeman's "memory had faded some over those twenty years by the time he gave his statement in 2013, but there are two particular slides that are crystal clear in Eric's memory: the defendant choking Rayna Rison to death on March 26th of 1993, and then the two of them throwing her body into the pond where it would lie for a month."[25]

When it came time for Tompkins to reply to Fronk's prolonged opening pathos, he proved sharp and pointed—every bit the experienced trial attorney who could hold a jury in the palm of his hand. "That was a good story," he began. "The problem is it's not true. . . . The State and their story have a huge fatal flaw. The State's inspiration of all you heard, all you heard, is Rickey Hammons . . . a professional liar."

But while trying to focus on Hammons's credibility, Tompkins exposed a fatal flaw in the defense strategy. In speaking about Rickey's criminal past, the attorney told the jury, "Now, he didn't become a murderer until '98, '99. He lied then. Lied to the police."[26] But the jury would not hear precisely how he lied because Fronk objected. In a sidebar, the prosecutor complained that Tompkins was about to tell the jury "that [Hammons] lied to the police during the course of [his] murder investigation." In the motions in limine hearing, Judge Alevizos determined the unsavory details of Hammons's behavior should not be revealed, and the defense could not figure a way around that ruling—unaware of how reprehensible that behavior was.[27]

When Tompkins returned to his opening remarks, Alevizos did permit him to deride the Hammons pole barn story that would comprise most of Rickey's upcoming testimony. "It's a sophisticated lie; it's a good lie," he told the jury. "You know what I'd say a good lie is? . . . It's hard to catch. The evidence will show you this lie is hard to catch. . . . [It doesn't have] too much detail. It doesn't depend on anybody else corroborating [it]."

He next attacked Freeman as another type of liar—a scared one. "[He's] scared of not being on the police team, scared that Jason is going to try to hang this on him. The only evidence that you're going to hear from him, the only testimony . . . is what the police tell him. . . . His story is impossible. He talks about when and where and driving to different places. If you take the times and the facts that come in that Mr. Fronk talked about, when the coworker left work, and what time that was, and you compare it to Eric's story, it's impossible." Carrying on with that theme, Tompkins questioned Freeman's account of Rayna's "disposal" and abandonment of her car afterward as equally implausible. "One of the biggest things you'll notice about his story is the complete unbelievability of how it ends."

As for the State's other witnesses, Tompkins characterized them as liars too, but "paving to hell with their good intentions. These people, twenty years later, understandably may be confused, understandably may not get some things right, and they may get other things right, [and] may not be able to tell a full story completely accurately."

Having dispensed with the State's case, Tompkins turned to the heart of Jason's defense. "We believe the true story that this evidence will take you to points to another suspect. A man who admitted he molested Rayna when she was twelve, a man who got off probation for that crime a couple of months before she disappeared, a man who lied to the police about where he was while he knew the police were looking for her, hadn't found her yet, and a man who lied to the police about where he was when she disappeared after they found her body. That man was never tried. That man was her brother-in-law." Tompkins promised to show the evidence incriminating Ray McCarty was more plausible if the jury "tested" it against the State's evidence in Jason's indictment.

Finally, Tompkins would not let Fronk's dramatic reading become the last word in Jason's love letters to Rayna. "Listen to what Mr. Fronk said out of those letters," he implored the jurors. He then paraphrased the gist of young Jason's sentiments. "I want to go back out with you. That requires a future. I understand why you broke up with me. You made me feel secure. Why would you want to kill that person? I know you love Matt. I will protect you. That's not I-will-kill-you language."

Regarding the day's headline, Tompkins argued, "'If anything happens between you and Matt, give me a chance.' Jason's words. 'If I can't have you, nobody can.' [Those are] Eric Freeman's words, not Jason Tibbs's."[28]

After a break, the jury was introduced to the State's first witness, Eric M. Freeman. Jason and his lawyers had never figured out why he wanted to participate in the case against Tibbs. The two had some tiffs as teens, but nothing that should have motivated him to make such a grievous accusation against Jason or risk pretending to be his accomplice in a murder. It may have been Jason's wishful thinking, but when Eric took the stand, Jason says, "He seemed like he didn't want to be there." He had gained weight since Tibbs saw him last, and his hair had started receding, but he was still very recognizable. What had changed was his attitude. The angry edginess was gone. "He never looked at me. His eyes were shifting around everywhere else, and when the lawyers asked him a question, he seemed unsure and timid—like he was afraid of giving the wrong answer."

Freeman started by providing indisputable background information about how he showed up at La Porte High School for his senior year and met Jason when he began playing Fox Hunt after graduation. At the time, he was dating Jen Hammons and living in her family's home.

But soon, in ways that became increasingly glaring for Tibbs, he added embellishments that strayed further and further from the truth. Among the first lies that stood out was his claim that he saw Rayna playing Fox Hunt "a handful of times."[29] Although she expressed an interest in it, as far as Jason and Matt knew, she never played.[30]

But then his testimony veered much further from what Jason knew to be the truth. Jason remembered no interaction with Freeman of any kind on March 26. Instead, in the early evening, he was heading over to the trailer park—at the time when Rayna was abducted—so his friend James Amor could meet a cute girl. But on the stand, Freeman claimed that Jason used a CB radio to call him, asking for a ride. He said he heard the request on the Hammonses' "base station" inside their home.

Freeman testified that he "hopped in" Jen's silver 1986 Buick Century, picked Jason up at his home, and took him to the Pine Lake Animal Hospital.[31] In his police interviews, he at first said he dropped him off. Later, he claimed he sat in the Buick as the two had an uneventful conversation before they got inside. But during the trial, he testified, "They started arguing." After they got in the Buick, "They were arguing a lot more, and I was asked to pull over, and they started arguing more and more outside the vehicle."

The spot where this happened was also transformed since his last interviews from a vague intersection on Fail Road to "a cut out that had a little gravel in it." At the trial, for the first time, Freeman remembered "numerous cars had gone by" when he got out of the car and asked Jason and Rayna to get back inside. Fronk asked, "What happened next?"

Freeman replied, "They were continuing to argue. Then I seen him hit her and everything. And then, as I turned back around, he was on top of her, choking her." He added that she was fighting back, but he did not interfere. Instead, he got into the front seat of the Buick and "popped the trunk" but did no more because he was in "panic mode."

After Jason "threw her in the trunk," they drove to the Hammonses' home and backed into the pole barn. He said they got out of the car and argued.

"What were you saying to Jason?" Fronk asked.

"[I was] asking him what in the hell he did and why—and what was going on."

"Did he answer?"

"Yes, he did," Freeman said.

"What was his answer?"

"If I can't have her, nobody can."

Freeman said Jason opened the trunk, but he never looked inside. Then he testified, "We ended up leaving shortly thereafter to get her vehicle."

When they arrived at the animal hospital parking lot, Jason "hopped" into the LTD, and Freeman followed him to the pond. They parked the vehicles, he said, on a dirt trail along the north side.

As to what happened next, Freeman and Fronk had the following exchange:

> Q. So you got to this location where there was room—to park two cars. What did you do?
> A. We popped the trunk and carried her out to the pond.
> Q. You didn't drag her?
> A. No.
> Q. You carried her?
> A. Yes.
> Q. Did you help?
> A. Yes.
> Q. How did you carry her?
> A. I had her legs, and Jason had her around her shoulders. . . .
> Q. And you have her feet, and Jason has her round her shoulders. What did you do?

A. We got down towards the pond and everything, and we—one, two, three, heaved.

Q. What happened when you did that?

A. She went in the water.

Q. How did she land?

A. Face down. . . .

Q. Did you notice anything else before you left?

A. I noticed Jason putting some logs on her to weigh her down.

Q. What drew your attention to that?

A. The splashing sound.

Freeman testified that they then parted ways, and he had no idea what Tibbs did with the LTD, but Jason showed up at the Hammonses' house later that evening driving his father's pickup.

"I started hollering at him and asked—just gave him the letter jacket that was in the back seat of the car."

From then on, Freeman claimed, they only saw each other in passing, usually while playing Fox Hunt. Fronk asked, "When you ran into the defendant from time to time, playing Fox Hunt, did he ever say anything to you about it?"

Freeman replied, "He just asked me, 'Has anybody talked to you? Anybody said anything?'"

"What was your answer?"

"Nobody had said anything."

But Tibbs had no memory of running into Freeman "from time to time" after Rayna's abduction, and during his first interview with the police, Freeman explains why that was the case. By March 26, 1993, he had already moved to a horse farm in Merrillville, Indiana, where he worked with the woman he'd soon marry.[32]

Fronk's direct examination of Freeman skipped to 2008 and South Carolina, where the detectives interviewed him after hearing the Hammons pole barn story. "When they started to ask about Rayna or bodies in the trunk, what did you do?"

Freeman replied, "I skirted around the question. The attorney told me that they would grant me immunity if I gave them information pertaining to the case."

During this part of their exchange, Fronk and Freeman freely skipped back and forth between his three interviews with Airy and Williamson. In 2008, when they first met at a South Carolina police station for a recorded session, there was no mention of immunity, and Eric denied any involvement with Rayna's murder. The following remarks referred to an unusually long June 2013 session at the police station after Freeman signed the immunity agreement, which said he would not be prosecuted for any crime connected with Rayna's murder that he disclosed to police.[33]

> Q. So, how did that interview go?
> A. It was skittish [sic]. I beated [sic] around the bush. I didn't completely give everything in the beginning.
> Q. Now, part of the agreement was that you have to be truthful and honest and everything else. Otherwise, the agreement is meaningless.
> A. Right.
> Q. Did you understand that?
> A. Yes, I did.
> Q. Were you completely honest and truthful in that interview?
> A. At the end of it, yes.
> Q. What was going on at the start of it, Eric? Why was that so hard?
> A. I was just scared and nervous that I was still going to be tied—tied to this.
> Q. Were you scared and nervous that you were going to be seen as not being on the right team in this whole thing?
> A. Yes.
> Q. Now, the detectives, they told you, you know, we want you on our side, didn't they?
> A. Yes, they did.
> Q. Is being on their side—did that mean anything to you but apart from the fact that you had witnessed a crime and helped get rid of a body?
> A. It helped a little.
> Q. All right. If you hadn't been part of a crime [and] helped get rid of a body, would you have admitted doing that?
> A. No.

Fronk's extended discussion of immunity was understandable. For many jurors, a Get Out of Jail Free card raises questions about the witness's credibility. But other aspects of his questions should have raised red flags for the defense. The prosecutor was not only trying to inoculate his witness against prickly issues coming during cross-examination. He also inoculated the detectives who may have used coercive techniques during their interrogation, such as implying or threatening that immunity would only be given for testimony benefiting "our side."

But during Freeman's cross-examination, Tompkins chose not to focus on those issues. Instead, he reviewed the litany of discrepancies that ran throughout the three interviews in a scattershot fashion, an approach that may have been as confusing as it was damning. He focused first on answers given during the 2008 clueless interview when Freeman probably provided his most honest answers. These included not even knowing that Jason and Rayna had a relationship or that she worked at the animal hospital. As for Jen Hammons's Buick, during that first interview, he said he never saw a body in the trunk and never even remembered ever opening it.

Freeman acknowledged providing answers that continued to change during his 2008 and 2013 interviews and the 2014 deposition he gave the defense. But some of that updated testimony was particularly material to the State's case. In 2013, he had been adamant with the detectives that Jason and Rayna were not fighting in the animal hospital parking lot. But he had just told the jury that the two had been arguing *before* they entered the Buick.

Freeman also testified that he drove up Fail Road until Jason told him to stop. But during the deposition, he said Rayna was the one who asked him to pull over. "Two different stories," Tompkins charged. "They both asked me to stop the vehicle," Freeman replied. Tompkins shot back, "Three different stories."

There was more. In one interview, Freeman said he saw Jason choking Rayna in his rearview mirror.[34] In another, he said he didn't see him choking her until they were outside the car.[35] At one point, Freeman said he saw the body in the trunk but Jason was the one who opened it.[36] Then, he admitted opening the trunk but didn't see the body because it was under a blue tarp.[37] In the same June 2013 interview, he drove the Buick to the animal hospital to retrieve the LTD while leaving her body in the pole barn. Then he remembered he had made that trip with Rayna in the trunk. As Tompkins pinpointed each prevarication, Freeman agreed he had made it.

It's hard to know what the jury took from Freeman's feckless display. But the most telling revelation that Tompkins got out of him may have gone over their heads. Typically, when the government turns an accomplice into an informant, that person is given a wire or tapped phone call to get the individual they have targeted on tape in an incriminating comment. Freeman said the detectives never asked him to do that with Tibbs. But Tompkins did not tell the jury why the request would have been made and why it would have mattered.

Whatever points Tompkins may have thought he scored, his cross-examination missed three big ones. First were the unusual circumstances surrounding the immunity agreement—an omission that must have relieved Fronk. Second, Tompkins did not show the jury how the detectives played a role in Freeman's testimony by introducing him to information he didn't know. This would have required a dissection of the 2013 interviews that could have taken up a full day of testimony. If done properly, it could have broken Freeman on the stand. Just as important, the defense didn't introduce the transcripts of those sessions as evidence. While Fronk would have tried to block them at this point, Tompkins could have conducted an offer of proof for the trial record. An appellate court likely would not have ignored the detectives' illicit behavior during the June interview documented in the transcript.

For Jason, the next witness, Rickey Hammons, was not as recognizable as Freeman. The annoying little ferret had grown into a short and stocky thirty-six-year-old man. He had combed thin little bangs down his forehead to hide his receding hairline to the extent possible with a prison crew cut. Also, unlike Freeman, Hammons was preternaturally calm on the witness stand— as though he were a forensic expert who regularly testified in court. "Most people are nervous when they have to testify," Jason says. "But Hammons seemed to enjoy it. He didn't look at the lawyers. He looked at the jury like they were his audience and sometimes like he was toying with them."

Fronk began his direct examination by quickly dispensing with Hammons's criminal past, establishing he had been in prison for fifteen years after "a guilty plea to a charge of murder." The prosecutor then proposed, "Let's go back to 1993," when Rickey was fourteen.

When asked to describe a typical day, Hammons cracked, "Get up, go to school, when I wasn't expelled, come home, do chores, watch some TV, go to bed."

Fronk projected photos on a screen for the jurors to see the pole barn setting for Hammons's tale. Although there would be frequent mentions of the "loft," it was, in fact, no more than a wooden platform above the kennels and did not look very lofty from the shots exhibited in court. The defense could have asked if there was enough space above the kennels for Hammons to stand up and get the view that the State's case hinged on, but that question never arose.

From his first prison interview with the detectives to his testimony in Jason's trial, Rickey's story changed in subtle but telling ways—especially regarding why he was in the loft. "I was busy up there, hiding behind the hay bales getting high," he told Michigan City officer Mark Lachmund and Indiana state trooper Al Williamson.[38] Later, Williamson wondered why Tibbs and Freeman wouldn't have smelled the weed after they pulled in with the Buick. Hammons claimed the barn's ventilation would have been "pulling it right out."[39] But evidently, that explanation was not considered credible enough for Jason's trial. When Rickey took the stand, he had perfected his dope puffery. "I was in the loft area," he told the jurors. "I was *getting ready to smoke* a joint." (Italics added.)

After his slideshow about the pole barn, Fronk returned to the loft to set the scene, repeating, "Now, Mr. Hammons, you're up in the loft *getting ready* to smoke a joint." (Italics added.) A few minutes later, in case the jurors missed their "getting ready" remarks, Fronk made clear again his operative point about the joint. "Now, you said you had just lit up that joint." But then he asked, "Were you high?"

Hammons replied, "No."

Fronk then projected a black-and-white shot of the Buick Century with Jen Hammons standing in front of it, and Rickey confirmed that was the vehicle that backed into the pole barn. He next had Freeman getting out from behind the wheel and opening the trunk. "They started arguing," Rickey told the court, "Eric was asking him, you know, what the hell? What were you thinking? Why did you do that?"

When Fronk asked if it "was apparent to you what they were arguing about," Hammons replied, "As I looked down, yes. I mean, I started to become aware that, you know, there was a person in the trunk of the vehicle."

He later described that "person" in more detail. "She was an off-color, like—she wasn't moving. She was—I don't know. She didn't look like she had a lot of color in her face."

The nature of Rickey's description, emphasizing skin color, raised questions about the lighting inside the pole barn when the Buick supposedly backed inside. It had been another concern raised by Williamson when he first interviewed Hammons. Then, Rickey had insisted there was enough natural light to see Rayna in the trunk. But he also claimed the incident occurred after four thirty or five.[40] The detectives eventually realized the Buick's arrival would have been around 6:30 P.M. to comply with other witness testimony—fifteen minutes after sunset on an overcast night.[41] As a result, Rickey refined his testimony accordingly.

"Were the lights on in the barn?" Fronk asked.

Hammons answered, "Yes."

When asked about the demeanor of Tibbs and Freeman, Hammons said, "They were running around. It was like they were panicked." In terms of what they said, he testified, "They were arguing again. . . . Eric asked Jason, you know, 'Why did you do that' and—forgive my language—'Over some pussy.'"

Hammons said he heard them scraping around for something he assumed to be shovels. When he testified about their exit, he made another telling change from his first interview. He had then told the detectives that before Freeman and Tibbs left the pole barn, "Eric says, 'I know what we can do.'"

"Eric tells Jason?" Williamson asked.

Hammons replied, confirming he did mean Eric, "He says, 'I know what we can do.' And that's the last thing I heard them say before I heard . . . Eric get back in the car."[42]

But after Freeman's clueless interviews with Williamson and Airy, the detectives knew Hammons's first ending to his pole barn story would not fly. Probably as a result, Hammons made the following adjustment when he related the tale to Jason's jury:

> Eric was like, "I don't know what we're going to do. We can't stay here. She can't stay here. We got to leave. We got to get out of here."
>
> Mr. Tibbs said, "I know what we can do. I know what we can do."

> They shut the trunk, and Mr. Tibbs got in the—or Mr. Freeman got in the vehicle, Mr. Tibbs opened the door, and they left.

With the remainder of his direct examination, Fronk addressed the two questions he imagined jurors would pose about the bizarre story. Did Hammons know the girl who was supposedly in the trunk was Rayna Rison? Hammons told the court, "I remember the following day seeing the girl's picture in the paper that she was missing. It was that girl. I remember her face."

Why didn't he report the incident sooner? Rickey confessed, "I wasn't really that friendly with law enforcement at that age."

This reply only begged the question as to why he *ever* revealed his pole barn story. Fronk pitched the answer everyone would assume, "Now, with regard to [your coming forward], [are] you looking for anything out of that deal?"

"No," Hammons replied.

Fronk was not going to let Hammons's one-word denial suffice. Instead, he would milk the witness's self-professed selflessness even further.

"You understand that oftentimes when people write letters to law enforcement from prison, they are looking for something?" Fronk explained—no doubt speaking more to the jury than the witness.

"I understand," Hammons replied.

"Did you ask to be put on a different detail or duty or move to a different facility or anything like that?"

Hammons answered, "No," even though he sent his *Please Help Me* missive to Lachmund hours after their meeting in the Wabash Valley Correctional Facility.

Still, before he finished his direct examination, Fronk again played up the valor Hammons showed in coming forward with his pole barn story—as he did in his opening remarks.

> Q. When you cooperate with law enforcement and provide information, is that well received? Do your peers—your fellow inmates—do they like that?
> A. No.
> Q. What sort of stuff happens sometimes when guys do that stuff?
> A. You get beat up, get stabbed, get killed.
> Q. And even knowing that to be the case—because you'd have been in for about nine years by then?

A. Correct.

Q. You came forward with this information?

A. Yes.

Q. And you didn't ask for anything?

A. No.

Q. To this day, have you ever asked for anything in exchange for your testimony?

A. No.

Q. Is there any under-the-table deal or a wink or a nod or anything like that going on here?

A. No.

If Tompkins had studied Hammons's 2008 interview closely, he would have seen that the witness left several openings to impeach his testimony in Jason's trial. However, the Super Lawyer started with a fumble that made Jason wonder how familiar he was with the evidence. "In 2010, the State asked you about an interview you gave at Wabash Valley Correctional Facility," Tompkins said.

"Okay," Hammons replied.

"Do you recall at the beginning of that interview saying you wanted to speak off the record first?"

"No," Hammons replied. "In 2010? No."

When Tompkins approached with a transcript, it was left to his hostile witness to correct him. "Yes," Hammons said. "I remember this statement, but it's not from 2010."

"I'm sorry," Tompkins said. "My correction. March 10, 2008. My mistake." It was a minor flub, but it kept the attorney on his back foot for the rest of the cross-examination.

As for the transcript, asking the police to shut off the tape recorder at the start of the interview was an unusual, ominous request from the defense's perspective. During that time, the snitch and the detectives could have cut a deal in exchange for testimony that would incriminate Jason. But Tompkins never explained to the jury why an off-the-record conversation might have mattered. As he did throughout the trial, the lawyer let them fill in the blanks. Instead, he had Hammons repeat—twice—all the places he had been in the Indiana prison system. At one point, after reciting his multiple transfers,

Hammons said, "I see what you're getting at." But it's unlikely the jury did. Tompkins failed to suggest some of the moves were the reward Hammons received for his story about Jason. Somehow, with all the color-coded files in the van, the defense counsel and their paralegals could not produce the *Please Help Me* letter he sent to Lachmund after the Wabash Valley interview.

Similarly, Tompkins took Hammons through another lengthy setup without letting the jury hear his punchline. In this instance, he had him review the daily schedule of chores he performed for his parents and how they would have been known to Freeman. The lawyer had laid the foundation for an obvious question: Why would Eric have backed the car inside the pole barn without first checking for his girlfriend's annoying little brother since Freeman knew when he might be there? For some reason, Tompkins never explicitly asked the question.

What Tompkins did inquire about, over and over again, was whether Hammons had access to newspapers, trying to pin his "coming forward" with *The South Bend Tribune* article about the unsolved-homicides playing cards that would soon be distributed to Indiana's prisoners. The story mentioned inmates who cooperated with new information might receive sentence modifications. At the start of the cross-examination, Tompkins asked, "Back in 2008, you were in a facility that had newspapers, and you were reading them, correct?"

Hammons answered, "I was in a facility that had them, but I didn't have access to them."

Tompkins did not want to let up on this issue, although he didn't directly ask if Hammons had heard about the playing cards. He brought it up again as he was finishing the cross. "And you're sure you didn't have access to newspapers when you were down in Wabash in 2008?"

> A. Yes. Not on that unit.
> Q. My last question: Did you have access to newspapers when you were at Wabash in 2008?
> A. No, sir.
> Q. I'm not restricting you to a particular unit. Do you understand the question?
> A. Yes.

Tompkins succeeded in eliciting one response from Hammons that threatened severe damage to the State's case. He asked how long the "activity in the barn with Jason and Eric" lasted. Rickey replied, "Fifteen to twenty-five minutes," tying another milestone to the timeline associated with the State's charges, which the lawyer called "impossible" in his opening remarks.

In what would become a pattern for the trial, Fronk objected to any intimation that another man—namely Ray McCarty—had been arrested for Rayna's murder. During a sidebar, Tompkins explained why that mattered for Hammons if he genuinely believed Jason had been the killer. "Your Honor," he told the judge, "there is a significance in the character of a person who doesn't come forward, who allows someone else to get arrested." But even if Tompkins didn't mention McCarty by name, Alevizos would not allow any talk of another arrest. He ruled, "The prejudicial value is so great that I would sustain the objection to that."

The next witness to take the stand was utterly unrecognizable to Jason. When he last saw Patricia Umphrey, she was a pretty, petite woman with luxuriously combed and coiffed brown hair. At fifty-three years old, during his trial, he says, "She looked like she had lived a hard party life. She was very skinny, and her hair was stringy and streaked with gray. When she spoke, it was with one of those raspy smoker's voices you had trouble hearing."

Umphrey admitted that Jason was only an "occasional" visitor to her house as a friend of her son's friend. He stayed overnight at her home after "some CBers were chasing him in a car," then, despite the fact they barely knew each other, she claimed Jason talked to her about killing Rayna. When asked what he said, she replied, "That he loved her and if—there was an accident."

Suddenly, a State's witness suggested that Jason did not kill Rayna so no one else could have her. Instead, it was an accident. Tompkins leaped up to take full advantage of this unexpected break and asked for a sidebar. "Your Honor," he said. "Accident[?] We're way past that."

Alevizos sounded just as flummoxed. "What do you expect her answer to be?" he asked Fronk. If Jason had called the murder an accident, it was manslaughter and not homicide.

But the prosecutor batted that away by saying Jason's characterization of the murder as an accident to Umphrey was "self-serving." The judge then let him proceed with the following exchange:

Q. Did Jason tell you what the result of that accident was?
A. He did.
Q. What did he say?
A. That he did it.
Q. When he said, "He did it," what was he talking about?
A. Killed her.
Q. Did you tell him anything about that? Give him any suggestions or advice.
A. Told him he needed to talk to someone, get ahold of his parents, get some help.
Q. Did you let him stay at your house after that?
A. No.

With those answers and Umphrey's somnambulant demeanor, Fronk must have realized he was playing with fire if he kept her on the stand. But she had previously provided Airy with information about the location of the killing that had been crucial to fabricating the State's case. As the detective wrote in his supplement report, "Patricia stated that Jason advised [her] that [the murder happened] behind Rayna's car by the trunk on Fail Road after an argument."[43] Umphrey never had a chance to utter "Fail Road" before Fronk took his seat.

Scott Pejic rose for the cross-examination, making his first joust of the day before the jury. In a series of quick questions, he got Umphrey to acknowledge that "when Rayna Rison went missing," it was a "big deal" with "national attention." Then he said, "And there is no record of you ever coming forward until after Jason Tibbs is arrested." Fronk objected because the woman was unlikely to know "the record."

In the sidebar, Alevizos asked Pejic to "rephrase the question." As he would do through the early stages of the trial, the young lawyer responded to the judge like a submissive puppy dog. "I'll try to be better," he said and thanked the judge for overruling the objection. He then fumbled again, asking, "Are you aware of any record . . ." Fronk objected again, and there was another sidebar. Since there was no record of Umphrey doing anything, the judge told Pejic his question "assumes facts not in evidence." He added, "There is a right way to say that."

But Pejic abandoned his first thrust and asked instead about 2013, "last year." Umphrey said the police came to her after they spoke with her nephew, who was in prison with Rickey Hammons.

Before she left the stand, Pejic raised another salient point. "How many medications are you on?" he asked.

She replied, "Seventeen."

"How many times have you been hospitalized on the psychiatric floor of La Porte Hospital?"

"I couldn't tell you."

Although Umphrey could not have been a more disastrous witness, her son followed her to the stand as the State doubled down on her confession story. Lonnie Garner was another barely recognizable figure from Jason's past—with short-cropped hair and a scruffy beard. When Fronk asked if he was "hanging out with Jason Tibbs" in 1993, he replied, "Off and on, I'd see him."

The night Jason supposedly confessed to Umphrey, Garner testified, "I asked him what he had said to get Mom so upset. And he had said that he thinked [*sic*] that he murdered a girl."

When Pejic cross-examined him, he pulled out a deposition Garner gave six months earlier when he said that Jason did not *directly* talk to him about murdering a girl. When he heard that, he replied, "It was through words of the other guys." In the deposition, he admitted, "I guess it ain't clear to me exactly." Pejic also got Garner to acknowledge another Hammons connection— Lonnie's younger brother was friendly with Rickey when they lived around the corner.

For Jason, the day started like someone else's trial. Freeman, Hammons, Umphrey, Garner. He says, "I hardly knew these people." But the detectives from the first investigation must have been even more amazed. After years of digging and hundreds of interviews, none of these names had ever surfaced. They didn't just amount to a new orbit. They were a new constellation.

To someone unfamiliar with the McCarty indictment, it may have made sense. If Hahn and Boyd had never gotten to these people, no wonder they couldn't arrive at a satisfying solution to Rayna's murder. But for more experienced investigators, the State's crew of Johnny-come-lately witnesses, linked to one another through the Hammons family, were weaving a fever dream unsupported by any of the extensive forensic evidence collected in 1993—much like the psychics and jilted lover who came forward after Rayna first disappeared. Most surprising was the elevation of Umphrey and Garner into such positions of importance, given her mental state and his criminal background.

But for Fronk, Williamson, and Airy, the first four witnesses represented puzzle pieces that all had to fit—or get wedged—together if Freeman and Hammons were to be believed. Ironically, Umphrey never got to the critical information about the location of the killing she was supposed to impart on the stand. Still, the supposed crime scene on Fail Road originated in her interview with Airy. He forced it on Freeman and then watched it metastasize in ways that had the potential to demolish the State's case.

Throughout the proceedings, Jason furiously scribbled notes on his legal pad. Among the issues he raised was how Freeman barely knew Jason and how seldom they had been together. Even Eric admitted that in previous interviews. Why couldn't his lawyers ask questions to bring that out? But as they would do throughout the trial, Pejic and Tompkins would glance at his pad, maybe shake or nod their heads, but do nothing else in response. If Jason got upset about their inaction, Pejic, who sat beside him, would put a hand on his arm, Jason says, "To placate me." While his lawyers scored some points on the first day, Jason was disturbed by their performance. "Things happened that made me worry about their preparation." He shared his concerns with his mother that night, but Rachel had chatted with the lawyers outside of court. "They think everything is fine," she told her son. Then, echoing Tompkins, she added, "Just trust the process."

OLD EVIDENCE WITH NEW TWISTS

For the most part, witnesses who appeared later in the trial were not unfamiliar to Jason or the first investigation detectives, who themselves were among them. But what the civilians said on the stand often veered from what they initially told police in 1993. In many cases, Fronk and

Alevizos blocked them from the testimony that could either exonerate Jason or incriminate Ray McCarty. Some of the judge's rulings came in the motion of limine hearing before the trial started, but many happened in sidebars as Fronk objected throughout the proceedings. These meetings between lawyers and the judge, as is common, occurred where jurors couldn't hear them, when the jury wasn't present, or outside the courtroom.

After the first four witnesses, the rest of the State's case against Jason was roughly divided into four parts: the recovery of Rayna's body, car, and Matt's letterman jacket; the events surrounding her abduction in the animal hospital parking lot; Jason's alibi; and his supposedly suspicious role organizing her search parties.

Typically, the State's presentation of a victim's recovery is a gruesome show-and-tell that helps orient the jury to evidence collected around the crime scene. To provide narration, Fronk chose the retired evidence technician who took photographs of the operation. The jury saw various views of the pond and the mass of twigs, leaves, and branches under which Rayna had been submerged. Fronk then projected pictures taken on the day of her recovery with her sun-bleached jeans and bloated body still face down in the water and later, after it was brought to the shore to drain in a recovery bag. Another series of photos showed the rings on her swollen fingers.

During his cross-examination of the evidence technician, Pejic returned to Freeman's testimony about how he and Tibbs threw Rayna's body into the pond.

> Q. All right. Based on what you saw that day with your knowledge of the pond and the shoreline, would it have been possible for her to just have been one, two, three, heaved into the pond and land at that location?
> A. It's possible.
> Q. From the shoreline?
> A. Possibly.
> Q. Was there enough—would there had been enough room with all the branches and trees on the shoreline to do that?
> A. I'd have to say probably not.

Next, Pejic turned to the five-and-a-half-foot logs placed on Rayna to submerge her body. He asked, "Could that log have been thrown from the shoreline to land on Ms. Rison?"

"Possibly," the witness replied. "It would have been difficult for it to land particularly on her."

While Fronk made surprising choices about the witnesses he called, like Patricia Umphrey, his decisions not to bring certain parties to the stand were just as surprising and, perhaps, telling about their potential vulnerabilities during cross-examination. One such no-call was the man who discovered Rayna's body in the pond, James McWhirter. Although not in prison then, he had just been released six months earlier after serving forty-seven months for possessing and dealing a controlled substance. It had been his longest sentence to date. (He'd return to prison a year later for selling cocaine.[44]) Fronk or Airy may have also worried about the report from McCarty's neighbor about McWhirter being a friend of Ray's best friend.[45] This could have led to incriminating questions about Ray if McWhirter had been a witness. It may have also revealed Ray or his best friend—probably Charlie Allen—knew where Rayna was submerged.

In his stead, Fronk called McWhirter's daughter, Tracy Manns, who was fourteen when Rayna was discovered. "I was with my mom and my dad and my little brother, fishing, looking for turtles," she told the court.

Manns enthusiastically supplied the jury with details that had never appeared in the numerous newspaper and police reports about the event. "Well, me and my dad went back in the no-trespassing area. We always looked for turtles over there because that's where they mostly were. We used to find real big turtles, like real big [demonstrating]. And we started walking back along the shore, and I noticed a horrible smell. I could tell there was—something was dead."

Pursuing the smell, she said, "I looked in the water, and . . . the first thing I seen was a boot. And I followed it up and realized that it was a leg, and then, you know, I could see hair. It looked like seaweed, and I noticed it was a body. So I called my dad back, and I said, 'Dad, what is that?' And he said, 'It looks like a body.'"

If Pejic found anything suspicious in Manns's answers, he did not indicate that to the jurors. Nor did he ask why McWhirter wasn't there himself to testify. While her father told the police he had been to the pond five or six times at most, during cross-examination, the daughter said they had been there "somewhere between five and ten" times *that year*. When Pejic asked if there had been a "reward . . . for finding the body," Manns replied, "My parents had talked about it." When asked if she remembered how much, she answered, "I believe thirty or thirty-five thousand," adding, "I had called about it once. I'm not sure about my parents."

Although the State ostensibly brought in the next witness to testify about finding the letterman jacket, retired La Porte County patrolman Jim Jackson was more qualified to talk about Rayna's recovery than the evidence technician who took the photos. He and Joe Pavolka had donned scuba gear to pull the body from under the branches. Unlike Manns, Jackson never spoke of a smell. He also would have denied the body was as visible under the foliage as Manns had indicated. When interviewed today, he remembers, "You couldn't stand fifteen feet away and definitively tell that it was a body."[46]

His memory correlates with the account of the man McWhirter flagged down to witness his discovery. Like Jackson, he couldn't make out Rayna's body until McWhirter threw a rock in the water to direct him where to look.[47]

The retired county patrolman would have raised other issues about the crime scene that could have caused discomfort for Fronk and the McWhirter family. "It was not a highly used area," Jackson says today. "And that's why I always had a question in my own mind, 'Why was McWhirter fishing in there? What was his real point?' I don't know." Neither Jason's defense nor the State tried to answer that question during the trial.

Regarding the shoreline where Rayna was found, Jackson says, "You had to traverse through the woods [to get to the water], which was still thick with foliage, you know, brush and puckerbrush, you name it." Unlike the evidence technician, he would have denied that the body could have been heaved over that morass of vegetation. Instead, he believes the disarray of her clothes revealed how she was pulled and not thrown into the pond. "My opinion is somebody had her by the feet, and somebody else probably grabbed her by one arm. And then, for whatever reason, they grabbed the center of her bra and used that as a way to try to propel her into the water. . . . Because of the way the bra had been yanked up, one breast was pulled out [from under the bra]." (Ironically, later in the trial, the defense tried to call an evidence technician to discuss pulled versus thrown, but Alevizos wouldn't let him testify because he had no "specialized training" to form a conclusion. Also, he did not assist in recovery, so he couldn't discuss the evidence Jackson saw that indicated she was pulled.[48])

When Jackson took the stand, Fronk first focused on his role in finding the jacket the night of the *America's Most Wanted* broadcast. The prosecutor provided Jackson's report about the incident to refresh his memory. After describing the frost-covered jacket and the dump area where it was found hanging in a tree, Jackson identified Jason and his friend, Chris Frazier, as two of the civilians gawking at all the police cars lined up along the farm fields and wasteland—even though it was 11:00 P.M. on a Friday. Another officer testified he had searched the area the day before and had not seen the *Most Wanted* apparel. Jason's friends said they had been near the dump previously, but none said they saw him go off on his own there.

While Fronk suggested it was highly suspicious for Jason to appear, Tibbs says it was an unfortunate coincidence. Chris Frazier revealed during his direct examination, he lived a few hundred yards from the dump. In the hours before Patrolman Jackson arrived, Chris, Jason, and Vic Montorsi were together, drinking, picking up videos, and "mud bogging"—splashing through the soggy empty fields near the dump in their four-wheel-drive trucks. Frazier—who said he was too drunk to remember the evening—was of little help for either side. When Montorsi was called to the stand, he was asked to testify about Jason's alibi on March 26, and neither Fronk nor the defense asked him about the time he spent with Jason the night the letterman jacket was found.

Regarding the events surrounding Rayna's abduction in the animal hospital parking lot, no witness threatened the State's case more than the feisty fireplug Rene Gazarkiewicz. During the first investigation, police considered her to be a key witness. Her two early evening passes by the animal hospital provided the prosecution with unassailable milestones in the abduction timeline. But she also had vivid memories of Ray's blue Datsun station wagon with the rusted spots.[49] At one point, she described Rayna leaning so far through the driver's window of that car that her feet were off the ground.[50] Her testimony could turn into a minefield for the state. Strategically, Fronk may have decided she was too knowledgeable for him *not* to call her as his witness.

But once he got Gazarkiewicz going, there was no stopping her. As she explained to the jury, the times she provided were rock solid because they were set around getting cigarettes for her friend—who, she revealed, was disabled—and taking her daughter to the middle school Fun Night. Again, she recounted turning onto Pine Lake Avenue and getting blinded by the bright headlights of a "station wagon" in the exit lane of the animal hospital parking lot. When asked to describe the offending vehicle, she replied, "It's a blue four-door." Her mention of a vent in the rear driver's side window launched a time-tripping, free association reverie.

> When I was a child, when the parents smoked, they could vent the window in the front seat and put their ashes and their cigarette butts out that front vent window. But the passenger seats have vents back there, and the [blue four-door] had a rear [vent]—that's one thing that stuck in my mind—because that door was cracked open, but the dome light wasn't on. I just kept thinking, "You dumb"—excuse my language—"you dumb-ass kid. What are you doing? You're getting soaking wet." Because it was wet, drizzling, and it was a miserable night out. It was a Friday night. We were—I had to wait for traffic quite a bit that night because a bunch of La Porte people were going to the Michigan City [versus] La Porte basketball game. So I had a lot of traffic to wait on.

She repeated her story about Rayna leaning in the driver's side window but took off on one more tangent. "There was another person sitting in the passenger seat, and they had their brights on, which really—I don't know about anybody else, but that just irritates the you-know-what out of me to have brights in your eyes. That's the reason I actually paid attention to the car because they had their brights on."

With that comment, Fronk steered her back to the headlights. "Now, did you say anything about the shape of the headlights on that car?" he asked.

"They were side by side," she answered. "The headlights . . . were square."

For Fronk, Rene's ramble had finally hit pay dirt. Like Ray's Datsun, the Buick Century had square headlights stacked side by side. However, the Hammons car did not have the smaller yellow inner lights—Gazarkiewicz called them a "fog light thing" and didn't have "amber" lights on the side.

When Pejic had his shot at cross-examination, he spent as much time with Rene as any defense witness. He stressed again that the car she saw with the brights was "a blue station wagon." He had her use the court's Telestrator to sketch the configuration of the vehicles in the animal hospital parking lot and traffic on Pine Lake Avenue. Later, he had her draw the car's grille with the brights. ("I don't like drawing with my fingernails," she told the jury. "I feel like a three-year-old driving.")

With Rene's testimony, the defense counsel had a shot at landing their biggest blow of the trial. All they needed to follow through with an uppercut was to have her identify Ray's car. But Alevizos wouldn't allow it. At first, he didn't understand why that mattered. During the sidebar, he said, "I'm just trying to follow along. [Gazarkiewicz] identified Rayna's car and the other blocking it, which is the station wagon. . . . Why is that important? How is it relevant?"

"It's Ray's car," Tompkins replied.

Pejic had asked Gazarkiewicz if she could identify the station wagon "if I showed you a picture?"

"It's been twenty-one years," she answered, "but I think maybe I could."

When Pejic pulled out a photo of Ray's car, Fronk objected. In the sidebar, Alevizos thought he heard Rene say, "She didn't think she can [identify the car]." Fronk agreed.

Before Pejic could correct them, the judge said, "I'm sustaining [Fronk's objection] only because you're going to recall her anyway, and we will briefly discuss it then." But the defense never recalled Gazarkiewicz, and the jury never saw her identify Ray's car as the other vehicle near the parking lot when Rayna was abducted.

The State's following two witnesses proved more problematic for the defense. On March 26, both had passed the animal hospital within minutes of each other, shortly after 6:00 P.M., as their cars crawled through the slow-moving traffic on Pine Lake Avenue. Both had seen a young woman in a high school letterman jacket backing up toward the clinic and away from a young man in a baseball cap. Both believed they had been arguing. Both identified Rayna's LTD as one of the two cars parked alongside each other and pointed toward the exit.

When Pam Rosebaum first talked to Harold Hahn, she described the LTD as larger and lighter in color than the other car.[51] When interviewed by Arlie Boyd six weeks later, she said the smaller car was silver, and the young woman gestured to tell the young man to get away. She said he was five feet eight inches, not too much taller than she was.[52] On the witness stand in Jason's trial, she added that the male she saw was "about the same build as my husband and brother-in-law," who were "180 pounds." Ironically, he was the height of Ray McCarty, who weighed 170 pounds two years earlier.[53] Jason was no more than 150 pounds in those days. As for the cars, she continued to assert that the one parked alongside the LTD was silver— closer in color to the gray Hammons Buick than the blue Datsun—but "a little bit smaller." However, during cross-examination, she poured cold water onto everything else she said when asked about the weather on March 26. "It was pretty clear," she told Pejic. "I don't remember it raining or anything."

In 1993, Bryan Durham gave LPPD Detective Captain John Miller a more elaborate description of the combative couple than Rosebaum. He had the girl waving more dramatically. Unlike Pam, he did not think the couple was close in height. He saw the male as "lanky and tall [with a] clean-cut appearance [and hair that was] light brown to blonde in color." As an added odd detail, Durham believed he was wearing "football pants, tight jersey-type pants cut off below the knee." (The physical description matched Scott Scarborough, and the pants likely were the chaps he would have worn as a tree trimmer.)

Perhaps because he was so focused on the people, Durham was unsure about the vehicle descriptions. He identified one car as possibly an LTD— like Rayna's—but dark in color with a driver inside. He was not so sure about the other vehicle.[54]

But by the time he testified at the Tibbs trial, Durham's memory had radically changed in potentially devastating ways for Jason. Like other March 26 witnesses, he was headed to a school event with a child in his car, so he was sure of when he passed by the animal hospital. Also, he no longer talked of just one male confronting the "girl." Instead, he saw "two boys," and "she was arguing with one of the boys." Also, she was not waving her arms as if to say, "Leave me alone." She was "screaming" it.

Regarding the vehicles, he described Rayna's car as "cream-colored" instead of "dark." While he would not say the other car was the Buick Century, he did see a similarity in the grille area but conceded, "My focus was on the girl."

By repeatedly calling the two males "boys," Durham played right into the hands of the prosecution. "There was a taller boy and a shorter boy; one with dark hair that was closest to me, and the other blondish boy was the one that was arguing with the young girl." One of the two was now just "taller" instead of "lanky and tall," a description that did not apply to Freeman or Tibbs. But Durham's original account of the argument was not necessarily helpful to the prosecution because the "blondish boy" would have been Freeman, who had testified he stayed in the car.

But before he finished his direct examination, Fronk projected two pages of yearbook photos for the jury to see. One set was from La Porte High School, where Jason was the only dark-haired boy on the page. The second set was from the South Central high school where Freeman went. He was the only "blondish" boy on the page. In 2009, when interviewed by Airy, Durham circled Tibbs and Freeman, writing his initials and the identification date.

In forensic psychology circles, such photo lineups are notoriously inaccurate. As one expert in the field concluded, "Witnesses have a natural propensity to identify the person in the lineup who looks most like the perpetrator relative to the others. The problem with that is that if the real perp's not there, there's still somebody who looks more like the perpetrator than others."[55] Indeed, compared with the other individuals on the yearbook pages, Freeman most looked like Scarborough, and Jason most looked like Ray. But research aside, the impact of Durham's photo identification on the jury could not be minimized.

During his cross-examination, Pejic pinpointed all the discrepancies in the witness's testimony from what he said to the police in 1993 and the grand jury in 1998. Because of the motions in limine, he could only refer to the latter as "sworn testimony." Still, after having Durham look at one transcript, Pejic blurted out, "And you reviewed your grand jury testimony?"

Whether or not he was aware of his faux pas, the lawyer referred to the material properly moments later. "Would you agree with me that your memory was better when you spoke to the police in 1993 and offered sworn testimony in 1998 than it is now?" Durham agreed. He then admitted it was "a mistake" to say both males were outside the car. He further disclosed that when he picked out the yearbook photos, he did so based on "the eyes, the hair color, the shape of the face." But he agreed when Pejic said, "The people you saw in the parking lot appeared a lot older than the people whose photographs you were being shown."

After Pejic effectively unraveled Durham's updated account, Fronk did not do much to pull the threads back together during his redirect. He could only point out that Durham claimed to hear the screams in his *sworn* testimony.

When the jury went to lunch, the prosecutor approached the Court. "I'd like to discuss an issue," he said to Alevizos.

"What's that?" the judge asked.

"The fact that he said grand jury again."

While Pejic apologized, he added, "That's my first time."

But Fronk was not about to be mollified by an apology. Pejic's Durham demolition probably exacerbated his anger. "Your Honor, the Court issued an order signed October 22nd of 2014 granting the State's motions in limine regarding grand jury testimony, excluding any and all questioning, evidence, references to evidence, comment, testimony, or argument by counsel or witnesses relating to the empaneling of a grand jury, its findings, its indictment, so on and so forth. Both counsel now have violated this order of the Court."

"Are you moving for a mistrial?" Alevizos asked.

Fronk did not want that, but he suggested, "I think that the Court has within its power the ability to sanction counsel." Sanctions in Indiana courts can range from monetary fines to suspending a lawyer's license.

"Okay," the judge replied. "We'll do that if it happens again."

Now, it was Tompkins's turn to get on his high horse. While admitting to his own "grand jury" slip of the lip, he blamed the prosecution's "calling of witnesses in the most difficult way possible for the defense to prepare." Tompkins charged that they did not know about the appearances of some witnesses until they took the stand. "Those [slipups] are less likely if we were given a better opportunity to prepare and have our documents ready."

Fronk agreed to provide more notice, but his strategy was to keep Pejic and Tompkins off-balance by calling witnesses for the state whom the defense should have called—especially the ones who might have supported Jason's alibi.

One such witness was Chad Green, who had provided Jason with his ride to the trailer park. Still, Green's past behavior made his testimony unpredictable at best. Although related to Tibbs by marriage, Jason says he often had a chip on his shoulder, believing his friends took advantage of him because of his father's relative affluence—whether going out on the Greens' boat or asking Chad for rides in his Ford Tempo. Back in 1993, when first contacted by police a few days after Rayna's abduction, Green denied having picked up Jason and taken him to the trailer park with James Amor. He remembered driving around with Josh Jordan later and meeting Jason and James the next day to search for Rayna.[56] But after talking to Jason, Chad recalled picking up Tibbs and Amor and dropping them off at the trailer park. He said as much in a signed statement the next time he was picked up by the police, and Miller interviewed him.[57]

On the stand, Green could not remember what he did or said in 1993, even after Fronk gave him sworn testimony to refresh his memory. But the prosecutor most wanted the jury to hear one thing from Green. After his first interview with the police, when he said he wasn't with Jason, Chad testified, Jason "told me that I needed to go to the police and tell them that I was with him."

In his cross, Pejic wanted the jury to hear something else. "Let's get it straight," the lawyer said to Green. "Jason never told you to lie for him, right?"

Chad answered, "That's correct."

"And never asked you to be his alibi, right?"

"That's correct."

But Fronk chose to bolster Green's wishy-washy testimony with Harold Hahn. At sixty-eight, the retired detective was out of law enforcement and working as a supervisor at Home Depot. Fronk handed him the report he wrote after his 1993 interview with Jason on the evening of March 31 when the police unexpectedly hauled Jason down to the station for hours of questioning without letting him contact his parents. After he failed a polygraph—like Matt Elser—Tibbs had a contentious session with Hahn, who suspected Rayna was a runaway and the boyfriends were hiding what they knew. At Jason's trial, the retired detective reviewed the notes he took at the time, saying Jason was "nervous and shaken up."[58] Hahn also reported Jason telling him that on March 26, on his way to the trailer park between 5:30 and 6:00 P.M., he drove by the animal hospital with Vic Montorsi—not Green and Amor.

Hahn's account of the drive contrasted with what Jason told Detective Captain John Miller a few minutes later. Although Hahn initially denied it on the stand, the session with his boss was recorded. Miller then transcribed it himself.[59]

Soon after Hahn was dismissed, grizzly old John Miller took the stand. At seventy-seven, his hair had gone completely white, but his figure was still rotund. He confirmed that in his interview, Jason said Chad Green drove him and Amor to the trailer park, directly contradicting Hahn's report. But Fronk focused on two other matters in Miller's transcript. One was the time when Tibbs said he passed the animal hospital. He had told other detectives it was between five thirty and six. Miller transcribed 6:10. Also, Fronk asked, "Did [Tibbs] indicate in that statement that he didn't know Rayna's last name?"

Miller replied, "He did."

In his cross-examination, Pejic leafed through the transcript, pointing out blank underlines that showed "some parts that are omitted" and were later filled in with handwriting. Miller denied the writing was his, but when asked if it were an "accurate transcription," the retired detective replied, "It appears to be accurate," and maintained that opinion even as Pejic pointed out all the blanks. Since he retired long before, he had no idea whether the tape was retained, so there was no way to check the accuracy of his transcription.

But Miller did provide Pejic with one helpful sound bite when the lawyer asked, "His alibi checked out, right?"

The witness replied, "As far as I know. Yes, it was checked out."

Fronk objected, and Alevizos stopped any further questions about the previous investigation, calling it "overview testimony," that he had prohibited in his motions in limine ruling. But Pejic tried another bite at that apple after talking about all the state and local agencies involved in the 1993 investigation. He asked, "So everything checked out for Jason. Isn't that true?"

Miller replied, "It was in the process of being reviewed, correct."

"And during this process, Jason wasn't arrested, was he?"

"No, he was not."

"And there was another suspect, was there not?"

Fronk objected before Miller could answer. In a sidebar, the prosecutor charged the defense with trying to shoehorn Ray into the case through the detective. Alevizos agreed to let Pejic rephrase the question and proceed before the jury.

> Q. There were other suspects being looked at with respect to the disappearance of Ryana [sic] Rison?
> A. There were.
> Q. And there were other suspects who could not establish an alibi?
> A. That's possible. Right.
> Q. Is it possible there are other suspects that had an unverifiable alibi?
> A. That's true.

Despite Miller's vague remarks about clearing Jason's alibi, Fronk was outraged that the questions were asked and made them a topic of a prolonged sidebar outside the jury's presence. By getting Miller to comment on the previous investigation, the prosecutor charged, the defense was sneaking evidence into the trial that the judge had barred.

Once again, Alevizos dismissed the efforts of the 1993 detectives, particularly Miller, who retired before the year ended. "He's out the door when this happens. I doubt that John Miller even knew then that [Tibbs] was cleared. Now, he certainly doesn't know twenty-one years later."

However, the judge then upbraided Fronk. "The proper thing to have done would have been to object before Mr. Miller answered that question."

But Pejic protested that he should be allowed to impeach the current investigation by showing Airy and Williamson did not consider evidence developed two decades earlier. Alevizos shot back, "We're beyond impeachment [if you say] there was an additional investigation that cleared your guy."

The McCarty indictment continued to be the elephant in the room that the jury could not see but that weighed heavily on the prosecution. Many of the State's witnesses following Miller to the stand were called precisely to impeach the evidence that cleared Jason.

No witness could do more to support Jason's alibi than James Amor. He was the one who wanted to meet Misty Smith at her home in the trailer park, which is why Jason cooked up the scheme about tutoring her younger sister Jamie. Amor was the one who was driving around with Chad Green in his gray Ford Tempo when Misty's friend, Angie Vogel, reached out on the CB radio to say that Croc (Jason's handle) needed a ride. He and Chad then spent time with Jason at the Tibbses' house until the three drove to the trailer park. After Chad dropped them off, James and Jason stayed there with the girls until Peggy Johnson, Misty and Jamie's mother, kicked Amor out. When Chad picked him up, he left Jason behind to tutor Jamie. Amor confirmed this to Hahn in April 1993[60] and, unlike Chad, never changed his story.

But Pejic and Tompkins did not expect Fronk to call their best alibi witness, and they were caught on the back foot again. Amor never had a chance to review the report Hahn wrote about his interview with him, and he admitted on the stand that he had a hazy memory of all that transpired on March 26. While James remembered going to the trailer park, he was not "a hundred percent" sure how he got there. "It was twenty-two years ago," he told the court.

Regarding his ride, he said, "The absolute definitive memory that I have from that day, we were headed into town, and whoever we were with, we turned the CB on. . . . And someone asked Jason if Vic had gotten ahold of him. And Jason said, 'No, I haven't been on the radio.' And then he called out [on the CB] to try to get ahold of Vic, and Vic wasn't on anymore."

The only person Amor remembered at the destination was Misty Smith, the girl he wanted to meet. As for Jason's presence, again, he was "not a hundred percent [sure]." However, consistent with Tibbs's alibi, he recalled, "Jason didn't have a car at that time," and Amor slept over at Jason's house that night. They woke up briefly after Rachel Tibbs knocked on the door asking about Rayna and then went back to sleep when Jason said, "She probably ran off with her boyfriend."

Fronk assumed that Tibbs's lawyers had already shown Amor "your police reports and stuff that you made back in the day." He was surprised to hear James reply, "No. I haven't read them at all."

"I'm sorry, sir," the prosecutor said. "I thought you had that opportunity."

Jason listened to this exchange with dread. Amor was critical in verifying his alibi. He says, "Why didn't [Pejic and Tompkins] show him his 1993 interview before he took the stand? I couldn't believe it."

For Fronk, there was only one reason to introduce the report. He asked Amor, "Do you remember telling Sergeant Hahn on April 16th of '93 that Jason would like to be boyfriend and girlfriend again with Rayna?" Of course, the witness could not remember but agreed he said it after looking at the report. However, Fronk did not ask Amor to repeat the entire sentence: "Jason would like to be girlfriend boyfriend again but does not want to interfear [sic] with Matt and Rayna's relationship as he is close friends with both."[61] It was an omission the defense never tried to correct.

However, in his zealousness to prove that Jason was a lovelorn killer, Fronk committed one of the biggest blunders of the trial. The Hahn report he waved at Amor did much to support Jason's alibi.

When Tompkins attempted to show the document to the jury, Fronk objected. Despite his earlier reference to the report, the prosecutor was now dismissing it as hearsay. In a sidebar, Alevizos agreed. The judge said he would have sustained the objection and barred the report but added Fronk "kind of forfeited his right to object on the grounds he [was] trying to offer it himself." He later admonished the attorneys to review the rules on hearsay, which he had used to bar much of the defense evidence in his motions in limine ruling.

With the judge's rare approval on entering disputed evidence, Tompkins wrung every bit of information from Hahn's report that supported Jason's alibi: How James went to Jason's house to pick him up around 3:00 P.M. on March 26. How they next went to the trailer park so he could see Misty and how, after two hours, he left Jason behind to tutor Jamie when the girls' mother kicked James and Josh out of her house. Then afterward, Jason and James played Fox Hunt "until late that night," and Amor later slept over at Jason's house, where they didn't learn Rayna was missing until the next morning.

During the redirect, Fronk tried to blunt the impact of Hahn's report by asking, "You don't really have any memory of this particular report [and] these things?"

Amor replied, "I vaguely [remember]. Like I said, I know I went out to Misty and Jamie's house. I don't remember what time I got there. I don't remember exactly how I got there."

"Even if this were the gospel truth," Fronk began, diminishing the value of the report he had entered into evidence, "you weren't with Jason the whole night, were you?"

Amor answered, "Not the whole entire night."

If sloppy Harold Hahn had given to the defense with his report on the Amor interview, he took much more away with his account of what Jason said in 1993 after he failed the lie detector test. The detective wrote, "Jason was asked where he was at Friday, the evening Rayna turned up missing. Jason stated that he did drive by the animal hospital that night, and Vic Montorsey [sic] was with him."[62] Jason denies saying anything of the kind to Hahn, and extensive evidence supports him in that.

But Fronk treated *this* Hahn report as "gospel." After Amor, he called Montorsi to the stand. Like previous witnesses, Vic could not remember much of what had happened twenty-one years before. Alevizos allowed him to look at a signed statement from 1993 to refresh his memory, which included vignettes of mixed value for each side. But before he got off the stand, Fronk harked back to what Jason supposedly said to Hahn. "Okay. So is it your testimony that you were not with Jason Tibbs between 5:30 and 6:00 driving past Pine Lake Animal Hospital on March 26th of '93?"

"No, I was not," Montorsi replied, fully confident of that response because he was working at Dairy Queen.

With that answer, Fronk loaded a pistol he would fire in his closing argument. But Tompkins seemed oblivious to the potential harm and let Montorsi leave the stand after one unrelated question about whether Jason had asked Vic to lie or provide an alibi for him.

Arland Boyd next took the stand. Like the other detectives, he, too, had retired from law enforcement after spending more than three decades with the state police. Although nearly seventy years old and grayer, he was still trim. Now a long-distance runner, his name appeared in the papers associated with race results instead of murders or vocal performances.

Unlike other witnesses, Boyd had reviewed the report on his interview with Jason. During his direct examination, without looking at the document, he provided the times and places of Jason's alibi and the people he was with. However, Boyd did slip up by offering a time that didn't appear in his report. He had Jason arriving at the trailer park at 7:00 P.M. As Boyd's meticulous notes confirm, Jason never said that.[63] In his other interviews with the police, Jason indicated the time was closer to 6:00 P.M. During Indiana trials, jurors can ask questions, first screened by the judge, before a witness leaves the stand. One juror later noted the discrepancy in his trailer park arrival time, but Boyd stuck with 7:00 P.M.

Once again, Tompkins appeared to miss the significance of this crucial testimony and did not challenge Boyd about the trailer park arrival time. It was another seemingly small point that poked at Jason's credibility. Otherwise, given Boyd's experience investigating homicides, Tompkins could not have asked for a better witness to defend his client. Boyd says, "I was a prosecution witness, but a reluctant one. I just didn't believe he did it, and I can't say I believe it yet. We should have had a more extensive investigation of McCarty." Still, at the Tibbs trial, the retired Indiana state trooper came as close to exonerating Jason as anyone else who took the stand. Referring to Boyd's lengthy session questioning Jason in the presence of his mother and lawyer, Tompkins asked, "[Did you] consider him a viable suspect at the time of that interview . . . ?"

"Not at the time of the interview," Boyd replied. "Afterward, I didn't consider him a viable suspect."

Undoubtedly, Boyd's testimony made Fronk uncomfortable, but amazingly, during his cross-examination of Boyd, Tompkins made a comment that the prosecutor could use against his client later. The defense attorney had asked Boyd if Jason's reason for visiting the trailer park was "to tutor a girl." After the retired detective answered, "Yes," Tompkins said, "Now 'tutor' is code for making out, isn't it?"

"I wasn't sure what that actually meant," Boyd replied. "I took it that they were very good friends."

In a subtle but corrosive way, the lawyer's gratuitous remark only degraded Jason's alibi—even if it was only an awkward stab at humor. While Jason admitted the tutoring session was a ruse, it was done for Amor's sake and not his own. He wasn't making out with Jamie or her little sister. In fact, Tibbs had tutored the girls' friend in the past, which is why their mother kicked the other boys out of her home and let Jason stay—a fundamental ground truth for his alibi. He never left the trailer while someone else abducted, killed, and submerged Rayna in the pond. "Tutor is code" would be another tidbit Fronk could dredge up for his closing argument.

In his strategy to be the first to examine Jason's alibi witnesses, Fronk was most aggressive in calling Josh Jordan—Jason's oldest friend and one of the few who had not abandoned him after his arrest. In battling someone he deemed a "hostile witness," Fronk thought he had a secret weapon. A few weeks before the trial, Jason called Josh from a prison phone, and they spoke about his upcoming testimony. Knowing all prison calls are subject to recording, it was not a smart thing to do. Jason argues, "It wasn't like I said, 'You should say this or that.' I just reminded him who was with us that night, which is why Fronk never played that tape to the jury. He brought up the call to show that Josh was a dishonest witness."

But on the stand, Jordan didn't remember much of anything that happened on March 26. The same had been true in 1993, just a month after Rayna's disappearance, when he talked to Hahn. Even then, Josh only knew he was briefly at the trailer park with Jason but forgot who brought him and why they left.[64] Twenty years later, Jordan was even more bereft of the details.

During Jason's trial, Fronk tried to take advantage of Jordan's memory lapses. Although Josh never said Chad took him to the trailer park, he told Hahn he had been with Green at some point during the day. But Fronk twisted that comment by asking, "Then it was true that you and Chad Green took the defendant to a trailer park and dropped him off."

In fact, Jordan never said that to Hahn, but he replied, "As far as I can remember." Next, Fronk wanted Jordan to negate Amor's testimony too. "Is it true that during the time when you were speaking to the police, you never mentioned James Amor being around that Friday night?" he asked.

"No," Josh replied. "I don't think I did."

Frustrated with that response, Fronk asked, "As you sit here today, do you remember March 26th of 1993?"

Jordan answered, "Not real well. . . . Pretty much the only memory I got is from what I read from [Hahn's] report in '93."

In his cross-examination, Tompkins dispensed with the possibility that Jason had put words in Jordan's mouth during his call from prison. He asked, "If you [and Jason had] gotten together and put together a great story, it wouldn't be: 'There's almost nothing I can remember from '93?'"

"Yeah. Yeah," Josh said, not quite seeing where Tompkins was going, "but I wouldn't do that."

"I understand," the lawyer replied. He then asked, "But if you did, it wouldn't be 'I don't remember hardly anything,' would it?"

"No," Josh answered. "It would be everybody knows everything, and it's a perfect story."

But the prosecution's following witnesses did not admit, like Jordan, that they couldn't remember events from twenty-one years earlier. Instead, the defense had problems with phantom events they were convinced had actually happened. Surprisingly, Angie Vogel, who had been an essential part of Jason's alibi, had never been interviewed by detectives during the first investigation. Airy was the only officer she talked with, and Jason's lawyers had not contacted her before the trial. While she confirmed that Jason had sometimes tutored her in math, she had no memory of working with him to arrange the tryst between Amor and Misty Smith. Instead, Vogel said the only time she saw Jason on March 26 was later that night. She told the court, "We were at the Pineapple Bank parking lot waiting to play Fox Hunt." Vogel said that when Jason approached, "He had a piece of paper with a picture on it, and [he] handed it to us and said that this chick was missing?"

"And who was that chick?" Fronk asked.

"Rayna," she answered.

Her recollection tore against the grain of multiple witnesses—not just those who were with Jason before, during, and after Fox Hunt. A crucial piece of evidence could irrefutably dispute it—Bennie did not report Rayna as missing until ten thirty,[65] long after the game had begun, and the Rison family never organized or participated in search parties until the next day. Others could attest that Jason did not know Rayna was missing until the next day or, at the very least, did not claim he did when Matt, Lisa Dyer, and Wendy Rison gathered on his doorstep.[66]

But following Vogel to the stand were her mother and ex-sister-in-law. They, too, remembered Jason handing them flyers, although they were not as sure as Angie about the time and place.

Besides James Amor, no witnesses were more essential to Jason's alibi than the sisters Jamie Swisher and Misty Smith and their mother, Peggy Johnson. Fronk called the older woman first, and it was clear she had severe issues with her memory. When the prosecutor asked her address in the trailer park, she answered, "I cannot remember."

When he pressed her further, "What do you remember about March 26th of 1993?" she replied, "Not a thing."

During his cross-examination, Tompkins asked Johnson about her comment to Hahn "that Jason Tibbs was at your house between 6:00 and 9:00 P.M."

"Again, I do not remember," she replied.

"But you don't deny saying it back in April of 1993?" Tompkins asked.

"I'm not denying it," Johnson said, "But I don't remember."

Jason remembers that his lawyers learned that Johnson had a medical condition that could have accounted for her memory issues. The same could not have been said for her daughters, Jamie and Misty, who professed that they could not remember what happened twenty-one years ago. As with Jason's other alibi witnesses, his lawyers had not attempted to brief them before the trial.

While Jamie remembered that Airy and Williamson saw her in 2008 and reviewed Hahn's 1993 report, "I didn't recall anything that was said on those police reports." She did not even remember talking to the detective.

In fact, upon reflection in 2008, Swisher told the detectives that Hahn's report made sense for various reasons. Perhaps unhappy with that comment, Airy asked if Jamie would have lied for Jason's sake. He wrote, "Jamie advised that she would have and would not even ask why."[67]

When Fronk brought that comment up, Swisher denied she said it. The prosecutor tried to "admit the portion [from Airy's report] she denies making" to show she was lying on the stand. Tompkins objected, and Alevizos sustained. Ironically, with Airy's report, Fronk had opened the door to validating Hahn's account and further supporting Jason's alibi. Tompkins chose not to pursue that track during his cross-examination of Swisher.

Whether by design or accident because of availability, Fronk closed his case with the two witnesses closest to Rayna—her best friend, Lisa Dyer, and the youngest Rison daughter, Wendy. Both had since married and used their husbands' last names.

Although Lisa admitted on the stand that "she didn't particularly care for Jason," she could have easily been a defense witness. Along with Tibbs, she had been among the first to tell police that Ray had started assaulting Rayna again. But at Jason's trial, she provided stunning testimony in line with the women who swore that Jason handed out flyers to them on Friday night. At the time, she was working at the Dairy Queen with Vic Montorsi. "That [Friday] evening," she said, "after we were told that [Rayna] had not come home, we were asked to go on a search party that evening."

"Who asked you?" Fronk inquired.

"Jason Tibbs," she replied, recalling that he had formed a search party in the DQ parking lot, telling those assembled to go to the KOP preserve.

Fronk pressed her on the timing. "How certain are you that this was the night she went missing?"

Implying that she was certain, she replied, "I remember it being very foggy that night."

She also recalled, "The very next morning, we had met at the high school to go on the search that was organized [by her parents]." She did not mention or remember going to Jason's house afterward.

During his cross-examination, Pejic gently challenged her about foraging through the KOP's postapocalyptic wilderness on such a foggy night. Lisa could not be shaken from that memory—even though she didn't remember who else was with her. There were several avenues to impeach her testimony, but Pejic didn't take any of them.

The prosecution's last witness, Rayna's little sister, Wendy, left the jury with an emotional touchstone. Although somewhat curt and caustic about the victim when first interviewed by police twenty-one years earlier, she cried as she took the stand. But Fronk did not call her just to tug on the jurors' heartstrings. He had her hark back to one of the first interviews she gave the La Porte police. In his report on that session, a detective noted, "When asked about Ray McCarty, Wendy was very defensive of him and denied that he had ever attempted anything of a sexual nature with her. She felt that in regards to the molesting, Rayna 'did not tell the whole truth.'"

Instead of her brother-in-law, during that interview she directed her ire at Jason.[68] Through her tears, with Fronk leading the way twenty-one years later, she reprised the story about when she was in Rayna's car with her sister and Jason.

> Q. And where were you sitting?
> A. In the back seat.
> Q. Where was the defendant sitting?
> A. In the passenger seat.
> Q. Was Rayna driving?
> A. Yes, sir.
> Q. Just the three of you in the car?
> A. Yes, sir.
> Q. What did the defendant say?
> A. He was telling my sister how much he loved her and that he wanted to get back together with her.
> Q. Did he say anything about Matt?
> A. That he wanted her not to be with him anymore.

For Jason, this, like Lisa's Friday night search party, was another story that could be impeached in several ways. When Matt Elser was on the stand only a few days before, he told the court that Rayna "would prefer I drive most of the time we went places anyway." According to Jason, "She never drove me anywhere in her car. Not one time."

But despite Jason's scribbled notes and perhaps wary of the jury's sympathy for the sobbing sister, Pejic chose not to cross. "Thank you," he told the judge. "No questions. Thank you."

SPIN DOCTOR

During the third day of the State's case, an extended interlude was granted to Dr. Rick Hoover, the forensic pathologist who performed the autopsy on Rayna. Like many others in his field, the witness's demeanor could quickly shift from a chatty professor to a condescending wonk when confronted by a hostile attorney. Ironically, Rob Beckman was once a Hoover adversary who responded to this behavior with the most trenchant put-down. He was then a defense counsel in a homicide case and took issue with Hoover's testimony about an autopsy. Calling him a "professional witness," he charged, "You're bought and paid for by [the prosecution]." Beckman then cautioned the jury, "Remember, the pathologists themselves admit that their opinions need only be based on a 'reasonable degree of medical certainty,' whatever that means. As members of the jury, you have to be certain beyond a reasonable doubt."[69]

This reminder might have come in handy for John Tompkins as he sparred with Hoover in Jason Tibbs's 2014 trial. But for those familiar with Hoover's comments about Rayna Rison's death in 1993, even more remarkable was the extent to which his "reasonable degree of medical certainty" had shifted in the intervening years, with all sorts of "new" details about the victim's condition that cropped up like the fungus on one of his cadavers. Meanwhile, the greatest conundrum that had once hung over Rayna's autopsy mysteriously disappeared from his 2014 testimony, a shift Tompkins failed to pick up during his needling cross-examination.

When Hoover took the stand for the prosecution, Fronk led him through a lengthy debrief on his background and field. He started by asking, "What is your profession?"

Hoover replied, "I am a physician." He added, "I have specialized in the field of pathology, and I have subspecialized in the field of forensic pathology, so I'm a forensic pathologist." He received his medical degree from Indiana

University and was certified by the American Board of Pathology, which he described as "the highest degree of certification" in forensic pathology. In addition, he was a member of several associations that focus on science related to his practice. Hoover was employed by the South Bend Medical Foundation and subcontracted to do autopsies by the La Porte County Coroner.

As proof of his expertise, Hoover testified, "I have personally performed, at this stage, about 1,800 autopsies. I've also either taught or consulted on probably another four to five hundred. So it's a little over 2,000 autopsies I've been involved with closely."

After describing the typical autopsy, Hoover walked the jury through the report he wrote about Rayna Rison's examination on April 28, 1993. While most of her body "showed changes of a prolonged environment that was wet or aquatic," the portion of her back above the waterline exposed to sunlight "was dried and almost parchment-like."

When Fronk asked how the victim's submersion affected her corpse, Hoover replied with a detailed description of "hyperhydration of the cutaneous tissues." He explained, "After a period of around three or four weeks, actually the skin gets so hydrated, and there's decomposition that you can [then] pull the skin off the hands."

But despite this outward sign of decomposition, Hoover said his autopsy could still determine "the most significant thing externally, there was [sic] no signs of trauma. I didn't see any evidence of, say, severe beating, tears in the skin, or lacerations, no stab wounds, no gunshot wounds."

That Hoover found no evidence of "severe beating" must have sounded confusing for the jury. Only days before, they heard Freeman testify that he saw Tibbs "hit her and everything. And then, as I turned back around, he was on top of her, choking her."

"We might touch back on that subject," Fronk interjected, realizing that Hoover would have to address the contradiction between his findings and the star witness's testimony.

But a few minutes later, when displaying a ghastly shot of Rayna's face, Hoover again downplayed any outward signs of physical trauma. "You'll see a lot of swelling and protuberance around the face," he told the jury. "The face looks almost bloated. That's not because of swelling due to a person that's been beaten when they're alive. It's simply the gas in the body."

A few minutes later, he repeated, "I would say that the thing that is remarkable at this point is there is no evidence of trauma."

Then, perhaps mindful of where the prosecution was heading, Hoover started to back off the "remarkable," spinning an alternative explanation that could align with Freeman's story. "In decomposition, any kind of a minor trauma, like say there was a minor scrape or a tiny bruise on just the surface, decomposition will completely mask that." Although he never used the term "minor trauma" in his autopsy, when discussing the possibility of strangulation and the area around Rayna's neck, Hoover wrote, "The post-mortem changes [i.e., decomposition] would mask any minor hemorrhages noted within the cervical soft tissue and musculature."[70]

On the stand, Hoover made a lack of neck trauma sound like the norm for teen strangulation. "In young females," he said, asphyxiation is "a very common way of death. . . . A decomposed body will leave really no physical evidence."

As if that was not enough of a qualification for the prosecution, he spun even further by hinting at another reason why there was no external trauma. He told the jury, "If you have a physically superior assailant strangling a victim that's of lesser weight—let's say you were to strangle a child. . . . Probably the most common thing in a child strangulation is no marking at all because the child is unable to put up any kind of struggle."

Hoover went into another extended discourse on how someone could have strangled Rayna without snapping the horseshoe-shaped hyoid bone above her Adam's apple or the surrounding cartilage. It was another "remarkable thing." He explained, "It was remarkable because we didn't see trauma, but it was also remarkable because anatomically, she wouldn't have shown trauma that we would typically find in an asphyxia-type death." But then he explained that other young women in Rayna's age group have "pliable" hyoid bones that don't snap, even after they are removed during the autopsy.

As a final step in determining the cause of death, Hoover told the jury he had "to look at toxicology to rule out the possibility of poisoning." Then, in a comment that would have shocked everyone ever associated with the Rison investigation, he said, "There were no significant findings in the toxicology examination that would explain her death as well."

To say "there were no significant findings" in the toxicology screens was an outright lie. As he knew well, the findings of isopropyl alcohol in Rayna's system sparked multiple tests to confirm them.[71] The labs found the absence of acetone to be "abnormal" as well.[72] By not mentioning these findings, he may have tried to cover for himself by adding that the results did not "explain her death"—at least as far as he was concerned.

Still, Hoover conceded to the jury that he had to use a "process of elimination" to conclude, "The cause of death was determined to be asphyxia due to cervical compression, and the manner of death was homicide."

For any defense counsel remotely familiar with Hoover's autopsy or his communications about it, the testimony at Jason's trial left several gaping holes in his conclusions on the cause of death. But it would have been better yet for the defense to have its own highly regarded pathologist react to Hoover's comments on the type of physical trauma that would have resulted from the fight Freeman described, the rate of decomposition for a corpse submerged in water, and the significance of the victim's toxicology screens.

But despite the resources Jim Bruno had put at Jason's disposal, Tompkins decided he alone could best take on Hoover with his cross-examination. It was a confrontation that got testy from the get-go. The lawyer's first parry was to question the pathologist's expertise in performing an autopsy on this particular victim. He asked, "As of 1993 when you conducted this autopsy, how many autopsies had you conducted on teenage female victims, if you know or recall?"

Calling it "a silly question," Hoover said there was no way his agency kept track of victims by age, so he could only answer, "I don't know."

But Tompkins was not done with this line of questioning. "Back to your experience in '93, if you recall, how many autopsies had you performed on bodies that had experienced prolonged water exposure?"

There was another snarky back-and-forth where Tompkins said, "I don't want a guess. If you want to give me an estimate, that's fine."

"I would apologize to the Court for using the word 'guess,'" Hoover sneered. "If you would like to rephrase your questions or re-ask them, I will answer every question with an estimate."

Eventually, the pathologist estimated that he had done an autopsy for "twenty-five to thirty bodies that have been in a prolonged water environment."

In other words, it was a tiny fraction of all the autopsies he had performed, but Tompkins could not make much hay with that. Instead, he walked Hoover through a tedious explication of each medical term and description in the autopsy report that he projected on the screen with his highlights. "And I'm sorry, but . . . I'm not a doctor," he said at one point, "I need a little explanation of your terminology there, please."

His prolonged probing did yield some defense-friendly tidbits from the voluble witness, who, despite himself, was eager to show off his forensic acumen, even during cross-examination. "She didn't have any evidence of a broken nail. A typical finding that we look for, and we do find in a minority of cases. . . . If you struggle, you can break your nails, especially if you have longer nails in, say, a female. The nails can actually—if there's enough struggle—they can get ripped off. If they get ripped off, there will be a tear in the skin, and there can be bleeding that is in the tissue, and we might note that even in a decomposed person."

Like Rene Gazarkiewicz, once Hoover got going, there was no stopping him, and the information about the nails was the sort of oversharing that could make a prosecutor cringe. But if Tompkins had his own forensic pathologist, an opposing expert could have told the jury about the injuries that Rayna should have suffered in a struggle like the one Freeman described and how that trauma would have appeared—even after moderate decomposition.

Despite the contentious start to the cross-examination, it eventually became the witness's show. Tompkins let Hoover's autopsy lead the way for his questions and permitted the professorial pathologist to spiel out his answers—even though many were fraught with internal contradictions, which the attorney appeared incapable of drawing out for the jury. Tompkins took them on an extended fishing expedition, but he had no catch to show for their journey. Without his own expert, he had to rely on Hoover's process of elimination for Rayna's cause of death. It was a determination that even the smug witness had to admit was unsupported by forensic evidence.

GHOST OF A CHANCE

Jason's lawyers began his defense on the fifth day of the trial. Although he continued to scribble one or two pages of notes each session, Jason says, "I might as well have been a ghost. I can't remember them asking a witness one question I wanted to ask."

During the prosecution's case, the worst of his fears were realized. "I tried to tell them, 'We need to focus on where I was and what time I was there.' But they didn't even bother to prepare my best alibi witnesses. They were so convinced McCarty did it. They weren't worried about showing I didn't do it." But that plan A didn't work. His counsel's attempts to introduce incriminating evidence about McCarty were continuously stifled, and Jason felt they hadn't done enough to support his alibi during cross-examination.

The lawyers assured him things would change when they called their witnesses. But the first one proved a disaster. "Things seemed to go south from there," Jason remembers. "Before the end of the day, after one of their sidebars, Tompkins came back to the table and said to me under his breath, 'You're not going to receive a fair trial. This is about damage control now.'"

Tompkins intended to strike a blow at the most vulnerable part of the Hammons and Freeman testimony by making retired deputy sheriff Mark Ludlow the first defense witness. The star witnesses' stories mentioned a series of locations separated by several miles. The trips between those places and the related activities could have never been completed between the time Rayna was abducted and her LTD was first seen on N. 200 E.

At sixty-three, thin and gray-haired, Ludlow joined the parade of retired police officers who had already testified. Having been with the La Porte County sheriff's office for twenty-five years, he was well qualified to conduct a "time survey" covering the routes that would have been taken between each destination Freeman delineated. While he was at it, Tompkins had Ludlow include travel times between Jason's home, the animal hospital, and the trailer park. Each result of his time survey was displayed on a big map for the jury. As the lawyer instructed, Ludlow marked seven locations with letters and drew lines over roads between them, reporting how long it took him to drive each route between 6:00 and 8:00 P.M. But when it came to the trip between the Fail Road spot where Jason supposedly killed Rayna and the pole barn, Ludlow started shuffling through his notes. "I apologize," he told the court. "I did not have the distance and the time."

"And you shared your notes with me on these routes that you took, correct?" Tompkins asked, clearly taken aback. The lawyer tried to give the witness the notes he shared, but Fronk objected since that would have been leading the witness, and Alevizos agreed. Tompkins and Ludlow were then forced to complete their map without the most time-consuming leg of Jason's alleged circuit. Adding insult to injury, when jurors had a chance to question the witness, they had issues with some of his route choices and travel times. Tompkins attempted to recall Ludlow the next day, but Fronk objected again, citing a rule that "prohibits [Ludlow] from . . . taking the second bite out of the apple because he didn't do it right the first time."

Alevizos agreed. "Hey," he told Tompkins, "You put it out there. You live with it now."

The second and third witnesses were to be the most crucial cogs in Jason's slam dunk defense: Ray and Lori McCarty. At 49, Ray wore his hair in a buzz cut and appeared to have bulked up, but he walked gingerly to the front of the courtroom. He later explained he had surgery on his back for degenerated spinal disks, and the lawyers let him remain standing while he testified.

Before the jury returned to the courtroom, there was more wrangling between Fronk and Tompkins about what the defense could ask Ray. In the deposition Pejic took a few weeks earlier, McCarty admitted knowing two people charged him with assaulting Rayna again before she disappeared.[73]

Alevizos permitted Tompkins to ask the question and submit the deposition as evidence. But, unhappy with the decision, Fronk wanted to know, "Does counsel see that as a springboard to something else?" Tompkins promised to stick to the judge's rigorous guidelines—no mention of the grand jury or its McCarty indictment. But questions about Rayna's molestation and Ray's conviction for that could be fair game.

When the direct examination began, Tompkins started with March 26, 1993, and McCarty admitted he had been near the animal hospital with his "light blue" Datsun B210 at "5:40, 5:45 [P.M.]," supposedly to look at a house for sale.

At this dramatic moment, Alevizos lurched up from the bench. His diabetes had struck again. "I'm sorry. I'm sick," he said. "Just hold it right there." He bolted out of the courtroom to vomit and didn't return for several minutes.

After the judge returned, Tompkins resumed his questions about McCarty's vantage point on Warren Street. From there, Ray said, weather conditions were "pretty clear," and he could see the Pine Lake Animal Hospital. "I went over to [the animal hospital] to ask [Rayna]—because I noticed her car was there—and I asked her the question, 'Did she know where Lori might be.'" When he pulled his Datsun into the parking lot, "she was in the foyer, mopping or something. I don't know what she was doing." He claimed he saw no one else and no other parked cars besides the LTD. He then calmly used the court's Telestrator to draw where his Datsun was parked after he backed into the lot.

Then, treating McCarty as another witness instead of the potential perpetrator, Tompkins asked if he had seen the Hammons Buick Century, "You never saw a silver car pull into the clinic parking lot while you were there . . . or while you were leaving?"

"No," Ray answered.

At this point, Tompkins tried to enter a photo of Ray's Datsun into evidence, but the shot was taken at the police station and was covered with a patchwork of tape to guide lifts of fingerprints. Fronk believed that to be incriminating, and Alevizos agreed. The judge asked, "Do you have a different one? Didn't you have one the other day?"

Now annoyed because he had nothing handy, Pejic snarked, "I can't get in my time machine." Once again, the jury was blocked from seeing McCarty's spotted car.

Tompkins next tried to show that Ray provided multiple alibis, which implied a consciousness of guilt. However, the lawyer had to let the jury come to that conclusion on their own.

> Q. And, in fact, you've told three stories in addition to the one you just told us today?
> A. Yes, but close.
> Q. And you were telling those three stories to the police?
> A. Yes.
> Q. The police who were investigating the disappearance of Rayna?
> A. Yes.

Nothing about McCarty's multiple alibis was more incriminating than how he changed them after witnesses came forward to counter his previous stories. When Tompkins probed in that direction, Fronk objected, and Alevizos wouldn't allow the defense attorney to delve into his own witness's lies in any detail. McCarty admitted he lied once, and that was all the jury had to hear.

Tompkins returned to the subject later in his direct examination, but he went down an alley that did his client no favors.

> Q. Why were you lying to the police about where you were on the evening of March 26th, 1993?
> A. Because the police talked to my wife first to find out what I was doing or where my whereabouts was.
> Q. That's why you lied to the police because they talked to your wife first?
> A. Well, she already gave them where I was, the story. So it's kind of hard to go back and change what they've already asked. . . .
> Q. Why were you telling a lie?
> A. Because I picked up a female hitchhiker and didn't want to tell her that.
> Q. Okay. Why didn't you want to tell her that?
> A. Well, the track record between me and her wasn't always the best.
> Q. Okay. So you thought it might upset her?
> A. Yeah.

With this line of questioning, Tompkins hammered home the McCartys' excuse for his multiple alibis. The impetus for each change was not caused by witnesses coming forward to dispute him. They were strictly made not to upset his wife or get her into trouble with the police.

Besides the changing alibis, McCarty's sexual history with Rayna also implicated him in her murder. Because of an answer Ray gave in a defense deposition, Alevizos allowed Tompkins to ask, "At the time Rayna disappeared, you are aware she had made allegations you were making sexual advances towards her. Isn't that correct?"

At first, McCarty denied he was ever aware, but Tompkins showed him the deposition. "You answered, 'Yeah,' to that question [during the deposition], didn't you?"

"Yes," McCarty replied.

Now the door was open to the most damning information about Ray that the jury would hear. "You had previously pled guilty to raping Rayna Rison, isn't that true?"

McCarty answered, "No," as Fronk objected. Technically, Tompkins was wrong about the charge. The lawyer tried again, "You were charged with child molestation as a Class C Felony, correct?" But he was wrong a second time, as Ray pointed out. The charge had been negotiated down to a D Felony.[74]

This was the most explosive news of the day for younger journalists unfamiliar with the events surrounding Rayna's 1993 disappearance and Ray's 1998 indictment. One reporter titled her story, "Shocking testimony in La Porte County cold case trial."

Although Alevizos let Tompkins question McCarty about this sensitive topic, the lawyer missed several chances to bring out the malevolent side of his witness's character. While Ray knew about the class of his felony, he was surprisingly clueless about other aspects of his crime and punishment. When asked about Rayna's age at the time he molested her, he replied, "I'm not sure. I think thirteen, twelve, thirteen." She was twelve when he started,[75] and if he did fail to remember how young she was, then he revealed his denial about the harm caused by the molestation—one reason he got kicked out of therapy.

Ray was also uncertain about the conditions of his probation. Tompkins asked, "And do you recall whether there was a no-contact order or restriction for your contact with minors during your probation?"

McCarty answered, "Minors discluding [*sic*] family, I believe."

"But including Rayna Rison?"

Ray replied, "I don't believe so."

Surprised at his answer, Tompkins asked again.

> Q. And if, in fact, you were on probation, contact with her would have subjected you to a potential violation of that probation, right?
>
> A. I don't believe she was [included]. I think [I could see] immediate family. We could all still be together; Christmas, New Year's, all of that. I don't think [the no-contact condition] was like that, no.
>
> Q. But sexual contact with her wasn't allowed, was it?
>
> A. Correct.
>
> Q. So, that type of contact would have subjected you to potential violations of your probation and new charges?
>
> A. Correct.

In fact, McCarty's order of probation came with an addendum that stated, "The defendant shall have no contact or restricted contact with minor children unless monitored by the probation department via constant adult supervision." There was no exclusion for his family—even his own children—and if he violated that condition, "the Court may revoke the suspended sentence." McCarty signed the addendum along with his probation officer and the judge. His other condition above those signatures was "counseling," which stipulated no more than three unexcused absences.[76] His ejection from three different programs would have been equally "shocking" for the jury, the journalists, and most in attendance, but the lawyer never mentioned it.

Tompkins appeared unprepared to respond to McCarty's claim that he was not restricted from contact with Rayna. To set the witness straight, he should have had ready access to Ray's order of probation in the color-coded files. Tompkins next asked when the probation "actually ended," and Ray, who never took probation seriously, replied, "That I don't know exactly."

Besides bringing up the multiple alibis and the molestation conviction, Tompkins only landed disjointed jabs at his witness. He had Ray return to the

Telestrator to show where he once lived on Fail Road, a little more than a mile from the pond. The lawyer also asked if he visited Charlie Allen at any point on March 26. Ray denied that. Tompkins would later read Allen's sworn testimony to the court to impeach him. (Having fallen off a bucket truck while trimming trees fifteen years earlier, Allen claimed he sustained a head injury that prevented him from testifying about 1993 incidents. The defense had to settle for his confusing, contradictory comments to the grand jury in 1998.)

Before McCarty left the stand, Tompkins convened a sidebar to discuss "one last question" he wanted to ask. "That question is," he told the judge, "Have you ever gone to trial for killing Rayna Rison?"

Of course, Fronk objected, and Alevizos sustained. He ruled that the defense had presented no facts about McCarty's guilt in evidence—something the judge had prevented them from doing. Tompkins argued he could ask because of the jurors' voir dire form, where they had to indicate whether they knew if someone else had been indicted for Rayna's murder. "The State brought up the statement [in voir dire]," Tompkins said. His question, he claimed, would assure the jurors that McCarty never went to trial. "The jury has one chance [to know if he went to trial]," Tompkins argued. "I want to make it clear that that's not true." His sudden concern about McCarty's reputation sounded disingenuous at best.

But the indictment question on the voir dire form was not evidence. Alevizos did not want Tompkins to bring it up during cross-examination or in his closing argument. The defense could only work it into the trial record as an offer of proof. Should they lose the case, the appellate court could consider whether the judge made the right decision. That hearing took place the next day, outside the presence of the jurors. For Jason, these sessions were excruciating torture. "I was hearing all this evidence that could have been used to exonerate me, and I didn't understand why the jury couldn't hear it too. I kept pushing John and Scott to get this stuff in front of the jury because this was where the truth was."

But as Alevizos told Jason's lawyers, nothing about McCarty's investigation or indictment was relevant to Jason's trial unless "you have . . . a particular piece of evidence that you can link up [to] this case." But "this case" mainly comprised the stories that Hammons and Freeman fabricated. How could they be associated with the actual murder?

The one significant piece from the original investigation that could have linked Ray to the crime was the isopropyl alcohol found in Rayna's body. The same chemical was integral to McCarty's job as a dipper. But virtually everyone involved with Jason's trial and both investigations were clueless about what Ray did at Teledyne. For all his tedious scrutiny of Hoover's autopsy, Tompkins never mentioned the toxicology report while he had the forensic pathologist on the stand during his cross-examination.

Ray's changing alibis were another story. While Tompkins brought them up multiple times during McCarty's direct examination, he could never tell the jury what was most suspicious about his alterations. Pejic pinpointed their significance during a contentious sidebar with the judge and Fronk. "Back in 1993, Mr. McCarty was changing his alibis as different evidence came out." The defense should have been allowed to break that down for the jury.

"Yeah? And guess what?" Alevizos retorted. McCarty "admitted it."

"No," Pejic replied. "You wouldn't let us go there, Judge, because you said, well, he's impeached, and we can't get into the details. And that goes into [Ray's] consciousness of guilt, and that's always relevant."

But the judge's most egregious block came when he refused to enter thirteen-year-old Rayna's police statement about her molestation. "If I didn't do as [McCarty] asked of me, he would hurt me," she told the female detective. "And he said that if I ever told, he would KILL me."

Her signature appeared above the text: "This statement is the truth to the best of my knowledge, and I will read and sign it as the truth as I know it."[77] But Alevizos dismissed the document because it wasn't made "under oath." He added, "The whole issue doesn't relate, you know. Child molesting and murder is [sic] not the same thing. . . . It [should] not be shown to the jury."

Several hearsay exceptions should have allowed jurors to hear that evidence. Pejic cited the one for public records, but Federal Rule 807, known as "Residual Exception," seems to have been written for it. The first condition requires that "the statement is supported by sufficient guarantees of trustworthiness—after considering the totality of circumstances under which it was made and evidence, if any, corroborating the statement."[78] The circumstances could not have been more trustworthy since they were witnessed by at least one police officer and Rayna's parents. As for evidence, only hours before, the underage

THE CASE AGAINST JASON TIBBS

victim had undergone an abortion, and her abuser admitted paternity. But the second condition is even more applicable to Jason's case, which requires "it is more probative [provides supporting proof] on the point for which it is offered than any other evidence that the proponent can obtain through reasonable efforts." In direct contradiction to the judge's comment, Rayna's statement showed how Ray's "molesting" could have led him to murder.

Ultimately, the jury would only hear Tompkins question McCarty about his threats without using Rayna's statement to impeach his answers.

Q. Had you threatened or warned Rayna Rison about telling anybody . . .
A. No.
Q. . . . about any sexual contact with between you and her back in '89?
A. No.
Q. You hadn't?
A. No.
Q. You're sure about that?
A. Positive.

When Lori McCarty took the stand, there was no weeping like her little sister. Jason says, "She just had an expression on her face like she was angry with the world." At forty-seven, Lori had gotten heavier, with gray streaks through her unruly shoulder-length hair. "She looked kind of rough," Jason remembers, "like one of those ladies you see sitting on a lawn chair in a trailer park. She didn't do anything to dress up either. Just a shirt and slacks."

When Pejic questioned her, she often snapped back with her answers and, at one point, perhaps in a bid for sympathy, provided a reason for her failure to remember incidents surrounding Rayna's murder. "My life hasn't always been just a walk in the park," she told the lawyer. "I've had a lot of different stress from a lot of different angles, and I lost my son three years ago. So, therefore, my memory is not the best anymore." Her son, Hunter, had died in a motorcycle accident at the age of twenty-one.[79]

But for those familiar with the details of the first investigation, the things Lori claimed to forget were suspicious, and the things she remembered were even more so. When asked about the car she was driving on March 26, Lori replied, "I'm going to say it was the Tracer at the time." She was undoubtedly aware that

308

the defense would call Val Eilers, who saw her Sunbird and Ray's spotted Datsun on North 150 East when she likely brought him his waders. Eilers remembered that one car had a black leather "bra" that wrapped around the headlights and front bumper. After Pejic pressed her to admit she owned a silver Pontiac with a "bra" on it, he asked, "Is it possible you were driving that car on March 26th?" She answered, "It's possible."

Similarly, she lied about her exit from the Risons' house with the kids to refute her possible involvement with the 6:30 P.M. Eilers sighting. "Do you remember what time you left your parents' home?" Pejic asked.

Lori answered, "7:00 P.M."

"You sure?"

"Absolutely sure."

As Pejic knew, other witnesses had her leaving more than an hour earlier, including Matt Elser, Wendy, and Wendy's then-boyfriend. But there was only so much the lawyer could do to impeach Lori's testimony at this stage in the trial. Using Jason's defense to convict Ray McCarty was like introducing one play during the intermission of another.

When the questions turned to Ray, Lori proved to have a better memory than her husband on such things as when his child molesting probation was completed. But memories about what led to his conviction faded in and out for the witness in convenient ways.

> Q. How did you find out Ray molested Rayna?
> A. From my father.
> Q. And how did he find out?
> A. From a pregnancy test that came back positive.
> Q. So Ray impregnated Rayna?
> A. Yes.
> Q. Do you remember going to the police station with your father?
> A. I don't remember that, no.
> Q. Do you remember telling the police that Ray threatened to harm you and your daughter if Rayna ever told on him that he was molesting her?
> A. I don't remember that either.

Fronk jumped up to stop the proceedings for yet another heated sidebar. Outside the jury's hearing, he called the 1989 police report[80] about the threat

"Inadmissible." When Pejic responded with the legal grounds for bringing it up, the prosecutor spat back, "Bull crap."

Since Lori was unwilling to confirm that Ray had threatened her, Alevizos and Fronk believed the report alone was hearsay. The prosecutor implied Rayna was the "one person that can testify to that." But for Tompkins and Pejic, it established "a motive" and a warning for why McCarty would have killed his sister-in-law if she turned him in again. That could count as a hearsay exception.

As far as the judge was concerned, though, evidence dealing with the molestation was irrelevant. The defense was picking on a man who made a mistake and had done his time. He argued the State wasn't allowed to behave that way, so Jason's team couldn't either. "If [prosecutors] are going after somebody, they can't use prior bad acts. [This] is the exact same situation."

Blocked from any further attack on Ray's character during his direct with Lori, Pejic tried to dissect the relationship between the sisters in the days before Rayna was abducted. When he asked about "the fight" that grew out of arrangements for their cousin's abortion, Lori said she had no memory of that.

Pejic approached again to refresh Lori's memory with her sworn testimony from 1998.

> Q. So, do you remember testifying that the fight was a Thursday the week prior?
> A. That's what I said on the paper.
> Q. And it was a heated argument?
> A. Yes.
> Q. Do you remember why you were mad?
> A. Because Rayna was mad at me.
> Q. Did you scream back to her, "At least this other person didn't screw her brother-in-law."
> A. I could have. I don't remember that.
> Q. Do you ever remember receiving a letter from Rayna?
> A. Not that I can remember, no.

But Pejic kept pressing on the animosity between the sisters, and Lori could not help but spew the acerbic comments about the victim that shocked investigators in 1993.

> Q. Did you ever tell people that it was partially Rayna's fault for having been molested?
>
> A. I don't recall that.
>
> Q. Did you ever say it takes two?
>
> A. I may have.

Seeing where Pejic was headed, Fronk objected, trying to cut off this line of questions. During the sidebar he charged, "He's trying to make [Lori] out to be a bad person because of a 13-year-old girl [and] all that. We've gone through that situation. At this point, it's just smearing people."

But Pejic wasn't putting words in the witness's mouth. As she expressed her views on Rayna's molestation, Lori painted a venomous self-portrait. Pejic had another bomb he wanted to drop. In the sidebar, he told the judge he would bring up the stun gun that Ray bought the day after "the fight."

"There has been no stun gun involved at all in this crime," Alevizos shot back. Pejic explained how it could have been used to murder Rayna in the animal hospital parking lot, but the judge cut him off. "It's speculation. No stun gun." But perhaps stunned by Lori's previous answers about her sister, Alevizos told Pejic, "You may continue [that] line of questioning." With the judge's permission, the lawyer sliced back into Lori's excuse for why her husband assaulted a tween.

> Q. What could a 12- or 13-year-old girl have done to be partly responsible for having been molested by an adult?
>
> A. Because I knew the mentality of my sister.
>
> Q. Was she a worldly person?
>
> A. What do you mean by "worldly"?
>
> Q. Well, had you ever told anyone she was worldly, advanced beyond her years?
>
> A. She was very intelligent.
>
> Q. Well, what don't you understand about the question? She was 12- or 13-years-old.
>
> A. I don't know what you don't understand about the answer.
>
> Q. Well, indulge me. What was your answer again?
>
> A. I said that I knew my sister.
>
> Q. And what did you know about your sister?
>
> A. That she was a lot more mature than your average 12 and 13-year-old.

> Q. Do you have any training, education, or experience with psychiatry or psychology?
>
> A. No, I do not.
>
> Q. . . . So when you say Rayna was very mature—do you mean physically versus mentally?
>
> A. The whole package.
>
> Q. And that's just based on your observation?
>
> A. My observation. Yes.

With Lori on the stand, the defense could take another crack at how Ray defied the conditions of his child molesting probation. Bennie Rison often claimed he had been responsible for the no-contact order,[81] and Pejic referred to that condition of probation as "another rule that Raymond was supposed to follow [out of] respect [for] your father."

This Lori remembered. Rayna and Ray "were not to be alone together."

Now Pejic could set McCarty up for a perfect gotcha moment. He asked, "And had Raymond ever been alone with Rayna prior to her disappearance and after him being released from probation?"

"Only from what I know through hearsay," she replied with a legal savvy that may have gone over the jury's head but must have been appreciated by the judge and prosecutor.

However, Pejic had artfully brought up two of those light bulbs that so vexed Lori in the early days of the first investigation. According to Bennie, Ray was never supposed to be alone with Rayna, but after her LTD was found, McCarty fretted about the FBI finding his fingerprints on the car. To allay his fears, Ray and Lori claimed he had been alone with Rayna when they took a recent shopping trip in her LTD. Only later did they realize this incident would have violated Bennie's rule.

Pejic asked Lori, "Do you ever remember testifying that Rayna took Ray to the store on one occasion?" She replied that she didn't remember, but Lori conceded that she must have said it after the lawyer pulled up her grand jury testimony.

Still, no matter how cutting Pejic's line of attack on this point, it may have been too deep in the weeds for a juror to appreciate. Throughout his direct examination, Pejic had multiple opportunities to challenge Lori's memory lapses and lies, but observers needed a backstory to understand their significance. There was no time for that in an hour-long session.

Before Lori left the stand, Pejic returned to the charge about her husband, making him a prime suspect in 1993. Previously, he asked, was she told two people heard Rayna say that Ray was "making sexual advances towards her?"

"Yes, I was told about that," Lori replied.

Without mentioning "grand jury," Pejic reminded her that she said in sworn testimony, "[The sexual advances would have been made] after my husband was off probation, so it was between . . . January and March." As Pejic realized, Lori's statement betrayed some questionable thinking on her part. Even if Ray was off probation, wasn't he still prevented from sexually assaulting her sister?

The allegation about Ray assaulting Rayna again in 1993 was something Fronk couldn't leave unchallenged. During the cross-examination, he asked Lori how she learned these people had made those charges. She answered, "I was told through one of the investigators."

Fronk followed up, "Did [he] tell you who the people were that were making these allegations?"

Lori replied, "One of them was Jason Tibbs, but I don't recall who the other name was." She had conveniently forgotten the other name was Matt Elser, someone whose testimony earlier in the trial had gone unchallenged by either Fronk or the defense. He probably also left a positive impression on the jury. At first, Pejic did not attempt to fill in the blanks during his redirect of Lori, but after jury questions, he was allowed more redirect examination. He asked, "Had you ever been made aware that Matt Elser was the other person who had made an allegation?"

"It could have been," Lori answered, "but Jason's name is the only one that stood out in my mind."

Pejic also used his extra time to ask Lori for the birth dates of her sister and husband. Earlier, a juror had asked her "the age difference between Raymond and Rayna." She replied, "About ten years." But as jurors learned after Pejic's question, the gap was closer to eleven years than ten.

Like the reporter, jurors may have been shocked that Ray had molested Rayna. Likewise, Lori did not leave a good impression when she used her sister's maturity to minimize her husband's crime. But it was one thing to tarnish the McCartys' reputation. It was quite another to accuse Ray of murder. With their remaining witnesses, the defense had a twofold challenge. First, they needed to conduct an abbreviated homicide case against Ray to prove he was more a suspect in Rayna's murder than Jason. Second, they needed to show how that evidence was ignored in a second investigation laser-focused on convicting Jason, no matter how weak the case was against him.

Like the detectives did when they built their timeline in 1993, Pejic started with Roy West. In the early evening of March 26, he was the first to spot McCarty's spotted Datsun on the street perpendicular to the animal hospital. But there was a confusing element to his account that Pejic and Fronk both skated around. The man who got out of the blue station wagon was not Ray McCarty—or Jason Tibbs, for that matter. He was tall and thin with blonde hair—likely Scott Scarborough. While on the stand at Jason's trial, West was not asked to describe the man he met, only the blue station wagon the stranger was in with its loud muffler and the time of the encounter.

During the first investigation, Val Eilers, the defense's next witness, had implicated both Ray and Lori McCarty by the cars they drove. She not only identified Ray's spotted Datsun pulled to the side of the road on North 150 East at 6:30 P.M. She also remembered the second car with it had "something black across the front," like the leather bra on Lori's Sunbird. She repeated her sighting under Tompkins's direct examination with the same steady self-assurance she had shown through numerous interviews, depositions, and the grand jury. During his cross-examination, Fronk didn't try to shake Val from her certainty about seeing Ray's Datsun that night. Instead, he focused on her sighting of Lori's Sunbird. When the county detective first showed her that model and asked if that was the second car, he reported she had said, "Absolutely not." But on multiple occasions after, Eilers denied she said that and corrected the detective's report before she testified at the grand jury. During his redirect, Tompkins asked, "So even back in '93, when you talked to that officer, were you certain about the white vehicle and the blue vehicle that you saw?"

"Yes," Val replied, "I was." As she later conceded under more cross by Fronk, she wasn't *as* certain because there were more cars in the style and color of Lori's Sunbird than Ray's Datsun station wagon.

Although Val Eilers would have been an effective witness in Ray McCarty's trial, her testimony for Jason Tibbs must have seemed like an outlier to the jury. The defense counsel did not or could not connect the dots that would explain the significance of Ray and Lori's meeting at North 150 East at that time. Indeed, investigators failed to come up with a probable explanation in 1993—that she was there to give her husband his waders.

The minitrial against Ray continued with the appearance of retired City of La Porte detective Robert Schoff, who had been yanked off Rayna's case because he may have been leaking information about the investigation to the Rison family. Lori had used him as an intermediary when Ray's alibis abruptly changed, and Schoff dutifully made reports on each of those attempts. However, his most damaging testimony was hamstrung by Alevizos. Schoff remembered speaking to Ray only once about his alibi. His other conversations were with Lori, and the judge deemed that hearsay since she was talking about a third party—her husband. Fronk argued that there was no reason to delve further into all Ray's lies because he had admitted he lied so as not to upset his wife. After more sidebar wrangling, the most potent question Pejic could ask was, "During the course of your investigation, did you ever determine an alibi for Ray McCarty?" Schoff replied, "No."

In what must have seemed an odd line of questioning to the jurors, Pejic also asked Schoff about Bennie Rison's involvement with the investigation. "Did he have the run of the station?" Schoff had to review his grand jury testimony before he agreed he had made that comment. For those familiar with what happened behind the scenes of the Rison investigation, Bennie was known to be a distraction in his efforts to steer detectives away from Ray. But Pejic did not connect those dots for the jurors. They were left on their own to determine why that mattered.

The next witness also touched on a discovery from the first investigation that did not seem significant without context. Timothy Shortt was the La

Porte County patrolman who first identified Rayna's car when the LTD was abandoned on North 200 East. But coincidentally, his parents were close friends with Bennie and Karen Rison. At the funeral home, the night before Rayna's funeral, Lori took Shortt aside to tell him how the city police had seized their cars, but that Ray had her vacuum his Datsun first. Evidence technicians later noted that the hatchback area—where Ray had kept carcasses wrapped in a green blanket—looked suspiciously clean compared to the rest of the car's messy conditions.[82] While most of the hatchback detritus had been vacuumed away, green rayon fibers remained in the car and on Rayna's body. But Jason's lawyers could never share these details with the jury. After more back-and-forth with Alevizos about what constituted hearsay in Shortt's potential testimony, Pejic was only permitted to ask, "Did Lori McCarty ever advise you that she had cleaned or vacuumed out Ray McCarty's car?" To which he answered, "Yes." He was permitted to leave, and the court was adjourned for the day.

By any account, the defense's debut at the trial was an unmitigated disaster. Still, counsel planned to wrap up their case the next day when their star witness would be Brett Airy. Their chances for acquittal would depend on how well they eviscerated him and his investigation. The City of La Porte detective was another revealing no-call among the State's witnesses. He and Williamson had supposedly solved a cold case that eluded a generation of detectives before them, but the prosecutor asked neither one to testify how they did it. Once again, this raised suspicions about the tactics they used. But Fronk may have been more concerned about how the detectives would handle sustained hostile questions.

Before Airy took the stand, the defense called Beth York—a move they intended to corner the detective and undermine the most fragile part of his case. York lived around the corner from where Rayna's car was abandoned with the hood open. Returning from a South Bend wrestling event with her two sons, she had to swerve around the LTD and a smaller-sized pickup parked behind it on the side of the narrow road. Her testimony had been tested over multiple interviews, depositions, and the grand jury. What she saw through the fog on March 26 was much at odds with the Freeman story. No one knew better than Airy, who first

316

interviewed her in 2009. After he failed to convince Beth that she saw Jen Hammons's Buick Century and not a pickup, the detective went on a fruitless weeks-long quest to prove the truck the Yorks saw belonged to another Hammons houseguest.

York and her sons also saw two men by the vehicles. One was bent over as though he were looking under the hood. The other stood back by the pickup. Although York had described the one under the hood as looking like a woodsman when she testified before the grand jury, Alevizos blocked her from repeating that to Jason's jury because this detail may have come out while she was under hypnosis. Her sighting of the pickup—rather than the Buick Century—was not the only distressing part of her testimony for the prosecution. She could also say with certainty that her observations occurred before 7:00 P.M. because her sons still saw a few minutes of *Married . . . with Children* before the program ended.

When Airy first took the stand, it was for the trial's most extended offer of proof outside the jury's presence. In a test run to see what the judge would permit him to ask, Pejic probed how much Airy failed to review the evidence against Ray McCarty. While the detective claimed to have read "all the case reports," the raw material of the first investigation, he admitted he had not reviewed the "prior sworn statement testimony"—in other words, the grand jury testimony. It was either slipshod on his part or contemptuous of the proceedings that resulted in McCarty's indictment.

With that opening, Pejic went step-by-step to see if he had reviewed all the known evidence that incriminated Ray. The detective said he was aware of the ever-changing alibis and McCarty's efforts to get others to support his false claims, which he continued to make during interviews he gave months before the trial. Yet Airy chose not to interview McCarty until after he arrested Tibbs. Referring to the multiple alibis, Pejic asked, "With you being a police officer, are you familiar with the term consciousness of guilt?"

Airy replied, "No."

Pejic also tried a more direct attack, charging, "You chose to ignore the prior evidence that was elicited and discovered in the prior investigation" about the alibis.

"That he lied?" Airy asked.

"Yeah."

"People lie all the time."

Now abandoning all pretexts of a Q&A, Pejic replied to his witness, "I understand that, but you chose to ignore all of that evidence."

"It doesn't mean he committed a murder," Airy shot back.

But for Alevizos, none of this mattered. As far as the judge was concerned, the only evidence about the changing alibis came from other detectives' reports. "What do you want [Airy] to testify to," he asked Pejic, "a report that's based on another third party's [report]? The way you do this is you call those people, and you put them on the stand." In fact, Harold Hahn was the perfect witness to meet the judge's challenge. He had already appeared as a State witness. Pejic could have called him back to review his "Summ. of Ray's Stories" memo, which tried to keep track of McCarty's ever-changing alibis during the spring of 1993.[83]

But that was not an option Pejic chose to take. Instead, he argued that the third-party reports qualified as hearsay exceptions because they could "impeach" Airy's contention that he conducted a thorough investigation.

Alevizos didn't buy it. "You can ask him . . ., 'You didn't interview Ray McCarty?' Yeah, that's fine. Yeah. That goes to [thoroughness]. But all of this other stuff about the alibi being shot . . . [you] had Officer Schoff indicate that none of [the alibis] panned out. And if I were to allow you to go further into those, I'm certainly not going to do it through an officer reading twenty-year-old police reports based on what somebody else said. The way you do that is you . . . get those witnesses, and you put them on the stand here."

"But, Judge, it's [Airy's] investigation," Pejic pleaded. "He's responsible for going over those reports and him speaking—"

Alevizos shut him down. "None of that is coming in front of this jury unless it comes through the people who actually made those statements in those reports because that's how the law works."

Then, in a slap at the defense counsel's competence, he added, "You have every right to call those people. Bring them in as witnesses. You could have listed them in your list of sixty witnesses. Why you didn't, that's your decision, not mine."

Even if Pejic had called those witnesses who were still alive, would Alevizos have allowed them to testify if they had no memory of what happened decades ago? The judge answered that question a few moments later, saying, "You're trying to bring in evidence that Ray McCarty did it. . . . You need to do that by following the rules of evidence, not by doing double hearsay twenty years removed." But the entire trial hung on Alevizos's application of those rules and his unwillingness to consider hearsay exceptions—not on a lack of witnesses.

For all Pejic's defiance—no doubt fueled by frustration—he couldn't say the quiet part out loud—namely that the judge's rulings were driven, in part, by bias against the first investigation. But Fronk would say that for him. As the judge brought the offer of proof to a close, he relented a bit by letting Pejic nod to the previous investigation. "You can say [Ray McCarty's name] because that stuff is already out . . .," Alevizos told Pejic. "You can ask, 'Did you follow up on [his changing alibis]?' . . . Beyond that, you can't [ask for more details]."

Fronk then insisted that during cross-examination, he had the right to ask Airy if he determined, "The investigation was run to the ground on Ray McCarty. . . . The leads were exhausted." Alevizos agreed Airy could confirm that if he thought it was true.

But it was not true. The cause of death, Ray's whereabouts throughout the night on March 26, and the identity of his accomplice, Scott Scarborough, had yet to be determined in that investigation. Important leads had been ignored on Lori's complicity and McCarty's connection to the man who found Rayna's body. Moreover, multiple instances of unknown male DNA could have been identified using state-of-the-art techniques developed in later years. After he dropped the charges against Ray, it's unlikely that Beckman would have permitted a fresh set of eyes to finish the job if all roads again led to McCarty. But the mere fact that the prosecutor dropped the charges against Ray did not mean McCarty was cleared—especially because Beckman never gave a detailed reason for why he did it. However, in the sidebars, Alevizos and Fronk treated Beckman's decision as the equivalent of acquittal before a jury of McCarty's peers—a pillar of truth that couldn't be toppled in another proceeding.

When the jury returned to the courtroom, Pejic started the direct examination of Airy, now more hamstrung by the judge than he ever expected. But things would get even worse. Pejic planned to grill Airy about the June 2013 police interview with Eric Freeman, which had been pivotal in building the State's case. As Jason's lawyers discovered, the 140-page transcript of the recorded session revealed questionable tactics by the detectives. They were "spoon-feeding" him the information he would have known if he had assisted in Rayna's murder, and they were coercing him to stick with events consistent with Rickey Hammons's pole barn story.

But within moments, this cornerstone of the defense strategy crumbled to pieces with dire ramifications for Jason that extended beyond the trial. After Airy reviewed a bulky document and admitted it was the June 2013 transcript, the defense counsel moved to enter it as evidence. Fronk objected. "It's hearsay."

Pejic was incredulous. Airy's "there. He verified [the transcript]."

Alevizos didn't buy the hearsay objection but wouldn't let Pejic enter the interview as evidence. "You know what?" the judge asked rhetorically. "That could have been used to impeach Mr. Freeman. . . . I don't know how you can get it in through [Airy]."

Airy "was at the interview," Pejic replied. "I can't talk about the course of his investigation?"

"No," the judge answered. Fronk's objection was sustained.

Jason couldn't hear what they said in the sidebar, but he knew something was wrong. "Scott usually held himself pretty upright in almost a military way," he remembers. "But all of a sudden, his shoulders just slumped over." He ran his fingers through his thick black hair in another ominous sign. "I knew things weren't going our way when he did that to his hair."

Pejic's defeat at the sidebar would be compounded by what he didn't do. He should have made an offer of proof for the interview transcript and it would have been entered into the trial record. Then, at the very least, the appellate court would have to consider it during Jason's appeal. The police misconduct that it contained was too manifest to be ignored. But Pejic was now focused on salvaging something from Airy's direct examination— virtually his last chance to shift the momentum of the trial.

Regarding the Freeman interviews, Pejic could only serve the detective a thin gruel of questions with obvious answers. Did he ask Eric leading questions? Airy answered, "No." Did Williamson ask leading Eric Leading questions? Airy didn't remember. Why did Freeman radically change his story about March 26 from 2008 to 2013, even changing some parts of his story at different times in his June interview? Airy replied, "He was lying."

When answering questions about Hammons, the detective had no idea if he saw an article about the unsolved-homicides playing cards. "And you knew he was a confessed and convicted murderer?" Pejic asked. Airy said he did. Another question: "You knew he shot a kid seven times in the face?" Fronk objected. Alevizos sustained and had the question "stricken from the record" before the detective could answer. Airy said that as far as he and Williamson were concerned, Hammons "wasn't asking for anything" in return for his testimony, and he didn't know anything about him getting transferred from one prison to another closer to home as a result.

Regarding the McCarty investigation, Pejic stuck to the narrow scope of questions Alevizos dictated during the offer of proof. Airy was aware of Ray's changing alibis and never attempted to verify them. While Airy admitted talking to Rolling Prairie witnesses who encountered Rayna's car on March 26, he did not look to develop more evidence that could incriminate Ray, like asking if they heard a car with a loud muffler.

Seemingly out of the blue, Pejic asked, "Did you ever learn about any analyses that might have been done on fiber evidence?" Airy replied that he did. The lawyer then asked, "Did any of that fiber evidence lead to Jason?"

Before Airy could answer, Fronk objected, and another sidebar ensued. "I don't know anything about any fiber analysis," Alevizos snapped. Pejic tried to fill him in about the green fibers, but the judge dismissed it as hearsay unless the defense produced an expert to testify. Outside the jury's presence during the break, Pejic said he had an expert who could have commented on fiber evidence. However, the evidence technician was unavailable to testify before the proceedings ended that day.

When the trial resumed, Pejic continued to strike out time and again. With the judge's various restrictions, he couldn't get Airy to account for the unusual nature of the June 2013 interview or why it was so long.

But suddenly, when all hope seemed lost, Pejic unexpectedly stumbled into his side's most significant break in the trial. He started this line of questions by asking Airy if he conducted a "time survey" with the driving routes he got in Freeman's June 2013 confession. Airy said he did.

The lawyer followed up, "Did you reduce that time study to writing?"

"No," Airy replied.

Now smelling blood, Pejic asked, "And were you ever going to share those results of your time study with us?"

"No."

"We need a hearing outside the presence of the jury, Judge," Pejic said, and Alevizos dutifully complied.

When the jury was gone, Pejic continued to bore into Airy's time survey, which he said he conducted shortly after the June 2013 interview with Freeman. The detective related each route he timed but admitted he didn't account for interludes like Rayna's abduction and murder, the pole barn visit, or the victim's submersion in the pond. Even without all those events, the detective admitted, it still took him an hour to make those trips.

It was clear why the prosecution had not called Airy to the stand. Without realizing it, the callow young detective had thrown the defense a lifeline and enough rope to hang his investigation. Pejic would try to take full advantage.

> Q. Would you agree that that evidence that you uncovered by your time survey was favorable to Mr. Tibbs?
>
> A. No.
>
> Q. And why?
>
> A. Because it's an approximation. It was 20 years later. I don't know what the roads were in 1993. I don't know how fast they were driving.
>
> Q. Then why did you even do it?
>
> A. To see approximately what the—, the approximation. I don't know how fast they were going what time they left the clinic. There are so many variables that—

At this point, Pejic cut him off. They had all heard enough. The lawyer could now ask the judge for "latitude in questioning [Airy] about this matter."

A panic-stricken Fronk jumped up to protest. The defense "did a time study. . . . I didn't hear crap about that." Then he admitted he was the one who sent Airy out, implying it wasn't a time survey. "The fact that I sent a detective out to drive a route is part of trial prep—"

Alevizos cut in, "No. No. No. No." For once, the judge had enough of Fronk's "crap." The prosecutor and his detective were skipping over the third rail of a mistrial with what is known as a Brady rule violation. It occurs when the government fails to share anything it has found that could clear the defendant—in other words, exculpatory information.[84] Alevizos lectured Fronk that he had "every bit of a duty" to turn over anything "exculpatory."

The prosecutor fell back on his detective's weak argument. "There are so many variables involved here . . .," he said. "It's difficult to say whether or not it's exculpatory. I don't think, you know—"

But Alevizos cut him off again. He didn't want to know what Fronk was thinking. Instead, he asked, "Why would you think that that would be exculpatory, Mr. Pejic?"

"Because the route that Mr. Freeman offered them in this long interview is impossible," Pejic replied. He then walked the judge through each stop Freeman claimed to make, the various activities Airy didn't account for, and the stopover at the pole barn, which Freeman had said took a half hour. All had to happen between six and seven.

Alevizos remembered the bit about *Married . . . with Children* but otherwise seemed to be putting the impossible routes together for the first time.

Pejic summed up. "So this is a Brady violation. This is clearly exculpatory, and that's what we're here to discuss."

Alevizos asked Fronk to respond. Rather than comment on Airy's deception, the prosecutor questioned the accuracy of the witness sightings, but he did not receive any sympathy from the judge. "It should have been disclosed," Alevizos said, "so I'm going to give [Pejic] the latitude to get into it."

Knowing he had a losing hand in this argument, Fronk replied, "All right. It's the Court's discretion. Understood."

But it wasn't all right for Alevizos, who must have realized how close to the brink Fronk had been willing to go. "Otherwise," the judge told the prosecutor, "you have major constitutional problems."

When the jury returned to the courtroom, Pejic had carte blanche to drag Airy over the coals on his time survey. First, he had him admit he never turned it over to the prosecution or the defense. He then had him repeat the routes and distances he surveyed and all the activity times he left out. Finally, he asked, "Based upon your own time survey, wouldn't Eric Freeman's story be impossible?"

"There is [sic] too many variables to say whether it was impossible or not," Airy replied. "I don't know what time they left the clinic. I don't know how fast they were driving. I don't know what exact route they took. I don't know what the exact traffic was like on March 26, 1993. I don't know any of those things."

But, as Pejic soon got him to admit, Airy did know two of the most vital variables: when Rayna was last seen at the animal hospital and when her car was spotted on N. 200 E. Ironically, he pointed to Ray McCarty, the State's newfound fountain of truth. Airy ultimately conceded, from reports, that McCarty last saw Rayna in the animal hospital parking lot at 6:00 P.M.

Having extracted that start time from him, Pejic next asked, "What time did you allot for Rayna Rison's car being on [North] 200 East where it was ultimately found?"

"By 7:00," Airy answered.

"By 7:00?" Pejic asked again.

Airy nodded.

Pejic would not let this victorious moment pass without the opportunity to burnish it even more deeply in the jurors' consciousness. "I'll ask my question again. Wouldn't it be impossible to travel that route and get her car there by 7:00?"

Fronk jumped up to object, "Calls for speculation." Alevizos sustained, but the question now hung in the courtroom ether. When Pejic asked Airy why he didn't account for the "variables" during his time survey, the detective gave an obtuse reply: "I don't know what—I don't know how long they were at the pole barn exactly. I don't know how long they were at the clinic. I don't know how long the fight took place. I don't know any of those things. Those are all variables that I don't know."

They were all variables, but they would have all added time to his survey, not taken it away. Pejic did not feel he had to make that point. Instead, he asked whether Airy learned to conduct a proper time survey during his law enforcement training. The detective surprised him again by saying, "Not really.

No." But a few minutes later, Pejic got Airy to admit he was responsible for conducting a complete and thorough investigation. He could then ask, "Was there any reason why you quit that portion of your investigation as it relates to the time survey?"

Airy answered, "I can't drive 100 miles an hour to see if I can make it in an hour, and there are so many variables. There is no way I can conclusively say this happened or it didn't happen because it is twenty years later, and it's not the same night."

It was a weak reply that still didn't explain why his variables would not have added time to his survey, but Pejic let him off the ropes.

There were to be no further victories with Alevizos while Airy was on the stand. Pejic next wanted to ask him about unknown male DNA test results that he didn't try to match with a standard from Ray McCarty and the other tests that showed Jason was not a source. When the lawyer tried to enter the certificate of analysis from the Indiana State Police lab, Fronk objected because Airy didn't have the expertise to comment on it. More sidebar haggling ensued, where Tompkins joined in, arguing the results were exculpatory. But Alevizos wanted the Indiana State Police analyst who wrote the memo to testify before he'd enter it as evidence. "Nikki," Fronk chimed in. The judge assured the defense counsel they'd have no trouble getting her. "She's testified here a million times," he said.

Without the certificate of analysis, Pejic could only ask Airy about whose DNA he submitted to test against the evidence. While he provided standards from Tibbs and Freeman, the detective thought the lab already had McCarty's but didn't know for sure.

Similarly, because he couldn't pull up the June 2013 Freeman interview, Pejic lost a chance to catch Airy in a lie. The detective confirmed that Freeman had his cellphone number and email and denied that the two had "any communications [that] you haven't disclosed to us." But in that transcript there were two indications during the session where Williamson referred to an Airy call with Freeman that wasn't reported or recorded.

Pejic referred to another exchange between Airy and Freeman during an interview that must have sounded odd to the jury. He asked Airy, "Have you ever been made aware that pictures were requested [by Freeman]?"

The detective replied, "I believe he may have mentioned [pictures] in one interview to help jog his memory. He asked if we had pictures that—"

Pejic finished the thought, "You'd come over for a beer and, oops, you'd drop them, and he sees the pictures?"

"He said something like that," Airy conceded before Fronk could object. Alevizos sustained and ordered both the question and answer to be struck from the record.

With his cross, Fronk went through with his threat to impeach the first investigation. He asked Airy, "Isn't it true that you didn't attempt to quote, unquote, clear, or verify Ray McCarty's alibis because those leads had already been exhausted?"

"Yes," Airy replied as Pejic objected. In the sidebar, he argued that Schoff had testified the opposite was true.

"Yeah," Alevizos replied. "You know what? . . . When there is conflicting testimony, it is the exclusive purview of the jury to decide whom to believe."

At this stage, the defense had finally scored significant points, raising doubts about the second investigation. But the remaining testimony would not build on this triumph. Instead, disjointed as ever, the defense pivoted back to Ray McCarty's credibility. Turning on the wayback machine, Tompkins called Elvin "Bill" Keith to the stand. At seventy-one, the retired FBI agent was remarkably well preserved and steely as ever. "He was kind of ornery with Tompkins," Jason says. "I'm sure he was wondering why they never convicted Ray."

Still the consummate professional, Keith had reviewed his meticulous reports from the weeks before Rayna's body was found and his two sessions with McCarty. "As to the first interview," Tompkins asked, "what type of demeanor evidence were you able to observe?"

Keith replied, "The first thing, of course, is he was very, very nervous. And I got typical reactions that you'll get from someone who is not really that interested in cooperating with you—shifting eyes, moving fingers, kicking the foot. That sort of thing."

"From your training," Tompkins said, "what do those types of things indicate?"

Keith answered, "They indicate someone is not telling the truth." He added that McCarty became even more nervous as the interview went on. The next day, when they talked again, he noted that McCarty was still anxious, and his answers were inconsistent with what he had said previously.

"In relation to the investigation," Tompkins asked, "were the inconsistencies significant in your mind?"

"They were," Keith replied, and he could never resolve them.

During cross-examination, Fronk asked if it was only natural that McCarty would have been the prime suspect because "he had been convicted for molesting Rayna. . . . That's a no-brainer. You're going to look at that guy, right?"

"Absolutely," Keith replied.

Fronk's last question harked back to all the cops and prosecutors who felt they never had enough on Ray to arrest him. He asked, "Now, in the course of your work, did anybody report seeing Ray McCarty with Rayna, her car, or her body on or after March 26, 1993?"

Keith replied, "No."

The next witness, Mike Keeling, Ray's old cellmate, should have helped the defense counsel end their case with a bang since McCarty had confessed to him that he killed Rayna. Instead, Keeling was muzzled to incomprehensibility by the judge's hearsay restrictions, unable to say why he knew Ray or why he had been investigated. He could only testify that he sent a letter to the prosecuting attorney but could say nothing more about it.

The final witness, Charlie Allen, wasn't even in the courtroom. "Due to his memory loss because of his head injury," Tompkins explained, "the defense would next like to read in excerpts on Mr. Charles Allen's May 14, 1998 [grand jury] sworn statement." Pejic had the honor of playing befuddled Charlie while Tompkins took on the role of his inquisitor.

The lawyers' reading, coming at the end of an intense day, had all the ingredients for a forty-minute snooze fest. "You could see the jury didn't understand what it was about," Jason says. "They started out looking confused and just looked bored a few minutes into it." The reading introduced a new cast of characters—like Charlie's girlfriend, her job, his mother, his lawyer, and his friend Scott Scarborough—and plot twists that must have made jurors wonder why his sworn testimony was necessary. It was one thing for Allen to say he saw Ray on March 26 but quite another for him to substitute another unknown night and make several changes to the times McCarty came to the door—with and without a supposed unnamed companion.

If the jurors were not totally confused when the reading came to a close, Alevizos ensured they were when he explained, "This testimony was given as impeachment testimony of—" He stopped, now confused himself. Then added, "And not to be taken as evidence itself. It's for impeachment of Ray McCarty—" He stopped himself again, "No."

"Charles Allen," Fronk corrected.

"Of Charles Allen's testimony," Alevizos continued. He took a stab at explaining, "It's complicated because what happens is he—"

He stopped himself again and punted. "We'll get that as an instruction [tomorrow]."

It was still relatively early on Thursday, but the judge decided to punt the trial's closing too. His bailiff, who usually provided instructions, was out, and the closing arguments wouldn't start until 4:00, even if they tried to continue. He told the jury, "You'd be asked to deliberate through the night. Wouldn't you rather come in in the morning, hear closing arguments and final instructions, and have the whole day to deliberate tomorrow? I think counsel indicated that was their preference as well."

For once, Fronk and Tompkins agreed.

CLOSING CLAPTRAP

The next morning in court began with a brief discussion about the final instructions the judge would give the jury before their deliberations. At no point, Jason says, did his lawyers exude any sense of confidence or enthusiasm. "They were very reserved," he remembers, "like we were preparing for my funeral. I wasn't surprised by that. I knew I was screwed before they put on the defense."

After the jury entered the courtroom, final arguments began. During this trial segment, opposing attorneys get one more chance to review the trial's evidence and persuade the jury how it should be interpreted. It is a more freewheeling affair than anything previously presented, but it still has some limitations. In *People v. Ashwal*, a landmark case where a conviction was overturned, an appellate court determined that "summation is not an unbridled debate in which the restraints imposed at trial are cast aside so that counsel may employ all the rhetorical devices at his/her command."[85] In his closing argument, Fronk could not have been more unbridled, often stacking his rhetoric on questionable evidence. "I couldn't believe how he was running me into the ground," Jason says. "At one point, I whispered to Scott, 'How can he get away with saying this stuff?' and he answered, 'That's how it works.'"

However much Jason was upset by the prosecutor, the closing argument of his own attorney would prove even more wrongheaded and devastating.

Fronk started on an emotional high note as he did with his opening statement:

> A body lying on the gravel shoulder of the road. She's young and small in stature. A EURO [*sic*] sweatshirt and faded blue jeans, black ankle boots. Her light brown hair splayed around her on the ground, fighting for her life, clutching, grabbing, and grasping in his hands on her slender neck, strangling her. She looks up into the eyes of her killer, her friend. She doesn't understand. He swore he'd protect her. He said he loved her. Her pliable thyroid cartilage bends under the pressure of his hands, but it doesn't break. The sound of her heartbeat speeding up in panic, and then the dark veil of unconsciousness falls. Her young life fades, ebbs away, and death's prowler settles on the face of 16-year-old Rayna Rison. Jason Tibbs releases the clutch on her bruised neck and looks up at Eric Freeman, and says, pop the trunk. Why? Because if I can't have her, nobody can.

Once again, Fronk took artistic liberty, opening with assumptions not necessarily supported by the evidence or human anatomy. As the prosecution's esteemed forensic pathologist, Dr. Rick Hoover, repeatedly admitted, he could not determine whether Rayna's neck was "bruised."[86] Likewise, when Fronk referred to her "pliable thyroid cartilage," he should have said "pliable hyoid bone." All cartilage is pliable,[87] or we'd be as stiff as statues. While it's true that a young woman's hyoid bone may be so flexible it won't snap during strangulation,[88] it is equally true that there was virtually no physical sign that Rayna was strangled.

With this auspicious prelude, the prosecutor commenced his symphony of half-truths, internal contradictions, and hypocrisy. The principal target of his screed was Jason's alibi. Defense "counsel made . . . some suppositions that dozens of people would have had to have seen the defendant the night he was out running around if his story were true. Those dozens of people didn't appear." Fronk didn't add that he and Alevizos either blocked the jury from hearing their testimony or what they said in police reports at the time of the crime. But he did provide a convoluted reason why those alibi witnesses who did appear were not permitted to support Jason. "The fact that a witness on some prior occasion made a different statement or an inconsistent statement, and under the eyes of the law, making a statement one day and then coming in twenty years later and saying, 'I don't recall,' well, those are inconsistent [statements] because at the time you recall, and then you testify, and you don't. Under the eyes of the law, those are inconsistent statements." Elsewhere, he deems these "unrecallable statements"—as would be understandable after twenty-one years. But their appearance in 1993 police reports was insufficient to make them evidence because they were not sworn, as they would be in a trial or grand jury.

As for the supposedly consistent statements that did support Jason, he tried to protect the jury from those as well. "I didn't want you to fall into the same pit the police did back in 1993 where you hear maybe one story, and it sounds okay all on its own. I wanted you to have all of the information so that you would realize that the only consistency in the defendant's stories is the inconsistency. They don't match each other, and they don't match with anybody else."

The fault for some of the inconsistency, the prosecutor explained, was the antiquated and poorly organized nature of local law enforcement investigations in 1993. "Remember that the police officers were still dealing in an era of typewriters," he told the jurors. "So it's not like they put something on the computer and every terminal has it. They're typing on a piece of paper, and it goes in a file." He went on to criticize the circumstances surrounding the Rison investigation. "There [were] a lot of officers working on this case. It was like an all-hands-on-deck thing. You had multiple FBI agents, you had the state police, you had the city police, you had the county police, everybody wanting to bring Rayna home. But because of that, there was no central place for all of the information to go." As Fronk knew full well, there was one central place—the office of the La Porte County prosecuting attorney. Prosecutors and their investigators were assigned to collect and filter all tips and police reports.[89] There was also oversight from the Homicide Team and Indiana State Police Sergeant Arland Boyd.[90] Of course, critical information still slipped through the cracks, but it was nowhere near the chaos Fronk described.

But for all that was wrong with the 1993 police reports, Fronk still found some of their contents to be sacrosanct. In particular, there was one report from Harold Hahn where Jason said that Vic Montorsi took him to the trailer park and passed the Pine Lake Animal Hospital around 5:40.[91] This then contrasted with the comments he made to Detective Captain John Miller a few minutes later when he said he rode with Chad Green and passed the clinic at 6:10.[92]

Jason "was en route to a trailer to *tutor* some girls," the prosecutor said, taking the careless aside from Tompkins to skewer his client and cast further doubts on his credibility. "Now [the defense] counsel made some comments that tutor [is] just code for 'making out,' right? And I understand that if you're going to tell some girl's parents that that's what you're doing, you're going to go tutor her so you can come over and get permission to hang out with her. But when you're talking to the police, why wouldn't you just say I'm going to see a girl? Why would you put in that you're going to tutor her if it's just code for making out? That doesn't make any sense to me."

Jason's presence in the trailer park from around six until nine was essential to his alibi, but Fronk could crow, "Note that the alibi witnesses did not take the stand and say where Jason Tibbs was at shortly after 6:00 on March 26th of 1993. Not a one of them. He doesn't have an alibi. Their sworn testimony provides no alibi for the defendant." The prosecutor's sly "sworn testimony" qualification probably went over the jurors' heads. He referred to the grand jury where prosecutors felt no need to defend Jason's account of his whereabouts.

Jason's most important alibi witness, James Amor, did take the stand in his trial but was not adequately prepared by Jason's lawyers and was prevented from refreshing his memory. Fronk used his closing to belittle the witness.

"James Amor didn't recall March 26, 1993, very well. He remembers some things, though. He remembered being at the trailer, contrary to the girls' statements that it was actually Josh that was at the trailer. And, other than that, he didn't remember whether the defendant was there or not. He wasn't sure on that. He tells pretty much the same story as Josh." And what was wrong about Amor saying he didn't remember exactly what happened one night twenty-one years ago? Who does?

Fronk turned on Amor again for claiming a memory he did have from that night. Evidence from Rayna's LTD indicated that wet shoes or boots had been placed on newspapers under the front passenger seat. But James never remembered Jason having wet shoes and pants or changing out of them. "Isn't it interesting that . . . James Amor barely remembers anything from March 26th, [but] he doesn't remember the defendant having wet pants on that night?" If Amor was to have selective memory geared to helping the defense, why wouldn't he have claimed Jason was at the trailer park?

Fronk had commented on other "interesting" parts of the witness testimony. He told the jury, "I thought it was very interesting that all of those alibi witnesses, nobody recalled March 26th of 1993. But the [abduction] witnesses . . ., they remember driving past Pine Lake Animal Hospital and seeing two young men and a young lady, a lover's quarrel, an argument, two cars, the gray Buick Century, Rayna's tan car. They remember all of that, and they were just driving by." He later doubled down with the claim, "Nobody but nobody reported seeing a beat-up rusty blue Datsun mini-wagon in the Pine Lake Animal Hospital lot. Nobody saw that, but they saw that Buick and saw those two young men."

These were two more statements, supposedly based on evidence but replete with prevarication. The abduction witnesses did not *all* see the Buick Century. Rene Gazarkiewicz explicitly described the other car as a "blue station wagon" during her testimony. Although Fronk praised her "recall" as "pretty uncanny," the rear vent window she rhapsodized about and the headlights she drew on the Telestrator were more like the Datsun than the Buick. The prosecutor said Pam Rosebaum described the person she saw approaching Rayna as a "younger guy, but smaller in stature. It wasn't a big strapping factory worker, Ray McCarty." In fact, she saw someone like her brother-in-law, who was McCarty's height and weight. While Fronk repeated the claim that Bryan Durham "picked the defendant and Eric Freeman out of a yearbook," the witness admitted under cross-examination how his selection may have been influenced by having only one male with the respective hair colors he remembered on each page. He was also the only witness to say he saw two males in the parking lot with Rayna but then, under cross-examination, backed off that statement as well.

While Jason's alibis were supported by 1993 police reports, prosecution witnesses at his trial cited events without contemporaneous confirmation, which made them *more* credible for Fronk. These false memories included claims that Jason was passing out *Missing* flyers and organizing search parties in the DQ and Pineapple bank parking lots on March 26, even before anyone else knew Rayna was missing. Speaking about one of those witnesses, Fronk said, "She thought that was weird. [Rayna's] only been missing a couple of hours. How [does Jason] know she's missing? How [does Jason] know anybody did this?"

During Fronk's closing argument, no words were more damning than those Jason supposedly said in his 1993 police interviews. He spun one supposed statement into a cotton candy whorl of deceptive behavior. "You know, another interesting thing the defendant said when he talked to Detective Miller," he told the jury, "was despite the fact that he had dated Rayna, and despite the fact that they had been friends for years, and despite the fact he had written her these love letters, and despite the fact that he had given her this ring, he [didn't] know her last name."

This is why, Fronk argued, he didn't make a big thing about the ring found in Rayna's car that he impulsively gave her when he pulled it out of his pocket. "Jason Tibbs told Detective Boyd and Detective Miller that 'Yeah, yeah, that's my ring. Yep. I mean, I gave it to her just because she liked it. She liked to wear it.' It didn't mean anything, of course. He's distancing himself from her again." Fronk saw the same evil intent when Jason said his love letters had been written in eighth grade instead of ninth grade.

But in defending Freeman, Hammons, and McCarty, Fronk's argument scaled greater heights in hypocrisy and deception. A common theme for all three was that they were honorable and credible because they admitted their criminal guilt—unlike the defendant.

Fronk argued, "If the defendant had not put Eric Freeman in jeopardy by dragging him in to help him get rid of Rayna's body, if Eric hadn't agreed to do it, Eric Freeman would not take the stand and testify under oath that's what happened." Now confident that the 140-page transcript of the June 2013 interview would not be evidence, the prosecutor added, "There is no threat or coercion or enticement that's going to make a fellow do that. You've got no evidence whatsoever that such a thing happened."

His misrepresentation of the "physical evidence" continued when he said it "supports Eric Freeman . . . because the manner of death of Rayna Rison was by strangulation. Exactly the way Eric Freeman said it happened." Again, this is never what the slippery forensic pathologist said, and never once did Hoover's autopsy mention the word strangulation. On the stand, he admitted arriving at "asphyxia" as a cause of death through a "process of elimination." There was nothing "physical" that supported his determination.

Although Fronk portrayed Freeman's testimony as a beacon of truth, there were some ragged elements that he knew his closing argument needed to perfect. Such as "they tossed her into the water." Now, without support from any witness or physical evidence, he concocted a new post-toss scenario. "It's too shallow to submerge her body, so she had to be pushed out a little further where it's a little deeper where the logs could submerge her. She was moved to her place of location. She wasn't thrown to her place of location." It was "interesting" (to use one of his own terms) that Fronk couldn't even bring himself to say Jason was the one who "pushed" and "moved" her.

Of course, none of these details were mentioned by Freeman, and other elements of his story could not be perfected, but Fronk was willing to cut him a break he wouldn't give to Jason's alibi witnesses like James Amor. He told the jury, "I don't know that it's fair to Eric Freeman to allow everybody else to testify that, well, I remember this piece, and I remember this piece, but then require Eric Freeman's testimony or memory to be dead-solid perfect all the way through."

Fronk knew the jury would need special forbearance when considering Freeman's timeline for their murder story. Once again, the fact it was so dicey only added to his credibility. "Wouldn't he make sure it was airtight if he had some motive to do that?" As Airy showed, no one did more to disrupt Freeman's timeline than the abduction witnesses, who Fronk previously said were infallible. "But when it came to times," he said, "their memories are wrong. 'Twenty-one years ago, what time was it when this happened? I don't know.' Witnesses weren't very good on times. It's twenty-one years [ago]. I understand that."

The transformation of Rickey Hammons into a paragon of virtue was undoubtedly trickier for Fronk. He tried to get the messy details out of the way first. "Rickey Hammons committed a crime, and he pled guilty, and he's in prison," Fronk admitted. "You don't have to like him, but at least he pled guilty, and it says something about the man's character." Perhaps from a prosecutor's perspective, someone who pleads guilty is on a higher moral plane than an accused party who drags him through a trial. But wasn't this attitude counter to the presumption of innocence that Alevizos instructed the jurors about at the start of the proceedings?

Nevertheless, Fronk doubled down on his star witness's truthfulness, proclaiming, "There has been no evidence that Rickey Hammons is a professional liar. I don't recall any evidence at all that he's a liar." This assertion raised several questions. Would Alevizos have permitted that evidence? He shut down Tompkins when he attempted to provide details about Hammons's crime. Also, as Fronk must have known, there was so much more about Hammons's crime and its investigation that raised questions about his lying. The prosecutor must have been grateful for the defense team's deficient research that none had come out.

But Fronk's closing continued to tread into dangerous territory as he argued Rickey had "no motive" for providing his pole barn story. Picking up on his opening statement, he praised his witness as faultlessly generous in coming forward. "Rickey Hammons is not getting anything and will not accept anything for his testimony in this case," the prosecutor told the jury. This comment would later prove false. There is a chance that Fronk didn't know that. Still, he stressed again how courageous it was for Hammons to testify. "He put himself in peril. People that cooperate in prison with law enforcement put themselves in jeopardy of being beaten or killed."

A noble character alone could not account for Rickey's credibility. For that, Fronk relied on another questionable assertion. "Rickey Hammons corroborates Eric Freeman," he said, "and the two men haven't talked since 1993. Zero evidence [they have]." Furthermore, he claimed, the defense could not prove any "roundabout way that they communicated." But again, this was only because Jason's lawyers could not enter the June 2013 interview as evidence, which indicates three instances of "roundabout" communications—something Fronk must have known.

While Fronk portrayed Freeman and Hammons as objects of admiration, he wanted the jury to see Ray McCarty as an object of sympathy. He was innocent because his prior child molesting conviction made him look guilty. "He was a suspect [because of his] prior conduct." He was someone else Fronk saw deserving of credit because "he pled guilty. . . . You don't have to like him, but at least he's got that [plea] going for him." Because he had the guts to make that plea, Fronk argued, McCarty "knew he was a suspect as soon as he found out Rayna came up missing. Darn right, he was nervous when he was talking to the FBI. . . . Yeah, you're going to look really hard at Ray. He testified with the FBI agents, the city police, the county police, and the State police. They all looked really hard at Ray."

But then the prosecutor lied to the jury about what they found. "Despite all of the hard work by the law enforcement in this case, they were not able to prove—provide any evidence that Ray was involved." If they had not provided any evidence, how could Hedge have convened a grand jury, and how could that panel have indicted him? But Fronk's ability to get away with this falsehood was the fruit of Alevizos's rulings that prevented Jason's lawyers from mentioning the proceedings that resulted in Ray's arrest. It also permitted Fronk to repeat another lie: "Detective Airy testified that the reason he didn't investigate Ray was because there were no new leads, and all of that information that could be tracked down had been tracked down."

As for why this innocent man kept changing his alibis, Fronk tried to turn that argument back on the defense. "It's extremely inconsistent for the defense to monotonously repeat that Ray McCarty didn't have a good-faith alibi for March 26th when Jason Tibbs doesn't have an alibi for March 26th."

336

CLOSING CLAPTRAP

Of course, Jason would argue he did have one that never changed, but that was something for Tompkins to address in his closing argument.

Fronk returned to his lie that the first investigation "never led to any evidence that Ray McCarty killed Rayna Rison. You may be asked to speculate about some, but remember, reasonable doubt is not based on imagination or speculation." Still, as he wrapped up his remarks, Fronk could not help speculating about another reason why Ray couldn't have done it. "A deer hunter dumping a body could probably do better than 35 feet off of a main road in the county," he speculated, not mentioning, or perhaps not remembering, the foggy, muddy conditions on March 26. "A deer hunter could probably hide a body where the big deer hang out, where the briars and brambles are so thick that humans cannot walk in there."

But for all the evidence he supposedly accumulated against Jason, Fronk could not help but make Ray a part of his final comments, perhaps anticipating that an attack on McCarty would constitute most of his counterpart's closing argument.

> Ladies and gentlemen, the defense is going to ask you to make the same mistakes that officers made in 1993. A mistake that was easy to understand. Again, Law Enforcement 101. It's a no-brainer. The mistake of spending too much time with Ray McCarty and not enough time spent looking at Rayna's killer, Jason Tibbs. Rayna has waited 21 years for her killer to stand trial. Don't let that justice delayed become justice denied. This is the evidence that, when you consider it all together, you will realize that it proves the defendant, Jason Tibbs, guilty of murdering Rayna Rison on March 26th of 1993, and then you should return your verdict accordingly.

Before he started his closing argument, Tompkins asked the judge for a sidebar. The lawyer now wanted a hearing devoted to Ray's guilt because of the time Fronk dedicated to that in his remarks. "I believe they've opened a door . . . in their closing [that] we did not prove Ray McCarty guilty."

"No. I did not say that," Fronk shot back. "They spent this whole time blaming Ray McCarty, and the Court said that's not evidence. Him [sic] being a suspect isn't evidence. [The defense] said we're going to show another suspect."

But Fronk didn't need to reply. Alevizos was not going to change his mind about McCarty's guilt or the role it should play in the Tibbs trial. The judge intoned, "My evidentiary ruling stands."

In the opening lines of his closing argument, Tompkins promised to show the jury that "Rickey Hammons's story and Eric Freeman's story is impossible" and "there is a better suspect." But first, he addressed Fronk's emotional appeal. "The State started off right away, right at the beginning, tugging at your heartstrings, and that's easy to do in this case, in most murder cases, and certainly in almost every loss of life of a young woman." Then he added, "You'll get an instruction about that. You're not allowed to convict with sympathy, and they shouldn't be asking you to. . . . Nothing can make this story sadder than convicting the wrong person, [and] letting [off] a person who committed this murder."

While acknowledging Fronk's base tactics, Tompkins responded with the sort of dry, legalistic arguments that were sure to turn a jury off, at one point, saying, "We don't have to prove anything." In other words, proving guilt is the burden of the State. Such calculations may win the day in a classroom. Without practical guidance, they don't have much sway in deliberations.

But Tompkins couldn't help himself, offering a jumbled mini-lecture on the types of defenses.

> This defense is an innocence defense. There are two kinds of defenses you hear defense attorneys talk about: innocence and sufficiency. Did they have enough evidence? Is their case strong enough? Well, an innocence defense is always also a sufficiency defense, and you hope it would be because you would hope that the State can't build a strong enough case to convict an innocent person. You would hope that. That's not always true. You hear those stories. You hope it would be true all the time.
>
> Secondly, this is an injustice defense. We are defending the Constitution. We're defending it against detectives who run their own traffic studies and don't write it down and don't tell anybody about it. Because it doesn't fit their theory from their inspiration from a murderer, Rickey Hammons. That's injustice. That's our Constitution, and we're going to defend against it.

While defending the Constitution was a noble cause, it was unlikely to trump a juror's desire to convict should that person think Jason was guilty. Arguments about government overreach have their place in criminal defense, but more in cases like entrapment where the defendant accepts some level of guilt. This should not have been an issue in Jason's murder trial.

But after his reverie about legal tactics, Tompkins tore into Hammons with relish. "He's a skilled liar, and he's a manipulator. You heard the State say in their opening snitches get stitches, whatever. He didn't get stitches. He got transferred to a facility closer to his home. He got transferred from Southern Indiana back here in Westville months after he snitched. He wrote his letter in 2008." Tompkins then made a good point that he should have brought up in Hammons's cross-examination. "Can't tell you what he wanted in 2008, but he probably didn't count on the State not prosecuting this case until 2013 and trying it in 2014." It was a delay more rooted in La Porte prosecuting attorney politics than the development of new evidence, and undoubtedly frustrating for Hammons and his family.

Tompkins next tried to show why Hammons was a "skilled liar." He told the jury, "The State wants you to believe that because he admitted to bad facts that he was smoking a joint and looking at girly magazines, you should believe him more." As the lawyer argued, nothing about his pole barn incident was ever corroborated, and his account of Rayna's body wrapped in a blanket disputed Freeman's testimony that she was under a "blue tarp."

Less convincing was Tompkins's computation of the time Rickey typically spent on chores—forty-five minutes—when he started at four thirty and when the car arrived—somewhere between five fifteen and six. But did it matter if Rickey lingered on the loft for a few minutes? This began a troubling trend in the lawyer's closing argument. For some reason, he was taking the word of a villain in his narrative over the more reliable witnesses, who saw an abduction several minutes after 6:00 P.M. in the Pine Lake Animal Hospital. If the lawyer had used them as his North Star, the car would have arrived long after 7:00 P.M.

Tompkins pointed to two other instances of Hammons's behavior on the stand, which he probably blew out of proportion. First, Rickey gave one distance between the pole barn and his family's house in the deposition and changed it when he testified in the trial. But Tompkins never explained why that distance mattered. Secondly, he played up Rickey's comment, "I see where you're going," when the lawyer walked him through the transfers he received after he talked to the police about the pole barn. Hammons is "not listening to the question and answering the question. He's trying to figure out where the questions are going so he can stay ahead of the game." Perhaps true, but not necessarily an example of his lying.

Tompkins dug into Eric Freeman by appropriately characterizing him as a "scared liar." He asked the jury, "Why can't Eric remember the story exactly? Quite frankly, because he doesn't know everything the police does [*sic*]. It's a guessing game." But then, to prove his point, Tompkins served the jury an incomprehensible hash, mixing and matching Freeman's comments from interviews and trial testimony without offering any perspective.

Regarding his first interview, the lawyer charged, Freeman "starts out lying in '08. He says it's because he's worried about getting arrested. He doesn't want to cooperate." But Freeman did not lie in 2008. He didn't know what the police were talking about. It's Airy who said he lied.

Without explaining what changed, Tompkins skipped to the more suspicious second interview. "In '13, when they come back and talk to him, he's got immunity. Now, he's supposed to be cooperating, but . . . what he does in the 2013 interview when he's got immunity, he continues to lie. He continues to lie because now he's got to stay on that team." The lawyer's mention of "immunity" comes out of nowhere. Why did he get it, and what did it mean for his behavior during the June 2013 interview? The significance of staying on "the team," was probably lost on the jury because the defense could never show how it was used to coerce him. Even more confusing was the lawyer's comment, Freeman "continues to lie," when he should have said, "Now, with the immunity, Freeman starts to lie."

However, Tompkins did provide a plausible explanation for why Eric decided to cooperate. "He's scared of having it hung on him. That's what he said in the interview. He's not pinning this on me." But Tompkins did not lay a foundation for "He's not pinning this on me." Because the jury had not been exposed to the interview transcripts, they did not know that the detectives' fraudulent claims about Jason pinning things on Freeman were another tool for coercion.

Time and again, Tompkins dipped in and out of interviews, trying to show how malleable Freeman was in the hands of his interlocutors, but without preparing the jury with an explanation for what changed. In attacking Freeman's account of the murder, he told the jury, "One time [Freeman] says, Jason said, 'Stop here,' and that's where he stopped and the fight occurs. Another time he says—but not in Court—Rayna said to stop, and that's when they got out, and the fight occurred, and in Court, he said they both said stop."

Tompkins continued his confusing ways by returning to the abortive time survey to prove "how impossible" it would have been to make the trips and complete the deeds described by Freeman. He told the jurors they could refer to the incomplete exhibit the retired sheriff's deputy created, but they would only have access to that during deliberations. In his closing argument, Tompkins wanted the jury to keep track of what he said in their minds—a daunting request for most. "I'm going to talk about three routes—or three time frames on routes," he said. "I'm going to talk about reconstructing as best we can with what we know."

Over and over again, the lawyer promised, "I'm going to try to be fair." But from the start, he took his fairness to a self-destructive extreme. Rather than take the word of Rene Gazarkiewicz, who saw the abduction at 6:10, Tompkins relied on Ray McCarty and his claim that he last saw Rayna at 5:50. He then builds his timeline based on Freeman's claim that they drove up Fail Road. Again, "to be fair," instead of going up to East 1000 North, Tompkins let them stop at East 800 North. He then assumed Jason took five minutes to kill Rayna—a time that Hoover gave when asked how long a throat had to be compressed for asphyxiation. But why would Tompkins have even mentioned that if there was no evidence of strangulation?

Tompkins continued to time Freeman's route to the pole barn. Although Hammons said they were there for at least fifteen minutes, Tompkins again bent over backward to be fair and said ten minutes. He took verbal detours from his routes to explain the speed in his calculation, combined his scenarios, and reminded the jury how close Ray lived to the pond. ("Can't ignore that. Can't ignore that.") He swerved yet again to dispute Fronk's post-toss closing addendum. ("I'm going to stop on the timeline for a second to address the way I think it's important in another way.")

Somehow, Tompkins expected the jury to hang on during all the wild gyrations of his verbal time survey. Using his various "fair" calculations,

Tompkins determined, "At 7:22, Rayna's car is dropped. Why is that a problem? Well, it's a problem because of York, back between 6:30 and 7:00. So somewhere in here, we have York. She saw the car that night knew the time because of the TV show, before 7:00." Even if the jury could follow along, did the difference of twenty-two minutes make Freeman's route sound so "impossible"?

To sum up his case against Ray, Tompkins started with the accusations that Jason and Matt made about Ray abusing Rayna again. Incredibly, despite all the misbehavior in the State's closing argument, Fronk objected, decrying facts not in evidence and hearsay. Indeed, Pejic had forgotten to ask Elser about Ray's gropes when he was on the stand. Still, the information had already come out during Lori's testimony, and Alevizos let Tompkins continue. He focused on Ray's nervous behavior and multiple alibis before Rayna was found. He disputed the supposed cause for his changes. Why would "his wife . . . be upset if she found out about the female hitchhiker? How would that not upset her, given he molested and impregnated her younger sister?" But, if Tompkins had read the police reports, he would have discovered Lori was upset in 1989 when she first learned what Ray did to her sister. Into this muddle, Tompkins introduced the conflicting stories of Charles Allen that the defense lawyer read to the jury. They did more to cast doubt on the brain-damaged witness's credibility than incriminate Ray.

At this juncture, Tompkins failed to provide the jury with either a coherent dissection of the Freeman timeline or a convincing case for McCarty's guilt. Still, the most detrimental part of his closing argument was yet to come. "Let's get back to our defense of Jason Tibbs," he began, as though his previous comments were immaterial. "The State says he doesn't have a good alibi."

To this charge, Tompkins replied, "He doesn't have a good story. It's not a good story. He can't get it straight. In 2014, it's a mess. It was pretty much a mess in 1993."

Jason nearly jumped out of his skin as he listened at the defense table. It was bad enough to get run down by Fronk, but why was his defense attorney attacking his alibi? Unlike McCarty's, it never changed. "I looked at Scott and said, 'That's not true.' But he put that same placating hand on my shoulder as if to say, 'Hold on, hold on.'"

Somehow, for Tompkins, Jason proved his innocence by not having a good story. He argued, "On March 26, 1993, and the days that followed, Jason Tibbs wasn't thinking, 'I murdered that girl. I better get a good story,' because he didn't commit murder."

Tompkins didn't stop there. He barreled right into the most crucial part of the alibi. Jason "tells [the police] he goes to the trailer. Those people generally remembered he was there, [but they] couldn't fix times, couldn't make it exact. He didn't make a good story."

Jason did not need to make up a good story. The truth did just fine as long as he was allowed to present the evidence that Alevizos had blocked. But amazingly, Tompkins was not done tearing him down. He next repeated the false memories of those who claimed Jason told people Rayna was missing on Friday night. Jason "ran around town [saying], 'We got to search for her.' He went to the Pineapple Bank, 'We got to search for her.' He went to the DQ, 'We got to search for her.'"

Again, Tompkins argued this was a good thing. The lawyer may have demolished his client's alibi, but that didn't make Tibbs more guilty than the others searching for Rayna. "All of her band friends who showed up at the DQ, make them suspects, too . . .," he told the jury. "They wanted to search—their friends that were the Fox Hunters over at the Pineapple Bank—round them up."

Tompkins's comments were both a nightmare and a monumental betrayal. As Jason long suspected, his Super-Lawyer lawyer was unfamiliar with the record. There was absolutely no evidence of Friday night search parties organized by Jason or anyone else. Worse yet, if Tompkins harbored doubts about Jason's alibi or what he did on Friday night, why did he wait until the trial to bring them up? He could have had Pejic discuss them during one of his innumerable visits.

As if Tompkins hadn't done enough to cloud the jurors' minds, he added one more of his legalistic bromides that doused virtually everything else that came before it. "The defendant," he declared, "is not required to present any evidence to prove his innocence or to prove or explain anything."

Despite all the confusion he sowed, in closing, Tompkins implored the jury "to think of me again . . ., think of my voice and my argument [when] you go back to deliberate."

In the ten minutes he had for rebuttal, Fronk was only too happy to think of Tompkins's voice, replaying for the jury what his adversary said only moments ago. "You know, it's difficult talking out of both sides of your face," he cracked, "because Mr. Tompkins sure seems to hate liars. Sure seems to hate them. Then he stands up here and says, 'Yeah, Jason's story was a mess in '93. It's a mess in 2014. The witnesses, you know, it's stuff, you know, it's a mess, but that's okay.' It's all right for him. But he's the only one that gets a pass on inconsistencies. He's the only one that gets a pass on out-and-out lies."

But the "mess" was not Tompkins's only gift Fronk would use to bludgeon Jason. He told the jury, "Mr. Tompkins admitted that Jason Tibbs was looking for Rayna that night because he's such a Good Samaritan. But Tibbs said, 'I didn't find out till Saturday morning or maybe even Saturday night.' He's been sitting next to that liar the whole case."

Jason sat through the judge's instructions in a daze. He had low expectations when he started the day, but after his lawyer's closing fiasco, he felt the verdict was a foregone conclusion. After the jury left the courtroom for deliberations, he was escorted to the basement walkway that led to the jail's all-glass holding cell, where guards could make sure the prisoner didn't do anything to harm himself. It was only noon. He sat there for five hours— it seemed like only minutes—before they came to get him.

During the trial, Jason rarely looked over his shoulder to check out the expansive spectator gallery behind him. He knew there was plenty of media coverage because he couldn't escape it—even in jail. It was on the TV and radio with page-one headlines in the local newspapers. The courtroom was already packed when he arrived for the verdict. "They brought extra chairs, and people were still standing in the back," he remembers. One group in attendance caught his eye. "There was like a row of police officers I had probably offended at some point. They were all smirking when I looked at them, finally getting their pound of flesh."

Pejic was alone at the defense table. "I asked, 'Where is John?'" Jason remembers, and Scott said, 'He's on his way home. He had to be somewhere today.' That really irritated me. I felt they had thrown my case away, and now he didn't even have the courtesy to show up for the verdict."

But earlier in the day, before he left town, Tompkins did stop long enough to talk to a TV reporter outside the courtroom. "I trust the system," he told her. "I think [the jurors] got a fair representation on both sides of this case."[93]

When the jury filed in, Jason did see something unexpected. One young woman in the front row looked like she had been crying. He remembers, "They just couldn't look at me. I already didn't have much hope, but that kind of prepared me for the worst."

"Ladies and gentlemen of the jury, have you reached a verdict?" the judge asked.

"That's when Scott leaned over," Jason says, "and whispered, 'No matter what they decide, no negative reactions. Don't make it worse on yourself.'"

A woman stood up with a piece of paper and said, "We have, Your Honor."

The bailiff took it from her and handed it to the judge. He read, "We, the jury, find the defendant, Jason Tibbs, guilty of murder, a felony."

At that, Jason could hear his ex, Leslie, sob—though now entirely estranged from him and living with another man. When he turned toward his mother, Rachel was silent with her head bowed.

He looked back at the jury. He couldn't help but wonder if that young woman who had been crying thought he was guilty. But before he could say anything to his lawyer, Alevizos had asked the lawyers if they wanted to poll the jury. Pejic replied, "No, Your Honor."

After Jason was taken from the courtroom, his mother stayed behind to talk to their lawyer. Throughout the trial, she sat next to Pejic's mother, who continuously gave her an upbeat appraisal of the proceedings. Although Pejic's mother had been a nurse, she had another child who also practiced law and seemed very knowledgeable about courtroom affairs. But Mrs. Pejic was as shocked as Jason's mother when she heard the verdict. As they filed out of the courtroom, Rachel approached Pejic, expecting him to be sympathetic and even apologetic, but she found him curt instead. Rachel asked, "What's the next step?"

According to Rachel, he replied, "I don't know, but I don't think you can afford me for that."

WHAT SHOULD HAVE BEEN THE DEFENSE FOR JASON TIBBS

RAYNA RISON

FAMILY
- Bennie, Karen (parents)
- Lori, Wendy (sisters)

FRIENDS
- Matt Elser (boyfriend)
- Lisa Dyer
- Cheryl VanSchoyck

CITY OF LA PORTE POLICE DEPARTMENT
- Detective Brett Airy
- Detectives John Miller, Harold Hahn (retired)

MICHIGAN CITY POLICE DEPARTMENT
- Patrolman Michael Kellems*
- Detectives Dick Buell*, Larry Biggs*, John Kintzele*
- Detective Mark Lachmund

LA PORTE COUNTY
- Dr. Rick Hoover, Forensic Pathologist
- Sheriff's Deputy Mark Ludlow (retired)
- Sheriff Jim Arnold*
- Circuit Court Judge Thomas Alevizos

PROSECUTING ATTORNEYS
- Rob Beckman
- Chief Deputy Christopher Fronk

JASON TIBBS

FAMILY
- Rachel (mother)
- Leslie (wife, ex-wife)

LAWYERS
- Scott Pejic
- John Tompkins
- Craig Braje

FRIENDS AND COWORKERS
- Josh Jordan
- Jim, Nancy Bruno; daughter Jennifer Delrio (employers)
- James Amor
- Angie Vogel

FBI
- Douglas Deedrick, Trace Evidence Analyst
- Elvin "Bill" Keith

INDIANA STATE POLICE
- Sergeant Al Williamson
- Sergeant Arland Boyd (retired)

*INTRODUCED IN THIS CHAPTER

LORI AND RAY McCARTY

FAMILY
- Adrienne (daughter)
- Hunter (son)

CIVILIAN WITNESSES FROM 1ST INVESTIGATION
- Beth York; sons Kyle, Austin
- Rene Gazarkiewicz
- Beth York; Kyle, Austin (sons)
- Val Eilers
- Bryan Durham
- Vic Montorsi
- Misty Smith, Jamie Swisher (sisters); Peggy Johnson (mother)
- Chad Green

OTHER CIVILIAN WITNESSES
- Rickey J. Hammons Jr.
- Eric Freeman
- Patricia Umphrey

HAMMONS INVESTIGATION
- Rickey Hammons Sr., Judith (parents)
- Jen Hammons (sister)
- Dan Cassidy (victim)
- Bob Sheridan (coworker)

347

WHAT SHOULD HAVE BEEN THE DEFENSE FOR JASON TIBBS

When reviewing a trial transcript, it's easy to be a Monday morning quarterback for the losing side. On paper, glaring holes emerge in the opponent's case, along with missed opportunities for presenting points to sway the jury. But to be fair, any legal proceeding is like a living organism, subject to myriad interactions that the best-prepared attorney cannot control. The uncertainty starts with the judge and his or her behavior on the bench for any given day. The Court's interpretation of the rules may prove wrong and ultimately impact the jury but not prove wrong enough to result in a retrial. Witnesses, even under direct examination, may blurt out unexpected comments. The tactics of opposing counsel are another unpredictable factor. Like great athletes under pressure, the best trial lawyers can adjust on the fly and dispense with the playbook they thought would work before the gavel sounded. Some lawyers have this innate ability; most do not. Still, nothing prevents the jury—or even one member—from being disposed against the state or the defendant, no matter how much contrasting evidence is presented.

But even considering all these organic variables, the lawyers for Jason Tibbs fell far short of an adequate defense. Their failure was partly due to Judge Alevizos, who resolutely undermined their strategy to expose Ray McCarty as the real murderer. But when the court's questionable decisions defeated their plan A, they were not ready with a plan B, as Jason said. John Tompkins, the experienced member of Jason's legal team, once crowed to him, "We don't have to present a defense. It's [the State's] job to prove you're guilty. They have to prove their case." That may be legal theory, and the pablum defense counsel feeds juries at the outset of their case, but in reality, Jason's lawyers had to show why the state did not have a case. They had plenty of opportunities to do that, starting with the prosecution's star witnesses. Rickey Hammons was not just an unreliable truth-teller. He was extraordinarily unreliable, as the lawyers would have discovered if they had delved into the background of his murder case. By not properly entering Eric Freeman's June 2013 confession into evidence, the attorneys could not show how he was forced to provide details of a murder he knew nothing about. Besides attacking the witnesses' credibility, the lawyers also could have focused on the plentiful physical evidence contradicting the State's testimony. With Jim Bruno's resources and a little more persistence, they could have bolstered this argument with their own experts. They did pinpoint how an impossible timeline undercut the pole barn story, but they blundered fatally in their presentation. Just as bad, in his closing argument, Tompkins portrayed Jason's alibi as a "mess" when it was one of the strongest pillars of his defense.

THE "PATHOLOGICAL LIAR"

If an appellate court had any doubt about the centrality of Rickey J. Hammons to the State's case against Jason Tibbs, it would have had to look no further than a letter that the prosecutor, Christopher Fronk, sent to the trial's judge one year later. In requesting that Hammons receive a modification of his sentence for murder, he wrote,

> As you know, Mr. Hammons was a key witness in the successful murder prosecution of Jason Tibbs. His corroboration of a key portion of the State's most crucial witness was instrumental to the jury reaching a guilty verdict. In and of itself, that cooperation is worthy of significant consideration. However, that is not Mr. Hammons' most significant contribution to the cause of justice in this matter. That came back in 2008 when Mr. Hammons contacted Detective Mark Lachmund to bring Rayna Rison's murder case back from a cold case to a viable case. Without Hammons, Rayna Rison's killer would still be at large.

Hammons's role in convicting Jason was not the only reason Fronk believed he deserved the judge's leniency. He also cited his age at the time of the crime. As he reminded Alevizos, "The Court has noted numerous times that a nineteen-year-old is not operating with a fully developed brain. I believe drug use delays that development even further. Both were significant factors in Mr. Hammons' mental maturity at the time of his crime when he was 19."

In fact, when Rickey Hammons killed Danny Cassidy, he was twenty-one. The wrong age may have been an unintentional miscalculation on Fronk's part. Still, there is much about Rickey's crime and its investigation that the prosecutor may have wanted the judge to forget—or the jury not to hear—since it would have impeached "his significant contribution to the cause of justice" and destroyed any value he had as a witness for the State. Equally important is Detective Mark Lachmund's role as an investigator in the Cassidy case. He witnessed Rickey's serial deceptions and fabrications more than any other officer.

During their closing arguments, Fronk and Tompkins debated whether the State's "key witness" was lying. The prosecutor argued the defense presented no evidence that Hammons was a "professional liar." Tompkins replied that Hammons's prevarications on the stand proved he was a "skilled liar."

But if the jury had been presented with Rickey's behavior during the Cassidy investigation, they would have discovered another term more apt than "professional" or "skilled." Jennifer Hammons used it during a taped interview two days after Danny died. She had previously told a detective that her brother had a problem with telling the truth. Referring to the problem, the detective asked, "What was that?"

Jen replied that he was "a pathological liar."

"Why do you call him that?" was the response.

"That's what he is," she explained.[1]

A pathological liar is defined as a person with "a persistent, compulsive tendency to tell lies" and is often loosely applied to people caught in multiple duplicitous comments. But Jennifer's characterization of her brother was not an exaggeration. The lies he told throughout the Cassidy investigation, even after his guilty plea, were exceptional for their wealth of elaborate false details. Along the way, he accused innocent men of complicity in the murder and claimed they were involved in other serious crimes. Beyond the substance of his stories was how he told them, holding court with the detectives interrogating him and thriving on their attention. When they challenged him, he was strikingly unflappable until he was confronted with hard evidence that could not be denied. After it became clear that one bogus story was not getting any purchase, he pivoted to another, trying to lay fault at the feet of the victim. Even during his sentencing hearing, he persisted with a new tale when he turned to Cassidy's bereaved family and told them Danny "had another side to him you all didn't know."

Judge Alevizos would have probably found a way to bar or limit testimony related to the Cassidy homicide in Jason's trial as not relevant, but there would have been multiple ways around that ruling.

To fully plumb the depths of Rickey's deception during the Cassidy investigation, it helps to wade through his conversations with the police in the days that followed Danny's death in October 1999. Lachmund conducted Rickey's first interview with Patrolman Michael Kellems, who knew Hammons as the result of unspecified juvenile offenses. Rickey addressed the officer several times as "Mike." Informed that they had contacted him about Cassidy's homicide, Hammons expressed shock and dismay. When asked if he knew anyone who could have been involved from the dealership where Danny worked, he replied, "Dude, I don't." Then, according to the transcript, he "exhale[d a] breath" and dramatically added, "You just told me that my friend was fucking murdered and shit, dude."[2]

Throughout the session, Hammons mixed what seemed like candor with information the detectives soon discovered was false. When asked why he moved out of the Harbor dealership house, Rickey said, "My parents kind of needed more help back at [their] house. That was one thing."[3] (Actually, he moved to another friend's apartment.[4])

But then he spoke about the sum he owed Cassidy. "He wanted the money for the damage that [my] dog did to his car, and somebody had actually . . . broken into the house when he was on vacation, and somebody kicked some holes in the wall and threw some shit around, but they didn't steal nothing or anything. And . . . he's like, 'You're responsible. This is Harbor [dealership]'s house. . . .' He's like, 'You're going to have to move out.' So I said, 'Okay. [That's] understandable,' so I moved out."

When asked if he agreed on the amount he owed Cassidy for the damage to the house and his car, Hammons answered, "There is no agreement on paper. [Cassidy] said he wanted fifteen hundred dollars."

"Did you agree to that?" Lachmund asked.

"So, so," Hammons replied. "I was like, Danny, you know, just figure out what it costs to get it fixed and let me know. My mom told him the same thing. He was like, 'All right. . . .' The guy never got ahold of me again." Hammons elaborated later in the interview, "My mom called him one day, and they said they was going to take care of it; some amount that will settle it. He goes, 'If we gotta go through court, we'll go through court. If not, we'll settle out of court.'"[5]

Lachmund asked, "So you guys didn't actually fight or nothing like that?"

"Hell no," Rickey replied. "No. It wasn't that important."[6]

Even during this first day of their investigation, detectives learned Rickey rarely lied with a "yes" or "no" answer. Instead, he larded each falsehood with additional details. Hammons said he did not have a handgun—only a bow and arrow—but could access his father's .22 rifles to hunt squirrels, deer, and rabbits. When asked where he was when Danny was shot, Rickey claimed he was sleeping in the basement room of his parents' house but added he woke up briefly when they yelled for him to turn off the TV[7]—something the parents did not verify when interviewed separately from their son.[8]

As the taped interview closed, Patrolman Kellems inquired if Rickey had anything more to add. Hammons replied, "I've told you everything I know, Mike. I don't know what the hell is going on. You just told me that my best friend—well, not my best friend—the guy that I lived with is dead."[9]

But it only took hours before holes appeared in Rickey's story. The night of his interview, police learned Big Rickey had a semiautomatic pistol that shot the same caliber bullets that killed Cassidy. He told the police he bought four Russian-made Makarovs, and two were stolen.[10] The following morning, after detectives interviewed coworkers at Harbor Chevrolet, they learned that Hammons's $1,500 debt had not been settled with Cassidy, who was actively and angrily seeking repayment—even holding Hammons's bedroom set as ransom.[11] Rickey also didn't tell the police about his appearance at the dealership before anyone knew Danny had been killed. He asked the office manager for his paycheck. When she told Hammons he didn't have one coming, he responded with a "creepy attitude" and said Danny Cassidy assured him the dealership still owed Rickey money.[12]

In the afternoon, Lachmund and another detective arranged to pick up Rickey at his parents' house and interview him again. With the investigation tightening around him, Hammons spun a new tale in the county sheriff's interview room. As Lachmund wrote in his report, "Rickey . . . had felt that Harbor Chevrolet may have connections to organized crime . . . and that Danny Cassidy could have been 'tied in' with the syndicate." Hammons provided vague reasons for his suspicions: "employees [who] carried black briefcases and drove sporty new cars all the time" and "new vehicles [that] were transported to other dealerships [in the Chicago area]." He told the detectives, "It might be possible that the 'mob' took care of Danny," but didn't want to be recorded saying so because of "fear of retaliation from the 'mob.'" Lachmund wrote that he left the room "to substantiate Rickey's theory."[13]

Detective Dick Buell continued the interview. He reported Hammons said that Cassidy "always had large sums of money on his person" and was "always traveling to Chicago" on one of two boats. Rickey also claimed that Danny had "a shit load of money invested in stocks to the tune of $40,000 to $50,000." He figured Cassidy could only be getting those sums from the Mob. However, as the detectives discovered from banking records, Cassidy was nowhere near that flush. He had cashed out $13,000 in certificates of deposit earlier in the year and still owed $8,000 on his one boat, with no other apparent investments or savings.

Rickey's accusations about Mob influence at Harbor Chevrolet extended to the finance director, who told detectives he had lectured Danny about wasting his money drinking and gambling. According to Rickey, this executive "travels all over the world . . . , eats shrimp and crab, and is big into wine . . . and does cocaine." As for Bob Sheridan, Danny's mentor in sales, whom he called "Dad," Hammons said he, too, was involved in organized crime and, "if anyone shot Dan, Rickey believed that it would have been Bob Sheridan." To back up this charge, Rickey brought up an incident where

Sheridan reprimanded Danny for not doing proper paperwork. Hammons said that Cassidy responded by nearly throwing a chair at him.

As Lachmund rejoined the interview, Hammons continued with stories about people in "fancy cars with dark-tinted windows" picking up Cassidy. Buell wrote, "[Hammons] felt Dan was into something—whether it was dealing in dope or transporting guns to Harbor." He claimed the dealership's organized crime connections were known to their mutual friends, including Danny's cousin. Of course, none of these individuals confirmed Rickey's accusations about Harbor. Before he left the sheriff's department, Hammons agreed to take a voice stress analysis test in his response to two questions: *Do you know who killed Dan Cassidy?* and *Did you kill Dan Cassidy?* Before he failed, Rickey had two questions of his own for the detective administering the test: "Am I suspect? Do you guys think I killed Dan?" The detective told him that he was "a suspect."[14]

The next day, incriminating evidence continued to build against Hammons: first, from his sister's casino coworker who overheard Jen's phone call with her mother, Judith Hammons, saying she gave Rickey bullets shortly before the murder.[15] Later that evening, Jen admitted as much to detectives. During the session, she called her brother a "pathological liar" capable of killing someone. She also revealed that Hammons told her to lie when police asked if he had a handgun.[16]

Meanwhile, detectives were grilling Rickey in another room at the sheriff's department. Hearing that his sister was in the building, Hammons asked if he could talk to her. The detectives told him they wouldn't interrupt her interview. Other police talked to Big Rickey and Judith at the Hammonses' residence. They permitted them to search their son's basement bedroom, where the officers found an empty box for .380 caliber bullets.

Even with the likelihood that his family had given him up, during his interview, Rickey persisted in smearing the dealership and the murder victim. As Detective Sergeant Larry Biggs reported, "Again, Hammons went into a long explanation on his observations of Harbor Chevy being involved with organized crime figures and that he felt Cassidy was involved with them in some way. Hammons then began making comments that 'Dan Cassidy was not the nice guy everyone thought he was. . . . Just ask [his cousin]. He knows what a bastard Dan can be.'"[17]

By 10:40 P.M., Rickey was still at the sheriff's department, Biggs wrote, insisting that "someone connected to organized crime was responsible for killing Dan Cassidy. Each time, he attempted to be more convincing than the time before but still could not provide any legitimate reasoning for his allegations." As Biggs drove Hammons home, Rickey gave the sergeant a stark warning. "I'll bet you within the next two weeks, someone else will die over this." He agreed to disclose more the next day if they met at La Porte's Dairy Queen so the Mafia wouldn't observe him entering the sheriff's department.[18]

As agreed, at 1:00 P.M. the following afternoon, Biggs met with Hammons in the DQ parking lot. Perhaps realizing that Danny Cassidy's funeral procession would soon pass them by, Rickey insisted on driving to another location. When they parked, Hammons first wanted to know why he was a suspect. Although Biggs said he could not share all the developing evidence against him, he could mention Rickey's possession of the type of handgun and bullets that killed Danny—as confirmed by the rest of the Hammons family. According to Biggs, the officer's response "irritated" Hammons, and he resumed his spurious charges against Bob Sheridan, the sales manager, whom Danny called "Dad." When asked why Sheridan would have done it, Hammons replied, "I don't know. Maybe it's because [Cassidy] knew something he shouldn't have. Maybe he owed them money for drugs."

But Biggs had had enough of Rickey's Mob stories. He told him he only wanted to hear "why [you] killed Cassidy" and where he hid the murder weapon. This challenge made Hammons "visibly sweaty and extremely jumpy and nervous." Again, Rickey predicted the Mob would kill him next because of his "close association" with Cassidy. When Biggs told him he didn't believe that and asked how long Rickey would deny what the evidence proved, the sergeant wrote that he replied, "I didn't kill the fucker." If he had, he said, "I would have blown my fucking brains out by now." Hammons then took off in his car, with his tires squealing.[19]

Later that afternoon, the Michigan City detectives learned of Rickey's involvement in another criminal case when they interviewed the individual who rented Hammons a room in his apartment after Cassidy kicked him out. As before, Rickey did not pay rent or reimburse the cost of his long-distance phone calls, and the new landlord locked up some of his possessions to get the $350 Rickey owed him. But before that could happen, the apartment was set on fire, destroying its contents. When the detectives searched Rickey's basement bedroom in his parents' house, they found several items the landlord had held hostage.[20]

The significance of this arson and theft report would diminish when, a few hours later, a disheveled Hammons appeared at the sheriff's department. He demanded to see the La Porte County sheriff, Jim Arnold. Putting an abrupt halt to his Saturday evening activities, Arnold rushed to the station. As they waited with Rickey, detectives noted his soiled clothes and bloody hands. Sergeant Biggs asked if he had been in the woods, and he replied that he goes there "when he needs to be by himself and think." Biggs asked if he was ready to discuss the Cassidy homicide, and Hammons said, "No, man. I told you I didn't have anything to do with that."

Instead, after Sheriff Arnold arrived, Rickey reported disposing of pistols, rifles, and ammunition he "shouldn't have had." He gave a field behind a truck stop as the location. At 6:00 P.M., the sheriff marshaled two trucks and crews from a local fire department to provide lighting, and he assembled a band of detectives—including Michigan City officer Mark Lachmund—to aid in the search. It would prove a wild-goose chase. When brought to the fruitless scene, Rickey speculated that someone saw him toss the guns and recovered them before the police arrived.

After two hours, Sheriff Arnold called off the search. The exasperated detectives returned to the station with Rickey in tow.[21] There would be no more pussyfooting with the prime suspect. Sergeant John Kintzele, a no-nonsense detective who had taken charge of the investigation for the Michigan City police, would handle the latest interrogation. He was short and wiry, with a buzz cut, mustache, and lips pressed into a perpetual expression of skepticism. When Kintzele let loose with the evidence arrayed against him, Rickey responded by spitting out lies—big and small—like sparks from a grinding wheel.

As he later detailed in his supplement report, Kintzele told Rickey they had two witnesses who saw him with a handgun. Hammons replied that they saw him with a Lorcin, not a Makarov pistol. The sergeant wrote, "I explained to Rickey that I did not believe he was telling the truth." When the sergeant asked that he show him the gun, Hammons repeated the story about throwing it behind the truck stop. Kintzele asked him why he would have done that. He reported Hammons "had no reason. . . . I again told him that I thought he was lying. . . . I explained that I was not fooled by his stories about throwing guns in the field and that I knew he was involved in the shooting death of Danny Cassidy. Rickey paused for a moment. He then stated that . . . if he had killed Danny Cassidy and really thought that a policeman knew what he had done, that policeman would be next. Rickey was very calm and appeared very serious while making this statement. I asked Rickey if he was threatening me. He stated, 'No.'"

Hammons also denied stealing the Makarov from his parents. However, when they reported the burglary, Big Rickey and Judith listed other items missing besides the guns, including her Beanie Babies. One of Little Rickey's friends saw him pawn the stuffed animals to get cash for Chicago Cubs tickets. The sergeant reported, "I told [Hammons] I knew about the Beanie Babies." The detective next talked about the items his landlord had locked up as collateral for back rent payment and lost after someone broke into his apartment and set it on fire. Hammons claimed he took the items with him when he moved out. Kintzele wrote, "I informed him that what he was saying was not true. . . . I had seen the [items] in his room [in his parents' house], and I knew he had taken them back."

Now that the detective had cornered him with indisputable facts, Kintzele reported, "Rickey told me that he may go to prison for the rest of his life for theft, arson, burglary, and other things he had done, but he was not going to say that he had shot Danny. I again explained that I only wanted him to tell the truth."

Still, Hammons was not done with his bizarre lies. Attempting, for a moment, to appear sympathetic, Kintzele said, "I was sure what happened between him and Danny was very traumatic for him and probably the worst thing that happened in his life." But Rickey denied that would have been so. "He told me that he had been shot and stabbed before. I asked him where he was shot. He stated that he was shot in the leg. He then pointed to the inside of his left thigh. I asked him if he received medical treatment. He stated no. He claimed he took care of it himself. I told him that I thought he was lying."

Rickey then told Kintzele he was playing "mind games" with him. Hammons said he had "special training and knew the psychology behind the way we were treating him." When the sergeant asked where he got that training, Hammons refused to say and added, "It was not really important."

Since he was not under arrest, Rickey was free to leave the sheriff's department, but a few minutes later, on a hunch, Kintzele and another detective went to Danny Cassidy's grave site. They arrived to see the Red Chevy Lumina nearby, which sped off as soon as the driver—thought to be Hammons—spotted them.[22]

Over Sunday and Monday, the noose around Rickey's neck would grow tighter as the detectives tracked down the shops where he pawned his parents' stolen merchandise.[23] Soon afterward, his sister admitted Rickey never returned the .380 caliber bullets she gave him for his Makarov pistol.[24] On Tuesday morning at 1:42 A.M., Hammons made another impromptu visit to the La Porte County sheriff's department, demanding to see Sheriff Arnold, who arrived twenty minutes later. Lachmund, Biggs, and Kintzele were also mustered to the station. According to a report written by Biggs, "Rickey Hammons explained to the Sheriff that he felt that his life was in danger. He claimed that employees at Harbor Chevrolet were responsible for Daniel Cassidy's death and that he was concerned he would be the next person murdered."[25]

When Kintzele arrived, he found an inebriated Rickey in Arnold's office with his feet on the sheriff's desk. He had a bottle of Heineken in one hand and, with the other, flicked ashes from his cigarette on the carpet.

According to his report, Hammons told Kintzele, "He did not like me." Biggs and Kintzele then told Hammons that they confirmed he had pawned the items his parents reported stolen, except for the Makarov pistols.

Rickey had no response to that. Instead, he lectured the assembled detectives about how they had "fucked up" in their investigation and "only he knew where the gun was that killed Danny." He also claimed that only he had "hard evidence regarding who killed Danny." The murder, he said, was related to Harbor Chevy drug dealing and eight pounds of cocaine hidden in the hot tub at the house he shared with Cassidy. He warned the assembled police that his allegations were in a videotape he had already sent to the FBI and US Marshals, implying the local cops would look foolish if they didn't take him seriously.

Rickey then interrupted his harangue to say he needed to "take a piss." Biggs and Kintzele followed him into the restroom. When Hammons opened his belt, Kintzele half expected him to pull out a gun. When Rickey saw the detective observing him over his shoulder, he shouted, "Faggot." On his way out the door, Kintzele wrote, Hammons "struck me in the chest with a closed fist. He then pushed me as he made contact." Kintzele shoved him back. As the detectives yelled at Rickey to settle down, Biggs and Lachmund rushed in to subdue him, but Hammons broke away from them and yelled, "Fuck you guys." When Kintzele approached, he spat in his face. Finally, as Lachmund and Biggs held each arm, Kintzele "clamped" his hand over Rickey's nose and mouth. He wrote, "This caused Rickey's oxygen supply to diminish rapidly. . . . He stopped resisting and was escorted to the booking area by other officers."[26]

Hammons remained composed long enough to have a mug shot taken with a noticeable smirk.[27] But moments later, when asked to change into a jail jumpsuit, he became "combative" again, according to the report.[28] During the struggle, jail officers said they heard him comment about hurting himself and wanting to die. They had to use pepper spray to make him comply with orders to remove all his clothes—so he wouldn't have anything to hang himself with—and enter a padded cell.[29]

Meanwhile, at 3:45 A.M., Lachmund and two other detectives searched the Harbor Chevrolet house for a stash of cocaine behind the hot tub. It would prove to be another of Rickey's wild-goose chases.

Once Lachmund returned to the sheriff's department an hour later, he learned that Hammons had summoned him and Biggs.[30] Sheriff Arnold saw Hammons first and warned him, "If he played any games," he'd go right back to the padded cell.[31]

At 8:20 A.M., Lachmund and Biggs recorded another interview with Rickey Hammons, and in a matter of minutes, it turned into another rant about the nefarious activities at Harbor Chevrolet. Besides singling out managers like Bob Sheridan, Hammons charged one of the dealership owners with "drug trafficking." He forgot his last name, which was Italian, and referred to him as Geno.[32]

After that introduction, Hammons spun a new story with action and dialogue reminiscent of Al Pacino's starring role in *Scarface*. The night before Danny was killed, Hammons claimed he had stopped at the Blue Chip Casino when Geno and Sheridan ordered him to get into a silver Pontiac with four doors and a gray interior. "Do you recall the conversation between you and them?" Biggs asked.

"No," Rickey answered. "They just said, 'Get in. We're going for a ride.'"

They were headed to Cassidy's house, but Hammons saw them first park his car behind the K & M grocery store along the way. When they arrived at their destination, Hammons said he watched as Sheridan knocked, and Danny answered the door in his boxers—colored silver and black. After a few minutes, Hammons told the detectives, Cassidy got dressed and emerged from the house with Sheridan holding a gun on him.

"What's he doing with the gun?" Biggs asked.

"Kind of like, you know, signaling Danny," Hammons answered. "That's when I knew something was wrong."

"Now the four of you are in the car, and you're in the driveway. Do you recall the conversation and who was talking?" Biggs asked.

Hammons replied, "Geno turned around and looked at Danny and said, 'Where's his shit?'" Rickey explained that meant, "Where's the coke?"

When asked how Danny responded, Hammons answered, Cassidy "said he's not going to get it, and that it's nowhere to be found and . . . pretty much, 'Fuck off. You ain't gonna get it.'"

Hammons had Geno driving with one hand on the wheel and the other holding a gun. Rickey said Sheridan pulled out his revolver along the way and asked Danny "where he wanted to die." Cassidy replied, "Fuck you."

When they stopped at the bend on Orr Lake Road, Hammons said, Geno ordered them out of the car and then handed Hammons a TEC-9 handgun, which he described as a "machine pistol." However, he told the detective he did not know the caliber of the bullets inside. "Then what happens?" Biggs asked.

Rickey replied, "He told me I'm either going to kill Danny or Danny's going to kill me. And Danny said he wasn't going to kill me." Hammons then admitted to shooting Danny Cassidy in the chest, describing the "real weird sound" he made as he fell. "Like gurgling blood or some shit."

Rickey told the detectives how Sheridan approached after Cassidy hit the ground. "He said, 'That's not how you kill a man.' And then he grabbed the gun, and he kind of leaned over Danny and just started—"

Biggs interrupted at that point to have Rickey describe the area where Danny fell and the position his body was in. He then asked, "Can you give me a guess on how many times he fired the gun?"

Hammons replied, "Maybe six or seven. . . . Right at Danny's face."

"Was the gun close to Danny's face or at a distance?"

"It was real close."

After the shooting, Hammons said, Geno was "flippin'." He first yelled at Sheridan, "What are you doing, you fuckin' man, and all types of shit." He then looked at Hammons and said, "Don't say nothing. Just shut up. Just get in the car."

He told the detectives that before they left Sheridan leaned over Cassidy's body and spit in his face. Meanwhile, he claimed, Geno "threw something" into the lake. "Something made a big splash. Yes, most definitely." No doubt, Hammons was referring here to the murder weapon, perhaps expecting the police to search the lake as they did behind the truck stop.

Hammons next described Geno's roundabout escape route from Orr Lake to his Chevy Lumina in the grocery store parking lot, delineating each road and turn. When asked if there was any conversation along the way, Rickey replied, "They're saying if I tell anybody that they're going to kill my family. . . . They knew I had nieces and nephews, and they were going to start with them first."

Hammons said that when he got home he threw his BDU clothing in his mother's dirty clothes pile but later burned his boots in a barrel behind the pole barn. While Hammons may have intended that to be the end of his story, Biggs was not ready to end the interview. He asked Hammons to tell him what handguns he owned. While Hammons persisted in saying he threw all his guns behind the truck stop, Rickey finally admitted that a Makarov pistol had been in his possession, which he "stole back" from the landlord who had the fire. He claimed to have broken the gun apart with a hammer before Danny's murder so "if any kids found it, they couldn't use it." He threw the pieces behind a recycling center. As for the bullets he got from his sister Jen, he shot them at some trees near his parents' house.

When asked why he confessed, Rickey replied, "I just couldn't take it no more. Knowing." When asked if he wanted to add anything else to his statement, he said, "I didn't want to . . . shoot Danny. But they left me no choice." A few minutes later, he added, "I wish I would have just died, too. I'm sorry for his family. You can tell all my friends and my family and everybody. [But] it was me or him or then both of us."

During the interview, Lachmund and Biggs wanted Hammons to clarify something else—what happened between him and the detectives in the bathroom.

"You have to put down on tape what happened?" Hammons asked.

"Yeah," Biggs replied. During Hammons's response, Lachmund told him to put his head closer to the microphone.

When asked why he punched Kintzele, Hammons replied, "I just believe that the man offended me." Biggs wondered if the fight was due to his "frustration and the stress that you've encountered over the last several days." Rickey agreed and said the stress also contributed to his fight with the jail guards.

Biggs then asked, "Have you been mistreated by us at all in all the encounters that you've come in here to talk to us?"

Rickey replied, "No. Not really at all."

"Have we been disrespectful to you?"

"You haven't," Hammons said to Biggs and referring to Lachmund, "and Mark hasn't. No."

During their hour-long interview with Hammons, Biggs and Lachmund did elicit one salient piece of the truth—where he threw the murder weapon.[33] At 12:15 P.M., the detectives pulled Hammons out of jail and took him to the recycling center, where he led them to the woods on one side of the facility. They found the barrel and frame of a .380 Makarov semiautomatic pistol there. Rickey had smashed the barrel with a hammer, evidently trying to prevent ballistics tests that could match the bullets taken from Danny's body with the gun. The detectives next had Hammons return to the country road where they found Cassidy. While a video camera was running, he acted out the kill-Danny-or-get-killed crime scene he had elaborately described in his confession.[34]

By the time Hammons returned to jail, he had decided to talk to Biggs and Lachmund again. They said he should get some sleep instead. At 8:50 P.M., Lachmund and Biggs were back in an interview room with Rickey. He told them he had not been "totally honest" during his previous confession but was now ready to impart the "real truth."[35] After hearing this new version of the homicide, the detectives decided to arrange a third Hammons videotape recording, which commenced at 11:10 P.M.

In this confession, Rickey once again provided details on each friend he visited before the murder but added another stop at a bar and tallied all the alcohol he consumed. He also mentioned a return home where he changed into his BDU clothes. He said he then spent time with one more friend and left his home around 11:30 P.M. Biggs asked, "What happens next?"

"After that, I don't remember," Hammons replied. "The only thing that I remember after that is standing over the body of Daniel Cassidy . . . with a loaded handgun." Rickey claimed he could provide no more details about the actual shooting.

Biggs reminded him, "This afternoon, you told us that Cassidy stood in front of you [and] you had a gun in your hand. Is that correct?"

"Correct," Hammons replied, "but I was lying to you then."

When asked if he recalled pulling the trigger, Hammons said, "I just came to, and he was . . . he was dead, and I was standing over him."

Although he saw Danny's bloody body below him, he didn't know if he had any bullets left in his gun. Then Rickey said, "[I] freaked out and took off." He next drove to the Toll Road, explaining, "I didn't believe that I did it, and I just wanted to kill myself." He got out of his car and "sat in the middle of the Toll Road," but no vehicles appeared to run him over, so he returned home and "tried to go to sleep."

Rickey did not just draw a blank about the homicide. He told the detectives he didn't know why he would have done it.

"And you don't recall having a beef that . . . would provoke this?" Biggs asked.

"I don't know why it happened," Hammons replied.

When asked about the melodrama he depicted during the previous taping, Rickey explained, "I lied and said that Bobby and Geno were involved."

"Say that again?" Biggs asked.

"I lied and said that Bobby and Geno were involved."

"[And] one of them went in and brought Dan Cassidy out at gunpoint?" Biggs pressed. "That story is a lie?"

"Yes, sir," Rickey answered, no longer on a first-name basis with his interrogators.

"Being forced to ride with them to Orr Lake Road was a lie?"

"Yes, sir."

"Being forced at gunpoint to point a loaded gun at Dan Cassidy and pull the trigger was a lie?"

"Yes, sir."

"Okay. And nobody ever threatened to harm anyone in your family if you didn't kill Dan Cassidy. Is that correct?"

"Yes, sir."[36]

But more lies would still follow. Rickey claimed he did not remember visiting Cassidy's house or even meeting him that day. Hammons said he did not recall loading the gun, where he got the bullets, or the type he used[37]—though he would later disclose the .380 cartridge brand to other prisoners in the jail.[38]

After the tape recording was over, Biggs wrote in his report, "Hammons was told that his last two confessions did not appear to be totally truthful. That within the next twenty-four hours, investigators would probably seek a warrant for his arrest, charging him with murder. That each time he has provided a taped recorded statement, it becomes part of the investigative record. It was suggested to Hammons that he think about his future, and if he wished to talk to the investigators further, he should do so by written request. That the investigators were only interested in the truth."[39]

The next day, according to the summary report, Lachmund and another detective "greeted" Hammons at the jail and placed him under arrest for public intoxication, battery by body waste (for spitting at Kintzele), and murder.[40]

Still, despite his record of multiple false confessions and false accusations, Rickey was not done lying. The final target for his calumny was the victim, Danny Cassidy.

Fifteen hours after his previous late-night confession, Hammons asked to meet with detectives Lachmund and Biggs again for one more videotaped session. His arrest warrants with their affidavits of probable cause revealed his legal jeopardy. Rickey needed a new story to mitigate his sentence if not entirely exonerate him.

Yet again, after the taping started, Rickey was read his rights and agreed to talk without a lawyer. But this time, he began to cry and then pulled himself together. "Thought I was going to lose it there," he explained.

Lachmund asked, "You okay?"

Rickey responded with, "Uh huh."[41] He then recited his background and how he met Cassidy—information the detectives probably knew by heart. His new twist came with an event he said occurred in mid-August after he had been out drinking with Cassidy, and they came home with Steak 'n Shake take-out meals. After nearly passing out on the couch, he told the detectives, "I started to realize that I was being undressed. . . . I told him, 'No, no, no,' and he's like, 'Just don't move. . . .' And when I got up to go away, that's when [he] pushed back down on the couch. That's when I knew something was wrong. . . . I got up to leave again, and he grabbed me again. He threw me to the floor. [My] pants were jerked down around [my] ankles. I tried making it up the two steps into the kitchen [and] was pulled back, and I was raped."

When Biggs asked him what exactly he meant by that, Rickey replied, "He stuck his dick in my ass." Hammons said this was done while he still had his clothes on—with his pants below his knees—and Cassidy was wearing his shorts. Biggs asked if Danny used a lubricant or condom, and Rickey answered, "No, sir."

"Did you experience any pain?"

"Yes, sir."

According to Hammons, Cassidy left that night but returned the next day and "told me not to tell nobody." He said Danny "threatened me" to keep quiet "with my job, my friends, a bunch of shit. . . . [Also] I thought he would use physical force."

"If you told anyone?" Biggs asked.

"In such a way," Hammons replied. But then, despite the demand that Rickey not tell anyone, he said Danny threatened to tell his friends "me and him was gay."[42]

Rickey told the detectives that the incident was so traumatic he could not return to work for the rest of the week and only appeared at Harbor to pick up the Chevy Lumina Danny helped him get.[43]

On the night of the murder, Hammons said, Cassidy asked him to come over to the Harbor house to discuss paying for the damage that Rickey's dog did to Danny's car. He suspected he really wanted to talk about the rape, so he brought the handgun. "Not so much as to scare him but to know that I had protection."

Hammons claimed it wasn't long before "[Danny's] trying to talk me into having sex with him again," and he pulled out his gun.

"Are you mad?" Biggs asked.

"More scared than mad," Hammons replied.

"But if you're scared, why did you go there?"

"Don't know, really."

"Why not call him up on the phone?"

"I don't know," Hammons answered. "I was not thinking straight."

Rather than use his gun to flee the house, Hammons said that he ordered Cassidy to get dressed and ride in his car. He told Biggs he could drive while holding the gun on Danny. As they got to Orr Lake Road, he said Cassidy grabbed him in "my crotch area." He slammed the brakes and made Danny get out of the car. "I was just gonna fuckin' scare him and make him think about it," he told the detectives. "That's when he went to kiss me, and that's when I pointed the gun at him. And I shot. . . . Til the gun was empty."

Hammons said he put two or three rounds in Danny's face, but "I wasn't really keeping track."

Biggs, clearly skeptical, probed the nonsense in Rickey's new narrative. Among the items missing from the house was Danny's cordless phone, which Rickey admitted he took with him. "Why did you take that?" Biggs asked.

"Because I was just going to leave. I didn't want him to call the police, so I took the phone."

"Why didn't you just leave?"

"I don't know.

"Wasn't it just as easy to talk to him in his house than it would be to get him in your car and try to talk to him?"

367

Hammons replied that it didn't matter. "Either or," he said and repeated those words when a puzzled Biggs asked again.[44]

Although Biggs did not express any outrage in his report about the "third confession," the detectives' actions in the following twenty-four hours showed how anxious they were to dispute it. From jail, Hammons had already phoned his mutual friends with Cassidy to say he'd reveal the rape story and that it might make the papers.[45] The people he called were incredulous, as they told the detectives. Each one was asked to appear at the sheriff's department for a taped interview before the end of the day.[46] Summing up what the detectives heard about Danny's sexuality from his friends, Biggs pointed to his cousin, who "knew [Cassidy] his entire life and had never seen anything that would lead him to believe that Dan Cassidy was bisexual or homosexual."[47]

To further counter the rape story, the detectives checked his employment records at Harbor Chevrolet. Contrary to what he told Biggs and Lachmund, Hammons worked on the days after the alleged assault.[48]

During his incarceration in county jail, Hammons was only too happy to talk about his case, bragging that "he was in jail for murder." A guard overhead him telling another prisoner, "Cassidy had raped him when he was drunk," and that he was also "involved in some kind of child pornography." On the night of the murder, while driving on the country road, Cassidy "attempted to kiss [Hammons] and grope his genitals. . . . Hammons claimed that was more than he could take, so he shot Cassidy nine times. . . . If he would have brought more bullets [then] he would have shot Cassidy even more. . . . He shot Cassidy in the face so that the family could not have an open-casket funeral." The guard said he then added, "He did the world a favor." A county jail prisoner reported hearing something similar from Rickey and "did not know why Hammons told him . . . because no one in the [prison] block usually speaks about their cases, [but] Hammons was running around 'like a chicken with its head cut off' and talking about the case. Hammons told him, 'Once I get out, nobody will ever mess with me again because of what I did.'"[49]

But a few months later, after being assigned Craig Braje as a public defender, Rickey tried to discard all three confessions, charging that they were made while intoxicated or after he had been "physically assaulted" by the detectives and "suffered a psychological breakdown."[50]

After his motion to suppress statements was denied, in June 2000, Braje negotiated a plea agreement with him serving forty-five years for Cassidy's murder—a sentence that Rickey tried to modify ever after. At first, Rickey stuck with his rape charge.[51] Then, in 2008, he suddenly changed his tune after coming up with his pole barn sighting and accepted guilt for killing Danny without qualification.

Whether or not a deal was made for an early release in exchange for his testimony against Jason Tibbs, Hammons must have had that expectation when he first approached Mark Lachmund in 2008. Of all the Michigan City and La Porte County detectives involved in the Cassidy case, Lachmund had been most exposed to the twists and turns of Rickey's deception. Time and again, Hammons showed a propensity for making up preposterous stories to weasel his way out of judicial jeopardy. Lachmund could not have forgotten that.

But according to Jason, his lawyers never looked into the Cassidy case files. Instead, Pejic seemingly did no more than review the press clips about his trial. "When I asked Scott [Pejic] why Rickey killed that guy," Jason recalls, "he told me it had something to do with a homosexual rape."

If Jason's lawyers had delved into the background of the State's star witness, they had several avenues to present the jury with his propensity to lie. It could have come up in their cross-examination of Hammons and his sister. They could have asked her if she ever called her brother a pathological liar and what she meant by that. They could have asked Hammons if he had a habit of charging innocent men with serious crimes.

As another gateway to Hammons's lies, they could have called Mark Lachmund as a defense witness. Oddly, and perhaps tellingly, he was not a prosecution witness even though he was the first detective Hammons contacted with his supposed barn sighting of Rayna's dead body. Lachmund's prior experience with Hammons should have undercut any new story he had to tell. Jason's lawyers could have also subpoenaed the other Michigan City detectives who challenged Hammons's bizarre claims and allegations. Should Alevizos have blocked any of this testimony as irrelevant, the defense counsel would have ensured the appeals court saw it with an appropriate offer of proof. It's hard to believe that jurors would have taken Hammons's story about the pole barn seriously if they later heard even a portion of the lies he told in his own murder case.

THE PERJURY TWO-STEP

B rett Airy served two years as a patrolman before becoming a detective and received scant special instructions for that job. As he testified in Jason's trial, his training consisted of a class at the John Reid School of Interview Interrogation,[52] typically taught over four days.[53] In recent decades, research papers and government hearings have criticized the school's techniques as coercive and leading to false confessions. In response, Reid's leaders issued their own paper titled "Clarifying Misinformation about The Reid Technique," which argues their methods are "specifically designed to do everything possible to protect against a person making a false confession." As proof, they enumerate the guiding principles that appear in Reid's "training manual, courses and books." These include, at the very top of this list:

- Do not make any promises of leniency.
- Do not threaten the subject with any physical harm or inevitable consequences.
- Do not conduct interrogations for an excessively lengthy period of time.[54]

We cannot know whether these principles were stressed in Airy's training or how closely he listened to them if they were. However, we can be sure he violated these "guiding principles" in the false confession extracted from Eric Freeman on June 27, 2013, during an interview that lasted more than three and a half hours and was more indoctrination than interrogation. This pivotal event in the Jason Tibbs investigation was taped, and the 140-page transcript was made available to his defense counsel. Their failure to properly enter it as evidence during the trial is among the most egregious blunders of their representation. It provides remarkable documentation on how a hapless suspect with ultimate leniency—granted by legal immunity—can be talked into confirming a murder scenario he knows nothing about. Of course, Freeman's false confession posed no jeopardy for the confessor but had perilous consequences for Jason Tibbs.

The most charitable take on Indiana State Trooper Al Williamson and City of La Porte Detective Brett Airy is that they went into the June 2013 session somewhat believing Hammons's story and hoping Freeman would supply missing details. Perhaps they also hoped that a few secret interactions might refresh the supposed accomplice's memory beforehand. But the interlocutors quickly realized that Freeman was not fully read into the essential elements of Hammons's pole barn plot. Getting him there required a combination of cajoling and barefisted coercion. The detectives were also compelled to slip him crime scene details he apparently heard from them for the first time.

As the hours passed, the interrogators and their interviewee developed a dance-like routine to induce the perjury. Often, the first step was the promise of leniency, and the next step led Freeman where they wanted him to go. Should he stray too far from the choreography necessary for a Tibbs conviction, they could take a step backward, pointing to other supposed evidence, and pull him in that direction. Despite their best efforts to make the session look like a standard interview, their coaching and spoon-feeding are clear—sometimes to the extent that would be comic if another man's freedom wasn't at stake.

As a result, this one document could have upended the State's case if it had been carefully examined and dissected for the jury. It remains a remarkable example of how a truly clueless witness can be manipulated to meet the ends of the prosecution.

Immunity or Snake Eyes

For Jason and his attorneys, there was no doubt about why Rickey Hammons was willing to testify against him. As he had from the first day of incarceration, the convicted murderer was looking to reduce his sentence—much like any other prisoner. Eric Freeman was another story. Like Tibbs, he had no complicity in Rayna's murder. Why would he pretend he did and put an indelible stain on his reputation? Although Freeman no longer lived in the La Porte area, he was a google search away from his admitted participation in a notorious, heinous crime.

Part of the answer to this mystery could lie in the court files of the area where Freeman had lived for two decades. They show the domestic and financial turbulence that had entered his life months before his second interview. After April 2012, Freeman and his wife, Julie, could no longer

371

pay the $1,700 monthly payment for their mortgage. By December, the bank filed for foreclosure on the house he purchased in a sweetheart deal from the home builder, and he would eventually lose it. From the court affidavits, the Freemans appeared to have had no lawyers to defend them.[55] His marriage to Julie was slipping away too. On June 10, 2013, Julie Freeman filed for divorce.[56]

When Eric faced Airy and Williamson two weeks later, the groundwork had been laid for a different encounter than the one he had had five years earlier. In 2008, Freeman knew hardly anything about Rayna's murder and did not indicate his involvement. In 2013, the session started with his signature on an immunity agreement—an acknowledgment that he did know something.[57] It's not unusual for criminal accomplices to seek protection from the court in return for their testimony. However, several aspects of Freeman's immunity agreement were exceptional.

First, he received "transactional" immunity. Typically, such witnesses are given "use" immunity—anything they testify about cannot be used for their prosecution. For example, he could tell the court that he assisted in the abduction and murder of Rayna Rison and not be prosecuted for those crimes. However, if he ran over someone during his getaway and didn't testify about it, he could be charged with vehicular manslaughter for the hit-and-run. Transactional immunity protected him from any felony or misdemeanor associated with Rayna's homicide. This impenetrable witness shield is a prosecution tactic forbidden in federal cases and only dispensed rarely on the state level.[58]

Second, the agreement was negotiated with the La Porte prosecuting attorney by Craig Braje, who had previously represented Freeman's accuser, Rickey Hammons. According to Detective Airy's report, Freeman acknowledged retaining the Michigan City attorney in March 2013.[59] But La Porte County would not pick up Braje's exorbitant fees for a South Carolina resident. How Freeman paid for them remains in question since he couldn't afford a lawyer during his foreclosure or divorce. Another question would be why he would want to keep Braje on after he encouraged Freeman to take the polygraph in 2008, which his client failed.[60] As an experienced defense counsel, Braje should have known better than to let his client risk a faulty reading—a common occurrence.[61] Failing the test must have been disturbing for Freeman if he had considered himself innocent before he took it. His dire personal and financial straits might have made him susceptible to playing along with Hammons's story if someone else picked up his legal bills—namely, the Hammons family. But Freeman's association with Braje must have looked fishy at the last minute. When the witness signed the immunity agreement, he put "Waive" over the signature block on "Counsel for Eric M. Freeman."[62]

Representation and terms aside, nothing was more unusual about Freeman's immunity agreement than who was there to present it to him at the police department in Rock Hill, South Carolina. According to Airy's notes, the detectives were joined by La Porte County chief deputy attorney Christopher Fronk—not one of his assistants. Airy wrote, "Prosecutor Fronk met with Eric in a conference room at the police department. Prosecutor Fronk reviewed the immunity agreement with Eric, which he signed and waived legal counsel."[63] Details surrounding the detectives' interview were provided to Jason and his lawyers in the affidavit for probable cause for his arrest—but no mention was made of Fronk being present in South Carolina.[64]

It may be no surprise that the chief deputy prosecuting attorney would travel to South Carolina to present an immunity agreement to the key witness for such a notorious cold case. But it is odd that what he said to Freeman was not recorded or reported by Airy or Williamson. Jason's lawyers should have asked them during trial what they heard. As a result, we can only assume what Fronk said based on State Trooper Williamson's repeated warnings to Freeman during the interview about "rolling the dice." With transactional immunity, Eric would not be prosecuted for any crime associated with Rayna's murder—so long as he cooperated with the prosecution. However, if he diverged in any way from the prosecutor's "team"—another Williamson term—Freeman would be "rolling the dice."[65] If Freeman rolled snake eyes, no matter how ridiculous Hammons's pole barn story was, Freeman still stood a chance of being charged and even convicted.

Whatever Fronk told Freeman before the interview, there is even more mystery about why he did not lead the interrogation afterward since he had traveled all that way to be there. Although Fronk did not sit in the conference room, he still hovered nearby as an intimidating presence. Williamson had no compunction about reminding Freeman, "Um, like I said, the Deputy Prosecutor's sitting right outside if you have a question for him." Again, we can only surmise why Fronk didn't want to be part of the process. Perhaps he expected the detectives would behave in a way he didn't want to witness if called to testify about it later.

In any case, Freeman tried to be the epitome of the cooperative witness. As he indicated repeatedly, he did not want to roll the dice. But from the start, it was clear that Freeman was not read into all the quirky lies of Hammons's scenario. Freeman also thought he could provide some of his own spiffs to make the story more plausible. Little did he know his first two contributions to the storyline could blow the State's case sky high.

The Broke-down Buick

No element of Hammons's pole barn story was more essential than his sister Jen's gray Buick Century that some witnesses described as silver. This was the car Freeman drove without permission and where Little Rickey claimed he saw Rayna Rison's body in the trunk while smoking dope in the loft. This was also the car that Airy assiduously tried to place in the Pine Lake Animal Hospital parking lot or on North 200 East.

When the detectives started the interview, they tried to walk Freeman step-by-step through his supposed actions on the evening of March 26, 1993. He began by "remembering" that he had dropped Jason off at the animal hospital. It was one of those supposed memories that the detective would have to correct later because too many witnesses saw more than one male in the parking lot with Rayna—one in the car and one confronting her.

But the detectives' concern about the dropping-off detail was dwarfed by Freeman's answer to Williamson's follow-up question, "What were you driving?"

"Should've been driving a red Cavalier," Freeman replied, explaining that it was the car his grandfather let him use. The following fraught dialogue ensued:

Indiana State Police Detective Al Williamson (AW): Okay. Now I'll tell ya this: we have, um, evidence of a different vehicle that you were drivin' 'cause your statement of being with Jason there at that location is correct, but not in that vehicle.

Eric Freeman (EF): I wasn't drivin'. . . .

AW: Did you have access to any other vehicles at that time? Maybe yours was broke down. Maybe you were driving somebody else's vehicle.

EF: No, sir. I had, I was drivin' my red Cavalier, cause the Hammons's vehicle was in the pole barn broke down.

AW: And what was that vehicle?

EF: I wanna say it was a Buick Century.

AW: What color was that Buick Century?

EF: Grayish silver.

AW: Okay. Um, and again the, that vehicle was not broke down.

EF: It was in the pole barn.

AW: It may have been in the pole barn, but it was not broke down. It did break down later. You're correct.

EF: Okay.

AW: But at this time, the day Rayna came up missin', it was fully operative, and we do know that. We, we have testimony to that.

EF: Okay.[66]

Freeman's interview was not the first time the detectives heard about the "broke-down" Buick Century that some witnesses described as silver. Soon after Little Rickey provided police with his pole barn sighting, detectives found a big fray in his tangled web—probably first from the Hammons family. Little Rickey had claimed to see a car the family could have known wasn't working on March 26. In the evidence they collected, the detectives tried various means to show Big Rickey and Judith Hammons owned the Buick, including receipts for insurance and repairs. One postcard from a dealership parts department was even addressed to Freeman at the Hammonses' home address.[67]

However, the detectives used an interview and highly suspect evidence to establish the vehicle's working condition on March 26. In admitting the car's fragile condition, Judith explained that her brother-in-law would be enlisted to do the frequent repairs. When Airy talked to him, he claimed the car broke down on April 12 at the earliest—a little more than two weeks *after* Rayna's abduction.[68] As proof, he showed a notation in his checkbook ledger for $748.02 worth of parts from Johnson's Service. Airy made a copy of the page for his records.

However, the Johnson's Service line in the checkbook appears to be written over a previously erased entry—the only erasure on the page.[69] Unlike the other Buick evidence Airy collected, there is no receipt directly from the vendor, Johnson's Service.[70]

Airy brought up this suspicious evidence to get Freeman to stop talking about another car in the June 2013 interview. "We got documentation," the detective told Eric. "'Cause one, one of their relatives worked on the car and bought parts, and . . ."

But Freeman needed no more convincing. He finally relented, saying, "Okay. [If] ya'll have the evidence. . . ."[71]

No Place Like Home

In his dance with the detectives, Freeman did not just get off on the wrong foot with the car he was driving. The dates he gave when he stayed with the Hammons family were nearly as bad. This strained exchange started when Williamson asked, "So, where were you living back in March 1993?"

> EF: March of '93? I was livin' at my grandfather's. . . .
>
> AW: Were you there the whole month of March?
>
> EF: I honestly don't recall if I was there the whole month of March. I'm pretty sure I was there because . . . I lived with Jen until [the Hammons] kicked me out [in] January [1993]. Then I moved in with my grandfather.
>
> AW: Okay, why did they kick you out?
>
> EF: I wasn't bein' faithful or honest to Jen.
>
> AW: Okay.
>
> EF: Judy, her mother . . . did laundry and found a couple packs of rubbers.
>
> AW: Yeah, in your pocket?
>
> EF: Mm-hmm. In my vest.
>
> AW: Yeah. Okay. And that's what you stated before. Um, but [when] Rayna Rison came up missing, do you recall where you were living?
>
> EF: If I remember right, I was at my grandfather's house, living there. I lived there for about a month and a half.
>
> AW: Would it surprise you if you were living at the Hammons[es'] at that time?
>
> EF: No, I wasn't living at the Hammons[es']. That's because I went from the Hammons to my grandfather's to G Street [where his mother lived], and

in between my grandfather and G Street, I had talked to Jen, and we were trying to work things out.

AW: Okay.

EF: But I did not move back in.[72]

Freeman's actual residence on March 26, 1993, was another loose thread that could unravel Rickey's pole barn yarn. During his first interview in 2008, Freeman said he stayed with them for no more than six months, starting in June 1992, after he graduated from La Porte High School.[73] This date would have put his eviction from the Hammons household in January 1993 and three months before Rayna's abduction—at the latest.

Freeman's actual domicile on the night of Rayna's disappearance was another sensitive topic for the detectives. If Freeman lived with his grandfather on March 26—and not with the Hammons family—he would *not* have had access to the Buick. Given his infidelity with Jen, it's hard to believe the family would have welcomed him back inside their house, where he supposedly picked up a call from Jason on the CB base station.

At this point, Airy barged into Freeman's interview with the pole barn story crumbling before him. "At the time that this happened, you were still at the Hammons[es'] house," the detective told Freeman. "You, you told us that last time." Here, Airy referred to the 2008 interview, when Freeman said nothing of the kind.

But Eric would not argue with the detective about what he said. "[Then] I told you wrong," he replied. "I was not at [the Hammonses' house]. I was at . . . my grandfather's farm. . . . You can ask [my mother]."

Indeed, if they wanted to resolve any question about Freeman's residence, the detectives could have asked Eric's mother. She was still alive and in full possession of her senses. But Williamson wasn't going to do that. "We have documentation," he lied. "We've done our background, Eric. I'll tell ya that right now. It's undisputable [*sic*]. We know where you were at that time. You were at the Hammons[es'] house."

"I was living at the Hammons[es'] house?" Freeman asked.

Airy interjected. "Yeah."

"In March?" Eric asked.

"Yes," Williamson answered.

WHAT SHOULD HAVE BEEN THE DEFENSE FOR JASON TIBBS

Airy chimed in again to *mis*correct the record. "It was shortly after that . . . that you moved out."

Perhaps seeing a quizzical look on Freeman's face, Williamson attempted to explain how Eric could be so surprised about his residence. "You may be confusing years here. Like '92, '93, winter of one time versus spring of another." But Freeman would have needed a blow to the head and partial amnesia to mix up those years.[74] By the winter of 1993, he was living with another woman who would become his wife, and they would move to multiple places that the detectives could have verified in public directories. But as Freeman showed numerous times during the interview, he could be battered into saying what he knew was not true.

Jen Hammons was a different story. During Jason's trial, Fronk asked her, "How long did [Freeman] stay at your house?" She answered: "I don't remember."[75]

Coercion

In the first few minutes of the interview, the detectives and Freeman began dancing their two-step, which would continue throughout. Should Freeman blurt out unwanted information, he would hear that there is "evidence" contradicting his supposedly faulty memory. Should he persist with his argument, there would be subtle, then blatant warnings about the consequences he could face if he continued to be uncooperative. Eventually, Freeman would relent and step back, providing the so-called fact he did not know previously.

Williamson started the interview with stunning Orwellian doublespeak. "You can be truthful with us, be on our side," he told Freeman. "We'll be truthful with you. We'll be honest with you." But in *truth*, the detectives wanted anything but the truth if it was *not* on their side. That's why they didn't want to hear Eric was living with his grandfather on March 26 or driving his red Cavalier.

"Now, if you take the other avenue," Williamson warned, "That 'I-told-you-what-I-told-you' [during the March 18, 2008, interview, or] 'I-know-what-I-know'—now you're rolling the dice. You will be rolling the dice, and we don't want you to make the wrong decision. And [your] just showing up here today [shows] you're willing to cooperate."[76]

But what did Williamson mean by "cooperate," being "truthful," or "being on our side?" Early on, Freeman didn't get the message. When he clung to his version of the truth about where he lived on March 26—not what the detectives wanted to hear—Williamson let him know what was at stake. "I'll tell ya right now," he told Freeman. "We have evidence . . . as Detective Airy stated, that put you with Rayna Rison the day she came up missing. And we have evidence that puts you with her deceased body. Okay? I'm gonna tell ya that point-blank out front. We do."

Freeman replied, "Okay," but did not look as acquiescent as Williamson wanted.

"So, you have a confused look on your face," the state trooper noted.

"Yes, I do," Eric replied.

"I just want ya to think about it," Williamson said, referring to the so-called evidence about the deceased body. "We have enough to present that, okay?"

"Okay," Freeman responded.

"That's why we're offering you this immunity," Williamson said, perhaps echoing what Prosecutor Fronk told Eric before the interview began.[77] But in fact, the only evidence the detectives had putting Freeman with Rayna's dead body was Hammons's pole barn story. They also falsely indicated that Jason Tibbs had implicated him in the crime. Not once during the interview did Freeman ask to be presented with the sworn testimony that incriminated him—something a lawyer would have wanted to hear if Freeman had one with him in the conference room.

Realizing he couldn't argue with the detectives, Freeman tried another tactic—saying he couldn't remember.

In response, Williamson first tried to cajole him. "We don't want you to get mixed-up because of either you forgot something [or] you can't remember something," he said. Then, evidently referring to the immunity agreement, he added, "That's why we're here today throwin' this olive branch to you to say, 'Eric, now is the time.' So we want you to take care of you, [so] you won't have to see Brett [Airy] and I again."

At this stage, Williamson was not shy about invoking the name of the prosecutor sitting outside the door. "Now is the time that we'll walk out with Mr. Fronk and say, 'Ya know what? Eric, he's the man. He did the right thing. We know everything that happened. He told us the truth. This is where we're gonna go. He's on our team.'"[78]

But Freeman did not know the truth he was supposed to tell, and it wasn't long before he pleaded, "I mean, I don't remember this, okay? I mean, I would love to take a remember pill."

"And we'd love to give you one," Williamson replied. But a few minutes later, the state trooper was not so accommodating. "You're gonna have to stop doin' the 'I don't remember,'" he snapped, "because there is more that happened that night. I know it. You know it. Brett knows it. We know it. We've been workin' on this thing before we talked to you and even harder after we talked to you. Like I said, we can fill those gaps, but we want you with us."

With that, Freeman no longer offered resistance of any kind. Instead, he wanted the detectives to fill the yawning gaps for a nonexistent memory. In another pathetic plea, he said, "I wish y'all would show me what had happened to where . . . [my memory] would come back around or something."[79]

Williamson and Airy were only too willing to comply with that request. Thirteen times during the interview, Williamson offered Freeman some information to "jog your memory."

Words in His Mouth

To bolster Freeman's testimony during Jason's trial, Fronk repeatedly claimed that the only way Eric could have known about the alleged circumstances surrounding Rayna's murder was by participating in them. When Freeman was on the stand, the prosecutor asked, "When was the last time you spoke to Jen Hammons?" Freeman replied, "The last time I spoke to Jen would have been '93."[80]

But according to the transcript of the June 27, 2013, interview, Freeman spoke to Rickey's sister shortly before he met with the detectives. As Eric explained to the detectives, he was "tryin' to work with Jen" on what he should say. He would have had no better conduit for the pole barn story than Little Rickey's big sister.

The state trooper appeared to welcome their communication. "Jen and your statement mirror each other," Williamson said, "so I don't have a problem with that."[81]

The June 2013 transcript indicates Freeman also had unrecorded and unreported phone conversations with Airy.[82] Still, once he sat down in the South Carolina police station, he had only a broad outline of what he was supposed to say happened before and after the alleged stop at the pole barn. The detectives had not fleshed out all the details either. To an extent, they relied on Freeman to fill in the rest as long as his filler didn't conflict with Hammons and his associates.

But Eric Freeman did not have the creative powers of Little Rickey and repeatedly drew a blank. At times in the interview, when the detectives asked Freeman to get more specific, he'd say, "I don't know," and then, "Help me."[83] In response, Williamson would demur, saying, "I can't put words in your mouth. Brett can't put words in your mouth."[84]

But putting words in Freeman's mouth is exactly what they did—even with the most pivotal events. Often, they did so with the explanation they had evidence or that the material they were feeding him was "documented" when it was little more than something Hammons said or was needed to justify what he said. But sometimes their cues were grounded in evidence that Eric should have known if he had been involved.

Early in the interview, the detectives demonstrated their techniques when they pressed Freeman to tell them where he drove Jason and Rayna after he picked them up at the animal hospital in the Buick. His first response was, "I don't remember where we went." But Williamson would have none of that.

> AW: Okay. But we know, we all, we know you three left together.
> EF: I mean, the only place we would go would be back into town.
> AW: That didn't happen. You left her vehicle there, and we know that. Again, that's documented. But we need to know where you went because when she died, it was shortly thereafter. So it was a short time frame from when you left [the animal hospital] that Rayna died. So we need to know where you went. Did you go back to the Hammons[es']?
> EF: Well, if I didn't go back into La Porte, that's the only place I would go was back to the Hammons[es'].

But that was not the answer the detectives wanted to hear. Williamson made that clear, citing his undisclosed evidence, and Freeman was left to fumble with a multiple choice until his interrogators showed a sign of assent.

> AW: Eric, I know you know where you went. It's just gonna be tough for you to tell us. I know it's tough. Believe me, we know. You have to trust us, and I'm here to tell you you've got to trust us. So . . . if you went to [the Hammonses',] tell me you went to the [Hammonses']. If you went to Tibbs, tell me you went to Tibbs. If you went somewhere else, tell me you went somewhere else. We need to know where you went. I know you remember. You're not a bad person, Eric. This will all stop today.
>
> EF: Don't tell me we went to Fail Road.
>
> AW: This is where I want you to tell me. If you went to Fail Road, Eric, you went to Fail Road. Eric . . .
>
> EF: Yes?
>
> AW: . . . we know, okay? We know what happened. It wasn't supposed to happen. We know that. You were put in a bad position, in a bad way. This is your time to save your butt. Did you go to Fail Road?
>
> EF: We had to go to Fail Road.
>
> AW: Okay. What happened on Fail Road?[85]

Why did Freeman reluctantly bring up Fail Road? There is no evidence in the transcript that it was suggested to him. More likely, it was mentioned in one of the unreported and unrecorded conversations with either Jen Hammons or Airy. However he heard about it, Fail Road was the one reason the prosecution gave flaky Patricia Umphrey such a high profile. She told Airy that during Jason's supposed confession to her, Tibbs revealed, "He strangled that girl behind her car on Fail Road."[86]

Nothing Freeman allegedly witnessed was as critical to the State's case as the murder. But without help from the detectives, Freeman was at a loss to describe it. As Airy and Williamson discussed the crime scene with Freeman in the transcript, they sounded more like improv acting coaches than interlocutors.

> AW: When they were fighting, you said you got out and tried to break it up.
>
> EF: I tried to get Tibbs away from her.
>
> AW: Was she on the ground at that point, or was she standing?
>
> EF: I'd have to say she was on the ground.
>
> AW: What was he doin' to her?

EF: Hittin' her.

AW: And what else?

EF: (Unintelligible) chokin' her?

AW: Yeah. Was she on her back or on her stomach?

EF: On her back.

City of La Porte Detective Brett Airy (BA): Did you see her stop movin'?

AW: . . . Like Brett said . . ., was she still moving at that time?

EF: I don't think so.

BA: She was dead.

EF: Um, I don't know if she was dead, but she wasn't moving.

AW: We know she wasn't left there [on the road]. . . . How long did you go back and sit in the car before he told you to pop the trunk?

EF: Say that again?

AW: How long were you sitting . . . You went back into the car. You said he's on top of her. He's choking her. She's not moving. What did you do then?

EF: Went back [to the driver's seat] and popped the trunk.

Ironically, the detectives gave Freeman creative license to say that Tibbs put Rayna's body in the trunk while he remained in the driver's seat. At first, Airy tried to discourage this notion, explaining, "People are heavy. Even little people are heavy and awkward to pick up."

But Freeman stuck to his guns as Williamson reminded him, "You won't be in trouble."

Freeman insisted, "I don't recall helpin' him pick her up."

"Who put her in the trunk then?" Airy asked.

"Jason did," Freeman replied.

However, this explanation did not square with extensive testimony that the Buick was used for Fox Hunts. If the car had a CB radio, it also had a K40 trunk-mounted antenna. Freeman would have had to hold the trunk open for Jason, or the antenna would have forced it shut.

After Jason got into the car, Freeman had no idea where they went. "Help me out with some outline," he pleaded.

AW: Okay, you're going to go someplace that is safe for you and him.

EF: Goin' back to the Hammons[es'] then.

BA: Where at?

EF: Where at the Hammons[es']?

BA: Yeah. Where'd you go? Did you go to their house?

EF: Yeah.

BA: I mean, "Did you go? Is that when you were in the pole barn?"

EF: I don't know why we would have the car in the pole barn then.

Once again, the detectives had to jackhammer Freeman into Rickey's storyline. He would not have seen Rayna's body inside the trunk if the Buick had not backed into the pole barn. But here, too, Freeman was clueless, saying he must have parked at the top of the road leading to the Hammonses' house. The detectives next tried another tack.

AW: Where's a safe spot at the Hammons[es']?

EF: A safe spot at the Hammons[es']?

BA: Mm-hmm.

AW: 'Cause everybody's home.

BA: Where you could talk freely to Jason.

EF: Pole barn where the dogs are at.

BA: Mm-hmm.

Then, a prematurely triumphant Airy took his questions too far. "That's where you went?" he asked Freeman. "Do you remember driving into the pole barn?"

But Eric replied, "I don't remember or, or don't know, it's—"

"You do," Williamson shot back, not wanting him to go further. "It's just gonna take jogging to get out of your head."

While setting the scene inside the pole barn, the detectives' coaching reached a fevered pitch. As they did with their other cues, they kicked things off by claiming they had evidence that Freeman was angry at Tibbs for the situation he put him in. At first, Eric didn't know what they were talking about, but moments later, he played along.

AW: We can document you were pissed. We know this.

BA: There's evidence to coincide with what you're saying.

AW: Yup. As a matter of fact, you're yelling. We know this.

EF: I was yelling?

AW: Mm-hmm.

BA: Mm-hmm. You've been put in a bad situation.

AW: Yup.

EF: Who am I yelling at?

AW: Who's with ya?
EF: Tibbs.
BA: Know what you're yelling at?
EF: "What the fuck did you do?"
BA: Mm-hmm.
EF: Excuse my French.[87]

But Airy wanted him to say something else, and given the nature of his prompts, it could have been a line he rehearsed with Eric during one of his unreported and unrecorded calls.

> BA: Okay. Um, and what happened when you guys were inside the pole barn that you remember?
> EF: I was givin' him hell for what was goin' on and asked him what in the hell he was doin'.
> BA: Mm-hmm.
> EF: And he made the comment, "If I can't have her, nobody's gonna have her."
> BA: All right.[88]

Oddly enough, this line—*If I can't have her, nobody's gonna have her*—was not part of the Hammons urtext from his first interview with Lachmund and Williamson. Loquacious Little Rickey didn't have Tibbs saying anything about his motive for killing Rayna. He left that up to Freeman, telling the detectives, "Eric said something to Jason about some pussy. He said, 'Over some pussy,' like . . ., 'You did this over some pussy.' Over some jealousy, or over some uh, maybe she wouldn't give him some pussy or, I don't know."[89]

One can imagine how inconvenient it would be for a prosecutor to say the murder was "over some pussy," in his opening statement and closing argument. "If I can't have her, nobody's gonna have her" sounds like it was plucked from a soap opera, but it was not as offensive as repeated references to "pussy." Fronk could also tie the sentiment to Jason's lovelorn letter to Rayna, which the prosecution used as critical evidence in establishing a motive. But if Jason had said that line in the pole barn, why would Hammons have forgotten it?

According to the prosecution, Freeman did not just witness the murder. He also assisted in the disposal of Rayna's body. Still, according to the June

2013 transcript, he needed help providing essential details about events at the pond—or even how she got there.

Williamson tried to set the scene for Freeman after he left the pole barn with Tibbs. "We have Rayna's body in the trunk of the car . . .," he told Freeman. "What happens with Rayna's body?"

It's a question that would not have stumped a perpetrator for a second, but Freeman did not know the answer. Instead, Eric repeated Williamson's question, "What happens with Rayna's body?" The person transcribing Freeman's response from the tape adds a parenthetical comment: "talks very softly/quietly," like he was talking to himself.

Williamson prodded, "You remember. . . ."

But speaking softly again, Freeman repeated, "What happened to Rayna's body?"

"Did y'all leave it in the trunk of the car?" Williamson asked, starting to lose patience.

Airy next tried to get the ball rolling by scripting a line for Tibbs. "Jason said, 'We gotta get rid of her.'" But that didn't work either, and Freeman remained silent. Soon, Airy was pleading, "Y'all took her somewhere."

Eric finally spoke up to say, "I don't remember."

After telling Freeman to "take a deep breath," Williamson returned to his two-step, first assuring Eric he had nothing to fear. "Do you feel threatened that you are going to be arrested for what you have told us today?" he asked.

"No," Freeman answered.

"Good, because you're not," he said, then went to the next step. "Right now . . . you're gonna tell us what happened with her body. . . . Okay?"

"Okay," Freeman replied.

"So?"

But Eric didn't know. He asked, "Then help me to put—"

"Okay," Williamson said, cutting him off. "We're tryin'." Seconds later, he asked, "Do you know where her body was found?"

"It was in a pond," Freeman answered, adding, "A father and son found 'em a month later fishing."

Although he got some of the details wrong, Freeman's information about Rayna's discovery probably came from researching newspaper clips, which he said he did when first contacted by Airy in 2008. Williamson tried to backdate his knowledge to 1993, when the events unfolded. "You were following [the case because] it meant something to you. Because [you were thinking] like, 'Oh, shit.' Right?"

"Yeah," Freeman replied.

Williamson then picked up the thread. "You're right. She was found in that pond." But Freeman would soon frustrate him again.

> AW: How did she get in the pond?
> EF: I don't know.
> AW: Okay. Don't say you don't know. Let's not go in that direction. Correct?
> EF: I don't remember what [route I took] to the pond.
> AW: And what vehicle were you in when y'all took her to the pond?
> EF: The Buick.
> AW: Okay. Were you driving?
> EF: Yes.
> AW: Okay. Where was Jason?
> EF: Passenger seat.
> AW: Mm-hmm. Now, do you recall that night? Did you take her to the pond that night?
> EF: I don't recall if it was that night or the next day.
> AW: Okay. . . . Let's just "what-if." Okay? If it would've been the next day, where would her body have stayed?
> EF: The trunk.
> AW: Where? Where would the car have been parked?
> EF: In the pole barn.
> AW: Okay. Is that what happened? If it did, it did, Eric.
> EF: It sure seems like it.

Detective Airy did not like where Freeman was headed. He tried to steer him back on course with a few sanity-check questions.

> BA: You left the car parked in the pole barn with her body in it? In the trunk?
> EF: Yeah.
> BA: Till the next day?
> EF: Yeah.

With those answers, the detectives reached another junction in Freeman's interview that they couldn't pass. Too many witnesses had seen Rayna's abandoned LTD the night she was abducted. There was no way that Tibbs, by himself, could have put her in the Buick, left that car in the pole barn, and then moved Rayna's car from the animal hospital parking lot to North 200 East.

> AW: Okay, then that's . . . gonna open up a bunch of questions here, okay?
> EF: Okay.
> AW: Are you ready?
> EF: Yeah.
> AW: Ready as you'll ever be. Her car—
> EF: Her car?
> AW: Her car.
> EF: Her car that's still at the veterinarian's?
> BA: Correct. Y'all moved that car.
> AW: Again, we know a lot of things. We know when her car was recovered. We know when her car was seen.
> EF: So I took Tibbs back to get her car.
> BA: In what vehicle?
> EF: The Buick.
> AW: Okay. So, did you leave the Hammons[es']?
> EF: I had to leave the Hammons[es'] to get him over there to get her car.
> AW: Okay.
> BA: Was her body still in the trunk when you drove him over there?
> EF: No.
> AW: Okay, where's her body?
> EF: In the pole barn.

The detectives had to put the brakes on. There was no way this false Freeman memory could fly. Once again, Airy jumped in to set Eric straight.

> BA: Where'd you put her body in the pole barn?
> EF: Around some hay.
> BA: Are there hay bales in there?
> AW: Why would you do that, Eric? And, and again, if that's the truth and that's what happened, that's what happened.
> EF: Why would we?

At this point in the interview, Freeman pulled himself up short, as he did at other times—perhaps in response to a nonverbal signal like Airy or Williamson shaking his head. Eric then took a step back with a 180-degree turn.

> EF: No, we wouldn't [have] left her in there. That would have been. . . .
> BA: Did you take a different vehicle, then?
> EF: What do you mean, did we take another, different vehicle?
> BA: Well, if her body's still in the trunk and you didn't take the car with her body in the trunk to go get her car, you guys had to go get Rayna's car.
> AW: Would you have left that car in the, like Brett's saying, in the pole barn with her body in it and take a different vehicle to get Rayna's car?
> EF: I don't know what vehicle we would take because Rick had his truck, Judy had her car, and Tom had his truck.
> AW: Okay. . . . So the last thing you remember is when you left the Hammons[es'], what vehicle were you in, and where did you go?
> EF: What vehicle was I in?
> AW: Would it help you if I showed you a picture of Rayna's car?
> EF: I wasn't in Rayna's car.
> AW: No. No, I didn't say you were.
> EF: Right.
> AW: I'm just tryin' to jog your memory.
> BA: Do you remember seein' her car at the clinic?
> EF: Yes.
> AW: And you guys went back to the clinic to get her car?
> EF: Yes.
> BA: What kind of car was it?
> EF: Light . . . light-greenish.

Watching as their star witness dug a hole for himself, Detective Airy intervened with a suggestion for the state trooper. "You might want to pull that picture [of Rayna's car] out of there," he said, but Freeman kept floundering.

> EF: I wanna say a light green, four-door—
> BA: You know the make?
> AW: Bigger? Smaller? Mid-size?
> EF: It was . . . Hell, back then, I'd say it was a small mid-size. I mean, it was, wasn't very . . .

In fact, at eighteen feet in length, Rayna's 1984 LTD Crown Victoria was among the biggest cars made during the last two decades of the twentieth century. But then, Williamson cut Freeman off to show him a picture.

> AW: That's her car.
> EF: Huh?
> AW: That's her car. Now, [you didn't] look at the color because it's nighttime. It's a flash.
> EF: Understood. That was her car?
> BA: Yeah.
> AW: The color's distorted.
> EF: Okay. That ain't no small or mid-size, then.
> BA: No.[90]

In Williamson's words, he next tried to work on Freeman's "mind frame."

> AW: You're drivin' with her in, in the trunk of your car, and Tibbs has her car.
> EF: Right.
> AW: What's in your mind right now?
> EF: Where in the hell did we go?
> AW: What's in your mind back then?
> EF: I wanna get this [body] out of the trunk.

Despite the detectives' prompting, Williamson kept propping up the facade that information first came to them from Freeman. The state trooper proclaimed, "You know how we know you're tellin' the truth, Eric?"

"How?" Freeman replied.

"We DNA'd the keys," he answered, implying that Jason's DNA matched what they found on Rayna's car keys, so he must have been driving her car.[91] In fact, his DNA did not match what was found on the keys.[92]

But no amount of prompting could get Freeman to suggest their route to the pond. Eventually, Williamson was okay with that because Jason was "leading, and you're following." But once Jason and Eric supposedly reached their destination, the detectives needed to hear much more from Freeman, and another dance ensued.

AW: What happens at the pond? There's some significant things that we know . . . happened there. There's some very specific things there that are just unique to that location. Okay?

EF: Unique to that location.

AW: Yeah. That's the best way that I can put it, okay? Let's put it this way: when you got to the pond, did you help him take her out of the trunk?

Once again, when asked to contribute to the detectives' narrative, Freeman proved especially squeamish about touching the victim's body. The transcriber notes parenthetically that Eric "talks very quietly" when he responded, "I don't recall helpin' him."

But Williamson will have none of that. "If you did, Eric," he said, "you did." Airy chimed in to remind him where Rayna was. "If you did, it's [in] your car."

Of course, no one would forget removing a dead body, but the detectives resumed their disquisitions on the difficulties of lifting "dead weight" and why Freeman must have helped Tibbs.

AW: Like Brett said, he and I have moved numerous dead bodies in our life, okay?

BA: They're heavy.

AW: They're heavy and unbelievably awkward. And not to get morbid, but have you ever heard of rigor mortis? When rigor sets in, it's like a board. The rigor hadn't set in yet. Okay, cause she's still loose and pliable, we know that's even harder yet.

EF: Mm-hmm.

AW: That's why they call it dead weight.

EF: Yeah.

AW: So we know where her body was recovered. We know where the road is. With knowing those facts and knowing some of the things we know, did you help move her body from the trunk of the car to the pond?

EF: From what you all just described, I had to of.

Having bludgeoned Freeman into admitting he helped carry the body, the detectives next wanted to know how, but Eric still needed more prompting.

BA: Remember what you held on to, to get her over [to the pond]? Where did you grab her at to move her?

EF: No, I do not.

BA: Did you grab the head or feet?

EF: I wanna say the feet.

> BA: Do you remember what she had on?
> EF: No, I do not.
> BA: So you and Jason carried the body over to the pond? How'd she get in the pond?
> EF: One, two, three, heave.
> BA: All right.
> AW: Is that how you did it?
> EF: Yeah.
> AW: Did you drag her, or did you carry her there before you heaved?
> EF: Carried her there.[93]

As they did with his story about Jason putting Rayna in the trunk, the detectives granted Freeman the creative license to claim that he and Tibbs threw her body into the pond with just a "heave-ho." But heaving her body that far would have taken a superhuman effort. As the police who recovered Rayna's body testified, a mass of twigs, branches, and underbrush separated the shore from where she was submerged. That is why the recovery officers in scuba gear had to approach her corpse from the opposite side of the pond.[94]

Still, there were other memorable aspects to Rayna's submersion that the detectives had to hear from Freeman—their efforts to elicit an acceptable response most called their interrogation into question. Airy kicked off this part of the exchange.

> BA: Did you guys do anything else while you were out there? After you threw her in? Was she floating?
> EF: I, I don't recall if she was floating or if she was—
> AW: Did you hear a splash?
> EF: Yes.
> BA: Do you remember seein' her in the water?
> EF: Yes.
> BA: So she was floating then, or she sunk? Or was it somethin' else?
> EF: I remember seein' her. I remember hearin' the splash and seein' her in the water.
> BA: Face up or face down?
> EF: Down.
> BA: Did you guys do anything else there, like to the body?
> EF: I don't see why anybody would do anything. She was already in the water.

Suddenly, the detectives saw their interrogation drift sideways in the pond. They couldn't let Freeman get away with saying he and Tibbs didn't do "anything" to the body. How could a perpetrator forget the cross of tree limbs piled on Rayna? Airy jumped in with a pointed follow-up question on what they did to her body.

> BA: I mean, like, [did you] try to sink her or anything like that?
> EF: I don't—

Next, Williamson tried a leading question.

> AW: Did you or Jason go into the water afterward?
> EF: I did not go in the water.
> BA: Did Jason go in the water?
> EF: Yes.
> AW: What did he do?
> EF: It makes sense now.

Freeman's response—"It makes sense now"—was not an answer to Williamson's question. Instead, he appears to be reacting to something else— perhaps an Airy pantomime of pushing a body down. Freeman continued, "Tried to get her to go under the water so nobody would see her."

"How'd he do that?" Airy asked.

Freeman answered, "By puttin' a log on top of her, putting something on top of her."

Williamson chimed in with a question. "Did it work?"

Freeman replied, "No," perhaps prompted by having one of the detectives shake his head.

"Then what happened?" Williamson asked. He partly answered his own question by adding, "Face is in the water, puttin' a log on top of her."

Freeman again appeared to respond to a hand signal when he replied, "Seemed like he did that twice."

Williamson then had to ask another question to clarify. "Did [he] put [on] the same log or two different ones?"

Now getting the message, Freeman answered, "Two different ones."[95]

The Tell

Seemed like . . .

It seems . . .

I wanna say . . .

It doesn't take much digging or analysis to see significant areas in the June 2013 interview where Eric Freeman's testimony was influenced. In addition, Freeman inadvertently developed a verbal tic that betrayed the information force-fed by his interrogators. It's equivalent to what card sharps call a "tell" during a poker game when a raised eyebrow or some other expression can signal a good or bad hand. For Freeman, the tell was not so subtle. More than thirty times, he conditioned his answers with, "Seems like . . ." "Seemed like . . ." "I wanna say." The expression does not speak to confidence in what he's saying. On the contrary, it betrays uncertainty and an abject willingness to indulge the detectives, who often responded with affirmation—"Okay," "All right," "Yes"—after he parroted back what they wanted to hear.

These instances point to what became the most critical evidence from Freeman's testimony, revealing what he did *not* know before he sat down for the June 2013 interview. He had the following exchange with Williamson about the supposed fight he witnessed between Jason and Rayna before he killed her. (Bold in the next few excerpts is added emphasis.)

> AW: On that note . . . somethin' just came to me. Was he tryin' to come on to her while you're drivin' the car, and they're fightin' in the back seat?
>
> EF: He tried to come on to her whenever he had an opportunity.
>
> AW: Is that what started the fight?
>
> EF: **Seems like** what started the fight is because she didn't want to be with him.
>
> AW: All right. . . . When the fight occurred? Did it occur on Fail Road?
>
> EF: It **seems like** it did, yes.
>
> AW: Okay.[96]

Often the tell came after the detectives' prolonged badgering for Freeman to produce an acceptable response. To further reinforce the point, Airy had Freeman repeat it, but Eric couldn't help but insert the words that showed he didn't believe what he was saying.

BA: All right. So, just kinda to go over your statement . . ., do you remember where you were at when Tibbs hit you on the CB?

EF: **It seems** like I was at Jen and them's house.

BA: You were at Jen's house, and he hit you on the CB, and do you remember where he was at, where you picked him up from to take him to the animal clinic?

EF: **Seems like** he was at his house.

BA: Okay.[97]

Williamson had a similar back-and-forth with his interviewee when he led him through the divergent paths that Freeman and Jason allegedly took after submerging Rayna's body.

AW: You two are going back to your vehicles.

EF: Right.

AW: I'm sure there's words [you exchanged].

EF: There is.

AW: And what's bein' said?

EF: He's gotta get rid of the vehicle. And it **seems like** I went back to [the Hammonses'].

AW: Alone?

EF: Yes.

"Okay," Williamson replied to affirm Freeman was on the right track. Then he added a mutual pat on the back for their confabulation by saying, "We seemed to do pretty good at that.[98]

Cleanup

About two hours into the interview, Eric needed a bathroom break, and the tape recorder was shut off. While he was gone, the detectives probably reviewed their notes and felt another sort of urge to purge. Despite their best efforts, some things Freeman said earlier directly contradicted Rickey's story. At other times, after their manhandling, the witness contradicted comments he made moments before.

Before Freeman left the conference room for the day, they needed to clean up the unhelpful utterances. In at least one case, after he returned from the bathroom, Freeman made a "correction" without any prompting on tape. The problem may have been brought up to him before the detectives turned on the recorder. The clarification concerned why he was kicked out of the Hammonses' house. As Freeman indicated earlier, Judith Hammons found a condom in his vest pocket, which meant he was either having forbidden sex with her daughter or, more likely, with someone else. She confirmed this in previous interviews with detectives. But Rickey told a much more elaborate story to Lachmund and Williamson at the Wabash Valley Correctional Facility. It had him shirking his chores in the pole barn, which provoked Freeman to throw a "bag of feed' on him while Little Rickey was sleeping. Hammons claimed he then grabbed a twelve-gauge shotgun to confront his sister's boyfriend, a fight that convinced the parents to kick Eric out of the house.[99]

To clean up this discrepancy, the detectives had Freeman claim he returned to the Hammons household after he was kicked out for having the condom, which would have put him there when Rayna was abducted. "After [March 26]," Williamson asked, "how long did you stay at the Hammonses', live with the Hammonses, I should say?"

Freeman answered, "It wasn't much longer after that . . . , they asked me to leave again because me and little Rickey got into it again."[100]

The detectives also had other weightier topics to sanitize, such as how Eric and Jason transported Rayna and themselves to the pond. Williamson laid out the two "different ways" Freeman provided previously.

> AW: Earlier, when we talked about this, you said you guys picked up her car first, and you both drove out there. [Before that] you said you both drove out in the Buick. Do you recall which way it was?
>
> EF: We went to the clinic first. Then . . . I followed him out to the pond.
>
> AW: Either way is plausible.
>
> BA: You sure that's the way that happened?
>
> EF: That's the way it—
>
> BA: Okay.
>
> AW: And you followed him out to the pond?
>
> EF: Followed him out to the pond.

The detectives next needed to clean up where Freeman and Tibbs put the cars once they arrived at the pond. As with so much else, Freeman could not help. Williamson started by asking, "Where did you park the vehicle?"

Freeman answered, "On the side of the road."

But that wasn't what the state trooper wanted to hear. Williamson followed up, "Um, was it on the road? Off the road?"

Once again, Freeman floundered. "It was on and off the road," he said.

Neither answer worked. With hardly any shoulders by the pond, Range Road was too narrow for a car to park unobtrusively. The two vehicles would have drawn unwanted attention from passersby while the perpetrators were submerging Rayna. These were all factors Freeman would have remembered if he participated in the crime.

Williamson had to pull out a Google Earth map and ask, "Does that jog your memory at all?"

When Freeman reached over with a pen to ask a question, Airy said, "You don't have to mark it."

Williamson echoed more forcefully, "Don't mark it." Apparently, his marks could have betrayed his ignorance about the setting.

With the map, Freeman could see there was a dirt trail perpendicular to Range Road that ran along the side of the pond where Rayna's body was found. Referring to the map, Williamson tried to get Freeman to say how the cars were parked while they disposed of Rayna's body.

> AW: I mean, did you guys back into here? Pull into this little area where this—
> EF: Backed in.
> AW: You backed in?
> BA: . . . Okay. There's the pond. I don't know if you can see it from that little bit. It's on Range.
> AW: So if you backed into here—

But Freeman interrupted. Showing his unfamiliarity with the area, he pointed to some road, perhaps Range, asking, "And this is Fail?"

The detectives had to show him Fail was much farther away. Then, Williamson returned to the subject at hand.

> AW: But you said you backed into this area with the Buick?
> EF: Yes.

AW: . . . Where was the car, his car parked? If you're backed into here with this . . .

EF: Her car was parked right in here. [unintelligible, but perhaps he said: You can't] park two cars there.

AW: Okay. Did he pull in or back in?

EF: It seems like he just pulled in.[101]

The cleanup did not stop after Freeman left the South Carolina police station. Although earlier in the interview, Williamson had promised Freeman, "You won't have to see Brett and I again,"[102] Eric would hear from them two weeks later. After the detectives returned home and reviewed testimony from other witnesses, they realized they had much more work to do on Freeman's testimony. The call would turn into one part rehearsal, and one part attempted rewrite.

When Freeman came on the line, Airy tried to set the stage with their South Carolina two-step. "The main reason we wanted to talk to you is we just wanted to go over your statement with you and make sure we have it correct and accurate before we go on with everything and to just reiterate the immunity and make sure you understand the immunity is good for all charges and not just the murder charge but any other charges relating to this case you're immune from." As before, they would "reiterate" he had no charges to worry about as long as he provided the detectives with information they considered "correct and accurate" whether or not it was true.[103]

The detectives most needed to clean up one of Freeman's contributions to the narrative. It could prove fatal to the prosecution's case. When Williamson asked him where the killing occurred on Fail Road, Freeman replied that it happened at the intersection with East 1000 North. The location is near the area's most celebrated restaurant, the Heston Supper Club, where notables like Charlie Finley and Oprah regularly dined during the days when they lived in La Porte County.[104] Eric may have picked the spot because it was the only one he knew about on the northern reaches of Fail Road. If Freeman had been prompted to mention Fail Road to align with Umphrey's fanciful story about Jason's confession, Eric had improvised an intersection that made it untenable. Steady traffic would have passed by on a Friday night precisely because it was close to a popular restaurant. With no shoulder and only two lanes on that stretch of Fail, it's hard to believe no one would have noticed Jason beating and strangling Rayna on the side of the road during the several minutes it supposedly took to kill her. Second, even more problematic, the spot was twelve miles from the Pine Lake Animal Hospital. Between Rickey's pole barn fabrication and Eric's crime scene improvisation, the star witnesses were staging events that would have been impossible to reach within a reasonable time frame.

Airy proceeded with this part of the cleanup, seemingly confident he could sway Freeman in the direction he wanted, as the detectives did when he was face-to-face with them.

> BA: Okay, Eric, like I said, the most important thing is that we have a good location of where the murder actually occurred at.
> EF: Correct.
> BA: We need to know the truth about where the murder actually occurred at. Do you know where it actually occurred?
> EF: I can't see the road right on . . . No, Fail Road was where she was in the . . . the next road . . . Dog gone it, we had it on the map.

Airy tried to prod him away from his map marking, but Eric was not so pliable over the phone.

> BA: Are you sure you drove all the way out there? Because it's a bit of a drive to get all the way out there . . .
> EF: Yeah, we did go out there. I mean . . .

Since a gentle approach had not worked, the detective tried the more forceful tack while giving Eric the tacit approval to make up another location.

> BA: Okay, like I said, we know some things about what happened that night. You know, pretty well.
> EF: Right.
> BA: We just want to make sure that you are sure about that location because if it happened somewhere else, we need to know that. And it's fine

if it happened somewhere else. We just want to make sure that we have the right location of where this occurred.

But to the detective's chagrin, Freeman fixated on the Google Map he marked up that could later come back to haunt him. "I know it was on the map," he told Airy, "and I know we sat down, and you asked me to initial it and everything."

Airy could only muster a feeble reply, "Yeah, I remember that." But he tried again to indicate Freeman had a pass to change his mind. "If it happened at a different location, that's fine. We just needed to know that now before we—"

Freeman cut him off. "Not that I recall. No. I remember going out that way."

Airy tried one more time, "And you're confident that it was out there near 1000 North and Fail Road?"

"Yeah," Eric replied. "If I'm not mistaken, 1000 North takes you towards Heston."[105]

During the July call, Freeman was also reluctant to change his tune on events in the animal hospital parking lot before the abduction. The detectives had gravitated toward two witnesses—Bryan Durham and Pam Rosebaum—who remembered Rayna arguing with a young man they would identify as Jason. Their testimony clashed with Freeman's story that the argument between Jason and Rayna did not begin until they were in the Buick, which is why he claimed she entered willingly. This take was also at odds with Rayna's tendency to tell her loved ones when she would be late. If she had gotten in the car of her own volition, she would have first called home, knowing Matt was waiting for her there.

When Airy probed if the discussion between Jason and Rayna in the animal hospital parking lot was "heated," Freeman replied, "It didn't seem heated. It just seemed normal conversation."

The detective responded with the two-step, implying Eric had said something different in South Carolina. "The most important thing here is that we have a true and accurate account of what happened because before you said they were arguing out there." Airy then added something true: "Witnesses . . . saw that they were arguing out there in the parking lot."

The witness accounts did not get Freeman to change his story about when the argument started. He also did not take the cue when Airy referred yet again to the immunity agreement, suggesting it would be okay if he admitted to helping Jason subdue Rayna and force her into the Buick. "You're immune from any kidnapping or anything like that. . . . We just need to know the truth [about] how she got into the car."

"Right," Freeman replied, but as before, he pushed back on any suggestion he touched the victim. "I did not help or coerce her into the vehicle. From what I remember, she got into the vehicle."

"Did Jason pull her into the vehicle against her will?" Airy asked, grasping at one last straw. "You said that you didn't."

"No," Eric answered. "They both got into the backseat."[106]

By this time, it was clear that Freeman was not comfortable with playacting like Rickey. He had committed to the storyline he created with the detectives in South Carolina and would not budge from it over the phone.

Airy still tried to get an answer consistent with a detail that Hammons provided during his first interview. Evidently familiar with the fiber evidence that helped indict Ray McCarty, Rickey claimed a black-and-white checkerboard-colored blanket was wrapped around Rayna when he saw her in the trunk from his perch above the kennels. But Freeman said the body was covered by a blue tarp, something the family kept in the pole barn for such chores as raking leaves. While Eric admitted that Jen kept a blanket in the backseat, he did not remember what it looked like, unlike Rickey. Airy asked, "Was [the blanket] used at all with [Rayna's] body?"

"Not that I recall," Freeman replied. "No."[107]

Of all the topics covered in the July cleanup call, Airy most relentlessly pursued the possibility that Wiman's truck was involved in the disposal of Rayna's body. The York family sighting of the pickup on North 200 East undoubtedly played havoc with the detectives' Buick scenario.

Airy pounded out the two-step as never before. "Once again," he said once again, "just to reiterate the immunity. It's nothing that you're going to get in trouble for if that's what happened. . . . Just so we know, we have a true and accurate account of what happened that night."

After Freeman agreed that Wiman's truck was on the property, Airy added another oft-repeated refrain: "We don't want to put words in your mouth. We don't want anything like that. We just want to get a true statement from facts we know and from things from your statement that you did not seem real clear on."

But Freeman never said anything about driving Wiman's truck in South Carolina. Given the hostility between the two while they lived at the Hammonses' house, he was as clear about that as anything. Eric was equally clear over the phone when he said, "I really do not recall using Tom's truck."

Airy persisted, "Is it possible you used Tom's truck at any point during the night that this happened?" he asked.

"No," Freeman answered.[108]

But by the end of the call, Eric gave the detectives a glimmer of hope he might cave. "I'm sitting here second-guessing myself on Tom's vehicle," he said, probably wondering if Wiman had been battered like he was. "Did Tom say that I used his vehicle?"

"I can't tell you that," Airy replied, knowing full well that Wiman categorically denied letting Freeman drive his truck. In any case, he might as well have said, "No." Having previously faced the wrath of the ex-con, Eric would not tempt fate by crossing Wiman again. He stopped his second-guessing and denied he had driven the truck.[109]

Imperfect as it was, Freeman's testimony was still essential to the prosecution's case. The detectives' cleanup call with him would be their last interview before they arrested Jason seven weeks later.

Like the record of Hammons's pathological lying, the transcript of Freeman's June 27, 2013, interview should have been enough to devastate the State's case. As Airy's detective school warned, the excessive promises of leniency coupled with the warnings about "rolling the dice" affected a vulnerable personality like Freeman during the three-and-a-half-hour interrogation. The detectives' efforts to clean up his statement show their intention to tailor what Eric said in South Carolina to fit the preposterous pole barn story and much more reliable witnesses who couldn't be shaken out of their initial reports.

But here, too, Jason's lawyers fumbled the ball. If they had attempted to enter the 2013 interviews as evidence during the Freeman cross-examination, Alevizos might have sustained Fronk's hearsay objection. But an offer of proof would have forced appellate judges to consider the transcripts during deliberations. It's hard to believe they would have dismissed their importance.

THE STATE'S INCONVENIENT EVIDENCE

Despite all the hurdles that Judge Alevizos placed before the defense counsel in presenting their witness testimony, there remained unshakable evidence that he couldn't block. Foremost were the autopsy, the toxicology report, and letters forensic pathologist Dr. Rick Hoover exchanged with detectives during the first investigation. Tompkins tried to attack Hoover's credibility during cross-examination but was unfamiliar with the most problematic parts of the witness's record when he did so. The defense counsel should have called their experts in forensic pathology *and* forensic toxicology. Respected authorities in those fields would have focused on Hoover's deceptive spin—both what he said and didn't say—that Tompkins was incapable of challenging. The defense also had an opportunity to call in a third forensic expert, a leading analyst in his field who was intimately familiar with the case and renowned for his influence on juries; their failure to do so—and the reason why—was another maddening misstep by the defense.

For anyone familiar with the discussions between Dr. Hoover and the detectives in the weeks after Rayna's body was autopsied, nothing about his testimony in the Tibbs trial would have been more remarkable than the words that never crossed the forensic pathologist's lips: isopropyl alcohol, isopropanol, or IPA, the acronym associated with them. The names of the chemical hung over the first investigation like an unmoving slate-gray cloud. The detectives never knew enough about Ray's job to associate IPA with him. But apart from that, the investigation was dumbfounded by the two lingering mysteries surrounding the chemical: Why was such a large quantity present in Rayna's blood and gastric screens, and how had it gotten there?

No one was more stymied than Hoover. He put samples through multiple tests to make sure the results were accurate. Then he considered the potential gateways to her system: antemortem (AM), before her death, and postmortem (PM) after. The typical AM method studied by scientific literature was drinking, often by severe, desperate, or suicidal alcoholics.[110] A PM introduction could have come from contamination or the chemical reaction between the organs of a decomposing corpse and bacteria. But usually when alcohol is produced in these conditions, it's ethanol and not isopropanol, a distinctly different compound.[111]

After Hoover was confident in the results of his screens, he wrote City of La Porte detective Harold Hahn, "As I previously stated, interpretation of volatiles [e.g., IPA] in a postmortem sample is difficult, and this case has potentially been complicated by the fact that the analysis initially was not performed until several months following sample collection. Isopropanol, however, does not appear as a postmortem volatile from decomposition and, in my opinion, indicates premortem ingestion of Isopropyl Alcohol."[112]

When detectives continued to press him for a more definitive answer, he finally protested that he was a forensic pathologist and not a forensic toxicologist.[113] But five years later, as they prepared to indict Ray McCarty, prosecutors asked for Hoover's opinion again after they heard from a renowned toxicologist who believed that Rayna's IPA must have resulted from decomposition. Although still not fully committing to one side or the other, the South Bend doctor disputed the postmortem conclusion. It turned out that Hoover had been reading up on his forensic toxicology. As he wrote an inquiring prosecutor, "[My] literature research has turned out minimal information concerning postmortem levels of Isopropyl Alcohol in reference to postmortem decompositional changes." He argued that the IPA's source didn't matter because even if Rayna had ingested it before she died, the amount "detected" would have caused a "mild to moderate intoxicating effect and would not be expected to produce death."[114] He probably made the latter comment to minimize the importance of the IPA mystery, but he was wrong. Several studies showed that half the isopropanol in Rayna's system could still be fatal.[115]

But by the time Hoover talked to Airy in 2009, his opinion about the source of the IPA had evolved. In his notes on their meeting, the detective wrote, "Dr. Hoover stated that he knew that he originally thought that Rayna had ingested the Isopropanol before she died due to the high level, but now believed that the Isopropanol was present due to decomposition."[116]

In his testimony during the Tibbs trial, Hoover said the same but talked only of alcohol, not isopropyl alcohol, in a rambling response when asked if a toxicology report on Rayna ruled out a drug overdose. "There were some productions of alcohols," he told the court and then served up a jumbled word salad. "There was the presence of alcohol in the body. In a decomposed body, moderate decomposition, they really don't have any significance. We cannot interpret them. As the body, again, you know, alcohol, like the drinking alcohol, is simply made by letting yeast work on sugars. Our body doesn't know—the yeast doesn't know any difference between, say, us and grapes that are being fermented."[117]

Nothing in the prosecutor's question about a drug overdose should have prompted Hoover's ramble—other than he had isopropyl alcohol on his mind. However, in his example, *ethanol* is the alcohol created during decomposition, typically due to bacteria reacting with yeast secreted in the stomach.[118] Besides, any of these alcohol-producing reactions would require organs to putrefy, but in his autopsy, Hoover described "all of her normal organs" as still "perfect."[119]

Despite his supposed research, Hoover never delved into one unusual result from Rayna's toxicology tests that the labs tried to bring to his attention. As one blood and gastric screening report explained, "Isopropanol is converted to Acetone in humans, and in some cases, no Isopropanol will be present in the blood a few hours after ingestion." In other words, when people drink IPA, the chemical is quickly metabolized into acetone—sometimes so fast that no trace of isopropanol remains. The lab noted: "Acetone, an expected metabolite of Isopropyl Alcohol, is not [in] this specimen," a result called out by an asterisk with the all-caps footnote, "ABNORMAL."[120]

What Hoover did not recognize in or failed to report about the acetone reading was why Rayna did not metabolize IPA: she did not drink it. Instead, the chemical was likely inhaled, absorbed through her skin, or both. Compared to drinking IPA, relatively few studies exist on those other means of exposure. However, research has been done on animals that show a combination of transdermal transmission and inhalation can be nearly as toxic as swallowing the substance.[121] A rag soaked with IPA held over Rayna's mouth and nose would have provided the dual exposure. Her asthma would have only hastened suffocation.

If IPA had been the murder weapon, it would have accounted for the other glaring anomaly in the autopsy—the absence of physical trauma. In his autopsy, Hoover stressed at the top of his report, "No definitive evidence of injury is noted." Regarding the skin, he wrote, "The cutaneous surface demonstrates no evidence of lacerations, hemorrhage, contusion or ecchymoses [i.e., bruises]." Likewise, he saw no internal bleeding and "no evidence of gross hematoma formation about the head, with no evidence of subdural hematoma over the surface of the brain." While Hoover concluded that his autopsy could not provide "identifiable homicidal trauma," he did concede that could be due to "prolonged postmortem decomposition." In other words, the month Rayna was submerged in water wiped away the tiny broken blood vessels that would have pointed to her cause of death. In the process of elimination, Hoover chose "asphyxia due to compression," even though he admitted he had no "identifiable external trauma" to support that conclusion.[122]

But in 1993, when talking to investigators, Hoover was more plainspoken and definitive about the lack of trauma. As an evidence technician wrote when providing background on the murder for the FBI, "Her body showed no signs of defensive wounds or trauma usually associated with physical force beatings or strangulation."[123]

But "beatings and strangulation" are what Eric Freeman claimed he saw on Fail Road. Again, during his testimony in the Jason Tibbs trial, Hoover's opinion on trauma had evolved and became more definitive. During cross-examination, he explained, "Minor scrapes, superficial bruising would not be present that you can discern because of decomposition."[124]

While Tompkins tried to split hairs with Hoover on his definition of trauma, an experienced forensic pathologist might have questioned his response in two ways. First would have been the pathologist's characterization of wounds suffered in the fight Freeman described as "minor scrapes" and "superficial bruising." A head banged against the ground would leave abrasions on the skull and, potentially, a hematoma on the brain, which were not reported in Hoover's autopsy. The "defensive wounds" mentioned by the evidence technician would have come from Rayna fighting back or warding off blows. They typically create bruises on the hands and forearms that are not necessarily "superficial" for a frail young woman. Secondly, a forensic pathologist testifying for the defense would question the amount of decomposition that occurs after a month submerged in the pond. Research into corpse decomposition, known as taphonomy, shows that decay underwater can take *at least* twice as long as on dry land. It is even more prolonged in weather as cold as when Rayna was submerged (mostly midforties). Indeed, a month after her abduction, her body was still in the "bloat" stage when recovered, a process that would have ended in ten days if she had been found on land. In the next phase of decomposition—active decay—her organs would have started to rot,[125] but according to Hoover's autopsy, they were still intact.[126]

Of course, none of the issues about forensic pathology or taphonomy are cut and dried when debated by adversarial experts. Their impact on the jury often depends on the effectiveness of the witness's testimony and presentation materials. But if an expert had argued for the defense over decomposition and physical trauma issues, that authority would have had the advantage of using Hoover's own words against him.

Besides the autopsy and related screens, the most important physical evidence were the fibers and hairs analyzed by Douglas Deedrick at the FBI. Although his field had come under more scrutiny over the intervening years, the agent's findings were crucial factors in the decision to take Ray McCarty to trial and then to indict him.

But as the Jason Tibbs trial drew to a close, Tompkins and Pejic did not call him to the stand. As they confessed to the judge in a sidebar, they had not completed the necessary paperwork to permit Deedrick to discuss FBI records. It required an exchange of documents and government approvals that could take several weeks, if not months, provided there were no objections. "The FBI gave me the runaround," Tompkins complained to the judge, as though he was the first lawyer ever to encounter such bureaucratic behavior. "[Even though] we have a retired agent [referring to Deedrick]. They have a law that we have to follow. We have been trying for three weeks to comply with an email." Pejic then complained the FBI would not even give him Deedrick's contact information (which was readily available through his private consulting company, Deedrick Forensics, LLC) and couldn't get him to return his phone calls when he finally tracked him down.

Despite the lack of preparation on the lawyers' part, Alevizos was ready to be charitable. He offered to wait a few days for the "lab gal" from the Indiana State Police to testify about the unknown male DNA. She might have expertise in fiber evidence as well. If they called her to the stand, the judge said, "You can get it in that way." But when Alevizos asked the defense counsel if they would subpoena her, Pejic answered, "No." Tompkins then explained the lawyers had all agreed to wrap up their closing argument the next day.[127]

During his direct examination of Airy, Pejic still tried, in a ham-fisted way, to get Deedrick's evidence into the trial by asking, "During the course of your investigation in reviewing the reports, did you ever learn about fiber evidence?" When Fronk objected because Airy wasn't "competent" to answer questions on that topic, Pejic tried again. "Did you ever learn about any analyses that might have been done on fiber evidence?"

When the detective answered he did, the lawyer followed up, "And did any of that fiber evidence lead to Jason Tibbs?"

But that question was struck down again. During the sidebar, Pejic explained to the judge, "He is the lead detective of the entire case file. I'm asking if he knew of green fibers that were found in Ray McCarty's car." But without Deedrick's testimony, the fiber evidence amounted to "facts not in evidence."[128]

It was a subject Airy probably preferred not to discuss. When cherry-picking evidence from the first investigation, nothing showed Airy's bias more than another certificate of analysis from the Indiana State Police Laboratory Division. In the months before Jason's trial, these forms were used to submit Rison case items to confirm previous analyses and use new technology for additional insights. A January 17, 2014, certificate listed the most significant evidence screened by the FBI and used in Ray McCarty's indictment:

- The green fiber found on the letterman jacket,
- Rayna's E.U.R.O. sweatshirt, which also contained the green fiber,

• and the debris from under her car's steering wheel that had the clump of hair associated with McCarty.

However, this certificate did not ask for another analysis of the material. Instead, the ISP forensic scientist wrote, "The request for examination was withdrawn by Detective Brett Airy, La Porte City Police."[129]

THE UNTIMED TIMELINE

Much as Pejic and Tompkins believed that proof of Ray McCarty's guilt would ultimately vindicate Jason Tibbs in the jurors' eyes, they also felt confident one straightforward analysis would eviscerate the Freeman and Hammons stories. They called retired deputy sheriff Mark Ludlow as their first witness, expecting his "time survey" to deal the prosecution a fatal blow. Instead, his presentation to the jury was confusing, disjointed, and incomplete.

Ironically, the subject drew more blood with Airy on the stand when he admitted to Pejic that his own time survey didn't work with the star witnesses' accounts. For a few moments, with the judge on their side, the defense had the prosecution cornered as never before. Following the route laid out by Freeman, Airy took an hour to drive *without* including the time spent strangling Rayna, sitting in the pole barn, disposing of the body, and abandoning the car.

But Pejic let Airy off the ropes when he didn't challenge his argument about too many "variables" to conduct a time survey properly. While the whole trip took him an hour, he said, "I can't drive 100 miles an hour" to see if that's what it took.

In fact, Airy did know there was a problem with the murder scene location on Fail Road and E. 1000 N. that Freeman gave him. He tried to correct it during their July 2013 phone call. "Are you sure you drove all the way out there?" he asked Eric. "Because it's a bit of a drive to get all the way out there." But he failed to get him to change the location, and the State was stuck with it.[130]

Given the distance Freeman and Tibbs had to travel, Pejic tried to show it was impossible to do within the time frame set by other witnesses. But on the stand, Airy would not provide a time when his alleged abductors left the animal hospital parking lot. He dismissed witness testimony by arguing, "They all contradict each other. I mean, there is no cohesive . . . They're approximations between this time and that time."

Pejic next asked, "It was all between 6:00 and 6:20?"

"I believe one person said it could have been as late as 6:30," Airy replied, "but I mean, that could be."

"All right," Pejic conceded.

Airy wasn't finished. "They didn't know," he said. "It's approximate."

But while the detective claimed he couldn't determine a starting point, he would not fight the York family about the end point—when they first saw the LTD on North 200 East Rayna's car was found, Airy said, "by 7:00."

With that concession, Airy had pitched the defense a big juicy softball—underhand. During his closing argument, it was left for Tompkins to slam home the impossible timeline in a way that would make immediate sense to the jury. But right off the bat, the big-time trial attorney swung a mighty whiff, starting his routes from the animal hospital parking lot at 5:50—to be "more than fair to the State." Whose word did he take to support this time? Ray McCarty—the man he accused of being the *real* killer—because he was supposedly the last person to see Rayna. Throughout the trial, the defense tried to focus the jury on Ray's multiple lies regarding his alibi. Why would Jason's lawyers let McCarty determine such a crucial milestone?

Several uncompromised witnesses stuck in slow-moving traffic saw Rayna in the parking lot of the animal hospital after 6:00 P.M. Contrary to what Airy said, they did not all "contradict" themselves on this point. When interviewed a few days after the abduction, Kim Hackney said the cars exited at "exactly" 6:15, with their brights nearly blinding her. The officer interviewing Hackney added, "Very sure of this."[131] Four months later, when Arlie Boyd met with Hackney to confirm her critical sighting, he barely got her to budge on time. If not 6:15, she told him, 6:10—but no earlier.[132]

If Tompkins, in his closing argument, was going to concede a start time for Rayna's abductors, it should have been 6:10 and not 5:45. With the later time, Jason and Eric would have had only fifty minutes to accomplish all the criminal activity alleged in the Hammons and Freeman testimony. Tompkins could have then taken off fifteen minutes for their stay in the pole barn, the lowest amount estimated by Hammons, and after that deduction, only thirty-five minutes remained. If it improbably took only ten minutes to kill Rayna, submerge her body, and abandon her car, that would have left twenty-five minutes. The combined distance on Google Maps for all those places Hammons and Freeman had them go was forty-three miles. Ironically, just as Airy said on the stand, Tibbs and Freeman would have had to travel one hundred miles per hour—in dense fog, without obeying any stop signs or traffic lights—to reach the destinations in that time. It was one thing for the defense counsel to keep saying the Hammons/Freeman timeline was impossible. But it was another to explain why—*simply*.

DEFENDING THE ALIBI

During Tompkins's disastrous closing argument, he probably said nothing more damaging to his client than denigrating his alibi. Tibbs "doesn't have a good story," he told the jury. "It's not a good story. He can't get it straight. In 2014, it's a mess. It was pretty much a mess in 1993."

When compared to the other suspect in the case, Jason's alibi was anything but a mess. Unlike Ray McCarty, he did not make any significant changes to what he told the police in the days after Rayna's abduction. In 1993, his whereabouts throughout the evening of March 26 were corroborated by a dozen people, which is why experienced detectives like City of La Porte Captain John Miller and Indiana State Police Sergeant Arland Boyd were so quick to clear him as a suspect.

But Fronk begged to disagree in terms that would have concerned the jury if Jason's lawyers had effectively fought them. On the one hand, the prosecutor proclaimed, "Note that the alibi witnesses did not take the stand and say where Jason Tibbs was at shortly after 6:00 on March 26th of 1993. Not a one of them. He doesn't have an alibi."

More than "a one" would have testified about his alibi if permitted by the judge or properly prepared by Pejic and Tompkins. Incredibly, Fronk acknowledged that. "Many [of Jason's alibi witnesses] were confronted with their statements from 1993," he said. In other words, these witnesses were not asked to testify but "confronted."

He next stated something even more incomprehensible. "They didn't deny saying that in 1993, but that's not their sworn testimony." A follow-up question would be: *Then why did they say it in 1993?* Were they all trying to fool the police? And if they couldn't recall what they said, why couldn't they see the reports to refresh their memories? Fronk answered: "Those unrecallable statements in police reports from 1993 are not evidence except for purposes of credibility." If the statements were unrecallable, did that make them false? Can anyone, other than a practiced liar like Hammons, remember everything that happened one Friday night twenty-one years ago? Fronk's comment was precisely the sort of legal gibberish that makes average Americans doubt the fairness of their justice system. That Tompkins never went after the doublespeak in his closing argument defies common sense.

For Fronk, the attack on Jason's alibi was one of three legs on the stool holding up his case, along with the testimony of Hammons and Freeman. He hardly had any other evidence to provide significant support. To attack the account, the prosecutor employed three tactics. The first was to find and magnify the minor inconsistencies in what Jason did say in 1993 or, in as many as three cases, was wrongly reported to have said. The second was to block or obfuscate most of the testimony from other witnesses corroborating his alibi two decades before. By calling people who backed Jason's alibi as prosecution witnesses, he could discredit what they had to say before they could testify for the defense. Jason's lawyers were equally at fault for not preparing them before the trial, but they didn't expect Fronk to call them as his witnesses. Alevizos helped the prosecution by not letting the the jury see what they told police in 1993 during the trial. Because most police reports were not sworn statements, the judge considered them hearsay. Finally, depending on the false memories of what happened two decades before, Fronk introduced unfounded new accusations that Jason's lawyers never tried to rebut.

The cumulative effect of Fronk's tactics and Alevizos's rulings amounted to a cautionary tale about the dangers of trying cold cases. Jurors can be taken through the looking glass to a world where hazy, distorted recollections of what happened decades before become more valid than reports made at the time of the crime. Incredibly, Fronk tried to justify his upside-down perspective by disparaging the police who first investigated Rayna's murder. "Remember that the police officers were still dealing in an era of typewriters," he told the jurors. While some tips slipped through the cracks because the prosecuting attorney's staff didn't think they merited further investigation, that was certainly not the case with the alibis of Ray McCarty and Jason Tibbs.

It was incumbent for Tompkins to address the inconsistent molehills in Jason's alibi that Fronk turned into incriminating mountains during his closing argument. The trial would have been the best place to do it, and the defense had tools they did not employ. But Tompkins's closing argument could have also been used to expose the prosecutorial legerdemain. Instead, he shrugged it off and blamed Jason for not having "a good story."

When considering Jason's alibi and Fronk's efforts to tear it down, the jurors should have heard a response for each of the following:

Chad Green and the trip to the trailer park tutoring lesson. Jason has never changed the story about how he got to the trailer park. He could not take his father's truck, so his friend who arranged the meet-up, Angie Vogel, used her CB to contact his cousin Chad. He was driving around with Jason's friend James Amor. After the two arrived at the Tibbses' home, they all hung out for an hour and headed to the trailer park. At first, when interviewed by a detective, Green, who was always a truculent interviewee, said he did not remember driving with Jason. But a week later, he signed a statement with Captain Miller saying he drove out to Jason's house after hearing from Angie on the CB and picked him up to take him into town. Green later said he revised his statement after talking to Jason, and Fronk charged that Tibbs encouraged his erstwhile friend to lie. But James Amor was in the car with them. His interest in meeting a girl in the trailer park was the reason for the escapade, and he confirmed the trip during repeated interviews with the police in 1993, 2008, and 2009.

The time when Jason passed the animal hospital on the way to the trailer park. Here, Jason was *possibly* inconsistent. He told Hahn between 5:30 and 6:00, but moments later, during the taped interview with Miller, he was reported to have said, "I was supposed to have been [at the trailer park] at six, and we were running late, and I looked at my watch, and it was like 6:10, and Rayna's car was still at the animal hospital." Tibbs believes he told the detective "ten-to-six" and not "six-ten." (The tape of their conversation was not retained. More on Miller's transcription skills below.) But a month later, after having some time to think it over, Jason told Boyd that he "and Green had driven him by [the animal hospital at] approximately 5:40 P.M. on their way to the Deluxe [trailer park]." In any case, these times are not wildly inconsistent. The difference between them would not have encompassed the time it took to abduct Rayna, kill her, submerge her body, and abandon her car.

What happened at the trailer park. When interviewed by Hahn three weeks after Rayna's abduction, Misty Smith and Jamie Swisher both remembered Jason arriving at the trailer park between five and five thirty. Their mother, Peggy Johnson, told Hahn that Jason was there when she came home around 6:00 P.M. At first, she was angry to find him and two other boys with her daughters and no adults around. Although they claimed Jason was there to help with their homework, the girls were doing cartwheels on the front lawn with Angie Vogel when Johnson arrived. Johnson let Jason stay until 9:00 P.M. since she heard he had helped with Angie's homework in the past but sent the other two boys packing.

Johnson and her daughters gave Jason critical corroboration for his alibi, but their statements were not entirely accurate. They remembered Tibbs and Green arrived with Josh Jordan, not James Amor. But this was the first time the girls had met James. He was there briefly before their mother kicked him out, and Josh came later to pick Jason up. The girls were much more familiar with Josh, who usually hung around Jason. No wonder they were confused. However, Hahn also interviewed Amor, who confirmed he was at the trailer park with Jason. Fifteen years later, Jamie Swisher's memories were understandably sketchier. When questioned by Airy, she could not say for sure if Jason was at the trailer park on March 26 but said he was there on some night. The detective then read from Hahn's report, and she said it sounded like she provided that information but didn't remember talking to Hahn.[133] Peggy Johnson had no memory of anything that happened on March 26—something Fronk tried to exploit during the trial. However, if Johnson did have a medical condition, as Pejic told Jason, his lawyers had another option. They could have recited Hahn's report on his interview with her—much as they did with Charlie Allen's grand jury testimony.

Jason passed out flyers before anyone knew Rayna was missing.
This charge gave the defense an ideal opportunity to undermine Fronk's efforts to prioritize current hazy memories over reports taken at the time of the crime. Angie Vogel's false tale about Jason passing out Rayna Rison's *Missing* flyers on Friday, the night she was abducted, was one more bogus story that Fronk chose to highlight in his closing argument. Tibbs "went down to the Dairy Queen, organized a search down there, too . . . the night Rayna went missing, rounding up the search party to . . . search down at the KOP. There was talk of flyers. The Vogel ladies remember seeing the flyers." Jason's lawyers had ready access to the *Missing* flyers. They could have pulled one out while Angie Vogel was on the stand to have her acknowledge the item she said Jason was handing out. They could have cross-examined Lori, who had previously testified that no flyers were available on Friday night. Bennie printed them at his business in Elkhart and then distributed them in the high school parking lot on Saturday morning. According to Jason, the first time he saw them was when Rayna's friends gathered on his lawn.

If the defense had established the true origin and availability of the flyers, it would have provided a powerful rebuttal to the State's cold case. The very certainty of the "Vogel ladies" about seeing Jason with the flyers revealed the tricks memory can play on well-meaning people and how those can be manipulated by detectives and prosecutors when they don't have other evidence. But incredibly, in his closing argument, Tompkins treated those false memories as true.

Whether Vic Montorsi was along for the ride to the trailer park. The tiniest molehill that Fronk inflated into an enormous mountain was whether Jason claimed Montorsi traveled with him to the trailer park. Using this as his Perry Mason moment, Fronk blared, "Vic Montorsi testified that he was working at Dairy Queen from 4:00 to 10:30 that night. It would have been impossible—it was impossible—he did not drive the defendant past the Pine Lake Animal Hospital shortly before 6:00 P.M." This charge was drawn from a report written by City of La Porte detective Harold Hahn. He had Tibbs driving to the trailer park with Montorsi and no one else. Jason has denied he ever said it. Moments after talking to Hahn, during his taped interview with Miller, Jason told Hahn's boss he was with Green and Amor. He said the same when talking to Boyd one month later. For all Fronk's talk about the cops in 1993, their typewriters, and their other ancient ways, the prosecutor could not have been more cynical in making Hahn's error into Jason's incriminating behavior.

Whether Jason knew Rayna's last name. Fronk focused on another officer's clerical slip in an attempt to call Jason's character into question. John Miller admitted that he was the one who typed up his taped interview with Tibbs. A hard-bitten veteran on the verge of retirement, the detective captain probably had many more pressing chores. As a result, his interview manuscript did not display the skills of a master transcriber. Pejic pointed out that it had several blank underlines for phrases he did not hear the first time as he played the tape while typing. Besides the misspellings and typos, many words were missed entirely.

But one line, which Fronk picked out, seemed especially strange. Jason explained he had spoken earlier in the day with Lori.

"Who's Lori?" Miller asked.

Jason answered, "Rayna's sister, Lori."

Miller followed up with another question, "Last name[?]."

He typed Jason's reply: "I don't know here [*sic*] last name, all I know is her first name's Lori. I don't know *Rayna's* last name either." (Italics added.)

If, at that stage in the investigation, Miller didn't know Rayna's sister was Lori, he probably didn't know her husband was named Ray. If so, there is a good chance Miller may have heard "Rayna" or reflexively typed it when Jason said, "Ray." But for Fronk, this was no typo. Instead, it was a tacit admission of guilt on Jason's part. In high dudgeon, he charged that Tibbs pretended not to know her name "despite the fact that he had dated Rayna, and despite the fact that they had been friends for years, and despite the fact that he had given her this ring." He asked the jury, "Why was he trying to distance himself from Rayna?"

However minor each of these issues may have been on their own, together they undermined an alibi that should have been the most substantial part of Jason's defense. Worse yet, Tompkins mostly ignored the attacks or even agreed with some of them, despite sufficient evidence to clap back. That could not have sat well with the jurors.

A CASE OF FABRICATION AND INDOCTRINATION

Scott Pejic (*left*) wanted to be a defense counsel on a high-profile murder trial and brought in "Super Lawyer" John Tompkins (*middle*), who assured Jason his case was a "slam dunk." Photo: Pejic Law Group, Indiana Lawyer

City of La Porte detective Brett Airy (*right*) led the investigation against Jason. He had been frustrated when charges against Tibbs had been dropped in another crime. Photo: *La Porte County Herald-Dispatch*, Jessica Campbell

But Jason's attorneys were unprepared for Judge Thomas Alevizos's (*left*) rulings, which blocked incriminating evidence about Ray, or the tactics of prosecutor Christopher Fronk (*right*). Photos: *La Porte County Herald-Dispatch*, Erika C. Stallworth, Matt Fritz.

Jason believed he had been cleared long ago as a suspect in Rayna's murder. After his 2013 arrest, his mug shot helped transform his image from a hardworking family man into a monster. Photos: La Porte County Jail; LPHS, *El Pe*, 1992

Left: Some of the State's most problematic testimony came from Dr. Rick Hoover, who performed Rayna's autopsy. Jason's lawyers did not bring in their own expert to challenge him. Photo: South Bend Medical Foundation

Right: A key witness against Jason was Rickey Hammons, a convicted murderer in a despicable crime; he was three years younger than Tibbs. Photo: La Porte County Jail

Jason's attorneys also did not delve into the elaborate lies Hammons (*left*) told during the murder investigation of Danny Cassidy (*right*). Hammons's sister called Hammons "a pathological liar." Photos: La Porte County Jail, 1999; LPHS, *El Pe*, 1992.

WHAT SHOULD HAVE BEEN THE DEFENSE FOR JASON TIBBS

Hammons said he saw Jason with Eric Freeman, his older sister's boyfriend; Rayna's dead body was in the trunk of the sister's car after they backed into the family pole barn. Photo: Exhibits, State of Indiana Cause No. 46C01-1308—MR—278

Hammons claimed he was smoking dope in the loft and heard Freeman shout at Jason for killing Rayna "over some pussy." Jason barely knew Freeman and had never been alone with him. At eighteen, in his 1991 high school yearbook, and in a 2002 mug shot at twenty-nine. Photos: SCHS, 1991 *Orbit*; York County Sheriff's Office-Inmates

Over three hours, State Trooper Al Williamson fed Freeman details he didn't know about the murder. Jason's lawyers failed to enter a transcript of the taped session as evidence. Photo: Indiana State Police

Unlike after McCarty's indictment, the Rison family (Lori, Bennie, Karen, Wendy) was readily available for interviews after Jason's arrest, pleased it had "lifted the stigma" from Ray. Photo: *La Porte County Herald-Dispatch*, Matt Fritz

This check register was used by detectives as evidence that the Hammonses' Buick was not "broke down" on March 26. It shows a check for parts to repair the car in April, but on closer inspection, the entry was made over an erasure. There is no record of a receipt for those parts. Photo: Exhibits, State of Indiana

REVELATIONS

RAYNA RISON

FAMILY
- Bennie, Karen (parents)
- Lori, Wendy (sisters)

FRIENDS
- Matt Elser (boyfriend)

CITY OF LA PORTE POLICE DEPARTMENT
- Detective Brett Airy

MICHIGAN CITY POLICE DEPARTMENT
- Detective Mark Lachmund

LA PORTE COUNTY
- Circuit Court Judge Thomas Alevizos
- Chief Deputy Prosecuting Attorney Christopher Fronk

JASON TIBBS

FAMILY
- Rachel (mother, deceased)

LAWYERS
- Scott King*
- David Jones*
- Russell Brown* (appellate)
- Scott Pejic
- John Tompkins

EMPLOYERS
- Jim (deceased), Nancy Bruno; daughter Jennifer Delrio (employers)

FBI
- Douglas Deedrick, Trace Evidence Analyst

INDIANA STATE POLICE
- Sergeant Al Williamson

LORI AND RAY McCARTY

FAMILY
- Eric Chester Ray* (ex-son-in-law)
- Adrienne (daughter)
- Hunter (deceased)

CIVILIAN WITNESSES
- Rickey J. Hammons Jr.
- Eric Freeman
- Patricia Umphrey
- Jen Hammons (Rickey's sister)

*INTRODUCED IN THIS CHAPTER

FUNDAMENTAL ERROR

Six weeks after his conviction, Jason Tibbs returned to the courthouse for his sentencing. It was the most painful part of the prosecution. Before the lawyers and judge began the debate about his punishment, he first had to sit through victim impact statements from Rayna's family. As far as Jason was concerned, no one would have been more outraged by his presence in the dock than the victim. He had no doubt the Risons experienced legitimate grief about the murder. But he also believed they all knew who the real culprit was. In turn, they partly blamed Rayna's molestation charges for her own demise.

The first up was Bennie Rison, grayer and balder, but his eyes still fluttered shut as he spoke. Oddly enough, for someone so involved in the initial investigation that followed his daughter's death, this was his only appearance on the stand in Jason's proceedings.

True to the quirky behavior that bemused and bedeviled detectives, Bennie began his victim impact statement by playing a DVD. Although his comments should have been intended to sway the judge, he addressed his introduction to the assembled spectators as though they also had some role in the sentence. "You will hear the musical instruments that [Rayna] played. We will never hear her playing them again. Now, it's only memories that we see and hear in our minds, our hearts, DVDs, VHS tapes, and old photographs." Besides the marching band and orchestral performances, the video also showed scenes from birthday celebrations and when Matt Elser escorted Rayna to her last prom.

After the DVD ended, Bennie looked at Jason and blamed him for putting the family through "great heartache" by hiding Rayna's body in the pond. He then asked why Jason had not attended her funeral—"In fact, I went back and checked the funeral register"—even though "[you] professed through the whole trial how much you loved her."

Jason shook his head and whispered to Pejic, "They made sure I couldn't go." He was told the family didn't want him there because of what he said about Ray, but Bennie may not have known about the threat to beat him up if he did go, or he may have forgotten it.

Bennie closed by telling him, "My family has suffered the deepest grief and heartache for the past two decades that only those who have lost a child would know. Because of what you've done, your family is going to suffer the fate that ours has gone through."

Wendy was much harsher on Jason than her dad. When she had made up the story about Jason declaring his love for Rayna in the LTD while she sat in the back seat, he could never decide whether the little sister was truly in denial about Ray. But by his sentencing, Wendy was all in on Jason-did-it. "Eyes on me," she said during her victim impact statement and then asked, "If you really loved her, why would you kill her? How long had you planned this prior to leaving your house that fateful night? Why wasn't her friendship enough for you? Isn't that something better than nothing at all? Don't you wish you could have that now? Did you really think you were going get away with it?"

Later, she invoked the Freeman story about him strangling Rayna on the side of Fail Road.

Choking the life out of a beautiful, talented, gifted, loving, and hard-working, honest young woman who didn't love you. Those hands, hands of a killer, attached to you and you alone. Do you see the hands of a killer? Do you remember every time you look at them and what you did with them? Wrapping them around her small neck and gripping and tightening and clutching down on her throat, making it so she couldn't breathe? And Rayna looking up into your face, the face of her killer, and thinking of her family and friends and who she truly loved, and one of them wasn't you.

Wendy told the court that she had found a way to forgive Jason through her Christian faith, but then addressed the judge, "Even though I have forgiven him . . . do not find leniency on him. For twenty-one years, he lied about killing Rayna, and he still does to this day. He doesn't seem to have any remorse for what he did to her, killing her, dumping her body as if she were a piece of trash, and placing the blame on someone else."

But when it came to vitriol and bile, no victim impact statement would surpass that of Lori McCarty. "You decided my sister's fate on March 26, 1993, and twelve people have decided yours," she crowed to Jason. "It's not so comforting now, is it? You continued on with your life like nothing ever happened. You got married, had kids, continued to do whatever it is that you do to make yourself happy. What did my sister get for the last twenty-two years? She got cut from shoulder to shoulder, clear to the pubic bone, and organs removed, and photos taken and filed."

As it turned out, this was the more elevated part of Lori's statement. It would descend from there. "There is not enough hate in this world to compare to the sheer hatred I have for you," she told Jason. Her hatred did not blind her from the sentencing implications of a premeditated versus impulsive killing. "You had every intention of killing my beloved sister that night, and you know it," she said. A moment later, she asked, "Did you even look her in the eyes as you squeezed the last living breath out of her? You probably did then because you had the upper hand at the moment."

Even Tompkins had had enough. "Judge, I would object at this point. This is not victim impact."

"Excuse me," Lori sneered at the lawyer. "I'm making my statement."

"Overruled," Alevizos said and then sighed, "Let her have her say. Continue."

But much of what Lori had to say was not about her "beloved sister." Instead, she railed about the investigation and indictment that cost Ray "a good-paying job with great benefits," although she also said, "My husband may not be perfect, and he made his own mistakes, but he did not kill her."

For Lori, the most grievous harm from the murder had been inflicted on the McCartys. "My family was shunned and ridiculed because of your crime. I wasn't allowed to even say that Rayna was my sister because of you. My daughter was taunted and bullied in kindergarten because of your crime."

Her daughter, Adrienne, would have been another likely candidate for a victim impact statement. Although she was only six when Rayna died, friends said no one loved Rayna more. But Adrienne did not testify at the sentencing, leaving Lori to report, "My daughter is almost thirty years old and still has night terrors."

The rant continued, but again, Lori couldn't help but disparage the victim, saying, "Nothing will ever change for a sixteen-year-old girl who nobody knew until she made headlines in the newspaper." Like her poem at Rayna's funeral, it was an odd put-down at an odd time. Plenty of people knew and loved Rayna, which is what made her death so heartbreaking to the community.

If Jason got the sentence he deserved, Lori said, "I would have no problem flipping the switch, pushing the button, or pulling the trigger to get the so-called justice that my sister so deserves."

She was not finished. "You are nothing but a lying arrogant coward. . . . Only a man with a deep, dark secret to hide doesn't bother to show up at the funeral of the girl he supposedly loved. You loved her, but you couldn't remember her last name."

The taunts and insults finally got too much for even Alevizos to hear. Although there is no record of any action on his part in the official transcript, Jason remembers that the judge waved for her to stop, saying, "That's enough," under his breath. Lori ended with the threat, "I will be at every hearing from this day forward to make sure that you never see an early release. We can't just go dig Rayna up and get back to normal, so why should you? May God find mercy on your black soul because I never will."

Jason had to squelch his desire to return fire with fire, but he had crafted a sober response with his lawyers that Pejic encouraged him to keep.

> I'm going to start off by saying that I sympathize with the Rison family. No family should ever feel what it's like to lose a child. I can't imagine how your family has felt over the years. Having children of my own, I know

how it feels to be away from them, but to have them taken away is unimaginable. This crime was committed by someone not capable of knowing or understanding how it feels for a family. I'm not that person. This crime was not committed by me. Therefore, I cannot offer anything more than my condolences to your family for your loss. I cannot give you an apology or an explanation for something I was not involved with. . . . I will continue to assert my innocence and work to prove that I am not guilty of this crime so that I can rejoin my family and the investigation can resume to find the person who committed this.

After all the emotion vented by the Risons, to Jason's surprise, the judge settled into a dispassionate and technical discussion of sentencing guidelines with Fronk and Tompkins. He remembers, "For the first time during the whole process, Alevizos was being fair and impartial." When the session started, the judge acknowledged, "This crime allegedly occurred in 1993, and in 1993, the then-presumptive sentence for murder was forty [years]." After the victim impact statements and Jason's statement, Fronk had to provide aggravating factors that justified a longer sentence. The prosecutor grasped from a pile of disparate straws. Ironically, he claimed Jason caused the Rison family additional grief by fingering Ray, but Alevizos quickly batted that down. The molestation conviction would have made McCarty the prime suspect no matter what Jason said. Fronk pointed to Jason's juvenile record, the felony related to the auto parts store, and the circumstances around the murder—namely, submerging the body created more distress for the family. That theme had been a part of all the Rison victim impact statements, which the prosecutor probably orchestrated.

Tompkins, who appeared for sentencing, effectively argued that case law required much more severe aggravators to require harsher punishment and that none of Jason's prior convictions resulted from "crimes of violence." Alevizos agreed. Without further argument, the judge decreed, "I enter the finding of the jury was guilty. I enter that as a finding of guilt, find that you are guilty of murder, and sentence you to a determinate sentence of forty years in the Indiana Department of Corrections." He added that the sentence would be reduced by 484 days for the time Jason had already been incarcerated.

Before Alevizos adjourned, he looked at Jason and said, "It's my understanding you've already hired appellate counsel, and you seek to appeal." At that point, Jason's new lawyer, Scott King, stood up to identify himself as that counsel. His associate, Russell Brown, would do much of the work. Although well known in Northwestern Indiana as the former mayor of Gary, King was also esteemed as a defense attorney who, on appeal, had overturned wrongful convictions in the past. Although Pejic had told Jason's mother she couldn't afford him, Jim Bruno could. After the verdict, he told Jason, "We're still committed to getting you some justice," but he insisted on bringing in new attorneys to do it. Besides, if Jason lost his appeal in state courts, he would file a writ of habeas corpus in federal court, arguing he was "denied the effective assistance of counsel."[1]

In seeking relief for Jason's sentence in the Indiana Court of Appeals, King and Brown charged that "the trial court failed to allow him to present a complete defense." They focused on Alevizos blocking incriminating evidence about Ray McCarty's guilt and preventing Pejic from entering Freeman's June 2013 interview as evidence.[2] During embarrassing depositions with Pejic and Tompkins, the appellate lawyers got them to confess to the errors of their ways. Pejic indicated he had a dispute with Tompkins about whether they should seek to delay the trial until Deedrick, the FBI's fiber analyst, was available. He said Tompkins didn't think it was necessary. If the retired agent had indeed been unavailable, his grand jury testimony could have been read to the jury, but the lawyers did not consider that an alternative. Tompkins did minimize the significance of fiber evidence after the National Academy of Sciences cast doubt on the FBI's analytical techniques in a 2009 report,[3] but this would not have disqualified the significance of all the green acrylic fibers Deedrick found in Rayna's hair and Ray's vehicle, which they assumed had come from the blanket he used to wrap deer carcasses.

Regarding the June 2013 Freeman interview, Tompkins admitted, "I screwed up," when asked why he didn't enter it as evidence when cross-examining Freeman.[4] (Ironically, Alevizos, who berated Tompkins for most of the Tibbs trial, called this admission "noble."[5]) Pejic had next tried to enter the interview as evidence to impeach Detective Airy. After Alevizos blocked it, Pejic should have made an offer of proof. When asked during the appeal deposition why he hadn't, Pejic explained that he got "sidetracked" because the trial had gotten "very contentious with objections."[6] But he understood the price his client would pay for the negligence. The appellate court would not consider the crucial police interview as the basis for an appeal. The judges would first have to deem the omission a "fundamental error," which required a high standard—that it would have made the difference between an acquittal and a conviction.[7] Even more daunting, they had to make that determination without looking at the transcript.

Over the next six years, Jason's appeal wound through the Indiana appellate system. After it was denied each step of the way, the writ of habeas corpus for ineffective counsel went to the United States District Court, where it was rejected again in June 2023. All the denials had two themes in common. The first minimized the significance of fiber evidence, taking a cue from Tompkins's disparaging remarks about the NAS report. The second argued there was "overwhelming evidence" against Tibbs, citing the testimony of Hammons, Umphrey (the woman who claimed Jason confessed to her about an accident), Freeman, and the abduction witnesses. Some appellate decisions also questioned whether the June 2013 transcript would have made a difference. In direct examination, Freeman had already admitted he lied during some of his police interviews. Also, Airy did not deny that some of the detectives' questions may have been leading because of evidence they had from other witnesses. Nothing Alevizos let Pejic ask about the three-and-a-half-hour session made it seem very consequential.[8]

But Pejic never touched on the areas where Williamson and Airy coerced perjury from Freeman about such fundamental issues as the car he was driving or where he lived the night of Rayna's abduction. By not examining the transcript, the appellate judges also did not see the references to coaching Freeman received from Jen Hammons or the unreported and unrecorded call from Airy—despite Fronk's oft-repeated claim that there had been no "roundabout" communications with him.

Jason's appeal does not have to stop in federal court. He could start the long, arduous process again, arguing for his innocence. At the heart of this petition would be new evidence related to the impact of isopropyl alcohol on Rayna's death and the items with previously reported unknown male DNA. Even during Jason's 2014 trial, probabilistic genotyping[9] could have pulled out the individual genetic profiles mixed together in areas of Rayna's purse and her letterman jacket. More recent breakthroughs can derive DNA from hair samples, especially those with "root material" on the letterman jacket.[10] According to the Freeman testimony, he and Jason extensively handled that article of clothing. With the prototyping, they could be definitively excluded from the DNA taken from the coat and purse, which would cast further doubt on Eric's story. In addition, Ray's DNA could be connected to those samples. Even more revealing would be a DNA profile associated with McCarty's accomplice, Scott Scarborough. The tree-trimming coworker—a friend of both Ray and Charles Allen—had no connection to Jason or Freeman.

A positive development is that Jason may have a new set of lawyers to pursue another set of appeals based on innocence. The Notre Dame Law School's Exoneration Justice Clinic has considered taking on his case. The clinic describes its mission as "correcting the miscarriage of justice and investigating, litigating, and overturning wrongful convictions."

Given the time the appeal process takes, Jason Tibbs could be out of prison before it succeeds. With good behavior, Indiana state prisoners earn a year off for each year sentenced. Additional reductions come through completing classes determined to assist a prisoner with his employment prospects and family life. As a result, Jason should be released to a community program as early as 2028. In the meantime, as at Bruno Enterprises, he uses his certified trade skills to help his prison save on outside contractor fees with refrigeration, air conditioning, and electrical repairs.

Jason's greatest regret is that his mother and Jim Bruno did not live to see his exoneration. In 2017, at sixty-six, Rachel succumbed to a cascade of maladies, including internal injuries from a car accident, kidney failure, and pneumonia. "Right to the very last time I talked to her," Jason says, "she was hopeful I'd be getting out soon." In 2022, Bruno died after complications from back surgery.[11] Tibbs remains in close contact with his widow, Nancy, and their daughter, Jennifer, who now runs the family's business. The

Brunos continue to pay Jason's legal expenses. "If Jason wants a job here after he gets out," Jennifer says, "there's one waiting for him."[12]

RICKEY'S DEAL

For a few brief months at the end of 2015, Jason's appellate lawyers had a glimmer of hope that his conviction would be overturned and he would be granted a new trial. Their optimism was fed by Indiana's Rule 60(B), which provides "relief of justice" should "newly discovered evidence" prove so significant it would have altered the jury's verdict.[13]

Jason's lawyers had uncovered activity from Rickey Hammons that showed he expected a benefit in return for his pole barn testimony. It was a deal not disclosed during Jason's trial and denied by Hammons and Detective Airy. The State's appeals court convened a hearing to consider the findings, but the clock was ticking since Rule 60 determinations can be made no more than a year after sentencing. The good news was that Alevizos had to recuse himself since he potentially had a conflict if there was evidence he conspired with Fronk to reduce Hammons's sentence. The appellate court brought in an impartial judge to rule.[14]

A Hammons deal was no small matter in Jason's trial. Throughout the proceedings, the prosecutor harped on the selflessness and sanctity of Rickey Hammons's revelation that touched off the second investigation. In his closing argument, Fronk declared, "Rickey Hammons is not getting anything, will not accept anything for his testimony in this case."

However, undermining the purity of Rickey's intentions was a mysterious, unrecorded conversation with the detectives who first heard his story at the Wabash Valley Correctional Facility in 2008. Hammons asked them to turn off the tape, and the three spoke for five minutes. Rickey later claimed he took the time to tell Williamson and Lachmund that he wanted no benefit and was only revealing what happened in the pole barn to "do the right thing."

But soon after Jason's arrest in 2013, the Hammons family hired attorney David Jones for his sentence modification services. They had not employed a private lawyer since Rickey's arrest. In previous years,

Hammons had filed multiple motions pro se (acting as his own lawyer). Still, Jones advised Rickey to wait for the Tibbs trial to conclude before making any request to Judge Alevizos. When Fronk visited Hammons in prison to prep him for his testimony, Jones was with him for the session. Even the prosecutor admitted the intentions of the attorney and client were clear—that, at some point, they would seek sentence modification. Perhaps sensitive to the judge's sensibilities, Jones did not ask Alevizos for a hearing until August 2015, eight months after Jason received his sentence.[15] When the judge promptly denied the motion, the defense attorney texted Fronk. He had since become chief deputy prosecutor in the much bigger county of St. Joseph and was still well regarded by the judge.

Both Jones and Fronk testified during Jason's Rule 60(B) hearing. Although the attorneys had battled each other in court, they maintained a friendship outside of it. Fronk was working on his lawn when he received the text, which Jason's appellate lawyers had him produce as evidence. In the texts, Fronk did not hide his gratitude for Hammons bringing him the most celebrated case of his career. He texted in reply to Jones, "I was thinking about Rickey today while I was mowing. 'What can I do for that guy?' Also, I have a high school friend that writes novels. I was thinking this story would make a good, interesting book, right?" Fronk soon wrote a letter to Alevizos to "humbly ask the Court to please allow Mr. Hammons his day in court."

Jones and Fronk testified that they did not know that sentence modification rules had changed a few months before Rickey's lawyer filed his motion. Alevizos could no longer reduce Hammons's sentence. Nevertheless, the issue remained whether Rickey testified the way he did because he expected the judge would reward him.

During the hearing, Jason's appellate attorney, Scott King, could question Hammons under oath to see why he expected Alevizos to show him mercy. Although Rickey spoke better English than when he first entered prison, thanks to the college-level courses he took to earn time cuts, his seething insolence was still intact as he responded to King's questions. When told that serving forty-five years for murder was a minimum sentence for the crime, Rickey replied, "That's arguable," claiming, "I've seen people in Indiana get less. . . . I believe I probably could have gotten something less [from a] different legal defense strategy [and] maybe different circumstances."

When King asked to explain what he expected Alevizos could do for him, Hammons replied, "Let me break this down for you—simpler so you can understand it."

The judge then interjected, telling Rickey, "This isn't an idle conversation in a holding cell somewhere. You're in a court of law. Mr. King has been polite to you. You will be polite to Mr. King."

Eventually, Hammons insisted he only expected the judge to release him sooner to the Community Transition Program, where he could live at home with electronic monitoring. When King told him this option was typically offered six months before his release date, Rickey argued that placement wasn't automatic, which is why he needed a lawyer. "I'm a convicted murderer. I don't have anything coming from the DOC or from the courts for the most part, so unless I seek it out, I'm not going to get it."

But the question remained whether Williamson and Lachmund raised his expectations for leniency when he requested they turn off the tape recorder. King asked, "Was there any discussion with these detectives in any of these meetings regarding what, if any, benefit would come to you in exchange for the information you were providing?"

Hammons replied, "Detective Lachmund and Detective Williamson asked me what I wanted in return. I told them I didn't want anything whatsoever. Nothing."[16]

The Rule 60(B) hearing should have ended the day Hammons testified, but it was soon learned that Rickey was lying—as he did so many times before. The judge prompted the new development when he suggested they subpoena a video from Rickey's latest hearing before the Indiana Parole Board, where he made periodic requests for clemency. The recording revealed Hammons complained about promises made to him by Williamson and Airy. He said the detectives told him, "Guys get their sentences cut in half. Guys get deals all the time for this, you know. Do you know that that's an option?" He then claimed "they were rather shocked" when he didn't take them up on their offer.

A second Rule 60(B) hearing was convened, and King confronted Hammons with his comments before the parole board. He asked, "Did you ever, in any of your testimony, in trial, in deposition, or at any point, ever tell anyone about police officers offering you the benefit of a time reduction in exchange for your cooperation?"

"No. It was a given," Hammons replied. "I think everybody knows that. Obviously, the offer was there if I wanted it. I believe that was pretty much an assumption by everybody involved." As far as his testimony was concerned, "I didn't deny [an offer was made]. There was never any formal offer made. Had there been a formal offer made, I would have said, 'Yes, I was offered something.'"

King responded by asking, "So you were offered benefit, but it was verbal, not written. Is that your testimony?"

"No," Hammons answered. "I was not even formally, verbally offered any type of benefit. It was simply brought up that normally, people in my situation would ask for something and that that was possible. But I made it very clear to them that I did not want anything in return for the information that I had."[17]

Less than an hour later, Williamson took the stand to deny that either he or Lachmund said anything like "Guys get their sentences cut in half" after he turned the tape recorder off at the Wabash Valley Correctional Facility.[18] Undoubtedly, the question posed a delicate quandary for the state trooper. By calling Rickey Hammons a liar, he had undercut the credibility of a man who had been the bedrock of his most celebrated investigation—a case that won him plaudits, a promotion, and would surely be featured in his obituary when that time comes. However, throughout the Tibbs investigation, Williamson had also proved to be a liar.

Philosophy classes could be devoted to figuring out where the truth lay between the two men's testimonies and what was said after Hammons asked the detectives to turn off the tape recorder. But one assumption seems the most plausible. Rickey first asked what he could expect for solving the Rison homicide. Desperate for a break, the detectives provided their hyperbolic estimate that he could cut his sentence in half. In 2008, when he first came forward, that would have meant Hammons's release was just another year or so away. Cunning Rickey may have suggested that there be no "formal offer" so as not to jeopardize Jason's conviction. But as he blurted out in the Rule 60(B) hearing, it was "a given" he'd receive a benefit.[19]

In any case, Hammons's no-formal-offer claim did succeed in outfoxing Jason's appellate lawyers. Despite Rickey's comments to the parole board, the Rule 60(B) hearing judge denied the motion to overturn Jason's conviction. In his order, he explained that there was no firm evidence of an agreement between Hammons and the State that would have provided him with a benefit for his testimony.[20] However, in the process, Hammons may have outfoxed himself. Alevizos was on notice that any modification in Rickey's sentence would bring added scrutiny to the Tibbs case. As a result, he did not permit Hammons to enter the Community Transition Program until February 2019, eighteen months before his release date—ultimately a benefit of one year.[21]

At one point during the Rule 60 hearings, Hammons attested to his growth as a human being inside the prison walls. "I have matured as a person, and I have come a long way, which my IDOC [Indiana Department of Corrections] records will reflect. I truly believe I can re-enter society and be a productive, law-abiding member of my community."[22]

On October 4, 2019, eight months after Judge Alevizos released him to a community program, Rickey Hammons was arrested for violating his probation and incarcerated for eight days as punishment. He was reportedly found with a bag of knives and other nonballistic weapons in the house he shared with his ninety-year-old grandmother.[23]

THE LAST OF RAY

When an innocent man is convicted of a murder he did not commit, there is a dual miscarriage of justice. The State effectively releases an individual who can commit another violent act. A little more than three years after the Tibbs trial, Ray would nearly kill another in-law with his bare hands— the second husband of his daughter, Adrienne.

Her husband's beating was not the only example of Adrienne's dysfunctional relationship with her parents. In August 2000, Rayna's niece achieved her own troubling notoriety when the McCartys notified the police that their thirteen-year-old daughter was missing. Lori had dropped her off at a friend's La Porte house on Saturday evening, but the girl never entered the home and was last seen on Monday in front of the Pine Lake Animal Hospital, carrying a Walmart bag. The press did not refrain from mentioning the significance of that location and also revealed she had already been on probation for running away "on several different occasions." Ray had been released from jail a year earlier when Beckman dropped the charges against him. He told a reporter, "Just when you think your life is getting back in order, she does something like this. But she's good for the most part, she is."

"I'm very concerned now," Lori McCarty told *The South Bend Tribune*. "This is the longest she has been gone without calling. . . . All the times before, there was a reason in her mind for taking off. She was not angry or anything when she took off."[24] A day after the interview, a phone call helped police trace Adrienne to a supermarket parking lot, where she was picked up and sent to a juvenile detention center.[25]

Six years later, after sporadic stays with her grandparents, she left the McCarty home to move in with the man she'd marry at twenty.[26] By January 2018, she had divorced,[27] briefly married, and filed for dissolution again,[28] but was still living with her second husband, Eric Chester Ray. According to an arrest warrant filed by the St. Joseph County prosecuting attorney in February, the police were called to the Rays' house by a crying female. When New Carlisle police officer Ron Whitt arrived, a neighbor directed him to the kitchen:

> Officer Whitt noted . . . Mr. [Eric Chester] Ray . . . holding a towel over his face. There was a large pool of blood on the kitchen floor, with additional blood spattered around the area and blood smeared around a nearby trashcan. Officer Whitt noted that Mr. Ray was covered in blood and had severe swelling to both eyes and a laceration approximately two inches long beneath his left eye. Mr. Ray could not tell Officer Whitt what had happened to him as he had no recollection of the events. His facial swelling became so extreme that it became difficult for Mr. Ray to breathe and talk. Medics were called, and Mr. Ray was transported to Memorial Hospital in South Bend.

Officer Whitt found Adrienne in the living room in what he described as a "hysterical" condition. She said her husband had heard a noise in the kitchen and went to investigate. "Adrienne stated she then heard her father talking to her husband, and he sounded very angry. Adrienne stated she then heard the beating happen." Later, neighbors saw McCarty get into a "small older pickup" and speed away. When another officer visited Eric in the hospital, he had recovered enough to identify McCarty as the one who had assaulted him. The officer reported, "Mr. Ray was difficult to understand because of his inability to move his jaw." X-rays would show his father-in-law had shattered his nose and septum.

When officers went to Ray McCarty's home to arrest him, they found him only too happy to take credit for his handiwork, using Mixed Martial Arts terminology to explain his technique. "During an interview" with the police, the prosecutor wrote, "McCarty admitted to repeatedly striking Mr. Ray as he lay on the ground. McCarty stated that he is quite effective as a ground fighter due to his medical condition, which forces him to kneel instead of sitting on a chair. McCarty advised that he only used his fists to strike Mr. Ray and had a small injury on his right hand near his knuckles."

In requesting that McCarty be detained until bail was set, the prosecutor concluded, "McCarty is a danger to others and the community." Eventually, he'd be charged with a Felony 5 battery, defined as an offense resulting in serious bodily injury.[29]

Police never documented what touched off Ray's assault on his son-in-law. Some Rison family members said it was in retribution for Eric beating Adrienne, which is why she filed for divorce. But Eric told coworkers that McCarty had confessed to Adrienne and Hunter that he killed Rayna. During one dispute, Eric charged, his father-in-law drove him by the pond where Rayna was found and warned, "I already put one body in there, and I can put yours there, too." Eric implied he threatened to expose McCarty, and that is what nearly got him killed.[30]

Despite his notoriety, Ray McCarty's arrest for battery flew under the local media's radar. It would not come to light until four days later when McCarty slashed the median cubital vein in the crook of his arm while incarcerated. The St. Joseph County Jail had put him in a medical cell on a suicide watchlist. He had told a jail social worker he was depressed because of the recent death of his mother. The facility also cut off his daily medications, which included two pills for depression and one for pain relief. Guards were to check on him hourly but failed to do so from 11:00 A.M. until 1:40 P.M., when he had bled out from the self-inflicted wound. The newspapers then took notice, with one reporting on his death with the headline, "Former suspect in Rison killing dies in jail cell." A mug shot alongside the article presented Ray with a crew cut, a broad, fleshy face, and a full mountain-man beard—a photo that looked nothing like the swarthy young defendant from 1998.[31]

Nearly a year later, Ray's death was back in the news when it was reported that his estate had filed a federal lawsuit seeking compensation for his negligent treatment in jail. Over the years, the administration of the suit passed hands from Lori to Bennie and finally to Ray's sister Jane, who had left La Porte County decades before to live a prosperous life in the Indianapolis area. She would use an attorney near the state capital to negotiate with the county. In 2020, the estate agreed to a settlement amount of $290,000 from the county sheriff for Ray's "wrongful death." After payments for lawyers and expenses, including Ray's funeral, Lori received net proceeds of $160,000. As of this writing, she still lives in the Fish Lake home where her husband was arrested for Rayna's murder.

The funds were not all Ray left his wife. During a deposition, Lori testified that shortly before McCarty died in the medical jail cell, "He wrote in blood on the wall, 'I love my family.'"

SOURCES

Starting in January 2022, Hillel Levin interviewed Jason Tibbs during collect phone calls that he made from Indiana Department of Corrections facilities. These first took place in thirty-minute and then fifteen-minute increments and occurred as frequently as five days a week. Unless otherwise specified, Jason's quotes and perspectives originate from these interviews.

"2 Men Reportedly Seen near Teen-Ager's Car." *The South Bend Tribune*, March 30, 1993.

"400 Westmoreland Dr, Clover, SC." Scanned Property Card. York County Assessor, June 6, 2023. https://qpublic.schneidercorp.com/Application.aspx?AppID=862&LayerID=16113&PageTypeID=4&PageID=7174&KeyValue=3600000120.

"517 Haviland St." Property Record Card. La Porte County Assessor, 2022. https://beacon.schneidercorp.com/Application.aspx?AppID=205&LayerID=2736&PageTypeID=4&PageID=1531&Q=1498687543&KeyValue=460626353007000043.

"1408 D St., Specs and Transfer History." Property Record Card. La Porte County Assessor, March 27, 1998. https://beacon.schneidercorp.com/Application.aspx?AppID=205&LayerID=2736&PageTypeID=4&PageID=1531&Q=1498687543&KeyValue=460626353007000043.

"2501 S Taylor Rd, Specs and Transfer History." Property Record Card. La Porte County Assessor, March 27, 1998. https://beacon.schneidercorp.com/Application.aspx?AppID=205&LayerID=2736&PageTypeID=4&PageID=1531&Q=932128838&KeyValue=461217151003000055.

Aftowski, Barry. "Missing Person: Rison, Rayna—Stakeout of 517 Haviland St. (McCarty Home)—April 1, 1993, 1500–1800." Supplement Report. La Porte City Police Department, April 30, 1993.

Airy, Brett C. Eric Freeman Phone Interview (taped), July 11, 2013.

———. "Hammons Buick Receipts—Insurance," n.d.

———. "Homicide: Rison, Rayna—Investigation Supplement." Investigator's Supplement, April 7, 2008.

——— . "Kowalski, Raymond—Check Register March 15 to December 27, 1993, Showing April 23 Entry: Johnson's Service for $748.02.," n.d.

"Alevizos Named a Deputy Prosecutor." *The News-Dispatch* (Michigan City, IN), January 21, 1999.

Alevizos, Thomas. In Re: the Estate of Scottie L. Scarborough, No. 46C01-0809-ES-000133 (La Porte Circuit Court, March 15, 2011).

——— . Jason Tibbs v. State of Indiana—Order Denying Petition for Post-Conviction Relief, No. 46C0 1-1705-PC-9 (La Porte Circuit Court, December 7, 2018).

——— . State of Indiana v. Rickey Hammons #102425—Findings and Order for Community Transition Program, No. 46C01-9910-CF-000114 (La Porte Circuit Court, February 13, 2019).

——— . State of Indiana v. Scott L. Scarborough—Charges: Strangulation, Battery Domestic in Presence of a Child, Battery, No. 46C01-0808-FD-000495 (La Porte Circuit Court, January 9, 2009).

Alexander, Clayton Bert. "Ernest Rison Certificate of Death." Indiana State Department of Health, May 4, 1998.

Ames, Stephen R. "Homicide: Rison, Rayna—Items Collected from McCarty 1980 Datsun B210." Supplement Report. La Porte City Police Department, April 30, 1993.

——— . "Missing Person: Rison, Rayna—Located Jacket and Contents." Supplement Report. La Porte City Police Department, April 4, 1993.

——— . "To: Director, Federal Bureau of Investigation—Attention: FBI Lab—Items for FBI Lab Analysis," May 25, 1993.

Anderson, Richard L. "Record of Marriage—McWhirter to Salat." Marriage Certificate. Clerk of Court, La Porte County, December 4, 1976.

AP Wire Services. "Slain LaPorte Teen-Ager Buried as Search for Killer Continues." *The Times* (Hammond, IN), May 2, 1993. https://www.newspapers.com/image/310952957/.

Armstrong, Brian. State of Indiana v. Raymond C. McCarty—Petition Terminating Probation, No. 46C01-8912-CF-130 (La Porte Circuit Court, January 5, 1993).

Arndt, Greg. "Missing Person: Rison, Rayna—Interview with Kim Hackney." Supplement Report. La Porte City Police Department, March 31, 1993.

The Associated Press. "5-Year Investigation Brings Murder Charge." Post-Tribune (IN), May 29, 1998.

Automobile Catalog. "1984 Ford (USA) LTD Crown Victoria 4-Door Full Range Specs," n.d. Accessed May 9, 2023. https://www.automobile-catalog.com/make/ford_usa/ltd_crown_victoria/ltd_crown_victoria_base_4-door/1984.html#gsc.tab=0.

Babcock, Tobin L. "Murder: Cassidy, Daniel—Re: Accused: Rickey J. Hammons. His October 15 Comments to Other Prisoners about Gun and Bullets Used." Report Supplement. La Porte County Sheriff's Office, Jail Division, October 25, 1999.

Baker, Chris. "The Makarov: The AK of the Pistol World." *Lucky Gunner Lounge* (blog), November 1, 2021. https://www.luckygunner.com/lounge/the-makarov-the-ak-of-the-pistol-world/.

Baldini, Paul J. State of Indiana v. Raymond C. McCarty: Directing the Return of Restitution Money, No. 84-20K-143B (La Porte County Court, October 26, 1984).

SOURCES

Balthazor, Thomas. "To Brian Armstrong, Re: Ray McCarty Argumentative Behavior with Therapists at Psychology Associates," December 24, 1991.

———. "To Brian Armstrong, Re: Ray McCarty Discontinued from the Psychology Associates Program," July 27, 1992.

Bank of America, NA v. Eric M. Freeman; Julie M. Freeman—Foreclosure of Real Estate Mortgage, No. 2012CP4604371 (County of York Court of Common Pleas, March 17, 2014).

"Barbara Helen McWhirter 1993 Address." US Public Records Index, 1950–1993, Volume 1. Ancestry.com, n.d. Accessed November 9, 2023.

Bartlett Arborist Supply. "Solidur Felin Chainsaw Pants." Accessed November 9, 2023. https://www.bartlettman.com/products/solidur-felin-chainsaw-pants.

Barton, Gina. "Niles Teen's Killer Resentenced to Life—Becky Stowe's Killer Fails to Get Parole." *The South Bend Tribune*, February 15, 2000. https://www.newspapers.com/image/520227345/.

Bazemore, Harry L. "La Porte County Prisoner's Record—James F. McWhirter." La Porte County Police Department, May 5, 1980.

Beckman, Robert J. State of Indiana v. Rickey Hammons—Statement of Plea Agreement, No. 46C01-9910-CF-114 (La Porte Circuit Court, June 9, 2000).

———. State of Indiana v. Scott L. Scarborough—Request for Issuance of a Warrant of Arrest, No. 46C01-0808-FD-000495 (La Porte Circuit Court, August 15, 2008).

"Bennie Ray, Karen Rison Marriage Certificate." Indiana State Board of Health, May 30, 1964.

"Bennie Rison Addresses." US Public Records Index, 1950–1993, Volume 1. Ancestry.com, n.d. Accessed March 6, 2023. https://www.ancestry.com/discoveryui-content/view/297143084:1788.

Bergerson, Michael S. State of Indiana v. Raymond C. McCarty—Statement of Plea Agreement, No. 46C01-8912-CF-130 (La Porte Circuit Court, December 3, 1990).

Bernard, Roger. "Burglary—Resident, Accused: Jason Tibbs (Age 16)." Report Supplement. La Porte County Police Department, July 1991.

———. "Murder: Cassidy, Daniel—Witness Interview: Staff Sergeant J. R. Meyer." Report Supplement. La Porte County Sheriff's Department, October 18, 1999.

Bernth, Dennis. "Murder: Rison, Rayna—Interview with Rison Family." Case Report Supplement. La Porte County Police Department, n.d. Accessed April 29, 1993.

Biggs, Larry. "Murder: Cassidy, Daniel—Witness Interview: Brian Bowman on October 14, 1999, at 11:25 P.M." Interview Transcript. La Porte County Sheriff's Department, October 14, 1999.

———. "Murder: Cassidy, Daniel—Witness Interview: Dax A. Richter on October 14, 1999, at 10:50 P.M." Interview Transcript. La Porte County Sheriff's Department, October 14, 1999.

———. "Murder: Cassidy, Daniel—Witness Interview: R. Glassman on October 14, 1999, at 11:50 P.M." Interview Transcript. La Porte County Sheriff's Department, October 14, 1999.

———. "Murder: Cassidy, Daniel—Witness Interview: Rickey J. Hammons (with Lachmund) October 12, 1999, at 8:20 A.M." Interview Transcript. La Porte County Sheriff's Department, October 12, 1999.

———. "Murder: Cassidy, Daniel—Witness Interview: Rickey J. Hammons (with Lachmund) October 12, 1999, at 11:10 P.M." Interview Transcript. La Porte County Sheriff's Department, October 12, 1999.

———. "Murder: Cassidy, Daniel—Witness Interview: Rickey J. Hammons (with Lachmund) October 14, 1999, at 5:40 P.M." Interview Transcript. La Porte County Sheriff's Department, October 14, 1999.

Biggs, Larry A. "Crime Scene Summary—Daniel E. Cassidy Homicide." Report Supplement. La Porte County Sheriff's Department, October 6, 1999.

"Births—Adrienne McCarty." *The South Bend Tribune*, November 10, 1886.

Bishop, Amy. "From: Amy Bishop, Re: A Few Questions about Doug McGarvey [Her Father]," November 15, 2022.

Black, Lisa B. "Certificate of Analysis—Items Withdrawn for Analysis by Detective Brett Airy." Indiana State Police Laboratory Division, DNA/Serology Unit, January 17, 2014.

Bland, Terence. "Detectives Try Psychics When All Else Fails." *The South Bend Tribune*, February 18, 1996. https://www.newspapers.com/image/520227345/.

Boyd, Arland D. "Murder, Rayna Lynn Rison." Supplemental Case Report. Indiana State Police, August 5, 1993.

———. "Murder, Rayna Rison." Supplemental Case Report. Indiana State Police, February 2, 1994.

———. "Murder, Rayna Rison." Supplemental Case Report. Indiana State Police, March 18, 1994.

———. "Murder, Rayna Rison." Supplemental Case Report. Indiana State Police, May 20, 1994.

———. "Murder, Rayna Rison." Supplemental Case Report. Indiana State Police, June 28, 1994.

———. "Murder, Rayna Rison." Supplemental Case Report. Indiana State Police, October 11, 1994.

———. "Murder, Rayna Rison." Supplemental Case Report. Indiana State Police, April 3, 1995.

Bradford, Ken. "Psychic Says 'Gift' Isn't Always What People Expect." *The South Bend Tribune*, October 30, 1995. https://www.newspapers.com/image/520227345/.

Braje, Craig V. State of Indiana v. Rickey Hammons—Motion to Suppress Statements, No. 46C01-9910-CF-114 (La Porte Circuit Court, February 18, 2000).

"Bride-Elect Given Shower in South Bend." *The South Bend Tribune*, May 21, 1964. https://www.newspapers.com/image/515506476/.

Brown, Bob. "Police: Was Rison Drowned or Strangled." *The Times* (Hammond, IN), April 30, 1993. https://www.newspapers.com/image/310939855/.

Brown, Susan. "Grand Juries: Missing in Action." *The Times*, November 22, 1998. https://www.newspapers.com/image/310952957/.

Buckley, Joseph P. "Clarifying Misrepresentations About Law Enforcement Interrogation Techniques." John E. Reid and Associates, Inc., 2011. https://reid.com/resources/whats-new/2020-clarifying-misrepresentations-about-law-enforcement-interrogation-techniques.

Buell, Dick. "Murder: Cassidy, Daniel—Accused Rickey Hammons: Employment Records at Harbor Chevrolet." Report Supplement. La Porte County Police Department, October 26, 1999.

———. "Murder: Cassidy, Daniel—Witness Interview: George Stenslik." Report Supplement. La Porte County Police Department, October 18, 1999.

———. "Murder: Cassidy, Daniel—Witness Interview: Rick Flitter." Report Supplement. La Porte County Police Department, October 21, 1999.

———. "Murder: Cassidy, Daniel—Witness Interview: Rickey J. Hammons on October 7, 1999." Report Supplement. La Porte County Sheriff's Department, October 20, 1999.

———. "Murder: Cassidy, Daniel—Witness Interview: Robert Sheridan." Report Supplement. La Porte County Police Department, October 19, 1999.

———. "Murder: Cassidy, Daniel—Witness Interview: Ronda Reedy." Report Supplement. La Porte County Police Department, October 20, 1999.

Butcher, John. "Hostile Inmate: Hammons, Rickey." Case Report. La Porte County Sheriff's Office, Jail Division, October 12, 1999.

Cains, Lynn. "Missing Person: Rison, Rayna—Interview with Chad Green." Supplement Report. La Porte City Police Department, March 31, 1993.

———. "Missing Person: Rison, Rayna—Interview with JS." Supplement Report. La Porte City Police Department, March 30, 1993.

Cains, Lynn, Barry Aftowski, Thomas Thate, and Clyde R. Crass. "Missing Person: Rison, Rayna—Stakeout of 517 Haviland St. (McCarty Home)." Supplement Report. La Porte City Police Department, April 30, 1993.

"Cartilage: What It Is, Function & Types." Accessed November 18, 2023. https://my.clevelandclinic.org/health/body/23173-cartilage.

Caruso, James L. "Decomposition Changes in Bodies Recovered from Water." *Academic Forensic Pathology* 6, no. 1 (March 2016): 19–27. https://doi.org/10.23907/2016.003.

Cassidy, Julie A. State of Indiana v. Rickey Hammons—Victim's Impact Statement: Julie A. Cassidy, No. 46C01-9910-CF-114 (La Porte Circuit Court, August 10, 2000).

Chang, Annie. " 'If I Can't Have Her, Nobody Can': Testimony Begins in LaPorte Co. Cold Case Trial." *CBS—22 WSBT* (Mishawaka, IN), October 29, 2014.

———. "Jason Tibbs Found Guilty in Cold Case Murder of Rayna Rison." *CBS— 22 WSBT* (Mishawaka, IN), November 7, 2014.

"Cheryll Ann Morrison—Location: 114 M and A Farm Rd, Blacksburg, SC." Locations. Intelius, n.d.

Cooper, Gary. "Arrest for Battery—Ray McCarty." Arrest Report, June 8, 1984.

Corry, Janet. "Possible Sources of Ethanol Ante- and Post-mortem: Its Relationship to the Biochemistry and Microbiology of Decomposition." *Journal of Applied Bacteriology*, 44 (November 3, 1977).

Crass, Clyde R. "Rison, Rayna Homicide Investigation: Execution of Search Warrants 517 Haviland St." Supplement Report. La Porte City Police Department, April 29, 1993.

———. "Rison, Rayna Homicide Investigation: Interview with John Pursley." Supplement Report. La Porte City Police Department, April 30, 1993.

———. "Rison, Rayna Homicide Investigation: Interview with Scott McGovern." Supplement Report. La Porte City Police Department, May 5, 1993.

Cutler, Robert F. "Certificate of Death—Daniel E. Cassidy." D. Cassidy Certificate of Death. Indiana State Department of Health, October 6, 1999.

Damphousse, Kelly R. "Voice Stress Analysis: Only 15 Percent of Lies About Drug Use Detected in Field Test." National Institute of Justice, March 16, 2008. https://nij.ojp.gov/topics/articles/voice-stress-analysis-only-15-percent-lies-about-drug-use-detected-field-test.

"Death Penalty Could Be Sought." *The South Bend Tribune*, July 28, 1994.

Deedrick, Douglas. "Re: Raymond McCarty—Suspect; Rayna Rison—Victim; Homicide, Specimen: O-Mega Stun Gun," September 20, 1993.

———. "Re: Rayna Rison—Victim; Homicide, Communications Dated February 17, 1998, and April 21, 1998, and Communication Received April 10, 1998," May 19, 1998.

Dettmer, Sharon. "Courthouse Work Complete." *The South Bend Tribune*, December 15, 2006.

———. "Ex-Finley Estate up for Sale Again." *The South Bend Tribune*, October 22, 2001.

Deutsch, Linda. "Evidence Gets a Hair More Solid." *Associated Press*, July 1, 1995.

Dingman, Shantell. "In the Matter of State of Indiana v. Jason Tibbs—Pre-Sentence Investigation." La Porte Circuit Court, December 15, 2014.

Dixon, Ronald. "Record of Marriage—McCarty to Rison." Marriage Certificate. United Methodist Church, Rolling Prairie, IN: La Porte Circuit Court, August 24, 1985.

Dumollard, Carine, Jean-François Wiart, Florian Hakim, Christophe Demarly, Philippe Morbidelli, Delphine Allorge, and Jean-Michel Gaulier. "Putatively Lethal Ingestion of Isopropyl Alcohol-Related Case: Interpretation of Post-Mortem Isopropyl Alcohol and Acetone Concentrations Remains Challenging." *International Journal of Legal Medicine* 135, no. 1 (October 22, 2020): 175. https://doi.org/10.1007/s00414-020-02444-4.

Duran, Nicole. "Alevizos to Run for Prosecutor." *The News-Dispatch* (Michigan City, IN), November 20, 1997.

———. "Alevizos up in the Air about Political Future." *The News-Dispatch* (Michigan City, IN), January 22, 1998.

———. "Beckman Announces His Candidacy for Prosecutor." *The News-Dispatch* (Michigan City, IN), November 22, 1997.

———. "Candidates Philosophies Differ." *The News-Dispatch* (Michigan City, IN), October 11, 1998.

———. "City Votes Put Beckman on Top." *The News-Dispatch* (Michigan City, IN), May 6, 1998.

———. "Dems Sound off on Hedge." *The News-Dispatch* (Michigan City, IN), April 2, 1998.

———. "How Experienced Is Beckman?" *The News-Dispatch* (Michigan City, IN), October 22, 1998.

———. "Prosecutor Race Most Expensive." *The News-Dispatch* (Michigan City, IN), October 18, 1998.

Ebaugh, Alicia. "Beckman Apologizes—Remarks to Officer Made in Wake of Wife's Death." *The La Porte County Herald-Argus*, February 27, 2010.

———. "Prosecutor Called Out for Courtroom Remarks." *The La Porte County Herald-Argus*, April 10, 2010.

"Elmer Jerry Shreve—Locations." Locations. Intelius, n.d.

Elser, Matthew. "Matt Elser Love Letter to Rayna Rison," February 1993.

"Eric Matthew Freeman—Location: 114 M and A Farm Rd, Blacksburg, SC." Locations. Intelius, n.d. Accessed May 15, 2023.

"Eric Matthew Freeman—Location Report: 810 Deep Hollow Ct, Clover, SC." Locations. Intelius, June 18, 2023.

"Eric Matthew Freeman, Elizabeth Freeman—Ownership History: 254 Cedar Hollow Ln, Irmo, SC." Locations. Intelius, May 22, 2021.

Essling, Mark E. "Certificate of Death—Barbara Helen McWhirter." Certificate of Death. Indiana State Department of Health, April 3, 2009.

Everette, W. M. "Re: Larry Dewayne Hall," December 21, 1994.

Farnsley, Ann. In the Matter of Jason L. Tibbs, A Child Alleged to be a Delinquent—Victim Impact Statement, No. 46C01-9108-JD-151 (La Porte Circuit Court, December 17, 1991).

"Farrell McCleland 1950 Census Report." National Archives and Records Administration, Seventeenth Census of the United States 1950. Ancestry.com. https://www.ancestry.com/discoveryui-content/view/131635170:62308.

Field, Matt. "Szilagyi Edges out Beckman." *The News-Dispatch* (Michigan City, IN), May 5, 2010.

Flynn, Bridget. "Beckman Attacked for Stance on Drug Issues." *The News-Dispatch* (Michigan City, IN), February 4, 2010.

———. "Book: Former Janitor May Be Rayna Rison's Killer." *The News-Dispatch* (Michigan City, IN), June 6, 2010.

Ford, Marsha, Kathleen A. Delaney, Louis Ling, and Timothy Erickson. *Clinical Toxicology*. Philadelphia: Saunders, 2000.

"Freeman, Elizabeth L. Residence 2018–2020." US Index to Public Records, 1994–2019. Ancestry.com, n.d. Accessed November 9, 2023.

Fritz, Matt. "Szilagyi, Espar Trade Barbs." *The La Porte County Herald-Argus*, April 10, 2014.

———. "Szilagyi 'Numb' after Win." *The La Porte County Herald-Argus*, November 3, 2010.

"Fundamental Error." Wikipedia, April 30, 2023. https://en.wikipedia.org/w/index.php?title=Fundamental_error&oldid=1152522774#cite_note-4.

Gaekle, Robert. "Homicide: Rison, Rayna—Interview with Benny [sic] Rison and Wayne Zeman." Supplement Report. La Porte City Police Department, April 27, 1993.

Gaekle, Robert E. "Certificate of Death—Hunter C. McCarty." Certificate of Death. Indiana State Department of Health, August 9, 2011.

Gard, Jon. "Former Suspect in Rison Killing Dies in Jail Cell." *The La Porte County Herald-Argus*, February 27, 2018.

Gettinger, Robert S. State of Indiana in the Matter of the Search Warrant—Charles E. Allen (La Porte Circuit Court, April 7, 1998).

———. State of Indiana in the Matter of the Search Warrant—Raymond C. McCarty (La Porte Circuit Court, April 28, 1993).

———. State of Indiana in the Matter of the (Second) Search Warrant—Raymond C. McCarty (La Porte Circuit Court, June 16, 1993).

———. State of Indiana v. Raymond C. McCarty—Order of Probation (La Porte Circuit Court, January 7, 1991).

———. State of Indiana v. Raymond C. McCarty—Sentencing Order (La Porte Circuit Court, January 7, 1991).

Gonzalez, Gabrielle. "Attorney: Former Suspect's Alibis Were Faulty." *The La Porte County Herald-Argus*, January 16, 2014.

———. "Details Revealed in Tibbs Case." *The News-Dispatch* (Michigan City, IN), January 16, 2014.

———. "La Porte Man Charged with Murdering Wife." *The News-Dispatch* (Michigan City, IN), June 12, 2013.

———. "Rison Family Reacts to Tibbs' Arrest." *The News-Dispatch* (Michigan City, IN), August 25, 2013.

———. " 'There Is No Closure'—Rayna Rison's Family Looking Forward to Justice." *The La Porte County Herald-Argus*, August 24, 2013.

———. "Tibbs Denied Bond." *The La Porte County Herald-Argus*, January 17, 2014.

Gudas, Ray. "Jury Deliberating Lewis' Fate in Shooting Case." *The News-Dispatch* (Michigan City, IN), March 14, 1998.

Hahn, Harold J. "Missing Person: Rison, Rayna—Elizabeth York Statement." La Porte City Police Department, March 29, 1993.

———. "Missing Person: Rison, Rayna—Information from Billy Smith, Time and a Half Video Time Sheet." Supplement Report. La Porte City Police Department, May 3, 1993.

———. "Missing Person: Rison, Rayna—Interview with Austin York." Supplement Report. La Porte City Police Department, March 28, 1993.

———. "Missing Person: Rison, Rayna—Interview with James D. Amor." Supplement Report. La Porte City Police Department, April 16, 1993.

———. "Missing Person: Rison, Rayna—Interview with Jason Tibbs." Supplement Report. La Porte City Police Department, March 31, 1993.

———. "Missing Person: Rison, Rayna—Interview with Josh Jordan." Supplement Report. La Porte City Police Department, April 20, 1993.

———. "Missing Person: Rison, Rayna—Interview with Mark Stick." Supplement Report. La Porte City Police Department, April 1, 1993.

———. "Missing Person: Rison, Rayna—Interview with Matthew Elser." Supplement Report. La Porte City Police Department, March 31, 1993.

———. "Missing Person: Rison, Rayna—Interview with Pam Rosebaum." Supplement Report. La Porte City Police Department, March 31, 1993.

———. "Missing Person: Rison, Rayna—Interview with Raymond McCarty." Supplement Report. La Porte City Police Department, April 1, 1993.

———. "Missing Person: Rison, Rayna—Interview with Rene Gazarkiewicz." Supplement Report. La Porte City Police Department, April 1, 1993.

———. "Rison, Rayna Homicide Investigation: A/V Interview with Charles E. Allen 4." La Porte City Police Department, December 3, 1997.

———. "Rison, Rayna Homicide Investigation: Confidential Interviews with 'Nancy' (a Minor) and Her Parents." Supplement Report. La Porte City Police Department, October 20, 1994.

———. "Rison, Rayna Homicide Investigation: Consent to Search Information-Residence of 517 Haviland St." Supplement. La Porte City Police Department, May 12, 1998.

———. "Rison, Rayna Homicide Investigation: FBI Lab Update from Doug Deedrick." Supplement Report. La Porte City Police Department, June 11, 1993.

———. "Rison, Rayna Homicide Investigation: Information Body Search Warrant for Charles Allen." Supplement. La Porte City Police Department, April 7, 1998.

———. "Rison, Rayna Homicide Investigation: Information Harassment (R) McCarty, Raymond." Supplement Report. La Porte City Police Department, January 14, 1996.

———. "Rison, Rayna Homicide Investigation: Information Reference Lorie [sic] McCarty." Supplement Report. La Porte City Police Department, July 22, 1993.

———. "Rison, Rayna Homicide Investigation: Interview (Q&A) with Charles E. Allen." Supplement Report. La Porte City Police Department, February 7, 1994.

———. "Rison, Rayna Homicide Investigation: Interview with Allen Barkow." Supplement Report. La Porte City Police Department, May 14, 1993.

———. "Rison, Rayna Homicide Investigation: Interview with Andre Bridges." Supplement Report. La Porte City Police Department, November 17, 1994.

———. "Rison, Rayna Homicide Investigation: Interview with Ben Rison." La Porte City Police Department, January 23, 1994.

———. "Rison, Rayna Homicide Investigation: Interview with Brenda Pegg." Supplement Report. La Porte City Police Department, March 2, 1994.

———. "Rison, Rayna Homicide Investigation: Interview with Charles E. Allen." Supplement Report. La Porte City Police Department, May 3, 1993.

———. "Rison, Rayna Homicide Investigation: Interview with Charles E. Allen." Supplement Report. La Porte City Police Department, February 7, 1994.

———. "Rison, Rayna Homicide Investigation: Interview with Darold Willis." Supplement Report. La Porte City Police Department, July 7, 1993.

———. "Rison, Rayna Homicide Investigation: Interview with Gary Marshall." Supplement Report. La Porte City Police Department, April 20, 1993.

———. "Rison, Rayna Homicide Investigation: Interview with Jeanette Zellers." Supplement Report. La Porte City Police Department, March 29, 1994.

———. "Rison, Rayna Homicide Investigation: Interview with John Yates." Supplement Report. La Porte City Police Department, June 10, 1993.

———. "Rison, Rayna Homicide Investigation: Interview with Julie Sims." Supplement Report. La Porte City Police Department, March 1, 1994.

———. "Rison, Rayna Homicide Investigation: Interview with Karen Rison." La Porte City Police Department, May 26, 1993.

———. "Rison, Rayna Homicide Investigation: Interview with Lisa R. McKinney." Supplement Report. La Porte City Police Department, April 8, 1994.

———. "Rison, Rayna Homicide Investigation: Interview with Mary Beth Pienta." Supplement Report. La Porte City Police Department, July 12, 1995.

———. "Rison, Rayna Homicide Investigation: Interview with Mary Smutzer." Supplement Report. La Porte City Police Department, March 8, 1994.

———. "Rison, Rayna Homicide Investigation: Interview with Matthew Elser." Supplement Report. La Porte City Police Department, March 29, 1994.

. "Rison, Rayna Homicide Investigation: Interview with Michael A. Kepplin." Supplement Report. La Porte City Police Department, February 16, 1994.

. "Rison, Rayna Homicide Investigation: Interview with Patricia Walters." Supplement Report. La Porte City Police Department, March 1, 1994.

. "Rison, Rayna Homicide Investigation: Interview with Paula McCleland." Supplement Report. La Porte City Police Department, May 10, 1994.

. "Rison, Rayna Homicide Investigation: Interview with Richard Piechnik II." Supplement Report. La Porte City Police Department, May 28, 1993.

. "Rison, Rayna Homicide Investigation: Interview with Robin Dingman." Supplement Report. La Porte City Police Department, May 19, 1993.

. "Rison, Rayna Homicide Investigation: Interview with Rodney Rosenbaum." Supplement Report. La Porte City Police Department, August 11, 1993.

. "Rison, Rayna Homicide Investigation: Interview with Sharon Friend." Supplement Report. La Porte City Police Department, March 1, 1994.

. "Rison, Rayna Homicide Investigation: Interview with Sheila Albertson." Supplement Report. La Porte City Police Department, March 26, 1994.

. "Rison, Rayna Homicide Investigation: Interview with Sue Casper." Supplement Report. La Porte City Police Department, July 26, 1993.

. "Rison, Rayna Homicide Investigation: Interview with Tina M. Townsend." Supplement Report. La Porte City Police Department, June 3, 1993.

. "Rison, Rayna Homicide Investigation: Interview with Wendy Rison." La Porte City Police Department, May 28, 1993.

. "Rison, Rayna Homicide Investigation: Subpoena of Telephone Records." Supplement Report. La Porte City Police Department, May 12, 1993.

. "Rison, Rayna Homicide Investigation: Summary Information from SA Ken Temples, Danville Office FBI." Supplement Report. La Porte City Police Department, December 7, 1994.

. "Summ. of Ray's Stories," May 12, 1993.

. Tina Church, Private Investigator. Audio recording, January 16, 1996.

Hall, Larry Dewayne. "Handwritten List of His Potential Victims," n.d.

Haman, William C., and David A. Roth. "Cheryl K. VanSchoyck FBI Interview." FD-302. FBI, March 31, 1993.

. "Lisa Dyer FBI Interview." FD-302. FBI, April 9, 1993.

Hammons, Rick J. "To: Mr. Gillmore [sic]," October 26, 1999.

Hammons, Rickey. Rickey Hammons v. State of Indiana—Petition for Post-Conviction Relief (October 23, 2002).

. Rickey Hammons v. State of Indiana—Petition for Post-Conviction Relief, Motion for Change of Venue from Judge, n.d.

. "To: Lynne F. Spevak, Clerk of the La Porte Circuit Court, Re: Status on Change of Venue Request," September 3, 2002.

. "To: Mark Lachmund, Re: 'Help Me' Get Moved," March 13, 2008.

Heline, Marti Goodlad. "Close Friends Testify Maxy 'Strangled.' " *The South Bend Tribune*, July 13, 1983. https://www.newspapers.com/image/517723689/.

SOURCES

Hemphill, Pat. "Missing Person Report: Rison, Rayna Lynn." Case Report, March 26, 1993.

———. "Missing Person Report: Rison, Rayna Lynn—Various Interviews." Supplement Report, March 27, 1993.

Hess, Frederick G. "Murder: Cassidy, Daniel—Witness Interview: Rickey Hammons Sr. Re: Makarov Handgun." Report Supplement. La Porte County Sheriff's Department, October 8, 1999.

"Hill and Griffith Casting Solutions—Core Washes/Core Room—Isopropyl Alcohol Purity," Hill and Griffith, November 6, 2023. https://www.hillandgriffith.com/core-room-washes.

Hoover, Rick L. "Autopsy Report—Name: Rison, Rayna." Autopsy. Memorial Hospital, South Bend, IN. La Porte County Coroner: Barbara Houston, April 28, 1993.

———. "To: Kimberly A. Gudorf, Deputy Prosecuting Attorney—Re: Rayna Rison Post-Mortem Examination," April 9, 1998.

———. "To: Officer Harold Hahn—Re: Rayna Rison / Postmortem Toxicology," May 11, 1994.

Hughes, Virginia. "Why Police Lineups Will Never Be Perfect." *The Atlantic*, October 2, 2014. https://www.theatlantic.com/technology/archive/2014/10/the-evolving-science-of-police-lineups/381046/.

Humble, Charles. "To: Mike Spears, Subject: Matthew Elser & Jason Tibbs." Polygraph Results Analysis, April 1, 1993.

Ianson, Scott G. "Missing Person Report: Rison, Rayna L.—Doug McGarvey March 29 Tip at 8:05 P.M." Supplement Report, March 29, 1993.

Ihnat, Nicole. "Certificate of Analysis—Items Submitted for Analysis—File Number: 93L-800." Indiana State Police Laboratory Division, DNA/Serology Unit, September 30, 2008.

In Re: the Marriage of Adrienne M. Huegel and Michael E. Huegel, No. 46C01-1210-DR-000370 (La Porte Circuit Court, June 24, 2014).

In Re: the Marriage of Adrienne M. Ray and Eric C. Ray, No. 71D04-1801-DC-000072 (St. Joseph Superior Court 4, March 11, 2019).

Indiana Code Historical Statutes. "Indiana Code, Title 35: Criminal Law and Procedure, 1989: Chapter 2. Death Sentence and Sentences for Felonies and Habitual Offenders (ICT35-1989-030_35-43-7-5)," 1989. https://indianamemory.contentdm.oclc.org/digital/collection/IC/id/14821/rec/1.

Indiana Department of Correction. "IDOC: Wabash Valley Correctional Facility," 2023. https://www.in.gov/idoc/find-a-facility/adult/wabash-valley-correctional-facility/.

"Indiana Rules of Court—Rules of Trial Procedure—Rule 60. Relief from Judgment or Order: (B) Mistake—Excusable Neglect—Newly Discovered Evidence—Fraud, Etc." Indiana Judicial Branch, last updated April 2024. https://www.in.gov/courts/rules/trial_proc/index.htm#_Toc152229176.

"Jail Management Booking Form—Scott L. Scarborough." La Porte County Police Department, January 21, 1996.

Jason L. Tibbs v. Dennis Reagle—Petitioner's Supplemental Reply, No. 1:20-cv-01564-JMS-MJD (United States District Court Southern District of Indiana, Indianapolis Division, June 1, 2022).

Jason L. Tibbs v. State of Indiana—Rule 60(B) Hearing—Transcript II of II, Christine A. Kutanovski (Indiana Court of Appeals, 2015).

Jason L. Tibbs v. State of Indiana—Transcript I of II, Christine A. Kutanovski (Indiana Court of Appeals, 2015).

Jason L. Tibbs v. State of Indiana—Transcript II of II, Christine A. Kutanovski (Indiana Court of Appeals, 2015).

Jason Tibbs v. State of Indiana—Brief of Appellant, No. 46C01-1308-MR-278 (Indiana Court of Appeals, January 21, 2016).

Jason Tibbs v. State of Indiana—Memorandum Decision, No. 46A03-1501-CR-19 (Indiana Court of Appeals, September 8, 2016).

Jason Tibbs v. State of Indiana—Memorandum Decision, No. 46C01-1705-PC-9 (Indiana Court of Appeals, July 30, 2019).

Jenkins, Marilyn M. "Voice of the People: In Indiana, It's a Felony—Not 'an Affair,'" *The South Bend Tribune*, June 25, 1998.

"John E. Reid and Associates, Inc.," 2011. https://reid.com/programs.

Jones, Linda L. "Rayna Rison Remembered—Poems Honor the Dead Teen." *The South Bend Tribune*, May 2, 1993. https://www.newspapers.com/image/520251776/.

Jozaitis, Amanda. "Region Design Co.—Posts. [original mascot: slicer]. Facebook. *Region Design Company*, September 27, 2018. https://www.facebook.com/387379594978333/posts/we-felt-honored-that-la-porte-high-school-contacted-us-to-design-and-print-their/688541234862166/.

Kabacinski, Thomas. "Mischief/Damage—Victim: Milich, James; Accused: Tibbs, Jason L." Case Report. La Porte City Police Department, November 20, 1992.

Keeling, Michael. "To: John Lake, La Porte County Deputy Prosecuting Attorney, Re: Ray McCarty," April 11, 1999.

Keene, James, and Hillel Levin. *In with the Devil: A Fallen Hero, a Serial Killer, and a Dangerous Bargain for Redemption*. New York: St. Martin's Griffin, 2011.

Keith, Elvin W., III. "Bennie Ray Rison FBI Interview." FD-302. FBI, March 29, 1993.

———. "Bennie Ray Rison FBI Interview." FD-302. FBI, March 31, 1993.

———. "Bennie Ray Rison Interview." FD-302. FBI, April 2, 1993.

———. "Jennifer Lynn McCleland FBI Interview." FD-302. FBI, April 1, 1993.

———. "Lori Ann McCarty FBI Interview." FD-302. FBI, March 30, 1993.

———. "Mark A. Stick FBI Interview." FD-302. FBI, March 31, 1993.

———. "Raymond Clayton McCarty FBI Interview." FD-302. FBI, April 1, 1993.

Keith, Elvin W., III, and Michael Hanna. "Raymond Clayton McCarty Interview." FD-302. FBI, April 2, 1993.

Kemker, Wayne A. "Homicide: Rison, Rayna—Witness Interview: Val Eilers." Report Supplement. La Porte County Police Department, May 3, 1993.

———. "Rison, Rayna Homicide Investigation: Vehicle Search Warrant—Pontiac Silver '88 Sunbird." Physical Evidence Inventory. La Porte County Police Department, April 28, 1993.

King, Michael D. "Missing Person: Rison, Rayna—Shannon Siddall Interview." Supplement Report. La Porte City Police Department, April 28, 1993.

SOURCES

Kintzele, John F. "Victim: Cassidy, Daniel Jemiolo—Investigation Overview." Supplement Report. Michigan City Police Department, October 21, 1999.

———. "Victim: Cassidy, Daniel Jemiolo—Witness Interview: Brian Todd Bowman (Taped)." Interview Transcript. Michigan City Police Department, October 9, 1999.

Koehn, Linda J. "Child Molesting, Accused: Raymond C. McCarty." Report Supplement, December 19, 1989.

"La Porte County Prosecutor (Unopposed)." *The La Porte County Herald-Argus.* November 4, 2006.

La Porte County Sheriff. "Hammons, Rickey J.—RAP Sheet." La Porte County Sheriff's Office, October 11, 2019.

———. "McWhirter, James F.—RAP Sheet." La Porte County Sheriff's Office, June 24, 2022.

———. "Scarborough, Scott L.—RAP Sheet." La Porte County Sheriff's Office, July 14, 2022.

La Porte High School. *El Pe Yearbook 1962.* La Porte, IN, 1962.

———. *El Pe Yearbook 1984.* La Porte, IN, 1984.

———. *El Pe Yearbook 1985.* La Porte, IN, 1985.

———. *El Pe Yearbook 1992.* La Porte, IN, 1992.

"La Porte, Indiana." Wikipedia, n.d. Accessed October 15, 2023. https://en.wikipedia.org/w/index.php?title=La_Porte,_Indiana&oldid=1176803735.

"La Porte Indiana Sunset March 26, 1993." Google Search, November 14, 2023.

Lachmund, Mark. "Arrest Report: Rickey J. Hammons, on October 12, 1999—Mug Shot." La Porte County Sheriff's Office, October 12, 1999.

———. "Murder: Cassidy, Daniel—Witness Interview: Rickey J. Hammons on October 6, 1999." Interview Transcript. La Porte County Sheriff's Department, October 6, 1999.

———. "Murder: Cassidy, Daniel—Witness Interview: Rickey J. Hammons on October 7, 1999." Report Supplement. La Porte County Sheriff's Department, October 20, 1999.

———. "Murder: Rison, Rayna—Witness Interview: Ricky Hammons." Interview Transcript. La Porte County Sheriff's Department, March 10, 2008.

———. "Rayna Rison Homicide Investigation—Contact with Ricky [*sic*] Hammons." Case Report. La Porte County Sheriff's Department, March 18, 2008.

LaFrance, Catherine. "Officials Come Together to Help 'at-Risk' Teens." *The La Porte County Herald-Argus*, November 8, 2005.

"Lang Ready for Next Chapter." *Legal Monitor Worldwide*, December 31, 2014.

"La Porte County Prosecutor (Unopposed)," (November 2006). *The La Porte County Herald-Argus*, November 4, 2006.

"LaPorte County Courthouse," last updated November 23, 2020. https://www.hmdb.org/m.asp?m=43373.

"LaPorte County Prisoner's Record—Scott L. Scarborough." La Porte County Police Department, April 28, 1989.

"LaPorte County Prisoner's Record—Scott L. Scarborough Mug Shot." La Porte County Police Department, April 28, 1989.

"LaPorte Police Seek Leads in Rison Slaying." *The South Bend Tribune*, August 4, 1997.

Lee, David C. "Marriage License—Joseph E. Jemiolo, Janet M. Cassidy." The State of Colorado, City and County of Denver, September 11, 1973.

"Leslie Ann Dean—Birth Date." Personal Information. Intelius, n.d. Accessed December 30, 2021.

Levin, Hillel. "Calculation of Known Rayna Rison Interviews from March 26, 1993, to May 19, 1998." Spreadsheet, December 16, 2022. Levin, Hillel, Interview. Arland D. Boyd 1, September 27, 2022.

———. Arland D. Boyd 2, October 11, 2022.

———. Barbara H. Elliott, homeowner where Scott Scarborough died on the front lawn, September 7, 2022.

———. Chris Wallen, August 23, 2022.

———. Clifford Sheeler, November 3, 2022.

———. Confidential La Porte County Investigator, June 2023.

———. Daniel Jemiolo Cassidy relative, January 23, 2023.

———. Eric Ray coworker, August 2023.

———. Gary Marshall, July 11, 2022.

———. Gayla Moreau, July 19, 2022.

———. James McWhirter La Porte High School classmate, October 2022.

———. Jane Lindborg Wickstrom, September 14, 2022.

———. Jennifer Delrio, January 10, 2022.

———. Jim Jackson, November 7, 2022.

———. John Proud, September 30, 2022.

———. La Porte County Attorney (anonymous), June 13, 2022.

———. Lucas Scarborough, November 12, 2022.

———. Matthew Elser 1, February 18, 2023.

———. Matthew Elser 2, February 27, 2023.

———. Prisoner incarcerated with Hammons at Wabash Valley Correctional Facility, October 6, 2023.

———. Ray McCarty elementary school teacher, November 3, 2022.

———. Scott Duerring, April 4, 2023.

———. Scott Scarborough girlfriend 1, October 23, 2022.

———. Scott Scarborough girlfriend "Robin," September 29, 2022.

———. V. Michael Drayton, October 22, 2022.

LII/Legal Information Institute. "Brady Rule." Accessed November 18, 2023. https://www.law.cornell.edu/wex/brady_rule.

LII/Legal Information Institute. "Rule 807. Residual Exception." Accessed November 18, 2023. https://www.law.cornell.edu/rules/fre/rule_807.

LinkedIn. "Bennie Rison LinkedIn Profile," October 18, 2023. https://www.linkedin.com/in/bennie-rison-3a692481/.

"Lori A. McCarty Address." US Public Records Index, 1950–1993, Volume 1, n.d. Accessed December 29, 2021. https://www.ancestry.com/discoveryui-content/view/375328060:1788?tid=&pid=&queryId=5ad57fd7e486110784f30d16e4b1b8ac&_phsrc=bsx45&_phstart=successSource.

Lu, Jane. "The Datsun B210 Is an Unforgettable Classic." Jerry, June 27, 2022. https://

getjerry.com/insights/datsun-b210-unforgettable-classic.

McDermott, Melissa. "Assessment for Raymond C. McCarty." Assessment for La Porte County Court Adult Probation Department. Treatment Associates, February 25, 1991.

McVay, Rick. "Full Story of Beckman's Threats Not Told—Letter to Editor." *The News-Dispatch* (Michigan City, IN), May 29, 2010.

Macht, David I. "Isopropyl Alcohol, a Convenient Laboratory Anesthetic for Cats." *Proceedings of the Society for Experimental Biology and Medicine* 19, no. 2 (November 1, 1921): 85. https://doi.org/10.3181/00379727-19-44.

Maddux, Stan. "21 Years Separates LaPorte Family's Grief." *The South Bend Tribune*, October 14, 1999.

———. "House Struck by Motorist." *The La Porte County Herald-Argus*, March 19, 2009.

———. "La Porte Circuit Judge Thomas Alevizos Seeking Second Term." *La Porte County Herald-Dispatch*, February 11, 2012.

———. "LaPorte Police Chief Reflects on His Accomplishments." *The South Bend Tribune*, December 29, 1995.

———. "Man Charged with Murder." *The News-Dispatch* (Michigan City, IN), October 16, 1999.

———. "Man Gets 45 Years in Slaying." *The News-Dispatch* (Michigan City, IN), August 19, 2000.

———. "Mother Doubts Daughter Is a Runaway." *The South Bend Tribune*, August 24, 2000.

———. "Murder Victim Witnessed His Mother's Violent Death." *Post-Tribune* (IN), October 14, 1999.

———. "Prosecutor Links Ex-Boyfriend to Rison Murder." *The South Bend Tribune*, October 29, 2014.

———. "Rison Case—Five Years Later, Authorities Still Optimistic about Solution." *The News-Dispatch* (Michigan City, IN), April 9, 1998.

———. "Rison Murder Suspect Arraigned." *The News-Dispatch* (Michigan City, IN), June 2, 1998.

———. "Stigma of Murder Still Sticks." *Post-Tribune* (IN), August 26, 1999.

———. "Szilagyi Bested by Espar for LaPorte County Prosecutor's Race." *The Times* (Hammond, IN), May 7, 2014.

———. "Tibbs Gets 40 Years in '93 Rison Slaying." *The South Bend Tribune*, December 20, 2014.

Mair, Colleen. "100 Years for Child Molester." *The La Porte County Herald-Argus*, December 22, 2001.

Mandape, Sammed N., Kapema Bupe Kapema, Tiffany Duque, Amy Smuts, Jonathan L. King, Benjamin Crysup, Jianye Ge, Bruce Budowle, August E. Woerner. "Evaluating Probabilistic Genotyping for Low-Pass DNA Sequencing." *Forensic Science International Genetics Supplement Series* 8 (January 1, 2022): 112–114. Accessed November 20, 2023. https://nij.ojp.gov/library/publications/evaluating-probabilistic-genotyping-low-pass-dna-sequencing.

Margolick, David. "After 92 Days of Testimony, Simpson Prosecution Rests." *The New York Times*, July 7, 1995.

Marovich, Steve. "Homicide: Investigation Rison, Rayna—Interview with Trudy Hahn." Supplement Report. La Porte City Police Department, September 23, 1994.

————. "Missing Person: Rison, Rayna." Supplement Report. La Porte City Police Department, March 31, 1993.

————. "Missing Person: Rison, Rayna—Garry and Lois Bucher Interview." Supplement Report. La Porte City Police Department, March 31, 1993.

————. "Missing Person: Rison, Rayna—March 30 Tip Called in at 7:30 P.M." Supplement Report. La Porte City Police Department, March 30, 1993.

"Marriage License Applications—Huegel, Michael and Adrienne McCarty." *The South Bend Tribune*, July 22, 2007.

Martinez, T. T., R. W. Jaeger, F. J. deCastro, M. W. Thompson, and M. F. Hamilton. "A Comparison of the Absorption and Metabolism of Isopropyl Alcohol by Oral, Dermal and Inhalation Routes." *Veterinary and Human Toxicology* 28, no. 3 (June 1986): 233–236.

Matzke, Scott. "Victim: Cassidy, Daniel Jemiolo—Witness Interview: Jennifer Nicole Hammons on October 8. 1999." Interview Transcript. Michigan City Police Department, October 8, 1999.

————. "Victim: Cassidy, Daniel Jemiolo—Witness Interview: Ramona Gamez on October 8, 1999." Interview Transcript. Michigan City Police Department, October 8, 1999.

Medtox Laboratories. "Toxicology TDM (Therapeutic Drug Monitoring)—Patient Name: Rayna Rison, ID: 000039-001-00-8491." St. Paul, MN. For: La Porte Hospital, Clinical Laboratory, Attn: Dr. Jones, July 5, 1993.

Miller, John. "Missing Person: Rison, Rayna—Chad E. Green Statement." Statement. La Porte City Police Department, April 8, 1993.

————. "Missing Person: Rison, Rayna—Jason Tibbs Statement." Statement. La Porte City Police Department, March 31, 1993.

Miller, John, and Robert Schoff. "Death Investigation—Rison, Rayna Lynn—Body Recovery." Case Report. La Porte City Police Department, April 27, 1993.

Miller, John V. "Homicide: Rison, Rayna—Bryan Durham Interview." Supplement Report. La Porte City Police Department, May 13, 1993.

Mitchell, Larry. "Missing Person: Rison, Rayna—Calming down B. Rison at LPHS, Initial Interviews with: M. Ruminski, M. Elser, J. Tibbs (March 27, 1993)." Supplement Report. La Porte City Police Department, March 28, 1993.

Morse, Andrew J. "Domestic Battery—Scott (Scotty) Scarborough." Case Report. La Porte County Sheriff's Office, August 5, 2008.

"Murder: Daniel E. Cassidy Investigation—Photo Summary: Recently Cooked Chicken on Top of Stove (#140), A Pan of Cooked Macaroni on the Kitchen Counter (#143)." Interview Transcript. La Porte County Sheriff's Department, October 7, 1999.

Murphy, Heather. "Why This Scientist Keeps Receiving Packages of Serial Killers' Hair." *The New York Times*, September 16, 2019.

"Murphy Worker Files Job Bias Suit." *The South Bend Tribune*, March 19, 1977.

Nicholas, John. "Asphyxiation ruled in death." *The South Bend Tribune*, April 29, 1993.

————. "Brother-in-Law Charged in '93 Death: Prosecutor Cites New Evidence in Rison Slaying." *The South Bend Tribune*, May 29, 1998.

————. "Brother-in-Law Enters Innocent Plea in Rison Death." *The South Bend Tribune*, June 2, 1998.

———. "Demos Tap Cooley, Cooper for Council." *The South Bend Tribune*, May 4, 1994.

———. "Election Preview: Familiar Names on LaPorte Ballot: Several Races Have Rematches." *The South Bend Tribune*, November 1, 1998.

———. "Grand Jury Convened in 1993 LaPorte Slaying." *The South Bend Tribune*, May 7, 1998.

———. "Hedge, Herrbach Win Primaries." *The South Bend Tribune*, May 4, 1994.

———. "Hedge New Prosecutor." *The South Bend Tribune*, November 9, 1994. https://www.newspapers.com/image/520227345/.

———. "Hitchhiker Sought as Alibi in Killing of Rayna Rison." *The South Bend Tribune*, November 4, 1994.

———. "Lawyer Claims McCarty Innocent." *The South Bend Tribune*, May 31, 1998.

———. "Missing Girl Found in Michigan City." *The South Bend Tribune*, August 25, 2000.

———. "November 2002 Election Results—La Porte County Prosecuting Attorney." *The South Bend Tribune*, November 6, 2002.

———. "Officer Finds Rison's Jacket on Tree Limb, Reward Fund Reaches $31,000." *The South Bend Tribune*, April 5, 1993.

———. "Prosecutor Denies Rison Case Scheduled for Grand Jury." *The South Bend Tribune*, January 6, 1996.

———. "Teams Tackle Rison Case." *The South Bend Tribune*, April 11, 1993.

"November 2002 Election Results," (November 2002). *The South Bend Tribune*, November 6, 2002.

"Obituaries—Arland F. Farnsley." *The South Bend Tribune*, July 3, 1990.

"Obituary—Carolyn Theresa Kohley McCarty (1929-2017)," Find a Grave, August 19, 2017. https://www.findagrave.com/memorial/182531093/carolyn-theresa-mccarty.

"Obituary—Douglas N. McGarvey." *The Indianapolis Star*, September 7, 2017. https://www.newspapers.com/image/338199730/.

"Obituary—Ernest Rison Jr. (1939-2012)," Find a Grave, April 24, 2012. https://www.findagrave.com/memorial/89270603/ernest-rison.

"Obituary—Gayle Scarborough." *The South Bend Tribune*, September 24, 1984.

"Obituary—James David Bruno." *The La Porte County Herald-Argus*, February 8, 2022.

"Obituary—John R. Cassidy." *The South Bend Tribune*, April 27, 1994.

"Obituary—Julie McCarter Cross," Tribute Archive, July 21, 2020. https://www.tributearchive.com/obituaries/22329472/julie-mccarter-cross.

"Obituary—Stanley M. Salat." *The South Bend Tribune*, November 28, 1995.

"Obituary for Gene R. Samuelson." Frank L. Keszei Funeral Home, Inc., Essling Chapel, January 1, 2021. https://www.esslingfuneralhome.com/obituary/Gene-Samuelson.

"Obituary for James Donald Westmoreland." M. L. Ford & Sons Funeral Home, May 16, 2013. https://www.mlfordsons.com/obituary/James-Westmoreland.

"Obituary for Robert J. 'Rob' Beckman; Tribute Wall: Bill Nelson." Ott / Haverstock Funeral Chapel and Cremation Services, December 21, 2019. https://www.otthaverstock.com/obituary/Robert-Beckman.

"Offender Information System Conduct Summary—Hammons, Rickey." Indiana Department of Correction, October 22, 2009.

Our View. "Murder Charge Restores Community Confidence." *The South Bend Tribune*, June 4, 1998.

Palmer, Reginald Heber. *Foundry Practice: A Text Book for Molders, Students and Apprentices*. New York: Wiley, 1911.

Paul F. Boston Middle School. *Bostonian Yearbook*. La Porte, IN, 1988.

Pavolka, Joseph T. "Additional (Information—Rison Case) Continued: Beth York and Sons." Report Supplement. La Porte City Police Department, July 13, 1993.

———. "Additional to Case 9305-0542-M2 (Murder, Rayna Rison): Beth York." Report Supplement. La Porte County Police Department, August 31, 1993.

———. "Additional to Case 9305-0542-M2 (Murder, Rayna Rison): Richard Sarvis, Brent Glassman, Gerald and Diane Keehn." Report Supplement. La Porte County Police Department, September 1, 1993.

———. "Miscellaneous (Information—Rison Case)—Pickup, Sedan Sighting 9:50 P.M., March 26, 1993." Case Report. La Porte County Police Department, March 27, 1993.

"Paycheck Inquiry—Rick J Hammons." Payroll. Harbor Automotive Group, October 18, 1999.

People v. Ashwal, 39 N.Y.2d 105, April 1976. Accessed November 18, 2023. https://casetext.com/case/people-v-ashwal.

Pintal, Walter J. "To Brian Armstrong, Re: Ray McCarty Discharge from Swanson Center for Non-Compliance with Treatment," September 9, 1991.

Pliske, Thomas. "Number of Shootings Concerns Councilman." *The South Bend Tribune*, December 1, 1982.

"The Pole Barn vs The Timber Frame Barn," May 29, 2019. https://www.vermonttimberworks.com/blog/the-pole-barn-vs-the-timber-frame-barn/.

Pollanen, M. S., and D. A. Chiasson. "Fracture of the Hyoid Bone in Strangulation: Comparison of Fractured and Unfractured Hyoids from Victims of Strangulation." *Journal of Forensic Sciences* 41, no. 1 (January 1996): 110–113.

Porter, Don. "Teen's Lawyer Criticizes Limits on Defense in Slaying." *The South Bend Tribune*, July 18, 1998.

Post-Tribune Staff. "Mill Creek Man Faces '93 Charges in Rison Slaying." *Post-Tribune* (IN), May 30, 1998.

Przybyla, Daniel. "Oprah Quitting LaPorte." *The La Porte County Herald-Argus*, September 16, 2003.

"PubChem Compound Summary—Isopropyl Alcohol." PubChem, NIH—National Library of Medicine. Accessed November 6, 2023. https://pubchem.ncbi.nlm.nih.gov/compound/3776.

"Raymond C. McCarty—Locations." Locations. Intelius, n.d. Accessed January 18, 2023. https://www.intelius.com/dashboard/reports/c4d65187-9c1d-42f5-82cf-1f8743891566.

Raymond McCarty Arraignment. La Porte County Courthouse: WSBT-TV, Channel 22, 1998.

Richards, Rick A. "The LaPorte Casino Roller Rink—Still a Great Destination." *The Beacher* 27, no. 30, August 4, 2011.

Rison, Bennie. Rene Gazarkiewicz Interview (taped), October 11, 1995.

Rison, Bennie. "To: Parents and Friends—Request to Send Post Cards to Public Officials," January 1994.

SOURCES

Rison, Rayna. "To Matt Elser from Rayna Rison." Handwritten letter, March 18, 1993.

Ritter, George. "Murder: Cassidy, Daniel—Crime Scene, Initial Investigation." Report Supplement. La Porte County Police Department, October 6, 1999.

———. "Murder: Cassidy, Daniel—Investigative Summary October 06, 1999." Report Supplement. La Porte County Police Department, October 6, 1999.

———. "Murder: Cassidy, Daniel—October 7 Investigation Summary." Report Supplement. La Porte County Police Department, October 8, 1999.

———. "Murder: Cassidy, Daniel—October 8 Investigation Summary." Report Supplement. La Porte County Police Department, October 8, 1999.

———. "Murder: Cassidy, Daniel—October 9 Investigation Summary." Report Supplement. La Porte County Police Department, October 9, 1999.

———. "Murder: Cassidy, Daniel—October 12 Investigation Summary." Report Supplement. La Porte County Police Department, October 12, 1999.

———. "Murder: Cassidy, Daniel—October 13 Investigation Summary." Report Supplement. La Porte County Police Department, October 13, 1999.

———. "Murder: Cassidy, Daniel—Witness Interview: Brian Todd Bowman." Report Supplement. La Porte County Sheriff's Department, October 7, 1999.

———. "Murder: Cassidy, Daniel—Witness Interview: Julie Cassidy." Report Supplement. La Porte County Police Department, October 7, 1999.

———. "Murder: Cassidy, Daniel—Witness Interview: Kelly S. Loughlin." Report Supplement. La Porte County Police Department, October 8, 1999.

Rogers, Larry W. State of Indiana v. Raymond McCarty—Murder: Motion for Pre-trial Gag Order, No. 46C01-9805-CE-43 (La Porte Circuit Court, June 1, 1998).

Rolling Prairie High School. *Rolling Log Yearbook 1960*. Rolling Prairie, IN, 1960.

Ros, Pablo. "Will Inmates Put Cards on the Table?" *The South Bend Tribune*, February 18, 2008.

Roth, David A. "Dr. Gerald N. Wagner FBI Interview." FD-302. FBI, March 30, 1993.

Russell, Joyce. "Kingsbury Ordnance Plant Changed the Landscape of LaPorte County." *The Times of Northwest Indiana*, July 8, 2017.

Sanders, Thomas J. State of Indiana v. Raymond McCarty—Supplemental Affidavit in Support of Probable Cause, No. 71D03-1802-F5-000043 (St. Joseph Superior Court, February 23, 2018).

Schelling, Lee. "Beckman Firing Draws More Fire." *The News-Dispatch* (Michigan City, IN), August 16, 1997.

———. "Hedge Fires Beckman as Deputy Prosecutor." *The News-Dispatch* (Michigan City, IN), August 14, 1997.

Scherer, Terry. "Child Molesting Report, Accused: Raymond C. McCarty." La Porte City Police Department Report Supplement, December 18, 1989.

Schoff, Robert. "Death Investigation: Rison, Rayna—Interview with Judy Freeman Re: Ed Logan." Supplement Report. La Porte City Police Department, September 22, 1993.

———. "Death Investigation: Rison, Rayna—Interview with Noreen Molnar." Supplement Report. La Porte City Police Department, July 1, 1993.

———. "Death Investigation: Rison, Rayna—Lori McCarty Call at 7:30 P.M." Supplement Report. La Porte City Police Department, May 11, 1993.

———. "Missing Person: Rison, Rayna—Interview with Leah M. Pepples." Supplement Report. La Porte City Police Department, April 29, 1993.

———. "Missing Person: Rison, Rayna—Johnson Interview." Supplement Report. La Porte City Police Department, March 29, 1993.

———. "Missing Person: Rison, Rayna—Lisa Dyer Interview." Supplement Report. La Porte City Police Department, April 5, 1993.

———. "Missing Person: Rison, Rayna—Lori McCarty (Sister) Interview." Supplement Report. La Porte City Police Department, March 28, 1993.

———. "Missing Person: Rison, Rayna—Rayna Bedroom Search with Karen, Wendy Rison. They Submit Jason Tibbs's Letters. Schoff and Miller Find the Ones from Matt Elser." Supplement Report. La Porte City Police Department, April 8, 1993.

"Shooting Case Due for Probe." *The South Bend Tribune*, August 30, 1981.

Shortt, Timothy A. "Assistance Rendered—Victim Rayna L. Rison." Case Report. La Porte County Police Department, March 27, 1993.

Smith, John A. "Medical Certificate of Death—Farrell N. McCleland." Indiana State Board of Health, Division of Vital Records, March 17, 1969.

Smith, Mike. "On the Lookout." *Muncie Evening Press*, April 13, 1993.

Sobecki, Rhonda E. "Arrest Made in Rison Case." *The News-Dispatch* (Michigan City, IN), May 29, 1998.

———. "Beckman Edges Hedge." *The News-Dispatch* (Michigan City, IN), November 4, 1998.

———. "Grand Jury Called in Rison Case." *The News-Dispatch* (Michigan City, IN), May 7, 1998.

———. "Rison Murder Suspect Freed." *The News-Dispatch* (Michigan City, IN), August 14, 1998.

———. "Rison Murder Trial to Be Delayed until Fall." *The News-Dispatch* (Michigan City, IN), January 7, 1999.

South Carolina Department of Social Services. Freeman, Eric Matthew v. Wessinger, Claire R.—Final Decree of Divorce, No. 2017DR3600318 (Family Court, York County, South Carolina, January 29, 2018).

———. Freeman, Julie McCarter v. Freeman, Eric Matthew—Final Decree of Divorce, No. 2013DR4601222 (Family Court, York County, South Carolina, September 16, 2013).

———. Hawkins, William Neal v. Hawkins, Julie Elaine—Final Decree of Divorce, No. 1999DR4601183 (Family Court, York County, South Carolina August 27, 1999).

South Central High School. *1991 Orbit Yearbook*. Union Mills, IN, 1991.

———. *Orbit Yearbook 16*. Union Mills, IN, 1978.

———. *Orbit Yearbook 22*. Union Mills, IN, 1984.

Sprecher, James. "Coroner's Certificate of Death—Janet M. Jemiolo." Indiana State Board of Health, December 9, 1978.

Staff. "Voter Turnout Surprisingly High." *The News-Dispatch* (Michigan City, IN), November 5, 1998.

SOURCES

Stafford, Harold. "Seminar to Teach Police Techniques." *The South Bend Tribune*, June 8, 1990.

State of Indiana v. James F. McWhirter—Criminal Misdemeanor, No. 46D03-9301-CM-000113 (La Porte Superior Court 3, March 22, 1993).

State of Indiana v. Jason L. Tibbs—9-24-19-2/MA: Driving While Suspended 1, No. 46D03-9403-CM-000348 (La Porte Superior Court 3, March 24, 1994).

State of Indiana v. Jason L. Tibbs—9-24-19-2/MA: Driving While Suspended 2, No. 46D03-9404-CM-000477 (La Porte Superior Court 3, April 23, 1994).

State of Indiana v. Jason L. Tibbs—9-24-19-2/MA: Driving While Suspended 3, No. 46D03-9502-CM-000193 (La Porte Superior Court 3, February 18, 1995).

State of Indiana v. Jason L. Tibbs—9-24-19-2/MA: Driving While Suspended 4, No. 46D03-9606-CM-000852 (La Porte Superior Court 3, June 18, 1996).

State of Indiana v. Jason L. Tibbs—9-24-19-2/MA: Driving While Suspended 5, No. 46D03-9607-CM-000933 (La Porte Superior Court 3, June 28, 1996).

State of Indiana v. Jason L. Tibbs—Theft D Felony, No. 46D03-0301-FD-000133 (La Porte Superior Court 3, August 29, 2003).

State of Indiana v. Jason L. Tibbs—Theft D Felony (Dismissed without prejudice), No. 46D03-0907-FD-000344 (La Porte Superior Court 3, June 28, 2012).

State of Indiana v. Jason L. Tibbs—Theft D Felony (US Currency), No. 46D03-0011-FD-001572 (La Porte Superior Court 3, August 29, 2003).

State of Indiana v. Jason Tibbs—Murder, Christine A. Kutanovski (La Porte Circuit Court, 2014).

State of Indiana v. Jason Tibbs—Murder: Deposition of Ben [*sic*] Rison, Marilyn M. Jones (La Porte Circuit Court, 2014).

State of Indiana v. Jason Tibbs—Murder: Deposition of Eric Freeman, Marilyn M. Jones (La Porte Circuit Court, 2014).

State of Indiana v. Jason Tibbs—Murder: Deposition of Raymond McCarty, Marilyn M. Jones (La Porte Circuit Court, 2014).

State of Indiana v. Jason Tibbs—Murder: Hammons Pole Barn Photos DSC_0001-0058, No. 46C01-1308-MR-278 (La Porte Circuit Court, November 7, 2014).

State of Indiana v. Jason Tibbs—Murder: Pre-Jury Conference on Motions In Limine, Christine A. Espino (La Porte Circuit Court, 2014).

State of Indiana v. McWhirter, James E.—Theft D Felony, No. 46D04-8910-CF-1496 (La Porte Superior Court 4, November 20, 1989).

State of Indiana v. Rickey Hammons—Historical Record October 13, 1999–June 25, 2009, No. 46C01-9910-CF-114 (La Porte Circuit Court, June 25, 2009).

Strengthening Forensic Science in the United States: A Path Forward. Washington, DC: National Academies Press, 2009. https://doi.org/10.17226/12589.

Sullivan, John. "Autopsy Final Report—Cassidy, Daniel Evans." South Bend Medical Foundation, November 11, 1999.

"Szilagyi Joins Race for County Prosecutor." *The South Bend Tribune*, February 19, 1998.

Szilagyi, Robert. "Szilagyi Vows to Curtail Nepotism—Letter in Voice of the People." *The La Porte County Herald-Argus*, April 24, 2010.

SUBMERGED

Szilagyi, Robert C. State of Indiana v. Jason Tibbs—Murder: Affidavit for Probable Cause, No. 46C0-1308-MR-278 (La Porte Circuit Court, August 22, 2013).

———. "Transactional Immunity Agreement." Prosecuting Attorney, 32nd Judicial Circuit, n.d.
Thomas, LeRoy R. "Certificate of Death—James McWhirter." Certificate of Death. Indiana State Department of Health, September 9, 1968.
Thorp, John. "Additional: 9304-4268-M4 Rayna Rison—John Mitchell Interview." Report Supplement. La Porte County Police Department, May 5, 1993.
———. "Additional: 9304-4268-M4 Rayna Rison—Roy West, John Proud Interview." Report Supplement. La Porte County Police Department, April 29, 1993.
———. "Additional: 9304-4268-M4 Rayna Rison—Roy West Statement (Recorded)." Report Supplement. La Porte County Police Department, May 4, 1993.
———. "Additional: 9304-4268-M4 Rayna Rison—Tom Cassidy Interview." Report Supplement. La Porte County Police Department, May 12, 1993.
"Three Are Appointed to LaPorte County Prosecutor Staff." The South Bend Tribune, December 29, 1994.
Tibbs, Jason. "Jason Tibbs Love Letters to Rayna Rison," April 1991.
"Transactional Immunity for Witnesses—FindLaw." Last updated February 15, 2019. https:// www.findlaw.com/criminal/criminal-procedure/transactional-immunity-for-witnesses.html.
Troyer, Ronald L. In the Matter of Jason L. Tibbs, A Child Alleged to be a Delinquent— Pre-Dispositional Investigation, No. 46C01-9108-JD-151 (La Porte Circuit Court, November 15, 1991).
Trueblood, Larry D. "Rayna Rison Recovery—Personel [sic] at Scene." Supplement Report. La Porte County Police Department, April 27, 1993.
Tully, Matthew. "Crime Show Takes on Rison Case." Post-Tribune (IN), March 4, 1993.
———. "Scores Help Search for Teen." Post-Tribune (IN), March 28, 1993.
Tully, Matthew, and Lori Caldwell. "Anglers Find Body near Stream." Post-Tribune (IN), April 28, 1993.
"Two Use a Pen to Rob 41-Year-Old of $85." The South Bend Tribune, June 25, 1995.
"Union Mills Postmaster, McCarty, Dies." The South Bend Tribune, January 15, 1978.
Vale, Kellyn. "La Porte, a City Rich in History." La Porte County Life, January 14, 2019. https:// laportecounty.life/article/la-porte-a-city-rich-in-history/.
Walsh, Steve. "This Special Unit Gets Respect." The Vidette-Messenger of Porter County, February 10, 1991.
"Wedding Rings Out." The Vidette-Messenger of Porter County, November 21, 1972. https:// www.newspapers.com/image/333779557/.
Weliver, Geoffrey. "Child Molesting: Victim: Rayna Lynn Rison (13), Accused: Ray McCarty (24)." Case Report, December 18, 1989.
———. "Re: Rayna Rison Case—Chris Lewis Tip to Pavolka at 1645 Hrs about McWhirter Pickup Purchase Directed to Sgt. Hahn." Intelligence Report, July 2, 1994.
Wells Fargo Bank, NA v. Penny S. Scarborough, No. 46D02-0912-MF-000096 (La Porte Superior Court 2, June 22, 2010).
West, Roy, Sr. "RE: Individual You Saw on March 26, 1993," email, August 31, 2022.

458

SOURCES

Wilkerson, Jerry. "Neighborhood Butcher to Legendary Major League Baseball Club Owner." *The Arizona Daily Star*, January 31, 2001.

Williamson, Allen. "Murder Investigation, Rayna Lynn Rison—Eric Freeman Statement, March 18, 2008." Taped Statement Transcript. Indiana State Police, March 18, 2008.

———. "Murder Investigation, Rayna Lynn Rison—Eric Freeman Statement, June 27, 2013." Taped Statement Transcript. Indiana State Police, June 27, 2013.

WSBT-TV, Channel 22. "Raymond McCarty Arraignment—Video." June 1, 1998.

ENDNOTES

PROLOGUE

i   Post-Tribune Staff, "Mill Creek Man Faces '93 Charges."
ii   Sobecki, "Rison Murder Suspect Freed."
iii   Flynn, "Book: Former Janitor May Be Rayna Rison's Killer."
iv   "La Porte, Indiana."
v   Vale, "La Porte, a City Rich in History."
vi   Wilkerson, "Neighborhood Butcher to Legendary MLB Club Owner."
vii   Przybyla, "Oprah Quitting LaPorte."
viii   Tully, "Crime Show."
ix   Tully.
x   Gonzalez, "Rison Family Reacts."
xi   Maddux, "Tibbs Gets 40 Years."

RAY AND RAYNA

1   Paul F. Boston Middle School, *Bostonian Yearbook* 1988.
2   Paul F. Boston Middle School.
3   Richards, "LaPorte Casino Roller Rink."
4   Levin, Matthew Elser Interview #1 (February 18, 2023).
5   Boyd, "Rison Murder Report," (August 1993), 28.
6   "Raymond C. McCarty—Locations."
7   Levin, M. Elser 1.
8   Boyd, "Rison Murder Report," (August 1993), 28.
9   Bernth, "Interview with Rison Family," (April 29, 1993), 1.
10   Levin, M. Elser 1.
11   Keith, "Jennifer Lynn McCleland FBI Interview," (April 1993), 3.
12   La Porte High School, LPHS 1984 *Yearbook*.
13   Levin, M. Elser 1.
14   Levin, Gayla Moreau Interview (July 2022).
15   Levin, M. Elser 1.
16   Hahn, Tina Church Interview (January 1996).
17   "Farrell McCleland 1950 Census Report."
18   Smith, "Medical Death Certificate—Farrell McCleland."
19   Rolling Prairie High School, RPHS 1960 *Yearbook*, 16.
20   La Porte High School, LPHS 1962 *Yearbook*, 157.
21   "Bennie and Karen Rison Marriage Certificate."
22   "Obituary—Ernest Rison Sr."
23   Alexander, "Ernest Rison Certificate of Death."
24   "Bennie Rison LinkedIn Profile."
25   "Bride-Elect Given Shower in South Bend," 4.
26   "Bennie Rison Addresses." US Public Records Index, 1950–1993.
27   "Bennie Rison LinkedIn Profile."
28   La Porte High School, LPHS 1984 *Yearbook*, 43.
29   La Porte High School, 179.
30   "Union Mills Postmaster, McCarty, Dies," 44.
31   "Obituary—Carolyn McCarty."
32   Levin, G. Moreau.
33   McDermott, "Assessment for Raymond C. McCarty," (February 1991).
34   Levin, Ray McCarty Elementary School Teacher Interview (November 2022).
35   McDermott, "Assessment for R. McCarty."
36   "U. M. Postmaster, McCarty, Dies."
37   McDermott, "Assessment for R. McCarty."
38   South Central High School, SCHS 1984 *Yearbook*, 30.
39   South Central High School, 22.
40   Boyd, "Rison Murder Report," (August 1993), 11.
41   South Central High School, 47.
42   South Central High School, 22.
43   McDermott, "Assessment for R. McCarty."
44   "R. McCarty—Locations."
45   Cooper, "Arrest for Battery—Ray McCarty," 1984.
46   Baldini, Raymond McCarty Restitution, 1984.
47   "Lori A. McCarty Address," 1984.
48   Dixon, "Record of Marriage—McCarty to Rison."
49   McDermott, "Assessment for R. McCarty."
50   Hahn, Interview with Allen Barkow (May 1993).
51   Boyd, "Rison Murder Report," (August 1993), 22.
52   Boyd, "Rison Murder Report," (February 1994), 3.
53   Levin, Gary Marshall Interview (July 11, 2022).
54   Koehn, "Child Molesting, Accused: Raymond C. McCarty," (December 1989).
55   Weliver, "Child Molesting: Victim: Rayna Lynn Rison (13), Accused: Ray McCarty (24)," (December 18, 1989).
56   Bernth, "Rison Family Interview."
57   Weliver, "Child Molesting."
58   Rison, "To Matt Elser from Rayna Rison," March 18, 1993.
59   Airy, "Airy Supplement (Started April 7, 2008)," 3.
60   Levin, M. Elser 1.
61   "Births—Adrienne McCarty," 11.
62   McDermott, "Assessment for R. McCarty."
63   "Births—A. McCarty."
64   Boyd, "Rison Murder Report," (February 1994), 15–16.
65   Weliver, "Child Molesting."
66   Rison, "To Matt Elser."
67   Weliver, "Lewis Tip about McWhirter Pickup Purchase."
68   Koehn, "Molesting, Accused: R. McCarty."
69   Gaekle, "Certificate of Death—Hunter C. McCarty."
70   Koehn, "Molesting, Accused: R. McCarty."
71   Scherer, "Child Molesting Report, Accused: Raymond C. McCarty (December 18, 1989).
72   "Indiana Code, 1989 Sentences."
73   Bernth, "Rison Family Interview."
74   Keith, "J. McCleland FBI Interview."
75   McDermott, "Assessment for R. McCarty."

76 Rison, "To Matt Elser."
77 Bernth, "Rison Family Interview"; Boyd, "Rison Murder Report," (May 1994).
78 Haman and Roth, "Cheryl K. VanSchoyck FBI Interview," (March 1993).
79 Bergerson, Raymond C. McCarty—Statement of Plea Agreement (1990).
80 Gettinger, Raymond C. McCarty Order of Probation (1991).
81 Levin, Matthew Elser Interview #2 (February 27, 2023).
82 Marovich, "Missing Person Report," (March 31, 1993).
83 Hahn, Darold Willis Interview (July 1993).
84 McDermott, "Assessment for R. McCarty."
85 Levin, M. Elser 1.
86 Bernth, "Rison Family Interview."
87 Pintal, "Ray McCarty Discharge for Non-Compliance," (September 9, 1991).
88 Balthazor, "Ray McCarty Argumentative Behavior with Therapists," (December 24, 1991).
89 Balthazor, "Ray McCarty Discontinued from the Psychology Associates Program," (July 27, 1992).
90 Armstrong, Raymond C. McCarty—Petition Terminating Probation, (January 1993).
91 Levin, M. Elser 1.
92 Levin, M. Elser 2.
93 Jozaitis, "Region Design Co. [original mascot: slicer]," (September 2018).
94 La Porte High School, LPHS 1985 Yearbook.
95 Levin, M. Elser 2.
96 Bernth, "Rison Family Interview."
97 Haman and Roth, "VanSchoyck FBI Interview."
98 Boyd, "Rison Murder Report," (April 1995), 2.
99 Automobile Catalog. "1984 Ford LTD Specs."
100 Schoff, Leah Pepples Interview (April 1993).
101 Boyd, "Rison Murder Report," (April 1995).
102 Levin, M. Elser 2.
103 Cains, "Missing Person Report: JS Interview," (March 1993).
104 Levin, M. Elser 2.
105 Bernth, "Rison Family Interview."
106 Bernard, "Burglary—Resident, Accused: Jason Tibbs," (July 1991).
107 "Obituaries—Arland F. Farnsley," 19.
108 Farnsley, Jason L. Tibbs—Victim Impact Statement (December 17, 1991).
109 Bernard, "Burglary—J. Tibbs."
110 Farnsley, J. Tibbs—Victim Impact Statement.
111 Troyer, Jason L. Tibbs, Alleged Delinquent—Pre-Dispositional Investigation, (November 15, 1991).
112 Troyer.
113 Tibbs, "Jason Tibbs Love Letters to Rayna Rison," (April 1991).
114 Troyer, Tibbs—Pre-Dispositional Investigation.
115 Haman and Roth, "VanSchoyck FBI Interview."
116 Elser, "M. Elser Love Letter," February 1993.
117 Haman and Roth, "Lisa Dyer FBI Interview," (April 1993).
118 Levin, M. Elser 1.
119 Levin.
120 Schoff, "Lisa Dyer Interview," (April 1993).
121 Hahn, "Interview with Sharon Friend," (March 1994).
122 Keith, "J. McCleland FBI Interview."
123 Rison, "To Matt Elser."
124 Boyd, "Rison Murder Report," (August 1993), 46.
125 Hahn, "Interview with S. Friend."
126 Hahn, "Interview with Patricia Walters," (March 1994).
127 Cains, "Missing Person: JS Interview."
128 Levin, G. Moreau.

LOST AND FOUND

1 Boyd, "Rison Murder Report," (August 1993), 28.
2 Roth, "Dr. Gerald N. Wagner FBI Interview," (March 1993).
3 Haman and Roth, "VanSchoyck FBI Interview."
4 Bernth, "Rison Family Interview."
5 Roth, "Wagner FBI Interview."
6 Boyd, "Rison Murder Report," (February 1994).
7 Haman and Roth, "VanSchoyck FBI Interview."
8 Levin, M. Elser 1.
9 Boyd, "Rison Murder Report," (August 1993), 29.
10 Levin, M. Elser 1.
11 Hahn, "Interview with Richard Piechnik II," (May 1993); Hahn, "Interview with Wendy Rison," (May 1993).
12 Levin, M. Elser 1.
13 Hahn, Church Interview.
14 Levin, M. Elser 1.
15 Roth, "Wagner FBI Interview."
16 Hemphill, "Missing Person Report: Rison, Rayna Lynn," (March 26, 1993).
17 Tully, "Scores Help Search for Teen," (March 28,1993).
18 Mitchell, "Missing Person: Rison, Rayna—Calming down B. Rison, Interviews with M. Ruminski, M. Elser, J. Tibbs, (March 27, 1993)."
19 Gaekle, "Interview with B. Rison, W. Zeman," (April 1993).
20 Mitchell, "MP: Rison, R.—Calming down B. Rison," (March 27, 1993.)
21 Russell, "Kingsbury Ordnance Plant," (July 8, 2017).
22 Schoff, "Johnson Interview," (March 1993).
23 Hahn, "Elizabeth York Statement," (March 1993).
24 Shortt, "Assistance Rendered—Victim Rayna L. Rison," (March 27, 1993).
25 Stafford, "Seminar to Teach Police Techniques," (June 8, 1990).
26 Levin, Jim Jackson Interview (November 2022).
27 Hahn, "E. York Statement."
28 Hahn, "Interview with Austin York," (March 1993).
29 Hahn.
30 "2 Men Reportedly Seen," (March 30, 1993).
31 Pavolka, "Pickup, Sedan Sighting, March 26, 1993."
32 Pavolka, "Beth York and Sons," (July 1993); Pavolka, "Beth York," (August 1993).
33 Levin, G. Marshall.
34 "517 Haviland St.," 2022.
35 Schoff, "Lori McCarty (Sister) Interview," (March 28, 1993).
36 Mitchell, "MP: Rison, R.—Calming down B. Rison," (March 27, 1993.)
37 Schoff, "L. McCarty Interview."
38 Hahn, Church Interview.
39 Schoff, "L. McCarty Interview."
40 Keith, "Lori Ann McCarty FBI Interview," (March 30, 1993).
41 Bernth, "Rison Family Interview."
42 Hemphill, "Rison, Rayna Lynn—Various Interviews," (March 27, 1993).
43 Mitchell, "MP: Rison, R.—Calming down B. Rison," (March 27, 1993.)
44 Hahn, "Interview with Jason Tibbs," (March 31, 1993).
45 Humble, "Matthew Elser & Jason Tibbs," Polygraph Results Analysis (April 1, 1993).
46 Hahn, "Interview with J. Tibbs."
47 Levin, V. Michael Drayton Interview (October 2022).
48 Miller, "Jason Tibbs Statement," (March 31, 1993).
49 Boyd, "Rison Murder Report," (August 1993), 13.
50 Hahn, "Interview with Matthew Elser," (March 31, 1993).
51 Hemphill, "Rison, R.—Interviews," (March 27, 1993).
52 Keith, "Bennie Ray Rison FBI Interview," (March 29, 1993).
53 Keith, "Bennie Ray Rison FBI Interview 2," (March 31, 1993).
54 Keith, "Mark A. Stick FBI Interview," (March 31, 1993).
55 Keith, "Raymond Clayton McCarty FBI Interview," (April 1, 1993).
56 Levin, Clifford Sheeler Interview (November 2022).
57 Keith, "R. McCarty FBI Interview."
58 Keith, "M. Stick FBI Interview."
59 Hahn, "Interview with Mary Smutzer," (March 1994).
60 Keith, "R. McCarty FBI Interview."
61 Hahn, "Interview with Raymond McCarty," (April 1, 1993).
62 Keith, "R. McCarty FBI Interview."
63 Hahn, "Interview with R. McCarty."
64 Keith and Hanna, "Raymond Clayton McCarty Interview," (April 2, 1993).
65 Hahn, Church Interview.
66 Thorp, "Roy West, John Proud Interview," (April 1993).
67 Marovich, "Garry and Lois Bucher Interview," (March 31, 1993).
68 Keith and Hanna, "R. McCarty FBI Interview."
69 Tully, "Crime Show."
70 Nicholas, "Teams Tackle Rison Case," (April 1993); Levin, M. Elser 1.

71 Levin, G. Moreau.
72 Keith, "Bennie Ray Rison FBI Interview 3," (April 2, 1993).
73 Levin, J. Jackson.
74 Levin.
75 Ames, "Located Jacket and Contents," (April 1993).
76 Levin, J. Jackson.
77 Levin, Jennifer Lindborg Wickstrom Interview (September 2022).
78 Nicholas, "Officer Finds Rison's Jacket . . . Reward Fund," (April 1993).
79 Tully and Caldwell, "Anglers Find Body," (April 1993).
80 Nicholas, "Asphyxiation ruled in death," (April 29, 1993).
81 Trueblood, "Rayna Rison Recovery—Personel [sic] at Scene," (April 27, 1993).
82 State of Indiana v. Jason Tibbs, Kutanovski (2014), at 255–56.
83 La Porte County Sheriff, "McWhirter, James F.—RAP Sheet," (June 2022).
84 Miller and Schoff, "Rison, Rayna Lynn—Body Recovery," (April 27, 1993).
85 Schoff, "Interview—L. Pepples."
86 Boyd, "Rison Murder Report," (February 1994), 1.
87 Levin, J. Jackson.
88 Trueblood, "Personel [sic] at Scene," (April 1993).
89 Levin, J. Jackson.
90 Miller and Schoff, "Rison, R.—Body Recovery."

THE CASE AGAINST RAY

1 Boyd, "Rison Murder Report," (August 1993), 2.
2 Levin, Arland Boyd Interview 1 (September 2022).
3 Heline, "Wedding Rings Out," (November 21, 1972).
4 Boyd, "Rison Murder Report," (August 1993), 2.
5 Brown, "Police: Was Rison Drowned or Strangled," (April 1993).
6 Brown.
7 Boyd, "Rison Murder Report," (August 1993), 2.
8 Gettinger, Search Warrant [First]—Raymond McCarty (April 1993).
9 Boyd, "Rison Murder Report," (August 1993), 3.
10 Crass, "Execution of Search Warrants 517 Haviland St.," (April 1993).
11 Gettinger, Search Warrant [First]—R. McCarty.
12 Hahn, "Consent to Search," (May 1998).
13 Hahn, "Interview with Jeanette Zellers," (March 1994).
14 Ames, "Items Collected from McCarty Datsun," (April 1993).
15 Boyd, "Rison Murder Report," (February 1994), 3.
16 Levin, Arland Boyd Interview 2 (October 2022).
17 Deedrick, "Communications," (May 19, 1998).
18 Kemker, "Search Warrant—Pontiac Silver '88 Sunbird," (April 1993).
19 Levin, Arland Boyd Interview 2 (October 2022).
20 Boyd, "Rison Murder Report," (August 1993), 11–20.
21 Gaekle, "Interview with B. Rison, W. Zeman."
22 Gettinger, Raymond C. McCarty Sentencing Order (1991).
23 AP Wire Services, "Slain LaPorte Teen-Ager Buried," (May 1993).
24 Jones, "Rayna Rison Remembered," (May 1993).
25 Lu, "The Datsun B210 Is an Unforgettable Classic," (June 2022).
26 State of Indiana v. Jason Tibbs, Deposition of Ben[nie] Rison, Jones (2014).
27 Marovich, "Interview with Trudy Hahn," (September 1994).
28 Thorp, "R. West, J. Proud Interview," (April 1993).
29 Thorp, "Roy West Statement," (May 1993).
30 Hahn, "Interview with Pam Rosebaum," (March 1993).
31 Miller, "Bryan Durham Interview," (May 1993).
32 Boyd, "Rison Murder Report," (August 1993), 32–33; Hahn, "Interview with Rene Gazarkiewicz," (April 1993).
33 Boyd, "Rison Murder Report," (August 1993), 34; Arndt, "Interview with Kim Hackney," (March 1993).
34 Kemker, "Witness Interview: Val Eilers," (May 1993).
35 Hahn, "Interview with Sue Casper," (July 1993).
36 Levin, A. Boyd 1.
37 Boyd, "Rison Murder Report," (August 1993), 36–42.
38 Levin, A. Boyd 2.
39 Schoff, "Lori McCarty Call at 7:30 p.m.," (May 11, 1993).
40 Hahn, "Interview with Charles E. Allen 3," (February 7, 1994).
41 Thorp, "Tom Cassidy Interview," (May 1993).
42 Hahn, "Subpoena of Telephone Records," (May 1993).

43 Boyd, "Rison Murder Report," (August 1993), 42.
44 Cains et al., "Stakeout of 517 Haviland."
45 Gettinger, Search Warrant—Charles E. Allen (April 1998).
46 Hahn, "Interview with C. Allen 1."
47 Boyd, "Rison Murder Report," (August 1993), 21–25.
48 Levin, A. Boyd 2.
49 Boyd, "Rison Murder Report," (August 1993), 26.
50 Nicholas, "Prosecutor Denies."
51 Hoover, "Autopsy Report—Rison, Rayna," (April 1993).
52 Hoover, "Autopsy—Rison, R."
53 Hoover, "Autopsy—Rison, R."
54 Medtox Laboratories, "Toxicology—Rayna Rison," (July 1993).
55 Hoover, "To: Hahn Re: Rison Toxicology," (May 11, 1994).
56 Hahn, "Interview with Matthew Elser," (March 1993).
57 Medtox Laboratories, "Toxicology—R. Rison."
58 Hoover, "To: Hahn Re: Rison Toxicology."
59 Ames, "Items for FBI Lab Analysis," (May 25, 1993).
60 Deutsch, "Evidence Gets a Hair," (July 1995).
61 Margolick, "After 92 Days," (July 1995).
62 Hahn, "FBI Update from Doug Deedrick," (June 11, 1993).
63 Gettinger, (Second) Search Warrant—Raymond C. McCarty (June 1993).
64 Gettinger, at 3–4.
65 Hahn, "Interview with J. Zellers," (March 1994).
66 Deedrick, "Communications."
67 Hahn, "Interview with John Yates," (June 1993).
68 Crass, "Rison Homicide: Interview with John Pursely," (April 1993).
69 Hahn, "Interview with J. Yates."
70 Crass, "Rison Homicide: Interview with Scott McGovern," (May 1993).
71 Boyd, "Rison Murder Report," (February 1994).
72 Boyd, "Rison Murder Report," (August 1993), 42–48.
73 Hahn, "Information Reference L. McCarty," (July 1993).
74 Deedrick, "Communications."
75 Boyd, "Rison Murder Report," (August 1993), 47.
76 Levin, G. Moreau.
77 Boyd, "Rison Murder Report," (October 1994), 1–3; Levin, G. Moreau.
78 Hahn, "Interview with Paula McCleland," (May 1994).
79 Boyd, "Rison Murder Report," (May 1994), 6.
80 Boyd, "Rison Murder Report," (February 1994), 3; Boyd, "Rison Murder Report," (May 1994), 7; Boyd, "Rison Murder Report," (October 1994), 2; Hahn, "Interview with Lisa R. McKinney," (April 1994); Hahn, "Interview with Gary Marshall," (April 1993); Miller, "J. Tibbs Statement."
81 Hahn, "Interview with D. Willis."
82 Hahn, "Interview with R. Rosenbaum," (August 1993); Hahn, "Interview with C. Allen 3."
83 Boyd, "Rison Murder Report," (May 1994), 4–7.
84 Hahn, "Interview with Michael A. Kepplin," (February 1994).
85 Hahn, "Interview with Tina Townsend," (June 1993).
86 Schoff, "Interview with L. Pepples."
87 Boyd, "Rison Murder Report," (February 1994), 1.
88 Hahn, "Interview with Robin Dingman," (May 1993).
89 Hahn, "Billy Smith and Video Store Time Sheet," (May 1993).
90 Hahn, "Interview with J. Zellers."
91 Hahn, "Interview with Brenda Pegg," (March 1994).
92 Boyd, "Rison Murder Report," (February 1994), 4–7.
93 Hahn, "Interview with Sheila Albertson," (March 1994).
94 Boyd, "Rison Murder Report," (February 1994), 8–10.
95 Hahn, "Interview with P. Walters."
96 Levin, A. Boyd 2.
97 Hahn, "Interview with P. Walters."
98 Boyd, "Rison Murder Report," (March 1994).
99 Boyd, "Rison Murder Report," (February 1994), 3–5.
100 Boyd, "Rison Murder Report," (March 1994), 1–4.
101 Hahn, "Interview with C. Allen."
102 Rison, "To: Parents and Friends—Request," (January 1994).
103 Hahn, "Interview with B. Rison," (January 1994).
104 Boyd, "Rison Murder Report," (May 1994), 3–4.
105 Deedrick, "O-Mega Stun Gun," (September 20, 1993).
106 Boyd, "Rison Murder Report," (May 1994), 4.
107 Boyd, "Rison Murder Report," (March 1994), 3–4.
108 Levin, G. Moreau.
109 Schoff, "L. McCarty Interview."

110   Hahn, Church Interview.
111   Walsh, "This Special Unit Gets Respect," (February 1991); Smith, "On the Lookout," (April 1993); Pliske, "Number of Shootings Concerns Councilman," (December 1982).
112   Levin, A. Boyd 1.
113   Levin, Scott Duerring Interview (April 2023); Schoff, "Interview with Judy Freeman Re: Ed Logan," (September 1993).
114   Levin, A. Boyd 1.
115   Nicholas, "Hedge, Herrbach Win Primaries," (May 1994).
116   Marovich, "Interview with T. Hahn."
117   Boyd, "Rison Murder Report," (October 1994), 4.
118   Boyd, 5.
119   Boyd, 5.
120   Boyd, 1–2; Hahn, "Interviews with 'Nancy' and Her Parents," (October 1994).
121   Nicholas, "Hitchhiker Sought as Alibi," (November 1994).
122   Boyd, "Rison Murder Report," (April 1995), 7–8; Hahn, "Interview with Andre Bridges," (November 1994).
123   Nicholas, "Hedge New Prosecutor," (November 1994).
124   Levin, S. Duerring.
125   Levin, "Calculation of Known Rayna Rison Interviews," (December 2022).
126   Levin, A. Boyd 2.
127   Levin.
128   Levin, S. Duerring.
129   Levin, A. Boyd 2.
130   "Obituary for Gene Samuelson (January 2021)"; Maddux, "LaPorte Police Chief Reflects," (December 1995).
131   Maddux, "LaPorte Police Chief Reflects."
132   Hahn, Church Interview.
133   Rison, R. Gazarkiewicz Interview.
134   Hahn, "Interview with Mary Beth Pienta," (July 1995).
135   Rison, R. Gazarkiewicz Interview.
136   Porter, "Prosecutor Attacks T. Church," (July 1998).
137   The South Bend Tribune, "Murphy Worker Files Job Bias Suit," (March 1977).
138   Hahn, Church Interview.
139   Bradford, "Psychic Says," (October 1995).
140   Levin, J. Jackson.
141   Hahn, Church Interview.
142   Hahn, "Information Harassment McCarty, Raymond," (January 1996).
143   Hahn, Church Interview.
144   Schoff, "L. McCarty Interview," (July 1993).
145   Levin, Confidential La Porte Investigator Interview (June 2023).
146   Bland, "Detectives Try Psychics," (February 1996).
147   Bland.
148   "LaPorte Police Seek Leads," (August 1997).
149   Hahn, "A/V Interview with Charles E. Allen," (December 1997).
150   Levin, S. Duerring.
151   Deedrick, "Communications."
152   Nicholas, "Brother-in-Law Enters Innocent Plea," (June 1998).
153   Deedrick, "Communications."
154   Gettinger, Search Warrant—C. Allen (April 1998).
155   Hahn, "Body Search Warrant for Charles Allen," (April 1998).
156   Nicholas, "Prosecutor Denies."
157   Levin, S. Duerring.
158   "Lang Ready for Next Chapter," (December 2014).
159   Brown, "Grand Juries Missing in Action," (November 1998).
160   Levin, S. Duerring.
161   Deedrick, "Communications."
162   Keene and Levin, In with the Devil, (New York: St. Martin's Griffin, 2011).
163   Everette, W. M., Special Agent, "FBI Analysis of Hall Fingerprints (December 1994)," December 21, 1994.
164   Hahn, "L. Hall Background," (December 1994).
165   Keene and Levin, In with the Devil.
166   Hall, "Handwritten List of His Potential Victims."
167   Keene and Levin, In with the Devil.
168   Barton, "Niles Teen's Killer Resentenced to Life," (February 2000).
169   Flynn, "Former Janitor May Be Rayna Rison's Killer," (June 2010).

170   Everette, "Re: Larry Dewayne Hall," (December 1994).
171   Maddux, "Rison Case—Five Years Later," (April 1998).
172   Sobecki, "Grand Jury Called in Rison Case," (May 1998).
173   "2501 S Taylor Rd Transfer History," (March 1998).
174   Nicholas, "Brother-in-Law Charged in '93 Death," (May 1998).
175   Nicholas, "Lawyer Claims McCarty Innocent," (May 1998).
176   Nicholas, "Grand Jury Convened," (May 1998).
177   Jenkins, "In Indiana, It's a Felony Not 'an Affair,'" (June 1998).
178   Nicholas, "Brother-in-Law Enters Plea."
179   Sobecki, "Arrest Made in Rison Case," (May 29, 1998).
180   The Associated Press, "5-Year Investigation," (May 29, 1998).
181   Nicholas, "Brother-in-Law Charged," (May 1998).
182   Maddux, "Rison Murder Suspect," (June 1998).
183   WSBT-TV, Channel 22, "Raymond McCarty Arraignment—Video," (June 1, 1998).
184   Maddux, "Rison Murder Suspect Arraigned," (June 1998).
185   Rogers, Motion for Gag Order (June 1, 1998).
186   Maddux, "Rison Murder Suspect Arraigned."
187   Sobecki, "Beckman Edges Hedge," (November 1998).
188   Sobecki, "Rison Murder Suspect Freed."

THE CASE THAT SHOULD HAVE BEEN MADE AGAINST RAY

1   Hahn, "Interview with Mark Stick," (April 1993).
2   Levin, C. Sheeler.
3   Palmer, Foundry Practice (New York: Wiley, 1911).
4   Levin, C. Sheeler.
5   "PubChem Compound Summary—Isopropyl Alcohol."
6   "Hill and Griffith Isopropyl Alcohol Purity."
7   "PubChem—Isopropyl Alcohol."
8   Levin, Chris Wallen Interview (August 2022).
9   Ford et al., Clinical Toxicology (Philadelphia: Saunders, 2000), 669–770.
10   Macht, "Isopropyl Alcohol, a Convenient Laboratory Anesthetic for Cats," (November, 1921).
11   Ford et al., Clinical Toxicology, 669.
12   Ford et al., 770.
13   Levin, C. Wallen.
14   Keith, "M. Stick FBI Interview."
15   Boyd, "Rison Murder Report," (August 1993), 13.
16   Boyd, "Rison Murder Report," (March 1994), 12.
17   Boyd, "Rison Murder Report," (October 1994), 3.
18   Boyd, 3.
19   Levin, Lucas Scarborough Interview (November 2022).
20   South Central High School, SCHS 1978 Yearbook.
21   Levin, R. McCarty teacher (November 2022).
22   Levin, G. Marshall.
23   La Porte County Sheriff, "Scarborough, Scott L.—RAP Sheet," (July 2022).
24   "Obituary—Gayle Scarborough," (September 1984).
25   Alevizos, In Re: Estate of Scarborough (March 2011); Wells Fargo v. Scarborough (June 2010).
26   Levin, Scott Scarborough girlfriend 1 Interview (October 2022).
27   Levin.
28   Levin, L. Scarborough.
29   Levin, Scott Scarborough girlfriend "Robin" Interview (September 2022).
30   Morse, "Domestic Battery—Scott Scarborough," (August 2008).
31   Levin, L. Scarborough.
32   Morse, "Domestic Battery—S. Scarborough."
33   Alevizos, Scott Scarborough—Charges: Strangulation, Battery Domestic, Battery (January 2009).
34   Beckman, Scott Scarborough—Warrant of Arrest (August 2008).
35   Levin, L. Scarborough.
36   Levin, S. Scarborough girlfriend "Robin."
37   Levin, L. Scarborough.
38   Levin, Barbara H. Elliott Interview (September 2022).
39   Levin, S. Scarborough girlfriend 1.
40   Levin, S. Scarborough girlfriend "Robin."
41   Boyd, "Rison Murder Report," (August 1993), 25–26; Boyd, "Rison Murder Report," (March 1994), 10–11; Boyd, "Rison Murder Report," (June 1994), 1–2.
42   Boyd, "Rison Murder Report," (February 1994), 1.
43   Boyd, "Rison Murder Report," (August 1993), 22–23.

ENDNOTES

44 Hahn, "Interview with C. Allen 3."
45 Miller, "B. Durham Interview."
46 Bartlett Arborist Supply, "Solidur Felin Chainsaw Pants."
47 Levin, John Proud Interview (September 2022).
48 Thorp, "R. West Statement."
49 "Jail Management Booking Form—Scott L. Scarborough," (January 1996); "LaPorte County Prisoner's Record—Scott L. Scarborough," (April 1989).
50 "LaPorte County Prisoner's Record—Scott L. Scarborough Mug Shot," (April 1989).
51 West, "RE: Individual You Saw," email (August 2022).
52 Levin, L. Scarborough.
53 Aftowski, "Stakeout of 517 Haviland," (April 30, 1993).
54 Levin, L. Scarborough.
55 King, "Shannon Siddall Interview," (April 1993).
56 Rison, R. Gazarkiewicz Interview.
57 La Porte County Sheriff, "McWhirter, James F.—RAP Sheet," (June 2022).
58 Essling, "Certificate of Death—Barbara Helen McWhirter," (April 2009); Thomas, "Certificate of Death—James McWhirter," (September 1968).
59 Levin, James McWhirter classmate Interview (October 2022).
60 La Porte County Sheriff, "McWhirter—RAP Sheet."
61 "Obituary—Stanley Salat," (November 1995).
62 Bazemore, "La Porte County Prisoner's Record—James F. McWhirter," (May 1980).
63 "Obituary—Stanley Salat."
64 Anderson, "Record of Marriage—McWhirter to Salat," (December 1976).
65 Rison, R. Gazarkiewicz Interview.
66 La Porte County Sheriff, "McWhirter—RAP Sheet."
67 "1408 D St. Specs and Transfer History," (March 1998); "B. McWhirter Address," US Public Records Index, 1950–1993, Volume 1; Essling, "Certificate of Death—B. McWhirter."
68 Rison, R. Gazarkiewicz Interview.
69 Indiana v. McWhirter, James E.—Theft D Felony (November 1989).
70 Rison, R. Gazarkiewicz Interview.
71 La Porte County Sheriff, "McWhirter—RAP Sheet."
72 "Two Use a Pen to Rob," (June 1995).
73 Maddux, "House Struck by Motorist," (March 2009).
74 The South Bend Tribune, "Shooting case due for probe," (August 1981).
75 La Porte County Sheriff, "McWhirter—RAP Sheet."
76 "Obituary—Stanley Salat."
77 Indiana v. Tibbs, Kutanovski, at 262.
78 Rison, R. Gazarkiewicz Interview.
79 Boyd, "Rison Murder Report," (March 1994)," 3.
80 Boyd, "Rison Murder Report," (August 1993), 24.
81 State of Indiana v. James F. McWhirter—Criminal Misdemeanor (March 1993); "Elmer Jerry Shreve—Locations."
82 Weliver, "Lewis Tip about McWhirter Pickup Purchase."
83 Hahn, "Interview with C. Allen 3"; Hahn, "Interview with R. Rosenbaum"; Hahn, "Interview with D. Willis."
84 Hahn, "Interview with D. Willis."
85 La Porte County Sheriff, "McWhirter—RAP Sheet."
86 Levin, A. Boyd 2.
87 Hahn, "Interview with R. Dingman"; Hahn, "Interview with Karen Rison," (May 1993); Hahn, "Interview with Julie Sims," (March 1994); Hahn, "Interview with B. Pegg"; Hahn, "Interview with J. Zellers."
88 Nicholas, "Brother-in-Law Charged."
89 Hahn, "Interview with P. Walters."
90 Boyd, "Rison Murder Report," (March 1994), 15.
91 Levin, G. Moreau.
92 Boyd, "Rison Murder Report," (March 1994), 10.
93 Boyd, "Rison Murder Report," (October 1994), 2.
94 Levin, G. Moreau.
95 Keeling, "To: John Lake," (April 11, 1999).
96 Marovich, "Tip Called in at 7:30 p.m.," (March 1993).
97 Hahn, Church Interview.
98 Levin, A. Boyd 2.
99 Levin, G. Moreau.
100 Hahn, Church Interview.

101 Boyd, "Rison Murder Report," (August 1993), 40.
102 Levin, J. Jackson.
103 Levin, S. Scarborough girlfriend "Robin."
104 Hahn, "Interview with B. Pegg."
105 Boyd, "Rison Murder Report," (March 1994), 9.
106 Boyd, 6.
107 Levin, J. Jackson.
108 Thorp, "John Mitchell Interview," (May 1993).
109 Marovich, "G. & L. Interview."
110 Keith, "L. McCarty FBI Interview."
111 Miller, "J. Tibbs Statement."
112 Levin, A. Boyd 2.
113 "Obituary—Douglas McGarvey," (September 2017).
114 Bishop, "Re: A Few Questions about Doug McGarvey," (November 15, 2022).
115 Ianson, "Rison, Rayna L.—Doug McGarvey Tip," (March 29, 1993).
116 Bishop, "Questions about D. McGarvey."
117 Dettmer, "Ex-Finley Estate," (October 2001).
118 Pavolka, "Richard Sarvis, Brent Glassman, Gerald and Diane Keehn," (September 1993).
119 Haman and Roth, "VanSchoyck FBI Interview."
120 Indiana v. Tibbs, Kutanovski, at 316.
121 Levin, J. Lindborg Wickstrom.
122 Thorp, "J. Mitchell."

LIFTING THE STIGMA

1   Sobecki, "Rison Murder Suspect Freed."
2   Maddux, "Stigma of Murder," (August, 1999).
3   Our View, "Murder Charge Restores Community Confidence," (June 1998).
4   Levin, La Porte County Attorney 3 Interview (November 2023).
5   Sobecki, "Rison Murder Suspect Freed."
6   Levin, LPC Attorney 1 Interview (November 2023).
7   "Obituary for Robert J. 'Rob' Beckman; Tribute," (December 2019).
8   "Beckman Seeks Death Penalty."
9   Mair, "Beckman Asks 100-Year Sentence."
10 Flynn, "Beckman on Drug Issues."
11 LaFrance, "Beckman on 'at-Risk' Teens."
12 Haverstock Funeral Chapel and Cremation, "R. Beckman Tribute."
13 Duran, "Beckman's Experience."
14 "Hedge Appoints Beckmans."
15 Brown, "Grand Juries Missing (November 1998)."
16 Schelling, "Hedge Fires Beckman."
17 Levin, S. Duerring (April 2023).
18 Nicholas, "Beckman on Full-Time Prosecutors."
19 Levin, S. Duerring (April 2023).
20 Schelling, "Hedge Fires Beckman."
21 Levin, LPC Attorney 3.
22 Schelling, "Beckman Firing Draws Fire," (August 1997).
23 Schelling, "Hedge Fires Beckman," (August 1997).
24 Duran, "Beckman Announces His Candidacy," (November 1997).
25 "Szilagyi Joins Race for County Prosecutor," (February 1998).
26 Duran, "Prosecutor Race Most Expensive," (October 1998).
27 Duran, "Beckman Announces."
28 Duran, "Dems Sound off on Hedge," (April 1998).
29 Duran, "City Votes Put Beckman on Top," (May 1998).
30 Duran, "Prosecutor Race Most Expensive."
31 Duran, "Candidates Philosophies Differ," (October 1998); Duran, "How Experienced is Beckman," (October 1998).
32 Staff, "Voter Turnout Surprisingly High," (November 1998).
33 Sobecki, "Beckman Edges Hedge."
34 Sobecki, "Rison Murder Trial Delayed," (January 1999).
35 Sobecki, "Rison Murder Suspect Freed."
36 Levin, S. Duerring.
37 Sobecki, "Rison Murder Suspect Freed."
38 Levin, S. Duerring.
39 Sobecki, "Rison Murder Suspect Freed."
40 "November 2002 Election Results," (November 2002); "La Porte County Prosecutor (Unopposed)," (November 2006).
41 Maddux, "21 Years Separates LaPorte Family's Grief," (October 14, 1999).

42 Levin, Daniel Jemiolo Cassidy relative Interview (January 2023).
43 Lee, "Marriage License—Jemiolo, Cassidy," (September 1973).
44 Sprecher, "Coroner's Certificate of Death—Janet Jemiolo," (December 1978).
45 Levin, D. Cassidy relative.
46 Gonzalez, "La Porte Man Charged with Murdering Wife," (June 2013).
47 Maddux, "21 Years Separates LaPorte Family's Grief."
48 Cutler, "Certificate of Death—Daniel E. Cassidy," (October 1999).
49 La Porte High School, *El Pe 1992 Yearbook.*
50 Maddux, "21 Years Separates."
51 Kintzele, "Daniel Cassidy—Investigation Overview," (October 1999), 20.
52 "Obituary—John Cassidy," (April 1994).
53 Buell, "Interview: Robert Sheridan," (October 1999).
54 Buell, "Interview: Flitter," (October 1999).
55 Buell, "Interview: R. Sheridan."
56 Buell, "Interview: George Stenslik," (October 1999).
57 Ritter, "Witness Interview: Julie Cassidy," (October 1999).
58 Kintzele, "Cassidy—Investigation Overview," 1.
59 Sullivan, "Autopsy Report—Cassidy, Daniel Evans," (November 1999).
60 Buell, "Interview: Flitter."
61 Kintzele, "Cassidy—Investigation Overview," 20.
62 Buell, "Interview: Flitter."
63 Ritter, "Witness Interview: Kelly S. Loughlin," (October 1999).
64 Lachmund, "Rison Witness Interview: R. Hammons," (March 2008).
65 Lachmund, "Cassidy Witness Interview: Rickey J. Hammons," (October 6, 1999).
66 Ritter, "Witness Interview: Brian Todd Bowman," (October 7, 1999).
67 Buell, "Interview: Stenslik."
68 Ritter, "Witness Interview: B. Bowman."
69 Ritter, "Witness Interview: K. Loughlin."
70 Kintzele, "Witness Interview: Brian Todd Bowman," (October 9, 1999).
71 Kintzele, "Cassidy—Investigation Overview," 22.
72 Kintzele, 33.
73 Biggs, "Witness Interview: Dax A. Richter," (October 1999).
74 Ritter, "Witness Interview: K. Loughlin."
75 Matzke, "Witness Interview: Jennifer Nicole Hammons on October 8, 1999."
76 Biggs, "Witness Interview: Rickey J. Hammons (with Lachmund) October 12, 1999, at 8:20 a.m."
77 Buell, "Interview: Stenslik."
78 "Paycheck Inquiry—Rick J Hammons," (October 1999).
79 Biggs, "Witness Interview: D. Richter."
80 Kintzele, "Witness Interview: B. Bowman."
81 Bernard, "Murder: Cassidy, Daniel—Witness Interview: Staff Sergeant J. R. Meyer," (October 1999).
82 Kintzele, "Witness Interview: B. Bowman Taped."
83 Kintzele, "Cassidy—Investigation Overview," 8–9.
84 Biggs, "Witness Interview: D. Richter."
85 Buell, "Witness Interview: Flitter."
86 Buell, "Witness Interview: Stenslik."
87 Sullivan, "Autopsy Report—D. Cassidy."
88 "Cassidy Investigation—Photo Summary," (October 7, 1999).
89 Ritter, "Cassidy—Investigative Summary October 06, 1999."
90 Biggs, "Crime Scene Summary—Daniel E. Cassidy," (October 6, 1999).
91 Ritter, "Cassidy—Crime Scene," (October 6, 1999).
92 Buell, "Witness Interview: R. Sheridan."
93 Lachmund, "Cassidy Witness Interview: R. Hammons," (October 6, 1999).
94 Ritter, "Cassidy, Daniel—October 8 Investigation Summary," (October 1999).
95 Baker, "The Makarov," (November 2021).
96 Ritter, "Cassidy—October 8 Investigation Summary."
97 Maddux, "Man Charged with Murder," (October 1999).
98 Braje, *State of Indiana v. Rickey Hammons*—Motion to Suppress (February 2000).
99 Beckman, Rickey Hammons—Statement of Plea Agreement (June 2000).
100 Maddux, "Man Gets 45 Years," (August 2000).
101 *Cassidy, Indiana v. Hammons*—Victim Impact Statement: Julie A. Cassidy (August 2000).
102 Maddux, "Man Gets 45 Years."
103 Hammons, "To: Mr. Gillmore [sic]," (October 26, 1999).
104 *State of Indiana v. Rickey Hammons*—Historical Record to June 2009.
105 Hammons, R. *Hammons v. Indiana*—Petition for PCR (October 2002).
106 Hammons, R. *Hammons v. Indiana*—Motion for Change of Venue; Hammons, "To: Clerk Re: Change of Venue," (September 3, 2002).
107 "Offender Information System Conduct Summary—Hammons, Rickey," (October 2009).
108 Levin, Prisoner at Wabash Valley Interview (October 2023).
109 Ros, "Will Inmates Put Cards on the Table?" (February 2008).
110 Lachmund, "Contact with R. Hammons," (March 2008).
111 Dingman, "*Indiana v. Jason Tibbs*—Pre-Sentence Investigation," (December 2014).
112 "Leslie Ann Dean—Birth Date."
113 *State of Indiana v. Jason Tibbs*—Driving While Suspended 1 (March 1994); Tibbs Driving While Suspended 2 (April 1994); Tibbs Driving While Suspended 3 (February 1995); Tibbs Driving While Suspended 4 (June 1996); Tibbs Driving While Suspended 5 (June 1996).
114 *State of Indiana v. Jason Tibbs*—Theft D Felony (US Currency), (August 2003).
115 *Indiana v. Tibbs*—Theft D Felony.
116 Levin, M. Drayton (October 2022).
117 Airy, "Airy Supplement (Started April 7, 2008)," 13.
118 Levin, M. Drayton.
119 Lachmund, "Contact with R. Hammons."
120 Indiana Department of Correction. "IDOC: Wabash Valley Correctional Facility."
121 Gonzalez, "'There is no closure'—Rayna Rison's family looking forward to justice," (August 2013).
122 Lachmund, "Contact with R. Hammons."
123 "The Pole Barn vs The Timber Frame Barn."
124 *State of Indiana v. Jason Tibbs*—Hammons Pole Barn Photos, (November 2014).
125 Lachmund, "Rison Witness Interview: R. Hammons."
126 *Indiana v. Tibbs*—Hammons Pole Barn Photos.
127 Lachmund, "Rison Witness Interview: R. Hammons."
128 *Indiana v. Tibbs*—Hammons Pole Barn Photos.
129 "La Porte Indiana Sunset March 26, 1993." Google Search (November 2023).
130 Lachmund, "Rison Witness Interview: R. Hammons."
131 Kintzele, "Cassidy—Investigation Overview," 35–36.
132 Lachmund, "Rison Witness Interview: R. Hammons."
133 *Jason L. Tibbs v. State of Indiana*—Rule 60(B) Hearing (December 7, 2015), II of II, Kutanovski, at 76.
134 Hammons, "To: Mark Lachmund, Re: 'Help Me' Get Moved," (March 2008).
135 Airy, "Investigative Supplement," (April 7, 2008), 1.
136 *State of Indiana v. Jason Tibbs*—Deposition of Eric Freeman, Jones (2014) at 41; Williamson, "Eric Freeman Statement," (June 2013), 6–7.
137 *Indiana v. Tibbs*—Deposition of E. Freeman, Jones at 20.
138 Williamson, "E. Freeman Statement," 5.
139 South Central High School, SCHS 1991 *Yearbook*, 38.
140 Kabacinski, "Mischief/Damage—Victim: Milich, Accused: Tibbs," (November 1992).
141 Williamson, "E. Freeman Statement," 3.
142 "Cheryll Ann Morrison—Location: 114 M and A Farm Rd"; "Eric Matthew Freeman—Location: 114 M and A Farm Rd."
143 "Obituary—Julie McCarter Cross," (July 2020); "Freeman, Elizabeth L. Freeman Residence 2018–2020."
144 South Carolina Department of Social Services, *Hawkins, William Neal v. Hawkins, Julie Elaine*—Divorce (August 1999).
145 "Eric Matthew Freeman—Location Report: 810 Deep Hollow Ct," (June 18, 2023); "Eric Matthew Freeman Location: 810 Deep Hollow Ct," (n.d.).

ENDNOTES

146 South Carolina Department of Social Services, Hawkins Divorce (August 1999); South Carolina Department of Social Services, *Freeman, Julie McCarter v. Freeman, Eric Matthew*—Divorce (September 2013).
147 South Carolina Department of Social Services, *Freeman, Eric Matthew v. Wessinger, Claire R.*—Divorce (January 2018); "Eric Matthew Freeman, Elizabeth Freeman—Ownership History: 254 Cedar Hollow Ln," (May 22, 2021).
148 *Indiana v. Tibbs*—Deposition of E. Freeman, Jones at 11–15.
149 "Obituary for James Donald Westmoreland," (May 2013); *Indiana v. Tibbs*—Deposition of E. Freeman, Jones at 13.
150 York County Assessor, "400 Westmoreland Dr, Clover, SC."
151 Bank of America, Freeman foreclosure (March 2014).
152 Williamson, "Eric Freeman Statement," (March 2008), 1–2.
153 Lachmund, "Rison Witness Interview: R. Hammons," 48.
154 Williamson, "E. Freeman Statement," 4–5.
155 Williamson, 15.
156 Williamson, 45.
157 Williamson, 18.
158 Williamson, 20.
159 Williamson, 25–26.
160 Williamson, 32.
161 Williamson, 38.
162 Williamson, 39.
163 Williamson, 41.
164 Williamson, 51.
165 Williamson, 43.
166 Williamson, 43.
167 Williamson, 41.
168 Williamson, 55.
169 Airy, "Investigation Supplement," 9.
170 Hammons, *Hammons v. Indiana*—Petition for PCR.
171 Airy, "Investigation Supplement," 11–13.
172 Airy, 1–12.
173 Airy, 22–24.
174 Airy, 26–27.
175 Airy, 29–31.
176 Airy, 33–37.
177 Airy, 39–40.
178 Airy, 40.
179 Field, "Szilagyi Edges out Beckman," (May 2010).
180 Flynn, "Beckman Attacked for Stance on Drug Issues," (February 2010).
181 Ebaugh, "Prosecutor Called Out," (April 2010).
182 Szilagyi, "Szilagyi Vows to Curtail Nepotism," (April 2010).
183 Ebaugh, "Prosecutor Called Out."
184 Ebaugh, "Beckman Apologizes," (February 2010).
185 McVay, "Full Story of Beckman's Threats," (May 2010).
186 Field, "Szilagyi Edges out Beckman."
187 Fritz, "Szilagyi 'Numb' after Win," (November 2010).
188 Fritz, "Szilagyi, Espar Trade Barbs," (April 2014).
189 Maddux, "Szilagyi Bested by Espar," (May 2014).
190 "Obituary—James David Bruno," (February 2022).
191 Levin, Jennifer Delrio Interview (January 2022).
192 Levin.
193 Levin, M. Drayton.
194 *State of Indiana v. Jason Tibbs*—Theft D Felony (Dismissed), (June 28, 2012).
195 Levin, J. Delrio.

THE CASE AGAINST JASON TIBBS

1 Gonzalez, "Attorney: Former Suspect's Alibis Were Faulty," (January 2014).
2 Gonzalez, "Details Revealed in Tibbs Case," (January 2014).
3 Gonzalez, "Tibbs Denied Bond," (January 2014).
4 Levin, J. Delrio.
5 Dettmer, "Courthouse Work Complete," (December 2006); "LaPorte County Courthouse."
6 Levin, LPC Attorney 3.
7 Duran, "Alevizos to Run for Prosecutor," (November 1997).
8 Duran, "Alevizos up in the Air," (January 1998).
9 Duran, "Alevizos to Run for Prosecutor."
10 "Alevizos Named a Deputy Prosecutor," (January 1999).
11 Maddux, "La Porte Judge Alevizos Seeking Second Term," (February 11, 2012).
12 Levin, LPC Attorney 1.

13 *Indiana v. Tibbs*, Kutanovski, at 7.
14 *Indiana v. Tibbs*, Kutanovski, at 945.
15 *Indiana v. Tibbs*, Kutanovski, at 543.
16 State of Indiana v. Jason Tibbs, Motions In Limine Hearing, Espino (2014), at 25.
17 *Indiana v. Tibbs*, Motions In Limine Hearing, Espino, at 23.
18 *Indiana v. Tibbs*, Kutanovski, at 1,082.
19 *Indiana v. Tibbs*, Kutanovski, at 29.
20 Chang, "'If I Can't Have Her,'" (October 2014); Maddux, "Prosecutor Links Ex-Boyfriend," (October 2014).
21 Schoff, "Rayna Bedroom Search with Karen, Wendy," (April 1993).
22 *Indiana v. Tibbs*, Kutanovski, at 29.
23 *Indiana v. Tibbs*, Kutanovski, at 34.
24 *Indiana v. Tibbs*, Kutanovski, at 48–49.
25 *Indiana v. Tibbs*, Kutanovski, at 56–57.
26 *Indiana v. Tibbs*, Kutanovski, at 59.
27 *Indiana v. Tibbs*, Kutanovski, at 59.
28 *Indiana v. Tibbs*, Kutanovski, at 59–65.
29 *Indiana v. Tibbs*, Kutanovski, at 79.
30 Levin, M. Elser.
31 *Indiana v. Tibbs*, Kutanovski, at 80–81.
32 Williamson, "E. Freeman Statement," (March 2008), 7.
33 Szilagyi, "Transactional Immunity Agreement."
34 *Indiana v. Tibbs*—Deposition of E. Freeman, Jones at 31.
35 Williamson, "E. Freeman Statement," (June 2013), 48.
36 Williamson, 108.
37 Airy, Eric Freeman Phone Interview (July 2013), 9.
38 Lachmund, "Rison Witness Interview: R. Hammons," 16.
39 Lachmund, 66.
40 Lachmund, 29.
41 "La Porte Indiana Sunset March 26, 1993." Google Search.
42 Lachmund, "Rison Witness Interview: R. Hammons," 23.
43 Airy, "Investigation Supplement," 43.
44 La Porte County Sheriff, "McWhirter—RAP Sheet."
45 King, "Siddall Interview."
46 Levin, J. Jackson.
47 Trueblood, "Rayna Rison Recovery—Personel [sic] at Scene," (April 27, 1993).
48 Levin, J. Jackson.
49 Boyd, "Rison Murder Report," (August 1993), 33; Hahn, "Interview with R. Gazarkiewicz."
50 Rison, R. Gazarkiewicz Interview.
51 Hahn, "P. Rosebaum Interview."
52 Boyd, "Rison Murder Report," (August 1993), 35.
53 McDermott, "Assessment for R. McCarty."
54 Miller, "B. Durham."
55 Hughes, "Why Police Lineups Will Never Be Perfect," (October 2014).
56 Cains, "Interview with Chad Green," (March 1993).
57 Miller, "Chad E. Green Statement," (April 8, 1993).
58 Hahn, "Interview with J. Tibbs"; Hahn, "Interview with M. Elser."
59 Miller, "J. Tibbs Statement."
60 Hahn, "Interview with J. Amor."
61 Hahn.
62 Hahn, "Interview with J. Tibbs."
63 Boyd, "Rison Murder Report," (August 1993), 13–20.
64 Hahn, "Interview with J. Jordan."
65 Hemphill, "Missing Person Report: Rison, R."
66 Hahn, "Interview with J. Amor"; Levin, M. Elser 1.
67 Airy, "Investigation Supplement," 3–4.
68 Bernth, "Interview with Rison Family."
69 Gudas, "Jury Deliberating Lewis' Fate," (March 1998).
70 Hoover, "Autopsy—Rison, R."
71 Hoover, "To: Hahn Re: Rison Toxicology."
72 Medtox Laboratories, "Toxicology—R. Rison."
73 *State of Indiana v. Jason Tibbs*, Deposition of R. McCarty, Jones at 19.
74 Bergerson, R. McCarty—Plea Agreement.
75 McDermott, "Assessment for R. McCarty."
76 Gettinger, R. McCarty—Order of Probation.
77 Koehn, "Molesting, Accused: R. McCarty."
78 Legal Information Institute, "Rule 807, Residual Exception."

467

79 Gaekle, "Certificate of Death—H. McCarty."
80 Weliver, "Child Molesting."
81 Keith, "B. Rison FBI Interview 2."
82 Levin, A. Boyd 1.
83 Hahn, "Summ. of Ray's Stories," (May 1993).
84 Legal Information Institute, "Brady Rule."
85 *People v. Ashwal* (April 1976).
86 Hoover, "Autopsy—Rison, R."
87 "Cartilage: What It Is, Function & Types."
88 Pollanen and Chiasson, "Fracture of the Hyoid Bone in Strangulation," (January 1996).
89 Levin, S. Duerring.
90 Levin, A. Boyd 1.
91 Hahn, "Interview with J. Tibbs."
92 Miller, "J. Tibbs Statement."
93 Chang, "Jason Tibbs Found Guilty," (November 2014).

WHAT SHOULD HAVE BEEN THE DEFENSE FOR JASON TIBBS

1   Matzke, "Witness Interview: J. Hammons," 16.
2   Lachmund, "Cassidy Witness Interview: R. Hammons," (October 6, 1999), 17.
3   Lachmund, 8.
4   Kintzele, "Cassidy—Investigation Overview," 16.
5   Lachmund, "Cassidy Witness Interview: R. Hammons," (October 6, 1999), 8.
6   Lachmund, 22.
7   Lachmund, 12.
8   Ritter, "Cassidy—October 8 Investigation Summary," 9–10.
9   Lachmund, "Cassidy Witness Interview: R. Hammons," (October 6, 1999), 15.
10 Hess, "Witness Interview: R. Hammons Sr. Re: Makarov," (October 8, 1999); Ritter, "Cassidy, Daniel—October 7 Investigation Summary," (October 1999), 16.
11 Buell, "Witness Interview: Stenslik."
12 Buell, "Witness Interview: Ronda Reedy," (October 1999).
13 Lachmund, "Cassidy Witness Interview: Rickey J. Hammons on October 7, 1999."
14 Buell, "Witness Interview: Rickey J. Hammons," (October 1999).
15 Matzke, "Witness Interview: Ramona Gamez," (October 8, 1999).
16 Matzke, "Witness Interview: J. Hammons."
17 Ritter, "Cassidy—October 8 Investigation Summary," 9.
18 Ritter, 11.
19 Ritter, "Cassidy—October 9 Investigation Summary," (October 1999), 3–4.
20 Ritter, 4–5.
21 Ritter, 5–9.
22 Kintzele, "Cassidy—Investigation Overview," 25–28.
23 Kintzele, 30.
24 Ritter, "Cassidy—October 8 Investigation Summary," 9.
25 Ritter, "Cassidy, Daniel—October 12 Investigation Summary," (October 1999), 1.
26 Kintzele, "Cassidy—Investigation Overview," 35–36.
27 Lachmund, "Arrest Report: Rickey J. Hammons—Mug Shot," (October 1999).
28 Ritter, "Cassidy—October 12 Investigation Summary," 4.
29 Butcher, "Hostile Inmate: Hammons, Rickey," (October 1999).
30 Ritter, "Cassidy—October 12 Investigation Summary," 5.
31 Butcher, "Hostile Inmate: Hammons, Rickey."
32 Biggs, "Witness Interview: R. Hammons October 12, 1999 at 8:20 a.m.," 4.
33 Biggs, 14–47.
34 Ritter, "Cassidy—October 12 Investigation Summary," 8–9.
35 Ritter, 10.
36 Biggs, "Witness Interview: Rickey J. Hammons (with Lachmund) October 12, 1999, at 11:10 p.m.," (October 1999), 10–24.
37 Biggs, 22–25.
38 Babcock, "Cassidy, Daniel—Re: Accused: Rickey J. Hammons. Comments about Bullets," (October 15, 1999).
39 Ritter, "Cassidy—October 12 Investigation Summary," 11.
40 Ritter, "Cassidy, Daniel—October 13 Investigation Summary," (October 1999), 1.
41 Biggs, "Witness Interview: Rickey J. Hammons (with Lachmund) October 14, 1999, at 5:40 p.m.," (October 1999), 3.
42 Biggs, 6–25.
43 Biggs.
44 Biggs, 34–43.
45 Biggs, "Witness Interview: D. Richter."
46 Biggs, "Witness Interview: Brian Bowman," (October 1999); Biggs, "Witness Interview: D. Richter"; Biggs, "Witness Interview: R. Glassman," (October 1999).
47 Biggs, "Witness Interview: B. Bowman."
48 Buell, "Cassidy, Daniel—Rickey Hammons Employment Records," (October 1999).
49 Butcher, "Hostile Inmate: Hammons, R."
50 Braje, *Indiana v. Hammons* Motion to Suppress.
51 Hammons, "To Mr. Gillmore [sic]."
52 *Indiana v. Tibbs*, Kutanovski, at 1,092.
53 "John E. Reid and Associates, Inc."
54 Buckley, "Clarifying Misrepresentations About Interrogation Techniques," (2001).
55 Bank of America, Freeman foreclosure.
56 South Carolina Department of Social Services, Freeman, J. M. and E. M.—Divorce.
57 Szilagyi, "Transactional Immunity Agreement."
58 FindLaw, "Transactional Immunity," (February 2019).
59 Airy, "Investigation Supplement," 40.
60 Airy, 12.
61 Damphousse, "Voice Stress Analysis," (March 2008).
62 Szilagyi, "Transactional Immunity Agreement."
63 Airy, "Investigation Supplement," 41.
64 Szilagyi, *State of Indiana v. Jason Tibbs*—Affidavit for Probable Cause.
65 Williamson, "E. Freeman Statement," (June 2013), 3, 4, 26.
66 Williamson, 13–16.
67 Airy, "Hammons Buick Receipts."
68 Airy, "Investigation Supplement," 9–10.
69 Airy, "Kowalski, Raymond—Check Register," (1993).
70 Airy, "Hammons Buick Receipts."
71 Williamson, "E. Freeman Statement," (June 2013), 21.
72 Williamson, 10.
73 Williamson, "E. Freeman Statement," (March 2008), 4.
74 Williamson, "E. Freeman Statement," (June 2013), 19–21.
75 Indiana v. Tibbs, Christine A. Kutanovski, at 206.
76 Williamson, "E. Freeman Statement," (June 2013), 3–4.
77 Williamson, 11.
78 Williamson, 28–29.
79 Williamson, 27–29.
80 *Indiana v. Tibbs*, Kutanovski, at 105.
81 Williamson, "E. Freeman Statement," (June 2013), 38.
82 Williamson, 6, 28.
83 Williamson, 18, 43, 45, 50, 51, 57.
84 Williamson, 19.
85 Williamson, 34–36.
86 Airy, "Investigation Supplement," 43.
87 Williamson, "E. Freeman Statement," (June 2013), 46–54.
88 Williamson, 108.
89 Lachmund, "Rison Witness Interview: R. Hammons," 22.
90 Williamson, "E. Freeman Statement," (June 2013), 55–64.
91 Williamson, 67–68.
92 Ihnat, "Items Submitted for Analysis," (September 2008).
93 Williamson, "E. Freeman Statement," (June 2013), 70–72.
94 Levin, J. Jackson.
95 Williamson, "E. Freeman Statement," (June 2013), 72–74.
96 Williamson, 93.
97 Williamson, 99.
98 Williamson, 79.
99 Lachmund, "Rison Witness Interview: R. Hammons," 41.
100 Williamson, "E. Freeman Statement," (June 2013), 122.
101 Williamson, 116–30.
102 Williamson, 28.
103 Airy, E. Freeman Phone Interview, 1.
104 Levin, J. Jackson.
105 Airy, E. Freeman Phone Interview, 4–6.
106 Airy, 3–4.
107 Airy, 9.
108 Airy, 10–12.

109 Airy, 21.
110 Dumollard et al., "Putatively Lethal Ingestion of Isopropyl Alcohol-Related Case," (October 2020).
111 Corry, "Possible Sources of Ethanol," (November 1977).
112 Hoover, "To: Hahn Re: Rison Toxicology."
113 Levin, A. Boyd 1.
114 Hoover, "To: Gudorf Re: Rayna Rison Post-Mortem Examination," (April 9, 1998).
115 Ford et al., *Clinical Toxicology*.
116 Airy, "Investigation Supplement," 39–40.
117 *Indiana v. Tibbs*, Kutanovski, at 450–51.
118 Corry, "Possible Sources of Ethanol."
119 Hoover, "Autopsy—Rison, R."
120 Medtox Laboratories, "Toxicology—R. Rison."
121 Martinez et al., "A Comparison . . . Absorption and Metabolism of Isopropyl Alcohol," (June 1986).
122 Hoover, "Autopsy—Rison, R."
123 Ames, "Items for FBI Lab Analysis."
124 *Indiana v. Tibbs*, Kutanovski, at 215.
125 Caruso, "Decomposition in Water."
126 Hoover, M.D., "R. Rison Autopsy."
127 *Indiana v. Tibbs*, Kutanovski, at 1,184–86.
128 *Indiana v. Tibbs*, Kutanovski, at 1,108.
129 Black, "Certificate of Analysis—Items Withdrawn for Analysis by Airy," (January 2014).
130 Airy, E. Freeman Phone Interview, 5.
131 Arndt, "Interview with K. Hackney."
132 Boyd, "Rison Murder Report," (August 1993), 34.
133 Airy, "Investigation Supplement," 4.

REVELATIONS

1 *Jason L. Tibbs v. Dennis Reagle*—Petitioner's Supplemental Reply (June 1, 2022).
2 *Jason Tibbs v. State of Indiana*—Brief of Appellant, (January 21, 2016).
3 *Strengthening Forensic Science in the United States* (Washington, DC: National Academies Press, 2009).
4 *Jason L. Tibbs v. State of Indiana*—Transcript II of II, Kutanovski (December 7, 2015), at 80.
5 Alevizos, Tibbs Order Denying PCR in La Porte Circuit Court.
6 *Jason L. Tibbs v. State of Indiana*—Transcript II of II, Kutanovski at 39.
7 Wikipedia, "Fundamental Error," April 2023.
8 *Jason Tibbs v. State of Indiana*—Memorandum Decision (July 2019).
9 Mandape et al., "Evaluating Probabilistic Genotyping," (January 2022).
10 Murphy, "Why This Scientist," (September 16, 2019).
11 "Obituary—J. Bruno."
12 Levin, J. Delrio.
13 "Indiana Rules of Court—Rule 60. Relief from Judgment or Order: (B)," (April 2024).
14 *Jason L. Tibbs v. State of Indiana*—Rule 60(B) Hearing (November 30, 2015), I of II, Kutanovski, at 1.
15 *Tibbs v. Indiana*—Rule 60(B) Hearing, I of II, Kutanovski, at 108–10.
16 *Tibbs v. Indiana*—Rule 60(B) Hearing.
17 *Jason L. Tibbs v. State of Indiana*—Rule 60(B) Hearing (November 30, 2015), II of II, Kutanovski, at 31.
18 *Tibbs v. Indiana*—Rule 60(B) Hearing, II of II, Kutanovski, at 80.
19 *Tibbs v. Indiana*—Rule 60(B) Hearing.
20 *Jason Tibbs v. State of Indiana*—Memorandum Decision, (September 2016).
21 Alevizos, *State of Indiana v. Rickey Hammons*—Community Transition Program (February 2019).
22 *Jason L. Tibbs v. State of Indiana*—Rule 60(B) Hearing (December 7, 2015), II of II, Kutanovski, at 50.
23 La Porte County Sheriff, "Hammons, Rickey J.—RAP Sheet," (October 2019).
24 Maddux, "Mother Doubts Daughter Is a Runaway," (August 2000).
25 Nicholas, "Missing Girl Found in Michigan City," (August 2000).
26 "Marriage License Applications—Huegel, Michael and Adrienne McCarty," (July 2007).
27 In Re: the Marriage of Adrienne M. Huegel and Michael E. Huegel, (June 2014).
28 In Re: the Marriage of Adrienne M. Ray and Eric C. Ray, (March 2019).
29 Sanders, Chief Deputy Prosecuting Attorney, R. McCarty arrest probable cause affidavit (February 2018).
30 Levin, Eric Ray coworker Interview (August 2023).
31 Gard, "Former Suspect in Rison Killing Dies in Jail," (February 2018).

MAPS

MISSION IMPOSSIBLE: THE ALLEGED TIBBS AND FREEMAN ROUTES

Nothing does more to discredit the State's case against Jason Tibbs than the distances between the destinations involved in the testimony of the prosecution's star witnesses, Rickey Hammons and Eric Freeman. According to Freeman, he drove Tibbs and Rayna Rison **13 miles** from the Pine Lake Animal Hospital (PLAH) to a spot near the Heston Supper Club. He claimed the couple got out of the car—a 1986 Buick Century belonging to Hammons's sister—and Jason strangled Rayna by the side of the road. Freeman testified that Jason put her body in the Buick's trunk. They next rode **13 miles** to the Hammonses' pole barn, where Rickey said he was hiding in the loft. From that spot, he claimed to see Rayna's body when Freeman opened the trunk. They stayed at least **15 minutes**, Hammons claimed. Freeman had them traveling **4 miles** from the pole barn to PLAH to retrieve Rayna's Ford LTD. From there, they drove another **8 miles** to the pond, where they allegedly submerged the victim.

Therefore, Freeman had them traveling a total distance of **38 miles**. But other witnesses testified that Rayna was abducted no earlier than **6:10 P.M.**, and her LTD had been abandoned no later than **7:00 P.M.** Deductions can then be made for the time Jason allegedly spent at the murder scene and inside the pole barn. He and Freeman would have had the impossible task of driving more than **100 miles per hour** to reach all the destinations within **25 minutes**.

38 TOTAL MILES HAD TO BE DRIVEN IN 25 MINUTES

Animal Hospital to Heston Supper Club (13 miles)

Heston to Hammons Pole Barn (13 miles)

Pole Barn to Animal Hospital (4 miles)

Animal Hospital to Pond (8 miles)

DESTINATIONS

Animal Hospital

Hammons Pole Barn

Pond

Heston Supper Club

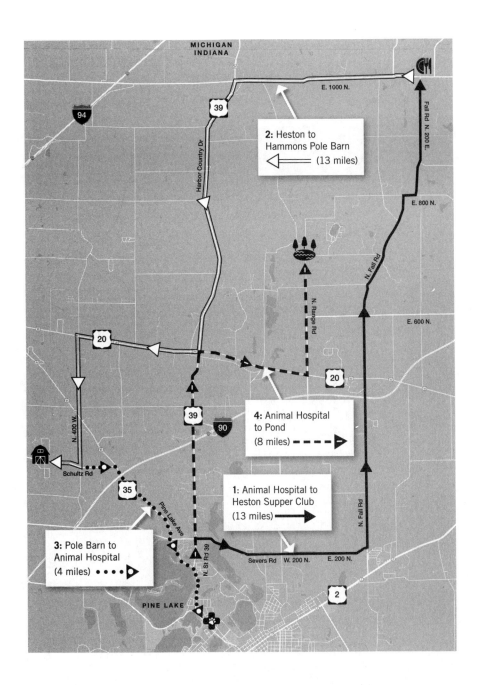

1) POSTABDUCTION ROUTES AND SIGHTINGS
6:10–6:25 P.M.

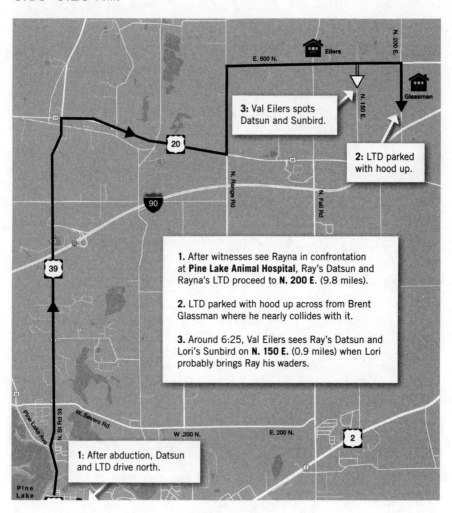

E. 600 N.   Eilers   N. 200 E.

3: Val Eilers spots Datsun and Sunbird.

Glassman

2: LTD parked with hood up.

N. 150 E.

20

N. Range Rd

90

N. Fall Rd

39

1. After witnesses see Rayna in confrontation at **Pine Lake Animal Hospital**, Ray's Datsun and Rayna's LTD proceed to **N. 200 E.** (9.8 miles).

2. LTD parked with hood up across from Brent Glassman where he nearly collides with it.

3. Around 6:25, Val Eilers sees Ray's Datsun and Lori's Sunbird on **N. 150 E.** (0.9 miles) when Lori probably brings Ray his waders.

Pine Lake Ave   N. St Rd 39   W. Severs Rd   W. .200 N.   E. 200 N.   2

1: After abduction, Datsun and LTD drive north.

Pine Lake

2) JUGGLING THE VEHICLES
6:25–6:40 P.M.

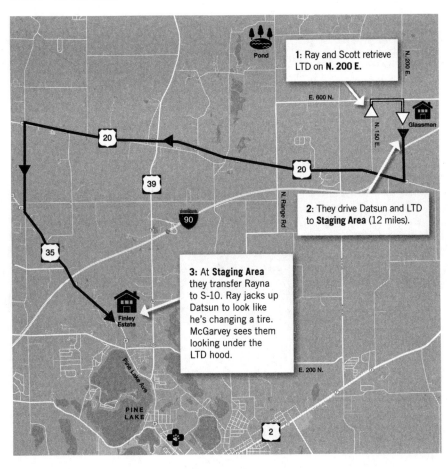

1: Ray and Scott retrieve LTD on **N. 200 E.**

2: They drive Datsun and LTD to **Staging Area** (12 miles).

3: At **Staging Area** they transfer Rayna to S-10. Ray jacks up Datsun to look like he's changing a tire. McGarvey sees them looking under the LTD hood.

3) CHECKING OUT THE POND, RETURNING THE LTD
6:38–6:55 P.M.

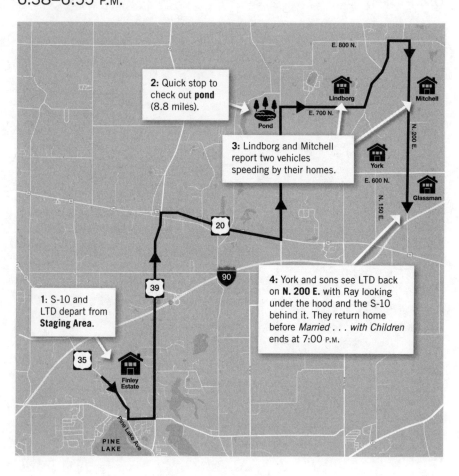

2: Quick stop to check out **pond** (8.8 miles).

3: Lindborg and Mitchell report two vehicles speeding by their homes.

1: S-10 and LTD depart from **Staging Area**.

4: York and sons see LTD back on **N. 200 E.** with Ray looking under the hood and the S-10 behind it. They return home before *Married . . . with Children* ends at 7:00 P.M.

E. 800 N.
Lindborg
Mitchell
E. 700 N.
Pond
York
E. 600 N.
Glassman
N. 200 E.
N. 150 E.
20
90
39
35
Finley Estate
Pine Lake Ave
PINE LAKE

4) SUBMERSION, RETURN HOME ROUTES
7:00–8:30 P.M.

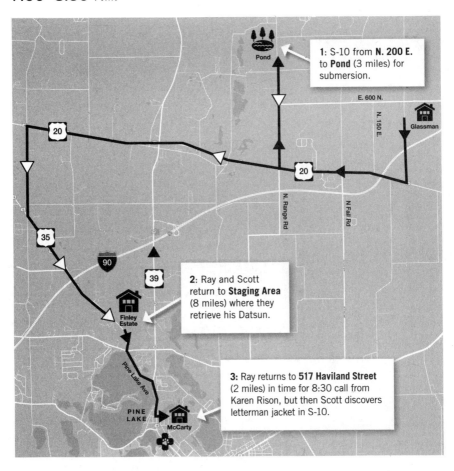

1: S-10 from **N. 200 E.** to **Pond** (3 miles) for submersion.

2: Ray and Scott return to **Staging Area** (8 miles) where they retrieve his Datsun.

3: Ray returns to **517 Haviland Street** (2 miles) in time for 8:30 call from Karen Rison, but then Scott discovers letterman jacket in S-10.

5) FAILED ATTEMPT TO RETURN JACKET TO RAYNA'S LTD
9:30–10:30 P.M.

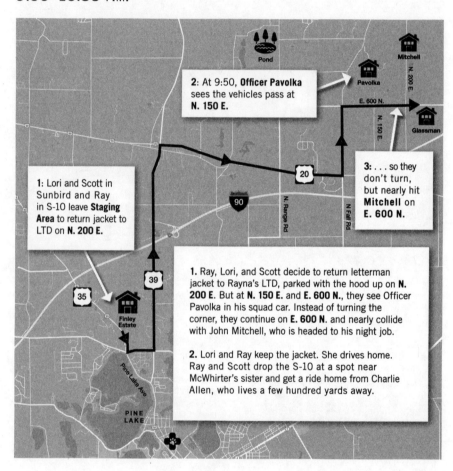

2: At 9:50, **Officer Pavolka** sees the vehicles pass at **N. 150 E.**

1: Lori and Scott in Sunbird and Ray in S-10 leave **Staging Area** to return jacket to LTD on **N. 200 E.**

3: . . . so they don't turn, but nearly hit **Mitchell** on **E. 600 N.**

1. Ray, Lori, and Scott decide to return letterman jacket to Rayna's LTD, parked with the hood up on **N. 200 E.** But at **N. 150 E.** and **E. 600 N.**, they see Officer Pavolka in his squad car. Instead of turning the corner, they continue on **E. 600 N.** and nearly collide with John Mitchell, who is headed to his night job.

2. Lori and Ray keep the jacket. She drives home. Ray and Scott drop the S-10 at a spot near McWhirter's sister and get a ride home from Charlie Allen, who lives a few hundred yards away.

INDEX

INDEX

ACKNOWLEDGMENTS

Submerged could not have been researched, written, or published without the help of the following:

First and foremost, I am most grateful to Jason Tibbs for his insight and patience with me, and his forbearance with injustice that would crush most others.

My literary agent, Nat Sobel of Sobel Weber Associates, is responsible for getting this book published by Crime Ink, where I've had the assistance of Otto Penzler, Charles Perry, Tom Wickersham, and Will Luckman. My books' media rights agent is Joel Gotler of the Intellectual Property Group. Eric Keller from Eric Keller Design provided the book's cover concept and maps with an assist from Kaitlyn Stancy's photography. Steve Simon of Acumen Probe advised me on public access to Indiana judicial files.

I appreciate all those who chose to speak with me for attribution, given the sensitivity that still surrounds the Rison case, including Arland Boyd, Jennifer Delrio, Mike Drayton, Scott Duerring, Matt Elser, Josh Jordan, Jane Lindborg, Gary Marshall, Gayla Moreau, Lucas Scarborough, Cliff Sheeler, Joe Walker, and Chris Wallens.

My research greatly benefited from the La Porte County Historical Society Museum, the La Porte County Public Library, and the Public Record Research System of the La Porte County Circuit Court and La Porte County Sheriff's Office.

Adam Hartford, Josh, and Jerry Daniel were extremely generous with their help down a particularly arduous blind alley.

For marketing assistance, I turned to Howard Diamond, Megan McConkey, Justin Garvin from Rise, a Quad Agency, and Joe Baugnet for their insight on Search Engine Optimization, and social media.

Mark Coe, Richard Rettenbacher, Don Marshall, David Johnson, and Gary Severyn from CTI Meeting Technology provided my tech support and experience with the National Library of Medicine for PubMed and PubChem.

As always, I appreciate my friend Tony Fitzpatrick, who inspires me each day to get behind the mule and plow.

Through these many years, I have prospered from the encouragement of my brothers Jay, Jonathan, and Wayne, and my local siblings Pat and Betsey. But none of this would be possible without my wife, Mary Jo, and my sons, Adam, Aaron, and Gabe.